The European Communities — of coal and steel, the Common Market and atomic energy — offer a unique organizational context for analyzing the growth of supranational law in Western Europe. They have given birth to independent legal orders which are essentially constitutional in nature and competitive with those of the six Member States. These legal orders break with the traditional concept of national sovereignty, including the restriction of applying international law in principle only to states. As result, Community law has become a potent instrument for the economic integration of the European Communities and the springboard for achieving the political unification of Western Europe.

This result has been due greatly to the creative jurisprudence of the Court of Justice. The Court, which is endowed with broad powers of judicial review, operates as guardian of the Treaties in the interpretation and application of Community law. It also exercises an arbiter function on the more delicate and fundamental conflict questions between the Member State legal orders and Community law. On these questions, the highly political basis of the Community becomes visible, and the Court must deal with the limits on the underlying Community consensus which forms the basis of the developing system of law. This book covers the first 15 years of the Court's jurisprudence. Part One sets forth the organizational framework of the Court, including the extent and nature of its jurisdiction and the political and comparative legal context of its decisions. In Part Two the author examines in depth the philosophical and institutional premises of judicial decision. Using the criteria developed there, Part Three then analyzes at length the Court's case law.

THE FUNCTION OF JUDICIAL DECISION IN EUROPEAN ECONOMIC INTEGRATION

THE FUNCTION OF JUDICIAL DECISION IN EUROPEAN ECONOMIC INTEGRATION

by

CLARENCE J. MANN

L.L.B., M.A. Econ. (Yale)

Dr. jur. (Bonn)

MARTINUS NIJHOFF – THE HAGUE – 1972

Softcover reprint of the hardcover 1st edition 1972

ISBN 978-94-011-8679-7 ISBN 978-94-011-9483-9 (eBook)
DOI 10.1007/978-94-011-9483-9

FOR MARIANNE

TABLE OF CONTENTS

PART TWO

THE THEORETICAL FOUNDATIONS OF JUDICIAL DECISION

PART THREE

THE JURISPRUDENCE OF THE COURT

ACKNOWLEDGEMENTS

This manuscript was completed in part fulfilment of the requirements for the Dr. jur. degree from the Rheinischen Friedrich-Wilhelms-Universität at Bonn, Germany. It analyzes the Court of Justice of the European Communities from an institutional viewpoint, combining the disciplines of law, political science and economics.

The research was conducted essentially at the Institute for International Law at the University of Bonn. I am most grateful to Professor Ulrich Scheuner, Director of this Institute, for his constant encouragement and generous gift of time and advice throughout an extended stay in Germany. Through his patient instruction I gained a valuable grounding in the public law traditions and institutions of the Continent.

The entire period of research in Germany, except for the concluding months when I served as Assistent in the Institute for International Law, was financed by the Alexander von Humboldt Foundation. The Foundation also assisted in the cost of publishing the manuscript. At every step of the way its generosity and personal interest were a constant source of aid and comfort.

Material for the manuscript was gathered also at the Max-Planck Institute for Foreign and Public Law and International Law in Heidelberg and at the Institute for Law of the European Communities at the University of Cologne. Upon returning to the United States I also received valuable assistance from the libraries of the Law Schools at the University of Chicago and the University of Michigan, where parts of the manuscript were expanded and revised. No decisions of the Court were considered beyond mid-1970.

This graduate study, however, would never have been undertaken without the early encouragement and counseling of Dr. Robert K. Woetzel, Professor of Political Science, at Boston College. I am indebted further to Professor Dr. Kurt Ballerstedt of Bonn University, who supported my interest in comparative law during an earlier visit to Bonn, and to Professor Dr. Ernst Friesenhahn of Bonn University, former Justice of the German Federal Constitutional Court, for his insights into German constitutional law.

Shakerwood
1971

FOREWORD

The present generation lives in a time of transition. The isolated national legal order, the supreme idea of 19th Century legal science, begins to be superseded by the evolution of a wider international and transnational network of legal rules and conceptions. With the recognition of a fundamental guarantee of human rights as a binding ingredient of the framework of international law, the strict separation of the internal system of the states from the international community is transcended. To this extent, the rules of international law now exercise a direct influence upon the national legal order. In some conventional arrangements safeguarding human rights, the individual is given direct access to international protection against his own state. The piercing of national borders by transnational norms finds its strongest expression in the formation of regional communities of states which seek to develop a common fund of legal rules, concepts and principles among their members. The leading role in this direction lies with European organizations. In the Community formed by the signatories of the European Convention on Human Rights, the members accept for themselves a standard of legal guarantees for fundamental rights of the individual laid down in the Convention. The organs of the Convention, including the Court and foremost the Commission, fulfill their tasks by measuring the national laws of the member states against the basic requirements embodied in the European Convention. In this way they contribute to the elaboration of a common body of fundamental principles recognized by the European Convention and forming something like a European public order.

A similar evolution, but in a much wider field and with even greater consequences, occurs in the European Communities. Their objective is to merge their member states into a real economic unit. This goal can only be achieved if the individual nations submit to common rules and principles which guide the process of breaking down national boundaries – not only in the domain of commercial and financial relations between individuals, but also in other directions such as the free exercise of professional services in every country, the prohibitions against restrictive trade practices or the elaboration of a common transport policy. In order to build common policy the organs of the Communities have developed general legal conceptions. These also may be applied within the internal legal order of each member state, upon which the execution of Community regulations often depends. The work of the European Communities, therefore, includes a great deal of comparative legal study and beyond that a readiness to evolve common legal conceptions and principles. The Rome Treaty itself demands that the laws of the member states should be "approximated" in so far as they directly affect the operation of the Common Market (Art. 100 EEC Treaty). The task of the Communities is made easier by the fact that the European countries have much in common in their legal traditions. Their legal systems have all undergone the influence of Roman law and its medieval continuation and of the school of rational natural law of the 17th and 18th Centuries, which formed the last generally accepted system of European legal thought before the divisive effect of 19th Century nationalism. When Great Britain joins the European Economic Community, the task of legal comparison and harmonization will become even more extended and interesting, leading to a real dialogue between Anglo-Saxon and Continental legal values and traditions.

In the process of legal integration the Court of Justice of the European Communities comes to play a major role. The Treaties of the European Economic Community, the European Coal and Steel Community and the European Atomic Energy Community lay down aims and principles for action only in general and often vague terms. It is left to the Court and its interpretation of the Treaty to develop the content of Community law and to fulfill thereby a task of political and legal integration. The analysis and description of this role of judicial decision – by framing a common legal basis for the Communities, evolving a consensus on it among the member states and developing workable rules for its implementation – constitutes the main subject of the work of Dr. Mann.

The book is not a systematic survey of the decisions of the Luxembourg Court; several such guides have already been published. Dr. Mann sets out to analyze, by an extensive and critical examination of the jurisprudence, the ways and methods by which the Court has succeeded in making so decisive a contribution to the elaboration of a new transnational legal order. The difficulties of this enterprise for the Court were formidable. Often the general terms in which the Treaty is clad do not give much assistance to the judges. They have had to formulate, always with due regard to the national legal systems and their common legal heritage on which the Treaties are founded, common standards of legal behaviour for the member states as well as for individuals. Also, as Dr. Mann points out, they have had to find a consensus among the nations for newly developed concepts and principles. The author explains, in three lengthy chapters of Part Three of his work, how the Court has unfolded the aims underlying the Treaties, set them into relation with each other and harmonized them. In that way they could be applied to individual decisions and cases. The author shows that the Court had to find a common expression for such important terms as fair competition, direct or indirect subvention or governmental assistance, discrimination and restrictive or improper practices whether by individuals or corporations. In some cases the Court took over and applied legal terms derived from a national system, like détournement de pouvoir, Marktbeherrschung, or "implied powers."

In a recent publication on "English and American Judges as Lawmakers" (Oxford 1969, p. 16), the author Louis E. Jeffe points out that modern legislation limits the range of the judicial legislative role. He adds, however, that in a time of change there is a peculiar opportunity and need for creative judicial activity. This coincides exactly with the situation of the Court of Justice. Its position is shaped by the demands which arise from the evolution of a European legal order. The task of determining the secondary law of the Communities is certainly granted by the Treaties, in the first place, to the central organs of the Communities. They issue the regulations and directives for the subjects of their legal systems. But these enactments by and large are strictly limited in character and do not contribute much to the evolution of the general terms and principles of the Treaties. They leave to the Court, therefore, the further elaboration of these basic provisions and goals. In another chapter the author analyzes the reasoning by which the judges arrive at such common standards and obtain their acceptance through the consensus of the nations forming the Communities. In a final chapter, the author sets forth the various tools and methods employed by the judges in developing practicable rules for implementing the basic Treaty provisions and goals.

While the author's training and practical experience belongs to American legal science, he studied Continental legal theory and practice during a sojourn of several years in Germany. He is able, therefore, to frame his examination of the decisions of the Court of Justice by a penetrating comparative analysis of the role of the judicial function in Anglo-Saxon and Continental legal theory. Stretching over a wide range of modern Continental legal theory, Dr. Mann is able to show how closely recent European legal thought approaches the English and American Common Law school in treating similar problems and ideas. This part of the book seems to me particularly suited for those familiar with Anglo-Saxon legal background to open the door to insights into the problems of the European Communities and to a better understanding of the methods of Continental legal reasoning. This book also may serve as a guide for English and American lawyers turning to the questions of European integration, as well as a source of inspiration for specialists in the law of the European Communities who will find here an extensive, critical and often entirely new evaluation of all the important decisions of the Court of Justice.

Bonn
October 1971

Ulrich Scheuner, Director
Institute for Public International Law,
Bonn University.

PART ONE

THE ORGANIZATIONAL FRAMEWORK OF THE COURT OF JUSTICE

"I send you enclos'd the propos'd new Federal Constitution for these States .... If it succeeds, I do not see why you might not in Europe carry the Project of good Henry the 4th into Execution, by forming a Federal Union and One Grand Republick of all its different States and Kingdoms, by means of a like Convention, for we had many Interests to reconcile."
Benjamin Franklin to Ferdinand Grand (in Paris), October 22, 1787.

With the establishment of the European Communities in the 1950's, a new era has dawned for the international community as well as for Western Europe. While the three economic Communities, of coal and steel, the Common Market and atomic energy, clearly fall short of the ecstatic idealism and hopes of those early years, it would be difficult to speculate what Western Europe would be today without them. In the first decade of the Common Market, inner-Community trade has more than tripled, Community trade with the rest of the world has nearly doubled and the gross national product of the Member States has increased more than sixty percent. Indeed, the economic advantages wrought by the Common Market were so unexpected that within two years after the Treaty of Rome was signed, it was decided to accelerate its formation. The customs union was completed on July 1, 1968, a full eighteen months ahead of schedule. The next major steps, as the summit meeting at The Hague in December 1969 well demonstrates, look toward a definitive financial arrangement for agriculture, an economic and monetary union with a common currency, an autonomous Community tax base and corresponding budgetary powers subject to parliamentary control. Common policies also must be developed for all the related economic sectors in order to remove the remaining obstacles to the free movement of labor, services and capital. Thus far, the economics of European integration has been impressive.

The really important question, however, is what Europe will make of its new-found wealth. Will it furnish the basis for a higher level of economic integration and, ultimately, political unification. Or will it be dissipated through political indifference, special interest pressures and latent nationalism in the Member States? The first signs since The Hague summit are hopeful. The European Economic Community completed its transitional phase on January 1, 1970. The negotiations with Britain, Ireland, Denmark and Norway have now reached a point that the enlargement of Community membership from six to ten countries can be expected with confidence within the next two years. Further, on February 8-9 the Council of Ministers agreed on an initial three-year stage, beginning January 1, 1971, for achieving an economic and monetary union within the Community by 1980. If so, then as Commission Member Ralf Dahrendorf recently declared, the 1970's will be a "European Decade."

The question of the future of Western Europe of course is a political one. The question is political, one of political organization with constitutional dimensions. It must be met not only with innovationary governmental structures on a supranational level, but also with structures capable of growth and of challenging the Member States with the need and direction for further development. These have emerged in the form of a Commission, of a Council of Ministers and a European Parliament and of a Court of Justice governing all three economic Communities. While these institutions constitute viable organs of independent Community action, they also represent the executive, legislative and judicial rudiments for a more consolidated form of political organization. That is to say, the potential for further political development exists, but it remains unrealized. The nature and extent of European integration has not yet been determined.

In this context what is the function, the enduring contribution, of judicial decision in European economic integration? What are the real limits and legitimate scope of that function? This can be determined only by examining, in theory and practice, the Court of Justice of the European Communities. Part One of this study sets forth the organizational context, both institutional and jurisdictional, of the Community Court. It further seeks to establish the evolutionary nature of the Community legal orders and the disciplined constitutional framework, including the division and balance of Community powers, within which the Court's mandate of judicial review is exercised. Given this organizational context, what are the tasks of the Court of Justice in the interpretation and application of Community law? These are established in Part Two through an examination of the theoretical foundations of judicial decision. Being derivatives of both the concept of law and its institutional setting, these tasks may be defined as the continuing search for purpose, authority and practicability in an imperfect and ever-developing positive law. It then remains, in Part Three, to consider these tasks in detail by an analysis of the Court's jurisprudence. This offers a test of the theory of judicial decision presented in Part Two, as well as an opportunity to assess the potential and concrete contribution of the Court of Justice to legal development and economic integration in the European Communities.

CHAPTER I

THE LEGAL CHARACTER OF THE COMMUNITIES

The legal character of the three European Communities has led to an endless controversy. While the Communities are based on international treaties, the subject matter of their regulation is most akin to that of municipal law. Further, taken individually the distinguishing marks of these Treaties may be found in various other international organizations, but taken as a whole the Treaties represent a distinct development in the history of international organizations. This development has been viewed from the standpoints of international, supranational, and federal organization,[1] a controversy which this study will not attempt to resolve. Rather, by comparing the Community[2] Treaties to municipal and international organization, it may be possible to pinpoint this development and to assess its essen-

[1] The literature on this question is already vast. Among those proceeding from the traditional international law view, see Bindschedler, *Rechtsfragen der europäischen Einigung,* 36f., 201, 204 (1954); Paul de Visscher, "La CECA et les Etats Membres," 2 *Actes Officiels du Congrès sur la CECA* (Stresa) 7, 34f. and following Ch. II (1957); and Scheuner, "Die Rechtsetzungsbefugnis internationaler Gemeinschaften," in *Festschrift Alfred Verdross,* 229, 230–34 (1960). Among those proceeding from a federal or federal-like view, especially during the early years of the ECSC, see La Pradelle, "Le Plan Schuman et les résistances de la souveraineté," 16/7 *Nouvelle Revue de l'Economie contemporaine,* 19 (1951); Ophüls, "Juristische Grundgedanken des Schumanplans," *N.J.W.*, 289 (1951), and, more recently, "Zwischen Völkerrecht und Staatlichem Recht," 4 *Juristen JB.,* 137, 151–56 (1963–64). Whichever of these starting points or emphases, the majority of writers arrive at some concept of 'supranational' organization. See references in Schlochauer, "Das Verhältnis des Rechts der EWG zu den nationalen Rechtsordnungen der Mitgliedstaaten," 11 *Arch. vr.* 1, 2 (1963–64); and Hoffman, "Das Verhältnis des Rechts der Europäischen Gemeinschaften zum Recht der Mitgliedstaaten, 13 *Die öff. Verw.,* 433f (1967). This means simply that the three Communities, although resting on international Treaties, possess a minimum of institutional structure and organizational autonomy and the authority to make laws which are directly binding on Member State authorities and individuals. See Secs. 2 and 4 of this Chapter.

[2] The term "Community," when employed here as an adjective and not otherwise stated, refers to all three European Communities.

tial importance for the function of the Court of Justice in the Communities.

In the field of international law, the Communities represent an advanced degree of international organization with which the international community has had little experience. The traditional form of international organization, with great variation from case to case, rests on a multilateral treaty offering membership to all States[3] interested in and willing to support the limited purposes which the organization serves. Such treaties typically establish a council of member-state representatives meeting periodically for consultation and decision-making, a permanent central office of some kind to advise the council and to administer and coordinate council decisions, and perhaps an assembly resembling a diplomatic conference, but with little or no legislative power.[4] Except for the League of Nations and the United Nations, which were established to serve broad peace-keeping purposes, international organizations generally have been limited to the gathering and distribution of certain information, to the solution of certain technical problems, e.g. coordinating mail and communication, or to the establishment of international standards in very limited areas, e.g. minimum labor standards. Decisions and policy of any importance typically are left to the council; its decisions either are reached unanimously or must be implemented by national legislation to be binding.[5]

The organization and the scope and intensity of Community powers break with this practice in several important ways. To the extent that they do, they call into question the general applicability to the Communities of traditional principles of international law. At the same time, they suggest a reason for drawing on municipal law principles, particularly those pertaining to constitutional interpretation, in the construction of the Treaties.

1. THE 'COMMUNITY' IDEA

The establishment of the European Coal and Steel Community (ECSC) in 1951 set in motion the first "supranational"[6] fusion of vital economic

[3] Eagleton, *International Government*, 179, (3rd. ed., 1957), emphasizes this "universal" element. International organizations and other non-State entities, as a "territory or group of territories" (World Meteorological Organization), are also occasionally accepted into membership. See Bowett, *The Law of International Institutions*, 101f. (1963).

[4] Compare the "deliberative" and "recommendatory" powers of the League of Nations and United Nations Assemblies. See Bowett, *op. cit.*, p. 42ff.

[5] Perhaps the two most important exceptions to this are the decree authority of the European Danube Commission (Paris Treaty of March 30, 1856, Art. 17) and the jurisdictional competence of the Rhine Commission, acting in an appellate capacity for decisions of its Court (Convention of Mannheim of Oct. 17, 1868, Art. 38).

[6] ECSC Art. 9, par. 6, as originally phrased, employed this term. The term, however, has been deleted by operation of the "fusion Treaty" discussed at note 32 *infra*.

powers among European States. Although the following initiative for political integration through a European Defense Community met defeat in the French Parliament, the advance toward European unity has been kept alive by a return to functional lines. On March 25, 1957, the six Member States of the ECSC – France, Germany, Italy and the three Benelux Countries – signed the Rome Treaties, bringing into existence the European Economic Community (EEC or Common Market) and the European Atomic Energy Community (Euratom). The most vague and yet perhaps the most valuable distinguishing mark of these Treaties lies in the idea of "community" which they embody. A sense of community – a consensus on some fundamental values and a willingness to enforce them – is the indisputable prerequisite for a viable legal order.[7] *Ubi societas ibi ius.* To what extent is this social consciousness reflected in the European Communities?

Tentatively, the answer must read: six geographically proximate States, with a common cultural heritage, have established through the Treaties certain common aims, to be achieved by common institutions on the basis of common markets. These Communities are at once too narrow and too broad to be fully grasped by the concept of "community" in international law. On the one hand, they do not embrace such fundamental functions as maintaining the peace or guaranteeing the political and territorial integrity of the Member States. They may be thought, however, to contribute greatly to these ends, for the new distribution of economic power among the Member States cannot fail to influence their political relations. On the other hand, they reach far into the reserved domain of the Member States. Proceeding from the concept of common markets, the Treaties mark-off important but limited aspects of Member State economies for common policy and control.

The scope of these markets is defined, in the case of the ECSC and Euratom, by reference to certain products and their producers[8] and, in much broader terms for the EEC, by reference to various economic sectors.[9] At the same time, whereas the ECSC emphasizes a common and competi-

[7] Lauterpacht-Oppenheim, *International Law,* vol. I, 11f (8th ed., 1955). Zimmern, "International Law and Social Consciousness," 20 *The Grotius Society,* 25, esp. 40–44 (1935) offers some critical insight into this question. See McDougal and Lasswell, "The Identification and Appraisal of Diverse Systems of Public Order," in McDougal and Associates, *Studies in World Public Order,* 3 (1960) and the notion of "public order" (p. 15f.).

[8] In particular, ECSC Arts. 80 and 81 and their references include coal, iron ore, steel and scrap. These terms are defined in Annexes I–III of the ECSC Treaty. See Judgment 9 and 12/60, 7 Rspr. 427, 461 (1961). See also Euratom Arts. 1 (2) and 2.

[9] See, in particular, EEC Art. 3.

tive market *throughout* the Member States, the EEC is restricted primarily to securing competition in *interstate* trade.[10] The concept of the market in the EEC, Bebr suggests,[11] is "somewhat less common and less competitive than that of the ECSC . . . The EEC seeks to bring about a rapprochement of national economies and markets . . ." This general difference, however, should not be exaggerated; a moment's reflection on the development of the Commerce Clause in United States constitutional and antitrust practice[12] suggests that, when the time is ripe, the "interstate" clause may prove a powerful ally in the extension of Community powers. Within these limits, but to differing degrees, these Treaties seek to establish the free flow of economic factors, goods and services by removing and preventing the establishment of Member State and private barriers to interstate and, where necessary, intra-state trade and competition.

The mere absence of trade restrictions, however, does not imply or secure economic integration. In contrast to the more limited customs union approach, the framers of the Treaties recognized the interdependence of social and economic policy for economic integration. Integration has come to mean more than merely larger markets; it entails the coalescence and assimilation of economic forces: not their mere addition, but their absolute intensification through a re-organization of their economic framework.[13] Thus, by the coordination or direction of Member State economic policy, the Communities seek to raise living standards,[14] rationalize and expand production and increase employment.[15] The greater scope of the EEC, however, permits it to go much further and aim, in addition, at a "harmonious development of economic activities, a continuous and balanced expansion, an increased stability, ... and closer relations between its Member States."[16] In view of the increasing interdependence of national economies, therefore, the Communities can offer economic advantages and control economic ef-

10 See ECSC Arts. 4, 65, 66 and 80; EEC Arts. 3(a), (c) and 3(f) in light of Art. 85 on market competition. The major exception to this may be found in EEC Article 7 which prohibits "any discrimination on the grounds of nationality."

11 Bebr, *Judicial Control of the European Communities,* 5 (1962).

12 See e. g. Ehmke, *Wirtschaft und Verfassung,* Ch. 1, esp. pp. 193–95 (1961).

13 Müller-Armack, "Fragen der Europäischen Integration," in *Festgabe Ludwig Erhard,* 531, 532–33 (1957). See also Meyer-Cording, "Die Europäische Integration als geistiger Entwicklungsprozess," 10 *Arch. VR.,* 42, 51–54 (1962–63); Hochbaum, *Das Diskriminierungs- und Subventionsverbot in der EGKS und EWG,* 43f (1962).

14 Euratom, being more limited, rests primarily on this goal and that of developing and controlling the commercial use of nuclear energy.

15 ECSC Arts 2 and 3; EEC Arts. 2 and 3.

16 EEC Art. 2, in part. This goal is spelled-out further in EEC Article 104, the so-called "magisches Dreieck" of high employment, stable prices and a balanced trade and payments account.

fects far beyond the reach of a single Member State. The whole is greater than the sum of its parts.

Proof of this lies in the contrasting structure of the ECSC and EEC.[17] The former establishes a highly normative framework for controlling and guiding the development of the strategically vital coal and steel industry. It establishes a common market, subject to certain transitional measures, with emphasis on market stability and efficient but guided growth. Being limited to only a few products, it is subject to fluctuating economic repercussions from sectors outside its control. The ECSC, therefore, has been compensated with a series of indirect and direct measures to influence the coal and steel industry, beginning with investment incentives and price subsidy and culminating in price-fixing and production quotas for times of economic crisis.[18] The exercise of these far-reaching powers in the various Treaty provisions, however, is tied to the realization of general objectives (ECSC Articles 2 and 3) in terms of a hierarchy of means (ECSC Articles 5 and 57). Combining a market economy with planning, the ECSC provides "a controlled system of free competition."[19]

In comparison, the EEC has been 'de-institutionalized'.[20] The enormous problems of integrating major economic sectors could not be so readily anticipated or even broadly resolved at the time the Treaty was written. The EEC Treaty, therefore, is primarily a transitional agreement, determining the specific stages of economic integration in the course of which concrete policies are to be developed by Member State representatives in the Council of Ministers. Originally, for instance, the Common Market was to be realized within 12 years, although provision was made in EEC Article 8 for extending this period if necessary. An extension was never required. To the contrary, within 2 years after the EEC was established the EEC Council accelerated the creation of the Common Market. As a result, by July 4, 1968, all inner-community tariffs and quantitative restrictions were re-

[17] Euratom meets problems entirely different from the ECSC and EEC, for the production and distribution of atomic energy is not burdened with the traditions and imperfections of an existing market structure. It was clear from the beginning that the commercial use of atomic energy must be made subject to strict controls.

[18] See ECSC Arts. 53 (subsidy arrangements), 54ff (investment and financial aid), 59f (production quotas and priorities) and 61f (price controls).

[19] Marjolin, *Europe and the United States in the World Economy*, 51 (1953). See also Meade and others, *Case Studies in European Economic Union*, 200–202 (1962).

[20] Meyer-Cording, *op. cit.*, p. 57. For this reason, the EEC Treaty – in comparison to the highly normative ECSC Treaty – has been termed a "traité cadre" or "skeletal" Treaty.

moved and the common customs vis-à-vis non-member States became fully applicable.[21]

The shift of decision-making power to the EEC Council[22] was attended by a general shift in economic philosophy. The broad scope of the Common Market made its economic structure susceptible to the more liberal "soziale Marktwirtschaft" philosophy of Alfred Müller-Armack.[23] It may be seen as the necessary prerequisite for economic integration on a broad scale.

> It may be taken as a proper assumption that – the more the different interests of the countries are subject to complicated centralized direction (Dirigismus), the more protective provisions and special regulations are created, the more States are forced to do things in the interest of their partners that they themselves would not like to do – a common market will have even significant antagonistic effects.[24]

Through this market structure, based on the full establishment of competition in interstate trade, private economic forces are released which have been long suppressed by national trade barriers and restrictions among private competitors. Whether in terms of the disciplined, guided coal and steel market or of the more liberal philosophy of the Common Market, therefore, both Communities introduce structural changes transcending the separate powers of the Member States.

This intense effort to forge Community policies out of previously separate national interests is further buttressed by a common cultural heritage.[25] Concretely seen, this is reflected in the legal systems of the Member States which, although varying greatly depending on the field of law, share common ideals and methods.[26] The *ius publicum europaeum* of the 17th through the 19th centuries formed the very basis of the present world-wide com-

[21] See the EEC Council Decision of July 26, 1966, in *Amtsblatt,* 2971 (September 21, 1966). Certain restrictions remain, however, as to agricultural products in Annex II of the EEC Treaty. Moreover, even as to the other products under the Treaty, trade may still be hampered by the public health provisions, technical requirements and customs procedures of the Member States.

[22] See Section 2 *infra.*

[23] Meyer-Cording, *op. cit.,* pp. 54–57.

[24] Müller-Armack, *op. cit.,* p. 534. It should be noted, however, that the Benelux Economic Union successfully developed on the basis of the relatively free market economy in Belgium and of the much more planned economy of Holland.

[25] Bonnefour, *L'Europe en face de son destin* (1952), sketches the historical development toward European unity. Cf. Beloff, *Europe and the Europeans* (1957).

[26] Strauss, *Fragen der Rechtsangleichung im Rahmen der Europäischen Gemeinschaften,* 9–11 (1959). Wieacker, *Privatrechtsgeschichte der Neuzeit* (1952), offers a thorough investigation of the intellectual background of German legal development in a European context.

munity of international law.[27] Its spirit emerges in the European Convention on Human Rights whose law and institutions define and defend in 14 European States, including 5 of the 6 Member States,[28] the fundamental requirements of democratic government.[29] Finally, as further evidence of an existing community, all six Member States have allied themselves in such collective defense efforts as the Western European Union and, with the exception of France's withdrawal, the North Atlantic Treaty Organization.

It may be concluded, therefore, that certain fundamental prerequisites for Community integration do exist among the six Member States. They are unique enough to suggest the danger of viewing the Communities simply as extensions of the international law community. They emphasize the need to view the Communities in their own terms, for each Community has meaning and effectiveness basically because of its peculiar relation to the six Member States. It remains to be seen, however, to what extent the Community institutions, the Community legal orders and the inner dynamics of economic integration can turn these prerequisites into a living and developing Community consensus.

2. COMMUNITY INDEPENDENCE IN POLICY FORMATION

The victory of the common interests of the European Communities over the special interests of individuals and Member States can be assured only through Community institutions. To this end, each Treaty originally established an Assembly of representatives chosen from the ranks of the national legislatures, a Court of Justice, a Council of Ministers representing the Member State governments, a High Authority (ECSC) or a Commission (EEC and Euratom) performing the executive and/or quasi-legislative function(s), and one or more consultative committees and specialized bodies.[30] In March 1957, with the formation of the EEC and Euratom, each of the

[27] See Carl Schmitt, *Der Nomos der Erde im Völkerrecht des Jus Publicum Europaeum,* Pt. III (1950).

[28] The Convention, which establishes a Commission and Court for implementing the particular rights, binds all the Member States of the Communities, except for France, plus Austria, Cyprus, Denmark, Greece, Iceland, Ireland, Norway, Sweden, Turkey and the United Kingdom.

[29] This prerequisite is stressed by point 2 in "Thesen der juristischen Arbeitsgruppe des 'Europäischen Kolloquiums'," 16 *Europa-Archiv,* 595f. (1961).

[30] These latter types of institutions reflect an attempt to represent in a consultative capacity the interests of producers, workers, consumers and the general interests in the Communities. Thus, ECSC Article 18 establishes a Consultative Committee, EEC Articles 4 and 193 and Euratom Article 165 an Economic and Social Committee. In addition, the EEC has a few highly specialized bodies, such as the European Investment Bank (Art. 129f) and the Monetary Committee (Art. 105(2)).

first two institutions was fused to create one General Assembly or European Parliament and one Court of Justice.[31] As of July 1, 1967, the same occurred for the policy-making and executive organs of the Communities.[32] On that day, one Council and one Commission of the European Communities emerged from its three counterparts. This represents thus far primarily an institutional simplification and reorganization,[33] for the powers and competence of each of these common Community organs continue to depend wholly on the provisions of the individual Treaties. For this reason, while this study adopts the new terminology, matters of substance remain essentially the same. Even the original terminology must be maintained where, as in Part Three, the jurisprudence of the Court of Justice is examined in detail.

This Section focuses attention on the powers possessed by the main policy-forming institutions of the Communities. (The Court of Justice is treated separately in the following Section.) At the present stage of Community development, this must exclude the European Parliament which remains of secondary importance. While the Rome Treaties call for parliamentary elections on the basis of "direct universal suffrage,"[34] that provision has not yet been implemented. Instead, representatives are chosen wholly by, and from, the individual Member State legislatures. Moreover, by virtue of the rather limited powers it possesses, the Parliament is little more than a deliberative and advisory body at the moment. Its major weapon – the power to dissolve the Commission[35] – is so extreme as to be of little use in the daily formation of Community policy. By continual prodding and the discreet deployment of its residual power to mobilize public opinion, however, the Parliament has steadily gained some influence, especially with the new Commission and its predecessors which lack the popular forum Parliament has to offer. Moreover, the Resolution of the Council of Ministers of December 1969 now grants Parliament increasingly effective budgetary control, particularly after 1975.

[31] Articles 1 through 4 of the Convention Relating to Certain Institutions Common to the European Communities, executed together with the Rome Treaties on March 25, 1957.

[32] See Articles 1 through 19 of the Treaty Establishing a Single Council and a Single Commission of the European Communities, signed April 8, 1965 (sometimes referred to as the "fusion Treaty") and concluded pursuant to Treaty amendment procedures set forth in ECSC Article 96, EEC Article 236 and Euratom Article 204.

[33] Articles 1, par. 2, and 9, par. 2, of the fusion Treaty expressly provide that each of these new bodies "shall exercise the powers and competences" devolving upon their original counterparts under the conditions laid down in the individual Treaties.

[34] EEC Art. 138(3) and Euratom Art. 108(3). This would be true also for the ECSC via Article 1 of the Convention cited in note 31 *supra*.

[35] See ECSC Article 24(2), as amended by the fusion Treaty, which corresponds now to EEC Article 144, par. 1, and Euratom Article 114, par. 1.

The crucial distinction to be kept in mind lies between the central organs of Community policy formation, the Council of Ministers and the Commission. The former represents the Member State governments, but at the same time is bound to the realization of Treaty objectives.[36] It must exercise its powers "in the manner provided" in the Treaties: [37] this may be, as in the ECSC, primarily "to harmonize" the action of the Commission with Member State governments or, as in the EEC, to take a most active policy-making hand in "ensuring the achievement of the objectives laid down in the Treaty." [38] The Commission like its predecessors, on the other hand, owes allegiance solely to the Communities. Although being primarily the executive organ of the Communities, it possesses some independent quasi-legislative powers and also participates to varying degrees in the exercise of other such powers by the Council. Despite these differences, as will be seen, the interdependence between these organs forms the heart of Community policy formation. For this reason, the Council and Commission "shall consult together and shall decide on methods of collaboration by mutual agreement." [39]

The nature and degree of Community independence in policy formation must be examined under two related standards: the degree of organizational autonomy and the scope of independent quasi-legislative powers.[40] Although neither of these standards has been fully realized in the Communities, both together are present to a degree far in advance of traditional international organization. The first of these two standards concerns only the Commission and its predecessors, for the Council is as much a creature of the Member States as of the Communities. This standard has two facets: the selection and loyalties of the members of the new Commission, and their independence from Member State directives. The Community character of this organ is guaranteed in that each State is assured one but no more than two of the nine members on the Commission; each member must be a national of some Member State.[41] These members, as well as the President and three Vice Presidents chosen from the ranks of the Commission, are appointed by the

[36] Friauf, *Die Staatenvertretung in supranationalen Gemeinschaften*, 127 (1960). See also EEC Commission, First Gen. Rep. 14 (German ed. 1958).

[37] ECSC Art. 26. See also Euratom Art. 115.

[38] EEC Art. 145.

[39] Article 15 of the fusion Treaty, now replacing EEC Article 162 and Euratom Article 131.

[40] Cf. Roselieb, "Zur Frage der Supranationalität," 12 *Österr. Z. öff. R.*, 461, 488–89 (1962–63), who distinguishes between "institutional" and "functional" independence. The latter encompasses the quasi-legislative powers discussed here.

[41] Art. 10(1) of the fusion Treaty.

unanimous agreement of the Member State governments; while in each case renewable, the terms of the members are four years and those of the officers are limited to two years.[42] During their terms of office, each member is expressly required to perform its duties, exclusive of all other paid or unpaid occupations, in complete independence from Member State governments and other influence, and "in the general interest of the Communities." The Member States, for their part, expressly undertake "to respect this principle and not to seek to influence the members of the Commission in the performance of their duties."[43] This organizational independence is safeguarded by the Court of Justice.[44] While these provisions do not distinguish the Commission from the institutional requirements of certain other international organizations, such as the Secretariat of the United Nations,[45] they do establish a fundamental prerequisite for independent policy formation within the Communities.

The second standard – the scope of independent quasi-legislative powers in the Communities – is considerably more complicated. To the extent that it is fulfilled, it distinguishes the Communities clearly from traditional international organization. Although somewhat imprecise and freighted with meaning, the term "quasi-legislative" usually refers to governmental powers which in their breadth and impact exceed the traditional scope of administrative or executive powers, but which have been entrusted to non-parliamentary bodies. It has been used by the Community Court and writers[46] to describe those economic powers of Community organs which, although broad, are not general in nature, for their exercise is bound closely in the Treaties by stipulated conditions and objectives. This, as will be seen, is most clearly true of certain independent powers of the Commission and its predecessor, the High Authority, under the ECSC Treaty.

[42] Arts. 11 and 14, par. 1, of the fusion Treaty. For a valuable discussion of the organization and internal working of the new Commission, see Knöpfle, "Organisation und Arbeitsweise der Gemeinsamen Kommission der Europäischen Gemeinschaften," 3 *Europarecht,* 30 (1968).

[43] Art. 10(2) of the fusion Treaty.

[44] Arts. 10(2), par. 3, and 13 of the fusion Treaty.

[45] United Nations Charter Art. 100. See Bowett, *The Law of International Institutions,* 82ff (1963).

[46] See Judgments 8/55, 2 Rspr. 197, 227 (1955–56); 18/57, 5 Rspr. 89, 112 (1958–59); and 20/59, 6 Rspr. 681, 713 (1960), speaking of "legislative power." See also Reuter, *La C.E.C.A.,* 99 (1953); Mathijsen, *Le Droit de la C.E.C.A.,* 47 (1958), speaking of a "veritable legislation"; Bebr, *Judicial Control of the European Communities,* 10–14, 38 (1962); Ophüls, "Deutsches Zustimmungsgesetz zum EWG-Vertrag teilweise verfassungswidrig *AWD,* 65, 67 (1964); and Catalano, in *Collège d'Europe, Droit Communautaire et Droit National,* 47f (1965), who considers it perfectly legitimate under Italian and German law to refer to EEC Regulations as "laws."

One further complication is that, depending on the Community in question, these powers are distributed variously among the Council and the Commission. Thus, it is necessary to determine not only who exercises them, but also to what extent they may be exercised independently of the Member States.[47] To the extent that the Commission has independent control over these powers, its supranational character is evident. And the more they are allocated to the unanimous decision of the Council, the more the character of these powers belongs to the traditional forms of international organization. Between these two extremes, moreover, lies a third group of quasi-legislative powers which can be exercised only by the Council and the Commission in combination. This is true, for instance, of the broad range of powers in the EEC where the Council and Commission hold a veto over each other. In that case, it is essential to consider the nature of the vote required in Council concurrence: as it departs from the strict requirement of unanimity, it tends to favor the supranational character of the Communities. In all three Communities, however, it is clear that as the scope of Community powers broadens to include greater segments of the national economies, the Council assumes an increasingly greater role in Community policy formation. A separate assessment of the quasi-legislative powers under the ECSC and the Rome Treaties is necessary to demonstrate their differing degrees of independence in Community policy formation.

In the ECSC, the Commission is "responsible for assuring the achievement of the purposes stated in the Treaty."[48] In most instances, these acts are independent entirely of the Council. In an executive capacity, the Commission can gather information from firms,[49] float bonds,[50] support private investment programs[51] and enforce prices and competition standards.[52] At the same time, in some matters of crucial economic importance, such as regulating monopolistic pricing practices,[53] cartels and combinations[54] and

[47] For this reason, the lengthier, more recent studies on Community powers of legislation have carefully distinguished between the various types of "legislation" and their nature. See Tosato, *I Regolamenti delle Comunità Europee*, Ch. 6 (1965); Wagner, *Grundbegriffe des Beschlussrechts der Europäischen Gemeinschaften*, esp. 257–82 (1965); Kovar, *Le pouvoir réglementaire de la CECA*, 325–28 (1964); and Rabe, *Das Verordnungsrecht der Europäischen Wirtschaftsgemeinschaft*, 23ff (1963).

[48] ECSC Art. 8.

[49] ECSC Art. 47.

[50] ECSC Art. 49 (2).

[51] ECSC Art. 54.

[52] ECSC Art. 61; and ECSC Arts. 65 (2), (3), (4) and (5), 66 and 67 (2) and (3).

[53] The Commission may define prohibited price discrimination pursuant to ECSC Article 60 (1).

[54] The Commission may define the control of an enterprise (ECSC Art. 66 (1)) and determine which agreements, decisions or practices of enterprises must be communi-

levying and collecting annual rates on enterprises,[55] the Commission possesses a quasi-legislative power conditioned only in some instances on previous consultation with the Council[56] and/or the Consultative Committee.[57] Nevertheless, the exercise of this power is carefully circumscribed by limited means in conjunction with general Treaty objectives.[58]

As the acts of the Commission depart from the tasks of eliminating restraints within the Treaty area and take on the more positive role of economic direction – such as aiding firms in periods of transition[59] setting production quotas,[60] distribution priorities[61] and export quotas[62] in times of crisis, and increasing taxes above the maximum rate[63] – only then does Council approval become mandatory. The degree of Council approval increases gradually, from absolute majority vote to unanimity,[64] the more directly Community acts touch other areas of the national economies or subject them to regulation. Thus, questions of tariff policy,[65] certain matters of Community financing for private firms,[66] the addition of new products to Community regulation,[67] measures to supplement the Treaty[68] the so-called "small Treaty revision"[69] and the admission of new Member States to the ECSC[70] are placed firmly in the hands of the Council, for they require unanimous approval. Despite the narrow confines of ECSC regulation and the reservation of certain matters to Council concurrence, therefore, the Commission possesses certain important quasi-legislative powers which it may exercise independently of both the Council and the Member States.

In the EEC and Euratom, on the other hand, the Commission emerged primarily as an executive body with little or no independent quasi-legisla-

cated to the Commission (ECSC Art. 65(3)) in order to prevent restrictive business practices under ECSC Article 65(1).

55 These rates may not exceed 1% of the average value of the various products under the Community jurisdiction, unless Council approval is first received. ECSC Arts. 49 and 50(2).

56 ECSC Arts. 60 (2) and 66 (1).

57 ECSC Art. 60 (2).

58 ECSC Arts. 2, 3 and 5.

59 ECSC Art. 56 (2) (b)

60 ECSC Art. 58 (1).

61 ECSC Arts. 59 (1) and (2).

62 ECSC Art. 59 (5).

63 ECSC Art. 50 (2).

64 ECSC Art. 28 defines the different degrees of Council approval.

65 ECSC Art. 72 (1).

66 ECSC Art. 54 (2).

67 ECSC Art. 81 (2).

68 ECSC Art. 95 (1).

69 ECSC Arts. 95 (3) and (4).

70 ECSC Art. 98.

tive power. In contrast to the ECSC, the center of power in the EEC and, to a lesser extent, in Euratom shifts to the Council. Whereas the Commission is given the narrower role of assuring "the functioning and development of the Common Market," [71] the Council is made explicitly responsible for the "achievement of the objectives laid down by the Treaty." [72] Absent a delegation of powers by the Council in the EEC and Euratom,[73] therefore, the Commission is deprived largely of those broad quasi-legislative powers it possesses in the ECSC.[74] They retain, however, an almost exclusive right to initiate the quasi-legislative powers of the Council and, thus, to control the course of Community policy. In this sense, they represent the driving power behind the Council, although the Council can check it at any time.

Despite this division of quasi-legislative powers between Council and Commission, the EEC has achieved on the whole a respectable degree of independent policy formation. This is reflected in the breadth of those EEC powers, which may be exercised only at the initiative of the Commission and frequently with only a simple or qualified majority vote of the Council. In the first place, the breadth and scope of the EEC – in contrast to both ECSC and Euratom [75] – means a broader quasi-legislative power [76] for the Council and possibly for the Commission should the Council chose to delegate it such power.[77] Thus, even a small degree of independence in policy-making carries a substantial impact. Secondly, the quasi-legislative power of the Council in the EEC [78] is bound, in most cases,[79] to the Commissions's pro-

[71] EEC Art. 155. See also Euratom Art. 124.

[72] EEC Art. 145. By comparison, in Euratom the Council (Art. 115) possesses a more modest general authority, resembling the ECSC.

[73] Such delegations are permitted under EEC Article 155 and Euratom Article 124. They have occurred on several occasions. See Rabe, *op. cit.* (n. 47), pp. 26 and 108–113 (1963); Roselieb, *op. cit.*, (n. 40), p. 502f.

[74] There are some minor exceptions e.g., EEC Article 48 (3) d).

[75] By and large, the executive powers prevail in Euratom. The Council, however, may modify the exclusive Community ownership of certain fissionable material (Euratom Art. 90), establish common custom tariffs for certain products and equipment (Euratom Art. 92, par. 2), grant certain fiscal advantages and some exemptions to joint enterprises (Euratom Art. 48) and take action in all those instances in which action appears necessary for the operation of the Treaty but is not provided for (Euratom Art. 203).

[76] Bebr, *op. cit.* (n. 46), p. 10.

[77] See note 73 *supra*.

[78] Euratom is similar. See note 75 *supra*.

[79] In the following few cases the Council is granted an independent power of decision: suspension of tariff reduction schedule during transition period only (EEC Art. 28); certain delicate aspects of the Community transportation policy (EEC Arts. 75(3) and 76); and granting reciprocal assistance to Member States having balance of payments difficulties (EEC Art. 108(2)).

posals. These cases include: modifications in the periodic reduction of tariffs[80] and in the percentage increase in global import quotas,[81] broad powers to elaborate the principles governing competition[82] and a "necessary and proper" clause as to acts whose necessity was not foreseen in the Treaty.[83] This right of initiative is safeguarded in the Treaties by permitting only a unanimous Council to amend a Commission proposal.[84] In effect, a Community will is expressed whether the Commission's proposals are accepted intact or amended, since political realities would rarely permit Community policy to represent more than a broad consensus of the Member States' interests.[85]

Finally, much of the EEC Council's quasi-legislative power in the EEC may be exercised by simple and qualified majorities.[86] Although the simple majority governs primarily questions of form, it does reach questions of substance:[87] e.g., measures effecting the free movement of labor[88] and establishing the conditions and limits for gathering information necessary to

[80] EEC Art. 14(7). During the transition period the Council alone may suspend this process, but after the transition period only on proposal of the Commission. See EEC Art. 28.

[81] EEC Art. 33(8).

[82] This includes not only defining the principles through Regulations or Directives (EEC Arts. 7, par. 2, and 87), but also establishing a system of fines and penalties (EEC Art. 87 (2) a)), determining their scope of application to the various economic sectors (EEC Art. 87(2) c)), defining "the respective responsibilities of the Commission and the Court of Justice" in applying these Regulations or Directives (EEC Art. 87(2) d)), and determining the relation of these acts to the Member States municipal law (EEC Art. 87(2) e)).

[83] EEC Art. 235.

[84] EEC Art. 149, par. 1, and Euratom Art. 119, par. 1.

[85] See Jaenicke, "Der Übernationale Charakter der EWG," 19 *Z. ausl. öff. R.* 153, 196 (1958), who sees in this power of amendment "eine notwendige Ergänzung" to the functions of the Community organs, "damit sich die Wirtschaftspolitik der Gemeinschaft veränderen oder unvorhergesehenen Situationen anpassen kann."

It has been contended, however, that this possibility of amendment, even by a unanimous Council, undermines the supranational character of the EEC by infringing on the Commission's exclusive right of initiative. This would permit a re-writing of the Commission's proposals in terms of the least common denominator of Member State interests. See Roselieb, *op. cit.* (n. 40), p. 517. Real as the danger may be, it must be remembered that the EEC Treaty leaves considerable room for political play. Indeed, this is the essence of economic integration. Should the Council stray from its Treaty obligations, however, it may be called to account before the Community Court. See text *infra*. Ch. II, Section 2.

[86] True also of Euratom; in stark contrast to the EEC, however, all of the Regulations of Euratom up to the spring of 1963 were promulgated by simple majority acts of the Council. See Roselieb, *id.*, p. 505.

[87] See Wohlfarth et al., *Die EWG: Kommentar zum Vertrag,* Art. 148, Anm. 2 (1960). A simple majority is a vote of 4 of the 6 Ministers in the Council.

[88] EEC Art. 49, in conjunction with Art. 148(1).

the tasks of the Commission.[89] A qualified majority[90] governs most Council decisions in the EEC concerning, among others, Regulations and Directives for removing discrimination on the basis of nationality,[91] for assisting in the adjustment of internal[92] and external[93] tariff problems, for regulating Member State subsidies to private firms[94] and for implementing the Social Fund.[95] Leaving to one side those matters subject to unanimous Council approval,[96] it is fair to conclude that the quasi-legislative powers of the Council in the EEC control important aspects of Member State economies. This became more evident as the EEC moved into the later stages of transition. As this occurred, the requirement of unanimity for many important Council decisions was reduced gradually to a qualified majority,[97] thereby abolishing the veto power of any one Member State and giving the Commission considerably more weight in Council decisions.

In Euratom, on the other hand, the prevalence of executive powers combined with the narrow scope of Treaty objectives requires a far more modest conclusion. Its "quasi-legislative" powers are limited to modifying the exclusive Community ownership of special fissionable material, establishing common customs tariffs for certain products and equipment essential for the production of atomic energy, and granting some fiscal advantages and other exemptions to joint enterprises.[98] It is by far the weakest of the three Communities.

As a whole, therefore, the ECSC and EEC possess a respectable degree of organizational autonomy and independent quasi-legislative powers. In view of their ability to promulgate Community policies, notwithstanding the special interests of a minority of Member States, they demonstrate a marked advance in international organization. From this standpoint, the absolute independence of one Community organ is not so important as the combined

[89] EEC Art. 213, in conjunction with Art. 148(1.)

[90] I.e., Member State votes are weighted (EEC Art. 148 and Euratom Art. 118) to reflect the economic and political importance of the States.

[91] EEC Art. 7(2) as the general provision: EEC Art. 79(3) in respect to transport.

[92] EEC Arts. 21(2), 14(2) c), (5).

[93] EEC Art. 21(1).

[94] EEC Art. 94.

[95] EEC Art. 127.

[96] See EEC Arts. 14(7), 51, 54(1), 59, par. 2, 63(1), 70(1), 87(1), 99, par. 2, 100, par. 1., 103(2), 235.

[97] See e.g., EEC Arts. 54(2), 56(2), 57(1), 63(2), 69 and 75(1). While the Luxembourg Agreement of January 29, 1966, has cast some doubt on the feasibility of majority decisions in the Council where "very important interests of one or more Member States are at stake" (see text *infra*, p. 38f.), nevertheless majority decisions even where allowed in the past have never been the practice of the Council.

[98] Euratom Articles 90, 92, par. 2, and 48, respectively.

capacity of all Community organs to define and execute a common policy. Thus, whereas the narrower quasi-legislative powers of the ECSC are located largely in the Commission, the broader EEC powers can be exercised generally only through the concurring action of the Commission and the Council. In the EEC the Council in turn is held in check not only through the exclusive right of the Commission to initiate most EEC policy, but also through requirement of a qualified or simple majority vote as well as through the control of judicial review. It must be concluded that both the ECSC and EEC have a claim to being "supranational."[99]

In any case, it is important to emphasize that effective international organization is scarcely a matter merely of the political independence of Community organs. The very loosening-up of the institutional structure, as pointed out in Section 1, may call forth constructive and integrating Community forces which would be stifled under another regime. Further, as Jaenicke points out,[100] the very essence of supranational organization – at least in the three European Economic Communities – is not establishing a super-state, but rather furthering the formation of common policies among the Member States and securing the unity and integrity of those already adopted. Indeed, a greater degree of policy-making independence for the Commission at this point in economic integration may not be desirable. In the absence of developed democratic institutions, including a directly elected parliament with legislative and investigative powers, it might well be imprudent to place such broad powers in the hands of more politically independent institutions. This is only to say that in international, as in all political organization, power and accountability are inseparable.

3. THE COMMUNITY LEGAL ORDERS

Despite the far-reaching independent decision-making powers of the Communities, their authority would be severely weakened without the development of Community legal orders. To meet this need, the Treaties establish a fundamental law secured by broad powers of judicial review. The

99 Roselieb, *op. cit.* (n. 40), pp. 516-18, refuses the EEC and Euratom supranational status because the Commissions do not have the degree and intensity of quasi-legislative ("functional") independence possessed by the High Authority. It must be granted that the independent policy-making powers of Euratom are reduced to an absolute minimum.

100 Jaenicke, *op. cit.* (n. 85), p. 196; and Hallstein, "Zu den Grundlagen und Verfassungsprinzipien der europäischen Gemeinschaften," in *Festschrift C. F. Ophüls,* 1, 17 (1965), who speaks of a Community "Willensbildungskompetenz."

essence of this law is constitutional,[101] for it governs the most fundamental relationships between Community organs, Member States and their nationals as to vital matters of economic policy. It does this by establishing common institutions for decision-making, securing the "rule of law" through elaborate means of judicial relief and vesting the Communities with a limited but autonomous capacity for legal development.

As to the first, the Treaties not only vest Community organs with those broad economic powers described above, but they also set the conditions and limits of their lawful exercise. This is especially clear in the ECSC where Community action under specific Treaty provisions is bound by the broad policy objectives and means of Articles 2 through 5.[102] The Treaties further establish the procedure for consultation and decision-making as well as a division and balance of powers among the Council, the Commission, the European Parliament and the Court of Justice.[103] In thus channelling decision-making, they further those stable expectations among Community participants which are so important for legal control. Finally, the Treaties establish the rights, privileges and immunities of Community personnel and property in the Member States[104] as well as the right of the Communities to maintain relations and conclude agreements with States and international organizations.[105]

As to the second, the Court of Justice of the European Communities is empowered to ensure "the respect for law in the interpretation and application" of the Treaties.[106] Its broad powers of judicial review, discussed in Chapter II, correspond to the proposal of the German delegation – with an eye to future European integration – to structure the ECSC according to the

101 See Scheuner, "Die Rechtsetzungbefugnis internationaler Gemeinschaften," in *Festschrift Alfred Verdross*, 229, 231 (1960); Mosler, "Der Vertrag der EGKS," 14 *Z. ausl. öff. R.*, 1, 32–39 (1951–52), in the context of the ECSC as a "lien fédéral"; Bebr, *Judicial Control of the European Communities*, 178 (1962), pointing out that "Community law operates almost exclusively within the domain of public law." The Community Court and Advocates-General make occasional reference to the "constitutionality" of Treaty norms and to the "constitutional" traits of the Treaties themselves. See e.g., Judgment 8/55, 2 Rspr. 197, 227 (1955–56); Conclusions of Adv.-Gen. Lagrange, Case 6/64, 10 Rspr. 1279, 1289 (1964).

102 Judgments 1/54, 1 Rspr. 1, 23f., 34 (1954–55), and its companion decision 2/54, 1 Rspr. 79 (1954–55); 8/57, 4 Rspr. 231, 251–55 (1958), and its companion decision 9/57, 4 Rspr. 381 (1958).

103 See text *supra*, Section 2; and Bebr, "The Balance of Power in the European Communities," 5 *European YB* 53 (1959).

104 ECSC Arts. 6, par. 3, and 76 (and Protocol); EEC Arts. 211 and 218 (and Protocol); Euratom Arts. 185 and 191 (and Protocol).

105 ECSC Arts. 6, pars. 1, 2 and 3, and 93 and 94; EEC Arts. 210 and 228–231; Euratom Arts. 185, 101 and 199–201.

106 ECSC Art. 31, EEC Art. 164, Euratom Art. 136.

"rule of law."[107] The persuasive argument for this proposal lies in the character of the Communities themselves. On the one hand, broad powers of judicial review were essential to ensure the unity and integrity of Community norms and policies vis-a-vis the special interests of Member States and individuals. The maintenance and continued growth of these legal orders, therefore, may be viewed as reflecting generally the extent of successful economic integration. On the other hand, the establishment of independent legal orders is a necessary check against the arbitrary exercise of Community powers. Only in the presence of such guarantees – especially in view of the rudimentary parliamentary control[108] – is it conceivable that States would permit the Community authorities to exercise important national powers.[109]

The jurisdiction and organization of the Court establish important advances over judicial control in the international community. Above all, except for certain matters of public liability, the Court possesses a jurisdictional monopoly over the interpretation of Community Law under the Rome Treaties – a monopoly which is somewhat relaxed, however, in the ECSC.[110] So far as a right of appeal exists, it is exclusive of all other judicial recourse.[111] Moreover, this jurisdiction is compulsory for all those subject to the Treaties. Member States have obligated themselves not to submit such disputes to any other tribunal, including the International Court of Justice.[112] They do not possess that jurisdictional option, therefore, which is open to them under Article 36 of the Statue of the International Court of Justice or under Article 46 of the European Convention of Human Rights.

Finally, in contrast to other international organizations, the Court is empowered to render binding decisions on questions of Treaty interpretation in disputes to which not only Community organs and Member States, but

107 Schlochauer, "Die Gerichtsbarkeit der EGKS," 3 *Arch. VR.*, 385, 386f. (1951–52). For a discussion of the premises and possibilities of a Supreme European Court with general jurisdiction, see Wiebringhaus, *Gerichtshof für Europa?* (1967).

108 *Ibid.*

109 See Bindschedler, *Rechtsfragen der Europäischen Einigung*, 93 (1954); Seeler, "Politische Integration und Gewaltenteilung," 15 *Europa-Archiv*, 13, 19f. (Part. I, 1960). This has a striking parallel in the United States, whose Supreme Court in its conception was due largely to the state's judges of that era who feared federal encroachment on state authority. Their belief, however, that the federal judicial power would be a rather mild check on state authority proved false. See Schmidhauser, *The Supreme Court as Final Arbiter in Federal-State Relations*, Ch. I (1958).

110 See discussion in text *infra*.

111 See Wohlfarth et al., *Die EWG: Kommentar zum Vertrag*, Art. 183. See also text *infra*, Ch. II, Section 2.

112 EEC Art. 219, Euratom Art. 193. ECSC Art. 87 is somewhat more narrowly worded. In any case, diplomatic settlement would not be excluded.

also enterprises, their associations and individuals are parties. By contrast, except for "advisory opinions" of the International Court of Justice,[113] the United Nations Charter makes no provision for its authoritative interpretation. Similarly, the specialized agencies have been authorized by the General Assembly to request "advisory opinions" on questions arising under their charters, but they may not themselves bring a dispute with a Member State before that Court.[114] In practice, however, these agencies most commonly refer disputes concerning the interpretation of their charters to non-judicial organs, typically within their own organizations.[115] The jurisdiction of the Community Court, therefore, permits it to guard the integrity and unity of Treaty interpretation.[116]

From the viewpoint of judicial organization, the Community Court differs notably from international courts and reflects more the structure of municipal courts. The Court is composed of seven judges, elected for a term of six years by the unanimous decision of the governments of the Member States.[117] This latter requirement, although considerably stricter than that for the International Court of Justice,[118] may be explained by the compulsory jurisdiction of the Community Court over matters of crucial importance to the Member States. The Community Court, however, is independent of Member State directives and of any one Member State's representation.[119] There is

[113] United Nations Charter Art. 96(1).

[114] See Bowett, *The Law of International Institutions,* 125–28, 229–233 (1963). This is a "derivative right" conferred by the General Assembly under Art. 96(2) of the United Nations Charter and extended to all specialized agencies except the Universal Postal Union.

[115] Hexner, "Interpretation by International Organizations of their Basic Instruments," 53 *Amer. J. Int. L.,* 341, 343f. (1959), offers four distinguishing marks of interpretation by international organizations: 1) undertaken by their own executive organs and not by an external tribunal, 2) employed preventively and not merely to resolve contentious disputes, 3) may be exclusive as to questions arising between organs and Member States as well as between Member States only, and 4) an interested party, i.e. the executive organ, is typically the judge.

[116] See text *infra,* Chapter II, Section 2.

[117] ECSC Art. 32b, par. 1, EEC Art. 167, par. 1, Euratom Art. 139, par. 1. Some voices have been raised against the six year term of office, arguing that this impairs the independence of the judges. See discussion of Bächle, *Die Rechtsstellung der Richter am Gerichtshof der Europäischen Gemeinschaften,* 126ff (1961). Such limited terms of office, however, are not unknown among the Member States; all or most of the constitutional judges in Italy and Germany are elected for a term of 12 and 8 years respectively.

[118] ICJ Stat., Art. 10, requires only an absolute majority of votes in the General Assembly and Security Council.

[119] ECSC Art. 32b, par. 1, and Stat. of the Court Arts. 2–4, 19, par. 4; EEC Art. 167, par. 1, and Stat. of the Court Arts. 2–4 and 16, par. 4; Euratom Art. 139, par. 1, and Stat. of the Court Arts. 2–4 and 16, par. 4. Although the Treaties appear to permit

no requirement, as there is for the International Court of Justice[120] or for the European Court of Human Rights,[121] that either all of the Member States or the Member State who are parties to an action be represented on the Court. Further, following continental practice but in contrast to that of the International Court of Justice[122] and of common law countries, the Community Court delivers its judgment as a collegiate body. At the early stage of Community development, as former President of the Court A. M. Donner has explained, it is hoped that this "ensures opinions that are understandable throughout the Communities and contributes to the establishment of a common fund of legal notions and principles."[123]

The Community Court is also assisted by two Advocates General. Their function is "to present publicly, with complete impartiality and independence, reasoned conclusions on cases submitted to the Court . . ."[124] Unlike any position in international and most municipal judicature, the Advocate-General is similar to the French commissaire du Gouvernement at the Conseil d'Etat.[125] Although neither judge nor prosecutor nor a participant in the deliberations and vote of the Court, his legally non-binding conclusions are published following the Court's decision and may raise points or arguments not considered either by the parties or by the Court. Since the Community judicature lacks an appellate system, the conclusions of the Advocates-General offer an independent argument for the Court to consider in tackling complex issues.[126] In the course of judicial decisions, therefore, the conclusions of the Advocates-General may have important influence on legal development.

Finally, the Community legal orders demonstrate a third constitutional element. Despite the elaborate framework of Treaty norms, the Community legal orders would be robbed of durability were there no institutionalized

the judges (and Advocates-General) to be chosen from nationals other than from Member States, Article 3, par. 3, of these Statutes implicitly rule this out. Moreover, by informal agreement, the six governments have carefully distributed the various judicial and para-judicial positions to maintain a certain balance of representation among the Member States. See Feld, *The Court of the European Communities,* 17f (1964), and Scheingold, *The Rule of Law in European Integration* 25–35 (1965). It is far from clear, however, that this has had any influence on particular decisions of the Community Court.

120 ICJ Stat., Art. 31.

121 *European Convention on Human Rights,* Art. 43.

122 ICJ Stat., Art. 57.

123 Donner, "The European Court of Justice," 59 *Law Soc. Gaz.,* 444, 445 (1962).

124 ECSC Art. 32a, par. 2; EEC Art. 166, par. 2; Euratom Art. 138, par. 2.

125 Hamson, *Executive Discretion and Judicial Control,* 79–81 (1954).

126 Donner, *op. cit.,* p. 445.

means for legal development.[127] These means do not merely distinguish the Community legal orders from the generally static character of international treaties, but they further impress them with the stamp of viability. Legal orders meant to endure must possess sufficient autonomy to enable them to adapt to unforeseen and changing circumstances. This potential for legal development is embodied above all in the quasi-legislative powers of the Council, and the Commission, discussed is Section 2. In this context, it is important to note that the Treaty norms are of such breadth and generality that their very application calls for imaginative creative judgment. This is inherent in the formulation of economic decisions which are based on the uncertain assessment of economic conditions and trends and must often strike a balance between conflicting economic objectives. A glance at the policy aims listed in ECSC Article 3 offers an insight into the enormity of this task. Further, where stipulated Treaty powers do not permit necessary Community action, they may – within limits – be adapted or altered. Thus, without deferring to the Member State legislatures, the Community organs acting together may undertake limited Treaty revision.[128]

In the last instance, however, it is the Community Court which must judge the legality of Community acts, practices and limited Treaty revision. Its decisions will reflect the actual growth of a "Community law." This is a law composed of norms which are immediately applicable not only to Community organs and Member States, but also to nationals in the Member States.[129] That is, whether by the self-executing effect of Treaty provisions[130] or by the implementing regulations and other acts of Community organs and Member State authorities, Community law creates rights and duties for private enterprises, associations and individuals. Moreover, this is

[127] Whereas Mathijsen, *Le Droit de la C.E.C.A.*, Ch. I and V (1958), has demonstrated that legal development is a central attribute of the ECSC Treaty, it has further been noted that legal development is an essential attribute of constitutional law in contrast to international treaty law. See, e.g., Scheuner, *op. cit.* (n. 101), p. 231.

[128] ECSC Art. 95, EEC Art. 235, Euratom Art. 203, See text *infra*, Ch. II, Section 2.

[129] For a discussion of the different types of Community norms, see Bebr, *op. cit.* (n. 101), pp. 41–57; Ophüls, "Die Geltungsnormen des Europäischen Gemeinschaftsrechts," in *Festschrift Riese*, 1 (1964); and the Conclusions of *Adv.-Gen.* Lagrange in Case 6/64, 10 Rspr. 1279, 1286f (1964).

[130] The Court has had occasion to declare certain Treaty norms directly applicable to nationals of the Member States, thereby establishing rights of individuals against their own national authorities. See, e.g., Judgment 7 and 9/54, 2 Rspr. 53, 90f (1955–56) (re ECSC Art. 4); Judgment 13/61, 8 Rspr. 97, 111 (1962) (re EEC Art. 85(1)); Judgment 26/62, 9 Rspr. 3 (1963) (re EEC Art. 12); Judgment 6/64, 10 Rspr. 1251 (1964) (re EEC Arts. 53 and 37, par. 2); Judgments 57/65, 12 Rspr. 257 (1966) (re EEC Art. 95, par. 1); Judgment 27/67, 14 Rspr. 333, 346f (1968) (re EEC Art. 95, par. 2); and Judgment 13/68, 14 Rspr. 679, 693f (1968) (re EEC Arts. 31 and 32, par. 1).

a law which proceeds from the Treaties, is elaborated through the exercise of quasi-legislative Community powers, but is constantly subject to the review and control of the Community Court. The broad and, to a large extent, exclusive jurisdiction of the Court in this respect contributes greatly both to the unity and integrity of the Community legal orders.[131] For the time being, each Treaty establishes its own jurisdiction and legal order. Nevertheless, judicial interpretation by a Court common to all the Communities will lead gradually to a common fund of legal knowledge, applicable within limits to all three Communities.

By its very nature, Community law cannot be assigned either to the international or municipal sphere. The questions it raises are not so easily mastered. While resting on international Treaties, it reaches far into the traditional domain of State powers. Most of the principles of international law are neither concerned nor adequate to deal, for instance, with the complexities of economic regulation. Nor are the legal concepts and practice of the Member States in this vast field in agreement.[132] Rather, the Court is forced to develop its own sources and principles – drawing as required and appropriate from both bodies of law.[133] The Court becomes unavoidably a participant, therefore, in a developing body of Community law. This law is unique to the needs and realities of European economic integration.

4. CONFLICT BETWEEN COMMUNITY AND MEMBER STATE LAW

Further, the Communities are distinguished from almost all international organizations by the relation of Community law to national law and the direct operation of both upon individuals in the Member States. The Community Treaties embody not only legal provisions which are directly binding on Community organs and the Member States, but also on individuals within the jurisdiction of the Member States. The first two types of legal provisions are found in most international organizations and do not raise peculiar prob-

[131] See text *infra*. Ch. II, Section 2.

[132] Hochbaum, *Das Diskriminierungs- und Subventionsverbot in der EGKS und EWG,* 21, 30 (1962), concludes that neither the concept of "discrimination" nor that of "subvention" possesses a common and established meaning or understanding among the Member States.

[133] The frequent attempts to treat this problem by assigning Community law or parts of it to differing fields of law, e.g. international law, municipal law or some *sui generis* category, have not proved particularly fruitful. Rather, they are, as Jaenicke suggests, "mehr von theoretischer als von praktischer Bedeutung." In "Völkerrechtsquellen," 3 Strupp-Schlochauer, *Wörterbuch des Völkerrechts,* 773 (2d ed., 1962). See also Schlochauer, "Das Verhältnis des Rechts der EWG zu den nationalen Rechtsordnungen der Mitgliedstaaten," 11 *Arch. VR.,* 1–4 (1963–64).

lems for the Communities. Therefore, they will not be discussed here. The third type of legal provision,[134] however, subjects the individual to other – the Community – legal orders which are unfolding complementary to those of the Member States. Since the binding effect of Community law on individuals is directly related to the extent to which the national legal orders have limited their traditional spheres of powers and undertaken to support Community regulation, it is important to examine the basis of such national obligations.

The legal orders of the Communities rest squarely on international Treaties. They were ratified by Member State legislatures as ordinary treaties and not, as is characteristic of national constitutions, by specially convened constitutive assemblies. Their binding force, therefore, must be sought in the relationship of international to national law. This relationship is viewed differently, according to whether one accepts the monist or dualist standpoint. No attempt will be made to examine this dispute, but only to note that in many cases for reasons of comity, enlightened self-interest or a growing – if only reluctant – realization of interdependence, even States proceeding from a dualist standpoint recognize certain important exceptions to their position.[135] These same reasons would suggest why the Member States should take a similar view toward the very economically beneficial Community Treaties. As a matter of fact, however, the broad economic powers bestowed by the Treaties have been the traditional reserve of State regulation. Because of this and the fact that the dualist position appears to be supported on the whole by the preponderance of jurists and practice in the Member States,[136] it will be employed here as the point of departure. This means in effect that while the Treaties fully obligate Member States under principles of international law, a conflict can arise between Community law and the Member State legal orders. To ascertain the nature of this conflict, it is necessary to consider first the Treaty obligations undertaken and the extent to which these obligations are recognized as fully binding by the constitutional practice in the six States. Following this, the means for obviating or mitigating this conflict will be considered briefly.

As to the first point, the Treaties themselves, viewed in their entirety, can not be said to establish the supremacy of Community law over municipal

[134] See note 130 *supra*.

[135] Lauterpacht-Oppenheim, *International Law*, vol. I, p. 44f (8th ed., 1954).

[136] Schlochauer, "Das Verhältnis des Rechts der EWG zu den nationalen Rechtsordnungen der Mitgliedstaaten," 11 *Arch. VR.*, 1, 15–17, 25–28 (1963–64); Ipsen, "Das Verhältnis des Rechts der europäischen Gemeinschaften zum nationalen Recht," in *Aktuelle Fragen des Europäischen Gemeinschaftsrechts*, 1, 2–4 (1965).

law. The very absence of express agreement in the Treaties to that or equal effect speaks against such a revolutionary presumption.[137] This silence is especially striking in light of the fact that the Communities lack both their own court system and executive offices in the Member States to ensure the unbiased enforcement of Community decisions.[138] Further, despite the fact that all the Member States have made constitutional provision for the transfer of sovereign rights to international or supranational organizations,[139] the abdication of important State powers can not be thereby implied. In the first place, this would raise weighty constitutional questions in the Member States, which in many cases can be resolved only by constitutional amendment. This is particularly true for the division and balance of powers in a federal State, such as the Federal Republic of Germany.[140] At the very least,

137 Münch, "Die Abgrenzung des Rechtsbereiches der supranationalen Gemeinschaft gegenüber dem innerstaatlichen Recht," 2 *Ber. deutsch. Ges. VR.*, 73, 77 (1957); Scheuner, "Die Rechtsetzungsbefugnis internationaler Gemeinschaften." in *Festschrift Alfred Verdross*, 229, 241 (1960); Schlochauer, *id.*, p. 27; Carstens, "Der Rang europäischer Verordnungen gegenüber deutschen Rechtsnormen," in *Festschrift Otto Riese* 65, 71 (1964); and Steindorff, *Rechtsschutz und Verfahren im Recht der europäischen Gemeinschaften* 49 (1964).

But cf. Ipsen, *id.*, p. 17ff, who sees Treaty recognition of the primacy of Community law over national legislation in EEC Article 189, paragraph 2: "Regulations shall have general application. They shall be binding in every respect and directly applicable in each Member State." While this provision indeed constitutes "a value and quality characterization of Community Regulations," as Ipsen contends, to say that a Regulation is generally and directly applicable is not the same as saying that it is supreme over national law. To reach the latter conclusion, Ipsen must supplement the language of that Article with the principle of effectiveness in Community law. While such reasoning is persuasive (see discussion in text *infra*, p. 378ff), it is by no means conclusive. It fails to explain why the authors of the Treaties, if they had intended the absolute supremacy of Community law, did not resolve such an important question with clear- cut language in a less obstrusive provision of the Treaty, like EEC Article 5.

138 It should be kept in mind that besides the vertical type of federalism in the United States, exhibiting parallel federal and state authorities, there exists also a horizontal type as found in the Federal Republic of Germany. Under this second type, which is the pattern for the Communities, the individual states supply the bulk of the administrative machinery.

139 German Basic Law Art. 24(1) and Italian Constitution Art. 11 (by way of interpretation) existed at the time all three Treaties were signed, whereas the remaining four Member States introduced these provisions later; Belgium Constitution Art. 25, Luxembourg Constitution Art. 49, Netherlands Constitution Art. 67 (Art. 60g of the 1953 Constitution) and French Constitution of 1958 Art. 53 (read together with the still valid Preamble, par. 15, of the 1946 Constitution.

140 Anxiety has been expressed that the Communities occasion an unhealthy shift of State power to the executive branch of the Member State governments, because the Council is composed of the ministers from the Member States. In Germany, the Government is obligated by law to inform the Federal Parliament before it commits itself in the Council of Ministers. Art. 2, Gesetz zu den Verträgen vom 25. März 1957 zur Gründung der EWG und EAG vom 27. Juli 1957. 1957 *Bundesgesetzblatt*, Pt. II/1,

the constitutions of the Member States establish limits to such an absolute transfer of sovereign powers.[141] Of the six States, only the Netherlands has taken the giant step of expressly permitting the transfer to international organizations of powers which deviate from constitutional provisions – and then only if both legislative chambers by a two-thirds vote consider that "the development of the international order requires this."[142] Finally, the Communities lack not only well developed parliamentary control, as pointed out in Section 2, but also the constitutional restraints of a bill of rights. As such, the transfer of vital sovereign powers to relatively autonomous Community organs would be imprudent and should not be lightly assumed.[143]

To what extent, then, does the constitutional practice of the Member States grant the Treaties a preferred position in their legal systems? The Constitution of the Netherlands presents the least difficulty. By a 1953 constitutional amendment, the self-executing provisions of international treaties as well as the legislative, administrative and judicial acts made pursuant to these treaties are made supreme over all prior and subsequent national legislation.[144] In effect, they are also supreme over the Netherlands Constitution, since "the courts are not competent to judge the constitutionality of agreements,"[145] but must apply them faithfully as the highest law of the land. Luxembourg has achieved the same result, although without the aid of a supremacy clause on the Dutch model. By a gradual evolution of its jurisprudence, the courts have come to regard the self-executing provisions of international treaties as supreme over antecedent and subsequent national legislation.[146] Although such provisions would appear to be inferior to the

No. 23, p. 753. See Holch, "Der Bundesrat zur Rechtsetzung der Europäischen Gemeinschaften," 4 *Europarecht* 213f (1969). See also the more recent Decision of the Finance Court of Rhineland/Palatinate (Nov. 14, 1963), challenging the constitutionality of the EEC Treaty for failure to observe the principle of the division of powers. Discussed in text *infra*, p. 418f.

[141] See, e.g., *German Basic Law* Art. 79(3), which provides that the basic constitutional guarantees of federal political structure and individual rights can not be amended.

[142] Netherlands Constitution Art. 63.

[143] Jaenicke, in "Aussprache," 2 *Ber. deutsch. Ges. VR.*, 132 (1957); Thieme, "Das Grundgesetz und die öffentliche Gewalt internationaler Staatengemeinschaften," 18 *VVdStRL*, 50, 73–75 (1960); Carstens, *op. cit.* (n. 137), p. 73.

[144] Netherlands Constitution Art. 66, as amended. For a discussion of this constitutional development, see Bauer, "Die niederländische Verfassungsänderung von 1956," 18 *Z. ausl. öff. R.*, 137 (1957–58); van Panhuys, "The Netherlands Constitution and International Law." 47 *Amer. J. Int. L.*, 537 (1953).

[145] Netherlands Constitution Art. 60, para. 3.

[146] See the Decisions of the Conseil d'Etat (Comité du contentieux) of July 28, 1951, 15 Pas. Lux. Juris. 263, 268 (1950–53); and of the Cour supérieur de justice (Cass. crim.) of July 14, 1954, 16 Pas. Lux. Juris. 150, 152 (1954–56). For this development, see P. de Visscher, "La C.E.C.A. et les Etats membres," 2 *Actes du Congrès sur la CECA* (Stresa), 7, 47 (1957); Bebr, *Judicial Control of the European Communities,*

constitution itself, the authority of this jurisprudence is ensured by the absence of constitutional review and the independence of the judiciary from the executive and legislature in treaty interpretation.

In France, both under the Constitutions of the Fourth and Fifth Republic, international treaties prevail over prior and subsequent national legislation.[147] The 1958 Constitution, however, introduces two changes which noticeably weaken the strong internationalist spirit of its predecessor. In the first place, although Article 55 grants international treaties an "autorité supérieure à celle des lois," it neglects to clarify to what extent subsequent legislation may unilaterally abrogate, modify or suspend a treaty or certain of its provisions. Article 28 of the 1946 Constitution expressly permitted this only "à la suite d'une dénonciation régulière, notifiée par voie diplomatique." Since the French judge is generally adverse to declaring the supremacy of treaties over French law,[148] he may well resort to a narrow treaty interpretation[149] or, as is usual when some doubt as to the meaning of a treaty arises, follow the interpretation of the Ministry of Foreign Affairs.[150] Indeed, in a

218f (1962); and Pescatore, "L'autorité en droit interne des Traités internationaux," 18 *Pas. Lux. Juris.*, 99 and 106ff (1962), a more recent review of which may be found in 5 *Europarecht* 56, 74–76 (1970).

[147] Dinh, "La Constitution de 1958 et le Droit international," 75 *Rev. dr. pub. sci. pol.* 515, 551–54 (1959); deVisscher, *id.* pp. 47–50; Bebr, *id.*, p. 219f and Schilling, *Völkerrecht und Staatliches Recht in Frankreich* 167 (1964). The relevant provisions are Arts. 26 and 28 of the 1946 Constitution, and Arts. 54 and 55 of the 1958 Constitution. See also Pescatore, "Die unmittelbare Anwendung der europäischen Verträge durch die staatlichen Gerichte," 5 *Europarecht* 56, 67f (1970).

[148] Bebr, *id.*, p. 220; Schilling, *id.*, p. 112f. In France, in any case, two theories still compete concerning the primacy of international treaties in the national legal order. Whereas the one establishes the supremacy of treaties by reference to the Constitution of 1946, the other emphasizes that French courts lack the competence to assert the supremacy of treaties just as they lack the power of judicial review in constitutional law. See Lussan and Martin, "La CEE, source de droit," Dalloz: *Chron. juris.*, 111 (1957) and, more recently, Lagrange, "La primauté du Droit communautaire sur le Droit national," in *Collège d'Europe, Droit communautaire et droit national,* 21, 37f (1965); and also Virole, J., "Questions posées par l'interprétation du Traité . . . CEE à propos de la nationalisation de l'électricité en Italie," 1 *Rev. trim. dr. europ.* 369, 376 (1965).

[149] Cf., eg., the Decision of the Conseil d'Etat in *Société de pétroles Shell-Berre and Others* (June 19, 1964), reported in 80 *Rev. dr. pub. sci. pol.*, 1019 (1964), and discussed in text *supra,* p. 388; and its Decision in *Jammes et Fédération des Associations viticoles de France* (May 23, 1969), reported in *Jurisclasseur périodique,* No. 16020 (1969).

[150] Bebr, *op. cit.* p. 220f; Schilling, *op. cit.*, pp. 120–23, 157 and 160; and Chevallier, "Le juge français et le Droit communautaire," in Donner et al., *Le juge national et le Droit communautaire,* 17, 21f (1966). It would be premature to suggest, as do Bebr and Chevallier, that this long-established practice, which is the result of a strict separation of powers principle, will be drastically changed by the "preliminary question" procedure, discussed in text *infra,* p. 67ff. By use of the "acte clair" doctrine (see discussion in text *infra,* p. 69 at notes 97 and 98, and p. 387ff), national courts themselves

most recent decision, the Conseil d'Etat decided in effect that Regulation No. 19 of the EEC had been negated by subsequent French legislation. The cryptic opinion of this highest administrative law tribunal was based implicitly on the principle of *lex posterior derogat legi priori,* ignoring altogether Article 55 of the French Constitution.[151]

Moreover, the deference of French courts to their Foreign Ministry in treaty interpretation becomes especially important in view of the new requirement of treaty reciprocity. Article 55 further strengthens the hand of the executive in treaty interpretation by conditioning the enforcement of treaties on their reciprocal application in other signatory States. Although this provision would seem to be superfluous in the light of recognized principles of international law,[152] it fully accords with the new political awareness of the Fifth Republic. It vests the President of the Republic, as "le garant de l'indépendance nationale, de l'intégrité du territoire, du respect des accords de Communauté et des traités,"[153] with a politically useful weapon.[154] In the absence of constitutional review, the standard of "reciprocity" is not that of international or even constitutional law, but of the Ministry for Foreign Affairs. Considering the divergent constitutional practice in the six Member States,[155] therefore, the formal superiority of treaties under the 1958 Constitution could become a potent diplomatic lever in the hands of the French Government.

subject the "preliminary question" procedure to a preliminary interpretation of their own. ECSC Article 41, in any case, does not extend the "preliminary question" procedure to matters of interpretation, but is limited to questions concerning the validity of Community acts. The former presumably remain in the hands of the French Ministry of Foreign Affairs.

151 Decision of March 1, 1968: *Syndicat général des fabricants de semoules de France,* reported in 3 Europarecht 317 (1968). As Constantinesco points out in his analysis and critical comment to this decision (3 Europarecht 318, 323–26), the opinion of the Conseil d'Etat does not depart from its traditional position in this respect. See also the discussion in text *infra,* p. 388ff, and the critical comment of the new Commission, in *Amtsblatt,* No. C 71 (July 17, 1968).

152 See Dahm, *Völkerrecht,* vol. III, p. 133f (1961); Schwarzenberger, *Manual of International Law,* 157 (4th ed., 1960); Lauterpacht-Oppenheim, *op. cit.,* (n. 135), pp. 930–33, 945–49.

153 Constitution of 1958, Art. 5, par. 2. See also Art. 16, stipulating special powers. As to the new position of the executive, as a guiding idea in the 1958 Constitution, see de Laubadère, "La Constitution française 1958," 20 *Z. ausl. öff. R.,* 506, 514–28 (1959–60).

154 Schilling, *op. cit.,* (n. 147), pp. 155, 160. See also Bülow, "Das Verhältnis des Rechts der europäischen Gemeinschaften zum nationalen Recht," in *Aktuelle Fragen des Europäischen Gemeinschaftsrechts,* 28, 35 (1965).

155 As to the applicability of the "reciprocity clause" in cases where only *some* of the treaty partners grant a treaty precedence over subsequent national legislation, see C. Rousseau, "La Constitution de 1958 et les traités internationaux," in *Mélanges Président Basdevant,* 463, esp. 471f (1960).

By contrast to France, international treaties in Germany have force and effect equal only to national legislation.[156] Pursuant to the general principle *lex posterior derogat legi priori,* they enjoy unquestioned application over prior legislation only.[157] Article 24(1) of the Basic Law, permitting the Federal Government to transfer sovereign rights to international ("zwischenstaatlichen") organizations, facilitates the undertaking of international obligations but does not overcome the established dualist position. This became evident in the constitutional debate surrounding the European Defense Community Treaty and the resulting amendment of Article 79(1) of the Constitution.[158] Attempts have been made to counter this conclusion by drawing on Article 25 of the Basic Law. Pursuant to that provision, "general principles of international law are a constituent part of Federal law," create immediate rights and obligations for individuals and take precedence over national law. By virtue of the principle of *pacta sunt servanda,* it is argued, Community law enjoys a preferred position vis-a-vis prior and subsequent federal legislation.[159] These attempts have clearly been rejected, however, by distinguishing between "general principles" and treaty agreements.[160]

Nevertheless, German law in this area is in the throes of rapid development. Thus, a recent study has revealed that the opinion of leading jurists is moving away from a strict transformation theory in favor of an execution theory ("Vollzugstheorie") of treaty application. According to the latter, the validity of treaty-implementing legislation is traced not to the legislative act

[156] See 6 BVerfG 290, 295 (1957) (Verfassungsbeschwerde re: deutsch-schweizerisches Abkommen); 6 BVerfG 309, 363 (1957) (Reichskonkordatsstreit); and BGH Judgment of December 13, 1961, 24 N.J.W. 1115, 1116 (1962). These decisions reflect the dominant position in the literature. See, e.g., Maunz-Dürig, *Grundgesetz Kommentar,* Randnr. 30 zu Art. 25 (2nd ed. 1964); and Schlochauer, *op. cit.* (n. 136), pp. 18–20.

[157] But cf. Ipsen, *op. cit.* (n. 136), p. 23f, who rejects the application of this general principle to the relationship of Community and Member State law because the two originate from different legislative sources. See also Steindorff, *Rechtsschutz und Verfahren im Recht der europäischen Gemeinschaften,* 47 (1964). However true this view may be, it can not resolve the question of primacy in cases of irreconcilable conflict.

[158] See Maunz-Dürig, *op. cit.,* Randnr. 11 zu Art. 79. As to the general acceptance of the dualist position in German court decisions and the literature, see Boehmer, *Der völkerrechtliche Vertrag im deutschen Recht,* 32–36 (1965); and Schlochauer, *op. cit.* (n. 136), p. 15f.

[159] Münch, "Staatsverfassungen und Friedenspolitik," 50 *Friedenswarte,* 346, 350 (1950/51); Münch, "Droit international et Droit interne d'après la Constitution de Bonn," 15 *Rev. int. franç. dr. gens,* 5, 14 (1950); Grewe, "Die auswärtige Gewalt der Bundesrepublik," 12 *VVdStRL,* 129, 149 (1954); and v. Mangoldt-Klein, *Das Bonner Grundgesetz, Kommentar,* Anm. III, 2b. zu Art. 25 (2nd ed. 1957).

[160] 6 *BVerfG* 309, 363 (1957). See also Pigorsch, *Die Einordnung völkerrechtlicher Normen in das Recht der Bundesrepublik Deutschland,* 88ff (1959); and Partsch (Berichterstatter), "Die Anwendung des Völkerrechts im innerstaatlichen Recht: Überprüfung der Transformationslehre," in 6 *Ber. deutsch. Ges. VR.* 72ff (1964).

itself, but to the treaty norms which it merely executes.[161] Although the "Vollzugstheorie" is thought to offer a more consistent theory, which contributes to a greater degree of harmony between municipal and international law in certain respects, its position as to the relationship of international treaties and national legislation does not at this time differ in result from that of the transformation theory.[162] More important than this, however, is recent recognition by the Federal Constitutional Court that the EEC embraces a distinct and autonomous legal order of its own, whose acts "neither need be ratified . . . nor can they be nullified" by the Member States.[163] Although that Court has studiously avoided a decision on the merits of the question, its *dicta* well reflects a growing consensus among German jurists. It remains to be seen whether and to what extent the autonomy of the Community legal orders also entails their supremacy over national law. Thus far at least, the Federal Finance Court of Appeals has assumed the identity and refused to apply the new German turnover tax to the extent it infringes EEC Article 95.[164]

Under the Italian Constitution, as in Germany, international treaties also have the same force and effect as national legislation. While Italy, pursuant to Article 11 of her Constitution, may limit her sovereignty by a delegation of powers to international organizations, this does not entail the supremacy of Community law. Indeed, as the Corte Costituzionale made clear in the famous *E.N.E.L.* Decision, Article 11 is only a permissive norm which can "endow the ordinary law which makes the Treaty operative [in Italy] no greater legal effect than that which inheres in its legal source." Though Italy must honor its international obligations, still the EEC Treaty like national legislation is subject to the principle *lex posterior derogat legi priori.*[165]

[161] The present discussion concerning the "Vollzugstheorie" appears to have been stimulated by Professor Mosler's critique of the transformation theory. See Mosler, *Das Völkerrecht in der Praxis der deutschen Gerichte,* 13–19 (1957). It is further discussed in the Report of Partsch, *id.*, pp. 19–24, where it has received broad acceptance among German jurists.

[162] Boehmer, *op. cit.* (n. 158), pp. 106-8. But cf. Pescatore, *op. cit.* (n. 147), p. 64f.

[163] Decision of October 18, 1967, reported in 3 *Europarecht* 134 (1968) and discussed in text *infra,* p. 422f.

[164] BFH Judgment of July 11, 1968 – VII 156/65, reported in 3 *Europarecht* 394, 397 and 401f (1968). See discussion in text *infra,* p. 424f. But cf. the early decision of the Bundesgerichtshof, 30 BGHZ 74 (1959), which denied the capacity of ECSC Articles 4b) and 60 to create rights under German civil law in a case concerning alleged illegal price discrimination. For comment, see Schloh, 9 *JB. int. R.*, 92 (1961).

[165] Decision No. 14 of March 7, 1964, reported in 87 *Il Foro Italiano,* Pt. I, Sp. 465 (1964); in *AWD,* 219 (1964); and in 2 *C.M.L. Rev.*, 224 (1964). See discussion in text *infra,* p. 405. For a survey of Italian law on this point, see Neri, "Le Juge italien et le Droit communautaire et l'ordre juridique interne," in Donner et al., *Le Juge national et le Droit Communautaire,* 77–81 (1966); and Pescatore, *op. cit.* (n. 147), p. 72f.

This outspoken position of the Corte Costituzionale struck a major blow at the authority of Community law, for the interpretation of treaties is exclusively in the hands of the judiciary and the judiciary possesses the power of judicial review. Nevertheless, a more recent decision of the Corte has recognized not only the unique and independent character of the Community legal orders, but also that at least in some procedural respects the Community legal orders need not coincide with the requirements of the Italian Constitution.[166]

Belgian constitutional practice is similar to that of Italy. The Constitution itself, which dates back to 1831 and was last revised in 1921, is silent on the point. By implication, however, judicial practice accords international treaties a legal effect equal only to national law and subject to the Constitution.[167] Though the Belgian judiciary has no power of judicial review, it does possess the exclusive authority to interpret treaties. While that authority, therefore, might be guided by the political objectives of the Community Treaties, a final resolution of the question most likely must await proposed revisions of the Constitution.[168]

From this brief survey, it is clear that the Treaties do not possess unquestioned priority over subsequent national legislation. The absence of an express or implied supremacy clause in the Treaties permits the force and effect of Community law to vary according to the constitutional practice of

But cf. the "dual function" theory of Catalano, which attributes to Article 11 of the Italian Constitution (set forth in note 418, p. 405 *infra*) both the mandate to delegate powers to international organizations as well as the corresponding authority to restrict national sovereignty. Catalano, "La position du Droit communautaire dans le droit des états membres," in *Collège d'Europe, Droit communautaire et droit national,* 55, 70 and 75ff (1965). See also Sico, "Considerazioni sull'interpretazione dell'art. 11 della Costituzione," 20 *Dir. int.,* 297, 306 n. 11 (1966), reviewing the positions of Migliazza, Tosato and Monaco, who agree with the reasoning or result of Catalano's view.

166 Decision No. 98 of December 16, 1965, reported in 2 *Europarecht* 146 (1966), upholding the constitutionality of ECSC Articles 41, 33, paragraph 2, and 92, last paragraph. See discussion in text *infra,* p. 426f.

167 See P. de Visscher, *op. cit.* (n. 146), pp. 48 and 50; Bebr, *op. cit.* (n. 145), p. 224; and *Commission d'étude interuniversitaire de l'institut royal des Relations internationales, Les Conséquences d'ordre interne de la participation de la belgique aux organisations internationales,* 172–75 (1964). But cf. Hayoit de Termicourt, "Le Conflit 'Traité – Loi interne'," 78 *Journal des Tribunaux* 481 (1963); and Waelbroeck, "Le Juge belge et le droit communautaire," in Donner et al., *op. cit.* (n. 163), pp. 31f, 33 and 37f, who takes the critical view in general of Hayoit de Termicourt. See also Pescatore, *op. cit.* (n. 147), pp. 60–63.

168 See the Commission report, *id.;* and the more recent critical examination for purposes of constitutional revision by Salmon and Suy, "La primauté du droit international sur le droit interne," in *Centres de droit international de l'Université de Bruxelles et de l'Université de Louvain, L'adaptation de la Constitution belge aux réalités internationales,* 67, 79–89 (1966).

the Member States. Whereas in the Netherlands and Luxembourg Community law enjoys a preferred position over national legislation, in France this is true only subject to the "act clair" doctrine of the Conseil d'Etat and under conditions which may be influenced by the political views of the executive. In Italy and Belgium, on the other hand, Community law is equal in status only to national legislation. That view too has prevailed in Germany, although most recently legal opinion has begun to consolidate in favor of treating Community law as supreme at least over national legislation. Depending on Member State constitutional practice, therefore, the Treaties establish decision-making powers and legal obligations which run not only parallel and complementary to, but also competitive with the legal orders of the Member States.[169] The Community Court has acknowledged as much in an early decision, declaring that "the municipal law . . . and the law of the EEC are two autonomous legal orders which are independent of each other."[170] Community law and national legislation may raise competing legal obligations for individuals in the Member States.

The very existence of this legal conflict is reflected in the possible means for its resolution. In the first place, despite the absence of a supremacy clause in the Treaties, the Member States expressly agree to "take all general or particular measures which are appropriate for ensuring the carrying out of the obligations arising out of the Treaty or resulting from the acts of the institutions of the Community" and to "abstain from any measures likely to jeopardize the attainment of the objectives of the Treaty."[171] To this end, the Council of Ministers represents not only the Member States, but also the Communities themselves. It has the task of harmonizing or coordinating Community and Member State economic policies.[172] A national counterpart to this is Article 2 of the German ratification law to the Rome Treaties, according to which the Bundestag and Bundesrat are to be informed before the Government commits itself in the Council of Ministers.[173] Ideally, therefore, the Member State governments will automatically adjust their laws to the developing law of the Communities.

This process of coordination and adjustment, however, was not entrusted

[169] Reuter, *La C.E.C.A.*, 100 (1953); Catalano, "Le Fonti normative della C.E.C.A.," 2 *Actes Officiels du Congrès sur la CECA* (Stresa), p. 249f; Schlochauer, *op. cit.* (n. 135), p. 29f.

[170] Judgment 13/61, 8 Rspr. 97, 110 (1962).

[171] EEC Art. 5, Euratom Art. 192, and the similar, although more detailed, ECSC Art. 86.

[172] See text *supra*, p. 12.

[173] See note 140 *supra*, which suggests that Art. 2 may well be a double-edged sword: used by the German Parliament either to further coordination or to oppose further integration.

solely to Member State authorities. The Treaties also establish certain procedures for ensuring the unity and integrity of Community law.[174] On the one hand, the "preliminary question" procedure obligates national courts to interrupt judicial proceedings and certify any question concerning the interpretation of Community law to the Community Court. This not only furthers the unity of Community law, but also permits national courts to inform themselves of their Treaty obligations before reaching a final decision on the case before them. It is only a procedure, however, governing the interpretation of Community law; as such it can not establish the priority of Community law as applied by national courts.[175] On the other hand, should it appear that national authorities have not respected their obligations under the Treaties, they may be called to account before the Community Court.[176] Even then, the Treaties take a cautious approach. They require a certain amount of prior consultation between the High Authority or Commission and the allegedly defaulting Member State government before judicial review is invoked. Furthermore, the Court decision merely establishes whether a Treaty violation exists; where sanctions are possible, as under ECSC Article 89, they do not result automatically, but must be instituted by a decision of the Council of Ministers. In any case, once the Court has affirmed a Treaty violation, the defaulting Member State has always conformed to the decision.

Finally, when an open conflict arises between Community and subsequent national legislation, it may be met in three ways. All three presuppose the coexistence of competing Community and national legal obligations for both individual nationals and Member State authorities alike. In the first place, whether based on a presumption of legislative intent or on some generally recognized principle such as *lex posterior generalis non derogat legi priori speciali,* national authorities may seek to mitigate the conflict by giving Community law the broadest possible force and effect.[177] Such approaches, however, are obviously limited in value and will not always be applicable.

174 See text *infra,* Ch. II, Section 2, for a more detailed discussion of the following two and other Community procedures.

175 The Community Court has made this clear in several recent decisions. See Judgments 100/63, 10 Rspr. 1213, 1230 (1964); 24/64, 10 Rspr. 1373, 1388 (1964); and 6/64, 10 Rspr. 1251, 1269 (1964). See also Ipsen, *op. cit.* (n. 137), p. 5ff.

176 See ECSC Art. 88, EEC Arts. 169 and 170, Euratom Arts. 141 and 142. See discussion in text *infra,* p. 63ff.

177 Lauterpacht-Oppenheim, *op. cit.* (n. 136), p. 42f. This presumption is expressly recognized by German courts. See Boehmer, *op. cit.,* (n. 158), p. 69f; Maunz-Dürig, *op. cit.* (n. 156), Randnr. 30 zu. Art. 25; and Schröcker, "Das vertragswidrige Gesetz," 73 *Deutsches Verwaltungsblatt,* 369, 372 and 374 (1958). French courts take a similar view. See Schilling, *op. cit.,* (n. 147), pp. 103–6.

Secondly, a less certain but perhaps more effective means to counter conflicting subsequent national legislation is the reactivation of those Community acts which such legislation negates. This approach of course would be relevant only for the quasi-legislation of Community organs – i.e., ECSC Decisions and EEC and Euratom Regulations and Decisions – which is directly applicable within the Member States. Assuming that this quasi-legislation possesses the same status in the Member States as the Treaties themselves,[178] the re-activated Community acts even under a dualistic theory would take precedence over prior national legislation so long as the basic decision-making powers of the Communities remain intact. Again, this could only be a stop-gap measure against a resolute Member State legislature.

In the last instance, however, an open conflict can be resolved in favor of the Communities only through the willing cooperation of the responsible Member State authorities. They determine the force and effect of Community law within their jurisdictions. When in case of conflict the Communities remain adamant, then – as Advocate-General Lagrange put it[179] – there remain only two possibilities for the Member States: either to bring their constitutions in accord with the Treaty or to revoke the Treaty. Nevertheless, the alternative will rarely be so clearly put. Until the Member States are prepared to stipulate categorically the supremacy of Community law, there will be haggling, negotiations, remonstrances, delays and occasional blank refusals to enforce fully or partially certain Community acts and Treaty provisions. The cumulative effect of such opposition over time could lead to a loss of Community authority and to the gradual dissolution of the Communities themselves. This is only to say that the binding effect of Community law – like the future of the Communities themselves – remains for the time being undetermined. It must await the outcome of Community integration. At the same time, this period of uncertainty does not disqualify Community organs, including the Court of Justice, and national authorities from asserting and granting the Community legal orders as much authority as possible. This is the very essence of co-existing – complementary and competing – Community and Member State legal orders.

[178] This view is generally accepted. See, e.g., Scheuner, *op. cit.* (n. 137), p. 241f; Bülow, *op. cit.* (n. 154), p. 53; Carstens, *op. cit.*, (n. 137), p. 74, citing Wagner, *Das Beschlussrecht der europäischen Gemeinschaften*, 331ff (1965); and Catalano, *La C.E.E. e l'Euratom* 60–69 (1957).

[179] Case 6/64, 10 Rspr. 1279, 1292 (1964).

5. THE DEVELOPMENT OF COMMUNITY CONSENSUS CONCLUSIONS

Finally, the Communities embrace a developing consensus which in its intensity is unique to international organization. It forms the necessary complement of the incomplete and contingent character of Community organization and authority – of the "Community" idea itself. Proceeding from the basis of international agreements within the framework of common markets, it possesses an inner dynamic which reaches far into the future relations of the Member States. "Because integration always means development," states Meyer-Cording,[180] "it involves a social process which is continually underway." The constant development of a Community consensus among Member State authorities, nationals and representatives is the key to the growth and establishment of Community legal orders over time.[181]

The inner dynamic of this consensus is reflected most clearly in its formal, substantive and result-oriented aspects. As to the first, the Treaties themselves establish the "title to rule,"[182] or a consensus as to the formal powers, institutions and procedures of decision-making in the Communities. As Sections 2 and 3 point out, this not only assures an essential minimum of integrity and unity for the common interests of the Community, but also institutionalizes a driving impulse for Community integration. The result is a degree of independence and continuity in Community decision-making which, as Ernst Haas explains,[183] tends to "upgrade the common interests" of the Member States. This tendency was reinforced as the EEC moved into the second and third stages of integration, for the voting requirement in the Council of Ministers on certain matters shifted from unanimity to a qualified or simple majority.[184] A relaxation of the voting requirement not only

[180] Meyer-Cording, "Die europäische Integration als geistiger Entwicklungsprozess," 10 *Arch. VR*. 42, 43 (1962); also in Festgabe Alfred Müller-Armack: *Wirtschaft, Gesellschaft und Kultur*, 291 (1961).

[181] See v. Simson, "Der politische Wille als Gegenstand der europäischen Gemeinschaftsverträge," in *Festschrift Otto Riese*, 83, 87 (1964), whose thesis runs: "Die 'Supra-nationalität' kann in dieser Sicht den gemeinsamen Willen der Staaten nicht ersetzen oder ihm entgegentreten, sondern sie operiert erst auf Grund dieses gemeinsamen Willens, und also auch nur insoweit und solange, als dieser gemeinsame Wille es zulässt."

[182] See Friedrich, *Man and His Government: An Empirical Theory of Politics*, Ch. 13 (1963).

[183] Haas, "International Integration: The European and the Universal Process," 15 *Int. Organ.*, 366, 368f (1961).

[184] This distinguishes the EEC from the ECSC and Euratom. In the following Treaty provisions the shift to simple or qualified majority vote occurred at the beginning of the second stage: EEC Art. 8(3); 33(8); 87(1) (after 3 years); 54(1) (2); 57(1) (2); 63(1) (2), 101, par. 2. Majority vote began in the third stage in the following cases:

strengthens the independence of the Council from the special interests of the Member States, but also adds new weight to the proposals of the Commission. Under the pressure of majority rule, the Ministers in the Council would be more inclined toward making concessions since the Commission's proposals can be amended only by unanimous vote.[185] These procedural modifications, therefore, help to mitigate the retrogressive tendencies present in the *ad hoc* decision-making of most international organizations.

Opposition to this built-in transition to majority rule accounts for a large part for President de Gaulle's boycott of the Council of Ministers. His policy of the "empty chair", beginning on July 1, 1965, arose in protest against the proposal of the EEC Commission to centralize administration of all customs duties within the Community and, concomitantly, to establish the control of the European Parliament over the Community budget. The Commission attempted, perhaps unwisely, to use the scheduled financial regulation for agriculture to force French approval of its provocative proposal.[186] As de Gaulle himself admitted, however, the Commission proposal was only the occasion for a more fundamental crisis; that lay in the Treaty requirement which soon would subject French interests in the Community to majority vote.[187] Due to the unity and perseverance of the other Member States, France returned to the Council seven months later without obtaining a change in EEC voting procedures. Nevertheless, the Luxembourg Agreement of January 29, 1966, between the Foreign Ministers of the Member States, cast some doubt on the feasibility of majority decisions in the Council where "very important interests of one or more Member States are at stake." In such cases, the Member State representatives would "endeavor, within a reasonable period of time, to reach a solution which is acceptable to all." Beyond this, France and the other five Member States could only "agree to disagree" as to the proper course to follow.[188] As a result, Community pro-

Art. 20, par. 3; 43(2); 44(5); 56(2); 69; 75(1); 112(1), par. 2. By the end of the three stage transitional period, the unanimous voting requirements of the Council have been modified, for the most part, into qualified majority votes.

[185] See Deringer (Generalberichterstatter), *Bericht zum Fünften Gesamtbericht über die Tätigkeit der EWG, Europ. Parlament Sitzungsdokument,* Nr. 74, p. 34 (Oct. 5, 1962).

[186] The financial regulation for agriculture, Regulation No. 25 of April 4, 1962, had established *in principle* the guidelines for the Community agricultural policy.

[187] See de Gaulle's Press Conference of September 9, 1965.

[188] For an account of this crisis and the Luxembourg Agreement, see Lindberg, "Integration as a Source of Stress on the European Community," 20 *Int. Organ.*, 233 (1966) Mosler, "Nationale und Gemeinschaftsinteressen im Verfahren des EWG-Ministerrats," 26 *Z. ausl. öff. R.*, 1 (1966); and Kaiser, "Das Europarecht in der Krise der Gemeinschaften," 1 *Europarecht*, 4 (1966).

cedures have remained intact, indeed the President of the Commission Jean Rey denied expressly before the European Parliament that the Luxembourg Agreement binds either the Commission or the Council.[189] Still, it would appear that the Commission and the Member States in the Council are "operating more cautiously than before." [190]

Secondly, the Communities embrace a developing consensus on matters of substance. This goes to the very heart of Community integration, for it encompasses not only the stated Treaty objectives but also the continuing struggle between the divergent political and economic viewpoints underlying the interpretative decisions of Community organs. This is especially true for the EEC – a "création continue" as Jean Monnet once called it – whose broad policies were left for articulation and implementation over the course of a 12 to 15 year transitional period.[191] As a result, the structural changes in Member State economies have been governed by a time table of programs and goals. This applies not only to the freeing of commerce and competition within the Community[192] and the erection of a common external tariff,[193] but also to the promulgation of Regulations and Directives for implementing general provisions in the Treaty. In successive stages, Community organs have become vested with increased tasks and powers and Member States have become subject correspondingly to new obligations.[194]

These ever-widening spheres of common economic policy have a cumulative or "spill-over" effect on Community integration. For, says Haas, "policies made pursuant to an initial task and grant of power can be made real only if the task itself is expanded . . . ."[195] Thus, while the continued growth of the Common Market rests upon the equality of economic conditions created by common policies, these common policies in turn are made necessary by the problems created in the integrating economic sectors and economics as a whole. As integral parts of the Community legal orders, the

[189] European Community No. 115, p. 17 (August 1968).

[190] Newhouse, *Collision in Brussels: The Common Market Crisis of 30 June 1965*, p. 167 (1967).

[191] See text *supra*, p. 8f.

[192] EEC Arts. 12ff. (Abolishing tariffs between Member States). Arts. 48–73 (freeing the movement of persons, services and capital) and Arts. 7, 85ff. 91, 92ff. (establishing a policy of competition).

[193] EEC Art. 18ff.

[194] See, e.g., EEC Arts. 20, pars. 2 and 3; 23f; 44, par. 4; 80, par. 1, and 95, par. 3; 88 and 87; and 119.

[195] Haas, *op. cit.* (n. 183), p. 368f. See also Haas, *The Uniting of Europe*, esp. Ch. 8 (1958).

achievement of these successive stages builds a floor beneath future development.

Despite appearances, however, the Treaties themselves have not established a substantive consensus. "It is not always sufficiently appreciated," emphasizes Meyer-Cording,[196] "that a community can not be created or maintained with legal means of organization alone. The rules and norms of organizational structure remain dead letters until and insofar as the ideational-spiritual accord and community of values is wanting." For this reason, the integration of Western Europe is not a mere matter of "social engineering" by a group of experts as it is sometimes represented.[197] Rather, as EEC Commission President Hallstein points out, European unification is "Politik, in welchen Verkleidungen und auf welchen Gebieten immer sie erscheint" – including that of "economic integration." [198] Precisely because the broad norms and programs of the Treaties embrace vital spheres of Member State economies, their interpretation by Community organs can not remain a matter of indifference to political leaders. The search for concrete content in ambiguous Treaty norms, therefore, occurs in the midst of a continuing struggle between divergent political and economic viewpoints.

This is apparent, in the first place, in the continuing contest between the "liberalist" and "dirigist" ideals of economic integration. Although the Treaties embody neither one extreme nor the other, in what proportions are they authorized and compatible with economic integration on the Community level? Whereas the French Socialists contend that "there is no alternative to a directed economy," since "the market can be extended not by liberalising but by organising,"[199] others take an equally strong free trade, free market economy position. Former West German Chancellor Erhard, while still Minister of Economics, declared before the European Parliament that competition –

196 Meyer-Cording, *op. cit.* (n. 180), p. 51.

197 E.g., Benoit, *Europe at Sixes and Sevens,* 242f (1961), has tended to overemphasize the role and function of technicians and specialists in bringing about European integration. Rather, as Nord has rightly pointed out, the task of European integration is one more for a gardener than an engineer. "In Search of a Political Framework for an Integrated Europe," in Haines, *European Integration,* 215, 219 (1957).

198 Hallstein, "Die echten Probleme der europäischen Integration," 37 *Kieler Vorträge,* 3 (Neue Folge, 1965).

199 André Philip, "Social Aspects of European Economic Co-operation," 76 *Int. Labour Rev.,* 244, 255 (1957). See also his *L'Europe unie et sa place dans l'Economie internationale* (1953), and M. Byé, "Freer Trade and Social Welfare," 77 *Int. Labour Rev.,* 38 (1958), who while not an advocate of centralized planning, recommends stepping-up state intervention.

quietly furthers the necessary adjustments, that is to say, by means of it the necessary responsiveness of the economy is maintained. By contrast, direct regulation and other types of economic planning appear to be very primitive and, in addition, tend to be centralistic .... When one ventures into economic planning and programming and becomes entangled in such kinds of calculation, the material data and factors advance more forcefully into the foreground. As a result, the danger increases that "man" loses, for he cannot be grasped with numbers.[200]

Further, this struggle is reflected in the debate concerning the nature of the Communities and the scope of their powers over the economic activities in the Member States. Here, the destinies and aspirations of Member State leaders come face-to-face with the integrating thrust of the Community organs. Are the Communities, like federal governments, empowered to exercise their powers exclusive of the Member States? Or, are the Communities like much traditional international organization, as President de Gaulle contended,[201] of mere "valeur technique, mais n'ont pas et ne peuvent avoir d'autorité et d'efficacité politique?" Whichever of these economic or political viewpoints is emphasized – and these are by no means exhaustive – it will exert considerable influence on the concrete formulation of Community policy and on Member State compliance. They appear time and again, expressly or implicitly, in the decisions of the Community organs, in the debates of the European Parliament and, indeed, in the briefs of counsel, the Conclusions of the Advocates-General and the reasoning of the Community Court of Justice.

Moreover, the resolution of substantive questions in the Treaties often colors the "title to rule" itself. Thus, the absence of a substantive consensus among the Member States in Council during the 1958–1959 coal crisis undermined the formal consensus in the ECSC Treaty. Since France, Germany and Italy – either out of dislike of "supranationalism" or "dirigisme"

[200] *Verhandlungen des Europäischen Parlaments,* 60, 63 (Nov. 19–23, 1962). See also Roepke, "Integration und Desintegration der internationalen Wirtschaft," in *Festgabe Ludwig Erhard,* 493 (1957), and M. Allais, "Fondements théoriques, perspectives et conditions d'un marché commun effectif," 68 *Rev. écon. pol.* 58, 65 (1958), who asserts that "pratiquement, la seule règle qui soit mutuellement acceptable pour une étroite co-opération économique entre des sociétés démocratiques est la règle de l'économie de marché." By and large, however, French economists appear to take a more dirigistic view of economic integration than, for instance, German economists.

[201] Press Conference of President de Gaulle, reported in *Le Monde,* Sept. 7, 1960, p. 4. See also Peyrefitte, "L'Avenir de l'Europe," in *Le Monde,* Sept. 14, 1960, p. 5. For equally critical views of such technocracy in general, see Erhard, "Was wird aus Europa?" *Handelsblatt* (Dec. 23 and 24, 1960).

or for reason of national advantage[202] – were unwilling to entrust a solution of the coal recession to the ECSC, the authorized Treaty measures proposed by the High Authority remained unrealized and Member State Treaty obligations unfulfilled.[203] This blatant failure of the ECSC prompted President de Gaulle shortly thereafter to remark: "So long as nothing serious happens, the Communities function without much difficulty. But let some dramatic situation arise, a great problem to resolve, and it becomes evident that only States and not an organ like the High Authority has influence over the various spheres of national life."[204] The developing consensus on Treaty substance, therefore, is nothing less than a comprehensive search for the meaning *and* authority of Community powers.

In the last instance, however, the development of Community consensus is a matter of concrete results. Support will accrue to the Communities only so far as their policies are felt to be good by individuals, groups and political representatives in the Member States and have proven themselves as such over time. As this occurs, the loyalties, expectations and business, professional and political activities will begin to shift from their distinct national settings toward a new Community centre.[205] For this reason, this third aspect of consensus is essentially pragmatic and can be measured only by a success standard which may well operate independently of both the stipulated agreement in the Treaties and the contest between the competing viewpoints just discussed. Even those who do not wholly agree with the political nature, the objectives and the policies of the Communities may be persuaded to tolerate or accept their results as good or irreversible. Depending on the various interests effected, therefore, the results of economic integration may ameliorate or accentuate the continuing struggle surrounding the development of Community powers and organization.

The initial interests involved were of course those of the Six Member

[202] Whereas Italy reaped large benefits from the low coal prices and Germany took its own measures while consulting the High Authority "only perfunctorily" (alarmed at the prospect of Community 'dirigisme'), France appears to have been motivated primarily by a dislike of supranationalism. See Meade et al., *Case Studies in European Economic Union,* 248–255 (1962).

[203] The High Authority was permitted only to resort to indirect measures, i.e., to assist in financing coal supplies out of its own coffers. Since such measures were obviously insufficient, direct measures under ECSC Articles 58 and 74 (cases of "manifest crisis") and also under Article 95 were proposed but rejected.

[204] Press Conference, *op. cit.*, p. 4.

[205] This corresponds to Haas' definition of "political integration." *Op. cit.* (n. 195), p. 16. See also Meyer-Cording, *op. cit.* (n. 180), p. 48: "Insbesondere erfordert eine wirkliche, echte Integration, dass man bereit ist, für die gemeinsamen Ziele und Zwecke Opfer zu bringen. Das gilt schon im nationalen Rahmen."

States. In signing the Treaties, they proceeded on the basis of those concrete political and economic advantages which the Communities would bring. Despite some recent comment of political leaders to the contrary, the expected benefits were considerable – though diverse – for all States involved. The ECSC negotiations turned on the basic plan of Robert Schuman, kept secret to the last minute, for a supranational authority. Whereas the breakdown of national trade barriers and increased competition meant cheaper production factors and larger markets for all Member States,[206] the political benefits of the two major steel-producing countries were of decisive importance.[207] For France, it made possible a step toward the solution of the Saar problem as well as the subjection of the German steel industry to common European supervision and measures of decartellization and deconcentration which would make war physically and spiritually impossible. By the same token, Germany would gain not only access to French markets for its highly competitive steel, but also a cessation of Allied economic controls and a position of equality for its coal and steel industry with the other Member States.

The EEC, corresponding to its much greater scope, makes even more visible the concrete benefits to be expected by the Member States. Taken as a whole, the EEC means the re-integration of national economies which in the course of increasing intra-European trade barriers between the First and Second World Wars had shifted their import trade greatly to non-industrialized economies. The accompanying systems of national preferences and discriminations entailed a decrease in competition and specialization which could not avoid having deleterious effects on the over-all growth and efficiency of European industry.[208] Thus, the broader EEC markets mean a predictable outlet for French agricultural products (employing 20% of the French Labor force), new possibilities for Dutch shipping and harbors and a stable market for at least a quarter of German export goods. Further, the EEC offers new hope for the structural problems in Belgium and Italy. Whereas Belgium, due to its natural location, may look forward to becoming an integral part of the Community industrial center, Italy receives an in-

206 The transition period, of course, raised considerable difficulties and, as in the Belgian coal fields, hardships which were eased to some extent by measures of investment and modernization as well as by efforts to close inefficient firms and retrain workers for other jobs.

207 See Haas, *op. cit.* (n. 195), pp. 241-48.

208 See Balassa, *The Theory of Economic Integration,* 5 (1962); and Sannwald and Stohler, *Wirtschaftliche Integration,* 8–14 (1958), on the "relative stagnation of Europe."

creased flow of capital for its developing industries and low-income areas.[209] Finally, the experience of the 1920's and 30's, followed by the break-up of world trade, is a near and constant reminder that small national economies are readily susceptible to the economic pressures and misfortunes of neighboring States. It has become increasingly clear during the present economic boom that inflation, just like depression, is readily exportable. The EEC Treaty considers this a matter of common interest and provides for coordinated policies among the Member States.[210]

Once the Communities have been established, however, their success and continued growth depends upon their ability not only to realize but also to expand and spread these initial expectations. Again, the "spill-over" effect is the essence of this dynamic. Whereas these expectations expand with the need to broaden and strengthen Community powers in an effort to preserve the benefits already achieved, they also spread as ever increasing numbers in the Member States participate in the benefits of Community policies and identify their futures with those of the Communities. In both cases the result is an increased willingness of individuals, groups and Member States to sacrifice national goals and values to the objectives of Community integration. The forces at work to reinforce these expectations are of course varied. Whether they are reactions to the stultifying effects of national autarchy, the evils of nationalism or the threat of Communism, or are responses to the appeal of a greater Europe, the preservation of a common heritage or the desire for greater personal opportunity or economic advantage, they all may find common cause in Community policies.

Above all, the Communities have released economic forces. While recognizing that these forces have only limited influence on the essentially political nature of Community integration,[211] they do possess a two-fold advantage in contributing to a developing Community consensus. In the first place, they focus concretely on the urgent needs and desires of the vast majority

[209] See Hallstein, *op. cit.* (n. 198), pp. 15-18. Lindberg, *The Political Dynamics of European Economic Integration,* Ch. 7 (1963), discusses the negotiating positions of the EEC Treaty partners.

[210] See Part III, Title II of the EEC Treaty.

[211] See Müller-Armack, "Fragen der Europäischen Integration," in *Festgabe Ludwig Erhard,* 531, 534 (1957), who points out that between the formation of the German Customs Union and the Federal German Empire stood the diplomacy of Bismark (and the power and prestige of Prussia). See also Keeton, "The Zollverein and the Common Market," 16 *Current Legal Problems,* 1 (1963). From a broader historical perspective, K. Polanyi, *The Great Transformation,* 56–57 (1944), attacks the view that market economies are *naturally* expansive.

of people.[212] In contrast to the more abstract political and cultural forces, the economic advantages arising from integration are often clearly evident from day-to-day in the households and firms of the Member States. While their effect may be positive or negative, depending on economic conditions, the competitive character of Western European economies and the immense opportunities for economies of scale and specialization suggest that in the near future at least the economic impulse will be positive.[213] During the first ten years of the EEC, inner-Community trade increased 338% in comparison with a world trade figure of 89%. At the same time Community trade with the rest of the world nearly doubled. The GNP of the Member States as an average grew by 60%, that of the United States by only 50%.[214]

Secondly, the economic impulse has the psychological advantage of avoiding a clear and present assault on national values. In his study of *The World and the West,* Arnold Toynbee has illustrated the impact and deceptiveness of Western technology on Eastern cultures.

> When a travelling culture-ray is diffracted into its component strands – technology, religion, politics, art, and so on – by the resistance of a foreign body social upon which it has impinged, its technological strand is apt to penetrate faster and farther than its religious strand; and this law can be formulated in more general terms. We can say that the penetrative power of a strand of cultural radiation is usually in inverse ratio to this strand's cultural value.[215]

Once the smallest breach has been made, however, the at first isolated economic splinter will tend to draw in after it the other component elements of the social system. Thus, the forced retreat from the political ideal of a European Defense Community to the economic integration of the EEC was viewed by many as the "backdoor" to a more gradual political integration which was at the same time politically acceptable. The very charge that the EEC may have become a "Europe des patrons" instead of a "Europe des patries"[216] suggests both the apolitical appeal and the seductive character of

212 Haas, *op. cit.* (n. 183), p. 372, points out that "the degree of functional specificity of the economic task is causally related to the intensity of integration ... Non-economic tasks have shown themselves much more barren."

213 See Balassa, *op. cit.* (n. 208), pp. 5f, 131–38, 159f, 170–72.

214 Information Memorandum of European Community Information Service, of June 14, 1968.

215 Toynbee, *The World and the West,* 68 (1953).

216 As Peyrefitte, *op. cit.* (n. 201), p. 1, points out: "Si l'Europe des patries est encore à faire, l'Europe des patrons se réalise déjà .... La structure de l'industrie européenne se transforme. Les producteurs adoptent une psychologie de grand marché." Indeed, much of the political pressure for the decision of May 1960 to accelerate the formation of the EEC customs union came from business circles. Their initial pessimism, as in

the economic impulse. The stimulation and channelling of economic forces may be seen, therefore, as a valuable counter-thrust to the traditional reluctance of national governments to transfer their sovereign powers to supranational authorities.

It would be a mistake, however, to suppose that the development of a Community consensus is automatic.[217] It embodies a dynamic core, but its fate rests with a long line of individual decisions by Community organs and Member States. Not the least of these decisions concerns the adequacy of existing Community organization as integration proceeds. The integration of economic sectors and of the economies as a whole calls for increased Community policy and regulation as the gradual transition from unanimous to majority decision-making in the Council suggests. Increased power, however, means increased responsibility toward the Member States and their populations. This implies a development of parliamentary powers as well as of a legal order capable of ensuring the rule of law within the Community and protecting it from the special interests of Member States and individuals.

CONCLUSIONS

From this analysis it is clear that the Communities occupy a unique position in the history of international organization. Although resting on international Treaties, they constitute disciplined institutional frameworks which bear the essential marks of a constitutional system. Their limited but vital powers reach far into the reserved domain of Member State economies, governing matters of economic and social policy with which international law and organization has had little or no experience. To a large extent, the formation and administration of this policy is entrusted to Community organs possessing a high degree of organizational autonomy. To ensure the integrity and unified exercise of Community powers, separate legal orders have been erected under the care and development of a common Court of

France, underwent a radical revision within two years after the opening of the Common Market. See Stein, "An American Lawyer Looks at the Common Market," in Stein and Nicholsen (eds.), *American Enterprise in the European Common Market,* 1, 12f (1960); and Lindberg, *The Political Dynamics of European Economic Integration,* 170f and Ch. 9 generally (1963).

[217] Hallstein, "Zu den Grundlagen und Verfassungsprinzipien der europäischen Gemeinschaften," in *Festschrift Carl Ophüls,* 1, 4 (1965). Moreover, as Etzioni has pointed out, an expansion of Community membership and the added heterogeneity of national interests which this implies would most likely increase the complexity and difficulty of consensus formation. "The Dialectics of Supranational Unification," 56 *Amer. Pol. Sci. Rev.,* 927, 931f (1962).

Justice vested with broad and exclusive powers of judicial review. These legal orders – composed of Treaty norms, the quasi-legislative and administrative acts of Community organs and the decisions of the Community Court – operate directly on individual nationals as well as on Community organs and Member States. Finally, in contrast to the expanding international legal community, the Communities proceed from a "Community" idea which embraces not only common markets and particular views of economic integration, but also a common cultural heritage which was once the center of the civilized world. Within this framework, the Community organs constitute an institutionalized impetus for continued Community integration, buttressed by varied and shifting social and economic forces in the Member States.

On the other hand, it is also clear that the Communities fall far short of federal government. Whether taken individually or as a whole, their powers are uniquely limited both as to scope, means and purposes. They are not authorized to deal with those basic questions of political and territorial integrity and of war and peace which are so characteristic of federal governments. Further, they lack a true legislative capacity as well as a parliament which is organized to represent an electorate and to initiate and control Community policy. The broader the powers granted the Communities, the more they are vested in the Council of Ministers and tied closely to the Member State governments. Finally, even where Community action is authorized under the Treaties, it is not "supreme" over the Member States. Rather, being based on international Treaties, it is contingent in the last instance on the constitutional practice of the Member States. In effect, therefore the Community legal orders are both complementary and competitive with those of the Member States and must depend to a large extent on Member State cooperation and support.

At the most, the Communities may be viewed as the uncertain beginning stage in a long process of federalism. Federalism, says Carl Friedrich,[218]

> should not be considered a term for a static pattern, designating a particular and precisely fixed devision of powers between governmental levels. Instead, federalism seems the most suitable term by which to designate the process of federalizing a political community, that is to say, the process by which a number of state political organizations, be they states or any other kind of associations, enter into arrangements for working out solutions, adapting joint policies and making joint decisions on joint problems. Or reversely, it is the process through which a hitherto unitary political community . . . becomes differentiated into a number of separate and distinct political communities . . . .

[218] Friedrich, "International Federalism in Theory and Practice," in Plischke (ed.), *Systems of Integrating the International Community,* 117, 126f (1964).

It is this process and not a static form of Community government – whether supranational or confederate – which is the central concern of this study. Standing astride both international and Member State law, the Communities embody legal orders in formation. Their dynamic underpinnings consist of a developing value consensus on the decisions-making powers, substantive policies and real effects of Community integration. This confronts the Community Court with a challenge for the creative development of Community law. What are the functions and tasks of judicial decision in this context?

CHAPTER II

THE JURISDICTION OF THE COURT

The Court of Justice of the European Communities is charged to "ensure the respect for law in the interpretation and application" of the Treaties.[1] As a general provision, this does not vest the Court with any particular jurisdiction in Community matters.[2] It does emphasize the crucial fact, however, that the Community Court is not a mere arbitral tribunal, but a court of law. Its jurisdiction is compulsory, its judgments are binding on the parties and its procedures are institutionalized. Moreover, the Court renders judgments through reasoned decisions within the constitutional framework of the Treaties, subject to the institutionalized discipline of a division of governmental functions and balance of powers. This framework lends judicial decision a continuity and permanency to a degree much greater than is found in the international community. It also establishes real limits to the judicial function and to the judicial development of Community law.

The essential foundation of the Court's jurisdiction is three-pronged. The treaty basis of Community law is reflected in the prominent if not decisive influence of the Member States over the course of Community development. These States not only participate directly in the political councils of Community decision, they also have broad access to the Court of Justice. Secondly, the major Community political institutions themselves may attack the legality of Community measures and Member State acts. Thus, the balance of powers is reinforced by the threat of judicial relief. Finally, individual nationals, firms and business associations in the Member States, all of which are subject to the direct application of Community law, have received limited constitutional safeguards in the form of rights of appeal against Community acts. These three bases of the Court's jurisdiction provide both the institu-

[1] ECSC Art. 31, EEC Art. 164, Euratom Art. 136.

[2] This view appears to be generally accepted. See, e.g., Valentine, *The Court of Justice of the European Communities*, vol. I, pp. 112 and 273f (1965); Groeben and Boeckh, *Kommentar zum EWG-Vertrag*, Anm. 2 zu Art. 164 (1960).

tional framework and the motivation for the judicial elaboration of vague and uncertain norms into meaningful and effective rules of Community law. They form the warp around which is woven a system of judicial control for the European Communities.

The literature frequently has tended to classify and analyze the Court's jurisdiction according to categories typical of municipal law.[3] Thus, the Court is said to exercise some international, constitutional, administrative and civil law jurisdiction and to act, in some cases, as a disciplinary and as an arbitral tribunal. This approach not only is useful for pedagogical and comparative law purposes, it further accords closely with those working concepts, especially in the field of administrative law, which guided the framers of the Treaties. In proceeding from these traditional legal categories, however, the danger exists of underestimating the unique character of the Court's jurisdiction in the service of the Community legal control and development. Just as it is misleading to identify Community acts with the administrative acts of municipal authorities,[4] it is also deceptive to explain the function of the Court's jurisdiction or its task of interpretation by reference primarily to considerations common to administrative courts.[5] While the Court has been endowed with the grounds of review and the procedural framework most nearly resembling the Conseil d'Etat, its object of review encompasses the scope and limits of Community powers as well as the division and balance of powers among Community organs and between the Communities and the Member States.[6] This jurisdiction, therefore, must be understood in terms of the unique nature of the Communities themselves. The Advocates-General have not hesitated to assess the extent of individuals' rights of appeal within the context of a "system of legal protection" in the Treaties.[7] Not unexpectedly, appeals common to administrative or inter-

[3] See, e.g., Schlochauer, "Die Gerichtsbarkeit der EGKS," 3 *Arch. VR.* 385 (1951–52); de Richemont, *La Cour de Justice,* 261ff (1954); Delvaux, *La Cour de Justice de la CECA,* (1956); van Houtte, "La Cour de Justice de la CECA," 2 *European Yearbook,* 183 (1956) ;Wohlfarth et al., *Die EWG, Kommentar zum Vertrag,* Vorb. 3 zu Art. 164 (1960); Feld, *The Court of the European Communities,* Ch. 3 (1964); and Colin, *Le Gouvernement des juges dans les Communautés Européennes,* Part I (1966).

[4] Bebr, *Judicial Control of the European Communities,* 38 (1962); also, Conclusions *of Adv-Gen.* Roemer in Case 7/54 and 9/54, 2 Rspr. 105, 122–23 (1955–56).

[5] Steindorff, *Die Nichtigkeitslage im Recht der EGKS,* 14–17 (1952), takes a doubtful position in this respect. See also Ule, "Verwaltungsgerichte überstaatlicher und internationaler Organisationen," 3 *Deutsches Verwaltungsblatt,* 491 (1953).

[6] Lagrange, "L'ordre juridique de la CECA vu à travers la jurisprudence de sa Cour de Justice," 64 *Rev. dr. pub. sci. pol.,* 841, 861f (1958).

[7] See, e.g., *Conclusions of Adv-Gen. Roemer,* in Case 73 and 74/63 10 Rspr. 33, 43 (1964).

national courts may, within the framework of the Communities, look more like constitutional control.[8]

The following discussion avoids such classifications by analyzing the Court's jurisdiction within its unique institutional framework. This requires, first of all, determining the scope of judicial authority to review alleged illegal acts under the Treaties. This authority is reflected in the differing grounds which may be raised by the several categories of parties on appeal. Following this, the basic considerations will be outlined which determine under what conditions and by which parties these grounds may be invoked. By this approach, it may be possible to determine the potential scope of the Court's contribution to legal development within the institutional balance of Community, Member States and private interests.

1. THE SCOPE OF JUDICIAL REVIEW

Judicial control in the Communities is fashioned to meet the requirements of political organization and economic regulation in new forms of international organization. The scope of review reflects a balance between two competing considerations. On the one hand, the absence of well-developed political controls in the Communities called for the broad exercise of judicial review in order to prevent the abuse of power by highly independent Community organs. The Court, Jean Monnet declared,[9] would be the "gardien de l'objectivité de la Haute Autorité." On the other hand, this unprecedented attempt at economic integration demanded the flexible management of Community powers. The decisions of Community organs must necessarily be based on the evaluation of economic facts, trends and situations for which no firm standards exist. Only to a limited extent are they accessible to legal analysis and the normative judgments of a Court. It was neither desirable nor intended to raise the Court above the Community executive and quasi-legislative organs "zum hoechsten Willensorgan in wirtschaftlichen Fragen."[10] A balance had to be sought, therefore, between strict adherence to standards of legality and the desire to curb the abuse of discretionary power.

8 See Lagrange, *op. cit.*, p. 861f. As noted above (p. 19), the Court has referred to appeals under ECSC Art. 33 against the High Authority as "constitutional."

9 Cited by Hallstein, *Der Schuman-Plan*, 23 (1951).

10 Amtliche Begründung des Montanvertrages, *Deutscher Bundestag-Drucksache*, Nr. 2401, p. 15 (1. Wahlperiode 1949, Anlage 3). See also Jaenicke, "Die EGKS, Struktur und Funktion ihrer Organe," 14 *Z. ausl. off. R.*, 727, 782 (1951–52); Jerusalem, *Das Recht der Montanunion*, 52f (1954). For a similar French view, see Rapport de la délégation française sur le Traité instituant la CECA 35f (Paris, 1951).

The balance struck is embodied for the most part in seven separate grounds of judicial review. Although reflecting the administrative judicature of all the Member States, they were taken essentially from that of the Conseil d'Etat, France's highest administrative court.[11] There, a sharp distinction is drawn between the *contentieux de pleine juridiction* and *pour excès de pouvoir*. These two may be distinguished in terms of both the object of litigation and the task of the judge.[12] The proceeding against *excès de pouvoir* [13] aims merely at ascertaining the legality of an administrative act according to rules of law, leaving the administration's sphere of discretion essentially untouched. This may occur on the basis of four separate grounds of appeal – incompetence, major violation of procedure, violation of law and *détournement de pouvoir* (misuse of discretion) – all of which have been incorporated in the Treaties as the cornerstone of judicial control.[14] The Court is authorized only to declare an illegal act null and void *erga omnes*, leaving to the appropriate authority the determination as to what further measures should be taken. This accords fully with the basic mandate of the Court "to ensure the respect for law" in the interpretation and application of the Treaties.

[11] The reasons for this are summarized in Becker, *Der Einfluss des französischen Verwaltungsrechts auf den Rechtsschutz in den Europäischen Gemeinschaften*, 141f (1963); Schlochauer, *op. cit.* (n. 3), p. 388.

[12] deLaubadère, *Traité Elémentaire de Droit Administratif*, vol. I, pp. 431–33 (3rd. ed. 1963); Duez-Debeyre, *Traité de Droit Administratif*, 334f (1952); and Becker, *id.*, p. 14f.

[13] This proceeding is discussed in Hamson, *Executive Discretion and Judicial Control*, 7–10 and 162–175 (1954); Freedeman, *The Conseil d'Etat in Modern France*, 133–38 (1961); de Laubadère, *id.*, vol. I, pp. 451–93; Steindorff, *op. cit.* (n. 5), pp. 53–83; and Becker, *id.*, pp. 14–16.

The classification "excès de pouvoir" is alien to Anglo-Saxon practice. It is translated by Freedeman, *id.*, as a "plea of ultra vires"; however, this term fails to convey either all the aspects or refinements of the French proceeding. The broader term "misuse of power" would more likely catch its many nuances. The French classification is followed by Belgium and, to some extent, Italy. Although neither Dutch nor German administrative law practice has formulated such a classification, comparable grounds of appeal are largely available. See Puget and Lévy, "Le Conseil d'Etat Néerlandais," in 3 *Conseil d'Etat, Etudes et Documents*, 150, 163 (1949); and Forsthoff, *Lehrbuch des Verwaltungsrechts*, vol. I, § 12 (8th ed. 1961); and Fromont, "Der Rechtsschutz gegen Massnahmen der Verwaltung im Europa der Sechs," 4 *Europarecht* 202, 209–212 (1969).

[14] ECSC Art. 33, EEC Art. 173 and Euratom Art. 146. For a discussion of these grounds, see generally, Steindorff, *op. cit.* (n. 5); Rolin, "Les recours en annulation et en cas de carence dans le droit de la CECA à la lumière de la jurisprudence, de la Cour de Justice des Communautés," 13 *Chron. pol. étr.*, 291 (1960); Valentine, "The Jurisdiction of the Court of Justice of the European Communities to Annul Executive Action," 36 *Brit. YB. Int. L.* 174 (1960); Bonaert et al., *Fragen der Nichtigkeits- und Untätigkeitsklagen nach dem Recht der EGKS* (1961); Bebr, *op. cit.* (n. 4), Ch. 4; and Becker, *op. cit.* (n. 11).

By contrast, the proceeding *de pleine juridiction* concerns the adjudication of individual rights, particularly in matters of public contracts or liability. Here, the judge is authorized to review exhaustively not only all questions of law, but also the facts, circumstances and behavior of the parties involved.[15] Since in this proceeding the judge must also replace or modify the annulled administrative act,[16] he is carried beyond the threshold of legality and into the realm of administrative discretion. This proceeding and two closely related grounds of the Treaties' own making, as will be seen, form the fifth, sixth and seventh grounds of appeal before the Community Court.

The first four grounds of the Court's jurisdiction go solely to the legality of the act in question. Illegal or, as the Court has put it,[17] "unconstitutional" acts are null and void, but their subsequent replacement or modification remains fully a matter for the Community organs which issued them.[18] The first two grounds of illegality – incompetence and major violation of procedure – establish a purely formal control over the legality of Community acts. Whereas the former controls the outer limits of a Community organ's authority to treat or act on a matter, the latter embraces those requirements by which a decision must be taken, such as matters of voting, publication and the procedures of hearings and consultation among Community organs.[19] It also includes the requirement of motivation, i.e. that quasi-legislative and executive acts of the Community organs be supported fully by stated reasons.[20] The High Authority, declared the Court,[21] must disclose "unequivocally and fully the factual and legal considerations" underlying its acts. Though not extending to the economic evaluations of the Community organs themselves, it opens decisions to scrutiny, making them thereby more accessible to attack on the merits.[22] The development and function of this requirement will be considered more closely in Chapter VII.[23] In any case, the ground of major procedural violation should not be confused with the American doctrine of "due process," which in time has come to embrace

[15] de Richemont, *op. cit.* (n. 3), p. 406.
[16] de Laubadère, *op. cit.*, p. 432; Duez-Debeyre, *op. cit.*, p. 335.
[17] See note 101 *supra*, p. 20.
[18] ECSC Art. 34, EEC Art. 176, Euratom Art. 149. The Court, however, may declare only a part of an act null and void.
[19] See text *supra*, Chapter I, Section 2, concerning the institutional check and balance among Community organs.
[20] ECSC Art. 15, EEC Art. 190, Euratom Art. 162.
[21] Judgment 2/56, 3 Rspr. 9, 38 (1957).
[22] See, e.g., Judgment 1/63, 9 Rspr. 653, 677 (1963).
[23] See text *infra*, pp. 480ff.

both substantive (e.g., discriminatory and arbitrary action) and procedural ("fair hearing," etc.) aspects. Instead, it follows the French concept of *vice de forme,* limited strictly to matters of form and procedure.

The third and fourth grounds of appeal – violation of the Treaty and *détournement de pouvoir* – go to the substance of the act or conduct in question. As to the third, an act is illegal if it violates provisions of a Treaty or "any rule of law relating to its application." The latter phrase, as will be seen in Chapters V and VI, encompasses not only general acts of the Community organs, but also those general principles of law implied by the Treaties and Community organization. The heavily normative character of the ECSC Treaty establishes especially stringent limits for the Commission;[24] the exercise of ECSC powers is circumscribed both by the fundamental objectives of Articles 2 and 3, the principles of market conduct in Article 4 and the limited means of market intervention stated in Article 5 as well as by the specific aims contained in the various provisions throughout the Treaty.[25] The interpretation of such general and at times conflicting Treaty objectives, which directly bind the Commission,[26] in itself grants the Court a central position in the development of Community law. In determining the existence of a Treaty violation, the Court must review the findings of facts which constitute the violation in light of the meaning of the Treaty provisions in question. Of course, the allegation of a Treaty violation may be raised not merely as to acts of the Community organs but also vis-à-vis the conduct of firms[27] and Member States.[28] In such cases, the scope of judicial review does not differ essentially from that presented here.

Furthermore, the determination of a Treaty violation may carry the Court into that sphere of economic evaluation which constitutes the basis of Community action. In theory, this ground of appeal does not authorize the Court to assess the consequences which a Community organ draws from its economic findings, but only to "ascertain" the facts and economic circumstances upon which a decision has been based.[29] In fact, however, the line is

[24] See ECSC Art. 8.

[25] See Chapter V, Section I *infra,* as to the role of these provisions in the jurisprudence of the Court. Cf. the classifications of Treaty provisions drawn up by Steindorff, "Die Vertragsziele der EGKS als Rechtsvorschriften und Richtlinien," 2 *Ber. deutsch. Ges. VR.* 94–100 (1957); and Bebr., *op. cit.* (n. 4), pp. 3–5.

[26] Judgments 1/54, 1 Rspr. 7, 23 (1954–55); 2/54, 1 Rspr. 79, 97 (1954–55); 7/54 and 9/54, 2 Rspr. 53, 90f (1955–56); 8/57, 4 Rspr. 231, 247 (1958). Judgments 9/57, 10/57, 12/57, 13/57 contain practically the same ruling. See also the Conclusions of *Adv.-Gen.,* Lagrange in Case 13/57, 4 Rspr. 317, 344f (1958).

[27] E.g., ECSC Art. 65 § 4.

[28] E.g., EEC Arts. 169 and 170; and Euratom Arts. 141 and 142.

[29] Judgment 6/54, 1 Rspr. 213, 235 (1955–56).

difficult to draw, since almost all Community powers are tied to legal conditions and limits which embody economic evaluations. This is particularly true of such indefinite legal concepts as "serious shortage" (ECSC Article 59), "decline in demand" (ECSC Article 58) and "distortion of competition" (EEC Article 85), which form the core of economic regulation.[30] The crucial point in establishing a Treaty violation is that while the Court must review economic findings of facts, it must not – unless expressly authorized – reach into the sphere of the Community organs' discretion and judge the advisability or opportuneness of measures taken. With this in mind, Advocate-General Lagrange pointed out in one case that the economic situation, which prompted the High Authority to select the measures that it did, "may be viewed so differently under the circumstances that the judge can not assume the responsibility of substituting his judgment for that of the executive."[31] Nevertheless, the determination of Treaty violations by the Court opens a broad range of economic questions to judicial normation.

The fourth major ground of appeal, *détournement de pouvoir*,[32] is aimed at controlling the misuse of discretionary powers by the Community organs. It should not be confused either with *l'abus de droit* in French and Swiss private law or with the "abuse of rights" in international law, though all three concepts share a core of common meaning.[33] Instead, it introduces a peculiar administrative law aspect into the scope of judicial review, having its counterpart with some variance in the law of all the Member States but its origins in the jurisprudence of the Conseil d'Etat.[34] Its function, as de-

[30] See Steindorff, *op. cit.* (n. 5), p. 136f; Bebr, *op. cit.* (n. 4), p. 95f. Cf. the critical position of Ehmke, "'Ermessen' und 'Unbestimmter Rechtsbegriff' im Verwaltungsrecht," in 230/231 *Recht und Staat in Geschichte und Gegenwart*, 29–31 and 46–51 (1960), who doubts the utility of attempting to separate the concept of discretion from that of "undetermined legal concept."

[31] Conclusions of *Adv-Gen.* Lagrange in Case 13/57, 4 Rspr. 317, 357f (1958).

[32] Due to the peculiarities of *détournement de pouvoir*, there is no corresponding ground in American or English administrative law practice. To avoid misunderstanding, therefore, the French term will be used throughout the text.

[33] See Roulet, *Le Caractère artificiel de la Théorie de l'abus de droit en Droit international public*, 13–23 and 41–44 (1958). In international law, the "abuse of rights" may be described as the application of a law or exercise of a right, generally recognized by the legal order, in a manner so arbitrary or disproportionate that it inflicts undue injury on others or the legitimate interests of the international community. See Lauterpacht-Oppenheim, *International Law*, vol. I, p. 345f (8th ed. 1955). But skeptical, see Roulet, *id.*, p. 149f. As to the employment of *détournement de pouvoir*, in reviewing acts of international organizations, see Fawcett, "Détournement de pouvoir by International Organizations" 33 *Brit. YB. Int. L.*, 311 (1957).

[34] Conclusions of *Adv-Gen.* Lagrange in Case 3/54, 1 Rspr. 157–79 (1954), who concludes after a detailed comparative study that the counterparts of *détournement de pouvoir* in the Member States do not differ essentially from each other. But see Daig,

fined there, neither permits a court to review the advisability or opportuneness of an administrative act, for this would undercut the essential sphere of executive discretion; nor to check the transgression of the limits of discretion, for this is a question of incompetence or violation of law.[35] In the practice of the Conseil d'Etat, the *détournement de pouvoir* is interpreted restrictively in favor of other grounds of illegality.[36]

Stated positively, the *détournement de pouvoir* is designed to nullify those acts within the authorized sphere of executive discretion which are undertaken, whether in good or bad faith, for the wrong or improper motives. Such acts may be characterized by the use of a public power to satisfy personal animosity, to favor the private interests of an official or a third party or to adopt a view of the public interest other than that provided in the law. Since motives are meaningfully reviewed, however, only in terms of the purposes of the power to be exercised, it is unavoidable that the subjective bearing of the executive in the act be compared with the objective references in the laws. A *détournement de pouvoir* may be said to exist, then, where the motives for executive action are found not to agree with the purpose of the power granted.[37] As Daig puts it:

> In all the Member State legal orders the Rechtsmissbrauch (*détournement de pouvoir*) serves the function of attacking not so much the illegal *content* as the faulty formation of the administrative act, that is to say, the decision-making process of the governmental authority.[38]

On this ground of appeal, therefore, the arbitrary use of administrative discretion is partially checked without the merits of the act itself being reviewed.

The Community Court has held largely to this central idea. A *détourne-*

"Die vier ersten Urteile des Gerichtshofes der Montanunion," 10 *Juristenzeitung,* 361, 369 (1955).

35 The German administrative law concept of discretionary control, however, would be broad enough in some cases to cover such a transgression, i.e. under the concept of Ermessensüberschreitung, if not Ermessenswillkür. See, e.g., Klinger, *Kommentar zur Verwaltungsgerichtsordnung,* § 42 G IV (1960); Lagrange, *id.,* pp. 176–78.

36 Lagrange, *id.,* p. 179, who contrasts this with the German and Italian practice.

37 A *détournement de pouvoir* is committed, says de Laubadère, *op. cit.* (n. 12), p. 479, "lorsqu'une autorité administrative accomplit un acte de sa compétence mais en vue d'un *but* autre que celui pour lequel l'acte pouvait légalement être accompli." See also, Garner, "French Administrative Law," 33 *Yale L. J.,* 597, 609 (1924); Hamson, *op. cit.,* (n. 13), pp. 166–69; and Freedeman, *op. cit.* (n. 13), p. 134f.

Further, only the dominant motive and not a secondary, even though illegal motive can make such an act illegal under French administrative practice. See Duez-Debeyre, *op. cit.* (n. 12), p. 393; and Judgment 1/54, 1 Rspr. 7, 34 (1954–55).

38 Daig, *op. cit.* (n. 34), p. 369f.

ment de pouvoir occurs, said the Court,[39] where the High Authority had exercised its power "for an objective other than the one for which the powers were granted." At the same time, the Court has adapted and broadened this ground to fit the requirements of the ECSC in a way which may not be warranted for the EEC.[40] Thus, the greater quasi-legislative powers of the Commission, within the highly normative structure of the ECSC, would seem to call for stricter judicial control. This is particularly true at the present stage of Community development because of the rudimentary nature of political control. Moreover, as will be discussed below,[41] private parties subject to the ECSC may challenge a general act of the Commission only on the ground of *détournement de pouvoir*. Under the EEC Treaty, by contrast, the right of appeal of private parties against general acts (Regulations) of the Commission and Council – although more generally limited than under the ECSC Treaty – is not concentrated on the ground of *détournement de pouvoir*. A liberal construction of this ground of review, therefore, accords with the felt need to grant private parties subject to ECSC regulation the broadest possible judicial relief.

Finally, the judicial development of the *détournement de pouvoir* has been encouraged also by the problem of proof. Thus, while the *détournement de pouvoir* may correctly be termed "the most powerful ground of illegality,"[42] this is true only potentially. Despite many attempts, only rarely has an allegation on this ground been successful.[43]. The difficulty often lies in showing that wrong or improper reasons motivated a Community act. Such motives, though present, may not sufficiently be evident either in the *travaux*

39 Judgment 6/54, 1 Rspr. 213, 239 (1954–55). See also Judgments 8/55, 2 Rspr. 297, 313f (1955–56); 8/57, 4 Rspr. 231, 253 (1958): the judicial control "consists in examining the objectives pursued and the purpose of the measure appealed." In Judgment 15/57, 4 Rspr. 159, 201 (1958), the Court illustrated its point: "It must be recognized that a *détournement de pouvoir* would have been possible if the High Authority, finding itself faced with a situation which necessitated the application of the procedure set out in Article 59, had nevertheless, in order to avoid the guarantees of Article 59, proceeded under Article 53b) and the financial arrangements which it contains."

40 See Bebr, *op. cit.* (n. 4), pp. 100–102.

41 See text *infra*, p. 80f.

42 Bebr, *op. cit.* (n. 4), p. 98.

43 See Judgment 9/56 (*Meroni & Co. S.p.A.* v. *High Authority*), 4 Rspr. 9, 44 (1958), and the companion case 10/56, 4 Rspr. 51 (1958), where the Court equated an unlawful delegation of High Authority powers with a *détournement de pouvoir*. The powers themselves were not questioned, only their mode of execution. Once the organizational error had been corrected, the program continued in force, unaltered in substance. See discussion in text *infra*, pp. 253ff and 311.

The ground of *détournement de pouvoir* has been invoked more successfully in attacks on administrative decisions falling under the Personnel Statute. See, e.g., 18 and 35/65, 12 Rspr. 153, 177f (1966).

préparatoires of the High Authority's decision or in the context of actions surrounding the decision. As a result, the Court has been willing to admit evidence of an objective violation of Treaty standards as proof of improper motivation.[44] Factual errors, of course, do not *ipso facto* prove the existence of a *détournement de pouvoir*. In addition, said the Court, it must be proven that "as a result of a grave lack of foresight or circumspection which amounts to a disregard of legal objectives, the High Authority pursued objectives other than those for which the powers were granted."[45] Nevertheless, this determination, that "a grave lack of foresight or circumspection" has occurred, may well draw the Court toward a closer scrutiny of the economic evaluations implied by the decision itself. Since the problem of evidence is as real under the Rome Treaties as under the ECSC Treaty, it is clear that at least in some respects there may be good reason for the Court to continue this development for all three Communities.

ECSC Article 33 deviates in another important respect from its counterparts in the Rome Treaties. By way of exception, when the Commission is alleged to have committed a *détournement de pouvoir* or to have "patently misconstrued" the Treaty or any rule of law concerning its application,[46] the Court may review "the evaluation of the situation resulting from the economic facts or circumstances in the light of which the decisions or recommendations were taken." This clause does not establish a special ground of appeal [47] or authorized the Court to determine the advisability or opportuneness of the Commission's acts, even though the review of such economic evaluations must reach deeply into its sphere of discretion. Rather, this broadened scope of judicial review is subsumed under the traditional grounds of violation of the Treaty and *détournement de pouvoir*. It may be invoked only if a misuse of ECSC powers is alleged, whether viewed objectively as a "patent misconstruction" of the Treaty, or subjectively as improper motives.[48] Once invoked, the Court may then "take into account structural and economic factors." [49]

44 See the insightful forecast of this development by Steindorff, *op. cit.* (n. 5), pp. 161–63. See also the Conclusions of *Adv-Gen.*, in Case 13/57, 4 Rspr. 317, 373 (1958); and Bebr, *op. cit.* (n. 4), p. 105f.

45 Judgment 8/55, 2 Rspr. 197, 317f (1955–56). See also Conclusions of *Adv-Gen.* Lagrange in Case 13/57, 4 Rspr. 317, 313f (1958).

46 This allegation need be supported only by *prima facie* evidence. See Judgment 6/54, 1 Rspr. 213, 237 (1954–55).

47 Conclusions of *Adv-Gen.* Roemer in Case 6/54, 1 Rspr. 241, 249f (1954–55).

48 Matthies, "Zur Nachprüfungsbefugnis des Gerichtshofs der Montanunion," 16 *Z. ausl. öff. R*, 427, 448f (1955–56). See also Steindorff, *op. cit.* (n. 5), pp. 137–40 and 161–63.

49 Judgment 6/54, 1 Rspr. 213, 236 (1954–55).

Nevertheless, the broadened scope of review which this clause establishes is circumscribed by its exceptional character. An act of the Commission must be upheld unless a comparison of the economic situation and the Commission's evaluation of it reveals either "a clear lack of necessity" for the measures taken ("patent misconstruction"),[50] or the use of powers "for a purpose other than the one for which they were given" (*détournement de pouvoir.*)[51] This clause reveals certain similarities to French and American administrative practice, where courts are prepared to broaden their scope of review in cases of flagrant illegality or of an increased need for judicial protection.[52] For the ECSC, it expresses a procedural compromise between an extensive judicial review of economic evaluations, which would displace the discretionary judgment of the Commission and the recognition that decisions based on economic evaluations within the framework of indefinite legal concepts can be only relatively right.[53] The obvious absence of a similar clause from the Rome Treaties (EEC Article 173 and Euratom Article 146) suggests a strict adherence to the objective standards of legality in judicial review. As if to ensure this, these Articles expressly direct the Court to "review the lawfulness" of Community acts. To meet the needs of legal protection, however, it is not inconceivable that in cases of flagrant misuse of power the Court could interpret liberally its powers of review.[54]

There remain, then, three further but closely related grounds of review established under the Treaties. They are aimed in varying degrees at the direct control of Community discretion. Not merely the legality of a Community act, but its advisability and opportuneness in the light of the Treaty provisions is subject to judicial review. Further, the decision of the Community Court may, to varying degrees, directly influence or fully displace that of the Community organs. Thus, in two cases – ECSC Article 66 § 5 (approval of mergers and acquisitions) and Article 95 ("small Treaty revisions") – the Court may review the decisions of Community organs with "full jurisdiction (pleine compétence) as to all matters of law and fact." Although in both cases the Court can only affirm or reject the Community

50 *Ibid.*, p. 238.

51 *Ibid.*, p. 239.

52 Steindorff, *id.* pp. 75, 95f, following a review of the practice of both countries; Steindorff, "Der unbestimmte Rechtsbegriff im Lichte der französischen und amerikanischen Verwaltungsrechtsprechung," 4 *Deutsches Verwaltungsblatt,* 110–114 (1954). For a statement of this position in recent American practice, see *Universal Camera Corp.* v. *NLRB,* 340 U.S. 474, 490 (1950), followed by *NLRB* v. *Babcock & Wilcox Co.* 351 U.S. 105, 112 (1955); *FTC* v. *Standard Oil Co.,* 355 U.S. 396, 400f (1958).

53 Schlochauer, *op. cit.* (n. 3), p. 405.

54 See Daig, "Die Gerichtsbarkeit in der EWG und EAG," 83 *Arch. öff. R.,* 132, 175 (1958).

act or proposal, the individualized character of the issues raised permit the Court an immense influence on Community discretion.

In another case, ECSC Article 37, the Court may be called to determine whether the action or inaction of the Commission "is of a nature to provoke fundamental and persistent disturbances" in the economies of the Member States. It must decide whether the decision of the Commission is "well-founded" (le bien-fondé). This constitutes a judgment embodying elements both of the proceeding *pour excès de pouvoir* and *de pleine juridiction*.[55] The Court's standards are those of "legality," but in the event of annulment the Commission must determine the appropriate measures to take "within the framework of the Court's judgment."

Finally, in certain other cases as ECSC Articles 88 and 36, EEC Article 172[56] and Euratom Article 144, the Court reviews decisions of the Community organs in *pleine juridiction*. The Court not only possesses full jurisdiction as to all questions of law and fact, but may make its own evaluations of the Community decisions and replace or modify them in terms of its findings.[57] In the Treaties, this proceeding is employed primarily to review the imposition of sanctions and claims of damages. As such, the subject of judicial review is not so much measures of economic regulation, but the sanctions following from its violation.[58]

The scope of judicial review in the European Communities, it may be concluded, closely accords with the grounds of appeal developed in the practice of the Conseil d'Etat. Through the jurisprudence of the Community Court, however, it has gradually received a character of its own. This is due, on the one hand, to the normative structure of the Treaties which bear important elements of constitutional organization. In the control of Community powers, the Court must rely primarily on standards of illegality. Even then, it has shown a decided preference for the first three grounds of appeal – incompetence, major violation of procedure and violation of the Treaty – and has been reluctant to extend its scope of review to economic evaluations, as is possible under ECSC Article 33, by considering the existence of either a *détournement de pouvoir* or a "patent misconstruction" of the Treaty. Such self-restraint is more typical of constitutional than administra-

[55] Conclusions of *Adv-Gen*. Lagrange in Case 2 and 3/60, 7 Rspr. 215, 326 (1961).

[56] See also Art. 17 of Regulation 17, implementing EEC Arts. 85f on the maintenance of competition.

[57] See text *supra*, p. 51f. At least under ECSC Art. 36, the appellant may raise all four grounds of legality mentioned in ECSC Art. 33. Judgment 2–10/63, 9 Rspr. 705, 738f (1963).

[58] Jaenicke, *op. cit.*, (n. 10), p. 782.

tive tribunals. In any case, only by way of exception and then primarily as to matters of sanctions is the Court authorized to proceed beyond questions of illegality into the area of Community discretion.

On the other hand, the scope of judicial review is also molded by the complexities of economic regulation. They call for flexibility in the formulation and execution of Community policy. Legal rules and principles can legitimately encompass only a small portion of economic activity without hindering the creative management of Community powers. Nevertheless, it must not be assumed, unless otherwise authorized, that the Court can fully avoid economic evaluations. While it may not presume to usurp the legitimate sphere of discretionary authority vested in the Community organs, the very nature of the questions facing the Court force it to rely in its judgments, if only implicitly, on certain value premises without which economic matters would be incomprehensible. These premises are not simply "existing" in the Treaty text, but form an integral part of judicial decisions. Legal interpretation, except in the most formalistic sense, can not ignore this fact. The Community Court, therefore, possesses a scope for review which permits it a formative function in the development of Community law. "Seine Rechtsprechung," as Walter Hallstein long ago observed,[59] "wird einen Schatz an gemeinsamer Rechts- und Wirtschaftsueberzeugung bilden."

2. THE FORMS OF APPEAL

An adequate appreciation of the Court's function in the development of Community law also requires an understanding of the rationale behind the forms of appeal. What are the leading and frequently competing considerations which they serve? To answer this, the forms of appeal will be presented in their institutional context. It reflects a triangle of interests: those of the Communities, of the Member State and of the private parties subject to the jurisdiction of both the Communities and their national authorities. Through the adjudication of conflicts arising among these interests, the Court becomes an active participant in the formation of those values underlying Community law.

Preserving the Unity and Integrity of Community Law

Since the Community legal orders are essential to the maintenance of Community authority, the preservation of their unity and integrity must be

[59] Hallstein, Discussion between Hallstein, Predoehl and Baade in Kiel, 2 *Kieler Vorträge*, 10 (Neue Folge, 1951).

a major aim of the Court's jurisdictional powers. On the one hand, to have left the interpretation of the Treaty provisions to the national courts, as was done with certain aspects of Treaty interpretation under the ECSC,[60] would have invited diverging national versions of Community law and a serious threat to the Communities themselves. On the other hand, to have reserved all disputes raising questions of Community law for determination by the Community Court, either *de novo* or on appeal from Member State courts, would have permitted the Court to determine the delicate relationship between Community and Member State laws. The Court would then have been authorized to dispose fully of those disputes between private parties and between Member States and private parties where Community and Member State laws potentially conflict. Whereas such broad jurisdiction would accord with a federal judicial system, it is fundamentally at odds with the complementary and competitive relationship between the Community and Member State legal orders.[61] Neither of these two approaches was adopted, although elements of both are contained in the Court's jurisdiction.

Instead, a jurisdictional compromise was drawn in which the unity and integrity of Community law could conceivably be preserved without transgressing the reserved domain of Member State legal orders. The first step towards this objective was to vest the Court with exclusive jurisdiction over those disputes whose determination is vital to the maintenance of Community authority. This encompasses primarily disputes over questions of Community public law. Thus, the Court is given exclusive jurisdiction[62] over matters of Community liability,[63] the interpretation and application of the Protocol concerning the Privileges and Immunities of the ECSC[64] and, most importantly, over the legality of acts of the Community organs.[65] Similarly, only the Court may settle disputes between the Member States[66] or between the Commission (or the High Authority) and the Member

60 See ESCS Art. 41, discussed *infra*, pp. 67–69.

61 See text *supra*, Chapter I, Section 4.

62 EEC Art. 183, Euratom Art. 155. A corresponding provision is lacking for the ECSC, although Article 43 is believed to imply this conclusion. See Wohlfarth, *op. cit.* (n. 3), Art. 183; Bebr, *op. cit.* (n. 4), pp. 178–80.

63 ECSC Arts. 34, 40, pars. 1–2; EEC Arts. 178, 215, par. 2; Euratom Arts. 151, 188, par. 2. See text *infra*, pp. 87f.

64 Art. 16 of the Protocol. See also that Protocol, Arts. 1 and 2, of EEC and Euratom Treaties.

65 ECSC Art. 33, EEC Art. 173, Euratom Art. 146.

66 EEC Art. 170, Euratom Art. 142. ECSC Art. 89, par. 1, is phrased much more broadly, extending the Court's jurisdiction to all disputes between Member States "concerning the application of the Treaty," which are not otherwise provided for in the Treaty.

States[67] concerning an alleged violation of a Treaty obligation by a Member State. Indeed, the Member States are expressly obligated not to submit a dispute concerning the interpretation and application of the Treaties to any method of settlement other than provided in the Treaties.[68] The Court may also be asked to arbitrate any dispute between Member States "in connection with the objects" of the Treaties, which is submitted to it under the terms of a compromise agreement.[69] Only rarely does its exclusive jurisdiction reach into the realm of Member State private law, as in determining the legality of agreements and combinations in restraint of competition.[70] Beyond this limited range of appeals, however, disputes raising questions of Community law – including those where the Community is a party litigant[71] – remain also within the jurisdiction of Member State courts.[72] Like the basic powers of the Communities, therefore, the Court's jurisdiction constitutes only an exception to the reserved domain of the Member States.

Especially important to the preservation of Treaty integrity is the obligatory adjudication of alleged Member State Treaty violations. It serves, observes Advocate-General Roemer,[73] "to guarantee a uniform and authentic Treaty interpretation." In this proceeding, the Treaty powers may be invoked by the Commission, the Council, a Member State or even private parties against the authors of the Treaties. Community interests and the special interests of the Member States threaten to collide. ECSC Article 88 authorizes the Commission to determine a Member State violation in a "reasoned decision" after giving the defaulting State an opportunity for comment. *This decision,* if appealed by the defaulting State within a period of two months, may be reviewed by the Court in *pleine juridiction.* As a result, the Court may not only annul or affirm the decision but even replace or modify it as the full examination of the Member State's conduct dictates.[74] Although only the Commission may invoke this proceeding, the

[67] ECSC Art. 88, EEC Art. 169, Euratom Art. 141.

[68] EEC Art. 219, Euratom Art. 193. ECSC Art. 87 is somewhat more narrowly worded. The Member States can not take their cases before the International Court of Justice, therefore, although diplomatic settlement would not be excluded.

[69] ECSC Art. 89, par. 2; EEC Art. 182; Euratom Art. 154.

[70] ECSC Arts. 65 § 4, 66 § 5, par. 2. As to the former provision, see Judgment 1/58, 5 Rspr. 43, 63, (1958–59); and EEC Regulation 17, implementing Arts. 85 and 86.

[71] E.g. questions of contractual obligation between the Communities and private parties. See text *infra,* p. 87f.

[72] See Matthies, "Das Recht der EGKS und die nationalen Gerichte der Mitgliedstaaten," 9 *Juristen Z.* 305, 307 (1954); and note 62 *supra.*

[73] Conclusions of *Adv-Gen.* Roemer in Case 20/59, 6 Rspr. 719, 727 (1960).

[74] See Judgment 3/59, 6 Rspr. 121, 138f (1960).

Council, a Member State or a private party may challenge the Commission's refusal to proceed against an alleged Member State violation.[75]

The Rome Treaties (EEC Articles 169 and 170, Euratom 141 and 142), on the other hand, authorize both the Commission and the Member States to proceed directly against alleged Member State violations.[76] In either case, an appeal to the Court must be preceded by a "reasoned opinion" of the Commission after giving the defaulting Member State the opportunity for comment. Again, in contrast to the ECSC Treaty, the initiating parties and not the defaulting Member State must bring the matter before the Court. By the same token, the subject of judicial review is not the "reasoned opinion" of the Commission in *pleine juridiction,* but the conduct of the defaulting Member State measured simply in law and in fact against the specific obligations of the Treaty. The Council and private parties may invoke this proceeding only indirectly by challenging the inaction of the Commission.[77]

In all three Communities, the defaulting Member State is given an opportunity to hear and comment on its alleged violation before the jurisdiction of the Court may be invoked. This introduces a preliminary period of negotiation, during which the Commission and the allegedly defaulting Member State may clarify their legal positions and the circumstances involved.[78] Both parties thereby are afforded an opportunity to correct any misconceptions and to modify or fully change their original positions. If the Member State complies, it is spared what might have been an embarrassing judicial contest. Insofar, this proceeding looks to the future – to persuading a defaulting Member State to correct its conduct – and not to punishing past action.[79] By institutionalizing such negotiation, this proceeding reflects a certain unmistakable restraint in dealing with the Member States that is not found, for instance, in appeals against the acts of Community organs.

75 ESCS Art. 35. See text *infra,* pp. 76f and 82f.

76 See also EEC Art. 93, for a special proceeding along these lines where unlawful Member State subvention is in question; and EEC Art. 180 (a), where the Board of Directors of the European Investment Bank are authorized to execute the powers of the Commission under EEC Art. 169.

Under the Euratom Treaty, the alleged violations of Member States may also be brought before the Court under specific provisions relating to Member State refusal to grant a license or cause it to be granted (Art. 21, par. 3), to Member State failure to take prescribed security measures (Art. 38, par. 3) or refusal to permit an inspection ordered by the Commission (Arts. 81, pars. 3 and 4, 82, par. 3), and to Member State failure to impose sanctions against private parties in their territory according to municipal law (Art. 145).

77 EEC Art. 175, Euratom Art. 148.

78 See Conclusions of *Adv-Gen.* Roemer in Case 20/59, 6 Rspr. 719, 728f (1961), and of *Adv-Gen.* Lagrange in Case 7/61, 7 Rspr. 723, 737 (1961), and Judgment 7/69, 16 Rspr. 111, 118 (1970).

79 Roemer, *id.,* p. 729; Lagrange, *id.,* p. 735f.

Whereas for the latter "time is of the essence" in bringing appeals, for the former negotiations may be drawn out months and even years.[80] In some respects, therefore, this proceeding is similar to the international treaty practice of combining binding judicial settlement with preliminary steps of conciliation.[81]

Even greater restraint is evident in levying Community sanctions against defaulting Member States. Whereas the Commission, under ECSC Article 88, may institute economic sanctions if its "reasoned decision" has not been respected by the defaulting Member State or rejected by the Community Court on appeal, it may do so only by a two-thirds vote of the Council. These sanctions may require the defaulting State to make money payments to the injured Member States or authorize the injured States to counteract the injuries by measures in deviation of ESCS Article 4. This decision to institute sanctions may, in turn, be reviewed by the Court in *pleine juridiction* upon appeal by the defaulting Member State. The corresponding provisions in the Rome Treaties, by contrast, fail to mention sanctions.[82] The Court is merely authorized to determine the existence of the violation; the defaulting Member State is then obligated to "take the measures required for the implementation of the judgment of the Court." [83] The Court itself has declared that it is not authorized to repeal the sovereign acts of a Member State in order to bring the Member State legal orders into agreement with the Treaties.[84] In a common enterprise like that of the Communities, however, where so much depends on Member State cooperation, too much weight should not be placed on formal sanctions. The potential loss of Member State prestige and of the broad range of economic advantages reaped continually from progressive integration, are the most effective sanctions at this stage in European economic integration.

Furthermore, the Treaties establish procedures for securing the vital interests of the Communities and the Member States against fundamental or threatening disturbances in the national economies. Although the authorized measures may well constitute exceptions to basic Treaty provisions, these procedures as such strengthen the Communities: they not only accord

[80] A good example will be found in Case 90 and 91/63, 10 Rspr. 1329 (1964), concerning illegal Member State levies on milk products, discussed in text *infra*, p. 327f.

[81] See Lauterpacht-Oppenheim, *International Law*, vol. II, pp. 90–96 (7th ed. 1952).

[82] This is only literally true since certain EEC provisions, such as Article 37(3) authorize the Commission to offset injurious measures of delinquent Member States by directing the injured Member States to retaliate in kind.

[83] EEC Art. 171, Euratom Art. 143.

[84] Judgment 6/60, 6 Rspr. 1163, 1184 (1960). See also Judgments 26/62, 9 Rspr. 1, 23 (1963); 100/63, 10 Rspr. 1213, 1230 (1964); 24/64, 10 Rspr. 1373, 1388 (1964).

with the political realities of the Member States, but also permit such emergencies to be regulated within the framework of the Communities. In the EEC, these procedures are numerous and varied, and subject only to the limited judicial review of "legality." Thus, a Member State, whose economy in an area or sector is threatened during the transitional period by serious and most likely presistent difficulties, may petition the Commission for the authorization to take appropriate protective measures in order to restore the situation or adapt the sector to the common market (EEC Article 226). Similarly, at the request of a Member State, the Council may decide by unanimous vote, if justified by "exceptional circumstances," that certain State subventions are compatible with the common market (EEC Article 93 (2), paragraph 2). In both cases, these decisions may be attacked presumably on the limited grounds of legality contained in EEC Article 173.[85] Furthermore, in accordance with the broad scope of the EEC common market, Articles 223 through 225 permit certain deviations from competitive conditions where they are necessary to protect the internal order or security of a Member State. The Commission or another Member State may appeal such measures to the Court, if it considers that they constitute an "improper use" of the powers stipulated by Articles 223 through 224. Again, the Court possesses no special authority to review the discretion of the Member States. In all these cases, however, the necessity of interpreting indefinite legal concepts will scarcely allow the Court to avoid considering the economic implication of the measures or decisions in question.

The limited scope of the ECSC emphasizes particularly the need for emergency provisions. Although operating solely within the coal and steel sectors, the ECSC policies may have far-reaching repercussions on the remainder of the national economies. Should the action or inaction of the High Authority threaten the economy of a Member State with "fundamental and persistent disturbances," therefore, that State may petition the High Authority to take the measures necessary to correct the situation while safeguarding "the essential interests of the Community" (ECSC Article 37). If no or inadequate measures are forthcoming, an appeal may be lodged with the Court. Such an appeal, says the Court[86] "requires an evaluation of the economic situation of the Member States, and necessitates further a review

[85] As to EEC Art. 226, see Bebr, *op. cit.* (n. 4), p. 155. Cf. Groeben, *op. cit.* (n. 2), Anm. 3 zu Art. 226. See also Wohlfarth, *op. cit.* (n. 3), Anm. 5 zu Art. 93, and Groeben, *id.* Anm. 4 zu Art. 93.

[86] Judgment 2 and 3/60, 7 Rspr. 281, 310 (1961), rejecting the implication in Judgment 3/59, 6 Rspr. 121, 139 (1960), that ECSC Art. 37 controls only the "legality" (Rechtmässigkeit) of the High Authority's decision.

of the question whether, under the circumstances, the measures taken constitute necessary and appropriate means." In thus reviewing the legality as well as the advisability and opportuneness ("Zweckmaessigkeit") of the measures, the Court is placed in an arbitral role.[87] Its judgment touches "the political responsibility of the High Authority and the Member State governments, especially as to a reconciliation between the special interests of a Member State and the general interests of the Community."[88] For this reason, however, its decisions are not simply "political" but "constitutional,"[89] designed to protect the essential interests of the Community while permitting the necessary and fitting assistance to the Member States.[90]

There remains still a broad range of questions as to the interpretation of Community law which arise in disputes before the courts of the Member States. These disputes concern, for instance, agreements between private parties or the enforcement of a Member State law, which draw an act of a Community organ or a provision of the Treaties into question. In order to secure the unity of Community law as well as the independence of the Community legal orders,[91] it was essential to establish a procedure by which such questions could be interpreted uniformly by the Community Court. At the same time, the Member States were not prepared to authorize the Community Court to determine the whole dispute, since this would have implied a judgment as to the supremacy of Community law. Instead, the Treaties embody a procedure which allows a "painless" accommodation[92] of the jurisprudence of the national courts to that of the Community Court. The national courts are authorized to suspend judgment in such cases and to certify the question of Community law to the Community Court for interpretation. This has the advantage of permitting national courts to avoid

[87] Ophüls, "Gerichtsbarkeit und Rechtsprechung im Schumanplan," 4 *N.J.W.* 693, 695 (1951), speaks of a "Politisch-Schiedsrichterliche" role for the Court; and Breitner, *Der Gerichtshof der Montangemeinschaft und seine Berufung bei fehlerhaften Organakten,* 72 (2nd. ed. 1954), of the political content of the economic disturbance. See also Rapport delégation française, *op. cit.* (n. 10), p. 42.

[88] Judgment 2 and 3/60, *op. cit.*, p. 310.

[89] See Moser, *Die Überstaatliche Gerichtsbarkeit der Montanunion,* 46 (1955); and Matthies, *op. cit.* (n. 48), p. 442f.

[90] Rupprecht, *Die Nachprüfungsbefugnis des Europäischen Gerichtshofes gegenüber Ermessenshandlungen der Exekutive in der Montanunion und der EWG,* 130 (1962), rightly suggests: "Man könnte von einem negativen Notstandsrecht sprechen, das Notstandsrecht des Staates wird zur Vermeidung eines Notstandes der Gemeinschaft verneint."

[91] Bebr, *op. cit.* (n. 4), pp. 179f and 225; Tomuschat, *Die gerichtliche Vorabentscheidung nach den Verträgen über die Europäischen Gemeinschaften,* 7f (1964). See also Judgments 13/61, 8 Rspr. 97, 111 (1962); and 26/62, 9 Rspr. 1, 25 (1963).

[92] Tomuschat, *id.*, p. 13.

decisions which are contrary to Community law without, however, transforming the Community Court into an appellate division of natural court decisions. The "preliminary question" procedure, therefore, effects a coordination – more than a subordination – of Member State with Community law.

The ECSC and Rome Treaties reflect two important differences in this procedure. ECSC Article 41 requires every national court to certify to the Community Court only those questions concerning the validity of acts (délibérations) of the Commission or Council.[93] The Rome Treaties (EEC Article 177, Euratom Article 150), on the other hand, extend the Court's jurisdictional monopoly to the interpretation of Treaty provisions and of certain statutes of institutions established by the Council as well as to questions concerning the validity and construction of acts of Community organs. The failure of ECSC Article 41 to cover questions of Treaty interpretation, where no act of a Community organ is involved, reveals an obvious weakness in the Court's jurisdiction.[94] Further, the Rome Treaties do not require every Member State court, but only those courts "from whose decision no appeal lies under municipal law"[95] to certify such questions to the Community Court. Lower courts may refer such questions, but only at their discretion. In view of the hierarchical arrangement of national court systems, this approach has the advantage of minimizing the work load of the Community Court without weakening the essential guarantee of uniformity in Community law interpretation.

The crucial fact remains, however, that under all three Treaties the Member State courts decide, presumably on or in the absence of a motion of a party,[96] whether a preliminary question has been "raised in a case." At first, Member State courts showed a reluctance to refer even the most obvious questions of Community law to the Court. By ignoring the question of Com-

[93] It must be doubted that the term "deliberations" refers to any but binding acts of the High Authority or Council. See Amtliche Begründung, *op. cit.* (n. 10), p. 17. Otherwise, there would be no need for a decision of the Community Court on the question.

[94] Bebr, *op. cit.* (n. 4), p. 182f, suggests that the national courts might, in certain cases, submit questions as to Treaty interpretation to the High Authority. He finds some legal basis for this in ECSC Article 90. But cf. Steindorff, "Die europäischen Gemeinschaften in der Rechtsprechung," 8 *Arch. VR.* 426, 430 (1959–60). See also Dumon, "Le Renvoi préjudiciel (Art. 41 CECA, 177 CEE et 150 CEA)," in *Collège d'Europe, Droit communautaire et droit national,* 197, 266 (1965).

[95] As to which national courts this would include, see Bebr, *ibid.,* pp. 181–91; Tomuschat, *op. cit.,* pp. 40–56, who lists the courts which would qualify; Dumon, *id.,* pp. 213–32; and Daig, "Aktuelle Fragen der Vorabentscheidungen nach Art. 177 EWGV," 3 Europarecht 259, 268ff (1968).

[96] Daig, "Die Gerichtsbarkeit in EWG und Euratom," 83 *Arch. öff. R.* 132, 196 (1958); Bebr, *id.,* p. 194; and Tomuschat, *id.,* pp. 68–72.

munity law at hand[97] or by tacitly interpreting the Treaty in order to conclude that no question of Community law was raised,[98] the Member State courts clearly circumvented their Treaty obligations. Although this reluctance has dwindled with time, an equally serious threat has arisen more recently in the briefs of Member State governments before national courts contending that provisions of national laws should be applied without reference to corresponding or potentially conflicting Treaty provisions.[99] Thus, true as it is that the Community Court possesses exclusive jurisdiction over questions of Community law and that its interpretation of such questions is binding,[100] this in no way resolves the fundamental relationship between Community and Member State law. EEC Article 177, concludes the Community Court,[101] "proceeds from a clear separation of the tasks of national courts and the Court of Justice. It authorizes the Court neither to decide the concrete case [before the national court] nor to review the reasons and purposes of the request for interpretation." The temptation of the national

[97] See, e.g., Decision of the Hoge Raad (Jan. 13, 1961), in *K.I.M.* c. *Sieverding*, 1 *Soc. Econ. Wetgeving* (Europa) 315 (1961), concerning a dispute over the validity of a price-fixing agreement in which a violation of EEC Article 85 was charged. And see also the more recent Decision of the Conseil d'Etat of March 1, 1968 (*Syndicat général des fabricants de semoules de France*), discussed *supra* in text, p. 30.

[98] See, e.g., Decision "Sarotti IV" of the Oberlandesgericht Düsseldorf (Oct. 21, 1958) – ZW 47/58, reported in Wirtschaft und Wettbewerb: Entscheidungssammlung OLG I, p. 263 (1959), concerning the validity of a price-fixing agreement which the court determined did not affect trade between the Member States within the meaning of EEC Article 85. See also the more recent decisions of the French Cour de Cassation (Ch. Crim.), of June 29, 1966, reported in *Rec. Dalloz: Chron. juris.* No. 35, p. 595 (Oct. 26, 1966); and of the Conseil d'Etat (*S.A. des Etablissements Petit-Jean et autres* and *Jammes et Fédération des Associations viticoles de France*), reported in l'Actualité Juridique, Droit Administratif No. 5, p. 285 (1967), and in *Jurisclasseur périodique*, No. 16020 (1969), respectively, and which cite the EEC Treaty and the Community Court's jurisprudence. These decisions are also reported in part in 2 *Europarecht* 152 and 245 (1967), and the latter is discussed there, together with other similar decisions of the Conseil d'Etat, at p. 246f.

[99] See Judgment 6/64, 10 Rspr. 1251, 1261f (1964); and 20/64, 11–3 Rspr. 6 (1965) (position of the French Government).

[100] This is the only meaningful justification for establishing such a procedure. The literature generally supports this view. See, e.g., de Richemont, *op. cit.* (n. 3), p. 336; Ballerstedt, *Übernationale und nationale Marktordnung*, 18 (1955); Ophüls, "Zwischen Völkerrecht und staatlichem Recht – Grundfragen des europäischen Rechts," 4 *Juristen JB.* 137, 159 (1963–64); Schlochauer, "Das Verhältnis des Rechts der EWG zu der nationalen Rechtsordnung der Mitgliedstaaten," 11 *Arch. VR.*, 1, 29 (1963–64); Tomuschat, *op. cit.* (n. 91), p. 171f; Bebr, *op. cit.*, (n. 4), 198; Donner, "The Court of Justice of the European Communities," *Int. Comp. L. Qu.*, Supp. 66, 71 (No. 1, 1961); van den Heuvel, *Prejudiciële vragen en bevoegdheidsproblemen in het Europese recht*, 58 (1962); Catalano, *Manuale di Diritto Comunità Europee*, 112f (1965).

[101] Judgment 6/64, 10 Rspr., 1251, 1269 (1964). See also Judgments 24/64, 10 Rspr. 1373, 1388 (1964), and 20/64, 11 Rspr. (1965).

courts to give way to the argument of Member State governments, therefore, is all the more dangerous because it permits national authorities, including the courts, to quietly avoid facing a conflict with Community law. Should Member State courts succumb to this temptation, the remaining judicial remedy would be for the Commission or another Member State to charge the delinquent State with the violation of a Treaty obligation.[102]

The jurisdiction of the Community Court, therefore, reflects to a large extent the existence of parallel legal orders between the Communities and Member States. The care with which the jurisdictional line is drawn demonstrates a delicate balance between competing legal orders in which the question of supremacy has been left open for the moment, awaiting the process of Community integration and the test of time. Although in the last instance the resolution of this question is not exclusively within the power of any court, much less the Court of the Communities, the latter is not without influence on legal development. It may, as will be seen in Chapter VI, contribute to a limited but active extent in asserting the authority of Community law.

Maintaining the Limits and Balance of Powers Within the Communities

The Treaties further provide for the direct appeal of acts of Community organs. While these acts may, under specific conditions, be challenged by private associations, enterprises and individuals, the discussion now is concerned with those actions in which the litigants are Member States and/or Community organs.[103] They deserve special treatment, for they emphasize the major role of both the Member States and the Community political institutions in the judicial process and its contribution to the check and balance of Community powers.[104] In contrast to constitutional practice in the United States,[105] the Treaties have introduced "abstract norm control"

[102] See Bebr, *op. cit.* (n. 4), p. 197; Tomuschat, *op. cit.* (n. 91) p. 13f.; and EEC Commission, Answer to Written Question No. 100, point 7, in *Amtsblatt,* Nr. 270 (Nov. 8, 1967).

[103] The right of third party intervention in a suit before the Court will not be treated. See Stats. of the Court: ECSC Art. 34, EEC Art. 37, Euratom Art. 38; and Bebr, *op. cit.* (n. 4), pp. 168–77; Valentine, *The Court of Justice of the European Communities,* vol. I, pp. 57–60.

[104] This "balance of powers" should not be identified with its counterpart on the national level. Although both share some characteristics in common, in the Communities the political organization is only rudimentary and the Member State play a major role in the formation and execution of Community policy.

[105] According to United States practice, individual states like private litigants must show a legally protected, usually proprietary, interest in order to challenge acts or

as found in some of the Member States, notably Germany and Italy.[106] Unlike private parties, the litigants in this proceeding need not show injury or an aggrieved interest as a condition of appeal. Such an interest is irrefutably presumed. Moreover, these litigants have constant access to the judicial process,[107] for the jurisdiction of the Community Court is obligatory. This proceeding has the advantage of permitting crucial issues to be fought out as they arise by the major Community powers rather than leaving them to the vicissitudes of private litigants and their immediate interests. Nevertheless, it can easily thrust the Community Court into the midst of a political controversy, since parties who have failed in political battle may well turn to judicial action.[108] The Court, therefore, may well become the arbiter in the balance and check of Community powers as well as the guardian of the unity and integrity of Community law.

The chief protagonists among the organs of each Community are the Council of Ministers and the Commission, the latter embodying the "supranational" character of the Communities and the former speaking for the special interests of the Member States as well as the common Community interests. The rudimentary political control of the European Parliament leaves it with little direct influence on the determination of Community action.[109] Partially to offset this weak political control and to help maintain the prescribed balance of powers, the Court has been empowered to review the acts of Community organs.[110] Within the framework of abstract norm control in the Treaties, this judicial review may be exercised both repressive-

legislation of the Federal Government. See *Massachusetts* v. *Mellon,* 262 U.S. 447 (1923), in which Massachusetts' standing to challenge the constitutionality of federal appropriations was denied.

[106] See the contributions of Friesenhahn, "Die Verfassungsgerichtsbarkeit in der Bundesrepublik Deutschland," pp. 91f, 108f and 122–28, and of Sandulli, "Die Verfassungsgerichtsbarkeit in Italien," pp. 310–13, in Mosler, (ed.) *Verfassungsgerichtsbarkeit in der Gegenwart* (1962). German constitutional practice distinguishes between "abstract" and "concrete" judicial review, both of which may lead to binding decisions. While the latter arises out of contentious proceedings (*ibid.,* pp. 731–33), the former may be invoked by an organ of government independent of a specific and proven interest in the cause of action. (*ibid.,* pp. 728–33).

[107] Of course, certain procedures and time limits must be respected in the specific appeals.

[108] See Gebhard Mueller (former President of the German Constitutional Court), "Ansprache bei Amtseinführung am 13. Februar 1959," in *Das Bundesverfassungsgericht,* 13, 16f (1963); and Rupp, "Judicial Review in the Federal Republic of Germany," 9 *Amer. J. Comp. L.,* 29, 43f (1960).

[109] See text *supra,* Chapter I, Section 2.

[110] As a court of last resort, says Colin, the Community Court is "the only true counterweight" to the exercise of Community powers by the Council and the Commission. *Op. cit.* (n. 3), p. 512.

ly on binding acts and preventively on proposed acts of Community organs.[111]

The preventive norm control averts embarrassing the Communities as to acts which can only with great difficulty be retracted. As has just been noted, the "preliminary question" proceeding fulfills this function where questions of Treaty law are raised in disputes before national courts. In such cases, the Community Court is not authorized to decide the concrete case, but only to give "an abstract interpretation" of the Community act or Treaty text in question.[112] Such control is equally valuable in areas of Community policy-making. Thus, international agreements between the EEC[113] and third states or international organizations may, before their conclusion, be appealed by the Council, the Commission or a Member State (EEC Article 228). If the Court finds the agreement to be incompatible with the provisions of the Treaty, it may be concluded only after Member States have amended the Treaty. Although the Euratom Treaty does not provide for judicial review in such cases,[114] it does require Member States to submit the drafts of contemplated international agreements, which concern the sphere of the Treaty's application, to the Commission for approval (Euratom Article 103). If they are found to infringe on the Treaty, the Member State may either alter them to meet the Commission's objections or petition the Court to overrule the Commission. A negative opinion of the Court is binding on the Member States, so that the proposed agreements may not be concluded unless modified.

Finally, the preventive norm control plays a crucial role in the "small Treaty revision" of ECSC Article 95, paragraphs 3 and 4. Unlike the other Treaty revision procedures,[115] which call for a unanimous vote of the Council, or the major Treaty amendment by the consent of the Member State Parliaments,[116] the "small Treaty revision" requires a qualified majority vote only of the Council (five-sixths) and of the Parliament (three-fourths). It is the joint product of all the Community organs; proposed by common agreement of the Commission and Council, then laid before the Court for review and, if found to agree with the Treaty, presented to the Parliament for approval or rejection. The relaxed vote of a qualified majori-

[111] See discussion in Mosler, *op. cit.*, p. 746ff.

[112] Conclusions of *Adv-Gen.* Lagrange in Case 75/63, 10 Rspr. 403, 406f (1964).

[113] Such agreements are negotiated by the Commission and concluded by the Council after consulting the Parliament.

[114] See Euratom Article 101, which does not expressly stipulate that such agreements bind the Member States as does EEC Article 228(2).

[115] See ECSC Art. 95, pars. 1 and 2; EEC Art. 235; Euratom Art. 203.

[116] ECSC Art. 96, EEC Art. 236, Euratom Art. 204.

ty, therefore, is held in check by judicial control, for the Court is empowered to review the proposed revision as to all questions of fact and law. It is called upon to determine whether, in order to cope with "unforeseen difficulties" or "a profound change in the economic or technical conditions directly affecting" the Community market, a revision of Commission powers would impair the basic Treaty objectives (Articles 2 through 4) or alter the distribution of powers among the Community organs (Article 7). While it may not substitute its discretion for that of the Community organs by amending the proposal,[117] a negative opinion of the Court would block the revision and at the same time imply those modifications which would make the proposal legally acceptable.[118] Preventive norm control within the context of the "small Treaty revision," therefore, forms a uniquely constitutional task.[119] Not only are the questions subject to reasoned binding decisions based on the Treaty, but the legal principles at stake concern the organization and basic objectives of the Community.

Nevertheless, in the Communities as in the Member States,[120] preventive norm control is only the exception and not the rule. Most typically, the object of abstract norm control is a "binding act" of a Community organ.[121] Under the ECSC Treaty this means Decisions and Recommendations, but not Opinions.[122] Whereas Decisions are binding in every respect and Opinions not at all, Recommendations are binding only as to the objectives to be attained, leaving the choice of the appropriate means to the addressee (Article 14). The Rome Treaties (EEC Article 189, Euratom Article 161) chose

[117] See Carstens, "Die kleine Revision des Vertrages über die EGKS," 21 *Z. aus. öff. R.* 1, 26 (1961), who, in reference to United States constitutional practice, argues that the proposed revision should be construed with a view to upholding it so far as possible.

[118] See, eg., the negative opinion of the Court on a proposed revision of ECSC Article 56. After modification, it was accepted by the Court. 5 Rspr. 553 (1958–59). See Carstens, *id.* pp. 26–37.

[119] Carstens, *id.*, p. 24, correctly points out that this veto role of the Community Court is essentially different from the purely advisory role of national courts in similar cases, e.g. the Conseil d'Etat and the Staatsgerichtshof of Land Rheinland-Pfalz.

[120] See Mosler, *op. cit.* (n. 106), p. 728f and the individual country reports.

[121] Except for the proceedings under preventive norm control, just discussed, only "binding acts" may be appealed. Judgment 1 and 14/57, 3 Rspr. 213, 233 (1957). See also Judgment 8/55, 2 Rspr. 197, 224 (1955–56). By negative phrasing, however, the Rome Treaties appear to permit a more liberal interpretation of such acts. EEC Arts. 173 and 175, and Euratom Arts. 146 and 148.

[122] ECSC Art. 54, par. 5, constitutes the one exceptional case in which Opinions are weighted as Decisions. See Judgment 1 and 14/57, 3 Rspr. 213, 235 (1957), and Conclusions of *Adv-Gen.* Lagrange, *ibid.*, p. 243f. Cf. also Judgments 54/65 ,12 Rspr. 529, 544 (1966), and 23, 24 and 52/63, 9 Rspr. 471 (1963), discussing the nature of a "genuine Decision" in the ECSC.

a different classification in order to account for the broader objectives of the EEC Treaty and the greater need for the flexible management of Treaty powers. Regulations, Directives and Decisions are all binding, but not Recommendations or Opinions. Whereas Regulations are binding in every respect and directly applicable in the Member States and Decisions are binding in every respect for the named addressees only, Directives bind only named Member States as to the goal to be achieved, leaving to national authorities the choice of the appropriate form and means.

Despite the clarity with which these distinctions are drawn, the matter is more complicated in practice. Not only are the Treaties frequently unclear in specific provisions as to which type of act is appropriate, but the same type of act may vary in quality depending on the Community organ which issues it. Thus, many Regulations of the EEC Council are of a quasi-legislative character and may not simply be equated in authority with the more typically administrative Regulations of the Commission.[123] Furthermore, as will be discussed below,[124] the character of the act in question is decisive for determining the scope of private parties' rights of appeal. For the Community organs and Member States, however, all "binding acts" are as a rule subject to appeal.

Within the context of abstract norm control, therefore, the judicial review of Community acts occurs for the most part in adversary proceedings, on appeal by the Commission, the Council or a Member State. Only exceptionally may the European Parliament or its acts be drawn into litigation.[125] The chief distinction may be drawn in terms of those four grounds of appeal presented above – incompetence, major violation of procedure, violation of the Treaty and *détournement de pouvoir*. Whereas under ECSC Article 38 the first two are the sole grounds of appeal by the Commission and Member States against the alleged illegal acts (délibérations) of the Council or Parliament, under EEC Article 173 and Euratom Article 146 the acts of the Council, like the Commission, are subject to appeal on all four grounds, and those of the Parliament not at all.

[123] Bebr, *op. cit.* (n. 4), pp. 52–54.

[124] See the text *infra*, p. 80f. Because the nature of the Community act is so crucial to judicial relief, the Court has been careful to look behind the Commission's label to see if a Decision in fact is at stake. See, e.g., Judgments 16 and 17/62, 8 Rspr. 969 (1962); 8–11/66, 13 Rspr. 99 (1967); and 30/67, 14 Rspr. 173 (1968), and the accompanying Conclusions of the Advocates-General.

[125] Whereas ECSC Article 38 permits acts of the Parliament ("Assembly") to be appealed but grants the Parliament itself no right of appeal, the Rome Treaties, at least by implication from EEC Article 175 and Euratom Article 148, permit exactly the converse of this.

The reasons for this shift between the ECSC and Rome Treaties are two-fold. First, the limited grounds of appeal in the ECSC Treaty reflect the political character of the Council and Parliament, whose acts were recognized from the beginning to be improper subjects for review on the merits.[126] A second reason comes to light by comparing the ECSC with the Rome Treaties. In the latter, the Council emerges as the powerful administrator and, to some extent, legislator of the Communities, so that the rule of law demands a more extensive judicial control. This is further substantiated by the requirement that the acts of the Council in the Rome Treaties, like those of the Commission be motivated.[127] This requirement etablishes a certain control over those quasi-legislative acts which are not subject to closer political control. Failure to motivate a decision adequately is ground for annulment as a major violation of procedure. Although the two formal grounds of incompetence and major violation of procedure offer only a limited degree of judicial control,[128] they establish a minimum for preserving the proper interplay between the Community organs. Not unexpectedly, they assume a more important function in the Rome Treaties where the complicated division of powers between the Council and the Commission raises complex questions of competence.

The cornerstone of abstract norm control in the Communities, however, is an appeal for annulment on the merits of a Community act, namely, on the grounds of *détournement de pouvoir* or of a violation of the Treaty or of any rule of law concerning its application. These grounds may be raised against acts of the Commission in the ECSC by the Council or a Member State and, under the Rome Treaties, against acts both of the Council and of the Commission by either the Council, the Commission or a Member State.[129] In broadening the grounds of appeal against the Council, the Rome Treaties take account of the increased importance of the Council in Community decision-making. On the other hand, this extended judicial review is held to strict standards of legality. No exception is made, as under ECSC Article 33, for the review of the economic situation upon which the Community acts rest in cases of *détournement de pouvoir* or a "patent misconstruction" of the Treaty. This restraint reflects the shift in power between the ECSC and Rome Treaties from the Commission to the Council. The

[126] Rapport délégation française, *op. cit.* (n. 10), p. 36f.

[127] ECSC Art. 15, EEC Art. 190, Euratom Art. 162.

[128] Thus far, no appeal has been brought against the Council or Parliament under ECSC Art. 38.

[129] ECSC Art. 33, EEC Art. 173, Euratom Art. 146.

enlarged policy-making role of the latter, as representatives of the Member States as well as of the Communities, is to be given freer hand.

In the appeal against inaction, a comparison between the ECSC and Rome Treaties is somewhat more complicated. This appeal is the complement of the appeal for annulment, as it charges the failure of a Community organ to act where inaction violates the Treaties. Since under all three Treaties the failure to issue a "binding act" is the object of litigation, an appeal against inaction requires some evidence, if only tacit, that a Community organ refuses to issue an act. As a result, the appellant must submit documentary evidence that an explicit request for action has been made.[130] If no answer is received within a period of two months following this request, a refusal to act will be inferred.[131]

At this point, however, the Treaties begin to differ. In the ECSC, the Court has tended to subsume the appeal against inaction under that for annulment, seeing the difference as between a negative and positive decision of the Commission.[132] This is understandable in that the parties as well as the grounds of appeal – violation of the Treaty and *détournement de pouvoir* – are identical in both provisions (ECSC Articles 33 and 35). This also implies that the broadened scope of review in appeals for annulment, i.e., cases of *détournement de pouvoir* or a "patent misconstruction" of the Treaty,[133] may be extended to appeals against inaction.

The Rome Treaties, on the other hand, appear to establish an independent action in the appeal against inaction (EEC Article 175, Euratom Article 148).[134] By contrast to ECSC Article 35, they speak only of a failure to act and thus avoid the question of a negative decision which has served to link ECSC Article 35 with Article 33. They further extend the circle of appellants beyond that in an appeal for annulment to "the other institutions of the Community." This evidently includes the Parliament but not the Court itself,[135] since such *ex officio* action of the Court is nowhere foreseen in the Treaties. Nor should it be lightly assumed that the Court has been made a judge in its own behalf. Finally, they refer solely to one ground of

130 Stats. of the Court: ECSC Art. 22, par. 2; EEC and Euratom Arts. 19, par. 2.

131 ECSC Art. 35, par. 3; EEC Art. 175, par. 2; Euratom Art. 148, par. 2.

132 Judgments 7 and 9/54, 2 Rspr. 53, 85–88 (1955–56); the Conclusions of *Adv-Gen.*, Roemer, *id.*, pp. 117f, 128f, and of *Adv-Gen.* Lagrange in Cases 32 and 33, 42/58, 5 Rspr. 325, 332–36 (1958–59); and Judgment 42 and 49/59, 7 Rspr. 109, 156 (1961). Bebr, *op. cit.* (n. 4), pp. 115-17, sharply attacks this position, arguing that ECSC Article 35 establishes independent grounds of appeal.

133 See text *supra* p. 58f.

134 Daig, *op. cit.* (n. 96), p. 178. See also Bebr, *op. cit.* (n. 4), p. 120f.

135 Wohlfarth, *op. cit.* (n. 3), Anm. 1 zu Art. 175; Bebr, *id.* p. 122f. But cf. Daig, *id.*, p. 178.

review, namely, a violation of the Treaty. This means that the broadened scope of review in ECSC Articles 33 and 35 has not been introduced into the Rome Treaties, even though the pragmatic growth of the Court's jurisprudence may take it in this direction.[136] At the same time, it is not clear whether the ground of Treaty violation mentioned in EEC Article 175 and Euratom Article 148 includes a *détournement de pouvoir*. Considering the breadth of discretion vested in the Commission and especially the Council, the inability to check such abuse of power would open a lacuna in judicial protection. Although recognizing the difficulty of proving a *détournement de pouvoir* in a case of inaction, it may and should, by a liberal interpretation, be included in the ground of Treaty violation.[137]

Further, the EEC Treaty also provides judicial protection against unauthorized acts of the European Investment Bank (Article 180). In the interest of a balanced and smooth development of the Common Market, the Bank is to facilitate the financing of certain projects by granting loans and guarantees on a non-profit-making basis (EEC Article 130). Under the conditions and on the grounds set forth in EEC Article 173, the "conclusions" of the Board of Governors may be appealed for annulment by the Member States, the Commission or the Directors of the Bank. Moreover, the "conclusions" of the Board of Directors of the Bank also may be appealed under the same conditions by either Member States or the Commission, but only on the ground of violation of those procedural requirements laid down in Article 21, paragraphs 2 and 5 through 7 of the Statute of the Bank. Here the right of appeal is limited solely to Member States or Community organs and no showing of an aggrieved interest is required.

Finally, the Treaties and their Protocols also regulate the disciplinary proceedings against members of the Commission and the Community Court. Being under the exclusive jurisdiction of the Community Court, these proceedings constitute not only a check on the misuse of power by Community organs, but also an important aspect of Community independence as a whole from the Member States. Thus, at the request of the Council or the Commission, members of the Commission may either be retired compulsorily or forfeit their rights to a pension or other benefits, but only for serious misconduct or for failure to fulfill the conditions required in the performance of their duties.[138] The removal of judges[139] and advocates-

136 See text *supra*, p. 58f.

137 Daig, *op. cit.* (n. 96), p. 179; Groeben, *op. cit.* (n. 2), Anm. 1 zu Art. 175.

138 Fusion Treaty Art. 11, cited in text *supra*, p. 11 at note 32.

139 Stat. of the Court, Art. 6, accompanying EEC and Euratom Treaties and replacing the Statute which originally governed the ECSC Treaty. See Convention Re-

general[140] may occur essentially under the same conditions, except that the proceeding may be initiated apparently by any of the Community organs, including the Court. A judgment of dismissal requires the unanimous opinion of the judges and the advocates-general so far as they are not defendants in the proceeding.

These several aspects of the Court's jurisdiction are directed primarily at maintaining responsible Community action. This means limiting Community powers in terms of Treaty norms and checking their exercise through an institutional balance of Community powers to which the Member States belong. This balance of powers is considerably more complicated in the EEC than in the ECSC, for in the former not one but two organs – namely, the Council and the Commission – possess major executive and, to differing extents, quasi-legislative powers. In either case, however, this balance reflects the constitutional dimensions of Community organization and the central function of the Court in helping to preserve it. It must be recalled, moreover, that the Communities are jurisdictionally separate from each other; they possess a common fund of experience, which may be reflected in the jurisprudence of the Court, but no forms of inter-Community judicial appeal. The progressive development of the Communities may be expected to increase the need for inter-Community coordination – as the fusion of the High Authority and Commissions clearly demonstrates – and to bring with it a corresponding need for inter-Community judicial relief.

Protecting the Rights of Private Parties

One of the most distinguishing characteristics of the Communities is their capacity to bind directly private enterprises, associations and individuals within the territory of the Member States. This binding effect may well result from the self-executing provisions of the Treaties[141] or from the quasi-legislative acts of Community organs. In the latter case, these acts may bind the legal subjects generally, as by declaring the prohibition of anticompetitive practices in EEC Article 85 to be inapplicable to certain groups of agreements.[142] They may also bind individually, as an ECSC Article 65 § 4

lating to Certain Institutions Common to the European Communities Arts. 3 and 4. See generally Bächle, Die *Rechtsstellung der Richter am Gerichtshof der Europäischen Gemeinschaften*, 69–79 (1961).

140 Stat. of the Court, Art. 8.

141 See note 130 *supra*, p. 24.

142 See, e.g., Regulation No. 67/67 of March 22, 1967, which pursuant to EEC Article 85(3) frees certain kinds of exclusive dealing agreements from the prohibition of EEC Article 85(1).

determination that an economic concentration is harmful to competition and must be dissolved. The failure to abide by such binding acts subjects an enterprise to enforcement procedures, including fining the delinquent party.[143] All decisions of the Court[144] as well as the acts of Community organs creating monetary obligations[145] are directly enforceable through the authorities of the Member States.[146]

As a corollary to this aspect of Community power, private enterprises, associations and individuals are granted a limited right of appeal before the Community Court. On the one hand, this constitutes a clear step beyond the contingent character of diplomatic protection so typical of international law.[147] As will be seen, private parties may attack the legality of acts of the Community organs as well as of their own and other Member State authorities. Only exceptionally have international treaties permitted such direct appeal before an international tribunal.[148] This procedure not only safeguards private rights in the Communities but, as Advocate-General Lagrange has put it,[149] ensures the "defense of the common interest." As ex-

143 ECSC Art. 66 § 5 and § 6; EEC Regulation 17, Arts. 15 and 16, in connection with EEC Art. 87 (2) a).

144 ECSC Art. 44, EEC. Art. 187, Euratom. Art. 159.

145 ECSC Art. 92, EEC Art. 192, Euratom Art. 164. In Judgment 4–13/59, 6 Rspr. 249, 288 (1960), the Court took the liberal position that the ECSC Article 92 does not contain an exhaustive enumeration of Treaty sanctions. The sanctions enforceable under Article 92 may also be implied from other Treaty provisions or powers. See also Conclusions of *Adv-Gen.* Roemer, *id.*, pp. 308–11.

146 Member State authorities may require no more than verification of the authenticity of the documents containing the act or judgment of the Community authority and must grant execution according to their own rules of civil procedure. See Judgment 108/63, 11 Rspr. 1, 13f (1965). See Osterheld, *Die Vollstreckung von Entscheidungen der EGKS in der Bundesrepublik Deutschland,* 70–84 (1954). The Community Court is not regarded as a foreign court in the Member States and its judgments may not be attacked collaterally nor are they subject to the exception of public policy in the Member State courts. Only the Community Court may suspend execution. See Mathijsen, *Le Droit de la C.E.C.A.*, 97 (1958); Stein and Nicholson (eds.), *American Enterprise in the European Common Market: A Legal Profile,* 464 (1960). For an exhaustive account of the legal status of foreign judgments in the six Member States as well as the EEC itself, see Mercier, *Effets internationaux des Jugements dans les Etats du Marché Commun* (1965).

147 Bandilla, *Das Klagerecht der Mitgliedstaaten der Europäischen Gemeinschaften gegen Durchgriffsakte,* 49–50 (1965).

148 For an exception, see *Steiner and Gross* v. *Polish State,* Case No. 188, Ann. Dig. (1927–28), where the Upper Silesian Arbitral Tribunal held that, under the terms of the Convention, it could entertain a claim by a Polish national as well as by a national of a third State, which was not a party to the Treaty, against the Polish State. See Lauterpacht-Oppenheim, *International Law,* vol. I, pp. 637–39 (8th ed. 1955); and Dahm, *Völkerrecht,* Vol. I, pp. 412–16 (1958).

149 Conclusions of *Adv-Gen.* Lagrange, in Case 8/55, 2 Rspr. 231, 251 (1955–56).

perience suggests, the Member States may not always be sufficiently interested to pursue violations of the Treaties.

On the other hand, the right of appeal of private parties is considerably more restricted than that of the Member States and Community organs. Even in the Member State legal orders, the existence of an unrestricted right of appeal for individuals against administrative or legislative acts is a rarity.[150] The Treaties restrict private parties' rights of appeal in terms of both the nature of the act in question, i.e., individual or general, and the status of the appellants. As to the latter, the status of the appellants may be determined in terms of an enumerated class of private parties, the existence of a certain "interest" or a combination of the two.[151] Only rarely is the enumeration of a class, such as "buyer," sufficient in itself.[152] Most typically, an aggrieved or affected interest is required.[153]

The Treaties, therefore, have followed the general policy of the Member States judicature, restricting the private right of appeal in the interest of stable and effective Community administration. Thus, while "any natural or legal person" may bring suit under the Rome Treaties, regardless of nationality or type of economic activity, he additionally must show a sufficient interest in the act at stake.[154] By contrast, ECSC Articles 33 and 35 narrow the circle of potential private party litigants to coal and steel enterprises and their associations, but demand likewise that an interest or injury of the part be involved.[155] In each case, it should be noted, the general requirement of "interest" possesses a built-in flexibility, for it is based upon judicial interpretation under concrete circumstances. This is important, because the notion of "interest," like that of economic integration, "is very relative and subject to evolution."[156] This enables it to keep with the ever-

[150] See the Conclusions of *Adv-Gen., Roemer,* in Case 7 and 9/54, 2 Rspr. 105, 121 (1955–56), concerning the requirements for private parties in French and German administrative law. In the latter country, for instance, Article 19(4) of the Basic Law guarantees every person *whose rights* have been violated by a public authority some form of judicial relief. Only by way of an exception, which is limited to the sphere of civil rights, may a person in the courts of some of the *Länder* of Germany bring a so-called "Popularklage" (independent of any actual injury) against an allegedly unconstitutional norm. See Maunz, *Deutsches Staatsrecht,* 123 and 239 (13th ed. 1964).

[151] See Conclusions of Roemer, *id.,* pp. 120–22.

[152] See ECSC Art. 63 § 2.

[153] ECSC Arts. 33, 35 and 66 § 5; EEC Arts. 173 and 175; Euratom Arts. 146 and 148.

[154] EEC and Euratom Art., *id.*

[155] ECSC Art. 80 defines these enterprises. See Bebr, *op. cit.* (n. 4), pp. 59–66.

[156] de Laubadère, *Traité Elementaire de Droit Administratif,* vol. I, p. 462 (3rd. ed. 1963). See also Conclusions of *Adv-Gen.* Lagrange, in Case 8/55, 2 Rspr. 231, 248 (1955–56); Bebr, *op. cit.* (n. 4), p. 73.

widening sphere of private interests caught-up in progressive Community integration.

The chief forms of judicial relief for private parties lie in the appeals for annulment and against inaction.[157] In appeals for annulment, private parties – like Community organs and Member States – may attack binding acts only. Their right of appeal is more limited, moreover, depending on whether a general or individual act of the Communities is in question.[158] An individual act – under the Rome Treaties, a Decision[159] – raises the presumption, apparently conclusive, that the addressees have a sufficient interest for appeal.[160] If the appellant is not the addressee, he may still be able to challenge an individual act addressed to another enterprise or even to a Member State,[161] if it is of "direct and specific concern to him."[162] In such cases, all four grounds of appeal – incompetence, major violation of procedure, violation of the Treaty and *détournement de pouvoir* – may be pleaded.

Only exceptionally may private parties appeal a general act or Regulation. According to ECSC Article 33, paragraph 2, an enterprise may attack a general act only for reason of a *détournement de pouvoir* of which it is the object or victim.[163] The *détournement de pouvoir*, therefore, must directly

157 See text *supra*, pp. 75–77.

158 The municipal law of the Member States also distinguishes variously between individual and general acts, but the existence of a true legislative function in these legal orders does not permit a useful comparison. See Bebr, *op. cit.* (n. 4), p. 41f; and Conclusions of *Adv-Gen.* Roemer, in Case 7 and 9/54, 2 Rspr. 105, 122 (1055–56).

159 The ECSC Treaty distinguishes between individual and general acts like the Rome Treaties between Decisions and Regulations. See text *supra*, p. 73f. In case of doubt, whether an individual or general act is in question, the Court will look primarily to content and not merely to form. See Judgments 8/55, 2 Rspr. 197, 225 (1955–56), and more recently, 55–59 and 61–63/63, 10 Rspr. 453, 492 (1964).

160 Whereas the Rome Treaties (EEC Art. 173, par. 2; Euratom Art. 146, para. 2) make this explicit, this may be deduced from ECSC Arts. 33, par. 2, and 36. See Conclusions of *Adv-Gen.* Roemer, in Case 7 and 9/54, 2 Rspr. 105, 121f (1955–56).

161 See Judgments 106 and 107/63, 11 Rspr. 547, 555f (1965); and 25/62, 9 Rspr. 211, 237 (1963), and the Conclusions of *Adv-Gen.* Roemer, *ibid.*, pp. 249–52. As Judgments 25/62, *id.*; 1/64, 10 Rspr. 883 (1964); and 38/64, 11 Rspr. 277 (1965), demonstrate, however, it may be practically impossible for private parties to show that they are directly and individually affected by a Decision directed to a Member State government.

162 EEC Art. 173, par. 2; Euratom Art. 146, par. 2. Implicit in ECSC Art. 33, par. 2, from concept of "interests affected." See Judgments 7 and 9/54, 2 Rspr. 53, 87 (1955–56); 24 and 34/58, 6 Rspr. 589, 615 (1960) (firms could appeal Decisions addressed to their competitors); and 30/59, 7 Rspr. 1, 39 (1961), declaring: "Contrary to the contentions of the appellees, the right of an enterprise to appeal does not depend on its being affected solely or almost alone by the individual Decision." But cf. Judgment 25/62, 9 Rspr. 211, 238f (1963), and Judgment 10 and 18/68, 15 Rspr. 459, 481f (1969).

163 ECSC Art. 33, par. 2, speaks of a "*détournement de pouvoir* affecting them." The enterprise may not be "affected" where the general act in question affects several

and specifically aggrieve an interest of the appellant. The Court has refused to create a special *détournement de pouvoir* of private parties, either by extending [164] or by narrowing [165] this ground of appeal. Rather, it has adopted a uniform concept for Article 33.[166] The language of the Rome Treaties, on the other hand, does not restrict private parties in their grounds of appeal against Regulations. Nevertheless, it obtains an even stricter result than the ECSC by narrowly defining the types of Regulations which may be challenged. Thus, while private parties may raise all four grounds of appeal, the Regulation challenged must be a "disguised Decision." That is to say, it must be "a Decision which, although in the form of a Regulation . . . , is of direct and individual concern to" the appellant. This would be true, says the Court,[167] only if the act affects him "due to certain personal traits or due to special circumstances which distinguish him from all other persons and thereby, in like manner, individualized him as the addressee." In contrast to ECSC Article 33, therefore, the Rome Treaties exclude an appeal against genuine Regulations.[168] This restriction of judicial relief may be justified only by weighting heavily the Community interest in unimpeded administrative activity.

The judicial protection of private parties is further strengthened by the appeal against inaction. Under all three Treaties, private parties with an aggrieved interest may attack the inaction of the Council or Commission as a Treaty violation,[169] after giving them notice and the opportunity to act.

enterprises (8 in all) "in equal measure." Judgment 55–59 and 61–63/63, 10 Rspr. 453, 493 (1964).

[164] See Daig, *op. cit.* (n. 34), p. 370.

[165] See argument of High Authority reported in Judgment 4/54, 1 Rspr. 189, 199 (1954–55); Conclusions of *Adv-Gen.* Lagrange, in Case 3/54, 1 Rspr. 151, 182f (1954–55), point out that this narrower concept would correspond most nearly to the viewpoint of the authors of the ECSC Treaty.

[166] Judgment 8/55, 2 Rspr. 197, 225–27 (1955–56).

[167] Judgment 40/64, 11 Rspr. 295, 311 (1965), following Judgments 38/64, 11 Rspr. 277 (1965) and 1/64, 10 Rspr. 887 (1964). See also Judgment 106 and 107/63, 11 Rspr. 547 (1965).

[168] See Judgments 16 and 17/62, 8 Rspr. 961, 978 (1962); 19–22/62, 8 Rspr. 1003, 1019f (1962). See also Judgment 30/67, 14 Rspr. 173, 181f (1963), denying that a disguised Decision resulted from territorial limitations on the application of a Regulation; and Judgments 30/67, 14 Rspr. 173, 183 (1968); 6/68, 14 Rspr. 611, 619–21 (1968); 63/69, 16 Rspr. 205, 210f (1970); 64/69, 16 Rspr. 221, 226f (1970); and 65/69, 16 Rspr. 229, 234 (1970), all denying that a measure loses its "general application" as a Regulation simply because it applies to identifiable persons and groups or has different effects for various legal entities, so long as the standards of application are objectively defined in accordance with the purposes to be served by the measure.

[169] See text *supra*, p. 76f, discussing the possibility that this ground be broadly interpreted to include *détournement de pouvoir.*

The Rome Treaties [170] restrict this right of appeal by requiring that the inaction alleged be the failure of the Council or Commission to address *to the appellant* an act other than a Recommendation or Opinion. Although this restriction applies also in an appeal for annulment, it notably prevents a private party from forcing the Commission to proceed against a defaulting Member State under EEC Article 169 (Euratom Article 141).[171] This is not the case under ECSC Article 35. Other than the requirement of "interest affected" [172] it makes no distinction between public and private appellants. A private party may attack the Commission for failing to issue a general or individual act, alleging that this failure violates a Treaty obligation or constitutes a *détournement de pouvoir*. To date most such appeals by private parties have attacked the failure of the Commission (i.e. its predecessor, the High Authority), pursuant to ECSC Article 88, to proceed against a defaulting Member State. Under the ECSC Treaty, therefore, enterprises are placed in the singular position of being able to force a supranational authority to proceed against a Treaty violation of their own Government or another Member State.[173]

Besides these general appeals for annulment and against inaction, private parties also are granted the right of appeal against Community acts in individual provisions scattered throughout the Treaties. These appeals primarily concern the regulation of competition and economic concentrations [174] and, as under the Euratom Treaty, the licensing and sub-licensing of patents and patent rights.[175] These provisions will not be treated specifically. It will only be noted that they may run parallel to [176] or be subsumed under [177] the general appeals for annulment or against inaction.

Were this an exhaustive account of the legal remedies of private parties against illegal acts of Community organs, it would be open to serious cri-

170 EEC Art. 175, par. 3; Euratom Art. 148, par. 3.

171 See Bebr, *op. cit.* (n. 4), p. 123f; and Judgment 48/65, 12 Rspr. 27, 39f (1966). The Court also has rejected attempts to use the appeal against inaction as a basis for attacking directly Decisions of the Commission. Judgment 10 and 18/68, 15 Rspr. 459, 483f (1969).

172 Although this requirement is not stated expressly in ECSC Article 35, the Court has construed it so. See note 161 *supra*.

173 See, e.g., Judgments 7 and 9/54, 2 Rspr. 53 (1955–56) (re Luxembourg levies on industrial coal); and 30/59, 7 Rspr. 1 (1961) (re German subvention of coal industry).

174 E.g., ECSC Arts. 63 § 2; 65 § 1, § 2 and § 4; and 66 § 5, par. 2; also EEC Regulation 17, Art. 17, implementing EEC Arts. 85 and 86.

175 Euratom Arts. 12, par. 2; and 18, par. 2.

176 E.g., ECSC Arts. 63 § 2, 66 § 5.

177 E.g., ECSC Art. 65 § 4. See Order of the Court 18/57, 3 Rspr. 247, 254f (1957) in conjunction with Judgment 18/57, 5 Rspr. 89, 11–13 (1958–59); and Valentine, *op. cit.*, (n. 2), vol. I, p. 245f.

ticism. Broad areas of Community regulation – including all Regulations issued under the Rome Treaties – would be closed to attack by private parties. This criticism, however, is greatly mitigated – if not overcome – by two procedures in which private parties may collaterally attack the validity of Community acts. Both perform the essential function of compensating for the restricted right of appeal of private parties under the appeal for annulment.[178]

The first and most general of these two, the "preliminary question" proceeding, has been discussed above. Here, all questions as to the validity of Community acts raised in disputes before national courts must be certified to the Community Court for determination. Under the Rome Treaties, this proceeding encompasses also all questions of Treaty interpretation as well as the interpretation of the statutes of any institutions created by the Council. The certification itself is not a right of the parties,[179] but a duty of the national courts – and under the Rome Treaties, only of the courts of last resort.

This proceeding differs in three important ways from a direct attack on the appeal for annulment. For one, private parties, including third parties outside Community jurisdiction, may obtain judicial relief even though they are otherwise barred from direct appeal – whether absolutely or due to the running of a time limit. Indeed, since Member State legislation may be attacked in this proceeding as contrary to Community law, such an attack may be more effective than if brought by the Commission itself. In this way, the individual can obtain immediate relief from the national court while the Commission can only obligate the Member State "to take the measures required for implementation of the Judgment of the Court."[180]

[178] This is particularly true for the more limited rights of private parties against acts of EEC organs. See Judgment 26/62, 9 Rspr. 1, 26 (1963; and also the Conclusions of *Adv-Gen.* Roemer in Case 10/56, 4 Rspr. 87, 102 (1958), and in Case 73 and 74/63, 10 Rspr. 33, 47 (1964).

[179] See Judgment 31 and 33/62, 8 Rspr. 1027, 1042f (1962), and Order of the Court, in Case 6/64, 10 Rspr. 1309 (1964), expressly rejecting plaintiff's right to certify directly a question to the Community Court via EEC Article 177. See also Judgment 44/65, 11 Rspr. 1267, 1275 (1965). The Federal Constitutional Court of Germany, moreover, has refused to interfere with a failure of the Finance Court under EEC Article 177. Decision of the BVerfG of Oct. 13, 1970.

[180] EEC Art. 171 and Euratom Art. 144. Pursuant to ECSC Article 88, moreover, sanctions against the defaulting Member State may be instituted only by two-thirds vote of the Council of Ministers. See also Judgments 7/61, 7 Rspr. 693, 715f (1961); and 28/67, 14 Rspr. 215, 233 (1968); and Judgment 9/70 (*Leberpfennig* Case), 16 Rspr. 825 (1970), holding that Decisions and Directives issued to Member State authorities could contain norms which are directly applicable to and create immediate rights for individual nationals. The Court, however, has refused to let this proceeding pre-empt an

Furthermore, the parties can not raise a preliminary question directly, but must await a dispute in a contentious proceeding before a national court. The possibility of relief, therefore, may be delayed while injury accumulates.

Finally, the effects of the Community Court's ruling also distinguish the "preliminary question" proceeding somewhat from the appeal for annulment. Although its ruling must be seen as fully binding on national courts as to the question of Community law,[181] the question remains as to its effect on a general act or Regulation drawn into question. Whether it should have an effect *erga omnes* or merely *inter partes* depends very much on the weight given the two competing considerations of equal justice and effective administration in the Communities. Whereas the former consideration emphasizes the lacuna in the legal protection of private parties which can be filled only by extending equally to all the benefits of a ruling that an act is "inapplicable,"[182] the latter stresses the "chaos and instability of administration" which would ensue if such a ruling, rendered after several years of enforcement, were generally binding for all.[183] Despite the confusion that might result in the short run, it is difficult to see how any effect except *erga omnes* can be justified with the "rule of law" in the Communities. In either case, however, the question remains open as to the obligation of Community organs resulting from such a ruling as well as to their liability for injury resulting from the illegal act.[184]

A more specific collateral attack against acts of Community organs, termed an "exception of illegality," is contained in ECSC Article 36, EEC Article 184 and Euratom Article 156. Under this proceeding, designed "to complete the judicial protection of enterprises,"[185] private parties may attack the legality of general acts or Regulations, *as applied to them,* in an appeal before the Community Court. Whereas the Rome Treaties extend this appeal to "any of the parties concerned" in a legal proceeding before the Community Court, the ECSC Treaty refers only to enterprises subject to pecuniary sanctions of the High Authority.[186] In either case, the parties

action by the Commission for Treaty violation under EEC Article 169. Judgment 31/69, 16 Rspr. 25, 33 (1970).

[181] See note 100 *supra.*

[182] See, e.g., Tomaschut, *op. cit.* (n. 91), pp. 174–80. Cf. also Dumon, *op. cit.* (n. 94), pp. 257–60.

[183] See, e.g., Bebr, *op. cit.* (n. 4), p. 199f.

[184] Cf. ECSC Art. 34, EEC Art. 174, Euratom Art. 147, controlling the effects of judgments of nullity against acts of Community organs. Only ECSC Article 34 provides expressly for compensation measures.

[185] Conclusions of *Adv-Gen.* Roemer in Case 10/56, 4 Rspr. 87, 102 (1958).

[186] The Court, however, has taken a liberal view of this qualification, permitting an attack against a general act even in cases where its implementation by an individual act

may invoke – without qualification – all four grounds set forth in the appeal for annulment. Under the ECSC Treaty, where sanctions are involved, the scope of review also extends to *pleine juridiction.*[187] In contrast to a direct appeal for annulment, "the legality of a general Decision can be alleged only so far as there exists a direct legal connection between the measure attacked and the general Decision."[188] Further, a judgment of the Court is effective only *inter partes* and *ex nunc*;[189] it does not annul the general act or Regulation as such, but only the specific act implementing or enforcing it. Its effect, therefore, is merely to exempt the immediate parties from application of the general act or Regulation.[190] Even this limited effect, however, can not avoid having far-reaching impact on the general validity of these acts. To mitigate such impact, the Court can declare – as is possible under an appeal for annulment[191] – only specific provisions to be "inapplicable" and thereby preserve as much as possible of the general act or Regulation. By this proceeding and that of "preliminary question," therefore, private parties have been restored much of the legal protection from which they are excluded under the appeal for annulment.

Finally, the Treaties also regulate Community liability and, except in cases of contractual liability, reserve such matters to the exclusive jurisdiction of the Community Court. Thus, the Court is exclusively competent to determine disputes between the Communities and their employees which involve pecuniary interests as well as other matters specified in the person-

is not by pecuniary sanction. See Judgments 9/56, 4 Rspr. 9, 26 (1958); 15/57, 4 Rspr. 159, 190 (1958); and Conclusions of *Adv-Gen.* Roemer in Case 10/56, 4 Rspr. 87, 102f (1958). But cf. Conclusions of *Adv-Gen.* Roemer in Case 41 and 50/59; 6 Rspr. 1055, 1064f. (1960).

[187] ECSC Art. 36, par. 2. Cf. EEC Art. 172, which authorizes the Council to vest the Court with powers of *pleine juridiction* in respect to the penalties prescribed in its Regulations. Cf. thereto Euratom Art. 144. See text *supra,* pp. 53 and 60.

[188] Judgment 21/64, 11 Rspr. 241, 259 (1965). What constitutes "a direct legal connection"? In Judgment 41 and 50/59, 6 Rspr. 1025, 1049ff, 1087 (1960), the Court said a party could not attack, by this proceeding, the mere "logical consequences" of a much earlier general act.

[189] See Judgments 9/56, 4 Rspr. 9, 27f (1958); 15/57, 4 Rspr. 159, 189f (1958). But cf., Wohlfarth, *op. cit.* (n. 3), Anm. 5 to Art. 184. A judgment under an appeal for annulment, however, has effect both *erga omnes* and *ex tunc*. See, e.g. Judgment 18/57, 5 Rspr. 89, 112 (1958–59).

[190] See Judgments 9/56, 4 Rspr. 9, 27 (1958); and 31 and 32/62, 8 Rspr. 1027, 1042 (1962). Cf., however, the somewhat enigmatic wording of the Court in Judgment 9/56, *id.*, p. 27f: "The annulment of an individual Decision, due to the illegality of a general Decision upon which it is based, does not alter the effect of the general Decision, *except* to the extent to which it has been made specific by the individual Decision which has been annulled."

[191] EEC Art. 174, Euratom Art. 147. Although not specifically stated in ECSC Art. 34, it may be deduced therefrom.

nel statutes of the three Communities.[192] The Court to date has rendered decisions in some 90 cases of this type. It may not only review the exercise of discretionary authority by a Community organ or agency, but may even set aside or alter their decisions. Further, the Court has exclusive jurisdiction over all disputes of Community tort (non-contractual) liability, whether resulting from an act of a Community employee[193] or of a Community organ.[194] This liability, however, is not so broadly worded in the ECSC Treaty as in the Rome Treaties.[195] Finally, the Court is also authorized to determine disputes over contracts, concluded by the Communities under public or private law, if this is stipulated by the parties in an arbitration clause.[196] Otherwise, these disputes fall within the jurisdiction of national courts,[197] at least for purposes of determining the liability of the parties.

As independent organizations, the Communities enjoy certain privileges and immunities, among which is full control over their assets. Execution against assets of the Communities within the territories of the Member States, therefore, must first be authorized by the Community Court.[198] The European Investment Bank is the notable exception to this rule. In an obvious attempt to enhance its credit-rating, the Bank is subject to suit in national courts and its assets liable to execution by the order of national courts.[199]

The judicial protection of private parties in the Communities, therefore, extends both to illegal acts of Community organs as well as to contractual and non-contractual liability of a civil law character. Especially the former reflects two competing considerations: the one favors effective and efficient administrative action and the other the full judicial relief for private injury. The balance struck exempts general acts or Regulations, for the most part,

192 Personnel Stats.: ECSC Art. 58 and Rome Treaties Art. 91. *Amtsblatt*, vol. I, pp. 1385–1460 (1962).

193 ECSC Art. 40, par. 2; EEC Arts. 178 and 215; Euratom Arts. 151 and 188.

194 ECSC Arts. 34 and 40, par. 1; EEC Arts. 176, 178 and 215; Euratom Arts. 149 and 151. Whereas ECSC Article 40 distinguishes between "official" and "personal" fault, the Rome Treaties speak generally of "non-contractual liability." The nature of this action is discussed in Judgment 5, 7 and 13–24/66, 13 Rspr. 331 (1967), involving the liability of the EEC Commission for the erroneous application of import restrictions.

195 See Kautzor-Schroeder, "Public Tort Liability Under the ECSC Treaty Compared with the Federal Tort Claims Act," 4 *Villanova L. Rev.*, 198, 235 (1958–59); and Much, *Die Amtshaftung im Recht der EGKS* (1952).

196 ECSC Art. 42, EEC Art. 181, Euratom Art. 153.

197 See note 62 *supra*.

198 Protocol Concerning the Privileges and Immunities of the ECSC, EEC and Euratom, Art. 1. See Judicial Decree 4/62, 8 Rspr. 87 (1962).

199 Protocol Concerning the European Investment Bank of the EEC, Art. 29.

from the direct attack of private parties. Such appeals are left primarily to the Member States and Community organs themselves. Instead, the judicial relief of private parties is tied to actual aggrieved interests and concentrated on the annulment of individual acts and sanctions and on compensating the damages resulting from illegal general or individual acts. The annulment of individual acts resting on general acts, however, can scarcely avoid undermining the authority of the latter. For this reason, it must be queried whether an immediate direct appeal against general acts would not have promoted greater legal certainty and effective administration than permitting an action, perhaps years later, against the results of such acts.[200]

CONCLUSIONS

The analysis of this Chapter has attempted to determine the jurisdictional scope of the Court of Justice for the development of the Community legal orders. The broad scope of judicial review, as reflected in the grounds of appeal, reveals the extent to which judicial decisions possess a formative function in legal development. While emphasis in the Communities has been placed on standards of legality, i.e., on the elaboration of principles of law based on the Treaties, the gradual formulation and maintenance of these standards can not ignore the value premises upon which they rest. The articulation of values and the elaboration of legal principles go hand in hand.

Judicial review in the Communities, moreover, occurs within an institutionalized framework of interests and powers, embracing Community organs, Member States and private parties. It reflects a broad range of competing considerations inherent to economic regulation and integration on the supranational level. Thus, the Court's jurisdiction is designed to ensure the unity and integrity of the Community legal orders whose far-reaching independence from the Member States is essential to supranational organization. Further, judicial control is aimed at delimiting Community powers and at maintaining a balance between the major institutions and powers of Community organization. Finally, the extension of judicial protection – restricted as it is – to individuals injured by Community acts discloses an initial attempt to establish those minimum standards of relief so fundamental to the rule of law. It constitutes further assurance that Community interests and procedures will not be sacrificed to the complacency of Member State governments.

Within the disciplined framework of Community organization, therefore,

200 Bebr, *op. cit.* (n. 4), p. 147f.

the Court possesses the jurisdictional authority to participate actively in legal development and the furtherance of Community integration. Though the constitutional organization of the Communities is in other respects somewhat rudimentary, the Court's broad powers of judicial review constitute both a safeguard for the determination of Treaty obligations as well as a potential for constitutional development. Indeed, it is this scope of judicial decision which establishes the essentially constitutional character of the Court's jurisprudence. It remains to be determined, however, in what sense the Court may pursue this active and creative function of judicial decision and the extent to which it has translated this function into reality.

PART TWO

THE THEORETICAL FOUNDATIONS OF JUDICIAL DECISION

> "The reconciliation of the irreconcilable, the merger of antitheses, the synthesis of opposites, these are the great problems of the law. 'Nomos,' one might fairly say, is the child of antinomies, and born of them travail." Benjamin Cardozo, The Paradoxes of Legal Science 4 (1928).

Having examined the Court of Justice of the European Communities within its organizational context, the framework has been set for considering the function of judicial decision in the development of Community law. Before proceeding to analyze the jurisprudence of the Court, however, it is necessary to determine the nature and scope of this function. What are the overriding tasks of a court and the parameters of judicial decision in the formation of a legal order? This is especially important where, as here, the Community Court possesses the mandate of judicial review. The answer to this question must be traced to the theory of judicial decision, which in turn is the resultant of two major factors: the concept of law and the institutional setting of judicial decision. Here two legal traditions meet. While continental jurisprudence, under the influence of rationalistic idealism, has tended to emphasize the philosophical basis and systematic analysis of the law, the common law has placed the court as an institution at the heart of legal development. Particularly in the United States, where judicial review and federalism have assumed such importance, judicial decision has been viewed as much as a product of its political milieu as of any particular concept of law. These traditional emphases of course cannot obscure the fact that both factors determine the course of judicial decision.

The Court of Justice and its jurisprudence must be examined in this light. A study of the concept of law reveals the extent and way in which law may be viewed as a dynamic and developing order in the Communities. Only in this context is it possible to determine the major tasks of judicial decision in the formation of Community law. These are, as will be seen, uniquely creative judicial tasks. Having determined this, the question remains how the Community Court responsibly can fulfill these tasks and make an enduring contribution to the constitutional development of the Communities.

In other words, if the Court of Justice is a potentially active and creative institution, what is the legitimate scope of the judicial function in legal development? For a court exercising the power of judicial review, this must be ascertained within the institutional framework of constitutional government. While the analysis in Part Two outlines a general theory of judicial decision, based broadly on a comparative study of theory and practice, it nevertheless is directed primarily at constitutional adjudication, including that conducted within the framework of the European Communities.

CHAPTER III

THE CONCEPT OF LAW IN JUDICIAL DECISION

The concept of law is as varied as the ends which it is thought to serve. However conceived – as an all-pervasive Reason in the nature of things (Montesquieu), as the "artificial Reason and Judgment" acquired through long study and experience and embodying the wisdom of successive generations (Coke), as an aggregate of rules or "commands of the sovereign" (Austin) or as "the prophecies of what the courts will do in fact" (Holmes) – each concept embodies a philosophy of its own. It not only explains the function of law, but also the nature and limits of law as a rational means of ordering human conduct. Moreover, the concept of law in turn determines the tasks of judicial decision. Thus, a static, formal or purely consensual concept of law, as is prevalent in the theories of legal positivism considered in this Chapter, may define judicial interpretation purely in terms of existing rules, system or power relationships. Yet if, as will be shown, law is much more than this, if indeed law is neither static nor purely formal, but a concrete system of values in the process of continuous reformulation and development, then what does this imply for judicial decision? The answer must be sought in those limits inherent in the nature of law. These are the limits to knowledge, authority and practicability. They are reflected in judicial decision and frame the major tasks of judicial interpretation.

1. THE CHALLENGE OF LEGAL POSITIVISM

Any present attempt of legal theory to renew the theoretical foundation of judicial decision must face up to the incisive challenge of legal positivism and overcome its weaknesses. Growing out of the reaction to 18th century natural law and the skepticism toward transcendental values in the law, legal positivism seeks to construct a scientific statement of law according to objectively knowable criteria. Although this takes many forms,[1] crucial to this

[1] In particular, that strand of legal positivism stemming from Auguste Comte, which

discussion is that brand of positivism, sometimes known as "analytical positivism," which stems from the philosophical bases of English pragmatism (H. L. A. Hart), of neo-Kantian thought (Hans Kelsen) and of the German rationalistic-deductive idealism found in *Begriffsjurisprudenz.*

The main thrust of this brand of positivism may be summarized under three propositions:[2] 1) there is no necessary or desirable connection between what law is and what it ought to be (or between law and morals in some sense); 2) laws are imperatives or authorized norms, rules or pronouncements which are coupled with a sanction and originate from a sovereign or authorized law-maker; 3) the study or analysis of legal concepts is worth pursuing divorced from historical and sociological inquiries into the causes, aims and social underpinnings of law. The crucial fact concerning these three propositions is that they are not severable from one another.[3] Rather, they constitute an integral whole, aimed at establishing law as a science and at curbing the arbitrary exercise of judicial power under the color of subjective or natural law preferences. Whether only one or both of these purposes is stressed, the last two propositions provide the essential organizational means (Proposition 2) and intellectual framework (Proposition 3) for structuring a system of law from which "higher law" values have been banished as objectively unascertainable. Taken together, these three propositions offer the means for establishing the finality, absolute authority and completeness of the law in its (decisional or statutory) written form.

Within this context, however, the concept of judicial decision varies radically. The following three theories may serve to demonstrate this as well as the intimate relationship between the concept of law and the theory of judicial decision.

Begriffsjurisprudenz

At one end of the positivist spectrum lies the concept of judicial decision generated by *Begriffsjurisprudenz.* It entails a severe formalization of the judicial function through the complete subordination of the judge to a rational-deductive legal system. Its philosophical origin may be traced to the

bases its analysis on the observation and ordering of natural scientific, psychological or sociological facts (Rechtstatsachen), will not be considered here.

[2] Hart, "Positivism and the Separation of Law and Morals," 71 *Harv. L. Rev.*, 593, 601f, n. 25 (1958), suggests five distinct bases for legal positivism. They are restated here essentially in three propositions.

[3] Cf., however, Hart, *id.*, p. 602, who argues that his five propositions are separable. Fuller, "Positivism and the Fidelity to Law – A Reply to Professor Hart," 71 *Harv. L. Rev.*, 630, 639f (1958), rejects Hart's contention.

rationalistic-deductive natural law idealism of Christian Wolff (1679–1754)[4] who, under the influence of Cartesian logic, sought to establish an exact, complete and systematic jurisprudence. Although these philosophical foundations were thoroughly shaken by Kant's epistemological critique, the systematic, rationalistic method remained intact and accessible to the new ethic of free will and moral autonomy.[5]

Evolving out of the early writings of Savigny,[6] *Begriffsjurisprudenz* received its most eloquent expression at the hands of the two Pandectists Puchta and Windscheid in the 19th century. It is a jurist's legal system which builds in pyramid fashion, with ever-increasing abstraction, from the more concrete legal concepts lying at its base. Conversely, proceeding from the most general concept at the apex, each subsumed concept contains all the attributes of its class plus at least one more. These legal concepts have not merely systematic and pedagogical value, but possess an independent life of their own and logical reality like that adhering to mathematical formulas by virtue of the mathematical structure of the world.

Because *Begriffsjurisprudenz* represents a complete (gapless) system, its logical application results in "right" and "just" decision for all conceivable cases. It became the theoretical prototype of code law thinking, exemplifying unity, clarity and simplicity.[7]

> In code law thinking firm rules of statutory application have been formed. Syllogistic deduction is so-to-speak provoked by the existence of major premises which permit subsumption, and the question of justice is transformed into a task of statutory construction so far as the principles of legal analysis contained in the code and its conceptual framework possess ultimate authority. And this is required in the interest of preserving the system, which is the most important thing for code law thinking but the least important for case law thinking.[8]

[4] See Wieacker, *Privatrechtsgeschichte der Neuzeit,* 192–194 (1952); Larenz, *Methodenlehre der Rechtswissenschaft,* 21f (1960); Coing, *Grundzüge der Rechtsphilosophie,* 151–156 (1950).

[5] See Wieacker, *id.,* p. 219f. In fact, Kant recognizes a large role for rational and systematic legislation. See *Die Metaphysik der Sitten,* Part I, esp. "Einleitung in die Rechtslehre," establishing the systematic framework for laws and condemning a purely empirical theory of law.

[6] Larenz, *op. cit.* (n. 4), p. 8f, points out that Savigny's very use of the term "philosophical" was not directed at any natural law theory, but rather at the systematic unifying ideal of jurisprudence.

[7] Carl J. Friedrich distinguishes between three types of codification movements: to digest, to reform and systematize and to revolutionize the law. Both the French and German codification movements turned out to be of the second type. See "Die ideologischen und philosophischen Voraussetzungen der Idee der Kodifizierung," in *Zur Theorie und Politik der Verfassungsordnung,* 57–69 (1963).

[8] Esser, *Grundsatz und Norm in der richterlichen Fortbildung des Privatrechts,* 220 (1956).

A strict distinction could thereby be drawn between the creative law-making function (Rechtsschoepfung) of the legislative and the juristic and judicial working-out and systematizing of statutory or code law (Rechtsfindung and Rechtsanwendung). Bound strictly to the logical application of prescribed norms, the judiciary was guaranteed both institutional independence and political neutrality.

Through the mode of code law *Begriffsjurisprudenz* has had wide influence throughout the world. The idea of "Systematik" lying at its core offers an attractive ordering and organizational quality for law in the throes of consolidation. This may explain its strong influence on continental public law,[9] as well as on John Austin who studied the Pandectists at the Universities of Bonn and Heidelberg. By overrating logic and system, however, it tends to underestimate the importance and contribution of "judge-made law" and "law-in-action" to legal development. They are at best disturbing elements in the maintenance of a "Systematik" for which "not one single conflict in doctrine and practice exists without creating the severest repercussions for the authority of the law."[10]

Begriffsjurisprudenz further tends to overlook those implied value premises upon which it was structured. The jurist, as Triepel warns,[11] is easily led "from the very beginning to put into a concept that which he later would like to withdraw, so that he surreptitiously obtains in good faith the desired result." In fact, concentrating on logic and system, *Begriffsjurisprudenz* gradually lost sight of all value foundation and, in the course of events, became a captive of "legislative positivism" ("Gesetzespositivismus")[12] Where the purpose of law is merely to mediate between the state and society or between a plurality of political interest groups, the judges could be bound even more unconditionally to the written law.[13] The methodological under-

[9] See e.g. R. Carré de Malberg, *Contribution à la Théorie générale de l'Etat,* vol. I, pp. 148–50 and 262–64 (1920); Laband, *Staatsrecht des Deutschen Reiches,* "Vorwort" (5th ed. 1964), establishing constitutional law not as the science of ends in any sense, but as the science of means and its constitutive elements.

[10] Esser, *op. cit.* (n. 8), pp. 220f and 254f.

[11] Triepel, *Staatsrecht und Politik,* 33 (1927). See also Ehrlich, *Die Juristische Logik,* 294 (1918), and *Scherz und Ernst in Jurisprudenz* (1st ed. 1885), who scathingly criticized this approach as a "conceptual heaven" (Begriffshimmel).

[12] See Wieacker, *op. cit.* (n. 4), pp. 271–74; Larenz, *op. cit.* (n. 4), p. 20f. This extreme position is best characterized in the writings of Bergbohm, who in his Jurisprudenz und Rechtsphilosophie 80 (1892) states: "nur was als Recht functioniert, das ist Recht, sonst nichts; und alles das ist Recht, ohne Ausnahme."

[13] It could even be made a judicial virtue to apply the law without regard to the just content of a law. See e.g. Radbruch, *Rechtsphilosophie,* 83f (3rd ed. 1932), whose position, however, underwent a substantial change with the experience of National Socialism.

pinnings of *Begriffsjurisprudenz* have outlasted the heyday of positivism and have lasting influence throughout Europe down to the present day. In a word: "The science of law . . . is systematic or it is nothing."[14]

Hans Kelsen

At the other end of the positivist spectrum lies Kelsen's concept of judicial decision. Based on the epistemological theory of Kant, Kelsen's *Pure Theory of Law* splits the legal world in two by a strict separation between "is" and "ought" judgments. While the science of law is by its nature limited to a knowledge of the structure of legal norms, namely, a formal normative logic similar in kind to a knowledge of geometric constructs, the factual world of legal content must be satisfied with a descriptive ("explikative") legal sociology.[15] Just as the jurist is guaranteed scientific objectivity and complete immunity from value-implicating observations, so long as he sticks to his "pure theory," just so he forfeits all this in attempting to assess the content of law, its proper interpretation or its accordance with justice.[16]

[14] H. J. Wolff, "Typen im Recht und in der Rechtswissenschaft," in *Studium Generale,* 195, 205 (1952). See also Wieacker, *op. cit.* (n. 4), pp. 193, 230 and 256f, who notes the great influence which strictly systematic methods still have today on German legal thinking and legal education; and Larenz, *op. cit.* (n. 4), p. 112, critical appraisal: "Die heute noch überwiegende Anfassung der deutschen Juristen geht dahin, dass es eine fertig bereitliegende Rechtsordnung gebe, die von dem Richter auf den einzelnen Fall nur "angewandt" zu werden brauche, um daraus mittels "Subsumtion" die richtige Entscheidung abzuleiten."

[15] Jurisprudence, states Kelsen, has "nur die Form einer Erscheinung zu berücksichtigen, mit deren Inhalt sich die Soziologie, die historisch-politischen Disziplinen zu befassen haben, einer Erscheinung, die man immerhin in ihrer Totalität als "Recht" bezeichnen mag, wenn man sich dann nur bewusst bleibt, dass der "Rechts"wissenschaft mit ihren spezifischen Erkenntnismitteln nur eine Seite dieser "Rechtserscheinung" zugänglich ist. Erkennt man aber, dass die Jurisprudenz die Form und nur die Form zu erfassen hat, dann darf man konsequenterweise in die Rechtsbegriffe keine anderen als formale Elemente aufnehmen." It might be considered "eine Geometrie der totalen Rechtserscheinung." "Die rein formalen Rechtsbegriffe als inhaltslosen Formeln für wertlos erklären, hiesse ebensoviel, wie die Begriffe der Geometrie verwerfen, weil sie lediglich die Formen der Körper erfassen, ohne über deren Inhalt etwas auszusagen." Kelsen, *Hauptprobleme der Staatsrechtslehre,* 92f (1911). See Ebenstein, *Die rechtsphilosophische Schule der Reinen Rechtslehre,* 24 (1938). Jurisprudence, however, is not mere "legal logic" ("Rechtslogik"), but the necessary forms of legal thought. See Kelsen, "Was ist die Reine Rechtslehre," in *Festgabe Z. Giacometti* 143, 149f (1953).

[16] "If the history of human thought proves anything," concludes Kelsen, "it is the futility of the attempt to establish, in the way of rational consideration, an absolutely correct standard of human behavior, and that means a standard of human behavior as the only just one, excluding the possibility of considering the opposite standard to be just too . . . only relative values are accessible to human reason." "What is Justice?" in

This purification of legal theory, however, is won only at the cost of relegating the content of law to the realm of politics, of ideology and power.[17]

The impact of this duality on judicial decision becomes dramatically clear within the framework of Kelson's *Stufenbau* theory. In the judicial process of norm concretization, the general language of the norm confronts the judge with several possible meanings, all of which are equally "right."

> If "interpretation" is understood as cognitive ascertainment of the meaning of the object that is to be interpreted, then the result of a legal interpretation can only be ascertaining the framework of the law to be interpreted, and thereby the cognition of several possibilities within that framework.[18]

Interpretation, therefore, requires the jurist "to leave to the law-applying organ the choice – determinable only on the basis of political considerations – between meanings which are equally possible as viewed from the science of law."[19]

In the end, judicial decision is reduced to a constitutive act of law-making (Zwangsakt), different only in degree from that of the legislature.[20] In fact, however, even the norm's supposed frame of reference is illusory, since the judicial choice creates valid law even if it "represents none of the meanings of the applicable legal norm which the science of law considers possible."[21] The only alternative for the jurist in such cases, concludes Kelsen,[22] is to admit "that by this act (Zwangsakt) new law has been created – though perhaps only for the concrete case in point." While this theory possesses the outspoken virtue of recognizing statutory imprecision and judicial creativity, it transforms judicial decision into little more than arbitrary pronouncements of judges.

Kelsen, *What is Justice? Collected Essays,* 1, 21 (1960). For this reason, any content can be law. Kelsen, *Pure Theory of Law,* 63–69 (transl. of the 2nd German Edition by Max Knight, 1967). "The legal scientist does not identify himself with any value, not even with the legal value he describes." *Pure Theory of Law, id.,* p. 68.

[17] See C. J. Friedrich, *The Philosophy of Law in Historical Perspective,* 175, 177 (Phoenix Paperback, 2nd ed., 1963).

[18] Kelsen, *Pure Theory of Law, op. cit.,* p. 351. See also, Kelsen, *The Law of the United Nations* xv (1951), and pp. 109 and 207 of that work for examples of this approach.

[19] Kelsen, "Was ist die Reine Rechtslehre," *op. cit.,* p. 152. See also his *Pure Theory of Law, op. cit.,* p. 351f.

[20] Kelsen, *Pure Theory of Law, id.,* p. 353.

[21] Kelsen, "Was ist die Reine Rechtslehre," *op. cit.,* p. 151.

[22] *Ibid.* See, for example, the Austrian Constitution of 1929 (re-introduced in 1945) Arts. 139 (2) and 140 (3) and (4), a product of Kelsen's thought, which permits the Constitutional Court to find an ordinance or law unconstitutional but, at the Court's discretion, to grant it legal effect for a future period up to 6 months or a year.

H.L.A.Hart

Finally, between these two extremes of analytical positivism lies the more moderate, pragmatic and convincing approach of H. L. A. Hart to judicial decision. It is built upon a critical reappraisal of Austinian theory. In recognizing that formalism, or conceptualism and rule-scepticism "are the Scylla and Charybdis of juristic theory,"[23] Hart clarifies the state of legal positivism today. His struggle to forge a more moderate theory, by tempering logic and system with the realities of legal rules and their unavoidable ambiguities, however, reveals in the most profound sense the inadequacies of legal positivism as well as its challenge to all other contenders. For these reasons, it is important to deal in more detail with *The Concept of Law*. It offers perhaps the most challenging contribution of analytical positivism in recent years.

At the center of Hart's thesis lies "the idea of a rule, without which we can not hope to elucidate even the most elementary forms of law."[24] In this idea he sees the means to meet the long-standing criticism of law as the command of the sovereign who is habitually obeyed. Austin has termed that concept "the key to the science of jurisprudence." A social rule, reasons Hart, embodies not only the "external" (observable) aspect of "regular uniform behavior" which is associated with social habit, but also three further qualities: the consciousness of a social standard and criticism toward deviational behavior, a justification ("good reason") for criticizing and punishing such deviations, and the recognition by "some at least" that the rule constitutes a "general standard to be followed by the group as a whole." They clarify what Hart calls the "internal aspect" of rules, whose essence lies *not* in a personal "feeling of compulsion," but in a "critical reflective attitude to certain patterns of behavior as a common standard."[25] This attitude is displayed "in criticism (including self-criticism), demands for conformity, and in acknowledgements that such criticism and demands are justified." These are characteristically expressed "in the normative terminology of 'ought,' 'must,' and 'should,' 'right' and 'wrong.' "[26]

The "internal aspect" of a rule, therefore, complements the one-sided (external) view of laws as merely habits of obedience. It hereby fairly accounts for the notion of rules as guides to personal conduct as well as for the continuity of authority and persistence of laws long after the death of the

[23] H. L. A. Hart, *The Concept of Law*, 113 (1961). For other critical comments on this positivist's approach, see Dworkin, "The Model of Rules," 35 *U. Chi. L. Rev.*, 14 (1967).

[24] Hart, *id.*, p. 78.

[25] *Ibid.*, pp. 54–56.

[26] *Ibid.*, p. 56.

law-maker and of the subjects who rendered him habitual obedience. At the outset, however, it should be noted that Hart speaks of "criticizing" and "justifying" *not* the rule itself, but rather deviating conduct *by reference to* the rule.[27] The rule itself can only be accepted (or not), in which case the "internal aspect" is merely descriptive of what happens. For this reason, Hart's use of "normative terminology" is purely a function of a rule's existence or, at the most, of its acceptance.

Nor does Hart move to correct this view in determining the origin and meaning of legal obligation. Obligation in general presupposes the "internal aspect" of rules, for the majority of people guide, rationalize and justify their daily actions by rules. Only in this way is one able to explain why an obligation persists even though the predicted sanctions (objective view) may not be imposed or the personal feelings of compulsion or fear of sanctions (subjective view) are absent in many individuals. At the same time, the statements "He ought to" and "He has an obligation to" are different in nature, even though both are based on rules. While the former evaluates acts in terms of any type of rule, the latter is used only "when the general demand for conformity is insistent and the social pressure brought to bear upon those who deviate or threaten to deviate is great."[28] A "legal" obligation then is said to arise only when, in the imposition of a rule, physical sanctions – whether highly organized or not – "are prominent or usual among the forms of pressure."[29]

By means of the "internal aspect" of rules as well as the "general demand for uniformity," therefore, Hart avoids that one-sided emphasis on sanctions as the basis of obligation which is characteristic of Austin and Kelsen.[30] He also incorporates the existing social tension between those who "accept and voluntarily co-operate in maintaining the rules" and those who

[27] "The most important of these factors which show that in acting we have applied a rule is that if our behavior is challenged we are disposed to justify it by reference to the rule: and the genuineness of our acceptance of the rule may be manifested not only in our past and subsequent general acknowledgments of it and conformity to it, but in our criticism of our own and others' deviation from it. On such or similar evidence we may indeed conclude that if, before our "unthinking" compliance with the rule, we had been asked to say what the right thing to do was and why, we would, if honest, have cited the rule in reply." *Ibid.*, p. 136f.

[28] *Ibid.*, p. 84.

[29] *Ibid.*

[30] Kelsen conceives all "genuine" laws to be conditional orders *to officials* to apply sanctions: "Law is the primary norm which stipulates the sanction." *General Theory of Law and the State*, 61 (1949). In this way, he clearly distinguishes his position from the crude "coercive orders" view of law, for it is not necessary that every breach of the law in fact be followed by a sanction. See also Kelsen, ***Pure Theory of Law, op. cit.*** (n. 16), pp. 33–37, 50f and 54.

"reject the rules and attend to them only from the external point of view as a sign of possible punishment."[31] Like his treatment of rules, however, Hart fails to reveal anything more than a purely factual basis for obligation. Thus, the "internal" meaning of a traffic signal is merely that drivers –

> look upon it as a signal for them to stop, and so a reason for stopping in conformity to rules which make stopping when the light is red a standard of behavior and an obligation.[32]

To acknowledge a legal obligation, therefore, is to accept a fact, i.e. the existence of a rule which guides individual conduct and is supported by general social pressure and the threat of physical sanctions – no more, no less!

The circularity of this reasoning becomes most apparent with the introduction of "secondary rules" (constitutional procedures). Their function is to identify, and thereby authorize, the proper primary rule to be applied ("rules of recognition"), the proper official to apply them and the procedure to be followed ("rules of adjudication"), and the means and process of legislation ("rules of change").[33] At this point a major transformation in the legal system occurs. While in a simple society, "where knowledge and understanding of the sources of law are widely diffused,"[34] the bulk of the population "might well"[35] both obey and accept the primary rules of conduct, in a complex modern society this would be only a fond hope. In the latter, no more than general obedience to primary rules, for whatever personal reason – insight, fear, coercion – is necessary for the existence of a legal system; "though in a healthy society [private citizens] will in fact often accept these rules as common standards of behavior and acknowledge an obligation to obey them, or even trace this obligation to a more general obligation to respect the constitution."[36]

Obedience, however, is not sufficient to describe the necessary bearing of the official towards secondary rules, because such rules furnish the "ultimate" criteria for assessing the validity of the primary rules. The courts, for instance, must regard a "rule of recognition" –

[31] Hart., *op. cit.*, p. 88.
[32] *Ibid.*, p. 87f.
[33] *Ibid.*, p. 89–96.
[34] *Ibid.*, p. 110.
[35] *Ibid.*, p. 111. However, in the simplest social structure, where there are no officials, the rules *must be* widely accepted. Otherwise "there could not logically be any rules." *Ibid.*, p. 114.
[36] *Ibid.*, p. 113.

> from the internal point of view as a public, common standard of correct judicial decision, and not as something which each judge merely obeys for his part only . . . . This is not merely a matter of the efficiency or health of the legal system, but is logically a necessary condition of our ability to speak of the existence of a single legal system . . . . The assertion that a legal system exists is therefore a Janusfaced statement looking both towards *obedience by ordinary citizens* and to the *acceptance by officials* of secondary rules as critical common standards of official behavior.[37]

As such, secondary rules are also "law" because they provide "a defining feature of a legal system." [38] Even in the "healthiest" of societies, however, their sole and "ultimate" basis is acceptance.

What does it mean for officials to "accept" secondary rules, to which in the end all else refers? On the one hand, Hart denies emphatically the rule-sceptic's view that the constitution is what the judges, or officialdom, say it is.[39] On the other hand, he argues that the "rule of recognition" – in contrast to a primary rule – "can neither be valid nor invalid but simply is accepted," like the standard metre bar in Paris.[40] "The assertion that it exists can only be an external statement of fact."[41] To require more would presuppose those pre-legal or meta-legal values which Hart – with one exception[42] – bans from the province of law. For officials to "appraise critically their own and each others' deviations as lapses,"[43] therefore, can mean no more than that they, individually and in concert, personally approve (or disapprove) each others' actions. The meaning of secondary rules becomes ultimately a question of officials agreeing or disagreeing, which in the latter case is resolved in a see-saw power play among governmental authorities.[44] Still, so long as they are tolerated, the judicial rulings are "final" – though perhaps not infallible.[45] In this context, "critical" and "correct" become irrelevant

[37] *Ibid.*, p. 112f. Emphasis added.

[38] *Ibid.*, p. 108.

[39] *Ibid.*, p. 141. "The adherence of the judge is required to maintain the standards, but the judge does not make them." *Ibid.*, p. 142.

[40] *Ibid.*, p. 105f.

[41] *Ibid.*, p. 107.

[42] Moral codes and legal systems alike contain "some form of prohibition of the use of violence, to persons or things, and requirements of truthfulness, fair dealing and respect for promises. These things, granted only certain very obvious truisms about human nature and the character of the physical world, can be seen in fact to be essential if human beings are to live continuously together in close proximity." *Ibid.*, p. 176, and also pp. 189–95.

[43] *Ibid.*, p. 113.

[44] *Ibid.*, pp. 141–50.

[45] *Ibid.*, p. 140f. "Whatever courts decide, both on matters lying within that part of the rule which seems plain to all, and those lying on its debatable border, stands till

terms, except in terms of political expediency or in some emotive sense. Like Kelsen, therefore, Hart does not seem able to avoid the conclusion that behind the positive law lies "the Gorgon head of power."

In his theory of judicial decision, however, Hart attempts to avoid just this and to establish at least some judicial references for "critical" and "correct" by returning to his notion of a rule. He proceeds from the fundamental conviction that (legal) rules embody "a core of certainty." At any given moment, he says,

> judges, even those of a supreme court, are parts of a system the rules of which are determinate enough at the centre to supply standards of correct judicial decision . . . .[46]

> [T]hough every rule may be doubtful at some points, it is indeed a necessary condition of a legal system existing, that every rule is [not] open to doubt on all points.[47]

Given this "core" of meaning, the judge may proceed by language analysis, subsumption and syllogistic reasoning.[48]

On the other hand, each rule also possesses a "fringe" or "a penumbra of doubt," which "imparts to all rules a fringe of vagueness or 'open texture'."[49] His favorite examples are such rules as: "no vehicle may be taken into the park." Due to the legislature's relative ignorance of fact and relative indeterminacy of aim, such language can only fix the "necessary conditions which anything must satisfy if it is to be within [the rule's] scope, and certain clear examples of what is certainly within its scope may be present to our minds."[50] While buses and autos are obviously included in the general terms, what about airplanes, bicycles and toy motor cars? At this point, where a statute's precise scope and ambit are in doubt, there is "no answer – only answers"[51] – and the judge exercises a "creative choice."[52] The uncertainty is resolved by ascertaining the legislative aim(s) from the terms of

altered by legislation; and over the interpretation of that courts will again have the same last authoritative voice."

46 *Ibid.*, p. 141f, and also pp. 127 and 132.

47 *Ibid.*, p. 148f. The author has taken the liberty of "correcting" what he believes to be an inaccurate phrasing of Professor Hart's point of view. The original reads: "... that not every rule is open to doubt on all points." See, e.g., Hart's concluding statement at p. 150.

48 *Ibid.*, p. 124.

49 *Ibid.*, p. 119f, and also p. 124f.

50 *Ibid.*, p. 125.

51 *Ibid.*, p. 147.

52 *Ibid.*, pp. 124, 126 and 149.

the rule itself – e.g. peace in the park – and then "choosing between the competing interests in the way which *best satisfies us*."[53]

This core-penumbral dichotomy well reflects the peculiar, language orientation of Hart's analysis. Despite the penumbra of doubt in every rule, the law possesses a determinate core. Indeed,

> the life of the law consists to a very large extent in the guidance both of officials and private individuals by determinate rules which unlike the applications of variable standards [e.g., "due care" or "reasonable"], do *not* require from them a fresh judgment from case to case.[54]

In this way, Hart seeks to establish a "settled" or "established" point of reference for judicial interpretation and to forge a theory lying somewhere between the logical formalism of, for instance, *Begriffsjurisprudenz* and the rule-scepticism of American "legal realism" [55] or the "Zwangsakt" theory of Kelsen. In fact, however, the former he locates in the "core," the latter at the "penumbra."

Even this modest attempt to establish objective points of judicial reference within the framework of legal positivism falls short of its mark. In the first place, even assuming all statutes or legal rules were of the relatively simple type which Hart suggests ("No vehicle may be taken into the park."), when does the judge apply "core" or "penumbral" analysis? If such analysis is to claim any more than pure descriptive value, it must deliver the means to answer this question. Otherwise, the existence of the "core" is solely a matter of personal discretion. Although giving no direct answer, Hart implies that if the "core" analysis does not prove satisfactory, i.e. if "the paradigm, clear cases" do not reveal a "certain choice," then the judge must turn to "penumbral" discretion. But what is a "satisfactory" choice in this context, except what pleases the judge or, in the last instance, officialdom in general? The resort to core-penumbra, therefore, serves only to shift the question before the court to another but equally inscrutable plane of analysis.

In the second place, even granting that "core" analysis constitutes an appropriate and necessary aspect of all interpretation, is it a sufficient judicial guideline within its own Hart-given sphere? Decidedly not. Without

[53] *Ibid.*, p. 126. Emphasis added.

[54] *Ibid.*, p. 132.

[55] See, e.g., Llewellyn, *The Bramble Bush*, 9 (2nd ed. 1951): "rules are important so far as they help you to predict what judges will do. That is all their importance except as pretty playthings." But cf. Llewellyn's view of this phrase, in his *Jurisprudence*, 152, n. 17 (1962).

at least reference to the purposes implicit in every statute, "core" analysis as such is useless.[56] Thus, it is not a mere matter of a vehicle *being* in the park, but rather what it is *doing* there (e.g., "backfiring," endangering lives, serving as a monument?)[57] A weighing up of social issues, which is the heart of teleological interpretation, is as necessary for the individual citizen as for the court, if either is to make heads-or-tails of a legal rule either at the first encounter or in varying circumstances. This "weighing-up," however, is exactly what Hart rejects for those "great areas of conduct" forming the "core" of a rule.[58]

Furthermore, the statutory examples Hart uses are disarmingly simple. No really crucial or complicated values are at stake, and the aims of such statutes, through their repeated application and the daily individual contact with them, have become a matter of common knowledge. Many – indeed, perhaps most – laws are not so simple, e.g., "Every contract or combination in restraint of trade and competition is illegal"; "Freedom of belief and of conscience is inviolable." In such cases, if there is any "core" meaning, it is a general purpose, whose content is not only vague but replete with value conflicts. The very "core" meaning must be developed and is neither clear nor plain in any language. This fact poses the crucial hurdle for any theory of judicial decision: how is the "core" meaning or major purpose of a law to be determined? For these reasons, therefore, Hart fails to make his "core" analysis a sufficient and operational concept of judicial decision. At the same time, he fails in the last possible attempt to establish an objective reference for such normative terminology as "correct," "critical" and "ought."

These three distinguished examples of legal positivism have failed to establish a workable and responsible framework of judicial decision. By strict adherence to system, pure theory or some notion of consent, they ultimately revert to a static formalism which leaves the creative aspect of judicial decision unexplained. On the one hand, the judge merely applies the existing and determinate legal concept, concretizes the given framework of the norm or subsumes the case at hand under the known "core" meaning of a rule. On the other hand, the judge creatively "fills gaps," legislates

[56] Lest this point be thought to exaggerate Hart's view, it should be noted that while Hart does mention "aims or purposes" in his book, in contrast to his prior article, he does so only fleetingly and with precious little weight in comparison with his language analysis. It may be earnestly doubted, therefore, that he takes it seriously. For his prior article, "Positivism and the Separation of Law and Morals," see 71 *Harv. L. Rev.*, 593, 606–15 (1958). See also Fuller, "Positivism and Fidelity to Law – A Reply to Professor Hart," 71 *Harv. L. Rev.*, 630, 661–69 (1958).

[57] Fuller, *id.*

[58] Hart, *op. cit.* (n. 23), p. 127.

("Zwangsakt") or chooses between the competing interests at the "penumbra" as best satisfies him. Such catchwords and phrases, as Esser observes,[59] "serve well to hide the methodological confusion in this area." However denoted, they are more descriptive than operational. Indeed, they represent what is left-over after the law has been otherwise defined. By teaching, therefore, that in the law as written there is nothing to create or that what has been created is final and unconditionally binding, the judicial development of the law is arrogated beyond rational criticism. At most, the law could be attacked from some extra-legal (e.g. ethical, moral, religious or sociological) standpoint, but this obviously would be legally irrelevant to a judicial decision wholly within the written law. If these theories fail, as this analysis concludes, it is not due to the absence of scholarship or intellectual precision, but to the very premises from which they proceed. For this reason, these premises must be more closely examined.

2. THE RATIONALITY OF JUDICIAL DECISION

Before turning to a critique of the major premises of analytical positivism, some introductory comments about the concept of judicial decision are in order. A proper understanding of judicial decision requires that it be viewed as a process. And this in two senses – as a process of creative decision and as a process of justification. In the first place, it constitutes a process of creative decision within the framework of the law as written. In every field of the law, says Esser,[60] it must be realized "that the formulation of the text itself never constitutes the totality of the positive law material." No matter how interstitial at first glance, value choices are always at stake in judicial decisions and gradually expand to influence the whole fabric of the law. Even a simple interpretation, says Larenz of code law construction, is "already 'in itself' the beginning of legal development (Rechtsfortbildung), though the interpreter is not himself aware of it." While the judge may feel constrained not to do this openly, "he generally does it anyway in disguise."[61] Moreover, the "mere" confirmation of existing rules is value

[59] Esser, *op. cit.* (n. 8), p. 120.

[60] Esser, *Grundsatz und Norm*, 95 (1956). See also, for the common law, Cardozo, *The Growth of the Law*, 37 (1924), and his *Nature of the Judicial Process*, 19 (1921): "Back of precedents are the basic juridical conceptions which are the postulates of legal reasoning . . . ."

[61] Larenz, *Methodenlehre der Rechtswissenschaft*, 273 and 277 (1960). See also Esser, *Grundsatz und Norm*, 119f (1956). That this view is generally recognized today on the Continent, see Larenz, *id.*, p. 275; also his "Kennzeichen geglückter richterlicher Rechtsfortbildungen," in 64 Schriftenreihe: *Jurist. Studiengesellschaft Karlsruhe*, 1

creative, for in rebuffing a challenge the authority of these rules is reinforced or their application is extended to new or varying fact situations.

In statutory construction, the potential for creative decision may be seen in three different but interrelated problems. Beginning with the most obvious, the judge must often deal with the latent ambiguities or vagueness of legal language. This may be simply a matter of logic or of word clarification; yet value predicates in the written law can rarely be mastered by formal rules.[62] They are potentially meaningful in many directions and especially in relation to a particular set of facts. In any case, the primary choice remains: an ambiguity does *or* does not exist. For this reason, this problem often shades over into another and the judge is drawn into a more profound consideration of legal values. This arises from the apparent divergence between the language and import, or between the letter and spirit of the text.[63] Here, either the law as written has not expressly provided for the case at hand or the question raised plainly reveals a discrepancy between the language and the intent of the legal norm. Such divergencies are often bridged by some method of interpretation. Still, as Cardozo points out, there are several, often conflicting methods, so that the one chosen may predetermine the decision itself.[64] For this reason, the method of interpretation is often chosen after first determining what the result should be. In that case, chides Radbruch: "The interpretation is the result of its result."[65]

Certainly, the choice (or mixture) of methods is no end in itself. It must be guided – and this is the most profound aspect of creative judicial activity – by deeper insights into the import or spirit of the particular norm in relation to the legal order as a whole.[66] At this point, the purpose of the law and

(1965); and Esser, *id.*, pp. 253f, 259f, 283f and 287 (1956). What has been said of code law is true *a fortiori* for the common law tradition. See, most recently, Llewellyn's "realistic" analysis of the many ways in which judges select and trim, restrict and expand as well as redirect and avoid precedents. *The Common Law Tradition: Deciding Appeals* 75–91 (1960), offering a list of no less than 64 techniques of this type.

[62] Larenz, *Methodenlehre der Rechtswissenschaft,* 215ff and 258 (1960). See also Toulmin, *The Uses of Argument,* Chs. IV and V (1958), who reveals in great detail the extreme limitations on the analytic ideal and formal logic in problem solving and the theory of knowledge.

[63] See Schneider, "Prinzipien der Verfassungsinterpretation," 20 *VVdStRL,* 1, 5 (1963).

[64] Cardozo, *The Nature of the Judicial Process,* 112 (1921). See also Esser, *op. cit.,* pp. 110–19; and Eichenberger, *Die richterliche Unabhängigkeit als staatsrechtliches Problem,* 204–14 (1960).

[65] Radbruch, *Einführung in die Rechtswissenschaft,* 161 (9th ed. 1952).

[66] Reference to the more general context of a law and the legal order as a whole is an accepted method of interpretation in both municipal and international law. See, e.g., Larenz, *op. cit.,* p. 250ff; and Bernhardt, *Die Auslegung völkerrechtlicher Verträge,* 81ff and 156ff (1963).

the criteria of judicial choice are themselves at issue. While this is most clearly evident in the broad-gauged phrasing of constitutional law, it is no less true for such concepts as "unfair discrimination" or "unjust enrichment in common and code law. Fundamental concepts have meaning not in isolation, but only in the wider context of the legal order and the values which law serves.[67] The question of legal meaning, therefore, cannot be divorced from the search for legal ends. Proceeding from the ambiguities and uncertainties in the written law, the judge is forced step-by-step toward the values and principles underlying the law – toward the law behind the law.

This creative pursuit of the law, however, cannot stand alone. It must be disciplined by reasoned opinions open to public scrutiny. In theory, it would not matter by what procedure or in what manner a decision is reached – whether by lot, intuition or merely judicial submission to the party line or social mores – so long as the procedure has community acceptance.[68] Yet in fact, few societies, and certainly none democratic, will long permit courts to render value judgments and decisions in peremptory and *ad hoc* fashion. This would appear and too easily turn arbitrary. Courts do, as Llewellyn aptly notes, possess a decisional leeway. But the leeway to *be* wrong "is not, let it be repeated, at all a leeway to *do wrong*."[69] Moreover, the naked procedure of adjudication, without the discipline of reasoned opinions, offers little leverage for organizing modern society. Though useful in resolving conflicts, it lacks the means to persuade the parties and to mobilize public support for judicial value judgments. The peace may be kept, at least for the time being, but without the capacity to articulate a workable body of law for the future. In order to be responsible as well as effective, therefore, the creative process of judicial decision must be disciplined.

This discipline, from the purely philosophical viewpoint of this Chapter, is termed the process of justification. Its benchmark is "deliberative choosing," embodying the creative as well as the disciplining elements of judicial decision. On the one hand, justification means giving all the (significant)

[67] See, in particular, Radbruch, *Rechtsphilosophie,* 215ff, esp. 218 (4th ed., 1950); and del Vecchio, "Les principes généraux du droit," in 2 *Rec. d'études Gény,* 69, 71ff (1934); and Esser in text *infra,* p. 112f.

[68] Wasserstrom, *The Judicial Decision,* 25ff (1961), introduces the useful distinction between the process of discovery and the process of justification. For purposes of this study, the process of discovery (i.e., the manner or procedure by which a decision is reached) is so fully dominated by as to be subsumed under the process of justification. For this distinction, see also Toulmin, *op. cit.,* p. 17; and Ladd, "The Place of Practical Reasoning in Judicial Decision," in Friedrich (ed.), *Rational Decision: Nomos,* VII 126, 134f (1964).

[69] Llewellyn, *op. cit.* (n. 61), p. 220.

reasons for and against a specific choice under the concrete circumstances. Though conceivably the reasons given might offer simply a defense *ex post* of a choice made by other means, rational decision-making demands that all reasons first be examined and weighed-up, and then a balance struck, based on the experience and insight of the judge. In this sense, jusitification is ends-means or practical reasoning, conducted under the constraints of time and the necessity for decision, where the good choice is judicial action most in accord with the ends of law.[70] On the other hand, the ultimate ends of law have not been concretely and finally formulated. Specific ends may be known or legislated with some precision, but like practical reasoning itself they take on their obligatory or "binding" quality only within the broader framework of the legal order as a whole and the basic values which it implies. As a result, justification reaches beyond the specific value choice and into the realm of speculative reasoning. It consists not only of reasoning *from* but also *about* the specific ends of law. Even more, this same speculative reasoning, though often in the form of *obiter dictum,* may act as "authority" or "precedent" for future decisions. The speculation of today becomes "settled law" tomorrow and the basis for practical reasoning. Proceeding from the law as written, therefore, the process of justification in judicial decision provides the nexus for legal development, combining the past with the future and specific judgments with the ultimate ends of law.

In light of this, what does it mean for judicial decisions to be "rational"? It must mean more – though certainly not less – than giving reasons, for specific reasons are not self-justifying. For this reason, the following analysis presents no catalogue of arguments and their uses in legal reasoning.[71] Further, it must mean more – though, again, not less – than being logical, for substance not form is the essence of judicial decisions. The more reasoning becomes logical in the formal sense, the less guidance it offers and relevance it has for decision-making.[72] Rather, from the standpoint of this Chapter, "rationality" must be defined in terms of the concept of law. This means determining the extent to which judicial reasoning, whether practical or speculative, meets the ultimate tasks of law. It is essential, therefore, to

[70] Aristotle speaks of the good state being "truth in agreement with right desire." For this and his discussion of practical reasoning generally, see the *Nicomachean Ethics,* 1109b(30)–1113b(3) and 1138b(18)–1139b(13); and *On the Motion of Animals,* 701aff. See also Ladd, *id.,* p. 132ff; and Anscombe, "Thought and Action in Aristotle," in Anscombe and others, *New Essays on Plato and Aristotle,* 143 (1965).

[71] A catalogue of this type, including such arguments as *a fortiori, a pari, a contrario* and from analogy, though not professing to be exhaustive, is presented by Perelman and Olbrechts-Tyteca, *Traité de l'Argumentation* 2 vols. (1958).

[72] See Toulmin, *op. cit.* (n. 62), Chs. IV and V.

lay bare those central purposes which are peculiar to the law as an ongoing enterprise.

What are these purposes, or tasks, which are the measure of the rationality of judicial decision – indeed, without which the very concept of law is violated? These can best be established by a critique of the three premises of analytical positivism set out at the beginning of this Chapter.[73] In this way, the one-sided static emphasis of these premises on the law as written can be juxtaposed to the constant search for purpose (and ultimately justice), reason and practicability in the law. This juxtaposition frames three basic, dynamic tensions inherent to the law, which in turn give rise both to the tasks of creative judicial decision and to the types of judicial reasoning which they entail. This will show why a study of the judicial process – which is both a creative process and a process of justification – cannot accept the finality or completeness of the law as written. That is the problem and not the premise of judicial decision; it is "an ever-present problem in jurisprudence and legal philosophy."[74] This analysis also will show why a study of the judicial process cannot be confined to the "gaps" or "penumbra" of the law as written. A review of the fatal shortcomings of analytical positivism reveals the full breadth as well as the inherent limits of rational judicial decision, and the potential in the law for continued growth and development.

Self-Critical Reasoning

The primary proposition of legal positivism disavows all "higher law" values as the basis for legal judgment. There is said to be no necessary, or perhaps even desirable, connection between law and morals or between law as it is and law as it ought to be. By this is meant not simply – as is undoubtedly true – that in a complex society many laws are founded on arbitrary distinctions, as is peculiar to certain tax or traffic regulations. Rather, the law as written is said to retain its validity undiminished, notwithstanding its repugnance to existing conceptions of "just order." Positivists, moreover, do not deny necessarily – aside from the "non-cognitivists" – that moral values may be known in some private sense. Indeed, through legislation and the so-called "gap," "Zwangsakt" or "penumbral" interpretation of judges,

73 See text *supra*, p. 94.

74 Lauterpacht, *The Function of Law in the International Community*, 60 (1933). For Lauterpacht and others, the problem of "non-liquet" in international law is the occasion for asserting the necessity of judicial creativity. See also Stone, "Non-Liquet and the Function of Law in the International Community," 35 *Brit. YB Int. L.*, 124 (1959); and Lauterpacht, "Some Observations on the Prohibition of 'Non-Liquet' and the Completeness of the Law," in *Symbolae Verzijl*, 196 (1958).

these values will often find their way into the law.[75] So far as this "incorporation" has not occurred *in fact,* however, moral values have no legal significance. Absent objective proof of these values, their exclusion from the law is to preserve not only its systematic or scientific integrity, but also – as Hart contends [76] – the critical capacity of those subject to its prescriptions.

As a result, this first premise implies an unbridgeable dichotomy between moral man and an amoral if not immoral law. Why, it must be queried, should the collective judgment of the law and of the judicial process not be subject to the same claims of morality as the private acts of men? That the former are attributable to authorized governmental agencies is no answer, for why should immoral acts of government be recognized? Further, though they in fact are enforced and though men are thereby obliged to act, it does not follow that they obligate men to obey and that they are worthy of the name "law." [77] Finally, while the law admittedly neither is identical with nor encompasses the full range of morality, neither does this conclusion entail the mutual exclusion of law and morality. The answer need not be "all" or "nothing." Rather, if the moral values in fact are incorporated gradually into the law, as the positivists grant, the logically prior question should read: *which* standards or *which* part of morality should the law embrace? This is the overriding question facing the judge and the process of judicial interpretation. The following discussion does not attempt to set forth the minimum morality of law, or the "morality that makes law possible." [78] It seeks simply, first by reviewing certain contemporary theorists and then by way of a more systematic analysis, to identify that tension in the law which marks the presence of higher law values and the continuing search for purpose. In turn, this search for purpose and, ultimately, of "just order" in the law entails a characteristic type of judicial reasoning and one of the overriding tasks of judicial interpretation.

I

Since the turn of this century, important advances have been made in articulating the process of judicial decision. While not overcoming the

[75] See, e.g., Austin, *Jurisprudence,* vol. I, Lectures 37 and 38, and vol. II, pp. 102, 989–1001 (4th ed., 1873), justifying the infusion of custom and "positive morality" in terms of "tacit" commands of the sovereign. And Hart, *The Concept of Law* 181f and 200f (1961).

[76] Hart, *id.,* pp. 203–7; and his "Positivism and the Separation of Law and Morals," 71 *Harv. L. Rev.,* 593, 620f (1958).

[77] Cf. Hart's distinction between "being obliged" and "obligation" as evidenced by discussion in the text *supra,* p. 99ff.

[78] See Fuller, *The Morality of Law,* Ch. II (1964).

skepticism toward an ascertainable system of natural law, they have demonstrated that a complete statement of the judicial process must encompass moral values lying outside the written law. The decisive breakthrough came with Gény's analysis of a century of legal development under the Code Civil. The purely formal and logical elements of the positive law, he concludes,

> are insufficient to satisfy the desiderata of law in action. The inevitable consequence is that the judicial process must look for the means needed to fulfill its mission outside of, and beyond, these elements.[79]

This judicial search for meaning, being neither purely receptive nor mechanical, is disciplined by *la libre recherche scientifique.* It is "free" because the application of abstract and incomplete legislative formulas to concrete problems is subject to no positive legal authority. At the same time, it is "scientific" research, for judicial decisions must be guided by objective criteria adapted to all the facts of social life.[80]

What are the nature and sources of these criteria? They are, says Gény, to be found in four *données,* "l'irréductible 'droit naturel'," embodying categories of considerations lying at the basis of all legal systems.[81] Whereas the données réelles (or naturelles) and *historiques* refer simply to the physical and historical facts of a given subject matter, the *données rationnelles* and *idéales* are the categories of judicial thought most appropriate and crucial to the regulation of social and moral conduct. Of these latter two, the *donné rationnel* offers the main guidelines for an objective elaboration of the law: being "the essential foundation of classical natural law, clearly divested of all other elements." These guidelines are universal and immutable precepts, "which reason derives from the nature of man and from his contact with the world." They are restricted, however, to that incontestable minimum which is immanent in the nature of things.[82]

Beyond these realities of life and history and the demands of reason lies the sphere of the *donné idéal:* "*desiderata,* more refined and more disputable,

[79] Gény, *Méthode d'Interprétation et sources en droit privé positif,* vol. II, p. 234 (2d ed. 1054), originally published in 1899. Though the English translation of the Louisiana State Law Institute is being used here, all citations are from the French edition of this work.

[80] *Ibid.,* pp. 75, 77–79 and the following discussion.

[81] See generally, Gény's latter work, *Science et Technique en droit privé positif,* vol. II, Ch. XIV (1927), originally published in 1913. These *données* (juridical "givens"), which complement and direct the molding of legal constructs (*construit*), are based on his study of the activity of the jurisconsults. *Ibid.,* vol. I, pp. 96–98.

[82] *Ibid.,* vol. II, pp. 380–84.

which are prompted by less clear aspirations."[83] These are considerations, unsettled and vague, "which are based on public attitudes or the present state of civilization." Here are concentrated the "moral or social aspirations of civilization and can be appreciated only in this respect." As such, they embody the "ceaseless progress of positive law," but are by nature the least scientific of all the *données*.[84] By thus combining the transcendent and the positive aspects of legal thought,[85] Gény has depicted the written law in evolution.[86] Indeed, "judicial decision (jurisprudence), studied in its evolution, is nothing else than the contemporary history of our positive law."[87] The law, fixed in time and place by the *données historiques,* is based on enduring physical and rational considerations but ever-striving toward the ideal precepts of mankind. In a word, therefore, the legitimate scope of judicial interpretation is: "Par le code civil, mais au-delà du code civil." [88]

In America, this analysis of Gény as well as of his European contemporaries has had considerable influence. It is reflected and often cited in writings of Pound and Cardozo. In attempting to articulate the competing values or interests in judicial decision, they focus largely on the *données idéales.* For Pound, the quest for a lasting concept of "just order" is futile.

[83] *Ibid.,* vol. II, p. 381f. This distinction between the *données rationelles* and *idéales* is meant to avoid the uncritical mingling of purely rational and speculative considerations.

[84] *Ibid.,* vol. II, pp. 384–89. The considerations of the *donné idéal,* says Gény, are "d'ordre physique, psychologique, moral, religieux, économique, politique, qui, sans déterminer, de façon nécessitante, de nouveaux préceptes de conduite sociale, en projettent, en quelque façon, l'inclinaison, ou, du moins, suggèrent la direction à suivre." *Ibid.,* p. 384.

[85] See Gény, *Méthode d'interprétation, op. cit.,* vol. II, pp. 91f and 100 and the discussion generally, pp. 93–144. Gény also speaks of combining pure and practical reason in legal interpretation. In fact, his whole theory, as he readily recognizes, is an outline of juridical epistemology. *Ibid.,* pp. 34f, 84–86; and *Science et Technique, op. cit.,* vol. I, p. 101 *et seq.* For a comparison of this attempt with that of Kelsen, see Sedláček, "L'oeuvre de François Gény et la science du Droit pure," in *Rec. d'études Fr. Gény,* vol. I, p. 277ff (1934).

[86] See, e.g., Gény, *Science et Technique, op. cit.,* vol. II, pp. 387f and 419f. Above all, says Gény, "positive law must remain alive. To live is to move and to change. In the case of law it is even more: it is to struggle toward a constant and perfect adaptation to the exigencies of society." *Méthode d'Interprétation, op. cit.,* vol. II, p. 225.

[87] *Ibid.,* p. 47.

[88] *Ibid.,* vol. II, p. 230. Legal interpretation, says Gény at another point, "far from being limited by the written law or by the narrow categories of abstract logic, can reach its full development and, so to speak, its proper level of culture only in the moral, social and economic environment which is the atmosphere of the world of law." *Ibid.,* vol. I, p. 220.

Probably the jurist can do no more than recognize the problem and conceive that it is put to him as a practical one of securing the whole scheme of social interests so far as he may; of maintaining a balance or a harmony or adjustment among them compatible with recognition of all of them.[89]

He, therefore, projects no hierarchy among his three classes of public (state), social ("public policy") and individual (private) interests,[90] although the interest in individual human life is "in some ways the most important of all."[91] In any case, Pound is clear that the most important task of the judge is "to induce a consciousness of the role of ideal pictures of the social and legal order both in decision and in declaring the law."[92]

Cardozo, following Gény more closely, sees the quest for justice as a constant part of judicial decision.[93] He too analyzes judicial decision in terms of social values, but consolidates this analysis into four methods of interpretation: philosophy (logic), history (evolution), tradition and sociology (teleology). Which of these methods should be employed in a given case and field of the law "must depend largely upon the comparative importance or value of the social interest that will be thereby promoted."[94] The judicial choice itself is a legislative choice and "demands the legislator's wisdom."[95] In a larger sense, it is guided by the method of sociology which "is the arbiter between other methods, determining in the last analysis the choice of each, weighing their competing claims, setting bounds to their pretensions, balancing and moderating and harmonizing them all."[96]

For both writers the objective is social integration – or, as Pound terms it, "social engineering" – and progress within the limits of legal certainty and continuity in the law. A balance among the conflicting values or interests, varying from field to field in the law, must be struck continually without purchasing any one at too high a price to the others.[97] "There is in truth,"

[89] Pound, *Jurisprudence*, vol. III, p. 330f (1959).

[90] "Interests," says Pound, are not group demands or desires, but "the strivings of men, in, or . . . through, groups and associations and relations to satisfy certain demands or desires." "The law does not create these interests. It finds them pressing for recognition and security." *Ibid.*, pp. 17 and 21.

[91] *Ibid.*, p. 315. Pound also defines this as the "social interest in the individual life" or "in the individual moral and social life."

[92] Pound, "The Theory of Judicial Decision," 36 *Harv. L. Rev.*, 940, 958 (1923).

[93] Cardozo, *The Nature of the Judicial Process*, 74f, 132–141 (1921), citing Gény. "The modern philosophy of law," says Cardozo, "recognizes that there is only *one* law, the positive law, but it seeks its ideal side, and its enduring idea." *Ibid.*, p. 132f.

[94] *Ibid.*, p. 112.

[95] *Ibid.*, p. 115.

[96] *Ibid.*, p. 98.

[97] Pound, *op. cit.*, vol. III, p. 331f. See Cardozo, *id.*, pp. 94f, 98, 102f, 108f, 112f and 120–23.

says Cardozo, "nothing revolutionary or even novel in this view of the judicial function. It is the way that courts have gone about their business for centuries in the development of the common law."[98]

In Germany, earlier than in America, the spirit of a *libre recherche scientifique* was also underway. Both in the various stages of *Interessenjurisprudenz* and in the more radical form of the *Freirechtslehre,*[99] the creative task of the judge was coming to the fore. In theory at least, conceptualistic positivism was clearly on the retreat by the early years of the 20th century. The social facts and interests of these theories, however, do not speak for themselves. They require judicial interest-balancing and this in turn simply emphasizes the search for legal principles behind the written text. This insight was soon to follow. As part of the revival of natural law thinking since 1945,[100] it has received full expression in Esser's comparative study of the judicial process in the common and code law traditions.[101]

Like Gény, Esser rejects the unqualified claims of continental code law to completeness. The creative task of the judge arises from the fragmentary character of the positive law.[102] In both legal systems, he points out,

> the "interpretation" of a text is not the *beginning* of a process of understanding, but is dependent for its part on experience and knowledge of the purpose of the legal order – from the perspective of historically existing, though not at all "positive", legal principles.[103]

Unlike Gény, however, Esser locates judge-made law not just at the periphery and in the gaps of the written text: "Every *interpretation* constitutes a union of *lex scripta* and *ius non scriptum,* which then produces the actual positive norm ('law-in-action')."[104] What is the nature and function of

[98] Cardozo, *id.*, p. 116.

[99] Neither of these movements, in contrast to the theories of Gény, Pound and Cardozo, was concerned with ideal but only with the legislative, social or voluntaristic factors in the law. For a more recent discussion of these two movements, see Larenz, *Methodenlehre der Rechtswissenschaft,* 42ff (1960).

[100] See such samplings as Radbruch, "Erste Stellungnahme nach dem Zusammenbruch 1945" and "Gesetzliches Unrecht und übergesetzliches Recht," in his *Der Mensch im Recht* 105 and 111 (1957); Coing, *Die obersten Grundsätze des Rechts,* 64ff (1947); Bachof, *Verfassungswidrige Verfassungsnormen?* (1951); and Decisions of the Bundesgerichtshof, 11 BGZ Anhang 36ff (Sept. 6, 1953), and of the Bundesverfassungsgerichtshof, 1 BVerfG 14, 33 and 61f (1951) and 3 BVerfG 225, 231–36 (1953).

[101] Esser, *Grundsatz und Norm in der richterlichen Fortbildung des Privatrechts* (1956).

[102] *Ibid.*, pp. 94 and 262.

[103] *Ibid.*, p. 256.

[104] *Ibid.*, p. 287 (emphasis added). See also p. 253f.

these principles and how do they become an integral part of the positive legal order?

Their nature and function, Esser emphasizes, varies in the code and common law systems. In both, the more concrete and determinate statutory norms or rules-of-the-case must be distinguished from legal principles in general.[105] In the common law, on the one hand, principles are identified by their general if not abstract nature, serving primarily as "starting points" of legal reasoning and as summarizing statements of the *ratio juris*.[106] According to continental code law, on the other hand, principles possess more specific, dogmatic content. Their well-ordered function is not so much to direct the judicial search for normative content (for that is already there!), but to offer the bases, criteria and justification for applying specific norms to specific situations.[107] This difference – not, however, to be overdone[108] – suggests the more open or rhetorical approach of the common law, where existing legal rules are continually being varied, limited, expanded, refined, precised and re-integrated into the body of the law through the course of the cases.[109] It also indicates the tendency of the more closed or systematic code law approach to emphasize the constant content of its norms and their disciplined role in the legal order.[110] Like the legal systems which they portray, however, these two functions are simply complementary aspects of the same legal principles.[111] In both systems, "the principle governs the interpretation of norm and rule . . . ."[112] In both systems – albeit to differing degrees – system and rhetoric are indispensable to a viable legal order.

More important, for Esser, is to ascertain in what sense such principles are an integral and effective part of the law. Just as the content of norms and rules depends on legal principles, so also no principle operates creatively by itself.[113] Its effective value for a legal order depends on uniform recognition and elaboration through the cases as well as on a common tradi-

[105] *Ibid.*, pp. 3, 51f, 195 and 201. On this distinction, see also Pound, *An Introduction to the Philosophy of law*, 56f (Yale Paperbound 1959); and Dworkin, "The Model of Rules," 35 *U. Chic. L. Rev.*, 14, 22–29 (1967).

[106] *Ibid.*, Ch. X and esp. p. 185.

[107] *Ibid.*, Ch. IX and esp. p. 51f.

[108] *Ibid.*, pp. 223ff and 239ff, emphasizing the tendencies of both legal traditions to move toward each other.

[109] *Ibid.*, p. 184.

[110] *Ibid.*, pp. 218–20.

[111] *Ibid.*, p. 7, speaking of the complementing and competing roles of these two systems, which is "weithin ein notwendiger und schubweiser Stoffwechsel zwischen den Neuerfahrungen der Fallpraxis und den Formkraeften der Schule."

[112] *Ibid.*, p. 192f.

[113] *Ibid.*, pp. 69–72.

tion in juristic doctrine.[114] The logical and ontological value of a principle means little until it has been historically incorporated into the *corpus juris*.[115]

> Interpretation means here: the reciprocal adaptation of principle and text. For each in itself is only a fragment, because the "correct", the "reasonable", etc., is not of itself discernible, nor can concrete determinations function in terms of their purpose in the legal order without criteria.[116]

In both legal traditions – and not just in the common law – this "reciprocal adaptation" is largely judicial activity.[117] "Judicial activity," emphasizes Esser,[118] "means the constant renewal of communication between substantive ethical values (natural law elements, "irreductible droit naturel" in the sense of Gény) and the values of legal forms and institutions."

This entails no wholesale identification of law and ethics,[119] but the continual sifting, testing and integration of "higher law" values into the positive legal order through the mediating forms of "topical" reasoning. The specific *topoi,* as embodied in legal principles in formation, are modes of rhetoric, "the viewpoints for selecting legal values, the authorized and legal basis of argumentation."[120] They are pragmatic viewpoints of substantive justice – such as "good faith," "reasonableness," the "nature of the thing" and their modern counterparts – oriented on the problem at hand and lying outside the law as system, dogma and axiom.[121] Whether written or unwritten, whether matters of ethics, public policy or just common sense, they regulate the selection of the norm or rule and the shaping of the facts in the case.[122] As such, they "are part of this very [legal] order itself and, in the course of interpretation, are treated as applicable – and not still to be created – law."[123]

From this perspective, judicial decision is a gradual process of articulating principles and the values which they imply. It proceeds case-by-case and is disciplined and tested through the problem orientation of judicial reasoning.[124] Like the process of "overruling," the formulation of principle is not a spontaneous product of the moment. Rather, it

114 Summarized, *ibid.*, p. 336.
115 *Ibid.*, p. 41.
116 *Ibid.*, p. 262.
117 *Ibid.*, pp. 119f, 139–41, 151 and 262f and Chs. 9 and 10 generally.
118 *Ibid.*, p. 60.
119 *Ibid.*, p. 61ff.
120 *Ibid.*, p. 20. See discussion in text *infra*, p. 214ff.
121 *Ibid.*, pp. 44–48 and 53–58.
122 *Ibid.*, pp. 53 and also 192f and 207.
123 *Ibid.*, p. 94.
124 *Ibid.*, p. 6.

arises from a longer subsurface process in which the still unformed principle in question emerges through the inadequacies of decisions validly rendered, and is heralded by equally valid counter-arguments and dissenting opinions. At this point, the *inventio* of a till then unformed idea suddenly takes on a convincing formulation which distinguishes it from mere interpretation and the construction of positive law materials.[125]

Nor are these principles, once formulated, final. "The principle is 'always underway,' "[126] based on current philosophical perspectives and social needs. As an integral part of natural law, principles may be eternal; as elements of the positive law they are not. "They take part in the change of the value order and of the structure of this system."[127]

In both the code and common law, therefore, the content of norm and rule is determined by the "functional unity" of principle and the casuistic of judicial decision.[128] As this suggests, legal principles should not be confused with legal rules, at least not in the technical sense of the latter. As *ratio legis,* however, principles may well be classified as positive law, "which are expressed through interpretation and become transformed thereby onto a more concrete plane."[129] Moreover, in keeping with the introduction to this Section, this emphasizes further the formative role of judicial decision as essentially a process of justification. Interpretation means not merely understanding the text as it is, but developing it (Fortbildung), completing it and, if necessary, even correcting it.[130] "Juristische Interpretation," declares Esser in words which this whole study echoes, "ist nicht Nachdenken des Vorgedachten, sondern Zu-Ende-Denken eines Gedachten – ja . . . Zu-Ende-Denken eines weltueberall Gedachten."[131]

II

These related approaches of Gény, Pound, Cardozo and Esser deny the strict separation of the ideal and the real, of the moral and the positive ele-

[125] *Ibid.*, p. 54. See also the description of this process by Cardozo, *The Nature of the Judicial Process,* 48 (1921).

[126] Esser, *id.*, p. 280.

[127] *Ibid.*, p. 327.

[128] *Ibid.*, pp. 275 and also 219.

[129] *Ibid.*, p. 94.

[130] Esser, *id.*, p. 260. See also Holmes, *The Common Law,* 35 (1881), who concludes that, in substance, "the growth of the law is legislative . . . . It is legislative in *its grounds*." Emphasis added.

[131] Esser, *id.*, p. 260 and also p. 262f. In translation Esser's prose reads: "Judicial interpretation is not reflecting on a prior idea, but thinking through an idea to its completion . . . indeed . . . thinking through a worldwide idea."

ments in law. They are striking evidence of the failure of legal positivism to adequately explain the judicial process. Are they, however, more than evidence? Do they focus on a central and necessary quality of law or only on a peripheral and isolated aspect, or on a mere technical imperfection of judicial decision? The answer hinges on the notion of legal obligation.

Both Hart and Kelsen, for instance, affirm the primacy of legal obligation for the concept of law, but in a way which empties obligation both of enduring and concrete meaning. Thus, Hart locates obligation in the *existence* of a rule supported by a general and insistent demand for conformity or, in a complex modern society, by the general obedience of ordinary citizens and "the acceptance by officials of secondary rules as critical common standards of official behavior."[132] Accordingly, obligation would be no more than the facts of obedience and consent – like adherence to the standard metre bar in Paris.

With Kelsen, it must be denied that normative rules can be derived from such facts.[133] It is true, as Hart contends, men may and do obey for many reasons other than the rightness or justness of the law or legal system, e.g., the threat or use of force, whim, personal advantage and social pressure. But this does not explain why they should or ought to obey. This is the essence of obligation, going qualitatively beyond a mere linguistic or emotive "description" of what men mean when they say "I am obligated." Moreover, while the majority or even a governing minority may consent to the laws, consent alone would be a capricious basis for legal obligation. However we may choose to define the law, says Brierly,

> an essential part of the function of law must be to limit the wills of those to whom its precepts are addressed, and its binding force cannot possibly by derived from the wills that it limits. A self-imposed limitation is no true limitation at all, but a contradiction in terms.[134]

From the mere fact of obedience or act of consent, therefore, individuals can create legal obligations neither for themselves nor, even less, for others.[135]

[132] These conclusions are based on the discussion in text *supra*, p. 101f.

[133] See Kelsen, *Pure Theory of Law*, 4ff (transl. of the 2nd German Edition by May Knight, 1967).

[134] Brierly, "The Basis of Obligation in International Law, in Lauterpacht (ed.), *The Basis of Obligation in International Law* 1, 14 (1958).

[135] "Es müsste seltsam anmuten," says Kelsen, "wenn man die subjektive, individuelle *Rechtspflicht* eines einzelnen auf die Anerkennung gründen wolle, die nicht von ihm selbst, sondern von der Majorität seiner Genossen, also von anderen, ausgegangen ist." *Hauptprobleme der Staatsrechtslehre*, 367 (2nd ed. 1960).

Kelsen, on the other hand, manages to preserve the normative quality of law, which he espouses, only by emptying it of all value content. While positing the basis of obligation and the legal system as a whole on an objectively ascertainable "Grundnorm," [136] he ascribes it purely formal binding effect. "For it must be emphasized that only the validity and not the content of the legal order can be derived from the Grundnorm." [137] This is precisely the difficulty. For if the value content and the normative form of law, like "is" and "ought" judgments, belong to mutually exclusive realms – and if, as rightly follows, a normative statement can be derived only from another normative statement – then it is impossible for legal content to have any obligatory quality at all.[138] The particular rules of a functioning legal system would be no more than normative fictions with "power politics" content. The "dualism" in theory becomes unavoidable for practice.

The notion of obligation cannot be meaningfully explained in this fashion. It is neither fact nor fiction, but the essential distinction between law and the mailed fist. Whatever the content of natural law theory over the course of centuries, it is living testimony to the idea that law is not identical with command and coercion. In the confrontation of natural and positive law, observes Welzel,

> the conviction is expressed throughout history most emphatically and persistently that, in the social relations of men, something exists beyond mere coercion due to dominant power or action according to established custom. Something exists that – independent of command and custom – *obligates* us in our most inner being to certain acts. The idea of unconditionally *being obligated* (Verpflichtet-Seins) is the core and lasting truth content of natural law.[139]

[136] See discussion in text *supra*, p. 97f; and Kelsen, *op. cit.* (n. 132), p. 7f.

[137] *Ibid.*, p. 224 and also pp. 69–71 and 223–26. See also Kelsen, *General Theory of Law and State*, 113 (1949): "Legal norms may have any kind of content."

[138] See the recent critique of Welzel, *An den Grenzen des Rechts: Die Frage nach der Rechtsgeltung*, 27–29 (1966). "Entscheidend ist," says Welzel, "dass in seinem Verlauf der Sollensbegriff seinen Ausgangsinhalt völlig verliert, und zwar unmittelbar, nachdem Kelsen die Disparität des Sollens vom Sein am *ethischen* Sollen aufgezeigt hat! An die Stelle eines aus der Ethik stammenden und in ihr allein aufzeigbaren Grundbegriffes setzt Kelsen eine gedankliche "Hypothese," genauer und präziser: die *Fiktion* einer Norm, die, wie er neuestens lehrt, auf einen fiktiven Willensakt zurückgeht."

[139] Welzel, *Naturrecht und Materiale Gerechtigkeit*, 237f (4th ed. 1962). See also Strauss, *Natural Right and History*, 6 and 100 (1953): "Once we realize that the principles of our actions have no other support than our blind choice, we really do not believe in them any more. We cannot wholeheartedly act upon them any more. We cannot live any more as responsible beings . . . The disagreement regarding the principles of justice thus seems to reveal a genuine perplexity aroused by a divination or insufficient grasp of natural right – a perplexity caused by something self-subsistent or natural that eludes human grasp."

This notion of obligation, reaching beyond the factual realm, locates man as a responsible being at the center of law.[140] Not by force, but by reason of values which in themselves are just, can man be obligated. This is not to identify the spheres of law and morality, for the question of *which values* has not yet been reached. And once it has, not all private values need necessarily be public values; there is a legitimate – though certainly no absolute – distinction between the two. Rather, this notion of legal obligation is simply the recognition that man's striving for truth cannot be compartmentalized.[141] His search for justice in legal society is the undeniable counterpart of his search for morality in private life.

Nevertheless, the rejection of legal positivism does not reestablish a natural-law value hierarchy. Legal theorists have had to recognize that a system of values is not susceptible to incontestable and demonstrable proof, whether in terms of logic or experience. While it is possible, with the help of logic, to demonstrate inconsistencies within any given value system, this does not apply to the ultimate principles which the system premises.[142] This must be true *a fortiori* for value choices in the sphere of judicial decision – of human action or practical reason – where the system itself is incomplete or at least only abstractly relevant for the case at hand. Does this necessarily mean, however, that creative judicial decisions are simply arbitrary? If this were true, then positivism would have been rejected only for a crass judicial voluntarism. It would, in effect, be asserting the necessity of a value reference for legal obligation without objectively knowable value content. This is the dilemma of modern legal theory, forced to recognize the modest limits of human knowledge without sliding into value nihilism.

This dilemma gives rise to a dynamic tension in the law between the imperfection of the written norm and the uncertainty as to its just or ideal

140 *Ibid.*, pp. 237–40. See also Welzel, *op. cit.*, *(An den Grenzen)*, pp. 29–32; and del Vecchio, *Die Gerechtigkeit*, 117 (2d German ed., 1950). Cf. Fuller, *The Morality of Law*, 186 (1964); and his "Freedom – A Suggested Analysis," 68 *Harv. L. Rev.*, 1305, 1313f (1955), who emphasizes the creative, choosing and purposive side of man's nature.

141 No one has done more than Fuller in recent years to make this interdependence between law and morality clear. See in particular his writings just mentioned, his "Positivism and Fidelity to Law – A reply to Professor Hart," 71 *Harv. L. Rev.*, 630 (1958); and his "Reason and Fiat in Case Law," 59 *Harv. L. Rev.*, 376, 380 (1946): "the basic problem of the judicial process remains that of discovering and applying those principles that will best promote the ends men seek by collective action."

142 See Viehweg, *Topik und Jurisprudenz*, 53–64 (1954), in his critique of attempts to construct axiomatic legal systems. It should be recalled that even in mathematics, the bastion of formal logic, Goedel's proof demonstrates certain inherent limitations in the axiomatic method which rule out any possibility that even the ordinary arithmetic of whole numbers can ever be fully systematized by this means. See Nagel and Newman, "Goedel's Proof," 194 *Scientific American*, 71 (1956).

content. It may be bridged – although never fully overcome – not by positing a complete value system,[143] but only by that self-critical search for purpose or ideal content which keeps the law sensitive to the requirements of "just order." In the sphere of practical reason, as Ch. Perelman so impressively contends, this means replacing closed value systems (philosophies premières) with the "philosophie régressive."[144] The latter is characterized by four principles. While acknowledging the continuing search for a total explanation of human experience (principe d'intégralité), it recognizes the impossibility of ever fully attaining this goal due to the existence of conflicting views (principe de dualité). New facts and experience are always presenting themselves, requiring the re-thinking and reappraisal of existing value systems. By way of corollary, therefore, no decision or insight is ever final or infallible, but subject constantly to review and being reversed (principe de réversibilité). The "philosophie régressive" recognizes only "an imperfect and ever perfectible knowledge, which seeks not the ideal of perfection but the ideal of progress."[145] For this reason, the model of philosophical thought is not that of the mathematician but of the judge, who must elaborate new law as well as apply existing law to concrete situations.[146]

The key to the "philosophie régressive," however, lies in the fourth principle, the "principe de responsabilité." It introduces the human and moral element into judicial decision. For, says Perelman, in the realm of practical reason, where knowledge is at best partial, "the thinker becomes involved by deciding. His ability, his sincerity, his integrity, in a word his responsibili-

[143] Several writers have noted the curious historical fact that once natural law reached its millennium in the Eighteenth Century and was incorporated into the constitutional law and codes of many countries, the creative tension between ideal and reality was dissolved and natural law sank without a fight below the intellectual horizons. See Pound, "The Theory of Judicial Decision," 36 *Harv. L. Rev.*, 641 (1923); Wieacker, *Privatrechtsgeschichte der Neuzeit,* 218 (1952); and Welzel, *op. cit.* (Naturrecht), p. 160.

[144] Perelman, "Philosophies premières et philosophie régressive," reprinted in the collection of essays of his and Olbrechts-Tyteca, *Rhétorique et Philosophie pour une Théorie de l'argumentation en philosophie,* 85 (1952). Whereas the diverse "philosophies premières" are competing total views of the world, the "philosophie régressive" attempts to account for the discord among these divergent views. "La philosophie régressive," says Perelman, "s'oppose au statut accordé par les philosophies premières à l'être nécessaire, à la vérité première et à la valeur absolue." *Ibid.*, p. 95.

[145] Perelman, *id.* (Philosophies premières), p. 106f. By "the ideal of progress," he means "non le fait de s'approcher de quelque perfection utopique, mais le fait de résorber les difficultés qui se présentent à l'aide d'un arbitrage constant, effectué par une société d'esprits libres, en interaction les uns avec les autres, des avantages et des inconvénients de toute prise de position devant l'ensemble des éléments de l'expérience." See also his "Opinions et vérité," in *Justice et Raison, id.*, p. 196ff.

[146] Perelman, *id.* (Philosophies premières), p. 99f.

ty, are at stake."[147] This entails the necessity *for* choosing, although not of the *choice* itself. Thus, absent a complete and objectively provable value system, the judge is presented with real value alternatives. This is what distinguishes him from the automat.[148] In a concrete case, he is not

> that anonymous being who simply prostrates himself before the responses which nature furnishes him; the creative scholar is a complete being who is involved in his activity, who thinks, who chooses, who decides. Rational activity is never that of a spectator.[149]

Real alternatives require real choice and the personal contribution of the judge to the search for justice.

Not only are the alternatives real, but some choice is unavoidable. We must not forget, observes Perelman,[150] that "within the realm of action, not to choose is still a choice, and that at times a graver risk is run by abstaining than by acting." For this reason, the value sceptic who rejects intelligent choice chooses anyway, or else delegates the decision to others. This is obviously true for the judge, and not simply because to pronounce a "non liquet" might be condemned as a denial of due process. Social conflict will be resolved one way or the other. Responsible judicial decision, therefore, means real and deliberate choice. It establishes an intimate solidarity between the judge and the judgment.

Responsible decision also means deliberated and not arbitrary choice. Precisely the danger of choice is partiality and a neglect of opposing viewpoints. The challenge for the just judge is to avoid this; he must choose, he is part of his choice, but his choice must be impartial. How to proceed? Of course, the "truth" or "justness" – and, for that matter, the falsity or injustice – of value choice can never be verified with the clarity of the natural sciences nor demonstrated in any absolute way; these are but vague and distant goals, the magnetic poles of the search for knowledge. Judicial choices, however, may be justified as "preferable" – as preferable to all other known alternatives. In judicial decision as everywhere, observes Perel-

[147] *Ibid.* See also Perelman, "La rôle de la décision dans la théorie de la connaissance," and "Rapports théoriques de la pensée et de l'action," in his *Justice et Raison, id.*, pp. 121ff and 175ff.

[148] In his *Law and the Social Order*, 242 (1933), M. R. Cohen points out that in a completely determinate system there is no essential difference between "is" and "ought" propositions, meaning that it would serve no useful purpose to assert how any two elements of such a system "ought" to fit together.

[149] Perelman, "La quête du rationnel," in his *Rhétorique et Philosophie, op. cit.*, p. 113f.

[150] Perelman, *op. cit.* (Philosophies premières), p. 100.

man,[151] "human knowledge never begins at zero, with a tabula rasa." Rather, the judge proceeds from the traditional framework, accepted knowledge and precedents and asks whether there are sufficient reasons to warrant adopting a new position. This is the elementary requirement of justice, that men in like circumstances be treated alike.[152] It further reflects the very nature of human knowledge: that to a large extent, to turn a phrase of C. S. Peirce, thought is "mind hidebound by habit." [153] Practical reason, therefore, must be built upon existing knowledge and practice.

Moreover, the "preferable" must not only be chosen. It must also be justified. Here the judge reaches beyond mere emotion, beyond the toss-up of "simply choosing" [154] – avoiding the extremes of dogmatism and scepticism, total system and absolute chaos – and into the realm of the reasoned and reasonable decision. "To reason," emphasizes Perelman throughout his writings, "is not merely to verify and to demonstrate, but also to deliberate, to criticize, and to justify; to give reasons for and against; in a word, to argue."[155] To argue is not to demonstrate the "true" or the "just," for arguments are never correct or incorrect, but strong or weak and relevant or irrelevant. Rather, to argue is to oppose real or potential criticism, i.e., "to show that the choice or decision in question is above criticism, and especially above any criticism one might advance from possible alternatives."[156] It is that "dialectical" reasoning which Aristotle examines in "The Topics" and demonstrates in his "Rhetoric," but rehabilitated and elaborated for the modern social sciences.[157]

Still, the question remains: *when* is a choice "preferable," a preference "justified" and the justification "reasonable"? "In the last instance, it is man," concludes Perelman,[158] "who is judge of his choice and of the choice of other men, both his collaborators and his opponents, judging at once the

[151] Perelman, "Opinions et vérité" and "Ce qu'une réflexion sur le droit peut apporter au philosophe," in his *Justice et Raison, op. cit.*, pp. 203 and 249f.

[152] See in particular Perelman, "L'idéal de rationalité et la règle de justice," 55 *Bull. de la Société française de philosophie,* 1, 2, 13f, 40, 46f (Jan–March, 1961).

[153] See Peirce, "The Law of Mind," reprinted in part in J. Buchler (ed.) *Philosophical Writings of Peirce,* 339, 350f (Dover ed. 1955).

[154] Or, in the psychological language of Hart, choosing "in a way which best satisfies us." See text *supra,* p. 103f.

[155] Perelman, "Justice and Justification," 10 *Natural L. Forum,* 1, 5 (1965).

[156] *Ibid.,* p. 6. See also Perelman, "Jugements de valeur, justification et argumentation," in his *Justice et Raison, op. cit.,* p. 234ff.

[157] See particularly Perelman and Olbrechts-Tyteca, *La Nouvelle Rhétorique, op. cit.,* which presents a whole list of arguments and techniques in this tradition. See also Viehweg, *Topik und Jurisprudenz* (1954); J. Stone's survey, *Legal System and Lawyers' Reasoning,* 332–35 (1964); and discussion in text *infra,* p. 214ff.

[158] Perelman, *op. cit.* (Philosophies premières), p. 98.

choice and the man who chooses." The heart of justification, therefore, is not the strict or formal classical conception of rationality. It is not the narrow sphere of demonstrable proof. It is instead the search for human accord through reasoned decisions.

This accord is no mere agreement among like-minded men or dominant interests. This would violate the "principe d'intégralité," upon which the search for 'just order' is premised, by arbitrarily excluding the critics. The "philosophie régressive"

> cannot reply to the proponent or the philosophies premières "just this far and no further." He may not refuse to follow his adversary by arguing from evidence which limits the entire discussion. But he may refuse to admit that the implicit principles, once set forth, constitute the definitive and ultimate basis of his philosophy, and *a fortiori* of all philosophy.[159]

Rather, the accord here in question is among the *universal audience.* In the continuing search for purpose in the law, this is the audience which the judge must address. The audience judges the cogency of his arguments and the reasonableness of his claims.

What constitutes this audience? It is both norm and fact, having both an ideal and a concrete construction.[160] Ideally, it never actually exists but is an intellectual referent for all reasoning that attempts to transcend the time and place of a particular dispute. It is composed of all men, the common reason of the world. If the judge would satisfy this audience, especially on the most fundamental questions of a legal order, he must present a rhetoric worthy of the gods themselves.[161] Were this achieved, the difference between reasonableness and rationality would disappear, for "one passes from the reasonable to the rational by the elimination of ambiguity, by formalization and mechanization."[162] Once accord is universal, as on matters of formal logic, all doubt is erased and the reasonable becomes the rational.

As a matter of fact, however, the judge must settle for less. In the existing world legal community as in the "cité philosophique actuelle," it is clearly vain to hope of achieving universal accord on concrete matters of substance. Moreover, and this is simply the other side of the coin, the actual character

[159] *Ibid.*, p. 102.

[160] Perelman, *op. cit.* (n. 152) (L'idéal de rationalité), p. 42; and his "Acte et personne dans l'argumentation," in his *Rhétorique et Philosophie, op. cit.* (n. 144), p. 50f.

[161] Perelman, *id.* (L'idéal de rationalité), p. 21, making express reference to Plato's statement in the Phaedrus 273e.

[162] Perelman, *id.*, p. 43. This is a narrower sense of the term "rationality" than that employed throughout this study (see the introduction to this Section 2), as well as that employed elsewhere by Perelman.

of the audience which the judge addresses is historically, socially and culturally determined. The common reason which it possesses is not eternal:

> to the contrary, each epoch, each civilization, even each intellectual discipline has its conception of rationality, of the "conscience collective rationnelle" which must be addressed and whose adherence must be solicited.[163]

That is to say, there are neither gods nor a corresponding rhetoric. The judge must look to the best audience possible: to all those "whom common reason would define as well-informed and reasonable men."[164] By the same token, while judicial reasoning can rarely if ever attain universal accord, it can at least "prétendre s'adresser à l'universalité des esprits."[165] The judge, following this categorical imperative of practical reasoning, may present those arguments or reasons only which lay claim to universal recognition.

Does this audience, and the categorical imperative which it implies, reflect merely a success standard of judicial rationality? In a sense "yes," but one bent on the continuing search for purpose in the law. This search, which is both motivated and directed by the notion of justice, cannot be disembodied from the conflicting values of concrete disputes.[166] So long as genuine doubt exists in the minds of the universal audience, whether arising from experience or pangs of conscience, judicial reasoning must attempt to meet and remove it. Otherwise, its pretensions to universality are frivolous. Indeed, the judge cannot stop here. Being closest to the problems at hand, he may uncover weaknesses in legal argument not seen by others. Every potential criticism is an index of imperfection in the positive law. More importantly society is not always so open or so self-searching that minority opinion –

[163] Perelman, *op. cit.* (n. 149; La quête du rationnel), p. 119f.

[164] Perelman, "Justice and Justification," 10 *Natural L. Forum*, 1, 18 (1965). For further explanation of the notion of a "universal audience," see Perelman, "De la preuve en philosophie," in his *Rhétorique et Philosophie, op. cit.* (n. 144), p. 129; and his "L'idéal de rationalité . . . ," *op. cit.* (n. 152), p. 14f.

[165] Perelman, *op. cit.* (n. 149: La quête du rationnel), 119f. Similar, but truncated views of judicial rationality have also been put forth by Cardozo, *The Nature of the Judicial Process*, 88f (1921): for judgments in accordance with reason and justice, "the thing that counts is not what I believe to be right. It is what I may reasonably believe that some other man of normal intellect and conscience might reasonably look upon as right"; and also in the early essay of Carl Schmitt, *Gesetz und Urteil*, 71 (1912): "Eine richterliche Entscheidung ist heute dann richtig, wenn anzunehmen ist, dass ein anderer Richter ebenso entschieden hätte. 'Ein anderer Richter' bedeutet hier den empirischen Typus des modernen rechtsgelehrten Juristen." As to the latter, see Hofmann's recent discussion: *Legitimität gegen Legalität – Der Weg der politischen Philosophie Carl Schmitts*, 32–35 (1964). See also Perelman, "De la preuve en philosophie," *id.*, p. 129.

[166] Perelman, *op. cit.* (n. 152: L'idéal de rationalité), p. 21.

however intelligent and telling – receives a full and fair hearing in ruling circles, the literature and litigation. It must be searched out, articulated and continually integrated into the legal order. If, as Leo Strauss has rightly pointed out, "the emergence of the idea of natural right presupposes . . . the doubt of authority,"[167] then minority opinion virtually becomes the conscience of the law.

This doubt, to varying degrees, is intrinsic to the universal audience. It attains its ultimate measure in the idea of justice which epitomizes – and in fact functions – as "the symbol of criticism in and for the law."[168] As a result, the inherent limits on human knowledge in the law, from which such doubt derives, necessitates the continuous exercise of *self-critical reasoning* in judicial decisions. This reasoning is neither self-destructive nor purely negative. It is but a candid and continuing reappraisal of the law as written in an effort to articulate those underlying value premises which obligate in and of themselves. It proceeds from the written text, judicial precedents and the existing legal tradition and value framework, yet recognizes their fragmentary and imperfect character. Above all, the judge himself must be aware of his and society's biases, as well as of the inarticulated value premises which they imply, lest the law be reduced to an ideology of the dominant morality. "Only a step," warns Perelman,[169] "separates the philosopher-king and the armed prophet from the tyrant, and a clear conscience makes a tyrant only more tyrannical." Unavoidably, therefore, the just judge is an activist. He must sound the battle cry against every ideology which attempts to usurp the function of the universal audience.[170] He is also the partisan of the law in its truest sense. His is the relentless search for the premises of "just order."

[167] Strauss, *op. cit.* (n. 139), p. 84. See also pp. 90–93, where he discusses the distinction between nature and convention, between *physis* and *nomos*, between reason and authority.

[168] Garlan, *Legal Realism and Justice*, 127f and 126 (1941).

[169] Perelman, *op. cit.* (n. 164: Justice and Justification), p. 11.

[170] In terms directed not specifically at the judge, Welzel speaks of the need to maintain "eine *geistige* Auseinandersetzung" in the law. *Op. cit.* (n. 138), p. 31f. And, within the framework of his relativism, Radbruch speaks of "den Aufruf zum Kampf gegen die Überzeugung des Gegners, deren Unbeweisbarkeit er [relativism] nachweist, und die Mahnung zur Achtung vor der Überzeugung des Gegners, deren Unwiderlegbarkeit er zeigt: Entschlossenheit zum Kampf auf der einen Seite, Duldsamkeit und Gerechtigkeit des Urteils auf der anderen – das ist die Moral des Relativismus." Radbruch, "Der Relativismus in der Rechtsphilosophie," in his *Der Mensch im Recht,* 80, 81 (2d ed. 1961). Within the framework of a thoroughgoing relativism which Radbruch espouses, however, it must be wondered whether an incapacitating value nihilism rather than a militant tolerance would not more likely result. See Strauss, *op. cit.* (n. 139), p. 6.

Persuasive Reasoning

The second proposition of analytical positivism deals with the question of authority in the law. It holds that laws are simply imperatives or authorized norms, rules or pronouncements which are coupled with a sanction and originate from a sovereign or authorized decision-maker. As to specific norms and decisions of governmental organs, on the one hand, the proposition is purely formal. They are "valid," "authorized" and "binding" – that is, "men ought to obey and apply the legal norms"[171] – if they have been issued or taken in accordance with the "Grundnorm" (Kelsen) or secondary rules (Hart). Each such rule has equal dignity and the same authority in the legal order, whatever its content or rationale. By this strict separation of legal form and substance, as Smend points out,[172] the existence of a law's authority is not a matter of degree, but only a categorical "yes" or "no." Nor are these positivists vitally concerned with the reasons for or the justification of a law; they are content with the mere fact that the legislature or court has declared a law or pronounced its validity. Accordingly, law becomes little more than the fiat of an authorized decision-maker.

Both Kelsen and Hart, on the other hand, do not deny the importance of the efficacy of law in general. Thus, Kelsen acknowledges that efficacy is a condition for the existence of a legal order, but is careful to distinguish this from the concept of validity. A single norm is then valid, even though generally disregarded in fact, if it belongs to a legal order which is on the whole respected.

> Thus, efficacy is a condition of validity; a condition, not the reason of validity. A norm is not valid *because* it is efficacious; it is valid *if* the order to which it belongs is, on the whole, efficacious.[173]

Kelsen does not explain, however, why a legal order would have any greater efficacy than its individual norms, nor why – as a corollary – the validity of any individual norm is any less a function of its own efficacy than of the efficacy of the legal order as a whole.[174] Once again, his concept of authority is all or nothing.

[171] Kelsen, *General Theory of Law and State*, 39 (1949).

[172] Smend, "Verfassung und Verfassungsrecht," in his *Staatsrechtliche Abhandlungen*, 119, 166 (1955).

[173] Kelsen, *op. cit.*, p. 42. See also pp. 39ff and 118ff.

[174] Kelsen, *op. cit.*, p. 119f, recognizes the notion of *desuetudo* by which a single norm may lose its validity. Apparently, this is an "authorized" means of negating norms via the growth of contradictory custom.

By comparison, Hart's approach is more flexible. For him, the efficacy of a legal order depends on the obedience of ordinary citizens to primary rules and on the acceptance by officials of secondary rules as common standards of procedure. Indeed, the latter "can neither be valid nor invalid but simply accepted."[175] In case of disagreement among officials, the legal system simply degenerates into a see-saw power play until accord has been reestablished in officialdom. In the end, the *ancien régime* either reappears or the system has been altered.[176] Law, however, has nothing more to say about this. For Hart as for Kelsen, therefore, the question of legal authority is reduced to formal validity and the facts of obedience and acceptance.

This one-sided emphasis on fiat and on the formal validity of judicial decision leaves the inner dynamic of the law unexplained. What – it must be asked – makes the relation of a norm to the legal system as a whole "authoritative"? Or, in terms more akin to Hart's theory, how does consent become an operative and integral part of judicial decision? To answer this, it is necessary to distinguish reason from fiat, from the assertion of power and the mere facts of obedience and acceptance. Authority in the law necessarily embraces both. Law, as Lon Fuller paraphrases Cardozo, is "by its limitations fiat, by its aspirations reason, and the whole view of it involve[s] a recognition of both its limitations and its aspirations."[177] These two aspects of authority frame the second inherent tension in the law. What are their nature and the character of the judicial reasoning which they entail?

Authority, says de Jouvenal, "is the ability to obtain assent." Or, in other words: "the efficient cause of voluntary agreement."[178] The stress here is not on the fact of assent or agreement, which is the product or basis of authority, but on the *capacity to create* this condition in others. Nor, by the same token, should the notion of authority be confused with that of legitimacy, i.e., why law or a legal order is just. Legitimacy ordinarily concerns the ultimate value bases of law and not simply its efficacy.[179] Indeed, the question of authority becomes acute only because ultimate values cannot be demonstrated with certainty. The question, therefore, is not why do I or why

175 Hart, *The Concept of Law*, 105f (1961). See the discussion in text *supra*, p. 101f.

176 Hart illustrates this case of disagreement by reference to a game and its rules. If the scorer makes aberrant rulings, then the players can either get themselves another scorer or play the scorer's game. There is apparently no room for true criticism and correction between the scorer and the players. *Ibid.*, p. 100f.

177 Fuller, "Reason and Fiat in Case Law," 59 *Harv. L. Rev.*, 376, 377 (1946).

178 de Jouvenel, *De la Souveraineté*, 45 and also 45–49 (1955).

179 Different again from the concepts both of authority and legitimacy, as used in this study, is the sociologically based "power to legitimate" or "legitimating function" of the judiciary described in Section 3 of the following Chapter.

should I obey, but how to gain assent on a given matter. Authority, as Carl Friedrich contends, "provides the bridge between power and justice."[180]

What is the nature of this bridge – of this capacity to gain assent for the law? de Jouvenal appears to emphasize mostly the quality of the person, the *auctor*. He is the composer or creator, the instigator or promoter and the guarantor or augmenter of assent.[181] While this quite aptly describes the active or dynamic quality of authority, for purposes of judicial decision it is more appropriate to emphasize the nature of the communication itself. This is the virtue of Friedrich's definition, derived from the verb *augere*, to augment: "*Auctoritas* thus supplements a mere act of the will by adding reasons to it."[182] What matters is not conclusive or demonstrable reasoning, but "the additional reasoning, the *more* of reasons that can be given for the communication of him who has authority."[183] It is, in short, "the capacity for reasoned elaboration" of a decision in terms of the opinions, values, beliefs, interests and needs of the community.[184] This capacity or potential to elaborate need not be exercised to be effective, but if challenged the person responsible must be able to support his communication "by valuational and instrumental reasoning."[185] For the judge, reasoned elaboration must constitute the heart of his decision. Every case is, in fact, a challenge of his capacity to reason upon values.

The type of reasoning which Friedrich, like Perelman,[186] has in mind does not belong either to mathematics or to formal logic. Rather, it is a reasoning "which relates actions to opinions and beliefs, and opinions and beliefs to values, however defined."[187] Nor, Friedrich insists, does it concern the fact of persuasion, i.e., of influencing the thinking and acting of others in some psychological way, though influence is often involved. If, instead, persuasion entails arguments which are worthy of persuading wise and prudent men or, in other words, means the capacity to gain communal assent for decisions by reasoned elaboration, then Friedrich's notion of reasoning would not differ appreciably from the techniques of rhetoric which Perelman dis-

[180] Friedrich, "Political Authority and Reasoning," in his *Man and His Government*, 216 and 218 (1963).

[181] de Jouvenel, *op. cit.*, p. 45f.

[182] Friedrich, *op. cit.*, p. 218f, although pointing out that this derivation has been disputed.

[183] *Ibid.*, p. 222.

[184] *Ibid.*, p. 226.

[185] *Ibid.*, p. 230.

[186] See discussion in text, *supra*, p. 123f.

[187] Friedrich, "Authority," in Friedrich (ed.), *Authority: Nomos*, I 28, 35 (1958), being substantially the same essay as the one appearing in his *Man and His Government, op. cit.*

cusses.[188] In fact, Friedrich does define his reasoning as "the ability to argue effectively and at greater length, to elaborate, in other words, in a way that makes sense."[189] Since what "makes sense" necessarily depends on the particular audience being addressed, he is led to qualify the function "reasoned elaboration" by the term "communal." Thus, to say that authority is being lost or disintegrating means that "the community is changing, and [the] capacity for *communal* reasoning is . . . declining."[190] The reasoning of the court in such cases, it may be said, is "no longer" cogent.

This "communal" quality of communication, which is so crucial for judicial decisions, explains why the capacity of courts to speak in persuasive terms varies enormously. It explains why judicial reasoning rarely falls in the logical categories of "true" or "false," but typically must be evaluated in degrees of cogency such as "forceful" or "weak."[191] A slight shift in community values and beliefs can destroy the tacit premises upon which the rationale of a decision has been built. Such a shift often entails a loss of authority for a specific decision or line of decisions and, perhaps, even for the court itself.

Thus, in the search for authority, the judge is not concerned with the "universal audience" of mankind as described above, but with the *real audience* or governing public(s) of a specific existing community.[192] This audience reflects the power realities of social organization upon which the authority of law depends. Obviously, in a pluralistic society with a democratic framework, "who governs" will be an audience of diverse and often conflicting publics acting for the most part in coalition. This explains why the rhetoric of judicial reasoning, being fashioned by judges who themselves reflect the divergent value frameworks of this coalition, is frequently a hodgepodge of arguments. However viable the ultimate consensus which unites this coalition, many specific issues have not been determined or will

188 "Rhetoric" in the classic concept of the Greeks, as Perelman employs the term, means "la manière de faire admettre sa pensée par autrui." It is a reasoning upon values in the form of argumentation. The more current view of rhetoric as the art of expression (eloquence, style, etc.) has only a subordinate role. Perelman, "L'idéal de rationalité et la règle de justice," 55 *Bull. Soc. Franc. phil.*, 1, 14 and 20f (Jan-March, 1961). See also the Introduction to his and Olbrechts-Tyteca, *La Nouvelle Rhétorique: Traité de l'argumentation,* vol. I (1958).

189 Friedrich, *op. cit.* (n. 180), p. 222.

190 *Ibid.*, p. 227.

191 Perelman, *op. cit.* (n. 188: L'idéal de rationalité), p. 14f, and his *La Nouvelle Rhétorique, op. cit.* (n. 188), pp. 1–83, esp. pp. 5–10.

192 In approaching the law essentially from the perspective of philosophy, Perelman (to the knowledge of this writer) has not drawn this distinction between the universal and the real audience. His notion of rhetoric, however, probably would encompass both audiences.

arise anew in the course of time and have to be fought out. Then too, the make-up of the coalition itself will alter depending on the issue in question.

The judicial capacity to reason persuasively on specific questions, therefore, reaches either inherent or established limits at some point. This is the area of fiat in the law. The established limits, as indicated above, are a function of the existing values and mores of a specific community. They arise, as Fuller points out, through "the force of established institutions" in an ongoing society.[193] Neither law nor judicial decision can operate in a historical vacuum; their aspirations of reason must be tailored to a given framework of values and beliefs. Consequently, the function of judicial reasoning in the search for authority is to relate a specific value judgment as cogently as possible to the underlying core of community values.

On the other hand, the capacity of a court to reason persuasively is inherently limited. This is not a function so much of community values as of the very nature of human knowledge. "There can be no absolute, no total, authority," notes Friedrich, "because there is not open to man any absolute truth or total reason."[194] Unable to demonstrate the concrete content of justice, the court must resort to the rhetoric of persuasion. Lacking conclusive arguments to persuade the real audience, moreover, judges must often conclude by fiat – fiat which the real audience at least will accept. "Vermag niemand festzustellen, was gerecht ist," observes Radbruch, "so muss jemand festsetzen, was rechtens sein soll."[195]

Authority in the law, therefore, must be understood in terms of its aspiration *and* its limitations. This is the source of the second major tension in the law – the tension between persuasive reason and fiat. It is the alternative to positivism's attempt to reduce authority to the mere fiat of an authorized decision-maker or the fact of efficacy. Further, it is a dynamic complement to the search for ideal content in the law. Because law tends to lose in authority to the extent that judicial decision cannot articulate and demonstrably rest on ultimate values, rhetoric is pressed into the task of persuading the community – within the framework of the legal discipline and the judicial process – that the laws are just and worthy of respect. This is not the self-critical reasoning in search of "just order," but the attempt to mobilize and consolidate public opinion, or at least the opinion of the governing public(s), in favor of judicial decisions. No legal community can long function where judicial decision is no more than *ipse dixit*. What cannot be established by

[193] Fuller, *op. cit.* (n. 177), p. 380.

[194] Friedrich, *op. cit.* (n. 180), p. 230.

[195] Radbruch, *Rechtsphilosophie,* 81 (3rd ed. 1932) ("If no one can determine what is just, then someone must establish what the law shall be.")

demonstrable proof must be buttressed by persuasion. Where the limits of persuasive reasoning are reached, however, fiat is unavoidable. At this point, the court must astutely avoid overreaching the existing community consensus to the extent of undermining its own authority and the legal order itself. The aspiration of reason has a here-and-now as well as a future.

Pragmatic Reasoning

The third fundamental proposition of analytical positivism holds that the study or analysis of legal concepts is worth pursuing, divorced from historical, economic, psychological and other types of inquiries into the causes, aims and social underpinnings of law. The law, that is to say, is treated as isolated from its social environment for purposes of analysis and classification.

The rationale for this separation has both functional and intellectual aspects. Functionally, it attempts to distinguish legal norms from social usage by emphasis on physical sanctions in the law. Legal norms are uniformly, if only potentially, backed up by the threat of coercion.[196] More important, perhaps, is the intellectual endeavor to establish law as a science independent of other social disciplines. While this aspect is not emphasized like the first in Hart's analysis, it is predominant in the other two types of analytical positivism discussed above. Thus, proponents of a *Begriffsjurisprudenz* work toward a "genealogy of concepts," which is abstracted from the "material evidence" of the law[197] and transformed into a logical, hierarchical juristic system reflecting the immanent reason in the law.[198] Kelsen, for his part, seeks system beyond the substantive realm of legal concepts in the "pure science" of law. Being purely a "science of norms" and not of sociology, it treats not the content but only the logical structure of legal norms.[199] To an even greater extent than *Begriffsjurisprudenz,* this *a priori* basis of Kelsen's "pure theory" is unable – indeed, is not meant – to take account of the law-in-action, of legal norms in application.[200] Whichever justification, whether functional or intellectual, this third proposition of analytical positivism ig-

196 See discussion in text *supra,* p. 99f. As is pointed out there, Hart supplements the "coercive orders" view of Kelsen with the "internal aspect" of legal rules.

197 The Pandectists, for instance, sought this evidence in custom as well as national legislation and the legal convictions (Rechtsüberzeugung) of the people.

198 See discussion in text *supra,* p. 95f.

199 See discussion in text *supra,* p. 97f.

200 But cf. Kelsen, *Reine Rechtslehre,* 19 (2nd ed. 1960), criticizing Alf Ross' contention that Kelsen's dualism prevents his theory from being even of the slightest value for the application of law.

nores or denies the interdependence of law and the social sciences and the latter's contribution to effective legal regulation.

The law, of course, can not be identified purely and simply as a normative science with the other social disciplines. For one, it possesses uniformly an essential element of coercion or threat of coercion. Even Ehrlich, despite his emphasis on actual social conduct and the inner order of groups as the basic and original form of law,[201] does not deny that "norms of judicial decisions" influence the conduct of men.[202] He and sociological jurisprudence since Montesquieu[203] have repeatedly demonstrated, however, that the threat or use of coercion is rarely sufficient to secure respect for law in practice. The law, says Pound,

> depends for its efficacy chiefly upon the extent to which it can identify social interests with individual advantage or interest and can rely upon individual initiative for enforcement of its precepts. Unless individuals can thus become enlisted in the service of the legal order the law in the books becomes academic. We get something quite different in action . . . .[204]

Due to the resistance of tradition, custom and other folkways as well as the egoism of human drives, therefore, the ability of coercion to secure social regulation and progress is seriously limited. Where principle is not at stake, the law must be shaped to accommodate and utilize these social realities and existing patterns of social control.

This interdependence of legal rules and social organization requires a corresponding method of legal analysis. Social goals and values can be legislated, but their realization depends for a large part on the practicability of the concrete rules shaped and developed through judicial decision. The norm and coercion, as Rudolf von Ihering urges, are "purely formal elements" of the law: "only through its content can we understand how the law serves society."[205] In his momentous conversion from *Begriffsjurisprudenz* during

[201] See Ehrlich, *Grundlegung der Soziologie des Rechts*, 1, 6, 15, 17, 31ff, 273f, 292, 393ff, Ch. XXI and the Vorwort generally (1929), contending that the centre of gravity of legal development lies not in legislation nor in juristic science or judicial decision, but in society itself.

[202] *Ibid.*, p. 7: "Surely no one denies that judicial decisions influence the conduct of men, but we must first of all inquire to what extent this is true and upon what circumstances it depends."

[203] See, e.g., Montesquieu's definition of "positive law" in Bk I, ch. 3 of his *Spirit of the Laws*, as well as the individual Books dealing with climate, geography, morals, commerce, population, etc. See also Ehrlich, "Montesquieu and Sociological Jurisprudence," 29 *Harv. L. Rev.* 582 (1915–16), praising Montesquieu's *Spirit of the Laws* like his *Persian Letters* for being "the first attempt to fashion a sociology of law."

[204] Pound, *Jurisprudence*, vol. III, p. 373 (1959). See also Ehrlich, *op. cit.*, p. 12f.

[205] Ihering, *Der Zweck im Recht*, vol. 1, p. 339 (4th ed. 1904).

the latter quarter of the nineteenth century, Ihering pioneered the search for new modes of juristic thought and legal methods.[206]

While styling his approach "social utilitarianism,"[207] Ihering's emphasis is neither the "mechanics" of Comte nor the individualistic hedonism of Bentham. It is rather orientation toward concrete purpose in the law. The function of law is not philosophical speculation in search of truth; rather, he contends, it is the more practical one of securing the essential standards of society.[208] For this reason, "the criterion of law is not the absolute one of truth, but the relative one of purpose."[209] By the same token, the criterion of legal analysis is the pragmatic one of "correctness," of ends-means reasoning. "The correctness of the content of the will is determined by its purpose."[210] And this in two senses. Normatively, "correctness" characterizes the concurrence of the will with that which should be, i.e., the written norm. Causally, it implies "the idea of direction, i.e., of the course which someone has to take in order to attain an end or goal."[211] Thus, despite his one-sided emphasis on utility, Ihering redirected jurisprudence toward the social function of law. He laid the basis for a teleological method of analysis by which the law could respond to the growing complexity of social control and the developing knowledge of sociological jurisprudence.

The rejection of the third proposition of analytical positivism demonstrates "the *practical* need," so strongly urged by Julius Stone, to pursue "the study of law in society."[212] This does not mean the assimilation of law by the social sciences or vice versa, since the law as a normative science for the control of human conduct cuts uniquely across all these varied disciplines. Its study, says Stone, is "a sort of specialization in nonspecialization."[213] Rather, the interdependence of law and the social sciences suggests the need to view legal rules, among other things, as means for achieving specific ends. Social goals and values can be legislated, but their realization depends for a

[206] See Pound, "The Scope and Purpose of Sociological Jurisprudence," 25 *Harv. L. Rev.*, 140ff (1911–12); and Larenz, *Methodenlehre der Rechtswissenschaft*, 62ff (1960).

[207] See Ihering, *op. cit.*, vol. 2, Vorrede, p. xiii, speaking of "gesellschaftlichen (objektiven) Utilitarismus."

[208] *Ibid.*, vol. 1, p. 345.

[209] *Ibid.*, pp. 342ff: "das ganze Recht ist nichts als eine einzige Zweckschöpfung." See also Holmes, "Law in Science and Science in Law," 12 *Harv. L. Rev.*, 443, 460 (1899): "the real justification of a rule of law, if there is one, is that it helps to bring about a social end which we desire . . . ."

[210] *Ibid.*, p. 340.

[211] *Ibid.*, p. 341.

[212] Stone, *Law and the Social Sciences in the Second Half Century*, 48 (1966).

[213] Stone, *id.*, p. 48.

large part on the practicability of the concrete rules selected or developed through case law.

It is necessary, therefore, to view the law as only one of various means of social control which can rarely be implemented effectively autonomous of the others. Further, the law must search beneath all doctrine and through the light of the available social knowledge for those key points in systems of action from which adjustments can effectively be made.[214] Whether the system in mind is the "market economy" or the institution of marriage, rules must be fashioned to the operative facts. Finally, the law must develop more meaningful categories, which both are informed through the social sciences and grasp society as a functioning unity.[215] These, then, are the sociological tasks of jurisprudence.

This "practical need" is the source of the third inherent tension in the law. The formulation of legal rules is caught between the almost infinite multiplicity of social facts and patterns and the necessity to reduce them to clear and general guides of conduct. The one demands fully individualized decisions, responsive to the particular circumstances and constant change in society; the other cries out for uniformity and simplicity of expression, conducive to predictability and certainty in the law.

As developed by Gény, this dichotomy is reflected in the contrasting categories of *donné* and *construit,* of science and technique in the law.[216] The *donné,* discussed above,[217] reveals the social basis of the law; the law, that is to say, must be shaped "such that it relates to the nature of things and, so far as possible, to their original state."[218] It is the task of legal science to penetrate and explain the basic elements in the life of the law.[219] The *construit,* on the other hand, is the result of legal technique attempting to organize these basic elements according to the needs of the legal order.[220] It is the "work of artificial if not arbitrary will, striving little by little to increase the sum of the *donné.*"[221] Typical of these techniques are concepts – but also legal fictions and presumptions – which attempt to impress on the disparate social facts a logical and cohesive form. In doing so, they necessarily

[214] *Ibid.*, p. 28f. See also Llewellyn, "The Normative, the Legal, and the Law-Jobs: The Problem of Juristic Method," 49 *Yale L. L.*, 1355, 1356f and 1373ff (1940).

[215] Stone, *id.*, p. 28.

[216] Gény, *Science et Technique en droit privé positif,* vol. I, p. 96ff and vol. IV, Ch. XXVI (1913).

[217] See text *supra,* p. 112f.

[218] Gény, *op. cit.*, vol. I, p. 97.

[219] *Ibid.*, p. 98f.

[220] *Ibid.*, pp. 96–100.

[221] *Ibid.*, p. 97.

distort, for to select and classify is to obscure some and to emphasize other data.[222]

The value and organizational effectiveness of such legal artifice depends on its ability to reflect and encompass the living and changing realities of the *donné*. To overemphasize the one leads to empty formulas.

> The realities have disappeared, the ideas tend to stiffen into words, judgments turn into formulas. The legal system takes the form of a comprehensive scheme of numerous and rigid compartments, separated by watertight partitions. The "esprit juridique" has vanquished the social material and subjected it imperiously, even capriciously, to its demands.[223]

To exaggerate the aspect of multiplicity, however, would stultify legal development and lead to the very dissolution of law as a normative order. Law-in-action must avoid both pitfalls.

This inherent tension in the law gives rise to the third judicial task, the search for practicability in the law. Thus, in order to avoid the extremes, on the one hand, of infinite multiplicity and change and, on the other, of purely rigid rules and formal concepts unresponsive to the realities of social life, the judge must seek to develop workable or manageable rules. This means rules with built-in flexibility, yet with operative criteria offering reasoned guidance for the fullest realization of legislated ends. For all the rule-skepticism attributed to him, this has been the relentless quest of Karl Llewellyn, America's most penetrating "legal realist."[224] His goal is not absolute certainty in the law, as some have wanted to contend,[225] but the "reasonable regularity" which is so necessary to legal guidance and judicial responsibility.[226] Having concluded that "*rules of law alone* do not, because they cannot, decide any appealed case *which has been worth both an appeal and a response*,"[227] he points out that the great body of the law has offered the

[222] See also Llewellyn, *Jurisprudence: Realism in Theory and Practice,* 27 and 96 (1962): "... to classify is to disturb. It is to build emphases, to create stresses, which obscure some of the data under observation and give fictitious value to others – a process which can be excused only insofar as it is necessary to the accomplishing of a purpose."

[223] Gény, *op. cit.*, vol. I, p. 114.

[224] See Garlan, *Legal Realism and Justice,* 4ff (1941); and Llewellyn, *The Common Law Tradition: Deciding Appeals,* App. B (1960); and his *Jurisprudence,* Essays 1, 2, 3 and 7 (1962).

[225] See, for instance, the critique of Clark and Trubek, "The Creative Role of the Judge: Restraint and Freedom in the Common Law Tradition," 71 *Yale L. J.*, 255, 267ff (1961–62).

[226] Llewellyn, *The Common Law Tradition, op. cit.*, p. 215f.

[227] *Ibid.*, p. 189.

lawyer who cares to look beneath the surface and the layman who needs to know a reasonable amount of guidance and predictability.

This guidance and predictability is the result of the judge-made rule with a "singing reason." This means a rule which "wears both a right situation-sense and a clear scope-criterion on its face." These are rules which are "relatively clear as to where and when they apply," are "shrewdly tailored to significant types of problem-situation" and "carry their reason on their face."[228] Further –

> Criterion and phrasing must guide immediately and effectively, in dealing with problem-facts. To this end, the reason is as essential as the rule; the reason indeed informs the rule, and it is the applicability of the reason which tests the applicability of the rule.[229]

Thus, "a 'rule' never rises to the full level of a rule, at all, except insofar as its sphere and criteria of application achieve a moderate clarity."[230]

To say that the rule is clear, but its application is not, simply is an untrue statement. If it only points to an issue and sets a goal, it does not do the very thing a rule of law is for, namely, "to produce a workable working measure for moving toward the desired goal or goals."

> A formula which does not guide its own application is not as yet a rule of law at all –

The judge must continue to reformulate.[231] The task of the judge in the Grand Style of Llewellyn, therefore, means "not the elimination of rules, but such setting of words and paper in perspective as can hugely step up their [rules'] power and effect."[232]

The judicial search for practicability, like the other two tasks of the judge discussed previously, is characterized also by a type of reasoning directed primarily at a particular audience. It is the *pragmatic reasoning* of means (legal rules) fashioned to the realization of specific values and ends. It is a way of reasoning, in the words of Llewellyn, that regards –

> the official formulation as a tool, not as a thing of value in itself; as a means without meaning save in terms of its workings, and of meaning in its working only when these last are compared with the results desired.[233]

[228] *Ibid.*, pp. 182 and 335.
[229] Llewellyn, *Jurisprudence, op. cit.*, p. 306.
[230] Llewellyn, *The Common Law Tradition, op. cit.*, p. 343f.
[231] *Ibid.*
[232] Llewellyn, *Jurisprudence, op. cit.*, p. 27.
[233] *Ibid.*, p. 26f.

This is the legacy of Ihering, combined with the practical insights of the social sciences. In the most concrete sense, it is lawyer's work: the "craft of doing and getting things done with the law."[234] In the colorful prose of Llewellyn, it is "horse sense," which is neither the sense of a horse nor ordinary common sense but "the extraordinary and uncommon kind of experience, sense, and intuition of . . . an old-fashioned skilled horse-trader in his dealings either with horses or with other horse traders."[235]

Moreover, like the other types of judicial reasoning, this pragmatic reasoning also is not disembodied but directed at a particular audience, the *controlled audience*. It is that group of persons, varying according to the subject matter or particular issue, who are concerned or interested because they are immediately affected by a specific norm. This audience is typical of the law, for most rules – however general as to the few they cover and the type of conduct in mind – are highly specialized when compared with the citizenry as a whole.[236] For instance, taxpayers with certain types of income, entrepreneurs undertaking price agreements with their competitors, businessmen making bulk sales, etc. Each forms a particularized and, at least in terms of the rule, a specialized audience whose actions the rule is meant to control. Insofar, the audience is the measure of the rule, for the rule must be shaped to offer the guidance and control necessary to achieve a certain end. The third inherent tension in the law, therefore, gives rise to the third judicial task, the search for practicability in the law. The essence of this task is pragmatic reasoning as measured by the controlled audience.

CONCLUSIONS

From this analysis of the concept of law, it may be concluded, law is neither final nor complete in its written form nor, to use Holmes' timeworn phrase, "a brooding omnipresence in the sky."[237] It embodies rather the continuing tensions between ideal and reality, between reason and fiat and between the multiplicity and change of social facts and patterns and the necessity for uniformity and certainty in rule shaping. These three tensions establish not only the dynamic character of the law, but also the unique tasks of the court in the search for purpose, authority and practicability in the law. Each task in turn is furthered by a type of judicial reasoning,

[234] *Ibid.*, pp. 318 (emphasis deleted) and 352ff. See also Llewellyn, "The Normative, the Legal and the Law-Jobs . . .," *op. cit.* (n. 214), p. 1373ff.

[235] Llewellyn, *The Common Law Tradition, op. cit.*, p. 200f.

[236] Llewellyn, *Jurisprudence, op. cit.*, p. 35.

[237] Justice Holmes dissenting in *So. Pacific Co.* v. *Jensen,* 244 U.S. 205, 222 (1917).

whether self-critical, persuasive or pragmatic, whose ultimate measure is the audience which it addresses. The law not only must seek to be just, it must also be admitted to be just as well as be tailored for effective application.

Taken together, these three types of reasoning compose a standard of rationality for judicial decision. Like the concept of law upon which it rests, this standard is never fully attained. Indeed, the imperfection of judicial reasoning stems not only from the inherent limits on knowledge, authority and practicability in the law, but also from a potential conflict among the judicial tasks themselves. The equities of a specific case, for instance, may well not offer the most practicable or the most persuasive solution. The proper aim of judicial decision is not to sever this Gordian knot of the law, but through judicial craftsmanship to reckon imaginatively with the tensions and potential conflicts which it entwines. This testifies to the unique contribution of each judicial decision to the continuing development of law. In the prose of Cardozo, "the inn that shelters for the night is not the journey's end. The law, like the traveller, must be ready for the morrow."[238]

[238] Cardozo, *The Growth of the Law*, 19f (1924).

CHAPTER IV

THE INSTITUTIONAL FOUNDATIONS OF JUDICIAL DECISION

Judicial decision is a function not only of the concept of law, but also of its institutional framework. While the concept of law establishes the tasks of the judge in the search for purpose, authority and practicability, these tasks must be precised and shaped further in the concrete setting of governmental powers. This is necessary, above all, because the creative process of judicial decision must be kept within the bounds of constitutional government. "It is by institutionalizing its power, in setting organic limits for it," observes Charles de Visscher, "that the State establishes the distinction between politics and law."[1] This principle has been exemplified clearly through the historical development of an independent judiciary. Independence has been accompanied by institutional limitations. Responsible judicial decision can be assured only by procedures and safeguards which depersonalize and circumscribe the exercise of judicial power.

An institutional analysis is necessary, moreover, because the judiciary does not and cannot bear the sole responsibility for the development of law. Courts are limited by their institutional design and by the appropriateness of this design to treat effectively the problem at hand. Traditionally, the lines of responsibility have been drawn within the disciplined framework of a tripartite division and balance of powers. The European Communities, no less than the Member States, reflect this pattern of constitutionalism. In addition, like some of the Member States, the Communities have taken the giant step of establishing a Court with broad powers of judicial review. With this act, the judiciary becomes the agency for interpreting and disciplining the institutional play of governmental powers. For this reason, especially, it must remain acutely aware of the proper scope and limits of its own function in relation to that of other branches of government.

The analysis of this Chapter is based essentially on the theory and prac-

[1] de Visscher, *Theory and Reality in Public International Law,* 91 (1957).

tice of judicial review by national courts. This is not to say, as previous Chapters have demonstrated, that comparisons of the Community Court with the International Court of Justice are useless. Their value is greatly reduced, however, because the international law system at present lacks the disciplined constitutional framework of the Communities as well as an analogous distribution of powers within the context of judicial review.[2] The constitutional courts of the United States and Germany, on the other hand, meet these requirements, and more.[3] The division of powers which they supervise embraces both the horizontal one of federal-state relationships as well as the vertical one among the various branches of government. Nevertheless, the powers of each are so circumscribed that their authority depends to a great extent on the willing cooperation of other governmental institutions. Thus, despite certain important organizational and jurisdictional differences,[4] the adjudication of the United States Supreme Court and the German Federal Constitutional Court will fairly reflect, though not at all perfectly, the tensions at work in the European Communities. What, it must be asked throughout this Chapter, is the unique character of judicial review that makes its creative decisions both a valuable and responsible contribution to legal development?

1. THE LEGACY OF MONTESQUIEU

The writings of Montesquieu have special significance for an analysis of the judicial power. Despite the historical bias of his conclusions, Montesquieu – in the wake of Bolingbroke and Locke[5] – saw the importance of institutionalized power for the establishment and maintenance of a *gouvernement modéré*, of responsible and limited government. What is more, he saw this in the context of human weakness and human dignity.[6] As a man of affairs, he recognized that the degeneration of even the best forms of government lies in the "eternal malady of man" to misuse power and the

[2] See Rosenne, *The Law and Practice of the International Court*, vol. I, p. 3 (1965).

[3] See Colin, *Le Gouvernement des juges dans les Communautés Européennes*, 36 (1966), who compares the Community Court favorably with the United States Supreme Court.

[4] By contrast with the Supreme Court, for instance, the jurisdiction of the Federal Constitutional Court is much broader (see note 106 in Chapter II) and its power of judicial review is expressly anchored in the German Basic Law.

[5] See, e.g., Kägi, *Zur Entstehung, Wandlung und Problematik des Gewaltenteilungsprinzip*, 41ff (1937).

[6] See, e.g., Forsthoff, "Zur Einführung," in his German translation of *De l'Esprit des Lois*, Vol. I, pp. xxvi–xxviii (1951).

law itself.[7] It was essential for the preservation of liberty, therefore, that the exercise of all governmental power be set within a framework of checks and balance.

The legacy of Montesquieu is above all this "règle de sagesse politique." By the prudent combination of governmental functions and political power, a constitution could be formed "such that no man shall be compelled to do things to which the law does not obligate him, nor forced to abstain from things which the law permits."[8] Through this rationalist's faith in the liberating capacity of the law and the moderating effect of institutionalized power on its potential misuse, liberty could be secured. An assessment of these aims in the light of subsequent developments in legal theory and of the rise of judicial review will help pinpoint the problem of responsible judicial decision in modern constitutional government.

The leitmotif of Montesquieu is the notion of *moderation* in its broadest and most profound sense. It reoccurs throughout his writings as a measure of man, of the laws and of governmental organization. As a human trait, it is reflected in the *noblesse oblige* of a far-sighted aristocracy[9] and in the democratic virtues of probity and temperance.[10] In political life, "even the highest refinement of reason is not always desirable and . . . it is better for men generally to adjust themselves to the mean than to the extreme."[11] Moreover, the laws – incorporating that "human reason governing all the people of the earth" – are an ideal reflection of human nature, but must be tailored to the physical conditions and social circumstances of each nation.[12] They counsel restraint. On the one hand, liberty does not consist in the right to do what one will. Where law governs, "liberty consists only in the power to do what one ought to will, and in not being constrained to do what one ought not to will."[13] On the other hand, morals and custom should not be changed by law – "this would be too much like tyranny" and would be likely to fail. Instead, this is a matter for education, where "people are induced to change themselves."[14]

7 Montesquieu, *Considérations sur la grandeur et la décadence des Romains*, Ch. VIII (1734).

8 Montesquieu, *De l'Esprit des Lois*, Bk. XI, ch. 4. The translation used here is taken in part from that of Thomas Nugent appearing in The Hafner Library of Classics (1949).

9 *Ibid.*, Bk. III, ch. 4.

10 *Ibid.*, Bk. III, ch. 3 and Bk. V, chs. 2–7.

11 *Ibid.*, Bk. XI, ch. 6 (next to last paragraph); and see also Bk. II, ch. 4.

12 *Ibid.*, Bk. I, ch. 3.

13 *Ibid.*, Bk. XI, ch. 3.

14 *Ibid.*, Bk. XIX, ch. 14.

All this would be futile, however, unless government is properly organized. Political liberty, Montesquieu contends, is not always found even in moderate forms of government – for "virtue itself has need of limits."[15] Rather, that moderation which is conducive to liberty will be found only in a *gouvernement modéré* where the inevitable abuse of unrestrained power is checked by power. The remedy lies in "a certain distribution of three powers," which he develops through a two-fold analysis of governmental institutions.[16] First, he distinguishes the legislative, executive and judicial functions. They form the conceptual framework of governmental activity and the necessary basis for an efficient and effective distribution of powers. He then proceeds, in terms of the existing political realities, to fuse the first two functions into a check and balance of social classes. While the legislature would have both aristocratically and more democratically representative assemblies, the executive power (essentially foreign policy) is entrusted to the monarch. The governmental functions and the political realities were thereby welded into institutions.

The judiciary, by contrast, is disestablished. Being otherwise "so terrible to mankind," its function is exercised independently of any one class or profession. Instead of standing tribunals with permanent appointments, Montesquieu envisages a constant change in the composition of the courts, similar to that of the English jury system. The result should be that "one fears the office, but not the officials."[17] The ingenuousness of this plan is further buttressed by a firm faith in the universal reason of the law. Given this, the judges simply could be strictly subordinated to the *ratio scripta* as enacted by parliament. They would be, so to speak, just "the mouth that pronounces the words of the law, mere passive beings, incapable of moderating either its force or rigor."[18] In terms of its governmental function, therefore, the judiciary is granted a distinct task and equal status with the other two branches. Deprived of a political basis, however, its power was thought to be "in some sense next to nothing."[19] By this discrete fusion of

[15] *Ibid.*, Bk. XI, ch. 4. The "virtue," which Montesquieu speaks of here, is the operational principle of democratic government, including love for the republic, for equality and sobriety as well as respect for laws and acting according to them.

[16] *Ibid.*, Bk. XI, ch. 6 (first paragraphs). See Krauss, "Die Gewaltengliederung bei Montesquieu," in *Festschrift Carl Schmitt*, 103 (1959).

[17] Montesquieu, *id.*, Bk. XI, ch .6 (pars. 14ff). It must be kept in mind that Montesquieu is concerned only with criminal and civil courts.

[18] *Ibid.*, Bk. XI, ch. 6 (par. 49).

[19] *Ibid.*, Bk. XI, ch. 6 (pars. 32 and also 14). In view of the apparent conflict in the idea that judicial power is both terrible and non-existent, Hauriou, *Principes de Droit public*, vol. I, p. 38 (2nd. ed. 1916) points out: "c'est-à-dire qu'elle est terrible comme pouvoir sur le justiciable, mais elle est nulle comme efficacité vis-à-vis des pouvoirs

governmental functions with political realities, Montesquieu attempts to preserve the principle of moderation throughout government.

Despite the obvious historical and jurisprudential limits of Montesquieu's premises, his conclusions offered an alluring distinction between "political" and "judicial" functions. Proceeding from this common source, the constitutional practice on the Continent and in the United States took divergent paths. The Continent, for its part, sharing a deep distrust of the judicial power,[20] took Montesquieu most literally. Starting from the ideal of a systematic codification of law, it fully subordinated the judiciary to parliament. The law (Gesetz, loi) – whether as the expression of the *volonté générale* or as the "carefully worked-out expression of the *a priori* idea of law"[21] – "was the Magna Charta of liberty, the judge being simply its obedient servant and executor."[22] Thus, in France – struggling to accommodate the political philosophies of Montesquieu and Rousseau – the former's "pouvoirs séparés collaborant" were transformed into "pouvoirs isolés,"[23] denying the very possibility of active judicial participation in a governmental check and balance of powers. In Germany, the dominant "esprit juriste" of the 19th century radically rationalized the governmental functions and fully subordinated the judiciary to the rational-deductive application of determinate norms.[24] Moreover, the turn to positivism merely bound the judge more securely to the written words of the statute.[25]

The United States, on the other hand, raised adjudication to the constitutional level. With a view to the needs of federal government[26] as well as

politiques de l'Etat, parce qu'elle n'a pas la puissance d'empêcher leur action." See Krauss, *op. cit.* (n. 16), p. 112f.

20 See, e.g., Plathner, *Der Kampf um die richterliche Unabhängigkeit bis zum Jahre 1848*, pp. 80ff and 140 (1935), pointing out that the battle to secure the independence of the judiciary was fought with the concept of a purely rational judicial function, simply subsuming specific cases under general laws in a mathematically precise way.

21 Eb. Schmidt, *Gesetz und Richter: Wert und Unwert des Positivismus* 7 (1952).

22 Bachof, "Die richterliche Kontrollfunktion im westdeutschen Verfassungsgefüge," in *Festschrift Hans Huber*, 26, 37 (1961).

23 See Kägi *op. cit.*, (n. 5), p. 88ff. The contrast between the ideas of Rousseau and Montesquieu are well reflected in Articles 3 and 16 of the "Déclaration des droits de l'homme et du citoyen" of 1789.

24 Kant developed a logical hierarchy of complementary governmental functions by reference to the three parts of a syllogism: parliament, as the source of all positive law, formulated the general principles; the administrative agencies bridge the gap from the general to the concrete situations; and the judiciary draws the conclusion for the individual case. *Metaphysik der Sitten*, Pt. I, pars. 45–48.

25 See text *supra*, p. 95f.

26 Whereas the nationalists in the Constitutional Convention proposed a congressional negative as the remedy for unconstitutional state legislation, the state rights supporters succeeded in passing their alternative of a federal judicial check. Their assump-

a firm faith in a known "higher law,"[27] the Supreme Court was thought necessary to ensure the supremacy of federal law and to preserve "certain exceptions to legislative authority."[28] Relying on the conclusions of "the celebrated Montesquieu," Hamilton argued that the Supreme Court was the best guardian of the Constitutoin vis-à-vis unlawful acts of the government." [I]n a government in which [the three branches] are separated from each other, the judiciary, from the nature of its functions, will always be the least dangerous to the political rights of the Constitution" – "is beyond comparison the weakest of the three departments of power" – having "neither FORCE nor WILL but merely judgment."[29] Should it exercise will instead of judgment, this would be to substitute its pleasure for that of the legislative body. That possibility, concludes Hamilton, "if it proved anything, would prove that there ought to be no judges distinct from that body."[30] As a uniquely limited institution, therefore, the Court was appropriate to exercise the power of judicial review.

The changing concept and function of law in the 19th century, however, undermined the rationalist's ideal of law lying at the heart of Montesquieu's theory of judicial power. In the first place, the theory and practice of judicial interpretation belie a rigid distinction between governmental functions. As the foregoing Chapter attempts to show, law does not possess that unambiguous, determinate character which can be mastered simply by the traditional tools of judicial interpretation. Rather, the judiciary is committed to a degree of value-choice and creative judgment which it may use for the creative development of the law or even to frustrate legislative attempts at reform.[31]

tion, however, that it would prove mild in comparison was soon to be disappointed. Schmidhauser, *The Supreme Court as Final Arbiter in Federal-State Relations,* Ch. I (1958).

[27] See, e.g., Corwin, "The 'Higher Law' Background of American Constitutional Law," 42 *Harv. L. Rev.,* 149–153, 379f and 394–409 (1929).

[28] *The Federalists Papers,* No. 78 (New American Library Ed., Paperback, 1961). This was neither then nor now, however, an unquestioned proposition.

[29] *Ibid.,* p. 465.

[30] *Ibid.,* p. 469.

[31] The opposition of the Supreme Court to the social reform legislation of the 1930's is well-known. Of courts not vested with judicial review, the creative role of the French Conseil d'Etat is perhaps best known and studied. See, e.g., Freedeman, *The Conseil d'Etat in Modern France,* Chs. 6 and 7 (1961); Hamson, *Executive Discretion and Judicial Control,* Chs. 1 and 4 (1954); Jeanneau, *Les Principes généraux du droit dans la jurisprudence administrative* (1954); and Rivero, "Le juge administratif: un juge qui gouverne," *Rec. Dalloz: Chron. juris.,* 21 (1951). In his *Judicial Review in the English-Speaking World,* 44 (1960), McWhinney has noted the resistance of the English judiciary to parliamentary reforms: "In fact, it is difficult to explain a good deal of judicial interpretation of legislation in the field of public law, except upon the assumption that the judges did not like what Parliament was doing, and sought to confine Parliament's activity to the narrowest possible area."

This tends to blur a strict distinction between the three branches of government as well as to emphasize the need for judicial self-restraint.

Furthermore, the consolidation of national power was accompanied by a shift in the nature of legislation which called for more effective constitutional control. The typical product of legislative discourse is clearly not general, abstract and enduring principles of a universal human reason, which merely crystallize the homogeneous qualities of particular situations. Under the increasing demand for social reform and welfare legislation, laws have become largely purposive instruments for the direction and organization of society and the protection of national (or regional or local) values.[32] If the function of law is to secure the essential standards of society, as Ihering contends, then "there is no legal rule which does not owe its origin to a purpose, i.e. to a practical motive."[33]

At the same time, the advent of the positive state has brought with it a flood of legislation together with the rapid growth of a complex administrative apparatus to implement and supervise its execution. The law has, in a sense, become "motorized."[34] Given this as well as the influence of special interests, occasional excesses of the popular will and the pressure of time in legislative and executive deliberations, the law as legislated and decreed may well work refractory to the "rule of law" and civil rights. The danger becomes particularly acute in the field of economic regulation,[35] where discretion is frequently broad and special interests most active. For these reasons as well as others, the shifting emphasis from *ratio* to *voluntas* in the law has stimulated a keen interest in the institution of judicial review.

From both conceptual and functional viewpoints, therefore, the judiciary has become a positive force in constitutional government. That once "so terrible" power, which was fit only to pronounce the *ratio* of the legislature, has become the very guardian of the constitution. The broad jurisdiction of the German Federal Constitutional Court and of the Italian and Austrian Constitutional Courts as well as of the Court of Justice of the European

[32] See Bachof, *op. cit., supra* (n. 22), pp. 38–41; Bockelmann, "Richter und Gesetz," in *Festschrift Rudolf Smend,* 23 (1952); Eb. Schmidt, *op. cit.* (n. 21), p. 9f; and the rather polemic study of Ripert, *Le déclin du droit* (1949).

[33] Ihering, *Der Zweck im Recht,* vol. I, pp. v, 345 and 359f (4th ed. 1904), who looked beyond the essentially individualistic premises of his contemporaries and saw the social function of law.

[34] See Carl Schmitt, *Die Lage der europäischen Rechtswissenschaft,* 18–21 (1950), speaking of "der motorisierte Gesetzgeber."

[35] See Hans Huber, "Grundsätze in der Auslegung der Wirtschaftsartikel," 10 *Wirtschaft und Recht,* 1, 3–5 (1958); Ballerstedt, "Über wirtschaftliche Massnahmegesetze," in *Festschrift Schmidt-Rimpler,* 369 (1957).

Communities are important instances of this.[36] In this capacity, the judiciary not merely interprets a statute, but checks or legitimates the executive or legislative will for the indefinite future. What is potentially at stake, as Holmes has so bluntly stated, "is a conflict between two social desires, each of which seeks to extend dominion over the case . . . ."[37] A confrontation of values is the essence of constitutional litigation.

For this reason, modern legal theory – especially on the constitutional level – faces the task of developing a judicial function which incorporates creative interpretation without abandoning either judicial independence or responsibility. For some, this task is impossible. Since value judgments by whatever branch of government can be little more than individual or collective preferences, judicial review is an invitation to judicial arbitrariness. The judicial veto, Judge Learned Hand contends, is no more than the *coup de main* of a third legislative chamber expressing what is "too strong for the judicial stomach . . . . It forbids making a different appraisal of values, which . . . is the essence of legislation."[38]

For others, the task is useless: judicial review does not help strengthen the constitutional foundation of a community. In a potent, frontal attack on judicial review in the United States, Commager could find no example in the first century-and-a-half of constitutional litigation where the Supreme Court secured the rights of minorities from congressional assault.[39] Nor is he convinced that there is anything uniquely judicial in constitutional decisions which could not better be left to the other branches of government.[40] A more recent Supreme Court study by a Swiss scholar has echoed essentially these conclusions.[41] Due to the shifting practice of the Court and to its frequent failure to establish definite normative content, judicial review has

[36] See Bachof, *op. cit.* (n. 22), p. 35ff, with respect to Germany. As to the jurisdiction of constitutional courts in Austria, Germany and Italy, see Mosler (ed.), *Verfassungsgerichtsbarkeit in der Gegenwart* (*Judicial Review in the Modern World*) (1962). For the discussion in Switzerland concerning extending judicial review of cantonal laws to federal laws, see Schindler, "Richterliches Prüfungsrecht und politischer Mehrheitswille: Erfahrungen der Vereinigten Staaten – Folgerungen für die Schweiz," 74 *Z. schweiz. R.*, 373 (1955); and Wolf, *Verfassungsgerichtsbarkeit und Verfassungstreue in den Vereinigten Staaten*, 228–237 (1961).

[37] Holmes, "Law in Science and Science in Law," 12 *Harv. L. Rev.*, 443, 460 (1899).

[38] Hand, *The Bill of Rights*, 55, 70, 37–39 (1960).

[39] Commager, *Majority Rule and Minority Rights*, 46–55 (1943). Indeed, Commager's findings show the Supreme Court at times frustrating congressional attempts to implement such rights. This conclusion obviously must be revised in the light of more recent Supreme Court decisions.

[40] *Ibid.*, pp. 42–46. Cf. also Laski, *The American Democracy*, 113f (1948); and Haines, *The American Doctrine of Judicial Supremacy*, Ch. XIV (2nd ed. 1932).

[41] Wolf, *Verfassungsgerichtsbarkeit und Verfassungstreue in den Vereinigten Staaten*, 228–230 (1961).

allegedly not contributed to strengthening either constitutional consciousness (Verfassungsbewusstsein) or fidelity (Verfassungstreue). Constitutional norms, he contends, embody for a large part political value concepts, which require for their construction a "statesmanlike" consideration of their political consequences: "The judge, therefore, cannot decide impassionately and abstractly, apart from the individual case and its concrete consequences; this forces the judge to become nothing less than untrue to himself and his office."[42]

These views rest on a rather narrow, if not static concept of the judicial function. They tend to forget that, however "political" constitutional questions may be, these same questions may have legitimate legal aspects.[43] Moreover, despite the shortcomings of a constitutional court in fact, the potential impact of judicial review on the public conscience undoubtedly far exceeds the occasions of its exercise. The very presence of this restraining power, observes Cardozo,[44] "tends to stabilize and rationalize the legislative judgment, to infuse it with the glow of principle, to hold the standard aloft and visible for those who must run the race and keep the faith."

Finally, a third group of writers accepts judicial review as necessary or even desirable, but considers it a "deviant institution" in democratic government. This may be so, on the one hand, because it operates counter-majoritarian.[45] Since all responsible power in democratic government proceeds from the people in assembly, Bickel contends

> that the policy-making power of representative institutions, born of the electoral process, is the distinguishing characteristic of the system .... Although democracy does not mean constant reconsideration of decisions once made, it does mean that a representative majority has the power to accomplish a reversal.[46]

If what is meant is a simple majority – Bickel does not make this clear – then the objection is obviously true. Judicial review undeniably represents

[42] *Ibid.*, p. 228. See also the opinion of some Swiss jurists, cited by Schindler, to the effect that so long as it cannot be shown that the government is not prepared to carry out the constitution, then there is no reason for judicial control. In any case, they argue, who is to say that any better or wiser men will sit on a constitutional court than are elected to political office. Schindler "Richterliches Pruefungsrecht und politischer Mehrheitswille," 74 *Z. schweiz. R.*, 289, 290 (1955).

[43] See Wengler, *Der Begriff des Politischen im internationalen Recht,* in Heft 189/190 *Recht und Staat,* 40ff (1956); Scheuner, "Der Bereich der Regierung" in *Festschrift Rudolf Smend,* 253, 295 (1952).

[44] Cardozo, *The Nature of the Judicial Process,* 92f (1921); and Schindler, *op. cit.* (n. 42), p. 302f.

[45] See Bickel, *The Least Dangerous Branch,* 16ff (1962); and Rostow, *The Sovereign Prerogative,* Chs. 5 and 6 (1962).

[46] Bickel, *id.*, pp. 17 and 19.

a certain distrust of majority opinion, but so does modern constitutional government – whether in terms of Locke, Montesquieu or, to a lesser extent, Kant – upon which judicial review rests. Not even Rousseau was content with the majority will as the expression of the *volonté générale*.[47] So far as the reference is to a qualified majority, however, the criticism loses most of its validity. Despite the difficulties involved, the decisions of constitutional courts can be reversed by constitutional amendment.

On the other hand, judicial review may also be termed a "deviant institution" should it begin to replace legislative responsibility.[48] Simply for reason of political expediency, however, the opposite would more likely occur; astute politicians will mind constitutional standards in order to get their laws past the courts.[49] The perverse effect would more probably ensue only if the court overstepped the limited scope of constitutional standards and entered the vast realm of legislative prerogative. Then, as James B. Thayer long ago warned, the legislature might well

> insensibly fall into a habit of assuming that whatever they could constitutionally do they may do, – as if honor and fair dealing and common honesty were not relevant to their inquiries. The people, all this while, become careless as to whom they send to the legislature . . . glad that these few wiser gentlemen on the bench are so ready to protect them against their more immediate representatives . . . .[50]

As a further danger, judicial review has the effect of correcting legislation "from the outside." Because of this, Thayer points out, the people "lose the political experience, and the moral education and stimulus that comes from fighting the question out in the ordinary way, and correcting their own errors." This tends "to dwarf the political capacity of the people, and to deaden its sense of moral responsibility."[51] Again, this is a clear warning against an overzealous judicializing of the political process, in which politics has nothing to gain and the judiciary everything to lose.[52] This assumes,

[47] For example Bk. II, chs. 3 and 6 of Rousseau's *Contrat social* states: "The general will is always right and tends to the public advantage; but it does not follow that the deliberations of the people are always equally correct. Of itself, the people will always the good, but of itself by no means always see it." See Friedrich, *The Philosophy of Law in Historical Perspective,* 123f (Phoenix ed. 1963).

[48] See Commager, *op. cit.* (n. 39), p. 76ff; Blachly and Oatman, "Some Consequences of Judicial Review," 1 *Z. ausl. öff. R.,* 500, 506 (1929); Hand, *op. cit.* (n. 38), p. 73f; and Thayer, cited *infra,* note 50.

[49] See Schindler, *op. cit.* (n. 42), p. 300.

[50] Thayer, *John Marshall,* 103f (1901). Cf. also Frankfurter, "John Marshall and The Judicial Function," 69 *Harv. L. Rev.,* 217, 232 (1955).

[51] Thayer, *id.,* p. 106f.

[52] This is the thesis which Carl Schmitt advances in his "Der Hüter der Verfassung," in Heft 1 *Beiträge zum öff. Recht der Gegenwart* (1931).

however, that the democratic process is existent and functioning and not deadlocked or frustrated. In any case, despite the real caveats which these criticisms raise, they say only that judicial review stands *potentially* in conflict with constitutional democracy.

These three views of judicial review present the challenge to a theory of judicial decision on the constitutional level. They do this by raising three questions which the following discussion will attempt to answer. For one, if the law is in continuous development and must be interpreted creatively, are judicial value-choices any more than personal preferences? Section 2 of the previous Chapter has answered this already to a large extent. For another, how can creative judicial decision make an enduring contribution to constitutional government? And finally, if the conflict between judicial review and the executive and legislative functions is only potential, what then is the unique and responsible sphere of the judicial function? Not unexpectedly, these questions share a common answer.

The legacy of Montesquieu, therefore, is a problem, a method of analysis and a guiding concept. The problem posed is that of judicial responsibility. Based on very particular historical and jurisprudential perspectives, however, Montesquieu's solution was rather limited. His goal of establishing an independent judiciary, free from the dominance of any one governmental power or social class, was rooted in his sublime faith in a universal and demonstrable *ratio* in the law. "He was a moralist," says Sabine,[53] "for whom the eternal verities had begun to wear thin but who lacked the constructive power to get on without them." Nevertheless, the disappearance of those particular premises of Montesquieu's thought has not diminished the validity of his institutional method of analysis. To the contrary, the rise of judicial review simply has emphasized the importance of this analytical approach. The fact remains that only by a prudent fusion of governmental functions with political reality can governmental power be effectively organized, distributed and limited. The sense of this institutional analysis, however, lies not in a mere check and balance of powers, but rather in that moderation of governmental power which it permits and furthers. The principle of moderation is the essence of the responsible exercise of all constitutional power – and above all of judicial review. It remains now to set the limits and legitimate scope of the judicial function in modern constitutional government.

[53] Sabine, *A History of Political Theory*, 558 (1950).

2. THE ILLUSION OF JUDICIAL NEUTRALITY

Traditional legal theory sees the essence of a responsible judicial function in an organizationally independent judiciary, bound to the interpretation of determinate norms. These are merely complementary aspects of one purpose, namely, to preserve the integrity and neutrality of the judiciary in the governmental context of political forces. Organizational independence permits that detachment necessary for the impartial administration and construction of the laws. The dedicated application of determinate laws, in turn, offers that intellectual purchase by which the judge is to secure himself to some great extent against biasing influences. As a corollary, those questions either assigned by the constitution to another branch of government *or* not governed by an existing norm are deemed "political" and without the purview of judicial concern. Whereas the former may be said to be permanently nonjusticiable, the latter remain nonjusticiable so long as a norm does not exist. An existing and determinate norm, or rule of law, is the exclusive basis for the exercise of the judicial function. It is said to be the guarantor of judicial independence and, therefore, will be more closely examined in the remainder of this Section.

At the outset, however, it should be forewarned that this theory offers only a purely formal delineation of the judicial function. On the one hand, it postulates precisely what is the heart of a constitutional dispute, namely, the established meaning of the norm in question. It thereby ignores the gradual process of case decision through which the uncertain content of constitutional provisions is developed. On the other hand, because of this emphasis on the determinate character of norms, the theory is highly skeptical of result-oriented decisions. Such decisions would tend to undermine the autonomy of the norm and obscure the nice distinction between the "political" and "legal" spheres. Nevertheless, as outlined in the previous Chapter and elaborated below in Section 3, consideration by the judiciary of the results or consequences of its decisions is an integral part of the continuing search for purpose, authority and practicability in the law. Though proponents of the traditional theory may not condemn judicial consideration of every type of consequence, they are uniformly critical – indeed, almost indignant – of the idea and methods of judicial compromise and self-restraint. For them, the judicial function is distinguished by the unyielding application of determinate norms.

The purely formal view of the judicial function, therefore, follows the letter and not the legacy of Montesquieu. The examples below are drawn from recent German and American writings in the theory of constitutional adjudication.

The Concept of Determinate Norms

The leading German – as well as Continental – theory proceeds from this formal distinction between "political" and "judicial" functions. Historically, its roots lie in the civil law codification movement of the 19th century where the "legal" sphere was circumscribed by the text of codes and well-defined rules of judicial construction.[54] It has been carried over, with little change, into the realm of constitutional adjudication. Conceptually drawn, this distinction makes the legislature, as the acting (handelnde) organ, and the judiciary, as the cognitive (erkenntnissprechende) organ, sovereign in its own sphere. Whereas the former creatively shapes and forms the law (Rechtsgestaltung) according to the demands of the political process, the latter determines the validity of legislation (Rechtsfeststellung) according to pre-scribed norms[55] whose content is *essentially determinate*.[56] "Never," says Professor Friesenhahn, a former Justice of the German Federal Constitutional Court, "is the Court authorized to exercise its volition on political matters or to form freely or to create new constitutional law."[57]

Determinate norms are the condition for the exercise of all judicial power, including that of the Federal Constitutional Court. To be "justiciable," a norm must be "as far as content is concerned, capable of more or less exact legal interpretation."[58] That is to say, the product of constitutional construction is not judge-made but *standing*-law – law already in existence.[59] Only in this sense is it possible to understand the view of Friesenhahn, for instance, "that the Court can only unfold what already is contained... in the

[54] See the discussion in text *supra*, p. 96f.

[55] For the concept and function of the "norm" in the code law tradition, see the discussion and references to Esser in text *supra*, p. 116f.

[56] See generally Eichenberger, *Die richterliche Unabhängigkeit als staatsrechtliches Problem*, 95–98 and 131–34 (1960). Cf. Esser, *Grundsatz und Norm*, Ch. 9 (1956).

[57] Friesenhahn, "Aufgabe und Funktion des Bundesverfassungsgerichts," 6 *Aus Politik und Zeitgeschichte*, 3, 15 (Feb. 10, 1965).

[58] Leibholz, *Politics and Law*, 274 (1965).

[59] *Ibid.*, p. 271f. The chapter from which these cites are taken is essentially a translation of an earlier article by Leibholz, "Der Status des Bundesverfassungsgerichts," in *Das Bundesverfassungsgericht*, 61 (1963). See also Friesenhahn, *op. cit.*, p. 18.

[60] Friesenhahn, "Wesen und Grenzen der Verfassungsgerichtsbarkeit," 73 *Z. schweiz. R.*, 129, 158 (1954). See also Leibholz, "Bericht an das Plenum des Bundesverfassungsgerichts zur 'Status'-Frage," in *Richard Thoma Gutachten* (1953), as reprinted in 6 JB oeff. R. 109, 126 at note 25 (1957).

Constitution."[60] Political questions, which are by definition non-justiciable, on the other hand, are those "which cannot be decided according to the rules of Law,"[61] i.e., "for whose decision no legal norms exist."[62] In such cases, contends Leibholz, the dispute is "about the law and not according to the law."[63] This formal distinction between "political" and "judicial" functions in German legal theory, therefore, rests on the idea of "determinate norms" to which the judge is unqualifiedly bound – sometimes called the *Normgebundenheitstheorie.*

Assuming for the moment the cogency of this distinction, its logical consequence is that "determinate norms" are to be applied without abatement and all other questions are non-justiciable. Proponents of this view fail to heed the warning, though they may well acknowledge the underlying premiset[64] of Triepel that "the nature of the constitution stands, to a certain degree, in contradiction to the nature of judicial review."[65] Even so-called "hoch-politische Angelegenheiten" – typical for constitutional provisions containing such concepts as "democracy," "freedom," "equality," etc. – allegedly can be legally domesticated and applied as uncompromisingly as any other legal rules.[66] As Leibholz puts it:

> It remains, however, of no importance whether a judge has to decide doubts and differences of opinions about a constitutional law or another law when he is judging a legal dispute. The values which a constitutional judge has to consider, when he is forming a judgment, only differ in the case of the constitutional administration of justice from those which the "ordinary" judge has to observe, in that the former are related to the legal decisions of the makers of the consti-

[61] Leibholz, *Politics and Law,* 275 (1965).

[62] E. Kaufmann, "Die Grenzen der Verfassungsgerichtsbarkeit," 9 *VVdStRL,* 1, 4 (1952). While granting that in one sense all legal norms can become "political" at one time or another, depending on the reaction of groups within society, he continues: "Aber das ist nicht der Sinn, in dem wir hier von politischen Fragen im Gegensatz zu Rechtsfragen sprechen. Füer uns ist allein wesentlich, ob auf einen Streitfall Rechtsnormen oder Normen anderer Art anzuwenden sind, unabhängig von jedem politischen Beigeschmack oder Nachgeschmack auszuschalten und nur das Recht zum Worte kommen zu lassen."

[63] Leibholz, *Politics and Law,* 275 (1965). See also Comments of Leibholz in 20 *VVdStRL,* 118f (1963); and Friesenhahn, *op. cit.* (n. 56), p. 18.

[64] See Leibholz, *Politics and Law,* 273 (1965), pointing out that "there exists in the political and legal sphere, between the political and legal questions, an inner tension, which, in the long run, cannot be removed."

[65] Triepel, "Wesen und Entwicklung der Staatsgerichtsbarkeit," 5 *VVdStRL,* 2, 7 (1929).

[66] Friesenhahn, *op. cit.,* (n. 60), pp. 150–52; and his other article, *op. cit.* (n. 57), pp. 15 and 18. See also Leibholz, *Politics and Law,* 275f; and his Comments in 10 *VVdStRL,* 118 (1963); and Kaufmann, *op. cit.* (n. 62), p. 5f.

tution, the latter, however, to those of that civil, criminal, or administrative law which has to be interpreted.[67]

This means, then, as Friesenhahn concludes,[68] that "absent an express exception for particular questions, even those constitutional law disputes giving rise to highly inflamed political controversies must be determined judicially." The "political questions" doctrine, as developed in the constitutional law practice of the United States, is considered inappropriate for the Federal Constitutional Court.[69]

Were the proponents of the *Normgebundenheitstheorie* claiming simply that the norm is the essential starting point for constitutional construction, there could be no quarrel. The norm, taken in its context, frames the judicial discussion as well as the decision itself. No theory of judicial decision can responsibly permit a court to render judgments which are incompatible with a decent respect for the language of the law. Proponents of this view, however, claim much more: they claim to present a comprehensive statement of the judicial function. They claim that prescribed determinate norms are not only the major premise of judicial activity, but also the sole measure of judicial decision and the guarantee of judicial neutrality. Such norms are the hand in the dike which holds back the sea of political compromise. The Court is thereby secure in the exercise of a purely legal (nonpolitical) function. It does not, says Friesenhahn,

participate in the creative formation of the political life of the nation. As an independent, neutral body, which renders decisions solely in terms of law (Gesetz und Recht), it determines the law with binding effect when it is disputed, doubted or under attack. In doing so, it bears no political responsibility, though its decisions may have great political significance.[70]

These words echo the warning of the President of the Staatsgerichtshof during the Weimar Government: "The repeated recommendations that the High Court consider the political consequences of its constitutional decisions

[67] Leibholz, *Politics and Law*, 275f.

[68] Friesenhahn, *op. cit.* (n. 60), p. 153.

[69] Leibholz, *Politics and Law*, 275; Friesenhahn, *op. cit.* (n. 60), p. 151f, and his other article, *op. cit.* (n. 57), p. 18, as well as his Comments in 20 *VVdStRL*, 121 (1963). See also the somewhat skeptical view of Rupp, "Some Remarks on Judicial Self-Restraint," 21 *Ohio St. L. J.*, 503, 510–15 (1960), also a Justice of the Federal Constitutional Court.

[70] Friesenhahn, *op. cit.* (n. 60), p. 158. See also Leibholz, *Politics and Law*, 279, speaking of a "politically neutral constitutional court, such as the Federal Constitutional Court."

place the axe at the root of its authority." [71] To resist this temptation, therefore, is thought to protect the normative enduring quality of constitutional law from the danger of dissolving into purely *ad hoc* ("dezisionistische") preferences of a court or its judges.[72]

Nevertheless, the cogency of the "political-legal" distinction and the judicial neutrality which it implies is no greater than the settled meaning or determinacy of the norm upon which it rests. At this point the purely formal and untenable basis of the theory becomes apparent. "Interpretation is decision," as Esser's comparative legal study so well demonstrates, "decision according to criteria which are not already present with the first word to be construed, but must be brought to the object by the interpreter . . . ." [73]

Proponents of the traditional theory often acknowledge, in fact, that the judge is vested with a certain creative task in ascertaining the content of the norms in question.[74] This is implied by Friesenhahn when he speaks of the "loosely woven formulation" of constitutional law which "leaves a great deal of room for interpretation." [75] Further, Leibholz refers to the "creative character" of judicial decisions which requires the Federal Constitutional Court "to participate . . . to a high degree in constitutional change." [76] It may even be admitted, as the Federal Constitutional Court has done,[77] that constitutional norms may be unconstitutional. In order to accomodate constitutional interpretation within the framework of "determinate norms," therefore, the proponents of this theory must *either* severely restrict the scope of constitutional adjudication to those few cases where formal rules of interpretation yield unambiguous answers *or else* expand the concept of "judiciability" to include creative judicial activity. Confronted with this alternative, they have – except for a brief period in the early Weimar years [78] –

[71] Simons, in Lammers and Simons, *Entscheidungssammlung,* Vol. IV, "Introduction," p. vii (1932).

[72] See Friesenhahn, *op. cit.* (n. 57), p. 14; and Kägi, *Die Verfassung als rechtliche Grundordnung des Staates,* Ch. 6 (1945). This is a reaction particularly to the extreme position of Carl Schmitt, discussed by Kägi, *id.* p. 139ff.

[73] Esser, *Grundsatz und Norm,* 258 (1956). See also Ehmke, "Prinzipien der Verfassungsinterpretation," 20 *VVdStRL,* 53, 55f (1963).

[74] See the survey of Eichenberger, *op. cit.* (n. 56), p. 134ff.

[75] Friesenhahn, *op. cit.* (n. 57), p. 18.

[76] Leibholz, *op. cit.* (n. 59), p. 62.

[77] See 1 BVerfG 14, 32 (1951); 2 BVerfG 237, 253 (1953); 3 BVerfG 225, 231ff (1953); and 4 BVerfG 294, 296 (1955). See also Bachof, *Verfassungswidrige Verfassungsnormen*? (1951).

[78] There was a lively discussion during the early Weimar years whether the provisions in Section II of the German Constitution, concerning the protection of individual rights, were concrete enough (no vaguer than the United States Bill of Rights) to permit their direct application, or simply program provisions to be implemented by the legis-

clearly chosen the latter course. In the same breath, however, they solemnly declare that the law applied is solely what "already exists." [79]

What brings this determinacy in constitutional norms which – though in some important sense the product of creative interpretation – dispels all doubt as to their meaning and proper application? For the *Normgebundenheitstheorie,* the answer lies primarily, if not wholly, in the "usual methods of constitutional interpretation," [80] namely, the grammatical, logical, historical and, above all, the systematic methods of statutory construction.[81] The first two are so obviously necessary, as well as typically inconclusive, that they require no further discussion. These together with the historical method, on the other hand, are heavily weighted by one group of writers [82] seeking to preserve the original intent or will of the founding fathers by clarification of the legal text. Only if these rules of interpretation "do not lead to a result" (nicht zum Ziele fuehrt), then "it is permissible to resort to the systematic context of the constitution." [83]

As a noted historian of the United States Supreme Court recently concluded, however, it is highly doubtful that on specific questions historical

lature. See Kägi, *op. cit.* (n. 72), pp. 131–34; and Rupp, "Judicial Review in the Federal Republic of Germany," 9 *Amer. J. Comp. L.*, 29, 31 (1960). The arguments employed at that time against the propriety of judicial interpretation were taken from the strict view of Montesquieu discussed in the previous Section. See Leibholz, *op. cit.* (n. 60), p. 123.

79 See Friesenhahn, *op. cit.* (n. 57), p. 18; and Leibholz, *op. cit.* (n. 59), p. 61f. Leibholz, for example argues in the same paragraph: "Der ermittelte Gehalt der verfassungsrechtlichen Normen verdeutlicht daher grundsätzlich nur bestehendes Verfassungsrecht. *Nur* ist dieses nicht in einem statischen Sinne als etwas fest Fixiertes zu begreifen . . . Insofern hat die Rechtssprechung des Bundesverfassungsgerichts . . . auch einen schöpferischen Charakter. *Nur* ändert diese Feststellung nichts daran, dass, soweit das Bundesverfassungsgericht Verfassungsrecht inhaltlich des näheren feststellt und konkretisiert, das richterlich 'erkannte' Verfassungsrecht den Charakter von Gerechtigkeit und Vernunft verkörpernden 'standing-law' und nicht von 'judge-made-law' hat." (Emphasis added.) But cf. Krüger, "Verfassungswandlung und Verfassungsgerichtsbarkeit," in *Festschrift Rudolf Smend,* 151 (1962), who has made a notable attempt to lay bare the difficulties of reconciling judicial creativity with the traditional approach to constitutional construction.

80 *Ibid.*, p. 274f. See also Friesenhahn, *op. cit.* (n. 57), p. 16; and cf. Esser, *Grundsatz und Norm,* 220 (1956), who makes clear the central role of rules of construction in code law.

81 See Leibholz, *id.*, p. 276; and the discussion of Schneider, "Prinzipien der Verfassungsinterpretation," 20 *VVdStRL,* 1, 6ff (1963).

82 See esp. Forsthoff, *Recht und Sprache, Prolegomena zu einer richterlichen Hermeneutik,* 46 (1940); his "Die Umbildung des Verfassungsgesetzes," in *Festschrift Carl Schmitt,* 35 (1959), and his "Zur Problematik der Verfassungsauslegung," 7 *Res publica,* 39f (1961), emphasizing the historical method. See also the views of Thoma in his Gutachten: *Die Rechtsstellung des Bundesverfassungsgerichts,* 23f (1953).

83 Forsthoff, *id.* (*Festschrift Carl Schmitt*), p. 40f.

research offers that certainty which this group so covets. "With adequate scholarship, the answer that must emerge in the vast majority of cases is no answer."[84] Above all, the resort to the traditional rules of interpretation offers no standards for determining *when* these very rules "do not lead to a result." Nor does it justify why so basic and enduring a document as a constitution should be colored by the limited insights and premises of certain selected method(s) of interpretation. In truth, this approach is a means of avoiding rather than tackling the problems of judicial creativity.

Perhaps the majority of German writers, however, acknowledge the general inadequacy of the traditional rules of interpretation to master constitutional norms. They take refuge in the notion of a constitutional "Systematik," which grasps the meaning of specific norms in light of the constitution as an integrated whole. The determinate character of these norms is to be preserved by reference to their *objective intent* as expressed in the full context of constitutional concepts, purposes and immanent values. The unifying premise of this "objective method" of interpretation lies in a value hierarchy, achieved through continuously working out and integrating the various constitutional provisions into a closed system.[85] "It involves," says Drath, ". . . a draft with normative character; it provides means for orienting [the judge] on specific questions of constitutional interpretation."[86]

In fact, the value hierarchy would be much more than a draft. By definition of the *Normgebundenheitstheorie* it embodies the *existing* normative content of the constitution.[87] Carried to its logical conclusion, this hierarchy would establish – on the basis of a given philosophical viewpoint, as that of Kant – certain substantive guiding principles of interpretation, as *in dubio pro libertate*.[88] While such general formulas are of little use in constitutional interpretation,[89] they well demonstrate the inarticulated value choices upon

[84] Bickel, *The Least Dangerous Branch,* 102 (1962). See also Esser, *Grundsatz und Norm,* 256, speaking of the general disappearance of the "Illusion einer historisch-genuinen Auslegungsmöglichkeit, welche auf die Lenkung und Anweisung durch aktuelle Rechtsgrundsätze verzichten könnte." In any case, says Esser (p. 258f), the isolated rules or means of interpretation offer no standards for interpretation.

[85] See the survey of Schneider, *op. cit.* (n. 81), p. 8ff.

[86] Drath, "Aussprache," in 20 *VVdStRL,* 109 and also 106f (1963). See also similar remarks of Dürig in the same "Aussprache," *ibid.,* p. 115, concluding: "Ich meine, dass das BVerfG seinen Weg zur Aufstellung eines positiven Wertkatechismus ruhig fortsetzen sollte. Die kommende Generation wird ihm dafuer dankbar sein."

[87] See note 83 *supra.*

[88] See, for instance, Schneider, *op. cit.* (n. 81), p. 27ff, who develops such a model.

[89] Cf. the doubts uttered by Scheuner, "Aussprache," 20 *VVdStRL,* 112 and 125f (1963).

which the value hierarchy ultimately must rest.[90] That is to say, this hierarchy of constitutional provisions is itself the product of constitutional construction. The "objective method" here described, therefore, is primarily a jurist's law, drawing the values of the prevailing philosophical system into the immanent structure of the constitution. Like the "Systematik" of *Begriffsjurisprudenz,*[91] it harbors the illusions of determinate norms in the fact of inarticulated value premises and of judicial neutrality aloof from the creative search for normative content.

In contrast to *Begriffsjurisprudenz,* however, proponents of this "Systematik" do not necessarily exclude considerations of political reality in the construction and application of the constitution.[92] A constitutional court, says Leibholz,

> must relate the norm to political reality . . . cannot simply behave indifferently toward the political order . . . [and] is required to draw the political consequences of its decisions into the sphere of its considerations, when there is a question of correctly construing provisions of the Constitution which require interpretation.[93]

Friesenhahn too speaks of "that unique interaction between constitutional law and political reality . . . , which may not be left out of consideration in applying constitutional law."[94] Indeed, by way of reinterpretation, a change in social conditions can even be said to work a change in the meaning of a particular norm.[95] Such admissions, realistic though they are, constitute an obvious breach in the autonomy of the norm, for now the norm must be interpreted and applied in the light of political realities. Precisely what kinds

[90] See the critique of Forsthoff, *op. cit.* (n. 82: Die Umbildung). By way of concrete example, see the inarticulated economic judgments made by the German Constitutional Court in the "Apotheke" Case, 7 BVerfG 377 (1958), discussed by Krüger, "Verfassungswandlung und Verfassungsgerichtsbarkeit," in *Festschrift Rudolf Smend,* 151, 167–69 (1962).

[91] See discussion in text *supra,* pp. 95–97.

[92] But cf. the sharp criticism of Richard Thoma, in his Gutachten, *op. cit.* (n. 60), pp. 170–72.

[93] Leibholz, *op. cit.* (n. 59), p. 70. See also Dürig in "Aussprache," 20 *VVdStRL,* 115 (1963): "Der Verfassungsrichter kommt m.E. ohne diesen ständigen Blick auf die Folgen seines Spruches nicht aus."

[94] Friesenhahn, *op. cit.* (n. 57), p. 18. He does not go on, however, to define more concretely just what this "interaction" consists of.

[95] See 7 BVerfG 342, 351 (1958); and 2 BVerfG 380, 401 (1953), where the Court declared: "Allerdings kann eine Verfassungsbestimmung einen Bedeutungswandel erfahren, wenn in ihrem Bereich neue, nicht vorausgesehene Tatbestände auftauchen oder bekannte Tatbestände durch ihre Einordnung in den Gesamtablauf einer Entwicklung in neuer Beziehung oder Bedeutung erscheinen." See also Leibholz, *op. cit.* (n. 59), p. 70. But cf. comment in note 98 *infra.*

of political realities is not revealed, though clearly from the above discussion[96] considerations of political expediency and judicial compromise would be excluded. Presumably, considerations of practicability in rule-shaping and of justice under the circumstances of the case would be allowed.[97] If so, then the concrete content of constitutional norms depends to some significant degree on the judicial appraisal of these realities. This appraisal in turn gives rise to value judgments for which the language of the norm is silent.[98]

Despite solemn claims to the contrary, therefore, the "usual methods of interpretation" do not render the content of constitutional norms determinate independent of judicial value judgments. To this extent there is no "existing law" clearly dispositive of the case in point, and the meaning of the norm is not determinate. This raises a final question which is most crucial to constitutional adjudication: when indeed are constitutional norms unambiguous enough to be determinate enough to be justiciable? Need an act, for instance, be explicitly condemned to be unconstitutional? Obviously not. Can a norm and its meaning be derived from reading several provisions together or from the general context of the constitution and its immanent values? According to the "Systematik" just discussed, apparently yes. By what ultimate standard then does a norm lack or possess determinacy?

The decisive factor, according to Leibholz, is the ability of the court to arrive at "a reasonable solution, based on a rule which in content can be more clearly defined."[99] That is to say, the intent of the legislature must be susceptible to a "legally reasonable interpretation" ("rechtlich vernuenftigen Auslegung").[100] Most recently, Friesenhahn has resorted to a related notion of "Evidenz." Only an apparent or clear ("evident") infringement of the constitution is unlawful, i.e., only if the content of a norm can be "sufficiently determined."[101] When the leading principles of the constitution are at

96 See text *supra*, p. 154f. See also Friesenhahn, *op. cit.* (n. 57), p. 18.

97 See text *supra*, pp. 154f and 159. As Leibholz states, a constitutional court must "relate the rules to political reality" and also "draw that interpretation of law into the ambit of his considerations which best does justice in consequence and meaning to the constitutional decision under consideration." *Politics and Law*, 276.

98 Any attempt to escape this conclusion by suggesting that the value judgments are simply the result of social change would reduce judicial interpretation to a determinism which is anathema to the law as normative science.

99 Leibholz, *Politics and Law*, 275.

100 Leibholz, *op. cit.* (n. 60), p. 126.

101 Friesenhahn, *Gutachtliche Stellungnahme zu den beim Bundesverfassungsgericht anhängigen Verfahren, die die Gewährung von Zuschüssen aus dem Bundeshaushaltsplan an die politischen Parteien zum Gegenstand haben*, 72 (mimeo, April 1966). The argument presented by Professor Friesenhahn is designed to demonstrate that the German Constitution contains no clearly definable norm which would forbid the German Parliament from appropriating money for the support of political parties.

issue, he argues by way of explanation,

> the Court may not simply impose its own interpretation (eigenwillige Deutung), but to a certain extent also must recognize a constitutional practice followed by a wide consensus of the political organs of government.[102]

In the last analysis, therefore, both writers must admit that the determinacy of the norm depends not so much on its prescribed content as on the *consensus of opinion* about that content. Terms such as "reasonable" or "clear" are after all purely conclusive, for they have no objective rule reference, least of all in the norm itself. At the most they indicate the status of existing opinion – whether juristic or public – on a given view. If this is the ultimate measure of determinacy, then the norm is a "sometime thing" whose content is by no means prescribed.

In conclusion, the theory of *Normgebundenheit* fails to offer an adequate explanation of the judicial process. It is simply an attempt to replace the question of what the norm means or should mean with rules of how it is to be construed – the "what" with the "how."[103] In clinging to the illusion of "determinate norms," on the one hand, its proponents cannot account for the full sweep of judicial creativity and for the problem of judicial responsibility which this implies. Thus, they are faced with the curious dilemma: though the norm purportedly is determinate, its meaning to a significant degree is not – the judicial decision purportedly is creative, but the law applied is already existing! This creates no small difficulty for German judicial theory. "Its correction," declares Esser, "entails a revolutionary program for our theory of legal sources, which can best be satisfied dogmatically by adding to our sources of law doctrine a legal discipline on the 'formation of law' (Rechtsbildungsrecht)."[104]

The concentration on system and unity in rules and doctrine, on the other hand, tends to underrate or ignore the indispensable search for consensus in constitutional law interpretation. Thus, in the words of Drath: "The problem of consensus on the content of constitutional law is secondary so long as it has no content at all."[105] Moreover, once the normative content has somehow been ascertained, then these same writers have no need for

Query: is this argument different in kind from that raised during the Weimar years against the propriety of judicial review? See note 78 *supra*.

[102] *Ibid.*

[103] Ehmke, *op. cit.* (n. 73), p. 61. See also Esser, *Grundsatz und Norm* 218–21 (1956). This, in essence, is Leo Strauss' conclusion and critique of modern political philosophy. Strauss, *What is Political Philosophy,* 79f (1959).

[104] Esser, *id.*, p. 120. See also Wieacker, *Gesetz und Richterkunst,* 15–17 (1957).

[105] Drath, "Aussprache," 20 *VVdStRL,* 109f (1963).

consensus. The mere existence of a "determinate norm" dispels all doubt as to its full and unqualified application. For them, judicial interpretation is purely an act of cognition. Nevertheless, as Ermacora warns, "the notion that the constitution possesses a unity exists only in scientific theory, but not in practical politics. Here the constitution appears more as a compromise, which simply hides the various political viewpoints only sooner or later to reappear."[106]

As this concluding paragraph indicates, the theory of judicial decision just presented, though predominant, is not unchallenged among German jurists. In particular, the studies of Esser and Viehweg, discussed elsewhere,[107] have led the way toward a growing reassessment of the traditional view. Undoubtedly, the introduction of judicial review with powers much broader than those, for instance, of the United States Supreme Court has been and will continue to be an impetus in this direction.

Neutral Principles of Law

The current American approach to constitutional construction accepts generally the judicial confrontation of values as the starting point for a theory of judicial decision. By its very nature, the common law mentality has been scarcely amenable to the systematic approach of code law thinking. The judge is forced to undertake a thorough analysis of previous precedents and piece together a "guiding principle" in light of the case before him, i.e., a principle which is never codified or complete, but always growing and in each case researched and re-thought anew.[108] In this spirit, the Supreme Court early declared "that its opinion upon the construction of the Constitution is always open to discussion when it is supposed to have been founded in error, and that its judicial authority should hereafter depend altogether on the force of the reasoning by which it is supported."[109] In fact, the Court has had to admit time and again – even if often reluctantly and only implicitly – that previous decisions were wrong.[110]

[106] Ermacora, "Aussprache," 20 *VVdStRL*, 111 (1963).

[107] See discussion in text *supra*, p. 115ff, and *infra*, p. 214ff. See also Ehmke, *op. cit.* (n. 73), pp. 59–72; Scheuner, "Aussprache," 20 *VVdStRL*, 108f. 111f and 125f; Ermacora, *Verfassungsrecht durch Richterspruch*, 30f (1960); and Bachof, *Summum Ius Summa Iniuria* (1963).

[108] See Cardozo, *The Nature of the Judicial Process*, 23, 28f, 102f and 116 (1921); Esser, *Grundsatz und Norm*, Ch. 10; and the discussion in text *supra*, p. 115ff.

[109] Chief Justice Taney, *Passenger Cases*, 48 U.S. (7 How.) 283, 470 (1849).

[110] See *Burnet* v. *Coronado Oil and Gas Co.*, 285 U.S. 393, 407–8 (1932), where Justice Brandeis, after pointing out 69 cases over-ruling earlier opinions, stated: "The Court bows to the lessons of experience and the force of better reasoning, recognizing

Furthermore, having experienced a period of dogmatic adherence to case doctrine for doctrine's sake, the onslaught of "legal realism" demonstrated poignantly the limits of rules and doctrine and the scope for judicial preferences in the preparation and reasoning of judicial decisions.[111] If according to "legal realism" rules were mostly "pretty playthings," then the Constitution might actually be merely what the judges say it is. This view, however, is neither satisfying nor helpful, for it does not offer the judge any standards except his whim or will.[112] Nor, as Hamilton argued,[113] does it help to distinguish the judiciary from the legislature. Nevertheless, the importance of "legal realism" is that it joined issue with the "found law" and "plain meaning" views of legal construction and forced judicial theory to come to grips with the realities of value choice.

The result has been a lively discussion in recent years on the nature and limits of judicial decision in constitutional interpretation.[114] The discussion stems from the continuing attempt to justify the exercise and scope of judicial review in democratic government, and leads of necessity to the question of how potentially competitive governmental institutions can be made complementary and responsible organs of government.[115] If, as Judge Hand would have it, the basis of judicial review lies solely in the requirement of effective federal government, i.e. that which is "essential to prevent the failure of the venture at hand," then its exercise for any reason other than "to distinguish *between* the frontiers of another department's authority" would not be more than a *coup de main*.[116] The preference of the Supreme Court simply would be pitted against the preference of the legislature.

Hand's view, argues Herbert Wechsler, cannot – that is, must not – be so, since the authority of judicial review is *not* a discretionary gloss of the Court. Instead, judicial review "is grounded in the language of the Constitution and

that the process of trial and error, so fruitful in the physical sciences, is appropriate also in the judicial function." See also Cardozo, *ibid.*, p. 150f, who urges "less hesitation in frank avowal and full abandonment" of obsolete or wrong rules.

111 See e.g. Cahn, "Fact-Skepticism and Fundamental Law," 33 *N.Y.U.L. Rev.*, 1 (1958); and Frank, *Courts on Trial*, Ch. 3 (1949).

112 "A mere empirical theory of law," as Kant scathingly remarks, "has (like the wooden head in the Phaedrus fable) a pretty head perhaps, but what a pity that it has no brain!" *Metaphysik der Sitten*, Pt. I. "Einleitung in die Rechtslehre" § B.

113 See text *supra* at note 30.

114 See Shapiro, *Law and Politics in the Supreme Court*, Ch. 1 (1964), for the general lines and literature of this discussion.

115 See the discussion of this question in text *supra*, pp. 148–151.

116 Hand, *the Bill of Rights*, 33f, 37f, 55f, and 70–72 (1960): the *Bill of Rights* must be read as "admonitory or hortatory, not definite enough to be guides on concrete occasions, prescribing no more than the temper of detachment, impartiality and an absence of self-directed bias that is the whole content of justice." Cf. text at note 78 *supra*.

is not a mere interpolation." [117] It is true, he continues, the Supreme Court *cannot escape* issues which are "political," i.e. involve a choice among competing values, for this is "reflected in the legislative or executive action in question, which the court must either condemn or condone." On the other hand, neither is it "free to function as a naked power organ," as an instrument of will and not of reason. Rather, "the main constituent of the judicial process is precisely that it must be genuinely principled, resting with respect to every step that is involved in reaching judgment on analysis and reasons quite transcending the immediate result that is achieved." [118] The courts must decide on grounds of principle, embodying "what surely are the main qualities of law, its generality and its neutrality." [119]

For Wechsler, then, "neutrality" does not refer to values. Value decisions are inescapable. The demand of neutrality, contends Wechsler, "is that a value and its measure be determined by a general analysis that gives no weight to accidents of application, finding a scope that is acceptable whatever interest, group, or person may assert the claim." The same neutrality must be assured "where there is a conflict among values having constitutional protection, calling for their ordering or their accomodation." [120]

What is important for the Supreme Court, therefore, is not the nature of the question before it. That will of course be "political." Crucial is the nature of the answer which a court of law may validly give. And that answer is "a principled decision," resting "on reasons with respect to all the issues in the case, reasons that in their generality and their neutrality transcend any immediate result that is involved." [121] "Neutral principles," by avoiding *ad hoc* decisions and expedient compromise to the situation of the parties in the case at hand, will produce a like decision – not necessarily result! – in like cases.[122] Thus, for Wechsler the 1954 School Segration Decisions rest

[117] Wechsler, "Toward Neutral Principles of Constitutional Law," 73 *Harv. L. Rev.*, 1, 3 (1959).

[118] *Ibid.*, p. 15.

[119] *Ibid.*, p. 16.

[120] Wechsler, *Principles, Politics and Fundamental Law*, xiii-xiv (1961).

[121] Wechsler, *op. cit.* (n. 117), p. 19. Cf. Hart. "Foreward: The Time Chart of the Justices," 73 *Harv. L. Rev.*, 84, 99 (1959): "Only opinions which are grounded in reason and not on mere fiat or precedent can do the job which the Supreme Court of the United States has to do." For the Court is "charged with the creative function of discerning afresh and of articulating and developing impersonal and durable principles of constitutional law and impersonal and durable principles for the interpretation of statutes and the resolution of difficult issues of decisional law."

[122] Although Wechsler contends that he does not wish to pose "an antithesis between 'making an enduring contribution to the quality of our society' and resting on 'neutral principles'," he concludes "that it is not enough that a decision makes such a contribution unless it also rests on neutral principles . . ." Due to the likely conflict between

on too narrow a ground to be neutrally principled. They turn on the deleterious effects which separate schools have upon black children. This ground is too narrow because it does not forbid "all racial lines in legislation," i.e. housing, marriage, etc., but restricts itself to public school segregation. It is also too narrow because, by resting primarily on effects reasoning, it merely usurps the state legislature's judgment that separate public schools, on balance, have better effects for both parties involved.[123] In such cases, where the Court cannot or is not prepared to formulate a "neutral principle," the legislative choice must stand.

Finally – like the proponents of "determinate norms," discussed above – Wechsler sees the judicial process in terms of unconditionally applicable principles. His "neutral principles" need not be inflexibly formulated nor considered infallible,[124] but once formulated they must be faithfully applied without abatement across-the-board to all comers. He too dissents from the pragmatic and somewhat discretionary lines of the "political questions" doctrine. He does not necessarily view the Court as unpolitical, but holds that the Court's denial to exercise the jurisdiction which it possesses must be based on "standards framed in neutral terms." He thereby converts the "political questions" doctrine from a device of judicial prudence and restraint, by which the Court in the past has attempted to stay free of the "political thicket," to a strict principle of division of powers. "[T]he only proper judgment that may lead to an abstention from decision is that the Constitution has committed the determination of the issue to another agency of government than the courts."[125] The same must be done, he argues, for other discretionary devices. The sole resort and protection of the judicial power lies in unyielding principles unconditionally applied.

The theory of "neutral principles," therefore, fully embraces the value choices which face a constitutional court. This distinguishes it from its Ger-

"neutral principles" and their undesirable results, Pollak rightly concludes, the judge's estimate of the likely impact on American life of a proposed constitutional decision would have to remain "a thing apart from the competing constitutional principles whose neutral accomodation yields one or another constitutional result." Where the two clash, "neutral principles" must win. See discussion in Pollak, "Constitutional Adjudication: Relative or Absolute Neutrality." *J. Pub. L.* 48, 60f and 53f (1962).

[123] Wechsler, *op. cit.* (n. 117), p. 33f. Pollack, "Racial Discrimination and Judicial Integrity: A Reply to Professor Wechsler," 108 *U. Pa. L. Rev.*, 1 (1959), argues that if Wechsler means only to eliminate *ad hoc* decisions through his "neutral principles," then the School Decision meets Wechsler's standard. Pollak concedes, however, that Wechsler may be after "bigger game," as indeed he appears to be, i.e. to eliminate result-oriented decisions altogether.

[124] Wechsler, *id.*, p. 31f.

[125] *Ibid.*, p. 9.

man counterpart discussed above. In order to avoid the extreme pitfalls of *ad hoc* "naked power" decisions, however, Wechsler adopts an equally rigid and unworkable position in the formulation and application of legal principles. In the first place, by focusing exclusively on internally consistent principles of law, he would severely restrict the scope of the judicial process. This is true, on the one hand, because only exceptionally is a court prepared to formulate principles which will yield defensible conclusions in all future imaginable cases.[126] "If we know anything at all about law," comments Eugene Rostow,[127] "we know that the goal which Professor Wechsler makes his only test for judicial propriety is impossible to achieve; that it never has been achieved by any common law court, nor by any other court; and that it can never be achieved, in the nature of the judicial process."

On the other hand, the goal of "neutral principles" offers no alternative means for developing the legal knowledge which is lacking. Instead, it raises a categorical imperative for judicial action which seeks to identify the "rule of the case" in every decision with general principles of constitutional law.[128] This ignores the crucial fact, which Esser so poignantly demonstrates in his comparison of code and common law systems,[129] that "the formulation of the principle constitutes a late stage in the juristic treatment of a problem." General legal principles, so far as they are ascertainable, are the guides – and not the concrete content – of judicial reasoning. Whereas principles are "the primary expression of value decision in the positive law, from which the applicable rule first obtains its legitimacy,"[130] rules of the case reflect the trial-and-error experience of the concrete problems. To simply identify the two is to ignore the fruitful tension between them and to seriously threaten legal development.

In the second place, Wechsler requires that his "neutral principles" – once formulated – be applied unremittingly in all cases. As others have

126 See criticism of Wechsler's position on this point by Bickel, *The Least Dangerous Branch*, 58, 63f and 69 (1962); Mueller and Schwarz, "The Principle of Neutral Principles," 7 *U.C.L.A. Intra. L. Rev.*, 571, 585f (1960); and Rostow, *the Sovereign Prerogative*, 38f (1962).

127 Rostow, *id.*, p. 32.

128 Esser, *Grundsatz und Norm*, 207f (1956), has pointed out that in both the common and code law traditions principles have a "systematizing" function. In the latter, however, this role is much more strictly disciplined. Wechsler's theory may be viewed as a step toward code law thinking by forcing the guiding principles to be formulated precisely in the "rule of the case."

129 *Ibid.*, p. 267.

130 *Ibid.*, p. 197. See also the discussion in text *supra*, p. 116f.

pointed out,[131] however, such an approach is not apt to stand the strain of an ongoing constitutional system. As Rostow puts it:

> Exercising high political powers, the Court must have a high sense of strategy and tactics. Its influence on our public life depends in large on the Court's skill in advocacy and its sensitivity to the powerful forces which from time to time, in different combinations, must resist its will. If the Court had in fact lived by Professor Wechsler's rule, it would have disappeared long ago from the stage of American life.[132]

Indeed, far from guaranteeing the neutrality of the Supreme Court in reaching value decision, Wechsler's theory may well constitute an invitation to judicial ideology. The discipline of reason which Wechsler so admirably respects, is often deceptive. "Even the highest refinement of reason," to recall the words of Montesquieu,[133] "is not always desirable." This is no less true for judges than for men in general. Clothed with the garb of "reasoned neutrality," they may more readily succumb to the myth of their own infallibility. Armed with the weapon of unyielding principles, they are more prone to overstep the prudent limits of judicial power. In order to avoid the danger of *ad hoc* decisions, the theory of "neutral principles" would subject the judiciary to a deceptive quest for certainty.

Despite their vastly differing legal traditions, the theories of "determinate norms" and "neutral principles" are amazingly alike. Both contain important elements of truth: whereas the language of the norm is the starting point for judicial interpretation, general reasoned principles epitomize the ultimate goal of the judicial process. Both, however, suffer the same deficiency. They are too narrowly conceived to account for that great expanse between the starting point and the ultimate goal which constitutes the very heart of the judicial process. They cannot account, in other words, for those imperfections in the law as a process of continuous development, which are reflected in the judicial search for purpose, authority and practicability. In their obeisance to certainty in the law, they fail to explain how it is that normative content and reasoned principles in fact arise only in the course of judicial decision. For this reason, discussion about the judicial process is

131 See e.g. Bickel, *op. cit.* (n. 126), p. 63f; and Miller and Howell, "The Myth of Neutrality in Constitutional Adjudication," 27 *U. Ch. L. Rev.*, 661, 687–89 (1959–60). But cf. Gunther, "The Subtle Vices of the 'Passive Virtues': A Comment on Principle and Expediency in Judicial Review," 64 *Colum. L. Rev.*, 1, 13–25 (1964).

132 Rostow, *op. cit.* p. 34.

133 See text *supra*, p. 116f.

blunted before it can begin. Moreover, due to an obsession with judicial neutrality, proponents of these two theories tend to ignore the real limits on the exercise of judicial review. Judicial neutrality, in contrast to organizational independence, is not a status that can be conferred simply by juridical dogma or legal theory. On the level of constitutional adjudication, where fundamental values are most obviously in issue, neutrality is a function of that consensus of opinion upon which these values rest. Whether neutrality is a desirable judicial objective need not be considered here. It is certainly a highly unlikely consequence of the theories just presented. The real question, in any case, is not neutrality but judicial responsibility. It can be answered only in an institutional context of judicial decision-making.

3. THE NATURE AND LIMITS OF THE JUDICIAL POWER

The judicial function, as just concluded, cannot be fully explained or properly distinguished in terms of determinate norms or reasoned principles. The purely formal criteria of these theories offer no insight into *either* the creative process of legal development through judicial decision *or* the responsible limits of that process. And yet, where the question in dispute goes to the very heart of a constitutional order, precisely these two matters are of vital importance. It may be contended, of course, that the proper scope of the judicial process is defined expressly or impliedly by the language and practice of the constitution. True as this may be, no definition will be precise enough to avoid the need for interpretation. Like other aspects of constitutional regulation, the division of powers also is subject to all the ambiguities of the written word as well as to the obvious limits on human foresight and experience.

Moreover, however detailed the division of powers may be drawn, constitutional provisions cannot capture and contain the essentially creative task of judicial interpretation. There are no concrete rules – least of all the formal concepts and criteria of the preceding Section – for ascertaining on specific questions when the creative task of interpretation has become a matter for legislation or administrative discretion rather than for judicial decision. This is the hard fact that blurs the neat but purely formal distinction between the judiciary and other branches of government. Finally and most important, there are limits to judicial decision that are independent of the lines set down in the constitution. This is only to say, with Professor Fuller, "that there are certain kinds of social tasks that are not suitable raw material for the adjudicative process."[134] To be effective within its peculiar

[134] Fuller, "Adjudication and the Rule of Law," 54 *Proc. Amer. Soc. Int. L.*, 1, 2 (1960).

institutional framework, a court must restrict itself to those aspects of a dispute which are susceptible of judicial treatment and resolution. Such restraint should be applied not only in fashioning judicial reasoning and the remedies of specific cases, but also as a general defense against improper attempts by the legislature to delegate its responsibilities to the judiciary. The failure to observe these limits must over time, if not in the immediate future, erode respect for the judiciary.

For these reasons, it is essential at this point to examine the nature and limits of the judicial power. This means translating those judicial tasks, presented in Section 2 of Chapter III, into institutional terms, following not only the analytical method of Montesquieu but also his guiding principle of "moderation."[135] In criticizing performance, Fuller suggests, look "to the aptness of the institutional design of the agency to perform the task assigned to it."[136] The question, therefore, is whether the judiciary, or perhaps another branch of government, is institutionally capable or better suited to treat a given problem.

The approach taken here does not deny the central role of norm and principle in the judicial function. It does recognize, however, that the normative content of both, as developed through judicial decision, is shaped materially by the institutional considerations set out below. These considerations are to a large extent the insight and experience gained from result-oriented jurisprudence. Furthermore, only by examining the judiciary in action, in terms of the realities of its institutional setting, is it possible to establish the responsible limits of creative judicial decision. Responsibility in decision-making cannot be determined *a priori*. In the context of a division and balance of powers, it must be measured by the feasible alternatives in the offing to resolve the problem at hand. This may at times require judicial activism or judicial restraint. By an institutional analysis, therefore, it can be shown that the judiciary not only acts but also is acted upon. To this extent, the tasks of judicial decision are a function of their institutional foundation.

The Power to Legitimate

What is the nature and source of judicial power at the level of constitutional adjudication? Some would flatly deny that such power exists – that the judiciary possesses any real power in government. The reasons for this are two at least, both of which have some basis in the writings of Montes-

135 See discussion of this principle in text *supra*, pp. 143–145 and 151.

136 Fuller, *The Morality of Law*, 176 (1964).

quieu. From a purely formal view of the judicial function, like the German theory discussed above,[137] the court merely interprets existing and determinate norms. This essentially cognitive activity reduces the court to a passive instrument of government, devoid of force and will and all political influence.

Another view proceeds from the concept of law as "command." The court, it may be argued, is not equipped to engage in a check and balance of political powers.[138] "The problem of the division of powers," says Hermann Jahrreiss,[139] "concerns only the force of command, . . . the acts of ruling, i.e., those commands which usually meet with success, or are obeyed." Since the judiciary can no more maintain law and order than full employment, it occupies only a subordinate position ("Hilfsgewalt") in government, merely assisting the real "political" powers. It may advise but in direct confrontation cannot check the other branches of government.

By exaggerating either the cognitive character of judicial decisions or the coercive element in the law, these views ignore the unique nature of judicial power. True enough, the judiciary does not control the purse or the sword, nor does it possess the legislature's immense facility to mobilize public opinion or the executive's built-in "chain of command" and enforcement agencies; yet its decisions are not deprived thereby of all but advisory effect in the play of governmental powers. In an institutional context, the weight of judicial decisions is enhanced not only by the formal authority of the judges and the cogency of their reasoning, but further by the station of the judiciary in the life of the nation as the appointed guardian of the legal order. By reason of the latter, the judiciary becomes identified with the realization and implementation of the law itself. The decisions of a constitutional court – far from being mere cognitive deductions from prescribed norms – take on the moral force of the "rule of law." More tangibly, the court becomes the ultimate tribunal for resolving conflicts on fundamental questions of law. For the sake of the legal system as a whole, loyalty to the law frequently will outweigh even widespread disenchantment with specific judicial decisions. Though men may not always regard the law as just, they still may hold it just to obey the law.[140]

137 See discussion in text *supra*, p. 153ff.

138 See discussion of Krauss, "Die Gewaltenteilung bei Montesquieu," in *Festschrift Carl Schmitt,* 103, 104 and 112f (1959). Some, like Learned Hand, *The Bill of Rights* (1960), also take a command view of the law, but do not see the judiciary as thereby powerless.

139 Jahrreiss, "Die Wesensverschiedenheit der Akte des Herrschers und das Problem der Gewaltenteilung," in his *Mensch und Staat,* 173, 182f (1959).

140 See de Visscher, *Theory and Reality in Public International Law,* 91 (1957).

By its very nature, as this suggests, the judiciary may possess a kind of power not found in other branches of government. In this context, therefore, the term "power" connotes much more than the idea of formal authority. Further, it embraces more than the persuasive reasoning of judicial decisions discussed above,[141] but without detracting from the search for authority. As used here, the term "power" means the real or actual ability of the judiciary or of one particular court, as a governmental institution, to influence others to act or to produce a result in keeping with the central tasks of judicial decision outlined in Chapter III. Within the context of judicial review, this means the ability to call forth and solidify support for governmental measures having only a tentative and uncertain acceptance. It also means the ability of the court to maintain its view and authority while vetoing politically popular acts. This goes to the sociological basis of judicial power. To the extent that the judiciary, in addition, thereby strengthens coordinated activity among the members and various organizations of society, it establishes an increased energy potential for the entire nation.[142]

The precise nature of this power is determined best perhaps by examining its source. There are two sources, one material and one formal. The latter is implied in the mandate of judicial review. Unlike other courts, a constitutional court may invalidate governmental acts incompatible with the constitution. Such a decision not merely interprets a statute and the constitution, but checks the executive or legislative will for an indefinite future time. The effects of this mandate are felt well beyond those limited number of cases where governmental acts are invalidated, for the very threat of judicial review will force legislators to be mindful of constitutional standards.[143]

Conversely, judicial review also entails the capacity to validate governmental acts. Since what is not invalidated upon judicial scrutiny will tend to be thought worthy of acceptance, or even justified, the power to validate may be said to be a function of the authority to invalidate. While this could be a danger to responsible government, as Thayer has warned,[144] it also constitutes an immense asset to the maintenance of a (constitutional) government with limited powers. Indeed, Charles Black contends,

> a case can be made for believing that the prime and most necessary function of the Court has been that of *validation*, not that of invalidation. What a government of limited powers needs, at the beginning and forever, is some means of satisfying the people that it has taken all steps humanly possible to stay within

141 See text *supra*, p. 128ff.
142 See Carlston, *Law and Structures of Social Action*, 14f (1956).
143 See discussion in text *supra*, at n. 49.
144 See text *supra*, at n. 50.

its powers. That is the condition of its legitimacy, and its legitimacy, in the long run, is the condition of its life. And the Court, through its history, has acted as the legitimator of the government. In a very real sense, the Government of the United States is based on the opinions of the Supreme Court.[145]

The formal power to validate, therefore, means "stamping governmental actions as legitimate." [146] The Supreme Court is the institutional means for "persuading the greater part of [the American] people that the principles of governmental limitation have been adhered to, notwithstanding differences of private opinion . . . ." [147] For Professor Black, the Court has put the sweetness into the air he breathes.

Professor Bickel follows Black's lead, but carefully notes that the power to legitimate must have a more independent basis. That power, he suggests, is not simply "the sweet odor of the Supreme Court":

Legitimacy, being the stability of a good government over time, is the fruit of consent to specific actions or to the authority to act; the consent to the exercise of authority, whether or not approved in each instance, of as unified a population as possible, but most importantly, of a present majority.[148]

As Bickel realizes, however, the "fruit of consent" may not be forthcoming unless the Court is capable of generating it. This, he believes, it can do. The Court is not only capable of "generating consent for hotly controverted legislative or executive measures; it has the subtler power of adding a certain impetus to measures that the majority enacts rather tentatively." [149] The Supreme Court, as the symbol of unity and continuity in American life, possesses such power because it "is felt to be good and has proven itself as such to generations past as well as in the present." [150] While this is undoubtedly true, neither Bickel nor Black explain how the Court could achieve such acceptance except as an historical accident. "Who can tell?" says Black. "Something clicks into place." [151] Were this in fact the only explanation, then the power of the Court would be as fickle as its source. Its source would be just happenstance. Consensus may establish the potential and outer limits of judicial power, but it is not its source. If judicial power exists, it must be made of sterner stuff.

There is indeed a more durable source of judicial power. It lies in the in-

[145] Black, *The People and the Court,* 53 (1960).
[146] *Ibid.*
[147] *Ibid.*, p. 43.
[148] Bickel, *The Least Dangerous Branch,* 30 (1962).
[149] *Ibid.*, p. 30f.
[150] *Ibid.*, p. 29.
[151] Black, *op. cit.*, p. 51.

stitutionalized process of adjudication through reasoned decisions. Within this context, judicial reasoning constitutes not merely a means of justification, or for reasoned elaboration in the search for authority, as described in Section 2 of Chapter III; it also embraces certain modes of social belief. As viewed from the sociology of Max Weber,[152] these modes represent three pure types of legitimacy, namely, tradition, charisma and legality, found at the root of all governmental action. They cannot be grasped from a dogmatic or speculative viewpoint, nor are they in themselves "right" or "true" bases of governmental action. They do not, moreover, depend on motives of expediency or habits of obedience in the populace,[153] for these lack the lasting and active character of a belief. Rather, being descriptive categories empirically derived from observable patterns of social action,[154] they constitute the sociological basis for adherence to the legal order as that order is embodied in the reasoning and decisions of governmental institutions. In this way the office and the process of judicial decision combine and fuse: the office dignifies the process, and the decisional reasoning in turn amplifies and gives concrete expression to the modes of belief. To the extent of this fusion, the judiciary takes on power independent of its formal authority.

This then is the material source of judicial power. While the modes of legitimacy inhere to some extent in the office and reasoning of all tribunals, they take on much greater significance in the context of judicial review. A brief sketch of these modes will illustrate this point. In the first place, the belief in tradition – in the validity of what has always been – may sanction in large measure the decisions of a constitutional court. It is reflected in the desire for continuity, and enhanced when, in contrast to the changing composition of legislative assemblies, judges are elected for life. It is an important part of the doctrine of precedent,[155] paying homage – in Cardozo's more palpable phrase – to "the power of the beaten track." Though this may be as for Herbert Spencer, the government of the living by the dead, still the

[152] See, in particularly, Weber, "Die drei reinen Typen der legitimen Herrschaft," 187 *Preussische Jahrbücher,* 1 (1922), reprinted in and discussed at length by Winckelmann, "Legitimitaet und Legalitaet" in Max Webers *Herrschaftssoziologie,* 25–43 and Appendix (1952). See also Weber, *The Theory of Social and Economic Organization,* 130–32 and 328ff (transl. by A. M. Henderson and Talcott Parsons, 1947), being Part I of Weber's *Wirtschaft und Gesellschaft* (1922).

[153] Weber, *The Theory of Social and Economic Organization,* 125 (1947).

[154] See Winckelmann, *op. cit.,* p. 26.

[155] As Holmes, "Law in Science and Science in Law," 12 *Harv. L. Rev.,* 443, 460 (1899), has put it: "the claim of our especial code to respect is simply that it exists, that it is the one to which we have become accustomed, and not that it represents an eternal principle . . . ."

conservatism of law and lawyers is no less real for all that.[156] This priority of the past in legal reasoning in writ large in a constitution whose value framework is meant to endure for generations. As the ultimate interpreter of the constitution, the court shares in the lasting quality of the values which it preserves.

The court also possesses a charismatic force in the life of a community.[157] As guardian of the constitution, it becomes identified with the ideals of law itself. A certain "noblesse de robe" may well develop,[158] invoking a latent faith in fundamental values and becoming the spokesman of their enduring quality. Professor Bickel appears to be thinking primarily of this mode of legitimacy. The Supreme Court, he says, personifies the Constitution which in America is the "symbol of nationhood, of continuity, of unity and common purpose." It is "defender of the faith, proclaimer and protector of the goals."[159] Further, "as an organ of government charged with translating principles into positive law," the Court in its decisions can speak directly to the nation over the heads of the political institutions. "No one should underestimate the dominion of ideas in a nation committed to the rule of principle as well as to majoritarian democracy."[160] Of the newfledged Constitutional Court of Germany, Rudolf Smend too concludes, it "champions the rule of law and justice by making the highest earthly values the basis of its decisions."[161] This faith in a higher law, says Thurman Arnold,

> made the Supreme Court the greatest unifying symbol in American government. Here was the one body which could still the constant debate, and represent to the country the ideal of a government of fundamental principles.[162]

[156] See Esser, *Grundsatz und Norm,* 82 (1956); Morgenthau, *Politics Among Nations,* 409f and 416 (4th ed. 1967); Krüger, "Verfassungswandlung und Verfassungsgerichtsbarkeit," in *Festschrift Rudolf Smend,* 151, 165f (1962); and Radbruch, *Der Geist des Englischen Rechts,* 11 (4th ed. 1956).

[157] Not merely the man on the white horse, institutions too may take on a charismatic force. See Weber, *op. cit.* (n. 153), p. 363ff, who speaks of charisma becoming "routinized"; and Winckelmann, *op. cit.*, p. 62.

[158] See Max Imboden, "Die Staatsformen," in his *Politische Systeme: Staatsformen,* 137, 163–178 (1964), whose theory of the separation of powers attempts to account for this aristocratic trait in the judiciary.

[159] Bickel, *op. cit.* (n. 148), p. 31.

[160] *Ibid.*, p. 188.

[161] Smend, "Das Bundesverfassungsgericht," *a Festvortrag in Das Bundesverfassungsgericht,* 23, 37 (1963).

[162] Arnold, *The Folklore of Capitalism,* 63f (Yale Paperbound 1961). See also Carl Friedrich, "The Constitution as a Political Force," in Eckstein and Apter (ed.), *Comparative Politics,* 133, 139 (1963): the constitution functions "as the most effective symbol of the unifying forces operative in a community."

A constitutional court, then, becomes keeper of the faith in constitutional values. As the ultimate interpreter of these values, it takes on a kind of oracular power.

Finally, in contrast to tradition and charisma, a third mode of legitimacy lies in the impersonal character of a highly rationalized, modern-day legal order. It consists of belief in the legality of patterns of substantive rules established by authorized decision-makers. The "office" of the judiciary is viewed apart from the personality and preferences of the judges, and its decisions are evaluated in terms of rational, intelligible and cogent elaborations of fundamental or constitutional principles. Thus, contrary to Carl Schmitt, "legality" encompasses more than purely organizational rules and formal validity.[163] It extends also to the substantive grounds, or principles, of judicial decisions. Moreover, what is important to "legality" as a mode of legitimacy is not how these principles were established originally, whether through coercion, the consensus of society or natural law reasoning, but that the decisions rendered in accordance with them bear the qualities of impartiality, disinterestedness and reasonedness which are the benchmark of objectivity. By virtue of its office and decisions, therefore, the court becomes a source of insight and enlightenment, or, to use the words of Henry Hart, the "voice of reason" itself.[164] It not only settles disputes, but also articulates and clarifies the basic value framework of the legal order, thereby projecting guidelines for social conduct as well. This has very practical advantages for complex industrialized societies where rationality itself becomes a prized object. Predictability is enhanced, expectations become more stable and the individual is given a greater measure of control over his social environment.

Real as these modes of legitimacy may be, they are subject to certain constraints.[165] In the first place, the social climate or mentality of a nation will not always be receptive to the one or the other. In a rapidly changing society where customary values cannot be adapted adequately, the legitimating belief in tradition may break. Similarly, if an unquestioned belief in certain common values is lacking or the symbols of unity and community are weak, a charismatic basis may be wanting. Indeed, not even the mode of "legality" may avail, if a sharp cleavage in fundamental values exists. How-

[163] Schmitt, *Legalität und Legitimität,* 14 (1932), contrasts the formality of legality with the substantive justification of legitimacy. See critique of Winckelmann, *op. cit.* (n. 152), p. 56ff.

[164] Hart, "Forward: The Time Chart of the Justices," 73 *Harv. L. Rev.*, 84, 99 (1959–60).

[165] See Winckelmann, *op. cit.* (n. 152), pp. 39–43, who points to the limiting effect of the very premises underlying the modes of legitimacy.

ever "objective" and "impartial" a decision and its procedures may be, it will always be susceptible to purely result-oriented criticism. Further, the belief in "legality" may suffer from a certain built-in tension, arising from "a kind of 'abstraction' of a part of the human individual from the concrete whole."[166] The office of the judge, for instance, must be abstracted from his person, his official opinion held aloof from his personal opinion. This distinction smarts as much under a common sense skepticism of its feasibility as under the occasional examples of its abuse in practice.

Secondly, though these modes of legitimacy are by no means mutually exclusive,[167] they also may set each other limits. This is because, as adjuncts of institutionalized judicial power, they are reflected variously in the methods of judicial interpretation. The legitimating mode of tradition, for instance, may best be invoked by the interpretational methods of history and custom, that of charisma by teleology and the adherence to current public policy, and that of legality by the methods of system and logic. Like these methods, moreover, the modes of legitimacy may vary in effectiveness by area of the law.[168] Thus, as Cardozo points out, the common law of property is rooted in tradition and must be understood primarily in terms of history.[166] In the field of constitutional law, on the other hand, the method of teleology may be most persuasive: there, "not the origin, but the goal, is the main thing."[170] Rules of economic regulation and commercial transactions, by contrast, are measured to a large extent by standards of efficiency, utility and predictability. Such standards, most nearly akin to the method of system and logic, are reflected in the mode of legality. Of course, these parallels between methods of interpretation and modes of legitimacy should not be overdrawn. They simply suggest how the latter may be projected concretely through the reasoning of the court. It is important to emphasize, for this reason, that the choice of the one may imply a choice of the other.

With this in mind, it is not improper to speak of a unique judicial power. It receives its form through the institution of judicial review, but its true source is the modes of legitimacy. Through them a constitutional court can evoke adherence to its value judgments and, in turn, legitimate existing governmental authorities, their policies and their decisions taken at first only tentatively. That such power is limited cannot be disputed, but that in

[166] See Parson's introductory comments to Weber, *op. cit.* (n. 153), pp. 68–71.

[167] See Weber, *id.*, pp. 117 and 329.

[168] See Cardozo, *The Nature of the Judicial Process*, 57f, 64f, 67 and 112f (1921); and Eichenberger, *Die richterliche Unabhängigkeit als staatsrechtliches Problem*, 204ff (1960).

[169] Cardozo, *id.*, p. 54f.

[170] *Ibid.*, p. 102 and also pp. 76 and 83–85.

itself is not decisive for this analysis. All governmental power, whether expressed in terms of coercion, material inducement or moral suasion, has limits. This the more so if society is dedicated to the "rule of law," and even if only because of enlightened self-interest. The crucial point is that, by virtue of these modes of legitimacy, the court possesses an independent and durable means for influencing others to act and for actively promoting values fundamental to the legal order.

Institutional Constraints

The guiding principle for the exercise of judicial power is judicial restraint or moderation. That is to say, for reasons of prudence set out below a constitutional court at times should not exercise its formal authority to the fullest extent in the case before it. Such power, says Rostow, "exists to be used at the right times, not lost in atrophy." A court "can be destroyed by the weakness as well as the recklessness of its members."[171] To avoid this and to test its timing, it must temper reason by experience, the application of rules and principles by their effects and the necessity for judicial relief by the alternatives at hand and the institutional constraints at work. These constraints may be peculiar to the judicial process, such as the dependence of the court on party initiative, the prejudicial effect (whether or not doctrinally established) of judicial decisions on future judgments and the inadequacy of judicial expertise and supervision to master the problems in point. They also may be external to that process, stemming from the inertia, lack of cooperation and jealousies of other branches of government. More important, the appropriateness and extent of judicial action must be weighed in the light of feasible alternatives. Adjudication is certainly not the only, nor always the best means of conflict resolution.

The following analysis outlines those considerations of prudence which should prompt the exercise of judicial restraint. It further presents some of the judicial techniques to accomplish this end. What results is not an elephantine version of the "political questions" doctrine, though the considerations set out below are clearly reflected in the premises of that doctrine. Nor does the following analysis offer that clear cut "political-legal" distinction so coveted by the proponents of a purely formal view of the judicial

[171] Eugene Rostow, *The Sovereign Prerogative*, 177f (1962). See also Roche, "Judicial Self-Restraint," 49 *Amer. Pol. Sci. Rev.*, 762, 772 (1955): "In short, judicial self-restraint and judicial power seem to be opposite sides of the same coin: it has been by judicious application of the former that the latter has been maintained."

function.[172] In an institutional context, this distinction can never be derived solely from existing norms or rules of law, however determinate. Thus, the absence of such a norm or rule may well be sufficient reason for refusing – at least on that particular point – to adjudicate a dispute. Yet it also may be occasion for creative judicial activity.[173] On the other hand, the mere existence of such a norm or rule does not prove conclusively that the judicial process can adequately deal with the problem at hand.[174] Certain aspects or even the whole of a problem may be qualitatively better treated by the administrative or the legislative process. In the last instance, the choice depends on an institutional analysis in light of the concrete circumstances of the case and the contours of the larger problem at stake.

Within the context of the judicial process, therefore, the notion of "political" is simply a conclusionary label. It represents those facets of questions whose determination is better left – at least for the moment – to other branches of government or the social process in general. It embraces several considerations, the most important of which is by no means the absence of a determinate norm. Given the immense scope of and necessity for creative judicial activity, this formal referent offers no judicial guideline at all. The court must look beyond it, to institutional considerations, in order to appreciate fully the real limits on its power. It must look to those institutional constraints peculiar to the overriding search for purpose, authority and practicability in the law.

I.

Judicial self-restraint is dictated, in the first place, by the search for pur-

[172] A matter also may be "political," it should be noted, because the legal principle at stake involves fundamental social values and principles of governmental organization, because the issues in dispute evoke volatile social consequences and/or because the judicial process is institutionally incapable of adequately treating the problem at hand. See also the discussion by Klein, *Bundesverfassungsgericht und richterliche Beurteilung politischer Fragen* (1966).

[173] See, for instance, the position of the German courts when faced with the failure of the German parliament to meet its deadline, as set by Article 117 I of the German Basic Law, to implement the Equality Clause for men and women. In refusing to postpone the deadline, the German Federal Constitutional Court declared the Equality Clause to be henceforth applicable and, had parliament not acted soon thereafter, laid the courts open to an immense job of law reformulation. Discussed by Esser, *Grundsatz und Norm,* 72f and 76–78 (1956).

[174] Though Chief Justice Marshall early stated, in *Cohens* v. *Virginia,* 19 U.S. 264, 404 (1821), that the Supreme Court "must take jurisdiction if it should," i.e. cannot "avoid a measure because it approaches the confines of the constitution," Bickel has concluded that Marshall's position "does not describe the system as it is or has been." Bickel, *The Least Dangerous Branch,* 261 (1962). See also Frankfurter, "John Marshall and the Judicial Function," 69 *Harv. L. Rev.,* 217, 227 (1955).

pose in the law. This search is generated, as previous discussion has indicated,[175] by the continuing tension between imperfection in the norm as written and the uncertainty as to its just or ideal content. Though dedicated ultimately to the realization of a just order, the law is confronted by inherent limits on human knowledge. By the very nature of law, the judiciary is committed to a relentless search for normative content and, consequently, for those fundamental values without which there is no obligation in the law but only the fact of obedience.

In institutional terms this presents a constitutional court with the following dilemma. It must guard the constitutional foundations of government, but it may do so only within the narrow confines of disputes initiated by the litigating parties. As a rule, it must decide the case before it, though full knowledge and experience is always lacking. It is obligated to maintain the self-critical development of the law, yet it cannot avoid legitimating the values which its decisions predicate. It is a leader of opinion on constitutional values; however, as Bickel says, "it must lead opinion, not merely impose its own."[176] Disputes must be settled, and critical discussion must continue.

How is this dilemma to be bridged? For Bickel,[177] the only solution can be for the court to decline to exercise the jurisdiction which is given. He sees the judicial process, as does Wechsler, solely in terms of fully principled decisions. The "paradox of all paradoxes ... is that the Court may only decide concrete cases and may not pronounce general principles at large; but it may decide a constitutional issue only on the basis of general principle."[178] Or, put another way, constitutional adjudication must be principled because it is binding; it is, however, in large part binding because it is principled.[179] And, like Wechsler, Bickel's principles are known and existing, necessarily reaching "far in the minds of men as well as in their immediate conduct, promising application in widening spheres."[180]

175 See text *supra*, p. 121ff.

176 Bickel, *The Least Dangerous Branch*, 239 (1962).

177 Despite appearances, it should be emphasized, Bickel is not concerned primarily with the search for knowledge through judicial decision. Instead, he tends to gloss over this aspect and concentrate on the single tension between principle and expediency in judicial review, i.e., the ability of a constitutional court to get "just" principles accepted. As a result, he presumes to know from the start which principles are "just."

178 *Ibid.*, p. 247.

179 *Ibid.*, p. 203.

180 *Ibid.*

By "principle" is meant general propositions, . . . organizing ideas of universal validity in the given universe of a culture and a place, ideas that are often grounded in ethical and moral presuppositions.[181]

Unlike Wechsler, on the other hand, Bickel contends that the requirement of principled decisions may dictate judicial inaction where the public is not prepared to accept the principle urged upon it. Should the Court, nevertheless, attempt to decide such cases, it must either risk jeopardizing its authority or, apparently, choose a false principle and unwarrantedly legitimate governmental acts in the eyes of the nation. For him, the judicial error in *Plessy* v. *Ferguson*,[182] which legitimated the state policy of segregated accomodations on railways, is not simply that the Court decided wrongly but that it decided at all![183] It not only decided, it further legitimated across-the-board the now infamous principle of "separate but equal." That decision, he concludes, "was no more defensible on principle then than it is now."[184] Instead, the Court should have refused to decide the case on some procedural ground, made clear that it was staying its hand and not legitimating, and given the political processes relatively free play.[185] Where principle is the sole measure of the judicial process, therefore, the legitimating aspect of judicial decisions often would require total judicial inaction on the dispute.

Such a view, however, greatly overestimates the sovereign sphere of judicial knowledge. "We do not," cautions Cardozo,[186] "pick our rules of law full-blossomed from the trees." As was pointed out above,[187] the formulation of principle is typically a late stage in the judicial treatment of a problem. To make this the prerequisite for judicial activity is to abandon the creative search for purpose which is the heart of the judicial process. Not judicial abstinence, but judicial engagement is the essence of this search.

Indeed, the history of the School Segregation litigation is a case in point. Neither *a priori* nor even on the basis of limited experience could the *Plessy* Court have ascertained whether "separate but equal" school facilities were compatible with the Equality Clause of the Fourteenth Amendment. *A priori,* a society *conceivably could* so develop that segrated schools were compatible with the ideals of a democratic society. And they certainly are not "inherently unequal," as the Supreme Court concludes in *Brown* v.

[181] *Ibid.*, p. 199.
[182] 163 U.S. 537 (1896).
[183] *Ibid.*, pp. 71 and 197.
[184] *Ibid.*, p. 71.
[185] *Ibid.*, pp. 70–72.
[186] Cardozo, *The Nature of the Judicial Process,* 103 (1921).
[187] See text *supra,* pp. 115–118.

Board of Education.[188] In many ways cultural autonomy is a recognized and legitimate value of a pluralistic society. Rather, segregated schools in American society proved over time to be a legally sanctioned institution[189] which operated oppressively, and without demonstrable state justification, on a racial minority.[190] This knowledge was not obtained through a disengaged judicial watching-and-waiting, but through a half century of litigation and judicial experience.[191] Only the results of "law-in-action," in the light of the maturing ideals of distributive justice, could determine in the end the concrete content of such broad constitutional provisions as the Equality Clause.

The lesson of *Plessy* is not so much that the Court decided wrongly, for infallibility tends to be a reoccurring phenomenon of judges and men alike. Nor is the difficulty, as Bickel would have it, that the Court decided the issue at all, for case decision is a primary source of judicial knowledge. The lesson of *Plessy* is that the Court too readily decided on general principles – principles so general that it was willing to draw analogies from every walk of life.[192] Instead of carefully narrowing the reasoning to the specific facts of the case, and of pointing out the uncertainties of the social values at stake, it raised "separate but equal" to a general constitutional standard. (Yet this is precisely what Bickel and Wechsler would have the Court do, except of course the principle espoused should be a "right" principle!) The Court's error, therefore, was the sin of pride: its opinion is burnished with uncritical and selfrighteous declarations of principle.[193] By its uncritical attitude, the Court contributed directly to an ideology of race relations which soothed the conscience of a nation for half a century.

The *Plessy* Decision is a paradigm case of why the judiciary must actively

188 *Brown* v. *Board of Education,* 347 U.S. 483, 495 (1954), reversing the doctrine in *Plessy* v. *Ferguson,* 163 U.S. 537 (1896).

189 The 14th Amendment applies only to "state action."

190 See the opinion drafted for the school segregation cases by Professor Pollak, "Racial Discrimination and Judicial Integrity: A Reply to Professor Wechsler," 108 *U. Pa. L. Rev.*, 1, 24–30 (1959).

191 See the conclusion of Rosenblum, *Law as a Political Instrument,* 38–69 (1955).

192 The Court points to social practice and laws concerning theater audiences, intermarriage and educational facilities. 163 U.S. 544f. This decision demonstrates well the pitfalls of letting the law be guided simply by the mores of the day, a view often espoused by analytical positivists.

193 By comparison, as Edmond Cahn points out, the *Brown* decision (cited *supra,* n. 188) and its companion case, *Bolling* v. *Sharpe,* 347 U.S., 497 (1954), were commendably bland. "Very wisely [Chief Justice Warren] declined the opportunity – one may say the temptation – to indulge in democratic rhetoric. There is not a word of reproach or provocation in either opinion. To his credit, the Chief Justice was less concerned with getting into the anthologies than with presenting the country with a model of rational calm." Cahn, *Confronting Injustice,* 330 (1966).

engage in decision-making, but scrupulously avoid "overcommitting the future."[194] Both can be accomplished by reasoning which is tailored closely to the facts of the case, yet critically aware of its underlying value premises. This means, in the biting words of Thurman Arnold, that "the opinion which 'illumines' the largest possible area of the law is not necessarily the wisest opinion."[195] Not only may it embarrass the court at a later time, it also may cut off discussion of crucial issues. The vaulting principles of Wechsler and Bickel reflect admirable goals, but goals must not be confused with the concrete articulation of normative content. Once clothed with the aura of constitutionality, principles tend to carry their own narcotic. Having decided in terms of principle, a moral is at stake. Judges are not then so easily moved to a candid reconsideration of their decisions in the light of cumulating experience.

Moreover, by reaching beyond the case at hand, general principles are in danger of losing contact with the conflicting values at stake. The more abstract the judicial reasoning, the less is knowledge informed by experience. In concentrating on the concrete problem of the case, on the other hand,

> there is real water in the cup and its presence there has put real lives at stake. That is why it is fitting that judges should whenever possible shy away from answers to suppositious cases; human wisdom is on its mettle only where there is a practical risk, which imports responsibility and the felt burden of a personal involvement.[196]

This is not simply a question of whether to follow a pragmatic rather than a systematic, or an inductive rather than a deductive approach to judicial decision. Rather, as Radbruch observes: it rightly emphasizes, "that the concrete necessity of deciding an actual case calls forth the creative energies of a judge to a much greater extent than occurs for the legislature in the formulation of a general rule of law."[197] That is to say that, when real issues are at stake, judicial decisions have "an actuality and a concrete character"

[194] The phrase was coined by Braden, "The Search for Objectivity in Constitutional Law," 57 *Yale L. J.*, 571, 577 (1947–48).

[195] Arnold, "Professor Hart's Theology," 73 *Harv. L. Rev.*, 1298, 1311f (1959–60).

[196] Cahn, *The Moral Decision: Right and Wrong in the Light of American Law*, 19 (1955).

[197] Radbruch, *Der Geist des Englischen Rechts*, 53 (4th ed. 1956). "The professor, the man of letters," says Holmes, "gives up one-half of life that his protected talent may grow and flower in peace. But to make up your mind at your peril upon a living question, for purposes of action, calls upon your whole nature." "Law in Science and Science in Law," 12 *Harv. L. Rev.*, 443, 452 (1899).

which abstract opinions can never have.[198] By trimming reasoning to the specific facts of the case, therefore, the court avoids the dangers of overgeneralization. This not only maximizes the responsible search for knowledge, but also constitutes the first line of judicial self-restraint.

A second and closely related mode of judicial self-restraint lies in the ability of courts to emphasize the *negative* rather than the positive aspect of legal knowledge. This approach is particularly valuable when very broad or new concepts of law are in question. In this way, for instance, the Federal Constitutional Court has attempted to move beyond a purely formal construction of the Equality Clause in Article 3 of the German Basic Law, without at the same time preempting the substantive question of distributive justice. In its Decision of December 17, 1953, it set out the boundaries of judicial review as follows:

> The principle of equality offers the Federal Constitutional Court no possibility of reviewing a statute from the viewpoint of "universal justice" and thereby substituting its own view of justice for that of the legislator. Rather, that principle leaves open to the legislator a wide area of discretion. The Federal Constitutional Court can only determine whether the outer limits of this area have been overstepped, and may not determine whether the legislator has in particular instances found the most suitable, the "most rational", or the "most just" solution . . . . If the solution adopted by the legislator is nonetheless compatible with the principle of equality, then it does not matter whether another more just or more reasonable solution would have been possible or would better accord with that principle.[199]

This "negative" approach – reflected not so much, for instance, in the notion of equality as of discriminatory and arbitrary acts – recognizes the obvious limits of judicial knowledge. For the meaning of justice is often clearest and best appreciated in its negation. It emphasizes, moreover, the necessary scope on such questions for legislative and executive prerogative. The search for justice can never be, either in theory or practice, the monopoly of the judiciary.

Such an approach places a heavy reliance on empirical knowledge gathered from experience and observation. In the law, as Edmond Cahn points out, general propositions "must ultimately succeed or fail in terms of their verifiable consequences . . . ."[200] An important vital source of this empirical

[198] Fitzmaurice, "Some Problems Regarding the Formal Sources of International Law," in *Symbolae Verzijl*, 153, 172 (1958).

[199] 3 BVerfG 162, 182 (1953). Cf. Garlan, *Legal Realism and Justice*, 121ff (1941).

[200] Cahn, *The Sense of Injustice* 12 (1949). Friedrich, "Justice: The Just Political Act," in Friedrich and Chapman (eds.), *Nomos VI: Justice*, 24, esp. 30 and 39f (1964); and his *The Philosophy of Law in History Perspective*, 199 (Paperback 1963).

guidance is what Cahn calls the "sense of injustice," being "not a state but a process, not a condition but an action." [201] It embraces those sympathetic reactions operative in the law, such as demands for equal treatment, proper desert of a wrongdoer, human dignity, conscientious adjudication and the fulfillment of common expectations. Without the discipline and information of reason, the "sense of injustice" would be little more than "the illiterate gropings of animal faith" or a supine reflection of the prevailing mores.[202] Through reason enlarged by the critical judgment of society, however, this empathy becomes the nerve and "cogent natural drive" toward a progressively better legal order.[203] The "sense of injustice" reveals the "active, vital and experimental" nature of the search for justice.[204] It permits a court to engage responsibly in decision-making without possessing the unpossessable, namely, a final knowledge of justice.

Maintaining the judicial search for knowledge may require further a calculated response to other branches of government. The objective is to avoid a precipitate or unnecessary foreclosure of discussion on critical issues. The German Federal Constitutional Court, for instance, has waited many months and even several years before handing down its decisions on certain cases. This apparent intentional delay, though never characterized as such, permits the Court to become better informed through the cumulation of a broad range of cases and comments on the question.[205] It may also permit the court to defer for a time to the political process with the view of avoiding an unwise or untimely judicial decision.[206]

201 *Ibid.*, p. 13. As to the "sense of injustice," see also Garlan, *Legal Realism and Justice*, 121ff (1941).

202 Cahn, *id.*, p. 26f. See also the criticism of J. Stone, *Human Law and Human Justice*, 316–321 (1965), as to the limits on the "sense of injustice."

203 Cahn, *id.*, p. 27.

204 *Ibid.*, p. 13.

205 See, e.g., the *Handwerk* Decisions in 13 BVerfG (1963), where the Constitutional Court delayed its judgments four to five years after presentation of argument and while the cases accumulated. See also the delay in the more recent church taxation decisions. The same result is achieved by the United States Supreme Court through use of its certiorari discretion.

206 In the delicate sphere of political controversies, the Federal Constitutional Court delayed its decision on the constitutionality of the E.D.C. Treaty some months in order to await the outcome of the political process within its own and the French legislature. Furthermore, in the Communist Party Case (5 BVerfG 85 (1956)), the Court delayed its decision five years before declaring the Party unconstitutional, all the while making inofficial inquiries with the government to see if it was really serious in prosecuting the case. The Communist Party had been losing ground rapidly and in all likelihood would have dropped below the five percent clause in the coming years and, therefore, be automatically excluded from the Bundestag. Since the government persisted in pressing its charges, however, the Court was forced finally to render a decision. See, as to both cases, McWhinney, *Constitutionalism in Germany*, 39f and 32–34 (1962).

To avoid unnecessarily foreclosuring discussion, moreover, a constitutional court generally should not determine issues on which the executive or legislature has taken no intentional position, no position at all, or at most only a tentative one. This may be achieved, for instance, by procedural techniques which nullify an act on formal grounds without prejudicing a reconsideration of its substance. This, as Bickel suggests,[207] is true of the delegation of powers doctrine. Though the court does not check the will of the legislature indefinitely, it may still force that body to reconsider the legislation in terms of new means and methods. At the same time, the court has the opportunity, via *obiter dictum,* of voicing its doubts and even offering suggestions on other, more substantive aspects at stake.

At other times, this same objective may better be achieved by the application of a judicial presumption toward legislative intent. Thus, when doubt exists as to the lawful intent or scope of a statute, the court may construe it narrowly to avoid conflicting with an international obligation [208] or construe it in keeping with the meaning of the constitution.[209] Not only does this approach avoid the need to face the constitutional issue which these doubts raise, it also keeps the discussion open for later rehearing and determination should the legislature decide to pursue the matter further. Judicial presumptions of other sorts may better account for certain biases built into a governmental institution. "There are times," observe Professors Wellington and Bickel,[210] when as a practical matter Congress may be able to act if the court does one thing but not if it does another." Where there was doubt, for instance, that the Mann Act, which forbids the interstate transportation of women for purposes of prostitution, was meant also to extend to purposes of polygamy, the narrower view should have been taken. Congress conceivably could always add polygamy to the list of crimes, but not *vice versa*: "can it be thought that any democratically elected institution in our society is free . . . to take action affirmatively to legalize polygamy?"[211]

Finally, there are issues also which reach beyond the proper sphere of judicial knowledge. They form a class of controversies which, says Justice Frankfurter, "do not lend themselves to judicial standards and judicial remedies."[212] In such cases prudence often dictates that courts reject the juris-

[207] See Bickel, *op. cit.* (n. 176), pp. 180f and 201f.

[208] See discussion in text *supra,* p. 35.

[209] See discussion in text *infra,* p. 300f.

[210] Bickel and Wellington, "Legislative Purpose and the Judicial Process," 71 *Harv. L. Rev.*, 1, 17 (1957).

[211] *Ibid.*, p. 17, n. 67.

[212] Justice Frankfurter dissenting, in *Baker* v. *Carr,* 369 U.S. 266, 280 (1962), discussed below.

diction that is given. Such are questions of political expediency, as who gets how much of the economic pie. Due to their very nature, these questions cannot be determined by rules and reason, but must be left to the ephemeral desires of men and the shifting coalitions of social forces. Similarly, the judiciary generally should refrain from determinations on foreign affairs,[213] for these too are governed by complex criteria which must be adaptable to the changing circumstances.

For different reasons, moreover, issues which rise to the level of pure political theory are not fit for judicial decision. A court is no philosopher king. Nor does it have the requisite wisdom to hew out the basic structure and organization of political institutions, or to resolve broad questions of political power, of sovereignty, of "the State as a State."[214] This is the twilight zone of the "political questions" doctrine, where the judiciary possesses neither the experience or insight adequately to deal with the issues, nor the process for appropriating the knowledge which is lacking. An attempt to set standards in spite of this leads the court down the byways of political ideology.

This states one horn of the dilemma facing the Supreme Court in the recent Reapportionment Cases. By taking jurisdiction of the question under the Equal Protection Clause of the 14th Amendment,[215] the Court drew itself into "a piece of political ideology"[216] which would not end till it had determined "what should constitute the proper composition of the legislatures of the fifty States."[217] In the lead-off decision of *Baker* v. *Carr,* Justice Frankfurter dissenting warned:

[213] This discretion as to foreign affairs, however, must not be confused with the judicial duty to apply the governing principles and treaties of international law.

[214] See *Pacific States Tel. & Tel. Co.* v. *Oregon,* 223 U.S. 118, 150 (1912), dismissing for want of jurisdiction a writ of error attacking a state license-tax statute enacted by an initiative procedure, on the claim that this mode of legislation was inconsistent with a Republican Form of Government and violated the Equal Protection Clause and other federal guarantees. The "essentially political nature" of the claim advanced, said the Court, lay in its assault "not on the tax as a tax, but on the State as a State."

[215] *Baker* v. *Carr,* 369 U.S. 186 (1962), reversing the lower court's decision that it lacked jurisdiction of the subject matter and that the complaint, attacking the Tennessee Apportionment Act of 1901 as in violation of the 14th Amendment, failed to state a claim upon which relief could be granted. Moreover, the Court found that plaintiffs had standing to challenge the Act and that the dispute itself was justiciable, i.e. did not fall within the purview of the "political questions" doctrine.

[216] Conclusion of Justice Harlan dissenting, in *Reynolds* v. *Sims,* 377 U.S. 589, 590 (1964), a sequel to the *Baker* v. *Carr* decision.

[217] Justice Frankfurter dissenting, in *Baker* v. *Carr,* 369 U.S. 269.

Even assuming the indispensable intellectual disinterestedness on the part of judges in such matters, they do not have accepted legal standards or criteria or even reliable analogies to draw upon for making judicial judgments. To charge courts with the task of accommodating the incommensurable factors of policy that underlie these mathematical puzzles is to attribute, however flatteringly, omnicompetence to judges.[218]

Nevertheless, in subsequent cases, the Court went on to determine that "our fundamental ideas of democratic government" demand the undiluted standard of equal population districts for members to *each* house of the State legislatures.[219] By "the constitutionally frail tautology that "equal" means "equal," [220] no room was left for that multitude of non-legal factors, such as geography, economics and urban-rural conflict, which have always influenced electoral apportionment. To equate the whole of democracy with majority-rule elections, Professor Shapiro criticizes, "represents naive political philosophy, bad political theory, and no political science."[221]

Arguably, on the other hand, the Court had to take jurisdiction under the circumstances. Given the practical impossibility for the majority of voters to change the existing legislative apportionment, was not judicial intervention the only real alternative?[222] Could the Court simply ignore a crazy quilt pattern of apportionment which, it concluded, "reflects *no* policy, but simply arbitrary and capricious action?"[223] Perhaps not, but neither has it the wisdom to choose among competing theories of political philosophy lying at the

[218] *Ibid.*, p. 268.

[219] Thus, in *Wesberry* v. *Sanders,* 376 U.S. 1 (1964), the standard "one man, one vote" for congressional elections, which the Court concluded was part of "our fundamental ideas of democratic government," was derived from a tenuous reading of American constitutional history and from the uncertain constitutional requirement that Representatives of the House be chosen "by the People of the several States." By virtue of the Equal Protection Clause of the 14th Amendment, this standard then was transplanted to both houses of the State legislatures, in *Reynolds* v. *Sims,* 377 U.S. 533 (1964); *WMCA, Inc. v. Lomenzo,* 377 U.S. 633 (1964); *Maryland Comm. for Fair Representation v. Tawes,* 377 U.S. 656 (1964); *Davis v. Mann,* 377 U.S. 678 (1964); *Roman* v. *Sincock,* 377 U.S. 695 (1964); *Lucas* v. *Forty-Fourth Gen. Assembly,* 377 U.S. 713 (1964).

[220] Justice Harlan dissenting, in *Reynolds* v. *Simms,* 377 U.S. 590. Just how frail this tautology is in historical perspective is well established in the dissenting opinions of Justice Harlan, *ibid.*, and of Justice Frankfurter, in *Baker* v. *Carr,* 369 U.S. 299–324.

[221] Martin Shapiro, *Law and Politics in the Supreme Court,* 250f (1964). See also Bickel, *Politics and the Warren Court,* 188 and 197 (1965).

[222] See the concurring opinion of Justice Clark, in *Baker* v. *Carr,* 369 U.S. 259, which points out not only that corrective state action was impractical under the circumstances, but also that although remedial action by Congress was theoretically possible, "to date, Congress has never undertaken such a task in any State."

[223] *Baker* v. *Carr,* 369 U.S. 226.

base of electoral reform. Indeed, contrary to the reasoning of the Court, this was not a classical problem of equal protection in a democracy, for not a minority but the majority of voters was the object of discrimination.[224] Their relief is ordinarily at the polls, refashioning the system to become responsive to their views. If by fit of circumstance the system itself has become subject to "a legislative strait jacket,"[225] then that strait jacket has to be broken and the sovereign prerogative returned to the citizens.

Not judicially legislated electoral standards but responsive procedures of constitutional amendment or of initiative and referendum were the demand of the day. The Court might have forced this issue, by focusing on the procedural deadlock rather than on the pernicious effects which it wrought.[226] Then an informed and civically active electorate could bring about the needed changes. If democratic government is the operative principle, then in the last instance the electorate must be left the veto on decisions of this magnitude. This principle demands judicial humility of an order so unmistakably expressed by Justice Holmes: "if my fellow citizens want to go to Hell I will help them. It's my job."[227]

At various points throughout the judicial process, therefore, the search for purpose in the law requires the exercise of judicial restraint. Depending on the circumstances, courts are equipped with a variety of techniques to make this possible, ranging from those of gradualism and delay to those of avoidance and, ultimately, to the more permanent doctrinal means for withholding decision altogether. When the court has reached the outer limits of judicial knowledge, only such restraint can avoid the imposition of a judicial ideology which stifles self-critical reasoning as well as legal development itself.

[224] As Justice Clark's opinion reveals, *ibid.*, p. 253, sixty percent of the voters of Tennessee elected only one-third of the State Senators.

[225] See Justice Clark's opinion, *ibid.*, p. 259.

[226] Whether the issue could have been, and should be, forced within the context of the Reapportionment Cases is of course open to some question. The Court would have had considerable leverage, however, since it could require elections-at-large until satisfactory procedures had been introduced. A similar approach apparently would have been acceptable to Justice Clark, since he dissented from the majority opinion in *Lucas v. Forty-Fourth Gen. Assembly of Colorado*, 377 U.S. 741, 742f, reasoning that Colorado's apportionment had been "adopted by the majority vote of every political subdivision in the State."

[227] Holmes, in *Holmes-Laski Letters*, vol. 1, p. 249 (1953). Further, as he states in *Holmes-Pollock Letters*, vol. 1, p. 163 (1941): "[T]he crowd if it knew more wouldn't want what it does – but that is immaterial."

II.

The second institutional constraint on the exercise of judicial power stems from the continuing tension in the law between reason and fiat. In the search for authority, the court's capacity to reason persuasively is constantly challenged by both the inherent and the established limits of fiat.[228] While inherent limits are peculiar to the very nature of human knowledge and thus to the judge himself, the latter are generated by the force of established values and institutions. These build the social consensus at the basis of all law, especially of law with constitutional proportions. Certainly in this respect, public law and international law closely correspond. In contrast to the relatively consolidated field of private law, where individual choice is widely respected through reciprocal modes of agreement, constitutional law organizes, channels and limits political power by common aims.[229] Where fundamental issues must be settled by common aims, authoritative decisions must necessarily rely on an active and current consensus.[230] Depending on the question at stake, as Section 5 of Chapter I has outlined for the European Communities, this consensus embraces several facets, including common procedures or institutions, substantive values as well as the beneficial effects which common policies call forth. Absent at least a tacit or potential consensus on fundamental issues, even the most valid exercise of judicial competence may be in vain. The common good, toward which law must constantly strive, "is an accepted and not a decreed good."[231]

For this reason, society may simply not be ready to believe that judicial decisions on fundamental values – however correct in terms of existing rules of law – are purely matters of legal interpretation. "A fundamental political tension," observes Charles de Visscher,[232] "cannot be appeased by inviting the antagonists to enact constitutional norms for their future relations." Neither logic, system nor reasoned principles can fully grasp the process of constitutional construction. At times, the logic of the constitution may be "the language of political battle."[233] Depending on the degree to which dis-

[228] See discussion in text *supra*, p. 129ff.

[229] This distinction, which is frequently emphasized in the public law literature both in America and on the Continent, has been most recently articulated by Fuller, "Forms and Limits of Adjudication," unpublished lecture delivered at The Center for the Study of Democratic Institutions (Santa Barbara, Cal., Dec. 29, 1958); and his "Freedom – A Suggested Analysis," 68 *Harv. L. Rev.*, 1305, 1316ff (1955).

[230] Cf. Miller and Howell, "The Myth of Neutrality in Constitutional Adjudication," 27 *U. Chi. L. Rev.*, 661, 689ff (1959–60).

[231] Ch. de Visscher, *Theory and Reality in Public International Law*, 71 (1957).

[232] *Ibid.*, p. 108.

[233] Miller and Howell, *op. cit.*, p. 689.

puted values are highly politicized, the judiciary may be drawn willy-nilly into the play of political forces and governmental powers.[234] Where political processes become unresponsive or deadlocked, the battleground may shift to the judiciary. This happens as a matter of course, for instance, in the Federal Republic of Germany where abstract norm control is a central feature of judicial review; having lost the battle in Parliament, a political party or agency of government may carry the matter directly to the Federal Constitutional Court.[235] This is no less true for minority groups in the United States, whose only feasible recourse against the majority will often be through the courts.[236]

Dissenting opinion, moreover, may reverberate and be amplified through other branches and agencies of government. These institutions, who jealously guard their traditional spheres of power, may see any attempt to curtail their views and prerogatives as a threat to their prestige as well as to their potential effectiveness.[237] This political sensitivity is reflected in the running battles between Congress and the Supreme Court. In such instances, Congressional reaction has taken the various forms of threats, attempts at impeachment, withdrawal of jurisdiction, the political evaluation and selection of Justices and attempts to pack the Court.[238] At times, the President has

234 See Truman, *The Governmental Process,* esp. pp. 488, 495ff (1951); Eichenberger, *Die richterliche Unabhängigkeit als staatsrechtliches Problem,* 133f (1960).

235 For a discussion of this judicial procedure, see discussion in text *supra,* p. 70f. As an example, see the litigation surrounding the adoption of the European Defense Community Treaty, discussed in McWhinney, *Constitutionalism in Germany,* 34–40 (1962); Loewenstein, "The Bonn Constitution and the European Defense Community Treaties," 64 *Yale L. J.,* 805, 809ff (1955); and Weber, "Die Vereinbarkeit des Verteidigungsbeitrags mit dem Grundgesetz," 78 *Arch. öff. R.,* 129 (1952).

236 The relation of interest groups to their access to the judicial process as well as to the functioning of the political process is discussed, e.g., by Murphy and Pritchett, *Courts, Judges and Politics,* Ch. 8 (1961); Vose, *Caucasians Only* (1959); and Schubert, *Constitutional Politics,* 69–88 (1960).

237 See Murphy, *Congress and the Court,* 257f (1962); Eichenberger, *op. cit.* (n. 234), p. 148.

238 See Murphy, *id.,* generally, for an analysis of the tension between Congress and the Supreme Court over the years. He concludes that in the exercise of judicial review over Congressional legislation, the Court has followed a pattern in periods of extreme tension: first, an advance in judicial policy, followed by a period of severe criticism by Congress coupled with threats of remedial and/or retaliatory legislative action, and finally a tactical (but only tactical!) retreat of the Court for a time. The latest example of this occurred in the 1950's, when Congress, stirred by a series of decisions on racial integration and national security (among others), barely failed to pass legislation curbing the Court's basic authority. *Ibid.,* pp. 245–47. With one exception (in 1802), however, "it is typical of previous Court conflicts that the President and Congress never joined together to press a serious assault on judicial power." *Ibid.,* p. 261f.

withheld his support of judicial decisions.[239] And, more recently, it has become abundantly clear the extent to which the lower federal and state courts can frustrate the spirit of Supreme Court decisions or delay their execution.[240] Even the short history of the Federal Constitutional Court of Germany reveals political influence in the selection of judges as well as the sensitivity of the Bundestag to judicial decisions.[241] Finally, it is a testimony to such political realities that the power of judicial review, which was not explicitly authorized in the United States and Weimar Constitutions, was established first in full support of federal legislative power.[242] Possessed of neither the purse nor the sword, the judiciary is also engaged in an "art of the possible."

The hasty formulation of general principles or perfection of normative content, therefore, may as well raise issues that tear a nation in two as lasting standards toward which men and government may aspire. Thus,

239 President Jackson flouted the decision of the Supreme Court, written by Chief Justice Marshall, in *Worcester* v. *Georgia* (1832), refusing to take action against the State of Georgia for disregarding the Treaty rights of Indians. Jackson was reported to have said: "John Marshall has made his decision, now let him enforce it." He was unwilling to allow the Court order to precipitate a national crisis. See Warren, *The Supreme Court in United States History,* vol. II, p. 218f. (1922).

At the outbreak of the Civil War, moreover, President Lincoln refused to execute the habeas corpus order of Chief Justice Taney in *Ex Parte Merryman,* Fed. Cases No. 9,487 (1861). See Murphy, *op. cit.*, pp. 31–33.

240 See Note, "Evasions of Supreme Court Mandates in Cases Remanded to State Courts since 1941," 67 *Harv. L. Rev.*, 1251–59 (1954).

241 The controversy surrounding the European Defense Community litigation, mentioned *supra* note 235, was accompanied by an attempt of the Adenauer Government to reduce the majority necessary for the election of Justices to the Federal Constitutional Court from a two-thirds to a simple majority. Although the Court's jurisdiction, unlike that of the United States Supreme Court, is firmly grounded in the Constitution, the Justices are elected only for a term of 8 years and not for life. The influence of political views in the selection of these Justices is readily admitted. See, e.g., Friesenhahn, "Aufgabe und Funktion des Bundesverfassungsgerichts," 6 *Aus Politik und Zeitgeschichte,* 3, 13 (Feb. 10, 1965).

See also the outspokenly critical attitude of the Adenauer Government vis-à-vis the Constitutional Court following the *Fernseh* Decision. Discussed by Meyer, "Die Reaktion auf das Fernsehurteil: Elemente der Verfassungswirklichkeit," in *Festschrift Ernst Friesenhahn,* 267 (Bonn Univ. mimeo. 1961).

242 The position of the Supreme Court in *Marbury* v. *Madison* (establishing judicial review) is an example of judicial triumph in a moment of weakness. See Kelly and Harbison, *The American Constitution,* 226–232 (1955). In the Weimar Republic, judicial review was first established by the decision of the *Reichtgericht in Zivilsachen,* vol. III, p. 320 (Nov. 4, 1925), in which the Court reviewed and affirmed the reevaluation law (Aufwertungsgesetzgebung) under the property rights guarantee of the Constitution. See Friesenhahn, "Die Verfassungsgerichtsbarkeit in der Bundesrepublik Deutschland," in Mosler (ed.), *Constitutional Review in the World Today,* 89, 96–98 (1962).

during the heated debate over slavery that raged the United States in the two decades preceding the Civil War, it was proposed to put the whole slavery question to the Supreme Court for final settlement. Indeed, the Senate passed just such a bill in 1848, but both sides were so fearful that the decision might go against them that it was defeated in the House.[243] Nevertheless, ten years later the Court took the opportunity to decide just such an issue. Although the Court had avoided deciding the matter in a previous case[244] and was on the verge of doing it again,[245] it changed its course and took the bull by its splintered horns.

In *Dred Scott* v. *Sandford,*[246] the Court not only held that the Negro had no rights as a "citizen" under the Constitution, but also marked the previously repealed Missouri Compromise as unconstitutional and a deprivation of property, i.e. of the right to slaves. It thereby nullified absolutely any future attempt to reach agreement between North and South. To the statement of President Buchanan that he would "cheerfully submit," whatever the decision of the Court might be, Horace Greeley retorted: "You may 'cheerfully submit' . . . but not one man who really desires the triumph of freedom over slavery in the territories will do so."[247] This Decision, says Swischer, "played an important part, not in postponing the conflict between the North and the South, but in bringing on the crisis."[248]

Crises of such fundamental proportions of course do not occur every day in constitutional litigation. Indeed, that is what makes judicial review a viable institution. Still, they dramatically demonstrate the potential danger of unbridled optimism over the capacity of a court to dispose authoritatively and finally of all questions of constitutional law properly before it. The possibility of such crises haunt every constitutional system. Thus, in Germany today, the tension between constitutional principle and political expediency have crystallized in the struggle for national reunification. The Basic Law of

243 See Warren, *op. cit.* (n. 239), pp. 480–87.

244 In *Strader* v. *Graham,* 10 How. 82 (1851), the question arose whether a slave taken into a State which the Missouri Compromise had declared to be free could claim his freedom. The Court refused to consider the status of slaves, ruling that this was a matter purely of state law.

245 An opinion, similar to that in *Strader, ibid.,* was apparently being prepared when the majority of the Justices learned that the dissenting opinions would cover broader aspects of Congressional control over slavery in the territories. Further, President Buchanan wrote Justice Grier, urging the Court to decide the case fully on the merits. See Swisher, *Roger B. Taney,* 496–500 (1936).

246 19 How. 393 (1857). For Background of the case, see Warren, *op. cit.* (n. 239), vol. III, Ch. 26.

247 See Swisher, *op. cit.* (n. 245), p. 502.

248 Swisher, *American Constitutional Development,* 251 (1943).

the Federal Republic, being by express stipulation a transitional constitutional order, politically commits and legally obligates the government "to seek energetically the unity of Germany."[249] And yet, without exception, governmental acts are bound by an extensive catalogue of individual and civil rights[250] which, if applied strictly, could well thwart politically desirable steps toward breaking down the barriers between the Federal Republic and the East Zone. Serious steps in this direction, entailing a demilitarization of the western zonal boundary, for instance, could scarcely be taken without guaranteeing, if only temporarily, the East Zone against a population flight and acts of subversion. Any intergovernmental agreement of understanding designed to return refugees and political fugitives to the East Zone government, however, would certainly impinge upon those fundamental rights in the Basic Law guaranteeing political asylum and the free movement of *all* Germans throughout the Federal Republic.[251]

In the event of litigation, such delicate issues of state diplomacy would appear to reach well into the realm of "political questions." In fact, the Federal Constitutional Court has recognized that the government must be allowed wide discretion in negotiating treaties which regulate the transition of occupied territory.[252] This was the subject of the Saar Treaty Decision, where the Court was called upon to determine whether a transitional agreement with the Western Powers, in particular France, was constitutional even though it did not fully secure to the Saar population certain of the fundamental rights safeguarded by the Basic Law.[253] While granting that "*every* exercise of State power in the Federal Republic of Germany is bound by the

[249] KPD Decision, 5 BVerfG 85, 127f (1956), citing the Preamble of the Basic Law.

[250] Saar Treaty Decision, 4 BVerfG 157, 169 (1955), citing Art. 20(3). These rights include not only those presented in the first 19 Articles of the Basic Law, but also by general consensus those contained in Articles 33, 38, 101(1) sentence 2, 103 and 104.

[251] Basic Law, Arts. 11 and 16(2) sent. 2. As to the scope of Art. 11, see 2 BVerfG 266, 277 (1953).

[252] Although the Basic Law does not state explicitly what the proper territorial boundaries of a reunited Germany shall be, the Federal Constitutional Court has interpreted this to be the boundaries of the German Reich as of December 31, 1937. Saar Treaty Decision, 4 BVerfG 164. The new agreement with Poland, if ratified by the German Parliament, would restrict somewhat the western boundaries of Germany.

[253] Although other violations of the Basic Law were alleged, the Court admitted only that the rights guaranteed in Article 20(2) concerning self-determination had not been fully realized by the Saar Treaty. These rights are especially protected, for Article 79(3) forbids their amendment.

[254] 4 BVerfG 169. Indeed, the Court stated that even the authorized discretion of the government ended, "where undeniable fundamental principles of the Basic Law were clearly violated," namely, if the essence of a civil or individual right (Art. 19(2)) or one of the principles of federal organization, the division of powers and democratic government (Art. 79(3)) were infringed. 4 BVerfG 169f.

Basic Law,"[254] the Court went on to point out that

political treaties, which reduce step-by-step a system of occupation without replacing it at the time with a fully new and permanent system, move far into a sphere which for a constitutional court is non-justiciable.[255]

Nevertheless, as the prevailing German view would have it,[256] the Court chose not to abstain from reviewing and deciding the question. Instead, it went on to develop a constitutional formula of political expediency which accounted for the lop-sided bargaining leverage of France as the occupying ally. In light of the political circumstances at the time, the Court was willing to view the agreement as constitutional so far as "the measures provided for by the Treaty were undertaken with the intention of . . . making it as constitutional as was politically possible, at least inasmuch as this was politically attainable."[257] This had been done and the Treaty was constitutional.

The Federal Constitutional Court, therefore, has avoided the uncompromising course of the Supreme Court in the *Dred Scott* Decision. Moreover, it has expressly recognized the tension between principle and expediency in delicate issues of natural policy. In doing so, however, it chose to justify rather than merely tolerate a result which by its own admission was largely beyond its proper sphere of control. This has the unwholesome effect of legitimating political expediency. Though expediency often may be necessary for viable government, it is quite another, self-defeating judicial step to incorporate it expressly into the constitution.[258]

This is the thrust of Bickel's thesis. Democratic government under law, he says, pulls in opposing directions.

If it carries the elements of explosion, it doesn't contain a critical mass of them. Yet if he critical mass is not to be reached, there must be an accommodation, a degree of concord between the diverging elements. Having been checked, should the people persist having been educated, should the people insist, must they not win over every fundamental principle save one – which is the principle that they must win? Are we sufficiently certain of the permanent validity of any other

[255] 4 BVerfG 169.

[256] See discussion in text *supra*, p. 154f.

[257] 4 BVerfG 169, also 170 and 178.

[258] Cf. *Korematsu* v. *United States*, 323 U.S. 214 (1944), where the Supreme Court, faced with the question of whether to pronounce on the constitutionality of a wartime exclusion order against Japanese-Americans, chose to condone the act essentially as a matter of military necessity. In his sharp dissent, Justice Jackson wrote: "But if we cannot confine military expedients by the Constitution, neither would I distort the Constitution to approve all that the military may deem expedient." *Ibid.*, p. 244f.

principle to be ready to impose it against a consistent and determined majority and could we do so for long? [259]

Given this alternative, Bickel's answer is a clear "No." A constitutional court, he concludes, "should declare as law only such principles as will – in time, but in a rather immediate foreseeable future – gain general assent." [260] For this reason, the timing of judicial decisions becomes crucial. Timing, however, is not of its own making, but an opportunity which a court prudently must utilize in the course of cases whose character and sequence depends wholly on party initiative. Faced then perchance with the tension between constitutional principle and public opinion, the judge often must find ways of issue avoidance or risk a loss of authority. "No society, certainly not a large and heterogeneous one," admonishes Bickel, "can fail in time to explode if it is deprived of the arts of compromise, if it knows no ways of muddling through." [261]

For Bickel, the arts of compromise permit the court "to evolve, to preserve, protect and defend principle." Indeed, the rendering of "principled adjudications" is the ultimate judicial function. Accordingly, a court may legitimate governmental acts on principle, it may also strike them down on principle. Or, it may do neither. It may "stay its hand" when the political processes are so deadlocked that principled judgment would not be viable, and in this way "maintain itself in the tension between principle and expediency."

If the institutions at last insist upon a course of action that cannot be accommodated to principle, it is no part of the function of the Court to bless it, however double-negatively.[262]

To this end, Bickel focuses on those judicial devices which "allow leeway to expediency without abandoning principle . . . and make possible a principled government." Such means of judicial non-decision range from the built-in discretion of certiorari procedure to the dismissal of appeals as well as denial of jurisdiction for lack of standing to sue and for lack of ripeness of

[259] Bickel, *The Least Dangerous Branch*, 27f (1962).

[260] *Ibid.*, p. 239. The importance as well as the perfidy of this kind of judicial assessment can be seen in the 1954 School Segregation Decisions. Due to national and presidential indifference in the months thereafter, there existed the real possibility that these Decisions would be frustrated in application and left to die. Not until the "Little Rock" incident in 1957, according to Bickel, was the national conscience seared to the point of supporting a serious effort at enforcement. *Ibid.*, Ch. 6.

[261] *Ibid.*, p. 64.

[262] *Ibid.*, pp. 188 and 69.

the issue for judicial determination; yet they go beyond these to encompass interpretational presumptions and specialized doctrine. The "political questions" doctrine, for instance, is simply the epitome of judicial self-restraint. To the extent that these devices necessarily depend on the exercise of judicial discretion, they are justified "as lesser rational alternatives to an otherwise unavoidable principled judgment, which would in turn be unwise in the given circumstances."[263] Their justification is ultimately the requirement of principled judicial decision.

Unfortunately, Bickel's whole concern is principled decision, though these principles to be viable must also have general public acceptance. However correctly he senses the tension at work in a constitutional democracy, his analysis greatly exaggerates the dichotomy between judicial opinion and public opinion, between principle and consent. He not only overestimates the sovereign sphere of judicial knowledge, as already discussed in the preceding section, but further ignores that judicial opinion – stripped of all legal doctrine – so often reflects the value discord in society. Judicial decision frequently involves several, conflicting values or principles, so that it embodies a compromise as much within the court as between the court and the public. As Chief Justice Stone replied to the criticism of an academic friend: "I should have preferred to have written your opinion than the one which will actually appear in the books. Had I done so I should have been in a minority of two or three, instead of a majority of six."[264]

As a result, given the demands for judicial compromise both within and without the court, the search for authority in the law may be served quite as well or better by reducing the size and blatancy of the judicial response as by rendering no opinion at all. Such is the nature of the *per curiam* opinion and of deliberate ambiguity in decisional reasoning, which permit the court to limit its exposure on controversial principles while mustering support on the basis of the decisional results.[265] Here brevity and ambiguity, like the

[263] *Ibid.*, pp. 71 and 206.

[264] Mason, *Harlan Fiske Stone*, 308 (1956). Cf. Murphy, "Courts as Small Groups," 79 *Harv. L. Rev.*, 1565, 1569 (1966), who concludes: "What may seem inscrutable wisdom to the traditional case analyst may only be deliberate ambiguity designed to accommodate by its very vagueness conflicting doctrines." Cf. further Murphy, "Marshaling the Court: Leadership, Bargaining and the Judicial Process," 29 *U. Chi. L. Rev.*, 640 (1962); and Arnold, "Professor Hart's Theology," 73 *Harv. L. Rev.*, 1298, 1311–13 (1960).

[265] See Deutsch, "Neutrality, Legitimacy, and the Supreme Court: Some Intersections Between Law and Political Science," 20 *Stan. L. Rev.*, 169, 219–221 and 228f (1968), who points out that Bickel's emphasis on principled decisions blinds him to the utility of the *per curiam* opinion as a mediating device. Curiously enough, Bickel affirms the sparse reasoning of the School Segregation Decisions, for "the less said the

devices of total judicial abstinence, also serve the need for consensus in the law.

To a large extent, therefore, the problem and not the premise of constitutional construction is the existence of at least a tacit or potential consensus on normative meaning. This consensus is rooted in the minds of the people as well as the judges, and is reflected most concretely in the major governmental institutions. In a study some years ago,[266] Robert Dahl concluded that the Supreme Court, in combination with the other two governmental branches and the aggregate of minorities which compose them, is part of an alliance of political leadership. His research shows that, against such a coalition, the Court can only delay policies for a relatively short period of time until the natural replacement of justices changes the "old guard." Should it attempt to fight the coalition, as in the Roosevelt era of the 1930's, or to make national policy absent a real or imminent coalition, as in the *Dred Scott* case, it is very likely to undermine its own power and lead to disaster. Working within a coalition, however, it is far from impotent. If the coalition is weak, it may even be able to "make" national policy. Within a coalition, it can always exert a certain influence on the formulation of fundamental values by reaffirming the basic procedures for resolving conflicts and legitimating "not simply the particular or parochial policies of the dominant political alliance, but . . . the basic pattern of behavior required for the operation of a democracy." An important task of a constitutional court, though by no means the whole of it, "is to confer legitimacy on the fundamental policies of the successful coalition."[267]

From an institutional perspective, then, consensus forms both the basis and the limits of judicial authority. Through persuasive reasoning a constitutional court may often strengthen, build on and expand this basis, but only to the extent permitted by the existing coalition and contours of social forces. This is the "aller de concert" in action, which Montesquieu so highly praised. Its success lies not in the application of unyielding principle but in the prudent, conscious and timely deployment of limited judicial power.

less chance of internal disagreement," and the smaller the target on the outside. "In sum, . . . here was a decision which, like a poem, 'should not mean/But be,' and . . . the Court saw this and acted on it." Bickel, *Politics and the Warren Court,* 212 (1965).

[266] Dahl, "Decision-Making in a Democracy: The Supreme Court as a National Policy-Maker," 6 *J. Pub. L.*, 279 (1957). Cf. also Schindler, "Richterliches Prüfungsrecht und politischer Mehrheitswille: Erfahrungen der Vereinigten Staaten – Folgerungen für die Schweiz," 74 *Z. schweiz. R.*, 289, 302ff (N.F. 1955).

[267] *Ibid.*, pp. 293–95. See also Miller and Howell, *op. cit.* (n. 230), p. 683ff, espousing a "purposive jurisprudence" for the Supreme Court.

III.

A third area of judicial self-restraint originates in the search for practicability in the law. The law, as outlined above,[268] is caught between the almost infinite multiplicity of social facts and patterns and the necessity to develop clear and general guides of conduct. This continuing tension in the law gives rise to the third judicial task of articulating workable or manageable rules which guide as they control, orienting on those key points in systems of social action from which adjustments can effectively be made. The well-shaped rule carries its reasoning on its face and, in this way, offers insight into its scope and goal.

Moreover, from an institutional point of view, it may also be argued that the articulation of intelligible and rational concrete rules is a source of judicial power. Especially in the regulation of complex economic activities, such rules are highly prized and their legitimacy grows with their increased rationality: not only are they more useful and accessible to the parties whose conduct they are meant to control, but they also contribute to the predictability and certainty of legal relationships.[269] Nevertheless, given the possibility to formulate clear, general and internally consistent rules, there remain real limits to the judicial capacity to make them workable in practice. What is the nature of these limits and the judicial techniques for meeting them?

At least three types of situations, by the very nature of the judicial process, set real limits to the articulation of manageable rules of law. In each case, the judicial task of rule-shaping becomes not merely difficult, but in some sense useless or self-defeating. For one, a case may be so individualized that it simply does not lend itself to generalization. That is to say, certain dominant or unique but material facts must either be ignored for the sake of the rule or the rule must be compromised for the sake of the facts. This is not only a question of the multiplicity or complexity of the facts involved, though this factor may well play some part. In the field of commercial transactions, for instance, the "equities" of the parties – however appealing – must often be subordinated to the needs of the system lest the system as a whole be undermined. The classical case, in the law of mortgages, pictures the prosperous banker foreclosing on poor widow Jones. While, it may be assumed, the just rule would grant the class of poor widows more lenient treatment, it would also tend to exclude them from the benefit of mortgages in the future. Moreover, granted the one exception, others would likely follow by analogy

[268] See discussion in text *supra*, p. 133ff.

[269] This type of legitimacy would most closely accord with the mode of legality, discussed in text *supra*, p. 175 .

for other needy classes, and the institution of mortgages would either fade away or be replaced by something else which would guarantee creditors the money loaned. "Hard cases," warned Justice Holmes, "make bad law."[270]

On other occasions, however, the incongruous facts cannot be ignored and the rule must necessarily suffer. This is frequently true in international law where, as Charles de Visscher puts it,

> a lack of solidarity and regularity . . . is accounted for now by natural differences, now by the strictly political and individualistic operation of power. This state of affairs becomes manifest in the predominance of particular over general situations. Typical relations, capable of being compared and assembled in common categories by processes of abstraction, are definitely rarer here than in the more evolved disciplines.[271]

The limits involved here, it should be emphasized, arise not simply from sovereign power acting defiantly, but from the difficulty of fairly incorporating the great variety of legitimate state interests in the rule at issue. From the very start and to a much greater degree than the national tribunals, "the international judge is faced with a fundamental question: On what level of generalization or individualization must the actual case before him be approached?"[272]

Secondly, the absence of a relatively stable or controllable context for the operation of a rule also may undermine judicial action. Too many variables, potentially in flux, greatly weaken and often destroy the intelligibility, utility and economy of rules. Not only is a court deprived of the capacity to formulate predictable decisional guidelines, but the case disposed of today may look quite differently tomorrow. A court is not in a position to intervene at will and readjust its prior decisions. Indeed, these decisions are *res judicata*. Nor is it procedurally, or institutionally, equipped to keep cases before it under continuous review and supervision.

In other words, courts are badly suited to treat what Fuller calls "polycentric problems."[273] These problems may be likened to a web: being pulled at one point or clipping one thread affects the configuration as a whole. These problems require overall planning for effective disposition, such as

[270] Dissenting opinion in *No. Sec. Co.* v. *United States,* 193 U.S. 197, 400f (1903). For further exploration of this point, see Radin, *The Law and Mr. Smith,* Ch. VI (1938); and Wasserstrom, *The Judicial Decision*, 140ff and 108ff (1961).

[271] Ch. de Visscher, *Theory and Reality in Public International Law,* 353 (1957).

[272] *Ibid.*

[273] Fuller, "Adjudication and the Rule of Law," 54 *Proc. Amer. Soc. Int. L.,* 1, 3f (1960), adapting a concept developed by Michael Polanyi, in his *The Logic of Liberty* (1951).

allocating air routes between cities or of radio and television channels among the population, drawing up collective bargaining agreements, designing a system of throughways into a metropolitan area, drawing international boundaries complicated by geography and ethnology and reapportioning election districts. The treatment of these problems piecemeal, as isolated issues come before the courts, would be plagued by both a lack of perspective and effective control. It would be like trying to erect a bridge solely from the viewpoint of the angle of two intersecting girders presented at random. Such problems can be treated more appropriately by managerial planning or by the spontaneous mutual adjustment of a free market system than by the relatively constricted perspective and procedures of the judicial process.[274]

Finally, judicial rule-making is limited also by the lack of expertise in many areas of the law. These inadequacies extend beyond the narrow confines of the "judicial notice" doctrine. Where conflict arises in the law, Cardozo remarks with his usual insight,

> a choice will be unintelligent unless we are informed which one of the conflicting rules has proved, in its operation, the most workable and useful. Some of the errors of courts have their origin in imperfect knowledge of the economic and social needs to which a decision will respond. In the complexities of modern life there is a constantly increasing need for resort by the judges to some fact-finding agency which will substitute exact knowledge of factual conditions for conjecture and impression.[275]

Obvious attempts to meet this problem may be seen in the innovatory organization of the independent regulatory commissions in the United States, and in the more judicially orthodox approach of the French Conseil d'Etat. While the former combine in various fashion rule-making, prosecution and adjudication,[276] the latter is both a consultative arm of the executive and the highest tribunal on matters of administrative law.[277] Each develops

[274] See Fuller, *id.*, p. 5. Cf. also Dahl and Lindblom, *Politics, Economics and Welfare* (1953), who survey various modes or procedures for decision-making in society.

[275] Cardozo, *The Growth of the Law*, 116f (1924). See also Justice Frankfurter's dissent in *Sherrer* v. *Sherrer*, 334 U.S. 343, 366 (1948), lamenting the Supreme Court's reversal of a State court's refusal to honor a sister State's divorce decree: "Only fragments of a social problem are seen through the narrow windows of a litigation. Had we innate or acquired understanding of a social problem in its entirety, we [still] would not have at our disposal adequate means for constructive solution."

[276] See Davis, *Administrative Law Treatise*, Ch. 13 (1958).

[277] See Hamson, *Executive Discretion and Judicial Control*, 45ff (1954); and Freedeman, *The Conseil d'Etat in Modern France*, 2ff (1961).

judicial expertise by close and continuous association with experienced specialists in the field.[278]

Nevertheless, there are limits even to such expertise. This is true, particularly in the field of competition regulation, for the evaluation of facts and patterns of conduct and the prediction of economic trends and consequences.[279] "Does anybody know," laments Justice Frankfurter, "when we have a case [under the Sherman Act], as we had one the other day, where we can go to find light on what the practical consequences of these decisions have been?. . . [T]o the extent that they may be relevant in deciding cases, they ought not to be left to the blind guessing of myself and others only a little less uninformed than I am."[280] And yet, this is just what frequently happens and courts must be prepared to meet such deficiencies in expert knowledge.

To meet any or all of these limitations in rule-making just discussed, however, does not mean to overcome them. In theory this may seem possible, but in practice it is not. At the most, judicial techniques can be developed simply to ameliorate or circumvent them. What is at play here, as Pound has pointed out, is a constant struggle in the law between rule and discretion – "a continual movement in legal history back and forth between wide discretion and strict detailed rule, . . . of administration of justice by law and administration of justice by the more or less trained intuition of experienced magistrates."[281] From an institutional point of view, the judicial techniques available may be divided into two general categories: those arising from the flexibility built into legal rules and concepts and those recognizing the proper sphere of discretion of other governmental institutions. These will be discussed in turn.

As to the first, the judiciary itself possesses a certain degree of discretion in case determination. This is obviously true in the selection and ordering

[278] Such association, however, must not be confused with the problem of the same person filling two distinct roles, such as judge and prosecutor or judge and administrator. As in the Conseil d'Etat, those in the judicial branch will simply have had the "experience of work at least in the advisory sections if not in the active administration also." Hamson, *id.*, pp. 93–96.

[279] See, e.g., the "rule of reason" or escape clauses built into the prohibitions of anticompetitive practices of the Communities. ECSC Art. 65 § 2 and EEC Art. 85(2).

[280] Frankfurter, *Some Observations on Supreme Court Litigation and Legal Education,* 17 (1953). See also Justice Harold Stephens, "What Courts Can Learn From Commissions," 21 *Amer. Bar Assoc. J.*, 141, 142 (1933).

[281] Pound, *An Introduction to the Philosophy of Law,* 54 (Yale Paperbound 1954). While Pound is emphasizing the difference "between justice without law, as it were, and justice according to law," the contrast is equally applicable to the narrower context in point here.

of the facts in question[282] and takes on major significance in the equitable pronouncements of a *praetor* or chancellor. Moreover, flexibility is built into abstract formulas, such as the legal standards of "good faith," "reasonableness," "prudence" and "diligence," which acquire high degrees of individualization in terms of specific circumstances. What is significant here, says Pound, "is not the fixed rule but the margin of discretion involved in the standard and its regard for the circumstances of the individual case."[283] Indeed, within the framework of French administrative law, the Conseil d'Etat has developed a veritable jurisprudence of abstractions. As Steindorff describes it, that Court limits itself

> to an evaluation of those recurring elements of the case which may be abstracted and tends to leave a part of the facts in question to administrative evaluation. This demonstrates the tendency to limit judicial activity to an evaluation of the logical elements contained in the administrative decisions, leaving the decisions themselves and the value judgments to public administration.[284]

Still, when the need for judicial relief is great, the Conseil d'Etat may descend from those Olympian heights and examine an administrative decision in all its legal and factual detail.[285]

This adherence to abstract standards and concepts, therefore, permits a court to individualize its decisions without overly prejudicing future cases. We need a theory, Pound has rightly pleaded, "which recognizes the administrative element as a legitimate part of the judicial function and insists that individualization in the application of legal precepts is no less important than the contents of those precepts themselves."[286]

Still, there are absolute limits to the practicability of legal rules and concepts as well as to the inventiveness of courts. That is to say, the judiciary may not be able to treat a particular problem or at least is significantly less able to do so than other governmental institutions. When these limits are reached, a court may well be advised to withdraw permanently from the field, leaving certain substantive considerations to the more skilled judgment and planning of other governmental institutions, and reserving to itself the review of only the minimum requirements of due process. Or, in the alternative, it may simply hold its answer in abeyance, maintaining judicial pressure on these other institutions until a workable rule is in sight.

282 See Pound, *id.*, pp. 56 and 59f; and Wasserstrom, *The Judicial Decision,* 14–22 (1961).
283 *Ibid.*, p. 58.
284 Steindorff, Die *Nichtigkeitsklage,* 64 (1952).
285 *Ibid.*, p. 72.
286 Pound, *op. cit.*, p. 60.

Two most poignant examples of such judicial self-restraint can be found in the case law of the Federal Constitutional Court of Germany.[287] In both cases, this Court upheld the constitutionality of the federal taxes in question, but for reasons and on conditions which recognize both the limits of rule practicability and the continuing responsibility of judicial review. This is not to contend that these judgments were the only possible or even the best dispositions of the cases in point. It does, however, demonstrate the sensitivity of high courts to the demands of practicability in the law.

In the Werkfernverkehrssteuer Judgment,[288] the plaintiff enterprises attacked a tax increase on long-haul trucking by them of their own products. The purpose of the tax, admittedly,[289] was to relieve an overburdening of the highways in favor of the federally owned railways as well as, to a lesser extent, independent long-haul trucking.[290] The increase, said the Court, constitutes "a measure of economic control (Lenkungsmassnahme) clothed in the garb of a tax law." [291] Moreover, this heavy taxation of the firms' own long-haul trucking, it conceded,

> lies on the boundary of what is constitutionally permissible, because it is not clear that – in the long run – the severe tax intervention in the "freedom of occupation" is of equally significant value for the common good.[292]

By the same token, the tax leads to "considerable differences in the burdens on enterprises doing their own long-haul trucking and independent long-haul truckers." This differential, the Court granted, "offers the latter . . . additional protection against competition." [293]

Still, the Court would "not yet" say that the tax violates either the rights to property, equal protection of the laws or the freedom of occupation under

[287] The Federal Constitutional Court has on various occasions affirmed the "principle of practicability" in upholding the constitutionality of federal laws. See, e.g., 11 BVerfG 139, 146f (1960); 12 BVerfG 151, 171f (1961); 17 BVerfG 337, 354 (1964); and other decisions of the Federal Finance Court cited by Padberg, *Die Rechtsprechung des Bundesfinanzhofes,* 204f (Bonn. Univ. Diss., 1965).

[288] Decision of May 22, 1963: 16 BVerfG 147 (1963), reported in 18 Der Betriebs-Berater 678 (1963).

[289] *Ibid.,* pp. 161f, 169–72, 176, 180 and 185.

[290] The relevant comparisons are between rail carriers, independent trucking lines and companies who are primarily manufacturers but who, in addition, haul their own goods. For tax purposes, federal law also distinguishes between long-hauls and short-hauls (up to 50 kilometers). The tax increase in question, which was passed in 1955, touched long-haul carriers of the last category only.

[291] 16 BVerfG 161.

[292] *Ibid.,* p. 187.

[293] *Ibid.,* p. 186.

Articles 14, 3 and 12 of the Basic Law. "Since the legislative decision has been taken only experimentally and in a most complex field, where the consequences of the transportation policy were not and are not yet fully known, the inequality must still be tolerated."[294] Nor, in view of the relatively short period (5 years) for assessing the consequences of the tax, had sufficient clarity been achieved "to enable the judge to declare the legislative norm unconstitutional." As a result, the legislature would be granted a longer period for "observing the effects of the specific measures which it had taken experimentally and in utilizing them for further determinations." Nevertheless, should these measures over the long run not serve the stated goals, the Court was prepared "to review again whether the special tax burden – at least at its present level – can still be upheld or whether the legislature must pursue its goals with other means that ensure with certainty a balanced intervention from all sides."[295] What had to be found were measures which were both "constitutional as well as effective means for stemming the amount of long-haul trucking."[296] Both are essential to the legislative formula.

In a more recent case, the Umsatzsteuer Judgment,[297] the Federal Constitutional Court was faced with the more agonizing problem of nullifying a tax law worth several billion dollars in collected revenues. The constitutional doubts concerned the different effects of the federal turnover tax on single-level and multiple-level enterprises. Although the law, as originally passed, had authorized the government to take compensatory measures, this provision was condemned in 1958 as an unconstitutional delegation of power.[298] As a result, the Federal Government was left with a statute which, in the words of the Court, no longer "met the legislature's own idea of a law which satisfied the equal protection requirement as to single and multiple-level enterprises." In addition, the resulting tax system

> tends in principle to burden multiple-level enterprises with less turnover tax costs than single-level enterprises and, therefore, to grant the former a competitive advantage . . . . [I]n this way, the [latter's] competitiveness is basically and decidedly impeded over the long run.[299]

[294] *Ibid.*

[295] *Ibid.*, p. 187f.

[296] *Ibid.*, p. 186.

[297] Decision of December 20, 1966, reported in Entscheidungen des BVerfG in systematischer Ordnung, vol. 3, Sec. 5 (1965–66), and, in part, in 20 *Die öff. Verw.*, 164 (1967).

[298] See 7 BVerfG 282 (1958).

[299] 20 *Die öff. Verw.*, 165f. For a more graphical comparison of this cascading type of tax with the new added value turnover tax in Germany, see Niehaus, "The New German Added Value Tax Law." 45 *Taxes – CCH*, 727 (1967).

Nevertheless, despite this fact and the failure of the legislature to correct this acknowledged deficiency during the succeeding eight years, the Court concluded: "at this time the law can be neither nullified nor can a violation of individual rights be established."[300]

The justification for this conclusion lay in the nature of the problem. On the one hand, to declare the legislature's classification unconstitutional would necessarily require the nullification of that part of the law in question.[301] According to the dominant view in Germany, this nullification would have retroactive effect and could not be limited *pro futuro*.[302] Partial nullification, moreover,

> would be only theoretically possible. Practically, due to the comprehensive character of the object taxed, there is no formula available for justiciably delimiting the invalid from the valid part of the law.[303]

On the other hand, to declare the whole turnover tax law invalid was also clearly out of the question. While this might be possible in simple cases, "here it would lead to the unbearable result that the law would be invalidated in an incomparably larger area having nothing at all to do with the question in point."[304] The "unbearable result," which the Court is alluding to, was apparently nothing less than state bankruptcy.[305]

As in the Werkfernverkehrssteuer Judgment, therefore, the law would remain valid for "a limited time." Because of the complexity of the problem

[300] 20 *Die öff. Verw.*, 166, col. 2.

[301] See Gesetz des BVerfG Art. 78, sent. 1; and the critique of Böckenförde, "Verfassungsinterpretation oder fiskalische Rücksichten?" 20 *Die öff. Verw.*, 157 (1967).

[302] See, e.g., 1 BVerfG 14, 37 (1951); and Friesenhahn, "Die Verfassungsgerichtsbarkeit in der Bundesrepublik Deutschland," in Mosler (ed.), *Verfassungsgerichtsbarkeit in der Gegenwart*, 89, 142f (1962). But cf. the critique of Böckenförde, *id.*, p. 158f, who advocates more flexible constitutional remedies which apparently, like the Austrian solution (see note 22 in text *supra*, Chapter III), would permit a nullification *pro futuro* of unconstitutional acts. Cf. also in this respect the more recent decision of the Supreme Court in *Linkletter* v. *Walker*, 381 U.S. 618 (1965), which asserts the general power of the Court to limit the effect of its decisions to prospective operation only. See hereto the critical appraisal of Mishkin, "The High Court, the Great Writ, and the Due Process of Time and Law," 79 *Harv. L. Rev.*, 56 (1965).

[303] 20 *Die öff. Verw.*, 166, col. 2.

[304] *Ibid.*

[305] Simply for damages arising from inequalities in competition between single-level and multi-level enterprises, compensation had been assessed at DM 10 billion. A nullification of the law would have run into several tens of billions of DM. See Böckenförde, *op. cit.*, p. 157f, who concludes, however: "Die fiskalischen Rücksichten haben dadurch bereits die Gesetzes- und Verfassungsinterpretation beeinflusst, die doch eigentlich davon unabhängig sein sollte."

and the difficulty of finding a suitable rule, this constitutional reprieve for the legislature had to be "measured generously."[306]

These cases serve to demonstrate how the search for practicability in the law may entail the exercise of judicial self-restraint. As with the other two judicial tasks discussed previously, this one too is confronted with real limitations. These, as has been seen, are the limits to rule individualization, to a stable or controllable context for rule operation and to judicial expertise in many areas of the law. These limitations may be ameliorated by built-in rule flexibility, but cannot by their very nature be overcome. Where such flexibility is absent or inadequate to the problem, as was the opinion of the Federal Constitutional Court in the cases above, it may be necessary to grant other governmental organs an added scope of discretion.

Moreover, the above cases demonstrate judicial sensitivity to the need for legislative as well as administrative experimentation, and to the immense difficulty of formulating workable rules to meet constitutional requirements in complex areas of regulation. In doing so, the Federal Constitutional Court has given a wide berth to legislative judgment, but acknowledged a time limit and the continuing potential for judicial review. It has, at the same time, discussed the nature of the criteria which the legislature must ultimately meet. In this way, judicial self-restraint is supplemented by activism which binds the Court and other governmental institutions in a dialogue about the kind of rule which would be both workable and constitutional. This constitutes prudent recognition of the limits of judicial power.

From this analysis, it is clear, the judiciary does not pronounce decisions in a vacuum. It must pursue its tasks of interpretation within an institutional context which at once bestows *and* limits the unique power of a constitutional court. Thus, by virtue both of its formal mandate of judicial review and of the modes of legitimacy intrinsic to its decisions, a court can evoke and solidify adherence to governmental decisions taken and policies advanced at first only tentatively. It can nurture a consensus thereby in support of that law which develops as a creative product of the judicial search for purpose and practicability. In this way, a constitutional court becomes an active and vital member of the existing concert of governmental powers, though its sphere of action is restricted functionally to the specific tasks of legal development.

Within this institutional context, a constitutional court faces both internal as well as external constraints on its power. The internal constraints are in-

[306] 20 *Die öff. Verw.*, 166, col. 2, and 167.

trinsic to the very tasks which a court must undertake. Because of its institutional design, an inappropriate or overextended use of judicial power is in some sense futile, or at least ultimately will serve to defeat the overriding tasks of judicial decision. Thus, the search for purpose will become sterile or ideologically rigid, consensus undermined or the rule unmanageable or empty. On the other hand, the external constraints may present a more immediate and tangible challenge. Faced with the certain and unyielding opposition of another branch of government or with the lethargy and disinterest of responsible segments of society, judicial indirection and compromise may offer at times the only feasible alternative for meaningful judicial action. Moreover, whether the constraint is internal or external, the appropriateness of judicial action must be weighed against the feasibility and certainty of action by other governmental agencies or by society in general.

Montesquieu's principle of moderation, therefore, is no mere maxim devoid of substance. Its operative content lies in those institutional considerations and judicial techniques or mediating devices of self-restraint just outlined, which in turn must be tailored to a court's peculiar legal tradition and institutional context. Being less a product of rules than of craftsmanship and statesmanship, the prudence which it dictates must be grasped through experience with judicial review and the deeper insights as to its function in constitutional democracy. Nor can it be contained by doctrine, like that of "political questions," unless the doctrine itself reflects both the functional and the empirical sources of that principle.[307] Prudence, like caution, in judicial practice "is a kind of noble fear,"[308] which by its nature must be result- and circumstance-oriented. Moreover, if the principle of moderation does have flesh and blood, then it is simply not true that the judge's "own sense of self-restraint" constitutes the only check upon the exercise of judicial review.[309] Appearances lie, even in the short run, for the imprudent de-

[307] Justice Frankfurter, in his dissenting opinion in *Baker* v. *Carr,* 369 U.S. (1962), in fact takes this broad view of the "political questions" doctrine, drawing on considerations as to the limits of judicial knowledge, authority and rule-shaping in rebutting the majority opinion of the Supreme Court. Cf. also Finkelstein, "Judicial Self-Limitation," 37 *Harv. L. Rev.,* 338 (1923–24), who views the doctrine primarily from an empirical viewpoint; and Scharpf, *Grenzen der richterlichen Verantwortung,* 404ff (1965), who concludes his exhaustive case law examination with a strictly functional view of the doctrine.

[308] Strauss, *Natural Right and History,* 206 (1953), discussing the meaning of "caution" when applied to practice or politics.

[309] The rejected assertion is by Chief Justice Stone dissenting, in *United States* v. *Butler,* 297 U.S. 1, 79 (1936). Indeed, the political repercussions of that decision well indicate how wrong he was. Cf. also a similar statement by Justice Geiger of the German Federal Constitutional Court, "Einige Probleme der Bundesverfassungsgerichtsbarkeit," 5 *Die öff. Verw.,* 481, 482 (1952).

cision of today will return to haunt the court tomorrow. Ultimately of course, as Llewellyn has warned, "a sustained course of extravagant judging will transgress limits of toleration which are as inescapable as they are undefined, unphrased."[310]

4. THE PROPER SCOPE OF THE JUDICIAL FUNCTION

Having established the nature and responsible limits of judicial power, it remains to determine the proper scope for the exercise of that power. This is to ask, what is the unique, overriding and enduring contribution of judicial review to constitutional government? Clearly, the judicial function cannot be restricted to the application of "determinate norms" or to the enunciation of "neutral principles," for these essentially static approaches to constitutional construction neither account for the creative process of judicial decision nor fairly appreciate the institutional constraints on that process, as reflected in the principle of moderation. Rather, as has been shown, precisely this process and these constraints establish the parameters of the judicial function. In a democracy, the two are bound together and ultimately bedded – like the law itself – in an evolving consensus of community values. Consensus is reflected not only institutionally, in the "aller de concert" of governmental powers just discussed, but also in those audiences or publics which underlie the rationality of judicial decision outlined in Chapter III. In the continuing search for purpose, authority and practicability in the law, therefore, consensus unites institutional with philosophical perspectives, the empirical with the rational parameters of judicial decision. What must now be elaborated is the origin of this consensus, and the unique and enduring contribution of judicial decision to its existence. This will establish the proper scope of the judicial function.

The Overriding Task of Judicial Decision

Judicial decision on the constitutional level, observes Cardozo, must be grasped in "le sens évolutif."[311] This is true for several reasons. In the first place, constitutional norms were born in compromise. They were designed to reconcile the diverging views of the founding fathers and to achieve con-

[310] Llewellyn, *The Common Law Tradition,* 220 (1960).

[311] Cardozo, *The Nature of the Judicial Process,* 85 (1921). See also Scheuner, "Die Auslegung verfassungsrechtlicher Leitsätze" 17–19 (*Rechtsgutachten,* 1952): "Der Blick der Auslegung ist hier nicht so sehr rückwärts auf Entstehungsgeschichte und Zeitmeinung als auf die Berücksichtigung der vorhandenen lebendigen Funktion der Ordnung, ihre Erhaltung und Fortentwicklung gerichtet."

sensus, but only so far as consensus was at that time possible. Quite frequently, as is apparent in the drafting of the Community Treaties,[312] ambiguous expressions are seized upon in order to resolve unyielding conflicts.

Secondly, most present situations facing the judiciary were simply not anticipated by the drafters. To refer these cases to the process of constitutional amendment would simply overtax the system, and would not necessarily lead to more meaningful guidelines for judicial decision. In fact, if it is clear that in most cases the constitutional fathers did not anticipate, indeed could not have anticipated present day conditions, then it must equally be clear that they knew this and wrote a constitution making it "possible for future battles to be fought out by men who, on both sides of contested issues, can in good faith profess allegiance to the organic law and to the regime established by it."[313]

In the third place, law like the society it reflects is caught up in a continuous process of development and change, embracing both values and institutions. "Viewed as positive law," says Rudolf Smend, "the constitution is not only norm but also reality.... This reality is constantly recreated through the continuing renewal of constitutional life."[314] If it is not to become irrelevant or to lose itself in abstractions, constitutional law must remain sensitive to the change at work in social and political institutions. The language of a constitution, therefore, is merely the historical residue and "temporary draft" of a legal order at one point in time.[315] In order to survive, it must be "language capable of growth."[316]

Above all, this evolutionary trait reflects the organic element, the cohesiveness and continuum peculiar to constitutional law. This is the element of consensus which nourishes the sense of unity and attachment in society and forms the viable basis of legitimacy in constitutional government.[317] Viewed statically, it connotes the general consent and accord in society among individuals, groups and governmental powers on at least certain

[312] See e.g. Hochbaum, *Das Diskriminierungs- und Subventionsverbot in der EGKS und EWG*, 33 (1962).

[313] Bickel, *The Least Dangerous Branch*, 105 (1962). See also his *Politics and the Warren Court*, 259–261 (1965), which amply demonstrates this development in the original understanding of the "equal protection" clause of the 14th Amendment.

[314] Smend, "Verfassung und Verfassungsrecht," in his *Staatsrechtliche Abhandlungen*, 119, 192 (1955).

[315] Bäumlin, *Staat, Recht und Geschichte*, 15–26 (1961).

[316] Bickel, *Politics and the Warren Court*, 260 (1965).

[317] See Ehmke, "Prinzipien der Verfassungsinterpretation," 20 *VVdStRL*, 53, 71f (1963); and Bickel, *id.*, p. 11: "The basis of all our law – rules of conduct, whether legislative, judicial or administrative in origin, behind which is the coercive power of the state – is consensual."

fundamental governing procedures and/or substantive values. These established solidarities in social sentiment and belief provide the necessary foundation on which the value creative decisions of a constitutional court must be built. In contrast to the proponents of determinate norms and neutral principles, Bickle clearly recognizes this fact. His single-minded emphasis on principle, however, tends to bisect the judicial process by pitting judicial opinion against public opinion, so as to frame that tension between principle and consent whose only solvent is judicial expediency. Little wonder, then, that Bickel labels judicial review a "deviant institution" in democratic government.[318]

Nevertheless, the mere fact of consent alone, or of an "aller de concert" of governmental powers, does not reflect or account for the evolutionary quality of constitutional law. Consent represents no more than a half-way house on the path of legal development, neither explaining nor elaborating the values it fosters, nor offering the essential rationale and guidelines for a changing society. As Holmes observes:

> We do not realize how large a part of our law is open to reconsideration upon a slight change in the habit of the public mind. No concrete proposition is self-evident, no matter how ready we may be to accept it . . . .[319]

By the same token, a slight change in the habit of the public mind tends also to work a change in the judicial mind. Judges too are products of their culture and the historicity of their social value framework. "Everybody knows," admits Bickel at one point, "that the lifetime of applied principle is often no longer than one or two generations." [320] If indeed this is the nature of those "enduring values" and "general propositions . . . of universal validity," which Bickel contends the court is charged "to evolve, preserve, protect and defend," [321] then the creative process of judicial decision must reach well beyond both principle and consent.

In dealing with the constitutional language that overlies unresolved conflicts, unanticipated problems and changing social values and institutions, therefore, a constitutional court must go to the source of that change which is common to both the judicial and the public mind. The common source of this change lies in the enlightenment of consent through the dynamic force of reasoned opinion. Both are found in the public mind, for without some accord there is no public to speak of, and without reason there is neither

[318] See discussion of Bickle's position in text *supra*, pp. 179f and 194–197.
[319] Holmes, "The Path of the Law," 10 *Harv. L. Rev.*, 457, 466 (1897).
[320] Bickel, *The Least Dangerous Branch*, 244 (1962).
[321] *Ibid.*, pp. 24, 188 and 199.

intelligent nor intelligible communication on fundamental values. Both inhere in the rationality of judicial decision, whose creative shaping of the law proceeds from reasoning directed at specific types of publics.[322] The court becomes the spokesman for and the advocate of the reasoned opinion of the larger community.

As this suggests, the standard of judicial rationality is set by the larger community. Thus, as already elaborated in Section 2 of chapter III, the self-critical reasoning of the judicial search for purpose in the law rests ultimately on the assent of the universal audience. The relentless demands of that public, however, commit the court to the unending pursuit of those value premises in the law which obligate in and of themselves. Adjudication, says Ehmke, constitutes "a struggle for the right understanding of the constitution, and . . . at the same time, a struggle for the right self-understanding of the community."[323] In the search for authority, moreover, the persuasive reasoning of judicial decision aims not merely at maintaining consent of the real audience for established values. It seeks further to enlighten and deepen this consent, and to expand it to embrace a greater range and evolving line of values. The constitution, in Rousseau's famous phrase, must indeed be graven not on "tablets of marble or brass, but on the hearts of the citizens."[324] Finally, through the mode of pragmatic reasoning, general constitutional norms and values are translated into workable rules of conduct. This reasoning too is oriented toward a particular audience and the unique character of consent which that audience implies. It is oriented toward those whom the rule must be shaped to control or regulate in order for law to be effective. In each of these cases, reason offers the new and evolving perspectives which must then be tested and often reformulated in light of the empirical standard of consent.

The consensus on which the law rests, therefore, has dynamic proportions. Being neither static nor blind, it fuses reason with consent. These form the twin roots of legitimate (constitutional) government.[325] Though limited

322 Both of which are discussed in Section 2 of Chapter III.

323 Ehmke, *op. cit.*, (n. 317), p. 69. This search for the basic constitutional premises (Vorverständnis) of the community, Ehmke points out, requires a judicial inquiry which combines both substantive political theory and practice. *Ibid.*, pp. 64f and 70. As to this latter point, see also Jackson, *The Supreme Court in The American System*, 57 (1958).

324 Rousseau, *Contrat social BK II*, ch. xii. See also Bickel, *op. cit.* (n. 320), p. 20, who emphasizes, with Learned Hand, that "coherent, stable – morally supportable – government is possible only on the basis of consent. . . ."

325 This is true both for classical and modern political theory. While the classics realized the necessity for consent, they gave distinct precedence to reason or wisdom in the rule of the wise and considered consent, as does Bickel apparently, to be largely a compromise with political reality. See Strauss, *Natural Right and History*, 140–42

in substance to the most fundamental values of political organization and human rights,[326] it must find support not only among governmental institutions and the public in general, but also among those particular types of publics or audiences just mentioned which nourish the rationality and responsible basis of legal development. Moreover, only a consensus in which these values continually are reinterpreted and reshaped, through testing judicial reasoning against public opinion, can preserve the enlightened basis of constitutional democracy.[327] Otherwise constitutional values would soon be buried and rendered ineffective by the onslaught of social change.[328]

As a result, the overriding task of judicial decision on the constitutional level is to maintain this evolving consensus on fundamental values. Not principle as such but reasoned decision in the relentless search for purpose, authority and practicability in the law frames this fruitful and vital exchange between judicial opinion and public opinion. And not reasoning in any fashion, or merely for the sake of logical analysis, but that self-critical, persuasive and pragmatic reasoning endemic to a just, authoritative and effective legal order. Here lies the enduring contribution of judicial review to constitutional government.

To this end a constitutional court must marshal and husband its legitimating power. In the creative development and ordering of fundamental political values, judicial power is neither exercised nor moderated for its own sake. The court has a distinct mission to perform. While other tribunals and lower courts sit primarily for the peaceful resolution of disputes, a constitutional court must seek essentially to secure and develop that constitutional consensus which frames and underpins that peaceful resolution. Above all, it must define and constantly focus society's attention on the underlying reoccurring questions of constitutional government.[329] The chief

(1953). John Locke's fertile admixture of reason (natural law) and consent (civil compact), on the other hand, provides that reason gives rise to a natural right whose violation no government could justify and no individual need accept. Second Treatise of Civil Government, particularly §§ 6, 8, 10, 22, 61, 95, 135, 147, 172 and 175.

[326] See Kägi, *Die Verfassung als rechtliche Grundordnung des Staates,* 70f (1945). But cf. the Greek conception of a constitution (politeia) which embodies the whole order of things in society, in Strauss, *id.*, pp. 135–37. See also discussion in text *supra,* Chapter I, Section 5.

[327] See Ehmke, *op. cit.* (n. 317), p. 68; and Jackson, *op. cit.* (n. 323), p. 82.

[328] Two poignant current examples of this are the problems of wiretapping and coerced confession.

[329] See Levi, "The Nature of Judicial Reasoning," 32 *U. Chi. L. Rev.*, 395, 408 (1965); and Schindler, "Richterliches Prüfungsrecht und politischer Mehrheitswille: Erfahrungen der Vereinigten Staaten – Folgerungen für die Schweiz," 74 *Z. schweiz. R.*, 289, 304 (N.F. 1955). Cf. also Garlan, *Legal Realism and Justice,* Ch. VI (1941), who points out that "justice" is essentially more of a question than an answer.

worth of judicial review, concludes Cardozo, lies in

> making vocal and audible the ideals that might otherwise be silenced, in giving them continuity of life and of expression, in guiding and directing choice within the limits where choice ranges.[330]

Not only must the court define the question and focus attention, it must also initiate inquiry and if necessary force discussion on these questions where discussion is lacking.

Where political processes are deadlocked, moreover, the court is not called so much to resolve issues. Rather, as Bickel contends, it should "do what it can to break that deadlock, so that the political institutions may make their decision before the [c]ourt is required to pass judgment" on the validity of the issue.[331] Faced at last with an unmistakable defiance of the constitution, the court may indeed have to exercise its veto power – all the while recognizing that the finality which the judicial veto imposes, though necessary under the circumstances, may well cut off significant discussion, inquiry and experimentation in that direction. While holding "the standard aloft and visible for those [political institutions] who must run the race and keep the faith," [332] the court must avoid that hardening of the legal arteries so anathema to continued development of the law.

To a great extent, therefore, asking the constitutional question and maintaining the discussion and inquiry overshadows the answer ultimately given. The answer, though nominally final in law, is ever subject to revision. No court possesses ultimate insight into the purpose, authority and practicability of law. Nor may a constitutional court claim a monopoly on what is known. Legislatures, reminds Cardozo, "are ultimate guardians of the liberties and welfare of the people in quite as great a degree as courts." [333] As the considerations underlying the principle of moderation evidence, the kinds of answers a court may give are circumscribed by both inherent and institutional constraints.

Nevertheless, by a prudent deployment of its powers, a constitutional court can offer that "sober second thought" on fundamental value questions which otherwise might well go unattended.[334] It can do this because, unlike other institutions of government, it is greatly insulated from

[330] Cardozo, *op. cit.* (n. 311), p. 94.

[331] Bickel, *op. cit.* (n. 320), p. 60.

[332] Cardozo, *op. cit.* (n. 311), p. 93.

[333] *Ibid.*, p. 90.

[334] The phrase is that of Chief Justice Stone, "The Common Law in the United States," 50 *Harv. L. Rev.*, 4, 25 (1936). See also Levi, *op. cit.* (n. 329), p. 408f; and Bickel, *op. cit.* (n. 320), p. 26.

the immediate pressures of time and popular opinion. Judges have, as Bickel points out, "the leisure, the training, and the insulation to follow the ways of the scholar in pursuing the ends of government." [335] As a caveat to Bickle's position, however, it must be noted that the "ways of the scholar" are not so much those of principled judgment as of searching reasoned inquiry. Judges further are disciplined uniquely by craft pressures and tradition, by highly structured proceedings and by the relentless demands of reasoned decision. These require full disclosure of the relevant facts and arguments and open the way for criticism and further inquiry.[336] Finally, in contrast to the broad-gauged legislative approach, the whole weight of the court's reasoning and examination is brought to bear on concrete issues. Courts must deal with "the flesh and blood of an actual case" which, as Bickel points out, "provides an extremely salutary proving ground for all abstractions." [337] As a result of these institutional traits, a constitutional court frequently may offer the only effective forum for raising and defining those enduring constitutional questions which underlie the daily flux of political life.

A Dialectic of Judicial Decision

Given this overriding responsibility and unique contribution of the judiciary to constitutional government, how is it to be implemented? What judicial approach to constitutional interpretation best ensures the effective but prudent deployment of limited judicial power? Certainly, the more common methods of legal construction, such as logic, history and "Systematik," offer no insight in this respect, for they are directed primarily at an interpretation of the text and not at defining the proper scope of the judicial function. The evolutionary character of constitutional law, and the judicial task which this implies, demand more. They call for a judicial style which focuses discussion and involves all governmental branches and the community at large in a continuing search for purpose, authority and practicability in the law. They also call for a decisional framework that disciplines discussion once begun and, within the institutional context of judicial review, permits decision without unnecessarily curtailing continued judicial inquiry and legal development.

This judicial style and decisional framework are well reflected in the

[335] Bickel, *id.*, p. 26.

[336] See Judge Traynor commenting on Breitel's presentation, in *Legal Institutions Today and Tomorrow*, 52f (1959).

[337] Bickel, *op. cit.* (n. 320), p. 26.

classic "dialectic" of Aristotle, as set forth in his *Topics* and *Rhetoric*.[338] His "dialectic" is essentially a disciplined discussion, "a process of criticism wherein lies the path to the principles of all inquiries." It not only offers "a plan of inquiry" for arguing about a proposed subject, it also facilitates a study of the philosophical sciences "because the ability to raise searching difficulties on both sides of a subject will make us detect more easily the truth and error about the several points that arise."[339] This style of analysis differs fundamentally from "demonstration" or "apodictic" reasoning which proceeds either from primary and true premises or from propositions based thereon. While the deductive method may be most appropriate for a science whose first principles have been established, absent such principles the "dialectic" must be employed to discover and test the outlines of a developing science and its premises.[340] Thus, dialectical reasoning proceeds not from truths, but from "opinions that are generally accepted," whether "by every one or by the majority or by the philosophers – i.e. by all, or by the majority, or by the most notable and illustrious of them."[341] It moves from opinion toward truth by opposing arguments and insights and by establishing agreement through persuasion.[342] In contrast to deductive logic, summarizes Viehweg, topical reasoning "is a meditative prologue whose task primarily is *inventio* and secondarily *conclusio*. First the topics must show how to find premises. Then logic takes and works them out."[343]

Basic to the "dialectic" is an earnest question or aporia, one which permits apparently of more than one answer. Such is inherent in the problems of justice, authority and practicability in the law, which arise and persist because they defy final resolution within a given value system. They arise in the course of judicial interpretation as question-begging or ambiguous con-

338 Aristotle's *Topics* (Topica), being books i–viii of the *Organon*, and his *Rhetoric* (Rhetorica) are taken from the Britannica Great Books Edition, vols. 8 and 9 (1952), as translated by W. A. Pickard-Cambridge and W. Rhys Roberts, respectively.

339 *Topics* 101a(25)–101b(4). For helpful discussions of the nature and function of the "dialectic," see E. Kapp, *Greek Foundations of Traditional Logic*, 4–17 and 67f (1942); H. D. P. Lee, *Zeno of Elea*, 113–23 (1936); G. Grote, *Aristotle*, vol. I, ch. ix (1872); and M. Adler, *Dialectic* (1927).

340 See Perelman, "The Dialectical Method and the Part Played by the Interlocutor in Dialogue," in his *The Idea of Justice and the Problem of Argument*, 161, 163 (1963).

341 *Topics* 100a(27)–100b(23).

342 See Strauss, *op. cit.* (n. 325), p. 80f; and Perelman, "The Social Context of Argumentation," in his *The Idea of Justice and the Problem of Argument*, 154, 158f (1963).

343 Viehweg, *Topik und Jurisprudenz*, 22 (1954). But cf. Sir David Ross, *Aristotle*, 59 (5th ed. 1949), who relegates the *Topics* to a by-gone mode of thought which Aristotle himself is said to have recognized in developing his *Analytics*. Admittedly, the view which Ross presses unfortunately has dominated scientific thought for the past three centuries. See Perelman and Olbrechts-Tyteca, *Traité de l'argumentation*, vol. I, pp. 1–13 (1958).

cepts and textual phrasing or as assumptions or implications essential to a coherent and meaningful understanding of the text.[344] They represent underlying and reoccurring problems of a culture whose consideration, as Aristotle would have it, "contributes either to choice and avoidance, or to truth and knowledge, . . . or as a help to the solution of some other such problem."[345]

They are earnest questions because substantial segments of society admittedly think them so and continue to press them and wrestle with them within the framework of constitutional adjudication.[346] Society eventually must admit its inability to comprehend and to resolve them completely by any one value system. They repeatedly appear in new forms and circumstances and in changing social contexts, and constantly impede logical reasoning forwards and backwards, both deduction and reduction.[347] As in constitutional litigation, therefore, the confrontation of opposing theses or values constitutes the nub of the "dialectic." In law as in philosophy, where knowledge is imperfect, incomplete and indemonstrable, the earnest question establishes the only meaningful unity.[348] It offers the primary and lasting source of disciplined inquiry.

Faced with an earnest question, the "dialectic" proceeds by way of the rhetorical topics. Being by definition a style of "problem thinking," it aims not at reformulating the problem to make it fit the logic of a given value system, but at moving toward a resolution of the problem by drawing on a variety of pragmatic viewpoints which may well reflect conflicting value systems. For this reason, as Viehweg so well phrases it, the "dialectic" effects a "Systemauslese" and not – as does the logic of a legal system – a "Problemauslese."[349] It does this by the use of *topoi,* the "commonplace rules" or "seats of arguments,"[350] from which reasoning from opinions on any problem can begin.

344 See discussion in text *supra,* pp. 106–108. See also Esser, *Grundsatz und Norm,* 62f (1956), who speaks of these loci in the text as "Umwandlungsstationen" in the positive law which may change over time in importance and function.

345 *Topics* 104b(1)–(3).

346 See Viehweg, *op. cit.,* pp. 17–22. See also Mannheim, "Die Bedeutung der Konkurrenz im Gebiete des Geistigen," *Züricher Referat* (1928), reprinted in Wolff (ed.), Karl Mannheim, *Wissenssoziologie – Auswahl aus dem Werk,* 566 (1964), and also his *Ideologie und Utopie,* Chs. 7 and 8 (3rd. ed. 1952), which emphasize the importance of social entities in the creation of social values.

347 Viehweg, *id.,* p. 21.

348 *Ibid.,* p. 68; and Bäumlin, *Staat, Recht und Geschichte,* 26–29 (1961), citing Viehweg extensively.

349 Viehweg, *id.,* p. 17. See also Esser, *op. cit.* (n. 344), p. 47.

350 The former phrase is used by Aristotle in his *Topics* 108b(34) and on other occasions; the latter phrase belongs to Cicero, *Topica* I, 7 and 8.

While Aristotle was concerned with the universally applicable *topoi,*[351] more specialized lines of reasoning also may arise within the framework of a particular science.[352] Such are the legal *topoi* of causation, foreseeability, due process, reliance interest and reasonableness which set important milestones in the search for purpose in the law.[353] Other lines of reasoning, such as those based on analogy or example, on adverse or desirable consequences and on preserving the integrity of the legal system,[354] contribute greatly to the rhetorical task in the search for authority. By the same token, the need for practicability in the law has been served by the specialized *topoi* of the *per se* rule, constructive notice and other types of inferences or presumptions. Indeed, in the broadest sense, each case decision taken in context offers a new insight and *topos* for the developing law. So long as such specialized lines of reasoning remain open to the more universal perspectives, the mediating *topoi* help preserve the growth potential and flexibility of the law.

At the same time, this judicial style and approach to interpretation does not dissolve the law into a scattering of unrelated considerations and decisions. Besides the earnest question itself, the "dialectic" is disciplined further by the historical context of the problem and its treatment. That is to say, the concrete formulation of normative content, including the reasons upon which it rests, evolves only over time in light of a given legal tradition or possibly statutory framework. Insofar law is history, for it is realized only in an historical context.[355] This implies not only, as already discussed

[351] Aristotle's *topoi,* which he meant to apply to all subjects, are based on his fundamental distinction between "definition," "property," "accident" and "genus," and reflect the considerations embodied by his ten classes of predicates, including quality, quantity, relation, place, time, position, state, etc. See his *Topics* 101b(11)–(37) and 103b(20)–104a(2).

[352] See, for instance, Cicero's *Topica,* developed at the behest of a jurist friend, whose list of topics includes: genus, kind, similarities, differences, contrasts, accompanying circumstances (prior, subsequent, contradictory), causes, effects and comparisons. Discussed by Viehweg, *op. cit.* (n. 343), pp. 10–13.

[353] Cf. Viehweg, *id.,* §§ 4–8; and Esser, *op. cit.* (n. 344), pp. 44–52 and 60–65. It should be noted that principles, as well as concepts and doctrines, can be carriers of legal *topoi.* See Dworkin, "The Model of Rules," 35 *U. Ch. L. Rev.,* 14, 25ff (1967), who sees principles as stating reasons which argue in one direction but do not necessitate a particular conclusion. They simply "incline a decision one way, though not conclusively, and they survive intact when they do not prevail." See also Esser, *id.,* pp. 20, 47f, 59–65 and 185.

[354] See Perelman and Olbrechts-Tyteca, *op. cit.* (n. 343), setting forth a long list and categories of rhetorical arguments. Aristotle expressly points out, it should be noted, that rhetoric "is an offshoot of dialectic and also of ethical studies.... As a matter of fact, it is a branch of dialectic and similar to it." *Rhetoric* 1356a(25)–(31).

[355] See Bäumlin, *op. cit.* (n. 348), pp. 15–26.

in this Section, that constitutional law and its underlying consensus are always open to further development, but also that there exists a residue of reasoning and common understanding about the problem from which judicial analysis can begin. The judge is never faced with a *tabula rasa.*[356] Rather, proceeding from the residue of prior reasoning, the topical insights produce new perspectives without impairing existing ones. That happens in this way, explains Viehweg:

> settled points are maintained but subjected to new perspectives, which often have arisen in totally different contexts. They offer the possibility of giving the old conceptions a new turn. Not every interpretation . . . does that, but each can do it. It is a part of topical reasoning and immensely appropriate for obtaining modification.[357]

Moreover, new perspectives once introduced must still run the gamut of public and professional approval. Modification in the law is realized only gradually, through the course of case decisions, as the new perspectives cumulate and are argued persuasively.[358] The historicity of the law and of the constitutional consensus upon which it rests, therefore, lends stability to the "dialectic" without stultifying continued legal development.

The heart of the "dialectic," of course, is discussion or "thinking in discourse." Here lies a third disciplining factor and the machinery for ensuring that all relevant arguments pro and con have been presented and considered. Here too lies the measure of the arguments themselves, for the discussants ultimately must decide whether new perspectives shall alter the established points of law. In "dialectic" a proposition holds against which no cogent arguments can be brought.[359] For this reason, it is of the utmost importance to identify the discussants and the framework of the discussion. 'Do not argue with every one, nor practice upon the man in the street," cautions Aristotle in concluding his *Topics,* "for there are some people with whom any argument is bound to degenerate." [360]

In the more traditional and consolidated field of private law, for instance, the "dialectic" occurs almost totally among the members of the courts and the legal profession. In this sphere of the law, the problems generally have been narrowed and closely defined over a long history of legal development.

[356] See discussion in text *supra,* p. 123f. See also Perelman, "Raison éternelle, Raison historique," in his *Justice et Raison,* 95, 100f (1963).

[357] Viehweg, *op. cit.* (n. 343), p. 24.

[358] See discussion in text *supra,* p. 117f.

[359] Adler, *op. cit.* (n. 339), p. 28.

[360] See Perelman, *op. cit.* (n. 340), esp. pp. 161–63 and 166f; and Perelman, *op. cit.* (n. 342), p. 156f.

Even then, the circle of discussants on any particular point may vary enormously, i.e. members of a court, the advocates between themselves, the court and the advocates, different levels of courts, courts over time and the courts and the legal profession and academic opinion. These varying circles of discussants are enlarged further by the practice of *amicus curiae* briefs,[362] third-party intervention[363] and dissenting and other non-binding opinions such as those of the Advocates-General of the Court of Justice of the European Communities.[364] Granting the purely "legal" orientation of these discussants, their presence in day-to-day judicial procedures helps avoid the crassest subjectivity in judicial decisions.[365]

On the level of constitutional litigation, however, the circle of discussants must expand to accord with the subject matter in issue. At this point, it is important to distinguish between the addressees of judicial reasoning and the circle of discussants. The addressees, on the one hand, consist of those various types of audiences or publics discussed in Section 2 of Chapter III. Each from its own perspective determines the rationality of judicial decision in the creative development of the law. While the standards of rationality which these audiences set are reflected functionally in the literature, political positions and the arguments before the courts, the audiences themselves are not normally represented personally or institutionally within the circle of discussants. Due to the very nature of social organization, the audiences are more abstractions than realities. The discussants, on the other hand, reflect social organization whether as public or private institutions or as independent representatives of special viewpoint.[366] Other than the discussants just listed, this circle of active participants clearly embraces the other governmental branches and agencies as well as state and local governments and major private organizations. In a representative sense, therefore, the "dialectic" on constitutional questions should embrace the community as a whole. A constitutional court, says Swisher of the Supreme Court,

361 *Topics* 164b(8)–(15).

362 The *amicus curiae* brief, presented by "a friend of the court," is permitted in many courts in the United States, including the Supreme Court.

363 The Court of Justice of the European Communities recognizes the right of third-party intervention. See ECSC Stat. of the Court Art. 34; EEC Stat. of the Court Art. 37; and Euratom Stat. of the Court Art. 38.

364 Although in contrast to common law practice the continental courts typically render their judgments as a collegial body only, the Court of Justice of the European Communities publishes the separate opinions of the Advocates-General. See discussion in text *supra*, p. 23. Cf. Nadelmann, "The Judicial Dissent," 8 *Amer. J. Comp. L.*, 415 (1959).

365 See Radbruch, *Einführung in die Rechtswissenschaft*, 165 (9th ed. 1952).

366 See Perelman, *op. cit.* (n. 342), p. 155f.

"must operate in a governmental and popular context already provided for it, and it cannot hope to escape from that context."[367]

Within this circle of discussants, a constitutional court assumes the classic role of the questioner. Though a partisan of the law, the court deigns to prove nothing.[368] Demonstrable proof is not in the nature of the problem. The overriding task of the court, within the context of the given case, is to raise and focus attention upon the earnest question(s) of constitutional law, to ensure that all the arguments on an issue have been presented and considered and to maintain the continuing search for purpose, authority and practicability in the law. Simply put, its task is to maintain discussion on those unresolved and unresolvable problems of constitutional law.[369] It can do this because, as pointed out earlier,[370] a nation committed to a constitution lays special significance on the institution and the decisions of the tribunal authorized to interpret it. While a court admittedly cannot initiate proceedings or pronounce opinions at large, it possesses great leeway in selecting the grounds of its decisions. Skilfully written decisions not only can identify the questions worthy of discussion, they also can force consideration of constitutional questions which society otherwise might overlook.[371] Thus, with the assistance of the legal profession, assuming the "role of interpreter to the public,"[372] a constitutional court is not without substantial influence in focusing and pressing inquiry. In that case, the Supreme Court justifiably may be called "an educational body" whose Justices "are inevitably teachers in a vital national seminar."[373] In the true sense of the word, of course, the teacher is also a serious student of the subject matter and is prepared to learn from all who offer new insights and experience. The teacher does not necessarily have the answers.

A constitutional court, moreover, not only must initiate and lead, it must also guide and maintain discussion on constitutional questions within the disciplined framework of the division and balance of governmental powers.

367 Swisher, *The Supreme Court in Modern Role,* 167 (1958).

368 See Grote, *op. cit.* (n. 339), p. 393; and Adler, *op. cit.* (n. 339), pp. 30–33.

369 Cf. Viehweg, *op. cit.* (n. 343), p. 32, speaks of the "besonderer, prämissensuchender Stil" of topical reasoning whose important function lies "im unablässigen Suchen des Rechten."

370 See discussion in text *supra,* p. 174f.

371 See Bickel, *The Least Dangerous Branch,* 188 (1962); and Schindler, "Richterliches Prüfungsrecht und politischer Mehrheitswille," 74 *Z. schweiz. R.*, 289, 304 (1955).

372 William C. Warren, "The Duty of Responsible Criticism," in *Legal Institutions Today and Tomorrow,* 323f (1959), reminding the lawyers that they exercise great influence in catalyzing public opinion. See also Cardozo, *The Nature of the Judicial Process,* 35 (1921).

373 Rostow, *The Sovereign Prerogative,* 167f (1962).

It must avoid judicial ideology as well as a hardening of the political arteries. The job of the Supreme Court in a perfectly real, concrete and developed controversy, as Bickel well notes, "is not to resolve issues on which the political processes are in deadlock, but to do what it can to break that deadlock so that the political institutions may make their decisions before the Court is required to pass judgment on their validity."[374]

For this reason, the timely application of judicial self-restraint, the decision of non-decision, often may be more important than the legitimation or invalidation of a measure on its merits. Indeed, by the prudent deployment of judicial techniques of non-decision, the court may stay its hand on the merits while remanding the issue back to the legislature or executive for renewed consideration.[375] At the same time, by the calculated use of *obiter dicta,* it may direct attention toward the critical issues at stake.[376] In this way, it may press a continuing dialogue between the major institutions of government through the medium of official decisions and acts. There are dozens of instances in United States history, says Bickel, when Congress and the Supreme Court have engaged in "responsive readings" of the developing law.[377] These may arise spontaneously, as the by-product of a judi-

[374] Bickel, *op. cit.*, p. 60. This is no less true of the International Court of Justice. See Rosenne, "The Court and the Judicial Process," 19 *Int. Organ.*, 518, 526f (1965), who discusses several cases in the last 20 years where disposition of the dispute on jurisdictional or procedural grounds, "sometimes on a narrow technical ground, sometimes on grounds more substantial and closer to the real dispute, merely laid the basis for a renewal of diplomatic negotiations leading to the ultimate negotiated settlement of the dispute."

[375] The idea of a judicial "remand function" has been raised by Bickel and Wellington, "Legislative Purpose and the Judicial Process: The Lincoln Mills Case," 71 *Harv. L. Rev.*, 1, 22–35 (1957); and has been discussed in other terms by Stone, "Non-Liquet and the Function of Law in the International Community," 35 *Brit. YB Int. L.*, 124, 148ff (1959), and Rosenne, *id.*, pp. 526–29.

An historical parallel to the "remand function" might be drawn to the institution of the "référé législatif," widespread in Europe prior to the 18th century. It required the judge, in case of doubt as to the meaning of the text, to consult with the monarch for his true intention. It was based, however, on a wholly different concept of government and of the judicial function. See Gény, *Méthode d'interprétation et sources en droit privé positif,* vol. I, p. 77ff (2nd ed. 1954); and Lukas, "Zur Lehre vom Willen des Gesetzgebers," in *Festgabe P. Laband,* vol. I, p. 397, 407ff (1908).

[376] Rosenne, *id.*, p. 528f, notes how the International Court of Justice has "treated the dispute 'once removed,' so to speak, from its original formulation," in order that it may "be fully aired in Court even when, on technical grounds, the judgment is limited to the minimum necessary to establish the inability of the Court to deal with the merits of the case."

[377] Bickel, *op. cit.* (n. 371), p. 206. See also Comment, "Deportation and Exclusion: A Continuing Dialogue between Congress and the Courts," 71 *Yale L. J.*, 760, 781f (1962).

cial decision; they also may be generated intentionally through procedural and doctrinal techniques of judicial self-restraint.[378] In effect, the court is abstaining in order to force or encourage "colloquies with political institution."[379]

As this suggests, therefore, the "dialectic" is devoid of neutral discussants. "Characteristic of this approach," says Viehweg, "is that it permits jurists to understand the law not as something merely to be endured, but as something which they continually and responsibly assist in forming. Their entire person participates in this, and 'their pride,' as Ihering says, is 'not merely intellectual but moral'."[380] This raises the last and most irradicable fact of interpretation: the existence of a value bias, of inarticulate value premises in judicial decision. "There is no objectivity in constitutional law," concludes Braden, "because there are no absolutes."[381] Or at least, it should be added, because no known absolutes have yet been demonstrated. This, however, constitutes neither weakness nor cause for disappointment, except for those who seek in the law a knowledge and certainty not present elsewhere in life. Rather, the recognition of value bias in judicial decision and the positive law lays the basis for genuine understanding and interpretation of the constitution.[382] The judge always approaches his task with a preconceived view of the text. It is only as incongruities or ambiquities between his view and the language of the text become evident that questions arise and inquiry becomes necessary. And only in confrontation with the historicity of the text is the value bias of the judge laid bare and opened to criticism. In practice, therefore, each judge would be required to acknowledge a "working philosophy"[383] to be tested and reevaluated in the light of case law experience. This also is a disciplining factor of the "dialectic."

In the last instance, therefore, the worth of the "dialectic" and of the

378 For the variety of techniques used, see discussion in text *supra*, pp. 185, 195f and 205f. See also Bickel, *id.*, Ch. 3; Rosenne, *op. cit.* (n. 374), pp. 527–29; and Gross, "Limitations upon the Judicial Function," 58 *Amer. J. Int. L.*, 415, 427 (1964).

379 Bickel, *id.*, p. 188.

380 Viehweg, *op. cit.* (n. 343), p. 32. Judges, as Chief Justice Warren has said, are "not monks or scientists, but participants in the living stream of our national life." Warren, "Law and the Future," 52 *Fortune*, 106 (November 1955). See also discussion in text *supra*, p. 122f.

381 Braden, "The Search for Objectivity in Constitutional Law," 57 *Yale L.J.*, 571, 594 (1948).

382 See Gadamer, *Wahrheit und Methode*, 250–90 (2nd ed. 1965), whose penetrating study of the historicity of all knowledge as well as of the process of interpretation is reflected in this and the following sentences of the text. See also Ehmke, "Prinzipien der Verfassungsinterpretation," 20 *VVdStRL*, 53, 64 and 70 (1963), acknowledging the existence of a value bias (Vor-Urteil) in constitutional interpretation.

383 The term is Braden's, *op. cit.*, p. 581, whose study reviews the working philo-

decisions to which it gives rise depends on the integrity and competence of the discussants. In particular this is true of the judges who are responsible for initiating and maintaining the discussion. Since judges must juggle outmoded concepts, then in the admonishing prose of Llewellyn let them do so consciously:

> Like Our Lady's Tumbler in the sweet medieval tale: let them turn on their juggling all that is best in them and all their skill . . . . Only . . . juggling too often *unawares,* they may be dupes of their own magic of yesterday, dupes of the game instead of its masters, and sometimes fail in their job because the wizard's hat they play before the multitude seems even to themselves to bring forth rabbits, white or pied, by some spontaneous generation.[384]

Even conscious juggling, however, is subject to error. In that case, says Ehmke, "things just turn out badly. A constitution, even one with judicial review, is not political life insurance."[385] Within the creative process of judicial decision there are no absolute standards from which to judge. Nor is there a transcendent loyalty to the statutory text or Gesetzestreue, or even to certain principles for the sake of the text.[386] There is only fidelity to the law, to the overriding search for purpose, authority and practicability in the law within the traditional and institutional framework of the existing legal order. In the end, this is the style of judicial decision that counts and the kind of self-discipline that must be fostered.

CONCLUSIONS

This analysis of the theoretical foundations of judicial decision has focused on the broad scope for judicial creativity in the law. This creativity is reflected in the rationality of judicial decision which has been defined in terms of three sometimes competing types of reasoning. Each type is directed at a unique judicial task: the self-critical search for purpose, the persuasive search for authority and the pragmatic search for practicability in the law. Not "determinate norms" or "neutral principles" of any kind, but reasoned decisions of this type are the heart of the judicial process. The reasoning of course must begin with the language of the positive law, and is

sophies of Chief Justice Stone, Justice Frankfurter and Justice Black as they state them and believe them. As he points out, while not all are so candid as Chief Justice Stone, every judge does at times seek to implement his personal creed.

384 Llewellyn, *Jurisprudence,* 90 and 92 (1962).

385 Ehmke, *op. cit.* (n. 382), p. 72.

386 See Esser, *op. cit.* (n. 344), p. 283, and also pp. 4, 119f and 148.

ultimately in search of lasting principles. Except in unusual cases, however, the one falls too short and the other too wide of the concrete situation confronting the judge. This is the nature of creative judicial decision.

The judiciary admittedly has no monopoly on the knowledge peculiar to these types of reasoning. This fact becomes crucial in the context of constitutional adjudication where fundamental political values are at stake. How can creative decisions, rendered in the course of judicial review, become responsible and unique contributions to constitutional government? Above all, the answer to this question entails a disciplined institutional framework, combined with the craft ideals and craftsmanship of the legal tradition. Only in the institutional context of a division and balance of governmental powers can the nature and limits of judicial power sufficiently be appreciated. This makes clear, at the same time, that a constitutional court not only has the power to act and legitimate governmental acts, but also is acted upon and constrained in its action. Within this context the overriding task of a constitutional court is not so much to resolve disputes as to initiate and press discussion on those earnest, underlying and enduring questions of constitutional law. It must use its limited power, in the classic style of the "dialectic," to maintain and further the development of that constitutional consensus embodying the continuing search for purpose, authority and practicability in the law. To this end and by the proper use of judicial techniques, the court may criticize prevailing opinion, it may focus discussion among the major political institutions and it even may check those views at least for a time. In this way, it helps bring a nation to full consciousness of the fundamental decisions being made. This is the enduring contribution of judicial review to constitutional government. Nevertheless, absent certain knowledge of the ends of law and given adamant public demand, a constitutional court ultimately must defer to the people's choice.

PART THREE

THE JURISPRUDENCE OF THE COURT

"L'interprétation ouvre un champ fertile à l'observation des démarches du raisonnement humain." Ch. de Visscher, Problèmes d'interprétation judiciaire en droit international public 12 (1963).

The previous Chapters have outlined the organizational structure of the European Communities and of the Court of Justice. They also have framed a theory of judicial decision. It is proposed now to test and develop this theory through the case law of the Community Court. This entails, first of all, tracing the course of the jurisprudence in terms of the chief tasks of judicial decision set forth in Chapter III. A chapter has been devoted to each task: the search for purpose, the search for authority and the search for practicability. Not all but certainly the most important of the 350 odd judgments of the Court, covering seventeen years from 1953 through mid-1970, are examined here. Only the numerous judgments of the Court on personnel matters, constituting perhaps one-fourth of the Court's case load, have been excluded generally from consideration. Not all the judgments are reviewed in any one chapter but rather in terms of the judicial task in question. In any case, so far as possible the judgments will be presented and evaluated in their context and through the words of the Court of Justice and the Advocates-General.

Moreover, the latter half of each chapter will develop the institutional framework of the Court's jurisprudence. In this way the tasks of the Court can be tested not only against the substantive product of lines of decisions, but also in terms of the real limits to judicial power. This is the point where the "dialectic" of judicial interpretation shifts from primarily an inner-judicial discourse to a circle of discussants including Community political organs and Member State authorities. No attempt is made now, it should be noted, to formulate more precisely the nature and limits of the Court's power. Its jurisdictional lines as well as its position in the historical and political context of the European Communities have been indicated already in Chapters I and II. Suffice it to summarize that the legitimating power of the Community Court and the institutional constraints operating upon it are not substantially different from those facing constitutional courts in a federal context. It must simply be recognized that the Court acts in a peculiar and, to some extent, unique institutional setting and that the underlying political tensions at work may on occasion be much greater in a "supranational" than in a national community. However this may be, it must be granted that the following chapters can neither prove nor disprove a theory of judicial decision. Rather, the theory developed in this study is intended to offer an explanatory framework of the jurisprudence of the Court of Justice as well as certain indices for evaluating the contribution of the Court to the development of Community law and economic integration. Ultimately, this analysis seeks to raise to consciousness the unexpressed premises of judicial decision-making in the European Communities.

CHAPTER V

THE SEARCH FOR PURPOSE

The search for purpose in the Treaties is a result of imperfection in the law as written. It originates in textual ambiguities and inconsistencies or in an apparent divergence between the language and import of a norm. Its roots, however, go much deeper. They lie in the very nature of law as a normative order, with real but unrealized and only vaguely ascertainable ideals. This gives rise, as Chapter III demonstrates, to a continuing tension between the norm as written and its ideal content. On concrete issues, it faces the Court of Justice with a choice between several possible textual meanings. This choice, on the one hand, can not be avoided simply by rules of interpretation. They offer, of course, valuable tools of legal reasoning.[1] So far as they serve to clarify the wording of the text or reflect logical reasoning, no court can do without them; they contribute to an economy of the judicial process and to the clarity of legal argument. Removed from their context, however, they tend to become artificial. "For as rule they are not the determining cause of judicial decision," observes Lauterpacht,[2] "but the form in which the judge cloaks a result arrived at by other means." On the other hand, the choice can not be explained or responsibly justified by the personal desires

[1] For general discussion of rules of interpretation as applied by the Community Court, see McMahon, "The Court of the European Communities; Judicial Interpretation and International Organization," 37 *Brit. YB Int. L.*, 320, 330–48 (1961); the discussion papers of Monaco, Bisdom and Wolf: "Auslegungsgrundsätze des Gerichtshofs," in *Zehn Jahre Rechtspechung des Gerichtshofs der Europäischen Gemeinschaften*, 177–192 (1965); Valentine, *The Court of Justice of the European Communities*, vol. I, Ch. 7 (1965); Breban, "Revue de jurisprudence de la Cour de Justice des Communautés européennes," 78 *Rev. dr. pub. sci. pol.*, 873, 877–80 (1962); Kreibaum, "Die Auslegung des Vertrages zur Begründung der EWG," 83 *Z. schweiz. R.*, 163 (1964); and Colin, *Le Gouvernement des juges dans les Communautés Européennes*, 119–26 (1966).

[2] Lauterpacht, "Restrictive Interpretation and the Principle of Effectiveness in the Interpretation of Treaties," 26 *Brit. YB Int. L.*, 48, 53 (1949). See also Esser, *Grundsatz und Norm*, 127f (1956).

of the judge or the purely obligatory character of judicial decision. If these, as might be countered, are but reality, then reality must be changed just that much. Such a view, says Charles de Visscher in criticism of Kelsen,[3] "est inacceptable pour qui le conçoit comme une discipline destinée à guider la conduite humaine." Instead, judicial choice points toward the deeper values and principles underlying the Treaties and Community organization. This Chapter is an inquiry into the methods employed in the judicial search for the basic premises of Treaty interpretation.

THE QUESTION OF METHODS

At least theoretically, the Community Court may emphasize one of three different methods in Treaty interpretation. In the code law tradition of the Continent, Peter Schneider distinguishes between the methods of language clarification, or a strict adherence to the legal text, and of determination of intent.[4] The latter may be subdivided into the subjective method or the historical will of the legislator, and the objective method or the systematic integration of the text as a whole. The objective method most clearly characterizes the constitutional practice in Germany and Switzerland today.[5] In international law, Fitzmaurice suggests a similar triangle of methods which he denotes as the "textual" or "ordinary meaning of the words" school, the "intent" or "founding fathers" school and the "teleological" or "aims and objects" school.[6] Whereas the International Court of Justice, like its predecessor, tends to favor the textual method, it has shown its willingness to take into consideration the broader context and purposes of treaties.[7]

These several methods, however, are by no means exclusive of each other. Indeed, beyond a certain point, there may be no practical difference between the "historical intent" and the "aims and objects" approaches.[8] Where legislative foresight is imperfect, disputes may often be resolved only by projecting the historical intent into the future. Further, should the actual intent not be ascertainable, the court may be called to apply what Lauterpacht terms "the overriding – the higher – common intention of the parties, not

[3] de Visscher, *Problèmes d'interprétation judiciaire en droit international public,* 14 (1963). For discussion of Kelsen's "Stufenbau" and "Zwangsakt" theory, see text *supra,* p. 97f.

[4] Schneider, "Prinzipien der Verfassungsinterpretation," 20 *VVdStRL,* 1, 6–9 (1963).

[5] *Ibid.,* pp. 9–13.

[6] Fitzmaurice, "The Law and Procedure of the International Court of Justice: Treaty Interpretation and Certain Other Treaty Points," 28 *Brit. YB Int. L.,* 1f (1952).

[7] *Ibid.,* p. 7ff. See also the more recent study of Bernhardt, *Die Auslegung völkerrechtlicher Verträge,* 81–97, 186f (1963).

[8] Fitzmaurice, *id.,* pp. 4f and 8. See also Schneider, *op. cit.,* p. 8f.

less real because it is necessarily implied." This "must be derived from the common intention of the treaty as a whole – from its policy, its object and its spirit."[9] At this point, the two methods scarcely differ at all.

The Community Court has shown little inclination to search for the historical intention of the Member States. Only rarely, in fact, has it alluded to the "common intention" of the drafters. When it has, it either has done so metaphorically,[10] has found it wanting[11] or has thereby confirmed that the alleged intent could not be contrary to an interpretation arrived at by other means.[12] The reasons for this reluctance are obvious. Multilateral treaties, especially those establishing an ongoing "supranational" organization with important powers of policy formation,[13] render the search for a common intention extremely difficult. The Treaty drafters simply could not have fully anticipated the changing demands of economic integration.[14] Furthermore, the *travaux préparatoires,* which constitute an important secondary source for ascertaining the will of the contracting parties, "are practically non-existent . . . or secret, (which amounts to the same thing)."[15] In interpreting the Personnel Statute, the Court took the principled position:[16]

> In the absence of *travaux préparatoires* clearly expressing the intentions of the authors of the provision, the Court can base its conclusions only upon the scope of the text in the form in which it has been drafted, and give it the meaning which flows naturally from a literal and logical interpretation.

In the case of textual ambiguity, therefore, the Court may resort only to the governmental reports which accompanied the Treaties during parliamentary ratification. Although varying considerably in length, they throw a certain light on specific provisions and are frequently cited by the litigating parties and Advocates-General.[17] They are of course "in no way binding"

[9] Lauterpacht, *op. cit.,* (n. 2), p. 81.

[10] See Judgment 3–18, 25 and 26/58, 6 Rspr. 373, 413f (1960).

[11] See Judgment 6/60, 6 Rspr. 1163, 1194 (1960).

[12] See Judgments 3/59, 6 Rspr. 121, 135f (1960); 3–18, 25 and 26/58, 6 Rspr. 373, 409f (1960); 30/59, 7 Rspr. 1, 45 (1961); 2 and 3/60, 7 Rspr. 281, 311 (1961); and 10/61, 8 Rspr. 1, 21 (1962).

[13] See text *supra,* p. 10ff, for a discussion of quasi-legislative powers in the Communities.

[14] See Bebr, "The Development of a Community Law by the Court of the European Coal and Steel Community," 42 *Minn. L. Rev.,* 845, 856f (1957–58).

[15] Conclusions of *Adv-Gen.* Lagrange, in Case 8/55, 2 Rspr. 231, 254 (1955–56).

[16] Judgment 15/60, 7 Rspr. 239, 262 (1961).

[17] See, e.g., Conclusions of *Adv-Gen.* Lagrange, in Cases 3/54, 1 Rspr. 151, 158 and 183 (1954–55); 8/55, 2 Rspr. 231, 254 (1955–56); 14/59, 5 Rspr. 501, 509 (1958–59); 2 and 3/60, 7 Rspr. 315, 327 (1961), and Conclusions of *Adv-Gen.* Roemer, in Cases 6/54, 1 Rspr. 241, 258 (1954–55); 1/55, 2 Rspr. 31, 37 (1955–56); 7 and 9/54,

and, like the *travaux préparatoires,* may be used only to clarify an unclear or ambiguous text.[18] The Court has cited them rarely and then only as supporting evidence.[19] Even assuming, as Lagrange contends,[20] that these reports were harmonized with each other to a certain extent, they still reveal varying emphases on specific Treaty provisions.[21] Further, they reflect not the course of the negotiations, but a public *exposé* of the opinions of individual delegations *following* the signing of the Treaties. As a result, they offer only a limited hope for ascertaining the actual intentions of the Member States.

Instead, the Court has adopted essentially an "objective" view of Treaty interpretation, combining elements both of the "textual" and "teleological" methods. As a rule, it begins with an examination of the specific text in question, apparently assuming that this most adequately reflects the intention of the Member States.[22] This means, in the first place, ascertaining the normal, ordinary or "customary use of the language," e.g., subvention,[23] and not necessarily its use in the law of the Member States. At times, this may require turning to the technical usage in a given industry.[24] And, due to the multiplicity of languages in the Communities, it may require also a comparison of the official texts or documents in question.[25] Linguistics, however, is not enough; as Lagrange contends,[26] the words must be seen in their context. Yet, on occasion, the Court has appeared overly impressed by a particular textual phrasing. Thus, since ECSC Article 60 § 2 states that the

2 Rspr. 105, 135 (1955–56); 27–29/58, 6 Rspr. 549, 568 (1960); 41 and 50/59, 6 Rspr. 1055, 1106 (1960); 13/60, 8 Rspr. 239, 280 (1962) (referring to *travaux préparatoires* of the ECSC Treaty).

18 Conclusions of *Adv-Gen.* Lagrange, in Case 8/55, *id.*, p. 254.

19 See, e.g., Judgments 6/60, 6 Rspr. 1163 1194f (1960); and 2 and 3/60, 7 Rspr. 281, 311 (1961).

20 Conclusions of *Adv-Gen.* Lagrange, in Case 8/55, *op. cit.*, p. 254.

21 Mathijsen, La C.E.C.A. 30f (1958); and Bebr, *op. cit.* (n. 14), p. 857.

22 See Judgments listed in note 12 *supra.*

23 Judgment 30/59, 7 Rspr. 1, 42f (1961).

24 Judgment 14/59, 5 Rspr. 465, 488 (1958–59).

25 Whereas the official language of the ECSC Treaty (Art. 100) is French, the EEC Treaty (Art. 248) is equally binding in German, French, Italian and Dutch. For a discussion of the language problem, see Ophüls, "Über die Auslegung der Europäischen Gemeinschaftsverträge" in *Festgabe Alfred Müller-Armack,* 279 (1961); Groeben-Boeckh, *Kommentar zum EWG-Vertrag,* Bem. zu Art. 248 (1960); and more generally Dölle, "Zur Problematik mehrsprachiger Gesetzes- und Vertragstexte" 26 *Rabels Z.*, 4 (1961). For language comparisons by the Community Court, see Judgments 5/55, 1 Rspr. 275, 290 (1954–55); 6/60, 6 Rspr. 1163, 1189 (1960); and 30/59, 7 Rspr. 1, 45 (1961). In interpreting a Decision of the Commission addressed to all Member States, the Court noted that all four official language versions must be considered. Judgment 29/69, 15 Rspr. 419, 424f (1969).

26 Conclusions of *Adv-Gen.* Lagrange, in Case 13/61, 8 Rspr. 119, 149f (1962).

prices of firms "must be published," it was held to establish an absolute obligation, permitting no exceptions or restrictions.[27] Or, conversely, the very absence of such obligatory wording in ECSC Article 70(2), for the publication of transport rates, shows "with certainty that this provision grants the High Authority no legislative power."[28]

Only rarely, however, has the Court been satisfied with such a limited perspective. While proceeding from the specific provisions in question, it is led by the major purposes of the Treaties. Thus, after its textual examination in Article 60, just mentioned, the Court further inquired into the *ratio legis* of the provision, to see if its construction "is not at variance with the objects of the Treaty or whether it can not be refuted by other considerations."[29] And, where doubt arose around the criterion of comparability for ECSC Article 4 c) "special burdens," it was deemed advisable to check "the results to which it leads against those which were intended by the Treaty."[30] Again and again, the Court has justified its conclusions by reading Community regulations in the light of Treaty articles,[31] by construing specific Treaty provisions in terms of major Treaty purposes[32] and, further, by checking its construction of major Treaty purposes against specific Treaty provisions.[33] This is necessary because, as the Court puts it, "the provisions of the Treaty form a whole; they complete and complement each other."[34] In sum, the proper scope and meaning of Treaty provisions must be determined "by the spirit of these provisions, by their systematic integration and by their terms."[35]

By the same token, the Court has not hesitated to elaborate those major Treaty purposes which guide its interpretation. For the ECSC, they are the

[27] Judgment 1/54, 1 Rspr. 1, 26 (1954–55).

[28] Judgment 20/59, 6 Rspr. 681, 707f (1960).

[29] Judgment 1/54, *op. cit.*, p. 31. See also Judgment 6/60, 6 Rspr. 1163, 1194f (1960).

[30] Judgment 7 and 9/54, 2 Rspr. 53, 91 (1955–56).

[31] Judgments 75/63, 10 Rspr. 379, 395f (1964); and 100/63, 10 Rspr. 1213, 1232f (1964), concerning the Social Security Reg. No. 3 of the EEC Council for migrant workers.

[32] Judgments 6/54, 1 Rspr. 213, 234f (1954–55); 3–18, 25 and 26/58, 6 Rspr. 373, 408f, 412–14 (1960); 27–29/58, 6 Rspr. 513, 536f, 539, 545 (1960); 30/59, 7 Rspr. 1, 44 (1961); 1/61 (Opinion), 7 Rspr. 523, 564–66 (1961); 9/61, 8 Rspr. 433, 476f (1962).

[33] Judgment 7 and 9/54, 2 Rspr. 53, 94–96 (1955–56).

[34] Judgment 9/61, 8 Rspr. 433, 477 (1962). See also Judgments 7 and 9/54, 2 Rspr. 53, 90f (1955–56); and 8/57, 5 Rspr. 231, 252 (1958); 27–29/58, 6 Rspr. 513, 536f (1960).

[35] Judgment 26/62, 9 Rspr. 1, 24 and 27 (1963). See also Judgments 2 and 3/60, 8 Rspr. 867, 882 (1962); 34/62, 9 Rspr. 287, 317 (1963); and 28/67, 14 Rspr. 215, 230 (1968) ("the wording . . . as well as the nature and spirit of the EEC Treaty must be used as a point of departure").

"articles philosophiques"[36] in Part I of the Treaty. In the very first Judgment,[37] these were defined as Articles 2, 3 and 4, constituting the "fundamental provisions establishing the common market and the objectives of the Community." To these was later added Article 5, governing the general means of market control.[38] These provisions, "being self-sufficient, . . . are immediately applicable" so far as they are not modified by other Treaty provisions; they "have equal binding force and must be read together if they are to be correctly applied."[39] For this reason, the express mention of only one of these Articles, e.g., Article 3, in a specific Treaty provision "does not release the High Authority from the obligation to respect the other articles of the Treaty and, in particular, Articles 2, 4 and 5, which with Article 3 . . . set out the fundamental purposes of the Community."[40] Where relevant and applicable, these major purposes bind directly not only the High Authority, but in general all organs of the Community[41] and the Member States.[42]

This same pattern appears in the shorter period of judicial experience with the EEC Treaty.[43] Despite its more skeletal context,[44] the Court has affirmed certain fundamental principles and procedures for erecting the Common Market. Thus, the various "stand still" provisions, whereby the Member States obligate themselves not to increase existing barriers to intra-Community trade, are absolutely and directly binding.

> From the clarity, certainty and unconditionality of Articles 9 and 12 and from the inherent logic of these provisions and of the entire Treaty, it is concluded that the proscription of new tariffs in conjunction with the principle of free trade represents a fundamental provision and that, therefore, all exceptions must be clearly stated and narrowly construed.[45]

Indeed, the EEC Article 12 "stand still" provision not only applies to manu-

[36] Rueff, "La Cour et l'économie politique," in *Zehn Jahre Rechtsprechung des Gerichtshofs der Europäischen Gemeinschaften,* 13, 15 (1965). See also Reuter, *La C.E.C.A.,* 176 (1953).

[37] Judgment 1/54, 1 Rspr. 7, 23 (1954–55).

[38] Judgment 8/57, 4 Rspr. 251f (1958). See also the identical language in Judgments 9–13/57, 4 Rspr. 299f, 403, 440, 478f and 518 (1958).

[39] *Ibid.*

[40] *Ibid.*

[41] Judgment 9/56, 4 Rspr. 7, 44 (1958) (re ECSC Art. 3). See also identical language of Judgment 10/56, 4 Rspr. (1958); and the Conclusions of *Adv-Gen.* Lagrange in Case 13/57, 4 Rspr. 317, 344–46 (1958).

[42] ECSC Art. 86(2). See Judgment 7 and 9/54, 2 Rspr. 53, 90f (1955–56) (re ECSC Art. 4). See also the Conclusions of *Adv-Gen.* Lagrange, *id.,* p. 344.

[43] No cases as yet have arisen under the Euratom Treaty.

[44] See discussion in text *supra,* p. 7ff.

[45] Judgment 2 and 3/62, 8 Rspr. 867, 882f (1962). See also Judgment 90 and 91/63, 10 Rspr. 1329, 1347 (1964).

factured products, it also constitutes "a necessary premise . . . for replacing the innerstate market regulations with a common organization of agricultural markets."[46] It states a categorical imperative which, when extended to quotas and similar quantitative restrictions (EEC Article 31), "permits of no exceptions, even of a partial character or limited in time."[47]

As a matter of method, therefore, the Court has adopted essentially a teleological approach to Treaty interpretation. It decides in terms of known Treaty objectives, but these in turn unfold in light of the "new objects or vistas" revealed through the operation of the Treaties.[48] This approach accords with the evolutionary quality of Community law, based not as the United Nations on "orders of coordination" but rather on "orders of integration."[49] The Community legal orders are designed not only to attain certain stated economic objectives, but to do so in an effort to integrate the substantially competing economies of the Member States. Integration is to be accomplished, moreover, not merely by the enlisted cooperation of national governments, but also through a disciplined procedural and institutional framework of government which is profoundly constitutional in nature.[50] As Advocate-General Lagrange has said of the ECSC in particular, the Communities resemble "much more a federal than an international organization."[51] As a result, the Court must be prepared in the course of judicial review to foster and maintain the development of Treaty objectives and the lines of growth necessary to constitutional government.

More fundamentally, of course, teleological interpretation is simply part of the larger search for purpose in the law. It proceeds by way of reasoned judicial decisions which, in their continuing self-critical search for Treaty content, focus the attention of jurists, Community and national authorities and, indeed, the Communities as a whole on the fundamental earnest questions of the Community legal orders. This search is framed and disciplined by the "dialectic" of judicial decision, outlined in in Section 4 of Chapter IV, and is nourished through the rhetorical topics and insights developed in the

[46] Judgment 90 and 91/63, *id.*, p. 1347.

[47] Judgment 7/61, 7 Rspr. 693, 718 (1961). See also Judgment 6/64, 10 Rspr. 1251, 1275 (1964) (re EEC Art. 37).

[48] Fitzmaurice, *op. cit.* (n. 6), p. 8 at note 2.

[49] C. de Visscher, *op. cit.* (n. 3), p. 153f, referring to the ECSC. See also the discussion in text *supra*, pp. 18f, 37ff and 46f.

[50] See discussion in text *supra*, pp. 19ff.

[51] Conclusions of *Adv-Gen*. Lagrange, in Case 8/55, 2 Rspr. 231, 266 (1955–56). See also his Conclusions, in Case 28–30/62, 9 Rspr. 85, 92 (1963); and his "L'ordre juridique de la C.E.C.A. vu à travers la jurisprudence de sa Cour de Justice," 64 *Rev. dr. pub. sci. pol.*, 841, 862f (1958).

course of adjudication.[52] As was indicated there, this overriding task of judicial decision has both substantive and institutional aspects.[53] These will be discussed separately in this Chapter. The former is characterized by the immediate engagement of the Court in a line of cases with a particular problem or set of problems. Through a gradual process of inclusion and exclusion, principles are formulated, tested and reappraised in light of varied and changing Community requirements and considerations. The emphasis here will be on the case law of the ECSC because of the relatively short period of EEC litigation. The institutional lines to be discussed in Section 2, on the other hand, reflect the real and the proper limits of judicial decision. There the Court is concerned, for a time or permanently, to abstain from substantive determinations in favor of other Community organs. Through the appropriate exercise of self-restraint, the Court avoids a premature or ill-advised judicial commitment in order not to restrict unnecessarily the process of issue resolution or to harden the lines of political discussion. Taken together, these two aspects reflect the scope and limits of judicial decision in the search for normative content.

1. THE SUBSTANTIVE LINES

The teleological method is often identified with arguments of efficacy or effectiveness. Thus, it may be said that the Court should not only ascertain and elaborate the major purposes of a Treaty, but also read in those provisions or powers necessary to implement these purposes. According to this method, says Fitzmaurice,

> a treaty must be interpreted – and not only interpreted, but as it were assisted or supplemented – by reference to its objects, principles, and purposes, as declared, known or to be presumed. In this way, gaps can be filled, corrections made, texts expanded or supplemented, always so long as this is consistent with, or in furtherance of, the objects, principles, and purposes in question.[54]

The definition will not be disputed here, for a term may mean whatever is ascribed to it. And there is good evidence that the method is often so defined.[55] Nevertheless, it by no means follows that every treaty purpose automatically implies the power necessary for its implementation. This would

[52] See discussion in text *supra*, p. 117f and p. 216f.

[53] Cf. Ehmke, "Prinzipien der Verfassungsinterpretation," 20 *VVdDStRL*, 53, 72–74 (1963), who draws a somewhat different distinction between substantive and functional aspects of constitutional interpretation.

[54] Fitzmaurice, *op. cit.* (n. 6), p. 8.

[55] See Fitzmaurice, *id.*, pp. 8 and 13ff; and also de Visscher, *op. cit.* (n. 3) p. 140ff. Cf. Lauterpacht, *op. cit.* (n. 2), p. 67ff; and Bernhardt, *op. cit.* (n. 7), p. 88ff.

be, as Lord McNair notes,[56] *a petitio principii:* "many treaties fail – and rightly fail – in their object by reason of the words used, and tribunals are properly reluctant to step in and modify or supplement the language of the treaty."[57] Further, the indiscriminate treatment of purpose and power may lead the judge to overreach the proper limits of the judicial function.[58] Judicial decision is not always the proper mode for legal development and change. It must respect the inherent and institutional limits of judicial knowledge[59] as well as the formal procedures for amendment and legal reform. To do otherwise would encourage the circumvention of common procedures and endanger the very authority of the Court.

A proper appreciation of the teleological method, therefore, requires a clear distinction between ascertaining the major purposes of the Treaties and determining the scope of the powers granted.[60] These constitute two separate and separable intellectual tasks of judicial interpretation, and may often be governed by differing considerations. This is especially important for the ECSC Treaty. It not only stipulates in some detail the general objectives (Article 2) and specific goals (Article 3) to be pursued, but must respect the partial character of coal and steel integration.[61] Even within the proper sphere of ECSC objectives, Treaty interpretation like Community policy is strongly influenced by the reserved powers of the Member States over their economies in general.[62] The realization of Community purposes, therefore, may well be limited by both the nature and scope of the powers granted. On occasion, the Community Court itself has refused "to judge the suitability"[63] or to supplement the language[64] of specific Treaty provisions which – rightly or wrongly – does not fully accord with certain Treaty purposes. Although in the cases there is no neat boundary between these two tasks of interpretation, the question of "implied powers" will be withheld for separate consideration. The distinction stands as a special reminder to the Court that the "constitutions" of the Communities are the products of international Treaties.

56 McNair, *The Law of Treaties,* 383 (1961).

57 See, e.g., ICJ Reports (Interpretation of the Treaty of Peace: Second Phase) 229 (1950); and ICJ Reports (U.S. Nationals in Morocco) 196, 199 (1952).

58 See Fitzmaurice, *op. cit.* (n. 6), p. 8; and Bernhardt, *op. cit.* (n. 7), p. 96f.

59 See discussion of these limits, *supra,* in Section 3 of Chapter IV.

60 Cf. Bernhardt, *op. cit.,* p. 89, n. 445, who, due to the absence of such a distinction in the literature, hesitates to use the term "teleological."

61 For discussion of this "partial character," see text *supra,* p. 6f.

62 See ECSC Arts. 26 and 67 and the cases discussed *infra,* p. 258ff.

63 Judgment 1/54, 1 Rspr. 7, 32 (1954–55), and discussion of Case *infra,* p. 243ff.

64 Judgments 20/59 and 25/59, 6 Rspr. 681 and 743 (1960), and discussion of these cases *infra,* pp. 294ff and 312ff.

Developing Major Treaty Purposes

"All interpretation," observes Charles de Visscher,[65] "is subject to a value order." In the ECSC, this value order is strikingly reflected in the major Treaty purposes of Articles 2, 3, 4 and 5. It would be naive, however, to assume that Treaty interpretation is thereby essentially simplified. These broad, often conflicting purposes must be translated into concrete decisions fixing the scope and content of the specific Treaty provisions. The law can not be satisfied with mere abstraction: "the law relies on decision and on action more than on intellectual speculation."[66] The task of the judge, says Advocate-General Lagrange,[67] "is not to erect theories but to determine the law." And yet, judicial interpretation cannot avoid a certain amount of intellectual speculation. Especially in constitutional adjudication, where fundamental values are at issue, judicial decisions are not only the products but also the precedents of legal orders in formation. The law, therefore, is informed through its major purposes, but these purposes must be articulated through specific provisions and concrete decisions. How is the Court to proceed?

One answer is offered by Ernst Steindorff.[68] In keeping with the "Systematik" of the German legal tradition,[69] he sees an immanent hierarchy among the major Treaty purposes. Despite declarations of the Community Court to the contrary,[70] Steindorff believes "that a series of questions can be differentiated in terms of various basic provisions and their legal consequences, and that this differentiation can be carried out in practice and cogently justified."[71] He then ranks ECSC Articles 2 through 5 in a descending order of importance: the fundamental *principles of the market* being first, the *Treaty goals* in the narrower sense coming next, followed by the *means* for achieving the first two.[72] In concrete cases, this hierarchy would be decisive,[73] considerably reducing the complexity of norm conflict.

[65] de Visscher, *op. cit.* (n. 3), p. 14.

[66] *Ibid.*

[67] Conclusions of *Adv-Gen*. Lagrange, in Case 8/55, 2 Rspr. 231, 234 (1955–56).

[68] Steindorff, "Die Vertragsziele der EGKS als Rechtsvorschriften und Richtlinien," 2 *Ber. deutsch. Ges. VR,* 94 (1957).

[69] For discussion of this tradition, see text *supra*, p. 94ff.

[70] E.g., Judgment 7 and 9/54, 2 Rspr. 53, 90 (1955–56). As to the EEC, see the Conclusions of *Adv-Gen*. Lagrange, in Case 13/63, 9 Rspr. 389, 394 (1963).

[71] Steindorff, *op. cit.*, p. 98.

[72] *Ibid.*, pp. 98–100.

[73] *Ibid.*, p. 102.

The primary norms in this hierarchy are determined by their direct contribution to the distinguishing trait of the ECSC, namely, the erection of a common market. Negatively seen,[74] these are the Article 4 provisions,[75] aimed at removing the barriers to the free distribution and movement of ECSC goods in Member State trade. Stated positively,[76] these include also Article 2, paragraph 2 obligating the Community to "progressively establish conditions which will *in themselves* ensure the most rational distribution of production at the highest possible level of productivity." (Emphasis supplied.) Thus, in contrast to purely liberalizing treaties, like GATT, a common market is to be established,

> which in and of itself furthers the rationalization of production and the optimalization of trade, replaces the initiatives of internationally collaborating governments and permits a counteraction to those initiatives subject to the requirement that fundamental disturbances in the national economics be avoided.[77]

The distinguishing mark and the "Mass der Dinge" in the ECSC, therefore, is the common market by which economic rationalization is actually compelled.[78]

By the same token, these market principles are seen as independent of the economic and social goals in Articles 2 and 3.[79]

Emphasizing generally economic expansion, increasing employment and a rising standard of living, Article 2, paragraph 2, reflects no more than

[74] *Ibid.*, p. 98.

[75] ECSC Art. 4 reads: "According with the conditions of this Treaty, the following practices are hereby abolished and prohibited within the Community as incompatible with the common market for coal and steel:

a) import and export duties, or charges with equivalent effect, and quantitative restrictions on the movement of goods;
b) measures or practices which discriminate between producers, or purchasers or consumers, especially as regards price and delivery terms and transport rates, as well as measures or practices which hinder the purchaser in the free choice of his supplier;
c) grants of subsidies or assistance by States or special financial burdens imposed by them in any form whatsoever;
d) restrictive practices aimed at allocating or exploiting markets."

[76] Steindorff, *op. cit.*, p. 98f.

[77] *Ibid.*, p. 99.

[78] *Ibid.*, pp. 99, 103.

[79] ECSC Art. 2, paragraph 1, reads: "The European Coal and Steel Community is charged with the duty of contributing to economic expansion, the growth of employment and a rising standard of living in the Member States, in harmony with the general economy of Member States and through the creation of a common market in accordance with the provisions of Article 4."

policies which the free world has long recognized.[80] Though more concretely defined in Article 3,[81] they are not only much less precise and clear but also less effective and more difficult to enforce than the fundamental market principles.[82] For these reasons, says Steindorff,[83] these goals can not constitute either the core or mainstay of supranational regulation in the ECSC. They must take their place behind the market principles.

Finally, Steindorff contends that the means to achieve these goals and to keep the market functioning must come last.[84] These "means," outlined in Article 5, condition the exercise of ECSC powers on "limited intervention." In particular, they obligate the Community to

> ensure the establishment, maintenance and observance of *normal conditions of competition* and interfere directly with production or the operation of the market only when circumstances make it imperative to do so.[85]

For Steindorff, the "principle of competition" is as such "not justiciable but is useful at most as a postulate: that principle permits varying legal policy

80 Steindorff, *op. cit.*, p. 103f.

81 ECSC Art. 3 reads: "The organs of the Community shall within the limits of their respective powers and in the common interest:
a) ensure a regular supply of the common market, taking account of the needs of third countries;
b) assure to all consumers in comparable situations within the common market equal access to the sources of production;
c) seek to establish the lowest possible prices under conditions which do not result in corresponding increases in the prices charged by the same enterprise in other transactions or in the general price level at other times, while allowing for the necessary amortization and providing opportunities for a normal return on invested capital;
d) seek to maintain conditions which will encourage enterprises to expand and improve their productive capacity and to follow a policy of rational, while avoiding a wasteful, exploitation of natural resources;
e) promote the improvement of living and working conditions for labor, such that these conditions, within the course of progress, will be equalized in each of the industries for which the Community is responsible;
f) promote the development of international trade and seek to ensure that proper limits are observed by prices charged on markets outside the Community;
g) promote the regular expansion and the modernization of production as well as the improvement of quality, so as to exclude protection from competing industries, unless it is justified by unlawful action by or on behalf of one of these firms."

82 Steindorff, *op. cit.* (n. 68), pp. 100, 103.

83 *Ibid.*, pp. 103–5.

84 *Ibid.*, p. 105.

85 Emphasis added. The other functions outlined in ECSC Art. 5 include: 1) gathering information, consulting and determining general goals, 2) making financial assistance available to firms for investment and to ease transition, 3) publishing the reasons for Community acts and taking the measures necessary to ensure the respect for Treaty provisions and 4) disposing of Community duties with the smallest possible administrative apparatus in close cooperation with the participating parties.

consequences."[86] As a result, the character of competition in the ECSC would depend first on the fundamental market principles in Article 4, such as non-discrimination.[87] Further, the legitimate sphere of Community intervention in the "normal conditions of competition" would be determined in terms of Treaty goals. For Steindorff, therefore, the concept of competition in the ECSC would be the product of the specific provisions in Articles 2, 3 and 4 and not, conversely, the principle from which rules of competition may be developed.[88]

Steindorff's analysis has the advantage of avoiding a particular ideology of competition. Considering the economic policies of the Member States, it can not be assumed, for instance, that fully free competition is a universally recognized value for all Western Europeans.[89] Lister points out:[90]

> Whereas concentrations and market dominating firms, as well as, restrictive agreements, are singled out for control in American anti-trust legislation, concentrations can not be dissolved in any member country of the Community under present legislation, although some of the abuses created by such firms are subject to some control in Germany, Belgium and the Netherlands.

While the anti-trust policy of the ECSC may be closer to American conceptions than to those existing in the Member States,[91] the individual provisions of the Treaty[92] as well as Article 5 itself suggest a compromise position between unrestricted competition and *dirigisme*. This position may be described, with Hallstein,[93] as "organisierte Konkurrenz" or, with Marjolin,[94] as "a controlled system of free competition" or, with Reuter,[95] as "regulated

[86] Steindorff, *op. cit.* (n. 68), p. 106.

[87] As to the relation between the concepts of "discrimination" and "competition" in ECSC Treaty interpretation, see Steindorff, "Der Begriff der Preisdiskriminierung im Recht der EGKS," 21 *Z. ausl. int. Priv. R.*, 270 (1956); and critique of this article by Mestmaecker, "Diskriminierung, Dirigismus und Wettbewerb," 7 *Wirtschaft und Wettbewerb*, 21 and 92 (1957).

[88] Steindorff, *op. cit.* (n. 68), p. 106.

[89] See Steindorff, *op. cit.* (n. 68), p. 283; Diebold, *The Schuman Plan*, 350f (1959); and Lister, *Europe's Coal and Steel Community*, 126f (1960). For a review of Member State anti-trust law, see Riesenfeld, "The Protection of Competition" in Stein and Nicholson, *American Enterprise in the European Common Market*, vol. II, pp. 207–94 (1960); and Blake (ed.), Business Regulation in the Common Market Nations, vols. I, II and III (1969).

[90] Lister, *id.*, p. 126.

[91] *Ibid.*, p. 129.

[92] See, e.g., ECSC Arts. 54, 57–59 and 61.

[93] Hallstein, *Der Schuman-Plan* 11, (1951).

[94] Marjolin, *Europe and the United States in the World Economy*, 51 (1953).

[95] Reuter, "Juridical and Institutional Aspects of the European Regional Communities," 26 *Law and Cont. Prob.*, 381 (1961).

competition or institutional markets." In any case, it appears most compatible with the *novum* of supranational economic regulation to assume that the Treaty fathers left open the question of a specific economic system.[96]

Despite the worth of this and other of Steindorff's considerations, however, his is an attempt to replace the economic postulate of competition with the juridical postulate of hierarchy. He professes the value of inductive reasoning,[97] but subordinates it to a hierarchy of Treaty purposes. As a tool or method of Treaty interpretation, this hierarchical approach manifests two serious weaknesses. First, in the endeavor to simplify Treaty interpretation, Steindorff emphasizes one Treaty objective, namely, economic rationality in Article 2, to the exclusion of all others. Yet the deductive value of this vague objective scarcely offers that degree of specificity which Steindorff seems to demand of his primary market principles. Indeed, if the theory on "workable competition" teaches anything, it is that the economic conditions which in themselves will "ensure the most rational distribution of production at the highest possible level of productivity" are only vaguely and approximately known.[98] It is obviously not fully compatible with other of his market principles, such as the prohibition of discrimination in Article 4 b) which tends to discourage price flexibility.[99]

Further, while economic rationality is certainly an important long run objective of ECSC integration, in the short-run it is not always compatible with the other goals of Articles 2 and 3. As the experience of national economies indicates, there is no reason to assume that the Community would always be willing or in a position to sacrifice such goals as high employment, regular market supply and the lowest possible price levels to economic rationality.[100] Instead, it is more likely that, from time to time, certain of the goals must be pursued at the cost of others, but that none will be granted permanent ascendancy. Taken together, they form, as it were, the welfare function or performance standards of the Community.[101] The emphasis

[96] Ophüls, "Juristische Grundgedanken des Schumanplans," 4 *NJW*, 289, 291 (1951); and Mestmäcker, *op. cit.* (n. 87), p. 33f.

[97] Steindorff, *op. cit.* (n. 68), p. 137, committing himself expressly to the approach of Esser, discussed in text *supra*, p. 115–118.

[98] See Kaysen and Turner, *Anti-Trust Policy: An Economic and Legal Analysis*, 52–56 (1959); and Ferguson's review of the theory on "workable competition" and of the underlying "theory of the second best," *A Macroeconomic Theory of Workable Competition* Chs. 1 and 2 (1964).

[99] See Bok, *The First Three Years of the Schuman Plan*, 35–37 (1955); and Meade, Liesner and Wells, *Case Studies in European Economic Union*, 258 (1962).

[100] See ECSC Arts. 2 and 3 in notes 78 and 80 *supra*.

[101] In a survey of the literature on "workable competition," Stephen Sosnick finds three types of standards for market policy: structural standards, standards of

among these goals may well shift according to the requirements of market conditions and the changing demands of economic integration. In each case, it is a matter of weighing the conflicting goals in question *at their margins* and determining whether the *increment* of one shall be purchased at the cost of the others.[102] Here, the Court is in the realm of Geny's *donné idéal* and of Pound's or Cardozo's value- or interest-balancing,[103] reflecting the somewhat vague and competing aspirations of ECSC integration. It remains to be seen just how the Court of Justice may take this into consideration.

Secondly, Steindorff's distinction between the market principles of Article 4 and the "means" of Article 5 is artificial. The provisions of Article 4 merely prohibit certain types of market behaviour, but can not fully explain those *conditions which in themselves compel* economic rationality. Yet this compulsion, says Steindorff,[104] is the distinguishing mark of the ECSC. If so, then it can be grasped, like the meaning of Article 4, only within the broader framework of a functioning price system which forces firms to compete on the basis of marginal costs. The nature and intensity of competition, of course, will vary with the structure of the market.[105] As the theory on "workable competition" suggests, this will depend on the size and number of firms, the price sensitivity of goods, the access to market information, firm mobility and the ease of market entry or the opening of fresh areas and types of competitive contact.[106] Thus, in a given industry, direct competition among firms is not the only possible, nor always the most effective means to enforce marginal cost pricing. In monopolistic and oligopolistic markets, price system controls also often include competitive bargaining among large buyers and sellers (e.g., via threats of substitution, of acquisi-

conduct and standards of performance. The goals of ECSC Articles 2 and 3 are found listed under the third type. Sosnick, "A Critique of Concepts of Workable Competition," 72 *Qu. J. Econ.*, 380 (1958).

102 For a pragmatic approach to decision-making on all levels, including the sphere of judicial decision and with particular reference to anti-trust policy, see Braybrooke and Lindblom, *A Strategy of Decision – Policy Evaluation as a Social Process*, Chs. 5 and 6 (1963).

103 See discussion in text *supra*, pp. 112–115.

104 Steindorff, *op. cit.* (n. 68), p. 98f, discussed in text *supra*, p. 237f.

105 "Market structure" here, with Kaysen and Turner, *op. cit.* (n. 98), p. 59, refers to "those conditions external to the firm which are relatively permanent or which change only slowly, and which affect, if they do not determine, the way the firm operates." Indeed, some conduct, like "administered prices," may be the product of market structure. See, e.g., the reasoning in Judgment 66/63, discussed *infra*, p. 283ff, and also the Commission's report on market concentration in EEC Bulletin 18ff (Feb. 1966). Market behavior, on the other hand, refers to the manipulation of this structure by individual firms or firms in concert. It must be doubted that Steindorff, *id.*, p. 99f, has kept this distinction clear.

106 See Sosnick's list of structural standards, *supra* note 101.

tion and of merger or integration), governmentally influenced or administered prices and governmental ownership.[107] All of these aspects of market control, it should be noted, are present to some extent in the European coal and steel industry.[108]

A functioning price system, therefore, constitutes much more than the mere absence of discriminatory acts, subventions and restrictive trade practices. It is a combination of those means of market control reflected in the structure of the market, and supplemented by standards of market behavior and, in some markets, by the constant presence of more direct governmental regulation and controls. Since ECSC Article 5 authorizes only "limited intervention," and then only by way of exception, in the "normal conditions of competition," direct controls clearly are not the solution intended for the Community coal and steel industry. Rather, the operational norm and standard of market control in the ECSC, as the standard for market intervention, is based on that combination of structural and behavioral means of market control which most effectively organize an industry in terms of marginal cost pricing. This norm is essentially the "normal conditions of competition," and furnishes the broader framework for making the behavioral controls of Article 4 effective and intelligible.

This critique of Steindorff's thesis rejects an immanent hierarchy among the major Treaty purposes. If such a value order is possible, then only after long years of judicial experience and not by way of theoretical construction. The supranational experiment of the ECSC can not be pressed so easily into pre-scribed juridical categories. Instead, the major purposes may be divided into *standards of market performance* or the Treaty goals of Articles 2 and 3, and *standards of market control* or the means for achieving these goals in Articles 4 and 5. Among the standards of market performance, that of economic rationality appears central, although it may not always and everywhere be preferred to the other goals. By the same token, among the standards of market control, preeminence must be given to "normal conditions of competition": it embodies those conditions of market organization which in themselves should permit the realization of the Treaty goals.

What is "normal," of course, depends greatly on the existing market structure and on the demands of market conditions and economic integration. The course of legal development in the ECSC reflects a continual testing and fashioning of the standards of market control, in particular the concept of "normal competition," against their ability to achieve a balanced

[107] See Dahl and Lindblom, *Politics, Economics and Welfare,* 173–202 (1953).

[108] See Lister, *op. cit.* (n. 89), pp. 187–201 and Ch. 8, describing the coal and steel industries in the Member States.

realization of the Community standards of market performance. Moreover, the relation is reciprocal. Just as the Treaty goals influence the means of market control, so these means will in part determine the extent to which the goals may legitimately be pursued.[109] Legal development proceeds not by a prescribed hierarchy, but by goals and means informing each other.

It remains, then, to test this hypothesis against judicial reasoning in the four major clusters of cases in ECSC litigation. They deal with the problems of establishing a common price system, ensuring orderly markets, removing discriminatory burdens and benefits, and ascertaining the nature of "normal competition." The common thread running through each series of cases is the development of legal principles informed by economic values. These values may be expressly stated in the major Treaty purposes or drawn from the general context of the Treaty as a whole. In general, the method of judicial interpretation is teleological, i.e., purpose- and value-oriented, and its mode is "topical." In focusing on the concrete problem, the Court reasons through *topoi* which discipline the discussion of economic considerations in terms of legal conceptions.[110] Insofar, the judicial method accords with the admonition of Advocate-General Lagrange,[111] that economic theory delivers no legal standards: "the jurist is more demanding or at least makes other demands, for he wishes to know on what fundamental conceptions the text in question rests." These conceptions, however, are not simply deductions from pre-scribed normative content, but the result of the continuing judicial development of major Treaty purposes.

1. A Common Price System

The underlying premise of an integrated market economy, as noted above, lies in a functioning price system which forces firms to compete on the basis of marginal costs. This constitutes the broader framework for fully understanding the means of market control in Articles 4 and 5. Not surprisingly, therefore, a cluster of three early cases concerns the erection of a common and unified price system in the European coal and steel industry. They deal with the questions of price publication in the steel industry and the use of price-setting powers by the High Authority (now merged into the new Commission) to offset, during the period of transition, a distorted price and

[109] Whereas their goals are broad, the Communities, it should be remembered, possess only limited powers. This fact is reflected in the grounds of appeal for incompetence and *détournement de pouvoir*, discussed in text *supra*, p. 55ff, as well as in the jurisprudence concerning "implied powers," discussed in text *infra*, p. 288ff.

[110] See the discussion of "topical" reasoning in text *supra*, p. 214ff.

[111] Conclusions of *Adv-Gen*. Lagrange, in Cases 8/57 and 9/57,4 Rspr. 317, 349 (1958).

market structure in the coal industry. While all three decisions serve the general aim of erecting a common price system, they are also characterized less by "topical" reasoning than by an unmistakable reserve toward underlying value considerations.

This is reflected, above all, in the Price Publication Cases,[112] the first to come before the Court. Under ECSC Article 60 § 2 a):

> The price lists and conditions of sale applied by enterprises within the common market must be made public to the extent and in the form prescribed by the High Authority . . . .

This constitutes an "immense revolution" for European coal and steel firms whose pricing practices amount to a long history of discriminatory and secret rebates, tailored to the demands of consumers.[113] Further, it constitutes one of Monnet's specific proposals and a basic bargained-for principle of market regulation between the French and Germans. As Haas puts it,[114] Article 60 "made 'non-discrimination' almost the equivalent of 'no price competition,' a deliberate device to limit the flow of German steel to the French market."

Such secret practices would not be altered except by legal enforcement. In May 1953, the High Authority issued a Decision requiring that steel producers sell only at those prices set out in their price lists.[115] The industry, however, had entered the post-Korean War period of declining demand. Prices were falling. Due to the tendency under oligopolistic market conditions for competitors to meet at once any price reductions, steel producers lowered their actual prices but were reluctant to lower their price schedules.[116] Moreover, strict price publication was difficult to enforce. The High Authority itself had come to regard its interpretation of Article 60 § 2 under the circumstances as too rigid. For this reason, the standard was

[112] Judgments 1/54, 2/54, 3/54 and 4/54, 1 Rspr. 7, 79, 131 and 189 (1954–55). This discussion is concerned only with 1/54 (*France* v. *High Authority*) and 2/54 (*Italy* v. *High Authority*). Since much of Judgment 1/54 is repeated in 2/54, all citations will be from 1/54.

[113] See Lister, *op. cit.* (n. 89), p. 208; Diebold, *op. cit.* (n. 89), pp. 262–266.

[114] Haas, *The Uniting of Europe,* 245 (1958).

[115] Decision No. 30–53 (May 2, 1953), in *Amtsblatt,* 109 (May 4, 1953). Article 3 of this Decision states, in part: "These prices, inclusive of delivery to the final destination, shall be calculated by adding to the conditions of the price lists: the costs of transport, charges or taxes payable by the purchaser, and by deducting discounts or rebates of which he has the benefit."

[116] See Bok, *op. cit.* (n. 99), pp. 35–38, who points out that clandestine and secret rebates amounted to as much as 20% for some products. See also, Diebold, *op. cit.* (n. 89), p. 258; Lister, *op. cit.* (n. 89), p. 205f; and Meade, *op. cit.* (n. 99), p. 256f.

relaxed and firms were allowed to deviate 2.5% from published price lists. Nevertheless, this margin of deviation, soon tabbed the "Monnet rebate," was opposed by both the Italian steel industry and the French and Italian Governments. Unable to block action in the Council of Ministers,[117] they carried the matter alternatively to the Court.

In a decision widely criticized for its formalistic reasoning,[118] the Court rejected the flexible rule adopted in the "Monnet rebate" in favor of a strict interpretation of Article 60 § 2 a). The language of that provision is "very clear," asserted the Court,[119] that price lists must be published and that "the price lists" are not mere informational documents but have the "character of an offer to contract on the basis of the prices which they set out." Since this means "the publication of exact prices in the form of list prices" *prior* to their application on the common market,[120] the High Authority possesses no power to permit deviations. Having reached this conclusion by textual analysis, the Court nevertheless buttresses its reasoning by reference to the several ends which strict and prior publication serves: 1) preventing prohibited practices as far as possible, 2) enabling buyers to acquaint themselves with the exact prices and also to participate in the regulation of discrimination and 3) enabling enterprises to align their prices.[121] What is most striking about these ends is that, contrary to Steindorff's thesis, they are not all to be found in Article 4 or even expressly among the major Treaty purposes in Articles 2 through 5. Price publication, to be sure, is a major aid to enforcing non-discrimination (Articles 4 b) and 60 § 1), but it is by no means its only purpose. The Court was careful to note,[122] contrary to the extreme contentions of the French Government,[123] that a violation of the price publication requirement did not necessarily entail a discriminatory practice. Price publication also facilitates the difficult task of obtaining reliable market information in a system accustomed to secret practices. It thereby

[117] Under ECSC Art. 60 § 2, the High Authority is required to consult but not to obtain the approval of the Council of Ministers. As to the motives of the French Government, see Scheingold, *The Rule of Law in European Integration,* 59f (1965).

[118] See, e.g., Deringer, "Monnet-Rabatt unzulaessig: die ersten Urteile des Gerichtshofes der Montanunion," 10 *Betriebs-Berater,* 78 (1955); and Jeantet, "Note doctrinale," 61 *Rev. dr. pub. sci. pol.,* 618 (1955). But cf. Daig, "Die vier ersten Urteile des Gerichtshofs des EGKS," 10 *Juristen Z.* 361, 366 (1955), in language similar to that cited *infra,* note 128.

[119] Judgment 1/54, 1 Rspr. 7, 27 (1954–55).

[120] *Ibid.,* pp. 27–29.

[121] *Ibid.,* p. 24f.

[122] *Ibid.,* p. 31.

[123] *Ibid.,* pp. 14–16.

furthers the "transparence du marché"[124] and the general alignment of prices.

In a system of competition among-the-few, however, price publication may also encourage price leadership and thereby curtail the free formation of prices.[125] The Court did not seriously examine or meet this contention, but simply attempted to sidestep it. First, there was no assurance that the "Monnet rebate" would fare any better.[126] Secondly, price publication according to Article 60 § 2 did not preclude the free movement of prices. "If the economic situation changes, the producers are forced to adapt their price lists and, in this way, 'the market forms the price.'"[127] Finally, even assuming another principle would be better, "it is not the task of the Court to give its opinion about the appropriateness of the system imposed by the Treaty or to suggest a revision of the Treaty . . ."[128] The Court was obviously unwilling, so early in the game and without clear cause, to tamper with one of the basic principles of German-French accord in the ECSC Treaty. Strict price publication, therefore, is only one means in service of several Treaty ends, but it is a necessary and indilutable means.[129] Beyond this point the Court did not go.

Two other cases further emphasize the importance of establishing a common price system within the ECSC. This time, however, they concern not a general Treaty rule but transitional measures. To what extent can the price-setting powers of the High Authority be exercised to offset a distorted market structure? In both cases, the power is affirmed: the Court assumes a wait-and-see posture, giving the High Authority the time and leeway to develop its own course of action. This is most apparent in *Netherlands* v. *High Authority*,[130] concerning the continuance of ceiling prices in the Ruhr and Nord et Pas-de-Calais coal fields. Although by 1954 ceiling prices could be abolished for the common market in general, this was impossible for these two largest coal fields in particular. Their existing market structure,[131] the High

[124] Rueff, "La Cour et l'économie politique," in *Zehn Jahre Rechtsprechung des Gerichtshofs der Europäischen Gemeinschaften*, 13, 19 (1965).

[125] Arguments of High Authority and Conclusions of *Adv-Gen*. Lagrange, in Case 1/54, *op. cit.*, pp. 18 and 57–64.

[126] Judgment 1/54, *id.*, p. 31f.

[127] *Ibid.*, p. 32.

[128] *Ibid.*, p. 31 and emphasized again on p. 32. See also Daig, *op. cit.* (n. 118), p. 366.

[129] Judgment 1/54, *id.*, p. 25. See also Judgment 29/67 (*Société de Wendel & Cie. SA v. Commission*), 14 Rspr. 391, 412–16 (1968), which rejects the attempt by a French seller to justify its failure to report rebates.

[130] Judgment 6/54, 1 Rspr. 211 (1954–55).

[131] In 1955, 26% of the combined German-Saar output, nearly all the French output and 42% of total ECSC output of coal was state-owned. Indeed, Belgium is the only Member State owning no coal mines. Lister, *op. cit.* (n. 89), p. 165. The coal

Authority believed with good justification,[132] could well resist the existing pressure of a buyers' market. GEORG alone, the common Ruhr agency, coordinated the sales of 50-odd mining companies which accounted for about 50% of total coal output in the ECSC.[133] In order to avoid the adverse repercussions of that market structure and to maintain the lowest prices possible, in accordance with Article 3 c), the High Authority invoked its price-setting powers under Article 61.[134]

The Dutch Government attacked that Decision as an unwarranted intervention in the market. It also maintained that the price-setting powers had been used inappropriately for counteracting illegal market restrictions. Instead, the High Authority should break up GEORG as Article 65 requires. The matter, as the Court knew and the High Authority contended, was not so simple. The still-existing sales and import cartels in France, Germany and Belgium formed an interlocking system of economic defense and attack.[135] Since time was needed to gather the necessary information and to undertake negotiations for dismantling these cartels, the Court gave the High Authority the benefit of the doubt. During the transition period, it concluded, the High Authority possessed a certain leeway in attacking such illegal organizations. Indeed, by way of negative pregnant, Article 12 of the Transitional Convention gave the High Authority the discretionary authority to grant them temporary approval.[136] Further, no one had challenged the fact that the coal organizations in question exercised a controlling influence on market prices or that price increases were likely. As a result, "no clear absence

market, in particular, was utterly dominated by the State-controlled Charbonnages de France and, in addition, by the ATIC (Association technique de l'importation charbonnière), which in effect was the sole French purchaser of imported coal until 1961. See Meade, *op. cit.* (n. 99), pp. 232–40; Lister, *id.*, Ch. 8; and the discussion in text *infra*, p. 271f.

While the Charbonnages de France is the only really important concentration of state-owned coal production in the ECSC, the balance would shift dramatically with the entry of England. Counting its nationalized industry, 70% of ECSC coal production would then be state-owned. See Lister, *id.*, p. 165. This would undoubtedly entail a reshaping of ECSC economic policy.

132 Judgment 6/54, *op. cit.*, pp. 227f, 229f.

133 In fact, GEORG (the shortened form for "Gemeinschaftsorganisation Ruhrkohle") handled only about 40 to 50% of total Ruhr output, but the bulk of the remainder never reached the market, being used either by the mines themselves or by vertically integrated consumers. See Meade, *op. cit.*, (n. 99), p. 240f, who also points out that in view of the uncompetitive position of the Belgian and the relative isolation of the French coal industry, this figure perhaps understates the strength of the Ruhr.

134 See Decision No. 18–54 (March 20, 1954), *Amtsblatt*, 267 (March 24, 1954).

135 See Meade, *op. cit.* (n. 99), pp. 232–248, esp. 239f; and also Diebold, *op. cit.* (n. 89), pp. 380–88, 395–98.

136 Judgment 6/54, *op. cit.*, p. 234f. See text *infra*, p. 477f.

of any need" for the High Authority's measures had been shown.[137] The Court thereby strengthened the bargaining position of the High Authority in dealing with the cartels,[138] but prudently reserved the legality of such trade restrictions as well as the lawful limits of Community intervention for later determination.

In the second case, *Fédération Charbonnière de Belgique* v. *High Authority*,[139] the Court was again faced with the exercise of price-setting powers in order to offset a distorted market structure. This time the transitional measures were aimed not at the powerful Ruhr, but at the weak and non-competitive Belgian coal industry.[140] Article 26 of the Transitional Convention provides, somewhat vaguely, for a "system of equalization" which was to enable Belgian coal prices to be brought gradually into line with those on the common market. While neglecting to prescribe the means for doing this, its aim was "to reduce Belgian coal prices to a level near that of the foreseeable costs of [coal] production at the end of the transitional period" and thereby "to ensure that the Belgian steel industry is not prevented . . . from being integrated into the common market. . . ." In agreement with the Belgian Government, the High Authority initially fixed Belgian coal prices at levels below the ruling market price and reimbursed the producers for the consequent losses. In the spring of 1955, however, this deficiency payments system was revised: in brief, coal prices were lowered and deficiency payments were made contingent on measures of rationalization and modernization.[141] Indeed, those coal producers who could face competition were to receive only reduced or no payments at all. Though this came at a time when the demand for coal, like the coal prices themselves, were rising generally, the Belgian producers were prompted to take their cause to the Court.

In contrast to the Price Publication Cases, the judicial reasoning is notably ends-oriented. Considering the competitively weak position of the Belgian coal position, said the Court, these measures are justified by their ability to "integrate the Belgian market into the common market."[142] The

137 *Ibid.*, p. 238.

138 See Scheingold, *op. cit.* (n. 117), p. 231.

139 Judgment 8/55, 2 Rspr. 197 and 297 (1955–56), the former page citation being from the Interim Order of the Court. Since judgment 9/55 (*Société des Charbonnages de Beeringen et al.* v. *High Authority*), 2 Rspr. 331 (1955–56), is substantially the same language, all citations from 8/55.

140 See discussion in Meade, *op. cit.* (n. 99), pp. 288–309.

141 Decision No. 25–55 (May 28, 1955) and High Authority Letter to Belgian Government (May 28, 1955), Amtsblatt 753 (May 31, 1955).

142 Judgment 6/54, *op. cit.*, p. 308. At p. 316, the Court states that the integration of the Belgian market "corresponds undoubtedly to the general conception of the Treaty."

recognized interests of coal consumers "makes it necessary that the lowering of Belgian prices to a level near the foreseeable costs of production should have its full effects to the exclusion of fluctuations on the Belgian market."[143] By the same token, these deficiency payments must be contingent on the relatively non-competitive position of the producers, else they would be transformed into mere subsidies.[144] Based on "implied powers" reasoning discussed below,[145] therefore, the High Authority possessed the power to set Belgian coal prices below the existing market price. In order to further a common price system and to achieve at the end of the transitional period an integrated market, the free formation of prices could be suspended temporarily on the Belgian coal market.[146]

In this first phase of ECSC litigation, considerations basic to the erection of a common price system dominate judicial decisions. This is a natural product of the Community task at hand. The judicial reasoning itself, however, is not at all uniform. It varies from the heavily textual analysis of the Price Publication Cases to the largely non-committal language of the *Netherlands* Judgment and then, dramatically, to the openly teleological approach in *Fédération Charbonnière.* The latter two are further characterized by typically transitional problems and their reasoning must be viewed in this context. They are less concerned with basic Treaty principles as with assuring the High Authority the necessary flexibility in establishing the common market. These early decisions, therefore, are characterized more by a variety of judicial approaches, all contributing to a common end, than by the development of a common judicial method.

II. Orderly Markets

An effectively functioning price system means more than simply common markets. "The Community," observes Meade[147] "has always aimed at creating 'orderly markets.'" More specifically, ECSC Article 3 a) and c) requires that the common market be ensured regular supplies at the lowest prices possible.[148] At the opening of the ECSC, however, these goals ap-

[143] *Ibid.*, p. 308.
[144] *Ibid.*, p. 322.
[145] See text *infra,* p. 293f.
[146] The problem of the Belgian coal industry, however, has not been so easily resolved. Between December 1959 and December 1962, the emergency measures of ECSC Art. 37 were invoked, thus isolating the Belgian market by quantitative restrictions on imports from the Member States. Experience has shown the ECSC that the Belgian coal problem could be solved not simply by modernizing, but only by an extensive closure of inefficient pits. See Meade, *op. cit.* (n. 99), pp. 303–309.
[147] *Ibid.*, p. 272.
[148] Article 3 cited in note 81 *supra.*

peared threatened by a shortage of scrap,[149] an important element in Community steel production. Although its overall deficit – about 3% of total requirements[150] – was small, it had to be made up by resort to the much more expensive and much less predictable world market. Depending on this marginal deficit, Community scrap prices were expected to fluctuate widely. For this reason, the High Authority encouraged the formation of a voluntary scrap import association among steel producers.[151] In brief, supplies purchased jointly abroad were to be sold on the common market at the average Community price; the difference between this and the import price was to be covered by a levy on scrap consumers, apportioned on the basis of each producer's total scrap purchases. As might have been expected, this voluntary plan proved unsuccessful.

In 1954, the Community turned to a compulsory fund based on the same principles.[152] Even the new estimates proved overly optimistic, so that economies in scrap consumption also had to be encouraged if the fund was to achieve its goals. At first, the High Authority employed investment opinions to promote the relative expansion of pig iron production as an alternative to scrap consumption.[153] When by 1955 this proved insufficient, observes Meade,[154] "the most obvious solution would appear to have been to abolish the fund altogether, for scrap prices would then have been so high as to have encouraged economy in use." Instead, the compulsory program was strengthened: a bonus was introduced for steel producers who reduced their reliance on scrap by an increased consumption of pig iron.[155] Still, the artificially low scrap prices continued to encourage scrap consumption. As the problem grew worse, the flat levy on scrap consumption was supplemented in 1957 by a surcharge on the increased consumption of scrap as compared to a base period.[156] What had begun as a compensation program for ensuring a regular scrap supply at ruling Community prices, therefore, had been transformed by its own logic, over the years, into a scheme of production

149 See Meade, *op. cit.*, pp. 269–272.

150 *Ibid.*, p. 272.

151 Decision No. 33–53 (May 19, 1953). Amtsblatt 137 (June 9, 1953). See ECSC Art. 53 a), upon which the plan was based.

152 Decision No. 22–54 (March 26, 1954), Amtsblatt 286 (March 30, 1954). See ECSC Art. 53 b), upon which the plan was based.

153 See ECSC Art. 54, § 4. In Judgment 1 and 14/57, 3 Rspr. 219 (1957), these opinions were held non-justiciable under ECSC Art. 33. Only opinions under ECSC Art. 54, § 5, can be challenged before the Court.

154 Meade, *op. cit.* (n. 99), p. 275.

155 Decision No. 14–55 (March 26, 1955), Amtsblatt 685 (March 30, 1955).

156 Decision No. 2–57 (Jan. 26, 1957), Amtsblatt 61 (Jan. 28, 1957).

bonuses and penalties.[157] In effect, the distorted price structure, which the program had produced, had to be offset by increasing measures of intervention in the free play of market forces.[158] Although the program was discontinued in December 1958 for lack of agreement in the Council of Ministers, it had long since given rise to a flourish of litigation.

The validity of the scrap program was attacked in three sets of cases[159] challenging the lawful limits of Community intervention in the common market. The litigation turned on the meaning of that "mysterious" Article 53 b)[160] which empowers the High Authority, by unanimous approval of the Council, "to create any financial arrangements [mécanismes financiers]" necessary to achieve the goals of Article 3 and in agreement with Article 65. The very ambiguity of this provision, as well as the important questions of market control which it raises, forced the Court to abandon its textual methods in search of underlying principles of Treaty interpretation. The mediating *topoi* between the economic considerations of "orderly markets" and the specific Treaty provisions are classical: "reasonableness," "arbitrariness," "common interest" and an "indirect-direct hierarchy" for measures of Community intervention.

In the first set of cases, represented by *Compagnie des Hauts Fourneaux de Chasse* v. *High Authority*,[161] the plaintiffs questioned the right of the High Authority to interfere with existing conditions of competition. In issue was the compulsory compensation program, with its bonus provision as it stood prior to its alteration in 1957. Chasse contended not only that its scrap consumption was not in effect a part of the scrap market being regulated, but also that the compensation program injured its competitive position in pig-iron production by artificially lowering the price of scrap and then by forcing Chasse to help subsidize this. Without going into the basis of the High Authority's powers as such, the Court fully rejects this attack.

157 A perusal of the motives of the successive Decisions, cited here, will reveal the gradual expansion in the emphases of the program from simply "orderly markets" to a more comprehensive view of the means of production.

158 Meade, *op. cit.* (n. 99), p. 279, suggests alternatively that a buffer stock would have promoted stable prices while avoiding the adverse effects on the price structure. Although the reasoning of the court which follows does not appear to exclude this possibility, it was never attempted by the Community.

159 The litigation on the various aspects of the scrap program has been voluminous. Only certain central issues are discussed here.

160 Reuter, "Les Interventions de la Haute Autorité," 5 *Actes officiels du Congrès sur la CECA* (Stresa) 1, 14 (1957).

161 Judgment 15/57, 4 Rspr. 159 (1958). Since the language of this Judgment concurs substantially with the companion Judgment 2/57 (same parties), 4 Rspr. 133 (1958), all citations from 15/57.

While the first contention is held to be unfounded in fact, the second is refuted by the very "reasonableness" of Community action in the "common interest." Only the second contention will be discussed here.

"The legality of High Authority acts," reasons the Court,[162] "does not depend on their absolute effectiveness in maintaining the pre-existing relationship between scrap and pig iron." To require the High Authority to prevent all repercussions of its scrap compensation program, which adversely affect the interests of pig-iron producers, would be excessive.[163]

> All economic legislation necessarily affects even the interests of those to whom the measures are not directly addressed. The application of the principles proposed by the plaintiffs would make illegal any intervention in the economic field believed necessary for safeguarding important interests, if it did not take into consideration all interests affected, however far removed they might be from the interests primarily in question.[164]

A public authority, continues the Court,[165] is required of course "to act with care and to intervene only after carefully considering the different interests involved, while limiting – as far as possible – the foreseeable injury to third parties." This the High Authority had done through bonuses to pig-iron producers. It could not be said, therefore, that "the system disregards the interests of pig-iron producers in any excessive or arbitrary way."[166] Instead, the High Authority has shown that these interests have been respected "in a reasonable and considered manner."[167]

Nor does the program infringe the concept of "common interest" in ECSC Article 3. Once again, the Court reasons more through *minimum standards* of "reasonableness" and "due care" than by any positive conception of "common interest." The High Authority in no way is obligated "to exercise its legislative powers only on the condition that no special interest is adversely affected." Indeed, legislation in the "common interest" means "the use of these powers, as the circumstances require, even to the detriment of certain special interests."[168] At the same time, the special interests may not be wholly disregarded or "more adversely affected than is reasonable to expect."

[162] Judgment 15/57, *id.*, p. 196.
[163] *Ibid.*, p. 193f.
[164] *Ibid.*, p. 194.
[165] *Ibid.*, p. 194.
[166] *Ibid.*, p. 195.
[167] *Ibid.*, p. 195f.
[168] *Ibid.*, p. 196f.

To the contrary, the High Authority is obligated to act with utmost care and circumspect in assessing and weighing the various and at times conflicting interests, and to avoid causing any greater damage than the nature of the decision to be taken requires.[169]

Enterprises, therefore, have no claim to the maintenance of the existing price structure, even if Community measures artificially influence their competitive position in the market.

On the very next day, in the second set of Scrap cases, this judicial approach is confirmed by express reference to the goals of Article 3. This Article, reasons the Court in *Meroni & Co. S.p.A.* v. *High Authority,*[170] contains "no less than eight distinct and very general goals, so that it is by no means certain that all can be pursued, under all circumstances, simultaneously and in their entirety." Rather, in pursuing its Treaty tasks, the *High Authority* must engage in

a *continuing reconciliation* of these individual goals and, where contradictions between them arise, grant to the one or the other that pre-eminence which *it considers* justified by the facts or economic circumstances of the decision taken.[171]

This reconciliation involves the exercise of a "true discretionary power" and must be sharply distinguished from "clearly defined powers of execution." Whereas the latter "are subject to strict control through objective criteria," the former "involve an extensive freedom of evaluation which, according to their exercise, permit the realization of a true economic policy." [172] Since this discretionary power to weigh and balance Article 3 goals has been vested by the Treaty in the High Authority (and other Community

[169] *Ibid.*, p. 196f.

[170] Judgment 9/56, 4 Rspr. 9, 43 (1958). Since language of the companion Judgment 10/56 (*Meroni & Co. Società in accomândita semplice* v. *High Authority*), 4 Rspr. 51 (1958), is substantially the same, all citations from 9/56.

[171] Judgment 9/56, *id.*, p. 43 (emphasis added). Rarely is a translation so important as here. The italicized phrase "continuing reconciliation" – in the French edition "la conciliation permanente" and in the German edition "dass diese Ziele ständig miteinander in Einklang gebracht werden sollen" – has been translated by some as "permanent reconciliation." See Valentine, *The Court of Justice of the European Communities*, vol. II, p. 477 (1965); and Scheingold, *op. cit.* (n. 117), p. 123. If, indeed, the High Authority were obligated to ensure a "permanent" reconciliation of even some Article 3 goals, this would soon impose a rigid regime on Community policy. Rather, as the German edition makes clear and the French edition would permit, the phrase "continuing reconciliation" is to be preferred. This interpretation allows Article 3 goals to be re-weighed and re-balanced as the changing and, many times, unforeseeable conditions of economic integration require.

[172] Judgment 9/56, *op. cit.*, p. 43 and also 46f.

organs), it may not be delegated to subordinate agencies.[173] In doing just this, within the framework of the scrap compensation program, the High Authority committed an unlawful delegation of powers. The Court thus discloses the very relativity of Treaty goals as well as the changing content of the "common interest" in Article 3. By emphasizing the broad scope of legislative discretion, it also signals the essentially limited scope of judicial review in interpreting Treaty goals.

Despite the *Meroni* Judgment, the scrap program itself had not been invalidated. *Meroni* simply annulled an individual Decision of the High Authority executing this program.[174] In any case, the grounds of annulment were more of form than substance,[175] being easily remedied by a new Decision which left the program intact.[176] The most penetrating attack on the scrap program arose in the third set of cases, challenging the general Decision of the High Authority to introduce penalties or surcharges on the increased consumption of scrap.[177] Thus, in *Groupement des Hauts Fourneaux et Aciéries Belges* v. *High Authority*,[178] the Court was called to determine, on the ground of a *détournement de pouvoir*,[179] whether the Treaty powers of Article 3 were being used for purposes other than those for which they were granted. This ground, in fact, defined the issues: the nature of the power being exercised and the purposes which it is meant to serve. The allegations of the plaintiffs are rejected and the Decision of the High Authority upheld.

By little more than assertion, the Court determines that the "financial arrangements" authorized by Article 53 b) serve "the transfer of resources, particularly in the form of compensations and subsidies."[180] In contrast to the employment of production quotas and allocation priorities in Articles 58 and 59, these are measures of "indirect" market control within the meaning of Article 57.

The subsidies do not affect prices directly, but rather the factors which contribute to their formation; hence, without interfering with the free determination of prices, these factors affect the level at which the price becomes established.

[173] *Ibid.*, p. 44.

[174] See ECSC Art. 36, discussed in text *supra*, p. 86f.

[175] An unlawful delegation of powers, although subsumed under the ground of *détournement de pouvoir*, has more the effects of a procedural irregularity. See Judgment 108/63, 11–1 Rspr. 1, 15 (1965).

[176] Decision No. 13–58 (July 24, 1958), Amtsblatt 269 (July 30, 1958).

[177] See note 156 *supra*, p. 250.

[178] Judgment 8/57, 4 Rspr. 231 (1958). Since the companion Judgments 9 through 13/57, 4 Rspr. (1958), are in substance similar, all citations from 8/57.

[179] See discussion of this ground in text *supra*, pp. 55–61.

[180] Judgment 8/57, *op. cit.*, p. 251.

By thus influencing the price level, the financial arrangements of Article 53 affect the other typical market factors, and particularly the supply and demand of the related products.[181]

Though "of an 'indirect' nature," therefore, the arrangements designated in Article 53 b) offer the High Authority a powerful and effective means of market intervention.[182]

The Court then turns to the purposes which these powers are intended to serve. Article 53 b) expressly refers to the goals of Article 3 and the other Treaty provisions, particularly Article 65.[183] Nevertheless, as a matter of principle, the exercise of Article 53 b) powers must respect *all* major Treaty purposes.

The express mention of Article 3 does not release the High Authority from the obligation to respect the other Articles of the Treaty, and in particular Articles 2, 4 and 5; with Article 3, they must always be respected because they set out the fundamental objectives of the Community. These provisions have equal binding force and must be read together if they are to be correctly applied.[184]

These Articles, being self-sufficient and immediately applicable,[185] determine "the erection, administration and orientation of the common market." [186]

Then, for the first time in the Court's jurisprudence, a distinction begins to appear between goals and means in the major Treaty purposes. The objectives of the Community are stated generally in the whole of Article 2.[187] This Article also establishes the broader context for interpreting Article 3, whose diverse goals "must be pursued exclusively in the common interest." [188] This entails, on the one hand – by a tacit adoption of the *Meroni* reasoning –

a certain reconciliation between the various goals of Article 3 because it is clearly impossible to achieve them all, each to its full extent. These goals contain general principles which must be realized and harmonized to the greatest extent possible.[189]

Where full harmony is impossible, "the one or the other of these goals must

[181] *Ibid.*
[182] *Ibid.*
[183] *Ibid.*
[184] *Ibid.*, p. 252.
[185] *Ibid.*
[186] *Ibid.*, p. 253.
[187] *Ibid.*, p. 253f. Article 2 is quoted in note 79 and in text at note 76 *supra*, p. 237.
[188] *Ibid.*, p. 259.
[189] *Ibid.*, pp. 252, also 254.

be given that temporary pre-eminence which the *High Authority* deems justified by the economic facts or circumstances . . . ."[190] Thus, the scrap program emphasizes the Article 3 a) and c) goals of "a regular scrap supply at a reasonable price."[191] Their choice may result in the sacrifice of certain other goals in Article 3 d) and g), namely, those aiming at the most rational use of natural resources as dictated by free market competition.[192] The very existence of the Community scrap shortage permitted *prima facie* the presumption that the choice of goals had not been based on an illegal motive.[193]

On the other hand, the overriding "common interest," which guides the choice of conflicting Article 3 goals, has its broader reference in Article 2. The "common interest," says the Court,

> in no way is limited to the sum of the particular interests of the coal and steel enterprises . . . it reaches beyond the circle of these interests and may be defined only in the context of the general objectives clearly specified in Article 2.[194]

As a result, Article 3 does not prevent the Community from emphasizing certain kinds of production, i.e., pig-iron production, "if the economic circumstances and the reasonably foreseeable development of market conditions appear to require this." In view of the serious scarcity of scrap, the challenged surcharges seek simply to encourage steel enterprises to make the most rational use of scrap.[195] This is compatible with Article 2. Where goal conflict is unavoidable, therefore, the legislative choice may be justified both *presumptively* in terms of a *prima facie* Community need, and by *positive reference* to the more general objectives in Article 2. Taken together, with the minimum standards of the *Chasse* Judgment, these are the three judicial viewpoints of the "common interest."

By contrast, Article 4, 5 and also 57 frame a three-stage hierarchy of market control. "The means (moyen) for achieving the objectives" in Article 2, said the Court,[196] "consist of the establishment of a common market under the conditions defined in Article 4 concerning the removal of hindrances to competition." These hindrances include import and export restrictions, restrictive and discriminatory business practices and state subsi-

[190] *Ibid.*, p. 254. Emphasis added.

[191] Motives of Decision No. 2–57, *op. cit.* (n. 156).

[192] Judgment 8/57, *op. cit.*, p. 258f. The Court rejected a conflict with the non-discrimination goal of Article 3 b). *Ibid.*, pp. 256–58. Article 3 is quoted in note 81 *supra.*

[193] *Ibid.*, p. 255.

[194] *Ibid.*, p. 259.

[195] *Ibid.*, p. 259f.

[196] *Ibid.*, p. 253.

dies or economic penalties. To this same end, moreover, "the Community must ensure the establishment, maintenance and observance of normal conditions of competition." [197] As specified in Article 5, further-reaching measures of Community control may be undertaken "only when the circumstances make that necessary." [198]

Moreover, Community intervention in the free play of competition must favor "indirect" over "direct" measures. This is the effect of Article 5, subject the principle set forth in Article 57.[199] The distinction itself "lies not in the goals pursued but in the means employed to attain these goals." [200] Thus, the "indirect" scrap penalty measures in question [196]

> offer the High Authority the means for altering *the effects* of the "normal conditions of competition," while at the same time ensuring the maintenance and respect for these conditions as required by Article 5.[201]

"By an appropriate use of these effective means of intervention," the High Authority could "ensure to a large extent the necessary reconciliation of the goals set out in Article 3 . . . ." [202] When viewed together, therefore, the various means of market control compose a hierarchy: beginning with the "normal conditions of competition" described in Articles 4 and 5, and proceeding to "indirect" and then to "direct" measures of market intervention only as the circumstances require.

The Scrap Cases set the emphasis of interpretation clearly on the major Treaty purposes. They do this through a variety of *topoi* which focus judicial reasoning and frame the relevant provisions into a coherent discussion. In particular, they begin to articulate a distinction between the Treaty goals of Articles 2 and 3 and the means of Articles 4 and 5. Whereas the means of market control are ordered hierarchically,[203] the diverse goals of market performance are subject to continuing reconciliation. Since the conflicting goals of Article 3 may not always be fully harmonized, some must at times be given preference over others. In such case, the guiding concept is the "common interest" set out in Article 3; it represents more than simply the sum of the particular interests, for it finds *positive* expression in the more general objectives of Article 2. As the Court fails to note, however, this reference merely shifts the task of reconciliation to a more general level: the

[197] *Ibid.*, p. 254.
[198] *Ibid.*, p. 254.
[199] *Ibid.*
[200] *Ibid.*, p. 260.
[201] *Ibid.*, p. 254f. Emphasis added.
[202] *Ibid.*, p. 254. See text *supra*, p. 250f.
[203] See further, the discussion of "implied powers" in text *infra*, p. 288ff.

goals of Article 3 are simply more concrete statements of the conflicts present in Article 2.

Not surprisingly, therefore, the Court offers no concrete formula or hierarchy for goal reconciliation. Instead, where Treaty goals are in conflict, the judicial approach is essentially restrained. So long as the legislative choice is neither excessive nor arbitrary, having met the *minimum standards* of "reasonableness" and "due care," as in the *Chasse* Judgment, the standard of "common interest" has adequately been respected. This same choice may also be justified further as in the *Belges* Judgment, by the judicial presumption that the economic facts and circumstances do not preclude *prima facie* the need for the Community action in question. In the realm of goal conflict, Advocate-General Lagrange cautions the Court,[204] "it is a question of moderation."

III. Special Burdens and Benefits

In the ECSC, the hallmark of the common market has been a "common" and "orderly" price system. Its erection has been ensured largely through measures of "direct" and "indirect" market intervention. By what principles is it to function? The preferred means of market control, as the *Belges* Judgment indicates,[205] are found in "the removal of hindrances to competition" (Article 4) and in "the establishment, maintenance and observance of normal conditions of competition" (Article 5). Following the chronology of the cases, the prohibitions of Article 4 – in particular of "discrimination" and "subventions" – will be treated first before proceeding to the more encompassing question of "normal competition." This approach reveals not only the course of inductive reasoning in judicial decision, but also the intrinsic relationship between the negative provisions or prohibitions of Article 4 b) and c) and the positive standard or dictate of Article 5.

The *nexus* between the two is the *topos* of "comparability." In other words, by what criterion are the burdens or benefits, imposed by Member States on Community enterprises, "special" or "discriminatory" and thereby unlawful? Further, due to the nature of the ECSC, this problem is complicated by the *topos* of "partial integration." At this point, the considerations – though not the conclusions – of Steindorff become important,[206] for Community policy comes face-to-face with the demands of Member State social policy. The limited scope of ECSC integration must respect the reserved

204 Conclusions of *Adv-Gen.* Lagrange, in Cases 8 through 13/57, 4 Rspr. 317, 345 (1958).

205 See text *supra*, pp. 254–257.

206 See text *supra*, p. 239f.

domain of the Member States. Through these two *topoi,* the ground is laid for the subsequent discussion of "normal competition" and "implied powers."

In the Luxembourg Coal Levies Judgment,[207] decided in the second year of litigation, Luxembourg steel producers challenged a governmental tax on industrial coal and coke consumption. The tax was raised to subsidize the price of coal sold for household use. Although Luxembourg itself produces no coal, it is an important steel-producing country. The tax, therefore, fell predominantly on Luxembourg steel producers. The appeal, challenging the High Authority's failure to proceed against the Luxembourg Government for a violation of ECSC Articles 4 b) and c),[208] was flatly rejected. Whether the coal levy constitutes a "special financial burden,"[209] the Court began, depends not simply upon the *firms affected* being in comparable situations. Since this would offer "only a relative and superficial standard," contingent on the firms in question, the "criterion of comparability" must be anchored in the Treaty and particularly in the Article 2 objective of economic rationality.[210] Accordingly, "production costs are based on productivity, i.e., on the natural and technical conditions peculiar to the individual producers." As a result, a financial burden may be "special" and prohibited by the Treaty,

> if, by affecting unequally the costs of producers in comparable situations, it introduces into the costs of production factors which are not related to productivity.[211]

Although "this criterion alone is not decisive,"[212] it establishes the basis of comparability.

Having emphasized this basis of comparability, the Court then disposes of the Case on totally other reasoning. First, while the coal levies introduce cost factors not related to productivity, they "affect all solid fuel *in Luxembourg* other than household fuel, whatever its origin." Thus, within the territorial jurisdiction of Luxembourg, the tax "affects equally all producers in the Community" who either sell or buy coal for industrial purposes.[213] Nor does the Treaty abrogate the right of Member States to levy social costs

207 Judgment 7 and 9/54 (*Groupement des industries sidérurgiques Luxembourgeoises* v. *High Authority*), 2 Rspr. 53 (1955–56).

208 The appeal against inaction is discussed in text *supra*, pp. 76f, 82f.

209 ECSC Art. 4c) is quoted in note 75 *supra*, p. 237.

210 Judgment 7 and 9/54, *op. cit.*, p. 91.

211 *Ibid.*, p. 92.

212 *Ibid.*, p. 92.

213 *Ibid.*, p. 93f. Emphasis added.

equally upon their nationals. Indeed, Article 26 confirms the primary responsibility of the Member States for "general economic policy"; Article 67, in authorizing the Community to offset measures of Member States which "have an appreciable effect on the conditions of competition in the coal and steel industry," recognizes that all discrimination is not necessarily prohibited by the Treaty.[214]

> The persistence of differences in competitive conditions, without implying a prohibited discrimination, is the necessary and inevitable consequence of only partially realized integration in the Treaty.[215]

As a result, the prohibition of discrimination under Article 4 b) "can not lead to the absolute equality of competitive conditions within the Community coal and steel industries," nor even to the abolition of all Member State intervention "which substantially increases the differences in the costs of production otherwise than through variations in productivity."[216]

In any case, concludes the Court,[217] none of the purposes of the levies in question "show any intention of influencing the interplay of competition." In fact, as Advocate-General Roemer points out,[218] the effect of the levies on the competitive position of Luxembourg steel in the Community was *de minimis*.[219] Whether for reason of territorial jurisdiction, partial integration or policy intent, therefore, the Court need never have considered the substantive criterion of comparability. Nevertheless, the *obiter dicta* serves a useful function. It focuses attention on the *topos* of "comparability" at an early stage in ECSC litigation, opening the matter up for discussion. The Court's language is vague, emphasizing the aspect of economic rationality in Article 2, while leaving elaboration for subsequent judicial decision.[220]

Four years later, in the German and French Rail Tariff Cases, the matter was again raised in earnest. The questions at issue were particularly sensitive because the railways, the most important carriers in the Community, are nationalized undertakings in all Member States. At the beginning of the ECSC, their rate structures constituted a maze of exceptions and special charges, designed to further special interests as well as social ends in the

[214] *Ibid.*, p. 95f.
[215] *Ibid.*, p. 96.
[216] *Ibid.*, p. 95f.
[217] *Ibid.*, p. 100.
[218] Conclusions of *Adv-Gen.* Roemer, in Case 7 and 9/54, *op. cit.*, p. 136.
[219] By order of the High Authority, however, the Luxembourg Government modified and then repealed these levies in September 1955.
[220] This prudent restraint of the Court, however, was criticized by Deringer, "Zur Auslegung des Montanvertrages," 6 *Wirtschaft und Wettbewerb*, 725, 730 (1956).

individual Member States.[221] While ECSC Article 70 expressly reserves transport policy to the Member States, it also forbids the employment of discriminatory tariffs based on nationality. Nevertheless, says Diebold, "the discrimination was simple and overt: foreign goods, or goods headed for a foreign destination, were often charged higher rates than domestic products."[222] In 1958, based on a study of the transport industry, the High Authority determined the legality of existing tariff exceptions, approving some and rejecting others.[223] The response was a wave of suits by German and French coal and steel firms; by joining, they were reduced to four, only two of which are important here.[224] As in the Luxembourg Coal Levies Judgment, the issue is discrimination for the sake of Member State social policy. The discrimination involved here, however, is not tax burdens but specially beneficial rail rates.

The essential difference between the two "special rate" cases considered here lies not so much in the contentions of the German and the French plaintiffs. While these parties sought a narrow construction of the principle of non-discrimination, the Court adopts the broader and more penetrating analysis of the High Authority. In both judgments, the attack on the Decisions of the High Authority is rejected as unfounded. Rather, the difference between these cases lies in the willingness of the Court to press the reasoning of the German Rail Tariff Case even further in the French Rail Tariff Case, toward the underlying criterion of comparability.

The Court begins, in both cases, by affirming the direct application of the principle of non-discrimination in Article 70 to transport rates. This principle, being simply "a concrete rule" derived from Article 4 b), is binding on the High Authority as well as on the Member States.[225]

> Article 4 b) prohibits measures "which discriminate between . . . consumers, especially as regards . . . transport rates." This prohibition, which forms an essential condition for the establishment and functioning of the common market,

[221] See Meade, *op. cit.* (n. 99), pp. 339–51; Lister, *op. cit.* (n. 89).

[222] Diebold, *id.*, p. 160.

[223] See Letters of the High Authority: to the German Government (Feb. 12, 1958), Amtsblatt 105 (March 3, 1958); to the French Government (Feb. 12, 1958), Amtsblatt 111 (March 3, 1958).

[224] Judgments 3–18, 25 and 26/58 (*Barbara Erzbergbau A.G. et al.* v. *High Authority*), 6 Rspr. 373 (1960); and 27–29/58 (*Compagnie des Hauts Fourneaux et Fonderies de Givors et al.* v. *High Authority*), 6 Rspr. 513 (1960). The other two Cases involved appeals by the German Government and certain French steel producers against the High Authority. See Judgments 19/58, 6 Rspr. 481 (1960), and 24 and 34/58, 6 Rspr. 589 (1960).

[225] Judgments 3–18, 25 and 26/58, *id.*, p. 408f; and 27–29/58, *id.*, p. 536f.

> permits exceptions and restrictions only insofar as this is expressly provided in the Treaty.[226]

As in the Luxembourg Coal Levies Judgment, however, the requirement of non-discrimination must be reconciled with the partial character of ECSC integration. Where Member State social policy is in question, the Court there concluded, Article 4 b) could neither establish the absolute equality of competitive conditions nor abolish all Member State interference.

This time, the emphasis falls in favor of the principle of non-discrimination. Although transport policy remains clearly in the hands of the Member States, the Treaty forbids discrimination on the basis of nationality. So long as transportation is not integrated into the common market, said the Court,[227]

> its individuality must be respected by limiting measures of [Community] intervention to those which are necessary to prevent the independence of the transport sector from frustrating the objectives of the Treaty.

For this reason, the Community itself is not in a position to pursue or even to condone, except in certain temporary political circumstances,[228] tariff policies based on social goals.[229]

Moreover, the concept of discrimination is essentially "objective." It does not, for instance, necessarily imply direct injury to third parties. "It would be arbitrary to limit the concept of discrimination only to those cases of unequal treatment where those involved actually suffer injury."[230] Nor does discrimination depend on the interests which special tariffs serve. It applies "to all special tariffs, whatever may be the intentions lying behind them," even to those tariffs "totally opposed to the interests of the enterprises being benefited." As a result, *all* special tariffs must be submitted to the High Authority for prior approval.[231] While Community control of transport policy has thus been limited to the prohibition of discrimination, that prohibition forms the least common denominator of economic integration.

Given this conclusion, Article 70, paragraph 4, clearly opposes a transport policy of industrial location for ECSC enterprises. The criterion of compa-

[226] Judgment 27–29/58, *id.*, p. 536.

[227] Judgments 3–18, 25 and 26/58, *id.*, pp. 409–11; and 27–29/58, *id.*, p. 537f.

[228] Judgments 3–18, 25 and 26/58, *id.*, p. 415f; and 27–29/58, *id.*, p. 540. One such exception exists for firms located in the vicinity of the German zonal boundary. See discussion in text *infra*, p. 265.

[229] Judgments 3–18, 25 and 26/58, *id.*, p. 410f; and 27–29/58, *id.*, p. 540.

[230] Judgment 3–18, 25 and 26/58, *id.*, p. 411.

[231] *Ibid.*, p. 412.

rability does not, contrary to the plaintiffs' contentions, extend to *all* conditions affecting firms, in particular to their place of production, the productiveness of the mines and regional disadvantages. Such a view, concludes the Court, would mean "that every enterprise would be comparable only with itself; the concept of 'comparable circumstances' and thereby of 'discrimination' would be devoid of meaning."[232] Rather, as the High Authority rightly asserts, this criterion must be oriented essentially from "the viewpoint of transportation."[233]

Furthermore, transport policies of industrial location "might well frustrate the realization of the common market." They are subject to the widely differing purposes which guide the transport policy in the Member States. Such diversity in market conditions would run fully contrary to Article 2, paragraph 2.

While expressing two reservations, this provision clearly states the *main goal of the common market,* according to which the general policy of the High Authority must seek – and also in the application of Article 70 – the progressive establishment of conditions which will in themselves ensure the most rational distribution of production.[234]

Of course, "this policy might force some enterprises, under circumstances, to alter or cease their business activity." These problems, however, have been regulated in the Transitional Convention and, in serious crisis situations, by Article 37.[235]

As a result, even if the Decisions of the High Authority, then under attack, would cause a temporary reduction in employment or certain firms to shut down, they would not violate Articles 2 and 3.

On the contrary, it can be claimed that these measures are necessary for the common market to attain its desired objectives, since this increases market resistance to crises by removing those firms which can not continue by their own means but solely by virtue of large and continuous subsidies.[236]

Still, the Court holds open an escape hatch, pointing out that no evidence of such crises has been offered and that, should they arise, this Judgment excludes neither a new request for special tariffs nor a new appeal to the

[232] *Ibid.*, p. 409; and Judgment 27–29/58, *id.*, p. 537.
[233] Judgments 3–18, 25 and 26/58, *id.*, p. 409; and 27–29/58, *id.*, p. 538.
[234] Judgments 3–18, 25 and 26/58, *id.*, p. 413; and 27–29/58, *id.*, p. 542f (emphasis added). ECSC Art. 70, § 4, it should be recalled, permits the approval of exceptional tariffs only if they accord with the principles of the Treaty.
[235] Judgments 3–18, 25 and 26/58, *op. cit.*, p. 413f; and 27–29/58, *op. cit.*, p. 543f.
[236] Judgments 3–18, 25 and 26/58, *id.*, p. 414; and 27–29/58, *id.*, p. 543.

Court.[237] Absent such crises, the main goal of economic rationality entails the removal of inefficient business activity in the common market.

The criterion of comparability, therefore, is not a formal but an operational principle of market control. It is based on those conditions which in themselves compel economic rationality at the cost of inefficient firms. What are these conditions and the nature of this compulsion? The Court moves to answer this in the French Rail Tariff Case. It takes up its discussion where the Luxembourg Coal Levies Judgment left off. The "most rational distribution of production," continues the Court, "is based particularly upon production costs resulting from differences in performance, i.e., from the natural and technical conditions of production and from the individual efforts of the various producers."[238] In particular,

> The common market rests on the *fundamental idea* that the competitive conditions of coal and steel enterprises should result from [these] natural and undistorted conditions of production.

Thus, every special tariff containing an element of subsidy "vitiates this fundamental idea, causing an artificial modification of the actual conditions of production."[239] The French rail tariffs in question, therefore, violated ECSC Article 4 c) as well as Articles 4 b) and 70, paragraph 1.

The Court rejects the contention, moreover, that the Decision of the High Authority infringes the Treaty goals of Articles 2 and 3. Thus, abolishing the special tariffs in question may well adversely affect the favored firms' access to sources of production (Article 3 b)), their price levels (Article 3 c)), the stimulus to their production (Article 3 d)) as well as the expansion and modernization of their production facilities (Article 3 g)). The goals in Articles 2 and 3, declares the Court in an obvious but tacit reference to the Scrap Cases, "can not all be attained simultaneously and to their full extent." To the contrary, they need only "have been reasonably respected in light of the peculiarities and possibilities of the given case, and pursued in order to realize the common interest as prescribed by Article 3, paragraph 1." The "common interest" requires looking beyond the mere sum of the individual Community enterprises to the general objectives of Article 2.[240] These objectives in turn rest on the principle of economic rationality and the natural undistorted conditions of production. In short, the Treaty goals are subject

[237] Judgments 3–18, 25 and 26/58, *id.*, p. 414f; and 27–29/58, *id.*, p. 543f.
[238] Judgment 27–29/58, *id.*, p. 540.
[239] *Ibid.*, pp. 539 and 545.
[240] *Ibid.*, pp. 544–46.

to "the *underlying principle of competition* which is the basis of the common market."[241]

The criterion of comparability in ECSC Articles 4 and 70, therefore, looks primarily toward the objective of economic rationality. Its *ratio* is the principle of free market competition. Nevertheless, as noted in the reasoning of both Rail Tariff Cases, even this overriding objective is subject to public policy exceptions. One such exception exists for steel firms located in the vicinity of the German zonal boundary. These firms, said the Court, suffer disadvantages "due to other than economic factors and, in particular, to current political circumstances which severed the enterprises from their market areas." In that case, subsidies of some form could be granted to enable these firms to adapt to the new conditions or to outlast an adverse situation which was not due to their fault.[242] In the more general terms of the French Rail Tariff Judgment, the special rates permitted by Article 70, paragraph 4, must "enable the benefiting enterprises to overcome temporary and exceptional difficulties caused by unforeseeable circumstances, which could have the effect that the production costs of the enterprises in question are no longer determined by natural market conditions."[243] The narrow application of this exception simply reemphasizes the overriding importance of the objective of economic rationality.

Eight years later, in an attack by the Dutch Government on special rail rates granted the Saar steel mills, the Court confirmed and applied this public policy exception.[244] The special rates were justified as an offsetting adjustment for the competitive disadvantage in transportation costs which the Saar mills suffered due to the canalization of the Main, Moselle and Neckar rivers. Based upon plans for another canal to connect the Saar with the Rhein, the German Government lowered the rail tariffs for the Saar to reflect the rates that would exist in fact were they competitive with the as yet non-existent Saar-Pfalz canal. Despite a delay of two years, these "Als-ob" ("just-as-if") tariffs were finally submitted to the High Authority for

241 *Ibid.*, p. 545.

242 Judgment 3–18, 25 and 26/58 (*Barbara-Erzbergbau A. G. et al.* v. *High Authority*), 6 Rspr. 373, 415f (1960). See also the Conclusions of *Adv-Gen.* Lagrange, *ibid.*, p. 455, discussing the question of a regional transport policy. Cf. EEC Articles 80 and 82, Judgment 1/69 (*Italy* v. *EC Commission*), 15 Rspr. 277, 283–286 (1969), and the accompanying Conclusions of Adv-Gen. Roemer, discussing the differences between ECSC and EEC rail tariff policy. The latter expressly requires the Commission to consider regional policy and other developmental factors in reaching its decisions.

243 Judgment 27–29/58, *op. cit.*, p. 540. See also Conclusions of *Adv-Gen.* Roemer, *ibid.*, pp. 570–72.

244 Judgment 28/66 (*Netherlands* v. *High Authority*), 14 Rspr. 1 (1968).

approval as prescribed by ECSC Article 70, paragraph 4.[245] Approval was given, but the Decision was subject to two conditions: the Saar rates would be extended to coal and steel products from other Member States, and the circumstances presently justifying the rate concessions must not change. The Decision could be rescinded for the failure of either condition.[246]

Upon review, the Decision was approved in principle but nullified because the conditions were unlimited in time. The Court built upon the formula developed in the French Rail Tariff Judgment. Permanent changes in the infrastructure of transportation, it cautioned, should not be confused with the perhaps more short-term economic consequences for the Saar steel industry. Appropriate assistance for a limited time would be authorized, if it would permit the Saar to overcome its difficulties or to adapt to the new conditions of production.[247] Furthermore, the Court grants, while the changes in infrastructure might have been foreseeable, they do not lie in the normal course of development but constitute a far more significant change which entails a new orientation of the economy.[248]

More importantly, however, the public policy exception can be justified because the objective of economic rationality does not constitute an unchanging quantity. "It embraces circumstances which – above all, over the course of time – are uncertain and changing."[249] Firms must of course be compelled to adapt their operations to the changed conditions of production, for this accords with the *primary* objective of economic rationality in the ECSC. This does not mean, however,

> that the social-political goals set forth in Article 2 of the Treaty must at all times take second place and may in no case determine Community acts. The general goals in Articles 2 and 3 can not all be attained simultaneously under all circumstances to the fullest extent. The Community, therefore, must provide continually for a balance between individual goals.

When conflict arises between these goals, "the Community must choose that one which in its opinion under the economic circumstances ought to receive precedence."[250] Special rail concessions, if appropriately conditioned and

[245] Originally the German Government justified its refusal to submit the rates for approval, arguing that they constituted measures for coordinating competition between different types of transportation and, therefore, were exempt from Community regulation by virtue of ECSC Article 70, paragraph 5.

[246] Decision No. 14–66 (July 20, 1966), *Amtsblatt*, Nr. 141 (August 2, 1966).

[247] Judgment 28/66, *op. cit.*, p. 18f.

[248] *Ibid.*, p. 19.

[249] *Ibid.*

[250] *Ibid.*, p. 20 Cf. Judgment 1/69, *op. cit.* (n. 242), pp. 292–294.

limited to a transitional period, "could well be the proper means" for overcoming the Saar difficulties and encouraging the most rapid adaptation to the new conditions of competition.

Once again the exception proves the rule. As the Scrap Cases of the preceding Subsection indicated, ECSC Articles 2 and 3 do not establish a definitive hierarchy of general Treaty objectives and individual goals. Rather, within the framework of both Articles, the Community must seek a continual adjustment under the prevailing economic circumstances of the problem in question. The admittedly primary objective of economic rationality must at times give way to special social-political ends. At the same time, the judicial ground for annulling the Decision gave the German Government clear warning. The proposed Saar-Pfalz canal could not be postponed much longer,[251] because the occasions for deviating from the objective of economic rationality were purely exceptional and limited strictly to a transitional period. "Just as if" conditions of competition could not replace the natural conditions on which the Treaty objectives were based. Exceptions would be permitted, therefore, only to enable the firms which were adversely affected to adapt their operations to the new conditions of competition. It is these conditions and the underlying principle of competition, as the French Rail Tariff Judgment so clearly states, that is the ultimate basis of Community policy.

The Court had confirmed this position in the Miners' Bonus Decision,[252] rendered less than a year after the French Rail Tariff Judgment. At issue was an attempt by the German Government to forestall the drift of miners into other occupations. A "shift bonus" from public funds, argued the Government, would not only raise the pay and prestige of underground miners, but also avoid "cost-push" inflation in the German economy as a whole.[253] The High Authority's consent was forthcoming, but only after the German Government agreed to offset this bonus by discontinuing its payments to the miners' insurance fund. Despite this concession, an association of Dutch coal producers attacked the failure of the High Authority to take action

[251] In February 1969, the West German Government announced plans to build this canal at a cost of some $600 million. CCH, Euromarket News p. 5 (Feb. 18, 1969). See also Wägenbaur, "Die Saar-Ausnahmetarife der Bundesbahn im Lichte der Rechtsprechung," 14 *AWD*, 140 (1968), predicting this result from the Court's Judgment.

[252] Judgment 30/59 (*De Gezamenlijke Steenkolenmijnen in Limburg* v. *High Authority*), 7 Rspr. 1 (1961).

[253] Since Ruhr prices, the only remaining coal prices under High Authority control, were to be freed in February 1956, the pressure for coal price increases was great in any case.

against the German Government.[254] The bonus, they alleged, constituted an illegal subsidy under ECSC Article 4 c).

As in previous cases, the Court again was called upon to demarcate the scope of Community provisions in light of the reserved sphere of Member State social policy. In stark contrast to the Luxembourg Coal Levies Judgment, however, what is involved here is not a special burden but a special benefit for the highly competitive Ruhr coal field. The parties and the intervening German Government presented the Court with a broad range of alternatives. Whereas the plaintiff and the High Authority agreed that the bonus contravenes Article 4 c) and the German Government flatly disputed this, both the High Authority and German Government believed that any illegal effects could be offset by other governmental measures. In principle, the Court adopts the plaintiff's position, but reserves for later development the extent to which the effects of subsidies might in fact be offset by other measures.

Illegal subsidies and other aid, the Court begins, constitute non-earned income in a business sense. It may be money or material assistance "lying outside a firm's remuneration for goods and services" or, in a broader sense, "means for the pursuit of stipulated goals which as a rule could not be achieved without outside help."[255] In either case, within the context of Article 2, they lead to prices

> which are not cost-determined and thereby to the maintenance or furtherance of economic activity which does not accord with the most rational distribution of production at the highest level of productivity.[256]

This is confirmed by reference to Article 5: "the creation of normal conditions of competition will undoubtedly be impeded if a part of the production costs are raised by parties other than buyers and consumers." Such assistance is illegal, therefore, not only because it contravenes the realization of one of the essential Treaty goals, but also because it is contrary to the normal conditions of competition.[257]

At the same time, contrary to the contentions of the German Government as well as to certain language in the Luxembourg Coal Levies Judgment,[258] ECSC Article 67 does not diminish the effect of Article 4 c). "It is true, in the last instance both pursue the same goal, for both provisions are to ensure

254 For discussion of this appeal, see text *supra,* pp. 76f and 82f.

255 Judgment 30/59, *op. cit.,* p. 42f. Cf. the discussion in text *infra,* p. 337ff, of the preferential interest rates of the French government.

256 *Ibid.,* p. 43.

257 *Ibid.,* p. 44.

258 See text *supra,* p. 260 at notes 214–16.

the 'creation, maintenance and respect of normal conditions of competition.'"[259] Nevertheless, they concern different matters and are governed by different procedures. The first aims at compensating and warding-off the adverse effects of national policy at work in spheres outside the ECSC. It reflects the "partial character" of ECSC integration, for the Member States retain control over their general economic policy (Article 26), social policy (Article 68 § 1) and fiscal policy.[260] Article 4 c), on the other hand, absolutely prohibits certain national interference "'within the Community,' i.e., within the substantive sphere of the Treaty's validity." Within this sphere, "the Community organs have exclusive competencc" over such matters as subventions, assistance and special burdens "of every form." "Precisely the strict phrasing of Article 4, permitting of no exceptions," concludes the Court, "underlines the exclusive jurisdiction of the Community within its sphere of competence." [261]

Despite its social aims, therefore, the miners' bonus constitutes an unlawful attempt to lower the costs of coal production. Through this artificial decrease in costs, the German coal industry "is placed in a privileged competitive position."[262] By comparison to the Luxembourg Coal Levies Case, this "privileged position" and not simply the pursuit of social aims marks the illegality of the miners' bonus. Furthermore, the German Government had not satisfactorily offset the illegal effects of this subvention. Had the Government really intended this, "then it is incomprehensible why it did not require the mining firms to reimburse this amount." Instead, its formula constitutes "only an approximate and uncertain relation" between the subvention and the suspended payments. The "general and absolute nature" of Article 4 c), however, is not satisfied by such approximations.[263] Could it be satisfied by a more exact formula? The Court never reaches the question.

The course of legal development, as these cases demonstrate, is both promoted and oriented primarily through "topical" reasoning. Such reasoning does not determine but simply disciplines the judicial choice. Thus, through the *topos* of "comparability" – raised first by *dicta* in the Luxembourg Coal Levies Judgment – the Court penetrates beneath the formal concepts of "discrimination" and "subvention" toward a substantive criterion. This it develops through the cases, first by emphasizing economic rationality as the main Treaty objective. This objective, however, at times

[259] Judgment 30/59, *op. cit.*, p. 47.
[260] *Ibid.*, pp. 48–50.
[261] *Ibid.*, p. 47.
[262] *Ibid.*, p. 56.
[263] *Ibid.*, p. 60.

must give way, if only temporarily, to social-political Community goals. The Court further articulates those market conditions essential to achieve this objective. They are, statically seen, the natural and undistorted conditions of production, exclusive of all means of outside assistance. They become operational and thereby compelling, however, through "the principle of competition which is the basis of the common market." Discriminatory measures and subvention are unlawful, therefore, because they distort the conditions of production, granting some firms a privileged competitive position.

The legitimate scope of Treaty provisions, moreover, is delimited by considerations of "partial integration." While the Community must respect the reserved domain of Member State social and economic policy, it must also be guaranteed the indispensable means for realizing Treaty goals. Though hesitant at first, the Court later finds the least common denominator of these competing considerations in the prohibitions of discrimination and subvention by the Member States. Indeed, these prohibitions extend not only to the integrated sector of coal and steel, but also to the unintegrated sector of transportation. This prevents the independence of the transport sector from frustrating the objectives of the Treaty.

IV. Normal Conditions of Competition

The course of "topical" reasoning in the previous cases has led judicial decision toward the unarticulated premises of Treaty interpretation. In considering the Treaty goals of Articles 2 and 3, the Court has emphasized economic rationality and stability in market organization. This fully accords with the observation of Diebold that, in establishing the ECSC, "people of a wide range of political opinions shared the view that markets should be 'organized' for stability and efficiency rather than left to the 'chaos' and 'waste' of 'atomistic competition.'"[264] As both the Scrap Cases and the Rail Tariff and Miners' Bonus Cases demonstrate,[265] however, these goals must accord with – if, indeed, they do not presuppose – an operational principle of market competition.

Furthermore, in considering the Treaty means of market control for attaining these goals, the Court has established its ultimate reference in those "normal conditions of competition" prescribed in Article 5. Whether as the basis for the criterion of comparability underlying Article 4 b) and c)[266] or as the primary norm in an "indirect-direct" hierarchy of measures of market

[264] Diebold, *op. cit.* (n. 89), p. 351.
[265] See text *supra*, pp. 256f, 264f and 268f.
[266] See text *supra*, p. 264f.

intervention,[267] the concept of competition constitutes the basis of the common market. Its articulation, therefore, raises chronologically the last and, in a real sense, the most profound *topos* of Treaty interpretation. What are those "normal" conditions of competition which in themselves compel economic rationality as well as permit the Community to realize its other major goals? What is "normal," as has been contended in the theory above,[268] depends on considerations of market structure, market behavior and market performance. These are the raw ingredients of "topical" reasoning in the cases which follow.

The occasions for judicial decision on this *topos* arose from the problem of market organization for the Ruhr enterprises. They embrace "the greatest concentrations of power in Europe's coal economy," says Diebold,[269] "and everyone else was to some extent dependent on them." The Ruhr produces one-half of the coal and almost one-third of the coke in the ECSC and accounts for 40% of its coal and 70% of its coke trade.[270] Since at the opening of the ECSC the Ruhr was dominated by GEORG, a common selling organization,[271] the fate of this cartel would most likely set the pattern for the entire common market. Competition among-the-few in the ECSC is of course far from any ideal of perfect competition. In most Member States at the opening of the ECSC, writes Diebold, "a few large steel firms stood head and shoulders above the others in size and market power. In coal, marketing was highly organized. In both fields governments owned firms or whole industries.[272]

Nevertheless, Article 4 d) is adamant that "restrictive practices aimed at the allocation or exploitation of the market" are prohibited. More precisely, Article 65 § 1 forbids all practices "which tend directly or indirectly to hinder, restrict or distort *the normal operation of competition* on the common market." (Emphasis added.) At the same time, in contrast to American antitrust practice, Article 65 § 2 authorizes the High Authority to approve certain "benevolent" cartels for purposes of product specialization and joint buying and selling, on the following conditions:

a) that such specialization or such joint buying or selling will contribute to a substantial improvement in the production or distribution of the products in question; and

267 See text *supra*, p. 256f.
268 See text *supra*, pp. 241–243.
269 Diebold, *op. cit.*, p. 390.
270 *Ibid.*
271 See text *supra*, p. 246f for discussion of GEORG in *Netherlands* v. *High Authority*.
272 Diebold, *op. cit.*, p. 351.

b) that the agreement in question is essential to achieve these results, and is no more restrictive than necessary for that purpose; and
c) that it is not capable of giving the enterprises concerned the power to determine prices, or to control or limit the production of marketing of a substantial part of the products in question on the common market, or of protecting them from effective competition by other enterprises within the common market.

In order to determine the legality of restrictive agreements and practices, therefore, some concept of "normal" or "effective" competition appears essential.

Precisely this concept was missing in the first Judgment under Article 65. In the *Geitling* Case,[273] the Court was finally called upon to determine the legality of the new Ruhr cartel arrangements. By 1956, following considerable negotiations, the High Authority had decided to break up GEORG but to replace it with three independent sales agencies.[274] A complete removal of joint-selling, it felt, would not only hinder specialization and the most economic distribution of production, but also, in times of excess demand, lead to inequalities in deliveries to merchants and consumers. Further, due to protected outlets and the lack of homogeneity in Ruhr coal, a fall in demand might well affect pits so unequally as to cause widely varying unemployment between the different mines and the accompanying social tensions. Each sales agency of 15 to 20 firms, therefore, constituted a compromise between the undesirable consequences of a fully atomized market and the aim of encouraging some measure of competition among Ruhr producers.

Ominously enough, the organizational and trading statutes of these three agencies were identical. Indeed, they had been jointly drafted and provided for certain common financial and technical organs. Furthermore, in order to ensure the orderly disposal of Ruhr coal during periods of market fluctuations, a Joint Office was established for negotiating sales to large consumers and for apportioning the supply of different kinds of coal.[275] While accepting all this, the High Authority objected in part to an additional clause restricting the access of wholesalers to Ruhr coal. Pursuant to that clause, any wholesaler wishing to trade with any of the Ruhr sales agencies would have had to have purchased in the previous year at least 75,000 tons of coal overall, 40,000 of which was sold in its own sales territory and 25,000 of which had been purchased from the Ruhr agencies. Of the 25,000 agency

[273] Judgment 2/56 ("*Geitling*" *Ruhrkohlenverkaufsgesellschaft mbH et al.* v. *High Authority*), 3 Rspr. 9 (1957).
[274] Decision No. 5–56 (Feb. 15, 1956), Amtsblatt 29 (March 13, 1956).
[275] See Meade, *op. cit.* (n. 99), p. 243f, for fuller discussion.

minimum at least 12,500 tons must have been purchased from *one* of the Ruhr agencies, and the other half from that or the other two agencies.[276] Some minimum requirements, the High Authority granted, were justifiable to promote the most rational distribution of coal,[277] but the agency requirement together with the "tying" provision was both discriminatory under ECSC Article 4 b) and more restrictive than warranted by Article 65 § 2. As a result, the access restrictions were approved only after the "tying" clause had been deleted, so that the minimum requirement for any one Ruhr agency amounted to 12,500 tons annually. This change was the source of Geitling's attack.

The Court upholds the High Authority on both counts. Yet its reasoning, formal and reserved, does not move beyond the narrow limits of the complaint. First, "by a purely legal assessment," the trading regulations constitute a restriction on competition under Article 65 § 1 and, to be lawful, must be approved by the High Authority under § 2. They allocate customers and markets and thereby are of a nature to restrict and distort competition between the different enterprises grouped within Geitling.

> [*A*]*ny limitation* upon the number of wholesalers allowed as direct customers restricts or distorts competition between the wholesalers, however many of them there may be.[278]

This reasoning, however, fully ignores the qualification in Article 65 § 1, that only those agreements are forbidden "which, directly or indirectly, tend to prevent, restrict or distort the normal operation of competition on the common market." Without further explanation, the Court adopts a *per se* rule for Article 65 § 1.

Secondly, by equally formal reasoning, the "tying" clause in particular is discriminatory and more restrictive than necessary. For one, it discriminates between the Ruhr and other coal fields as well as between wholesalers, depending on whether the latter have purchased additional quantities from one or the other of the two Ruhr agencies.[279] While this is undoubtedly true, the Court does not bother to explain those economic premises upon which this conclusion rests. For another, the "tying" clause is more restrictive than

[276] The relevant clause in the trading regulations reads: "That within that sales area [one of the seven areas into which the Community had been divided] the wholesaler must have had a minimum turnover of 25,000 metric tons of fuel obtained from any one or more of the three sales agencies, and of this 25,000 tons a minimum of 12,500 tons must have been obtained from 'Geitling.' " The other agencies had identical clauses.

[277] See Judgment 2/56, *op. cit.*, p. 43; and the motives of Decision No. 5–56, *op. cit.*

[278] Judgment 2/56, *id.*, p. 43. Emphasis added.

[279] *Ibid.*, p. 44f.

warranted by Article 65 § 2. At most, says the Court, this clause can be justified only as improving the distribution of all *Ruhr* coal; yet this improvement had already been secured by other arrangements which the High Authority approved.[280] Without reviewing either the economic considerations which the plaintiff raises[281] or those upon which the High Authority's Decision rests, the Court simply concludes that further-reaching restrictions than the High Authority has approved would compromise the independence of the Ruhr agencies without a corresponding improvement in distribution. This conclusion, asserts the Court, "follows directly from the wording of the ['tying'] clause in question and not from an assessment of the economic situation . . . ."[282]

So narrowly conceived, the Court's reasoning is as remarkable for what it says as for what it implies. Whereas Advocate-General Roemer, after considering the economic circumstances and justification for the "tying" clause, concludes simply and persuasively that Geitling did not carry its burden of proof,[283] the Court assumes a strictly *per se* attitude. It accomplishes this, on the one hand, by refusing to exercise its broadened scope of review under Article 33,[284] accepting unchallenged the economic evaluations of the High Authority. On the other hand, it ignores the concept of "normal competition" in Articles 5 and 65 § 1. As the theory of "workable competition" recognizes, however, categorical statements – like ideal models – do not necessarily reflect or comprehend the actual operation of competition in oligopolistic markets.[285] Indeed, by ignoring the economic circumstances, *per se* rules in particular may often be misleading. Ironically, the absolute damning of "all limitations" implies a radical view of free competition which can scarcely be squared with the Treaty as a whole. Although few would quarrel with the conclusions of the Judgment, it remains to be seen whether its reasoning will stand the test of time and litigation.

Neither the Ruhr nor the High Authority was ever really satisfied with the new cartel arrangements. Thus, on July 26, 1957, just five months after *Geitling,* the High Authority once again took the initiative. It reduced the minimum purchase requirements across-the-board for wholesalers dealing with the Ruhr sales agencies: from 75,000 to 60,000 tons overall, from 40,000 to 30,000 tons in the sales territory, and from 12,500 to 9,000 tons

280 *Ibid.*, p. 43.
281 See Conclusions of *Adv-Gen.* Roemer, *Ibid.*, p. 72.
282 *Ibid.*, p. 43f.
283 *Ibid.*, p. 74.
284 Discussed in text *supra*, p. 58f.
285 As to "workable competition," see text *supra*, p. 240.

for any one Ruhr agency.[286] This time, the Decision was attacked not by one of the three giant cartels, but by the Nold firm, a wholesaler of coal in Darmstadt. Due to a temporary postponement order,[287] however, the Court's decision was not forthcoming for almost two years. In the interim, it had become clear to the High Authority that the Ruhr agencies had not developed independently, but rather were pursuing a "uniform marketing policy in defiance of Treaty provisions."[288] Their price changes "had been uniform and simultaneous, and even at the distributive stage the High Authority's intentions had frequently been frustrated."[289] As a result, in February 1959, the life of the Ruhr cartels was extended by one year but their minimum purchase requirements were reduced further: the 60,000 ton overall requirement was abolished, and the 30,000 territorial and the 9,000 agency requirements were reduced respectively to 20,000 and 6,000 tons.[290]

One month later the *Nold* Case was decided.[291] In a curious twist, the Court struck down the High Authority's earlier Decisions for reason of inadequate motivation. Mere abstract statements that the Decisions had neither discriminatory nor anticompetitive effects, "as well as the absence of every justification for the altered quantitative restrictions," concluded the Court in a rather brief opinion, "do not make clear if the High Authority upon issuing the Decision in question also examined whether these restrictions are not more stringent than an evident improvement in distribution would require, pursuant to the object and purpose of Article 65 § 2 b)."[292] However true this might be, the Court had found no difficulty with the virtually identical Decision in the *Geitling* Judgment, although the motivation there was "more or less of the same extent and tenor as in *Nold*."[293] Indeed, the Decision in *Geitling*, according to the Court, had disclosed "unequivocally and fully the factual and legal considerations" on which it was based.[294] Advocate-General Roemer had been convinced of this for the Decisions in both the *Geitling* and *Nold* Cases.

This judicial enigma was compounded by the *Präsident* Judgment of a year later. Thus, in response to *Nold*, the High Authority immediately had issued a new Decision identical in content to its most recent reductions but

[286] Decisions No. 16 to 18–57 (July 26, 1957), Amtsblatt 319, 330 and 341 (August 10, 1957).
[287] Order of the Court 18/57, 3 Rspr. 247 (1957).
[288] High Authority, Seventh Gen. Rep. 172 (German ed. 1959).
[289] Meade, *op. cit.* (n. 99), p. 245.
[290] Decision No. 17–59 (Feb. 18, 1959), Amtsblatt 279 (March 7, 1959).
[291] Judgment 18/57 (*Firma I. Nold KG* v. *High Authority*), 5 Rspr. 89 (1958–59).
[292] *Ibid.*, p. 115.
[293] Bebr, *Judicial Control of the European Communities*, 88 (1962).
[294] Judgment 2/56, *op. cit.*, p. 38.

extensively motivated.[295] Upon appeal by the Ruhr sales agency "Präsident," they were annulled as before for insufficient motivation.[296] While openly admitting that the evaluation of the economic facts and circumstances surrounding the Decision "are partly removed from judicial review," the Court nevertheless concludes from this that "a substantiated motivation is indispensable" to assure complete compliance with the conditions of ECSC Article 65 § 2.[297] It then undertakes a most detailed and critical inquiry into the economic facts and circumstances supporting the Decision. Certain quantitative restrictions on wholesalers might be justified, but only if they promote "a noticeable improvement in the distribution" of coal. This was not the case for the minimum access restrictions in question. In particular, the 6,000 ton minimum for any one Ruhr agency could not be supported by reference to purchase requirements existing prior to the erection of the ECSC, "since considerable differences exist between the [economic] conditions prevailing then and now."[298]

The key to the marked shift in judicial doctrine must be traced to the substantive problem in issue, namely, the fate of the access requirements of the Ruhr cartels. In the *Nold* Judgment, the Court simply annulled minimum tonnage requirements which already had been reduced substantially by a subsequent Decision of the High Authority. Moreover, the ground of annulment was essentially formal, thus rejecting the Decision without prejudicing its reenactment on the merits. As the results of the *Präsident* Case indicate, however, judicial doctrine was being manipulated for a grander strategy. The Court's reasoning, which probed beneath the rationale of the motivation, made clear that "the time had come for the High Authority to cease chipping away at illegal operations."[299] By its terms, it appeared doubtful that anything more than the 6,000 ton minimum would be acceptable. Even that requirement would have to be adjusted and justified in terms of *prevailing* economic conditions. These change over time. It would seem, therefore, the Court was simply pacing the High Authority in the latter's search for a suitable organization for competition within the Ruhr.

The Ruhr producers, however, were determined to move in another direction.[300] They could argue, after all, that in the other three coal-producing Member States – France, Belgium and Holland – the coal industry was

295 Decision No. 36–59 (June 17, 1959), Amtsblatt 736 (July 1959).

296 Judgment 36–38 and 40/59 (*"Präsident" Ruhrkohlenverkaufsgesellschaft mbH et al.* v. *High Authority*), 6 Rspr. 891 (1960).

297 *Ibid.*, p. 921f.

298 *Ibid.*, p. 925.

299 Scheingold, *The Rule of Law in European Integration*, 239 (1965).

300 See Diebold, *op. cit.* (n. 89), p. 388; and Meade, *op. cit.* (n. 99), pp. 245–47.

either mostly state-controlled or highly cartellized.[301] Furthermore, by 1958 the coal surplus was becoming serious. Coal imports from third countries and competition from other fuels were making substantial inroads on the Community coal market. Meade writes:[302]

> In France and in the Netherlands demand for home-produced coal fell only a little, and stock changes kept within manageable limits. In Germany and in Belgium, on the other hand, the situation soon became serious. Between 1 January 1958 and the end of April 1959 stocks of coal and coke in Western Germany rose from 1.6 to 20 million tons and then amounted to 15 per cent of the 1958 level of coal output (132.6 million tons); in Belgium the position was even worse, for stocks rose from 1.7 to 7.9 million tons during the sixteen months in question and formed 29 per cent of the 1958 output (27.1 million tons) at the end of the period.

In early 1960, under considerable pressure from companies and unions, therefore, the German Government announced its support for a single Ruhr sales cartel.[303] Although the original wording of ECSC Article 65 § 2 would surely forbid such steps, there appeared a growing willingness among the Member States to support a "small Treaty revision."[304]

The essence of the proposed revision was to permit the formation of larger selling organizations. To accomplish this, the purposes for which "benevolent" cartels could be approved were to be broadened, the prohibition of "substantial market power" was to be relaxed and the High Authority was to be given greater supervisory powers to prevent the abuse of this increased economic power.[305] This would constitute a fundamental shift in the economic philosophy of the Treaty – from a prior or preventive control of the market through standards of market structure toward greater reliance on subsequent control of market behavior. The concept of market control in the ECSC, therefore, would be more closely aligned with the dominant economic philosophies in the Member States.[306]

The Court vetoed this attempt. While a "small Treaty revision" might well

[301] See Lister, *op. cit.* (n. 89), Ch. 8; Diebold, *id.*, pp. 395–98; and Meade, *id.*, pp. 232–35.

[302] Meade, *id.*, p. 248f. This development on the coal market may also be traced in the relevant sections of the Seventh through the Tenth General Reports of the High Authority.

[303] See Europe CECA (Agence internationale d'information pour la presse) p. 1 (March 4, 1960).

[304] This procedure is discussed in text *supra*, p. 24 and p. 72f.

[305] For the full text of this proposal, see Opinion of the Court 1/61, 7 Rspr. 551, 556–58 (1961).

[306] See discussion in text *supra*, p. 239f.

be justified by the economic difficulties in the coal market, the proposal itself was incompatible with the fundamental purposes of the Treaty. First, the proposed new purposes for approving "benevolent" cartels were so vague that they would grant the High Authority "new powers" rather than simply "adapt" the existing ones. Specifically, they would authorize the High Authority to approve "agreements *concerning* adjustments to new marketing conditions."[307] "In fact," observes the Court, "it would be difficult to imagine an agreement which would not fall within this category." As a result, the proposed revision would constitute not merely "a quantitative but also a qualitative modification of competences," fully contrary to Article 95. The powers would be simply without measurable limits.[308]

Secondly, the proposed revision unlawfully relaxed the prohibition of "substantial market power" in Article 65 § 2 c). This provision constitutes an absolutely inviolable condition for approving "benevolent" cartels, for it implements the general principle of Article 4 d).[309] Within the purposes of the Treaty, Article 65 § 2 c) ensures that

> no agreement will place a party, by virtue of his market power in a given sector, in a position to control the market of the products in question or, so far as these products are concerned, to hinder the attainment of Community objectives.[310]

Nor can the relaxation of this condition be offset "by competences which are not provided in Article 65, namely, the right and even the duty of subsequent control and the power of direct intervention."[311] Of course, "at least theoretically, [subsequent as well as prior control] can contribute equally to attaining Treaty objectives." In terms of High Authority powers, however, "there exists an essential difference between the two." For this reason, "such a modification of the existing Treaty system . . . would scarcely be a mere adaptation . . . of High Authority powers."[312] The Court gives notice, therefore, that market structure and not simply market behavior is an essential element of market control in the Community.

Having lost this battle and with little hope of getting a major Treaty amendment through the Member State parliaments, the three Ruhr selling agencies – "Geitling," "Mausegatt" and "Präsident" – made one last desperate appeal to the Court. They challenged the High Authority's refusal to

[307] See text of proposal in Opinion 1/61, *op. cit.*, pp. 556–58 and 562. Emphasis added.

[308] Opinion 1/61, *ibid.*, p. 561f.

[309] *Ibid.*, p. 564–66.

[310] *Ibid.*, p. 564.

[311] *Ibid.*, p. 565f.

[312] *Ibid.*, p. 565f.

approve a single Ruhr sales cartel.[313] In view of the Opinion on the "small Treaty revision," the main focus of their attack was Article 65 § 2 c).[314] This provision, they argued, should be construed narrowly, for it constitutes an exception to the general legality of "benevolent" cartels. Further, it should be grasped "qualitatively" in terms of the intensity of a cartel's market power and not, as the High Authority had done, purely "quantitatively" as a matter of market portion percentages. The power prohibited by Article 65 § 2 c), the plaintiffs argued, is monopoly power which permits a cartel to operate essentially independent of market demand and supply.[315] And, conversely:

> If . . . a substantial part of the products on the common market are regulated by a cartel agreement, while the cartel is forced to shape its price policy according to competitive products, then the cartel does not control the market.[316]

By this reasoning, the market portion prohibition of Article 65 § 2 c) would be relevant *only after* the existence of monopoly power had been established.[317] Such power is lacking, concluded the plaintiffs, since even a single Ruhr cartel still must compete with other ECSC coal fields, imported coal and oil.

Both the Advocate-General and the Court reject this position, but arrive at opposite conclusions. While the former would annul, the latter upholds the Decision of the High Authority. Fundamental to the reasoning of the Court, as well as to its concept of market structure, is the distinction between "price fixing" (fixer) and "price determination" (déterminer). The first is the result of agreement or organizational structure, the second of market power. Whereas both are prohibited in Article 65 § 1, only the second is unlawful for "benevolent" cartels under Article 65 § 2 c). A power of price determination, says the Court,[318] consists:

> in the capacity to set prices at a level which differs markedly from that which they would have reached had they been determined exclusively by competition.

This power of course "will be effective only so far as it succeeds in excluding the competitive pressure which leads to a reduction of list prices." [319] For the

[313] Judgment 13/60 (*"Geitling," "Mausegatt" and "Präsident" Ruhrkohlen-Verkaufsgesellschaften mbH* v. *High Authority*), 8 Rspr. 177 (1962). This was an appeal of the High Authority's Decision No. 16–60 (June 22, 1960), Amtsblatt 1014 (July 23, 1960).

[314] This Article is quoted in text *supra*, p. 271.

[315] Judgment 13/60, *op. cit.*, pp. 202 and 222.

[316] *Ibid.*, pp. 222 and also 201f.

[317] *Ibid.*, p. 201.

[318] *Ibid.*, p. 215.

[319] *Ibid.*, p. 217.

38 mining firms in the Ruhr, which embrace an appreciable amount of coal production, a single cartel would appear to be in that position.[320]

Nevertheless, even that market power would be ineffective, the Court adds, if competition from *outside* the Ruhr

> compelled the common sales organization to set its list price below the level which would result from the competition *among* Ruhr firms, were this competition not suppressed by a common sales organization.[321]

This is clearly not the case: in view of the high transport costs on coal, the geographical proximity of Ruhr coal producers and consumers offers "a noticeable protection against many other producers in the Community." Indeed, since the Ruhr possesses the lowest prices in the Community, its protected position is thereby strengthened.[322] Nor would imported coal or oil prevent a single Ruhr cartel from "freely choosing its list prices within certain limits."[323] A power of price determination, therefore, lies in the very "structure of the Ruhr area itself."[324] In reaching this conclusion, the Court is concerned not so much with the Community as a whole as with the impact of a single sales cartel on competition *within* the Ruhr.

Having determined the existence of market power, the next question is whether it embraces a substantial portion of the market. To answer this, the Court develops a sweeping theory of market structure in the ECSC.[325] At this point, the emphasis tacitly shifts from competition within the Ruhr to the energy market as a whole. It would be unrealistic, continues the Court, "to view the coal or energy market as an atomistic market of perfect competition." On this market, the few large producers are not freed of competition, "but by virtue of their size exert a not insignificant influence on the market price and are enabled thereby to pursue a genuine market policy."[326] As a result, they may "consciously align their behavior with that of their partners." Here lies a fundamental distinction from pure competition. It characterizes oligopolistic or imperfect competition on the coal and energy market:

> . . . [E]very seller calculates his decisions in terms of the probable behavior of his

[320] *Ibid.*, p. 217f.
[321] *Ibid.*, p. 218 Emphasis added.
[322] *Ibid.*, p. 219.
[323] *Ibid.*, p. 221. See also p. 222.
[324] *Ibid.*, p. 219.
[325] Maurice Bye, "l'Arrêt 13/60 du 18 Mai 1962 sur les comptoirs de la Ruhr," 26 *Droit social,* 257, 261f (1963), views this theory of the Court as a "régime sui generis."
[326] Judgment 13/60, *op. cit.*, p. 223.

competitors, for the simple reason that the behavior of his competitors is a direct response to his own.[327]

Thus, contrary to the contentions of the plaintiffs, market prices present no "insuperable barriers" but leave "an unclearly demarcated field of maneuver." Within this "zone of indeterminacy," the prices of firms are the result of market strategy and not simply a function of market prices.[328]

The existence of such oligopolistic power is both recognized and embraced by Treaty Articles 65 § 2. Indeed, it is a natural consequence of the technical and economic developments in the coal and steel industry.[329] However, it has its limits. These lie, as the previous Opinion of the Court made clear,[330] in the inviolable conditions of Article 65 § 2 c), aimed at preserving

that *minimum degree of competition* which is necessary to ensure respect for the fundamental requirements in Articles 2, 3, 4 and 5 and, especially in the future, to ensure the preservation and respect of normal conditions of competition.[331]

The circle has at last been closed. This "minimum degree," which is the heart of Article 65 § 2 c), constitutes the core of "normal competition" in the ECSC. It also determines the essential market structure for attaining the Treaty objectives. It is the common thread running through the major Treaty purposes in Articles 2, 3, 4 and 5.

What is this "minimum degree" in an oligopolistic market structure? The possession of market power, as the Court readily admits,[332] *is not* prohibited by Article 65 § 2 c) *unless* it embraces a substantial part of the products in question on the common market. The next task, therefore, is to determine the relevant market. Both the Court and Advocate-General Roemer adopt a *purely legal concept,*[333] namely, the entire ECSC common market for coal, without considering the extent or existence of effective competition among the individual coal fields.

This approach of Roemer is particularly questionable, who urges the Court to pursue "a dynamic interpretation and development" of market control "running parallel to economic development."[334] He contends that the High Authority has both overestimated the Ruhr's coal portion within the ECSC as well as underestimated the growing competition on the energy

327 *Ibid.*, p. 225f.
328 *Ibid.*, p. 226.
329 *Ibid.*, pp. 226f, 231.
330 See text *supra*, p. 277f.
331 *Ibid.*, p. 228 (emphasis added). See also p. 227.
332 *Ibid.*, p. 230.
333 *Ibid.*, pp. 231f, 235; Conclusions of *Adv-Gen.* Roemer, *ibid.*, p. 265.
334 Conclusions of *Adv-Gen.* Roemer, *id.*, pp. 279–82.

market between ECSC coal, imported coal and oil. On the one hand, if certain coal quantities, such as deliveries within integrated Ruhr enterprises, are to be excluded from market portion calculations, then the relevant market in question must be reduced just so much. While ignoring this fact, Roemer concludes that since the statistical error can not be corrected by the Court, the Decision must be remanded to the High Authority for recalculation.[335] On the other hand, if the concept "substantial portion" must be viewed in the context of competition on the energy market as a whole, then the relevant market must be expanded just so much. The term "substantial portion," says Roemer,[336] is an "undetermined legal concept" whose point of reference is the "normal competitive conditions" prescribed by ECSC Articles 5 and 65 § 1. The criterion of normality, however, has "fundamentally changed" since the time of the Community's formation in 1952.[337] The essential error of the High Authority, he concludes, lies in its failure to adapt the legal concept to the broadened scope of competition on the entire energy market.[338] Thus, although Roemer professes a purely legal view of the relevant market, denying it all "geographical or economic characteristics,"[339] he argues at every step from economic considerations.

For the Court, by contrast, these factual considerations do not play such a significant role. Article 65 § 2 c), it notes, is aimed not so much at the quantitative as at the structural characteristics of competition in the Community.[340]

> . . . [T]he *possibility* to determine the prices or control the market for a substantial portion of the products in question then exists, if the *effects* [of that control] are not of minor or subordinate proportions, but are of a kind to endanger that minimum degree of competition prescribed by the Treaty for the fulfillment of the Community tasks in Articles 2, 3, 4 and 5.[341]

Thus, while the statistics of the High Authority may be subject to some correction, the errors are *de minimis*.[342] Further, a single Ruhr cartel, embracing from 26.1 to 43.7% of total coal and coke production in the ECSC, would undoubtedly control a "substantial portion" of the market in question.[343] In competition among-the-few, however, "the influence of a selling organiza-

335 Conclusions, *id.*, p. 278.
336 *Ibid.*, p. 279.
337 *Ibid.*, pp. 280–82.
338 *Ibid.*, p. 282.
339 *Ibid.*, p. 265.
340 Judgment, *ibid.*, p. 235.
341 *Ibid.*, p. 231. Emphasis added.
342 *Ibid.*, pp. 232, 235.
343 *Ibid.*, p. 231f.

tion depends not so much on the product quantities which it controls as on those controlled by rival organizations."[344] Accordingly, Article 66 § 2 expressly authorizes the High Authority "to take the size of existing enterprises . . . into account."[345] In hard coal production, for instance, a single Ruhr cartel would be four times as large as any other coal field and twice as large as the Charbonnages de France, the next largest production unit in the Community. This "obvious disproportion" would lend a single Ruhr cartel great weight in competition among Community producers.[346] Its formation must, therefore, be rejected and the Decision of the High Authority upheld. The Court was prepared to respect "the dynamics of economic life," [347] but only within the framework of this concept of market structure.

It requires little imagination to determine the Ruhr's next step. With no hope of an improvement in the ECSC coal market, the High Authority was persuaded to form two instead of three selling agencies, each approximating the size of the Charbonnages de France.[348] Like their predecessors, their organizational structure and trading regulations were essentially identical. Further, the joint agencies – handling exports, market analysis, accounting and other technical operations – were preserved, but revised so as not to interfere with the independent market policies which the two agencies were to follow. To ensure this independence, the High Authority was to maintain "continuing surveillance" of the agencies' activities. Within a month after its release, this Decision of the High Authority was attacked by the Dutch Government, the major and perhaps sole remaining opponent to economic concentration in the Ruhr coal fields.[349] It charged that this "duopoly" arrangement would exclude, in fact, that indispensable "minimum degree of competition" on the coal market and that, further, the system of "continuing surveillance" constituted nothing less than what the Court had declared illegal in its Opinion on the "small Treaty revision" proposal to Article 65 § 2.

Once again, the Court upholds the High Authority. Proceeding from its

[344] *Ibid.*, p. 233.

[345] *Ibid.*, ECSC Art. 66 § 2, par. 2, reads: In evaluating the approval of a merger or acquisition, "the High Authority, according to the principle of non-discrimination in Article 4 b), is to take the size of existing enterprises of the same kind into account, so far as this is justified in order to avoid or compensate for disadvantages arising from inequalities in competitive conditions."

[346] *Ibid.*, p. 233.

[347] *Ibid.*, p. 228.

[348] Decision No. 5 and 6–63 (March 20, 1963), *Amtsblatt*, 1173 and 1191 (April 10, 1963).

[349] Judgment 66/63 (*Netherlands* v. *High Authority*), 10 Rspr. 1147 (1964).

legal concept of the relevant market, i.e., the entire common market of the six Member States, it admits that each of the two Ruhr agencies embraces "a not inconsiderable portion" of ECSC coal production. "[E]ach of them, however, is confronted in the same coal field and in other areas of the common market with economic units approximately equal in strength."[350] Still, the plaintiff had argued, the Charbonnages de France could scarcely serve as the measure of all things on the common market; this would transform the negative considerations of the previous Judgment into a positive thesis.[351] The Court was in no mood to quarrel. Despite the identity in size and structure of the two agencies, it reasons,

> In an oligopolistic market, the balance and independence of the large economic units active there can be furthered, if their economic power is comparable.[352]

Then, by simply ignoring all factual and economic analysis of the market and market power, it adopts the "rule of thumb" laid down in the previous judgment. Under Article 65 § 2 c),

> The size of a cartel becomes meaningful . . . only when compared with the size of the market and the size of other economic units, which are active there and are the present and future competitors of this cartel.[353]

The formation of the two Ruhr agencies is lawful, therefore, not so much because of their lack of market power, but because of the existence of countervailing power.[354] While appearing to draw purely the logical conclusions from its previous judgment, the Court indeed – as the Dutch Government warned – has turned a negative consideration into a positive thesis.

How was this thesis to be reconciled with that indispensable "minimum degree of competition" required by the Treaty? Its justification entails a noticeable attempt by the Court to bring its concepts of Community market control and market structure into line with accumulated experience and the changing demands of economic circumstances. First, in contrast to its Opinion on the "small Treaty revision,"[355] the Court appears more willing to accept a more extensive subsequent control of cartel conduct. While this

[350] *Ibid.*, p. 1182.
[351] *Ibid.*, p. 1169f.
[352] *Ibid.*, p. 1179.
[353] *Ibid.*, p. 1182.
[354] Cf. the more general theory of Galbraith, *American Capitalism: the Concept of Countervailing Power*, (1952); and the critical comments thereto of Kaysen and Turner, *Antitrust Policy*, 153 and 194 (1959).
[355] See discussion in text *supra*, p. 277f.

control does not extend nearly so far, e.g., to matters of price policy, as that in the proposed "small Treaty revision," the High Authority admits that it is more extensive than anything previously undertaken; this, however, is merely to account for "factors of uncertainty" in the High Authority's evaluations.[356] In any case, concludes the Court, the High Authority must have the right to keep watch on the conditions which it must impose on "benevolent" cartels. Moreover, the unwillingness of Ruhr cartels in the past to abide by such conditions "is sufficient in itself to justify these controls."[357] To an increasing extent, therefore, market control through market structure is to be supplemented by a closer scrutiny of abusive market behavior.

Secondly, in analyzing market structure, the Court's reasoning takes a most striking turn. In order to meet the new requirements of economic integration, the Court reformulates the concept of "normal competition" lying at the heart of ECSC market structure. Its reasoning is two-fold. On the one hand, it deemphasizes the rigidities in the existing price structure. The absence of price mobility as well as price differences among the Ruhr agencies does not prove that the requisite "minimum degree of competition" is lacking. In an oligopolistic market like the ECSC, where prices must be published and producers are large and few, prices "are almost inevitably characterized by great stability even though producers are actually in competition with each other."[358] This price stability is not contrary to the Treaty,

> if it is not the product of even tacit agreement, but of the free play of market forces and of the strategies of independent economic units with opposing interests.[359]

The language of "tacit agreement," though not further defined, is obviously directed at the uniform pricing policies of the three Ruhr agencies in previous years.[360] Does it also extend to price leadership and conscious parallelism of all kinds? Although the line is difficult to draw, this must be doubted.[361] Those pricing policies are to a large extent the unavoidable consequences of parallel organizational structure among the Ruhr agencies and of firm strategy in an oligopolistic market.[362] This structure and strategy not only have been held lawful, but are the premise of judicial reasoning.

On the other hand, the Court reorients the concept of "normal compe-

[356] Judgment 66/63, *op. cit.*, pp. 1161–63.
[357] *Ibid.*, p. 1177f.
[358] *Ibid.*, p. 1180.
[359] *Ibid.*, p. 1180.
[360] See text *supra*, pp. 272 and 275.
[361] But cf. Scheingold, *op. cit.* (n. 117), p. 254.
[362] See notes 98 and 105 *supra*, p. 240f, for economic theory on this point.

tition" within an expanded market reference. "The degree of competition desired by the Treaty," it continues, "may change with market conditions and the relative meaning of the various Treaty requirements." It is conceivable, therefore, that these changes would require measures of market reorganization which "take precedence over a large degree of competition . . ., without entailing the exclusion of all competition on the coal market."[363] As an integral part of the ECSC coal and steel market, these Ruhr agencies are faced increasingly with competition from other large scale economic units as well as substitute products. As a result, it is necessary to consider the growing

> importance of this viewpoint in assessing competition; moreover, this makes clear how important it is to take account of the general goals in Article 3.[364]

By virtue of changing economic circumstances in light of the shifting requirements of Treaty goals, therefore, the concept of "normal competition" may undergo a transformation. In thus extending the scope of the market to substitute and imported products, the Court has adopted the "dynamic" of Advocate-General Roemer in the previous judgment.[365]

By this two-fold analysis, Community law has been adapted to the changing requirements of economic integration. The standard of market structure and with it the concept of "normal competition" have been reformulated and, in addition, complemented by a more extensive control over market behavior. There has occurred a conscious shift of emphasis from preventive to subsequent means of market control. This offers an instructive example of legal development through judicial decision. It has occurred not by a unilateral decision of the Court, but in concert with the quasi-legislative organs of the Community. For this reason, the judicial reference to Article 3 goals, although abrupt, is pregnant with meaning. As the Scrap Cases demonstrate,[366] these goals are conflicting; their weighing and balancing is essentially a task for the High Authority. The High Authority Decision to reorganize the Ruhr obviously emphasizes the goals of full employment and a stable standard of living for the affected employees of the

[363] Judgment 66/63, *op. cit.*, p. 1180f.

[364] *Ibid.*, p. 1181.

[365] See Conclusions of *Adv-Gen.* Roemer, in Case 13/60, 8 Rspr. 239, 251, 282f (1962). In arguing for a broadened view of the relevant market, he concludes: "Und hier scheint mir am ehesten der Appell der Klägerinnen zur Befolgung einer dynamischen Rechtsauslegung und Rechtsfortbildung angebracht, die parallel geht zur wirtschaftlichen Entwicklung." See also text *supra*, p. 281 and at note 347.

[366] See text *supra*, pp. 253 and 255f.

coal industry at the cost of economic rationality.[367] Where fundamental questions of market organization are in issue, therefore, the Court wisely leaves the initiative to the High Authority.

Moreover, the essence of this judicial creativity lies not so much in the policy choice as in its justification. This justification is founded on "the relativity of the Treaty requirements" – or, better said, of the Treaty goals – as the standards of market performance. A shift in emphasis among these goals, due to the changing market circumstances, may require a reassessment of market structure and the concept of "normal competition." Thus, while the concept of "normal competition" – as reflected in the "minimum degree of competition" in Article 65 § 2 c) – constitutes an indispensable requirement for attaining Treaty goals, its content must be measured and moulded continuously in terms of these developing goals. Judicial justification, therefore, is neither value-neutral nor simply a reflection of economic circumstances. Such circumstances may indeed be the cause or occasion for judicial decision, but the reformulation by the Court reflects a shift in value emphasis. From this point of view, the fundamental principle of competition in the Treaty takes on new content. The virtue of the Court's decision lies in candidly recognizing this, while giving it reasoned elaboration. This is striking testimony to Holmes' thesis: that the judicial development of law may be logical in form, but "it is legislative in its grounds."[368]

The judicial development of major Treaty purposes, as this case analysis has attempted to demonstrate, proceeds teleologically by means of "topical" reasoning. Although at first reserved, the Court has pressed its search beyond the textual language of the individual provisions toward the fundamental premises of Treaty interpretation. Its reasoning neither pursues nor implies a hierarchical distinction of the Steindorffian variety. Rather, the Court articulates two groups of Treaty purposes – goals and means – each informing the other. On the one hand, the diverse and conflicting Treaty goals of Articles 2 and 3 are subject to continuous reconciliation in accordance with the changing requirements of economic integration. This is a task predominantly for the High Authority, being guided by the concept of the "common interest" and the minimum standards of "reasonableness" and "due care." On the other hand, the means of market control in Articles 4 and 5 are ordered

367 The Court euphemistically labels the reorganizational measures of the High Authority measures of "rationalization." Judgment 66/63, *op. cit.*, p. 1180. Instead, as Meade, *op. cit.* (n. 99), p. 247, points out, joint selling tends to protect inefficient pits, so that "market forces have a much reduced impact on the position of the individual undertakings."

368 Holmes, *The Common Law*, 35 (1881). See also discussion in text *supra*, p. 111ff.

hierarchically in terms of "normal conditions of competition," then "indirect" and finally "direct" measures of market intervention. The principle of competition is not only primary to this hierarchy, but also the ultimate criterion of comparability for the concepts of "discrimination" and "subvention" in Article 4. It is, however, an operational and not a static principle of interpretation. While embodying an indispensable "minimum degree of competition," its "normal" content must be continually tested and shaped against the developing goals of the ECSC. In essence, therefore, the *topos* of "normal competition" embodies the search for a workable economic philosophy in the ECSC, i.e., for those conditions which in themselves will permit a balanced realization of the Treaty goals. As such, this *topos* is for a functioning price system in the ECSC what "just order" is for the legal system as a whole.[369]

Of Powers Implied and Reserved

In a real sense, the concept of "implied powers" – or, in its more generalized form, of "necessary implication"[370] – establishes the farthest reach of the teleological method. As a *topos* of judicial interpretation, it constitutes ends-means reasoning. It tests legislative measures, which are necessary or appropriate for the achievement of constitutional ends, against the implied scope of enumerated (or delegated) governmental powers. This reasoning of course presumes, as is true of the federal governments in the United States and Germany, that governmental powers in some sense are limited. This is true in varying degrees for each of the European Communities, whose powers thus far are limited functionally to specific spheres of the Member State economies.[371] In fact, the Court took pains in the Miners' Bonus Case to set forth the premises for the concept of "enumerated powers" in the ECSC.[372] It has taken the opportunity on other occasions in the ECSC, discussed below, to develop "implied powers" reasoning.

369 See text *supra,* p. 270f.

370 See Bernhardt, *Die Auslegung völkerrechtlicher Verträge,* 97f (1963), discussing these two concepts in international law. But cf. Paul de Visscher, "La C.E.C.A. et les Etats membres," 2 *Actes Officiels du Congrès sur la C.E.C.A.*, 7, 37 (Stresa, 1957).

371 See, e.g., ECSC Arts 26, 67, 70 and 71; and also EEC Arts. 6(1), 36, 48(3) and (4), 55, 70(1), 73(2), 77, 85(1), 86, 92, 103(1), 105(1), 107(1), 118, par. 1, and 145, which are replete with negative pregnants as to "reserved powers," Member State commitments only as to the coordination of national policy and the limitation of EEC powers to matters affecting "interstate trade."

372 Judgment 30/59, 7 Rspr. 1, 48–51 (1961), discussed in text *supra,* p. 267ff. See also Werner von Simson, "Der Gerichtshof und unbestimmte Rechtsbegriffe," in *Zehn Jahre Rechtsprechung,* 396, 401 (1965), speaking of a Community "compétence d'attri-

The implied power's reasoning is two-fold: ascertaining the *content* of a power in terms of its purposes and delimiting its *scope* in terms of its organizational function. The one should not be confused with the other.[373] As a doctrine, it has been classically formulated by Chief Justice Marshall:[374]

> Let the end be legitimate, let it be within the scope of the constitution, and all means which are appropriate, which are plainly adapted to that end, which are not prohibited, but consist with the letter and the spirit of the constitution, are constitutional.

What is crucial is that "the power be given"; what is implied are the means appropriate "to facilitate its execution." The converse, however, can never be claimed, namely, "that these vast [federal] powers draw after them others of inferior importance, merely because they are inferior."[375] But what is the legitimate basis of the power implied? – a single provision of the constitution, several taken together ("resulting powers"), the general context of the constitution or, as Story suggests,[376] "the nature of political society."[377] Being largely a function of political solidarities,[378] the basis selected will profoundly reflect the character of political organization.

Even in international organization, where the concept of "implied powers" is hard-pressed by the dogma of sovereignty, the International Court of Justice has conceded its applicability.[379] In the Reparation for Injuries Decision, the Court searched the "purposes and functions" of the United Nations to determine whether, in case of a breach of obligation by a member State,

bution"; Pescatore's remarks therein, *ibid.*, p. 210f; and Conclusions of *Adv-Gen.* Roemer, in Case 41 and 50/59, 6 Rspr. 1069, 1080 and 1106 (1960), in Case 20/59, 6 Rspr. 681, 711 (1960), and of *Adv-Gen.* Lagrange, in Case 7/56 and 3–7/57, 3 Rspr. 154, 167 (1957).

373 See text *supra*, p. 234f.

374 *McCulloch* v. *Maryland*, 4 Wheat. 316, 421 (1819).

375 *Ibid.*, p. 407f.

376 Cited by Willoughby, *The Constitutional Law of the United States*, vol. I, p. 89 (2d ed. 1929).

377 For the "resulting powers" doctrine, see the opinion of Chief Justice Marshall in *Cohens* v. *Virginia*, 6 Wheat. 264 (1821); and also *United States* v. *Gettysburg Electric Ry. Co.*, 160 U.S. 668 (1895). *Dictum* expanding the basis of this doctrine even further may be found in the Legal Tender Cases, 12 Wall. 457, 554ff (1870).

The German Federal Constitutional Court, in one decision, 3 BVerfG 407, 421f (1954), suggests that a federal power may be implied not only as the "necessary presupposition" for exercising an existing competence, but also from the "nature of the federal tasks" themselves. For a survey, see Maunz-Dürig, *Kommentar zum Grundgesetz*, Art. 70, Randnr. 25–33 (1966).

378 See Bernhardt, *op. cit.*, p. 99. See also de Visscher, *Problèmes d'interprétation judiciaire en droit international public*, 153f and 156f (1963).

379 See generally, Bernhardt, *id.*, p. 97ff; and de Visscher, *id.*, p. 140ff.

that Organization could represent the interests of its agents before the International Court. In affirming the existence of this power, for which no express provisions provided, it reasoned:[380]

> Under international law, the Organization must be deemed to have those powers which, though not expressly provided in the Charter, are conferred upon it by necessary implication as being essential to the performance of its duties.

Similarly, in the Awards of Administrative Tribunal Case, the Court also implied the power of the General Assembly to establish a tribunal competent to render judgments binding on the United Nations in disputes arising out of contracts of services. Proceeding expressly from the reasoning in its previous Decision, the Court concludes that such a tribunal

> was essential to ensure the efficient working of the Secretariat and to give effect to the paramount consideration of securing the highest standards of efficiency, competence and integrity. Capacity to do this arises by necessary intendment out of the Charter.[381]

In both cases, the Court's reasoning followed the spirit of Marshall's; the powers implied are simply means to facilitate the execution of legitimate Charter purposes.

Despite this congruency in international and federal state judicial practice, the doctrine of "implied powers" can not be grasped abstractly. Its concrete formulation and application is a function of the purposes and structure of the governmental organization at hand. Not unexpectedly, therefore, the perhaps majority of writers who reject this doctrine for the European Communities argue from competing Treaty procedures.[382] ECSC Article 95,

380 ICJ Reports 173, 182f (1949). See also PCIJ Series B, No. 14 (European Commission of the Danube) 25f and 64 (1927). But cf. PCIJ Series A/B, No. 43 (Polish War Vessels in the Port of Danzig) 142, 145 and 147 (1951); and ICJ Reports (United States Nationals in Morocco) 176, 196 (1952).

381 ICJ Reports 47, 57 (1954).

382 See, e.g., Bindschedler, *Rechtsfragen der europäischen Einigung* 219 (1954); Lagrange, "Les Pouvoirs de la Haute Autorité et l'application du Traité de Paris," 67 *Rev. dr. pub. sci. pol.*, 40, 45ff (1961); Wohlfarth et al., *Kommentar zum EWG-Vertrag*, Anm. 7 zu Art. 235 (1960); and Rabe, *Das Verordnungsrecht der EWG*, 147ff (1963), with additional references. For literature supporting the "implied powers" doctrine in the Communities, see Ophüls, "Über die Auslegung der Europäischen Gemeinschaftsverträge," in *Festgabe Alfred Müller-Armack*, 279, 290 (1961); the Conclusions of *Adv-Gen.* Roemer, in Case 4–13/59, 6 Rspr. 295, 310 (1960); v. d. Heydte, "Die politischen Organe der EWG," 54 *Friedenswarte*, 1, 13 (1957–58); Daig, in Groeben-Boeckh, *Kommentar zum EWG-Vertrag*, Anm. 2 zu Art. 145 (1958), and his "Die Gerichtsbarkeit in der EWG und der europäischen Atomgemeinschaft," 83 *Arch. öff. R.*, 132, 152 (1958); Nicolaysen, "Zur Theorie von den implied powers in den Europäischen Gemeinschaften," 1 *Europarecht*, 129, 135 (1966); and the discussion of Rabe, *id.*, p. 150f.

paragraph 1, for instance,[383] authorizes the High Authority "in all cases not provided for" in the Treaty to issue those Decisions and Recommendations necessary to attain the major Treaty objectives in Articles 2 through 4; however, the unanimous consent of the Council of Ministers must be forthcoming and the principles of limited intervention in Article 5 respected. This procedure of Treaty complementation, it may be contended,[384] replaces judicial doctrine with a political decision. The solution is neat, but too nice for a document of constitutional proportions. Article 95, paragraph 1, does not purport to encompass even those cases not *expressly* "provided for" in the Treaty, nor can it legitimately do so if the effective functioning of the ECSC is not to be seriously encumbered or even endangered. To do so would entail those strict, literal and "sens clair" approaches to interpretation which the Court has rightly and unquestionably rejected.[385]

As Marshall's position shows, moreover, the "implied powers" doctrine is not meant to expand governmental powers. Its function is to "facilitate their execution," to grant the enumerated powers their full due. Nevertheless, it must be recognized that there are varying bases for implying such powers and that the line between powers implied and powers complemented is scarcely clear.[386] The task for the Court is to develop a basis for "implied powers" reasoning which respects the limits of partial integration and the delicate balance between Community and Member State jurisdiction. The problem, therefore, is not so much whether to affirm the "implied powers" doctrine, but to delimit the scope for its application in accordance with the nature of the ECSC.

What then is the nature of a Treaty power? On this the Court has taken a rather conceptualistic view. In approving the "small Treaty revision" of Article 56, it drew a sharp distinction between the "power" itself, i.e., reemployment assistance and investment aid, and the conditions for its exercise.[387] While under Article 95 the power can not be altered, its conditions

383 Cf. EEC Art. 235, Euratom Art. 203 and the ECSC Art. 95, par. 2, "small Treaty revision" procedure, discussed in text *supra*, p. 72f.

384 See Rabe, *op. cit.*, p. 157.

385 See discussion in text *supra*, p. 230f.

386 Nicolaysen, *op. cit.*, p. 131ff, attempts to distinguish the procedure in ECSC Article 95, par. 1, from the "implied powers" doctrine by relating the former to the general goals in Articles 2 through 4 and tying the latter to the more limited goals in the specific Treaty provisions. This distinction fails to take account, on the one hand, that some Treaty powers like Article 53 refer specifically to the general goals in Article 3 and, on the other, that the Court has consistently affirmed that the specific provisions must be read in the light of the major Treaty goals.

387 Opinions of the Court, 5 Rspr. 571, 577 (1958–59) and 1/60, 6 Rspr. 109, 116 (1960). The Court rejected the first submission of the High Authority, but approved it later as amended.

can and the power thereby "adapted" to new circumstances. By this reasoning, the ECSC firms have been forced to assume responsibility for unemployment arising not only from benefits accruing to the coal and steel industry, i.e., due to the establishment of the common market or to the introduction of technical processes or new equipment,[388] but also from the accidental and uninsured risks of market circumstances.[389] Re-employment financing and investment on these conditions, Carstens argues with some justification,[390] amounts to a fundamental change in Treaty philosophy and to an expansion of High Authority powers.

The judicial conceptualization which permitted this revision is all the more astounding as it contradicts the reasoning in an earlier case. In *Meroni & Co.* v. *High Authority,* the failure to subject the organs administering the scrap compensation program to adequate procedural conditions constituted an unlawful delegation of powers. The Court reasoned:

> If the organs in Brussels could make decisions free of the conditions which bind the High Authority in such cases, they would possess broader powers than the High Authority under the Treaty.[391]

This contradiction can not be cured simply by emphasizing the difference between substantive and procedural conditions, for the Court itself has implied that at least some rules of procedure may be revised under Article 95.[392] Nevertheless, the contradiction is more apparent than real; its cause, as a later Judgment indicates, is over-generalization. Thus, in its Opinion on the "small Treaty revision" of Article 65 § 2, the Court adheres to the distinction between "powers" and their conditions, but makes clear that there are different types of conditions.[393] The prohibition of substantial market power in ECSC Article 65 § 2 c), it concludes, is an unalterable condition for approving "benevolent" cartels. Its relaxation goes beyond the lawful limits of an Article 95 revision. The scope of Treaty powers, therefore, as the Court itself has experienced, can be ascertained only in the total context of Treaty provisions. If over-conceptualized or removed from this context, their interpretation may be too easily manipulated, tending to over- or underestimate their nature and scope.

388 See ECSC Art. 56 § 1, and Transitional Convention Art. 23.

389 See ECSC Art. 56 § 2, which is Art. 56 amendment.

390 Carstens, "Die kleine Revision des EGKS-Vertrags," 21 Z. *ausl. öff. R.* 1, 17–19 and 35ff (1961).

391 Judgment 9/56, 4 Rspr. 9, 40 (1958). Discussed also *supra,* p. 253f.

392 Opinion 1/60, 6 Rspr. 109, 116f (1960).

393 Opinion 1/61, 7 Rspr. 551, 566 and 569 (1961).

Such vacillation characterizes, to some extent, the Court's "implied powers" reasoning itself. Significantly, the Court has never justified the application of the doctrine within the broader context of Treaty revision procedures. The question of "implied powers" was raised first and most dramatically in *Fédération Charbonnière de Belgique* v. *High Authority*.[394] Did the High Authority have the power, under Article 26 of the Transitional Convention, to set Belgian coal prices (at a level below the prevailing market price)? Since the power was nowhere expressly given in this Article, the Court turns first to a consideration of Treaty purposes. The object of Article 26 was to integrate, from the beginning of the transitional period, the relatively inefficient Belgian coal industry *and thereby* the Belgian steel industry into the common market at price levels which approximate the foreseeable costs of production at the end of the transitional period. This goal, said the Court,[395] could not be achieved either by the free play of market forces or by indirect measures of coercion against uncooperative Belgian coal firms. Nor are the price-setting powers of ECSC Article 61 applicable to such situations.

Under these circumstances, "only the direct intervention of the High Authority is appropriate to ensure the realization" of Article 26.[396] While expressly rejecting an extensive construction of Article 26, the Court adopted

> a rule of interpretation, generally recognized in international as in municipal law, by which the provisions of an international treaty or law imply those provisions without which the former would be meaningless or could not be reasonably or usefully applied.[397]

This reasoning is confirmed by ECSC Article 8 which charges the High Authority "to ensure the attainment of Treaty goals according to the conditions of the Treaty." In order to fulfill this mandate, the High Authority "enjoys a certain autonomy in determining the implementing measures. . . ." [398]

Despite the general acclaim with which this reasoning was received among proponents of European integration, its rather unusual and narrow context must not be overlooked. First, the scope of the powers implied, as the Court points out,[399] "is restricted solely to the purpose" of realizing Article 26, a

[394] Judgment 8/55, 2 Rspr. 297 (1955–56), discussed in text *supra*, p. 248f.
[395] *Ibid.*, pp. 309–11.
[396] *Ibid.*, p. 311.
[397] *Ibid.*, p. 312.
[398] *Ibid.*, p. 312.
[399] *Ibid.*, p. 312.

transitional provision. Secondly, the power of the High Authority to set prices was not new to the Treaty; under the differing but more general conditions of Article 61, it is a permanent aspect of Community regulation. Finally, the measures were limited to the Belgian coal producers, the "problem children" of the ECSC. Not only was there little reason to expect objections from the Member States, but the Belgian Government had worked hand-in-hand with the High Authority to draft the measures.[400] It would be hasty, therefore, to generalize from this Judgment an "implied powers" doctrine for all aspects of Treaty powers.

Indeed, the limits of "implied powers" became painfully clear in the Road Tariff Publication Cases.[401] They were prompted by a Letter of the High Authority to the Member States, requiring trucking tariffs to be published in one of two alternative forms or communicated to the High Authority.[402] The High Authority based itself on ECSC Article 70, paragraph 3:

> The rates, prices and tariff provisions of all kinds; applied to the transport of coal and steel within and between Member States, shall be published or brought to the knowledge of the High Authority.

Since the negotiations for harmonizing transport rates throughout the common market had foundered,[403] this was an attempt to press for concrete action in the Member States. Holland and Italy, however, balked; since both had an interest in unpublished transport rates,[404] they contested the power of the High Authority to legislate the forms of transport tariff publication. While admitting that Article 70, paragraph 3, binds both the High Authority and the Member States, the Court denies that this provision endows the High Authority – either expressly or impliedly – with legislative power.

The Court's reasoning is in part unresponsive to the issues at stake as well

[400] See the consultation provisions in the Transitional Convention Arts. 25 and 26 § 4. The Belgian Government itself had already introduced certain rationalization measures. See Diebold, *The Schuman Plan,* 206 (1959). For a summary of the programs undertaken during the transitional period, see High Authority, Sixth Gen. Rep., vol. 2, pp. 28–51 (German ed. 1958).

[401] Judgments 20/59 (*Italy* v. *High Authority*), 6 Rspr. 681, (1960); and 25/59 (*Netherlands* v. *High Authority*), 6 Rspr. 743, (1960). Since the two Judgments are virtually identical, all citations from 20/59.

[402] See Art. 2 of Decision No. 18–59 (Feb. 18, 1959), Amtsblatt 287 (March 7, 1959).

[403] See High Authority, Seventh Gen. Rep. 193f (German ed. 1959); and Lister, *Europe's Coal and Steel Community,* 376 (1960).

[404] See Lister, *id.,* p. 375; Meade, Liesner and Wells, *Case Studies in European Economic Union,* 400f (1962); and Scheingold, *The Rule of Law in European Integration,* 153f (1965).

as fully at odds with the *Fédération Charbonnière* Judgment. In the first place, its approach is highly literal. Fully ignoring the purpose of the provisions in question, the Court points out that – unlike Article 60 § 2 a)[405] – Article 70, paragraph 3, is "silent as to the means of publication as well as to the measures of execution which they require . . . ."[406] Further, unlike Article 60 § 2 a), its implementation is not subject to a prior hearing of the Consultative Committee;[407] yet, in the *Fédération Charbonnière* Case, where further-reaching measures of High Authority intervention are in issue, a more blatant discrepancy in political control does not disturb the judicial conscience.[408] By virtue of this cursory reasoning the Court concludes that Article 70, paragraph 3, does not grant the High Authority legislative power of any sort.

Might not this power, however, be implied from other provisions *or even* from "the general context" of the Treaty?[409] The very way the question is worded suggests a judicial willingness to expand the "implied powers" basis, as laid down in *Fédération Charbonnière,* in the direction of "resulting powers." The Court answers its question negatively for the case at hand. Thus, it is unimportant that the publication of transport tariffs might well be a necessary complement of the strict requirement to publish product prices under Article 60 § 2 a). The latter simply does not apply to the former.[410] However necessary the publication transport tariff might be to further price alignment and market competition in general as well as to prevent price discrimination, ECSC Articles 4 b) and 70 cannot authorize "a preventive control by prescribing the manner of the publication of price lists or prices." The basis of the Court's reasoning is circular:

> Such a competence is exceptional and conditioned upon a renunciation by the Member States which in this case has occurred neither expressly nor implicitly.[411]

Moreover, the contention of the High Authority, that it had invoked Article 70 only after all attempts at negotiation among the Member States had failed, was never answered. Nevertheless, just such reasoning, i.e., that less

[405] In the Price Publication Cases, discussed *supra* in text at pp. 244–251. ECSC Art. 65 § 2a) was construed as requiring strict prior publication.

[406] Judgment 20/59, *op. cit.*, p. 707f.

[407] *Ibid.*, p. 708.

[408] See Judgment 8/55, 2 Rspr. 297, 310 (1955–56).

[409] Judgment 20/59, *op. cit.*, p. 708, invoking the "implied powers" principle but making no reference to *Fédération Charbonnière.*

[410] *Ibid.*, p. 708f.

[411] *Ibid.*, p. 710f.

forceful measures were inadequate, formed the core of judicial reasoning in *Fédération Charbonnière*.[412] By this unconvincing combination of literal, formal and circular reasoning, therefore, the Court has avoided the really crucial questions in issue. The doctrine of "implied powers" was affirmed in principle but then ignored.

Were the matter to end here,[413] it might well be doubted that the "implied powers" reasoning has a permanent place in the Court's jurisprudence. Indeed, the doctrine itself is expressly mentioned in only one other case, without however being applied.[414] Nevertheless, this or closely related reasoning has been employed in two other judgments on the scrap compensation program. In *Mannesmann A.G. et al.* v. *High Authority*,[415] the plaintiffs attacked individual Decisions of the High Authority to recover payments made to ECSC enterprises on the basis of fraudulent documents. Being themselves "good faith" purchasers,[416] the plaintiffs questioned the basic power of the High Authority to pass the Decisions. The formal competence to issue them, they asserted, was lacking: the only relevant provision was Article 92, but this simply determined the legal nature of enforceable Community decisions. While Advocate-General Roemer rejected this argument squarely on the "implied powers" reasoning of *Fédération Charbonnière*,[417] the Court avoided all reference by name. "It is erroneous," it said, "to assert that the ECSC Treaty enumerates exhaustively all cases concerning taxes, levies and fines." Rather, the Decisions in question rest not merely on Article 92, but on Article 53 which constitutes the basis of the scrap program.[418] Since within the framework of such compensation programs errors are unavoidable,

> it must be assumed that an obligation to make repayments *implies the authority* to make claims for restitution. Otherwise, the compensation regulations . . . could not be reasonably executed.

In order to recover erroneous payments, therefore, "an express authorization is not necessary."[419]

[412] Judgment 8/55, 2 Rspr. 297, 309–11 (1955–56).

[413] In fact, the discussion in the literature focuses wholly on the *Fédération Charbonnière* and Road Tariff Publication Cases.

[414] Judgment 7/56 and 3–7/57, 3 Rspr. 83, 122–25 (1957).

[415] Judgment 4–13/59, 6 Rspr. 249 (1960).

[416] The plaintiffs, all German steel producers, had relied on documents issued by the Dutch Economic Affairs Ministry.

[417] Conclusions of *Adv-Gen.* Roemer, in Case 4–13/59, *op. cit.*, p. 310.

[418] Judgment 4–13/59, *ibid.*, p. 288.

[419] *Ibid.*, p. 289 (emphasis added). For other reasons, however, the Court annulled the Decisions and released the plaintiffs from an obligation of repayment.

In a second case, the *Belges* Judgment discussed previously,[420] the Court employed a much more subtle variation on "implied powers" reasoning. In that case, it may be recalled, the scope of Article 53 b) – to create, with the unanimous approval of the Council of Ministers, "any financial arrangements" which are necessary to implement the goals of Article 3 and which accord with Article 65 – was again in question. While this provision might well, as the Court held, authorize compensation programs to achieve stability on the scrap market, did it also justify the introduction of production penalties in the form of surcharges on the increased consumption of scrap? The legitimate scope of this Article was not an idle question. As Advocate-General Lagrange put it: "we are touching here the basic concepts of economic power in the Treaty."[421]

The Court's reasoning is signal for the future development of Treaty powers. Unable to rely on the vague language of Article 53 b), it turns to more fundamental Treaty principles. First, the measure in question is necessary to the success of the scrap compensation program, for it "encourages steel enterprises to make the most rational use of scrap."[422] But is it not also, as Meade points out,[423] the unavoidable product of a distorted price structure which the scrap scheme itself created? Might not these distortions be avoided and the same ends better achieved simply by abolishing the compensation program? The Court does not consider these questions. The supplemental measure is purely instrumental to the original, legitimate aims of the High Authority's program.

Secondly, the surcharge is a legitimate means in itself for the pursuit of Article 53 aims. It conforms, in the words of Advocate-General Lagrange,[424] to a "true hierarchy of measures" in the Treaty for affecting production. For the Court, as has been discussed above,[425] this hierarchy is a basic principle of Treaty interpretation. Its essence, based on Articles 5 and 57, lies not in the major Treaty purposes pursued – for these are equally binding[426] – but in the means employed.[427] It is a hierarchy of "indirect-direct" measures of market intervention in which the former are not merely preferred to, but *required* by the latter.

420 Judgment 8/57, 4 Rspr. 231 (1958). See text *supra*, pp. 254–258.
421 Conclusions of *Adv-Gen*. Lagrange, *ibid.*, p. 353.
422 Judgment 8/57, *ibid.*, pp. 259f and also 259–67 and 265.
423 Meade, *op. cit.* (n. 404), pp. 275, 277–79.
424 Conclusions of *Adv-Gen*. Lagrange, in Case 8/57, *op. cit.*, pp. 353–58.
425 See text *supra*, p. 256f.
426 Judgment 8/57, *op. cit.*, p. 251f.
427 *Ibid.*, p. 260f.

If the High Authority was to avoid direct measures – as Article 57 obligates it to do – it could not escape the necessity and the duty of applying the procedure in Article 53 b). . . .[428]

The surcharge in question is an indirect measure, acting not on prices directly but on the "price-forming factors."[429] Of course, like a direct measure, it tends to modify the market structure. Nevertheless, whereas the former forcefully limits or excludes the freedom of the producer, the latter, "by creating the appropriate conditions, encourages them to choose voluntarily the line of action in keeping with the common interests of Article 3."[430] In accordance with this hierarchy of Treaty means of market control, therefore, the surcharge measure tends "to preserve existing conditions and to avoid the direct, immediate and rigorous application of Article 59" consumption quotas.[431]

By this reasoning, the Court has endowed the ECSC with broad powers of indirect market control. Given a legitimate Treaty goal, such powers may be implied from their ability to avoid the necessity for direct intervention. This is the exact converse of *Fédération Charbonnière* where the inefficacy of indirect measures of market control was reason for implying powers of direct control.[432] Indeed, in the *Belges* Judgment the Court has gone even further; it has employed, without label, the expanded basis put forward in the Road Tariff Publication Cases. The power implied is drawn not only from several provisions taken together, but also from a hierarchical principle of market control underlying the general context of the Treaty. The genius of the reasoning lies in transforming an apparent limitation on the use of direct measures of intervention into a justification for indirect measures. By the same token, the weakness of this reasoning lies in the negative pregnant: if indirect means are legitimate simply because they avoid the necessity for invoking more direct measures, where are their limits? Can it not be, as the plaintiffs contend, that some aspects of the market may not be regulated unless and until a manifest crisis requires direct intervention? If not, has not the Court claimed for the ECSC precisely what Marshall denied the Government of the United States, namely, that greater powers may draw after them inferior powers, merely because they are inferior? The answers to these questions must await judicial development.

The Court's "implied powers" reasoning is a forceful reflection on the

[428] *Ibid.*, p. 252 and also p. 254f.
[429] *Ibid.*, pp. 251, 260.
[430] *Ibid.*, p. 260f.
[431] *Ibid.*, p. 261.
[432] Judgment 8/55, 2 Rspr. 297, 309–11 (1955–56).

nature of Community organization. Although at times formal and overconceptualized, it recognizes the ECSC as an ongoing enterprise – "an order of integration," as Charles de Visscher puts it[433] – whose constitution must be interpreted to meet unforeseen and unforeseeable problems. The basis for the powers implied extends not only to one or more provisions, but also to the general context of the Treaty as a whole. Where important Community programs are at stake, therefore, the Court has been understandably reluctant to demand stringent adherence to the procedures of Article 95, paragraph 1, for complementing the Treaty. In providing this considerable leeway for the judicial development of Treaty powers, it simply has consummated the teleological method which it pursues in the interpretation of major Treaty purposes.

Nevertheless, while the potential of this method is great, its limits are real. Despite the beauty of the reasoning, acknowledged Treaty purposes may not always rest on plenary powers. In particular, as the Road Tariff Publication Judgments make clear, supranational organization must respect the reserved domain of the Member States. It is a sobering fact, indeed, that the Decisions of the High Authority upheld in the *Fédération Charbonnière* and *Belges* Judgments were supported – either tacitly or expressly – by the unanimous approval of the Member States. Not so in the Road Tariff Publication Cases: Italy and especially Holland were in strong dissent. Negotiations had collapsed because of the latter. While this does not excuse legalistic reasoning as subsequent discussion will show,[434] it does suggest the increasing need to rely on consensus in approaching the frontiers of Community powers. At that point, the search for meaning in the Treaties tends to overlap the search for authority.[435]

2. THE INSTITUTIONAL LINES

The search for Treaty content occurs not only through judicial decision, but also through judicial non-decision. The Court may engage directly, from case-to-case, in the elaboration of legal principles or it may stay its hand in favor of other Community organs. This self-restraint, as Chapter IV explains, is not simply the requirement of express provisions, but of a profound reflection on the nature and limits of the judicial function. In search of principle, the Court must avoid overcommitting the future of legal develop-

433 De Visscher, *op. cit.* (n. 378), p. 154.

434 See discussion in text *infra*, p. 312ff where the Road Tariff Publication Cases are viewed as a legitimate occasion for "judicial remand."

435 See discussion in text *infra*, p. 329ff.

ment in the European Communities. Being only one of several participants in legal development, it must respect the proper sphere of other governmental institutions – in particular, of the Commission and its predecessors as well as the Member States in council assembled. For reasons of prudence rather than Treaty command, therefore, the Court may – for a time or permanently – avoid adjudicating certain issues or types of issues. This judicial restraint, it is contended here, is not *contra legem,* but a legitimate gloss on the Treaty and the institutional balance of powers.

Delimiting the Judicial Function

Considering the highly normative character of the ECSC Treaty, judicial review would appear to reach deeply into the sphere of Community policy-making. While the Court is bound primarily to standards of "legality,"[436] it has declared the major Treaty purposes as well as the specific provisions of the Treaty to be binding directly on Community organs.[437] Lest the Court be raised to the position of a Community super-legislator, the very breadth and ambiguity of these purposes counsels restraint. The Court in fact has practiced restraint by the use of a presumption of constitutionality, a reserved sphere of legislative discretion and restrictions on the right of appeal. It has thereby recognized certain limits on the proper sphere of judicial knowledge.

As to the first, judicial self-restraint may be exercised by giving an act a favorable constitutional construction. Thus, where of two possible statutory interpretations one infringes the constitution, it is presumed that the legislature intended the other.[438] In such a case, says Ehmke,

> that intent must prevail which, as the objective intent of the statute, conforms to the constitution: substantively, because that statute is an integral part of and subordinate to the entire legal order; functionally [i.e., institutionally], because the Constitutional Court may nullify only those laws which are clearly unconstitutional.[439]

436 Discussed in text *supra,* pp. 51ff and 60f.

437 See text *supra,* p. 232.

438 While the "presumption of constitutionality" or "favorable constitutional construction" (verfassungskonforme Auslegung) has long been part of United States constitutional practice, it has also been adopted in German and Italian constitutional practice. For German practice, see Bender, "Inhalt und Grenzen des Gebots der Verfassungskonformen Gesetzesauslegung," 13 *Monats S. deutsches R.,* 441 (1959); and Maunz-Dürig, *Kommentar zum Grundgesetz,* Randnr. 24cc, 33, 36dd zu Art. 19 IV, Randnr. 67, 116bb zu Art. 20 and Randnr. 20d zu Art. 40 (1966). For Italian practice, see the judgments listed by Tomuschat, *Die gerichtliche Vorabentscheidung,* 160, n. 557 (1964).

439 Ehmke, "Prinzipien der Verfassungsinterpretation," 20 *VVdStRL,* 53, 74 (1963).

As a matter of technique, the court may proceed either by reading in a constitutional construction or, where the unconstitutional provision is legitimately separable from the act as a whole, by simply striking out this part. In either case, the judicial construction must not abuse but give reasonable effect to the legislative intent. Where this is not possible, the whole act should be condemned and left to a new legislative initiative.

Only recently has the Court begun to employ the first of these two techniques. In *Stauder* v. *Ulm,* it construed a Decision of the Commission, directed to the several Member States, to conform with "general principles of the Community legal order whose integrity the Court is bound to secure." Where doubt exists about the construction of a Decision, it stated, "the least burdensome construction should be given preference, if it is adequate to attain the goals which the Decision at issue is intended to serve." Burdensome for whom? Presumably for the German complainant who was required to divulge his name to grocers in order to receive a butter subsidy. Since the intent of the Commission as well as the language of 3 of the 4 official texts of the Decision allowed some leeway for interpretation, the Court adopted the broader construction. As a result, each Member State could determine how best to implement the Decision in accordance with its own laws. This avoids, the Court concludes, conflict with the "basic individual rights embodied in the general principles of the Community legal order." [439a] The Court, wisely enough, does not attempt at this point to set out in any detail what these "basic individual rights" might be.

There is no further evidence that the Court has adopted the technique of favorable constitutional construction. Indeed, its failure to do so, in construing the first proposal for a "small Treaty revision" of ECSC Article 56, was criticized by Carstens.[440] The new condition for exercising Treaty power, the Court held, "is so broadly formulated" that the High Authority could correct difficulties arising not "solely from a change in economic conditions," but also from the establishment of the common market. Insofar, the proposal exceeded the lawful limits of a "small Treaty revision." Still, as the Court itself admitted, "the possibility of such a [broad] application . . . must be excluded by the terms of the amendment

In international practice, if only from a substantive (materiell-rechtlichen) viewpoint, there also appears to be a presumption for treaty interpretation in favor of general international law. See Lauterpacht, *The Development of International Law by the International Court,* 27f (1958).

[439a] Judgment 29/69, 15 Rspr. 419, 424f (1969). See also the case note by Ehlermann, in 5 Europarecht 41 (1970).

[440] Carstens, "Die kleine Revision des EGKS-Vertrags," 21 Z. *ausl. öff. R.* 1, 36f (1961).

itself."[441] There would have been no particular danger, therefore, in curing this defect by a narrower construction in accordance with the Treaty.[442]

On the other hand, the Court has struck out illegal provisions in order to uphold an otherwise constitutional act. Thus, in upholding the Decision to re-divide the Ruhr into two coal selling agencies, the Court rejected the provision authorizing certain offices of the High Authority to determine, at their discretion, whether the subsequent practices and agreements of these cartels accord with their conditions of approval. Since those offices possess no independent authority under the Treaty, all such determinations must be reserved solely for collegial Decisions of the High Authority.[443] The same result could have been achieved while leaving the Decision undisturbed – as Advocate-General Lagrange chose to do – by simply noting that all acts of these offices must of course be published *as* Decisions of the High Authority. This would have preserved the right of appeal and the responsibility of the High Authority.[444] To some extent, therefore, these two techniques of constitutional construction are interchangeable.

A further exercise of judicial self-restraint lies in the Court's reluctance to weigh and balance conflicting Treaty goals. These goals, as in ECSC Article 3, are of course directly binding on the High Authority and must be interpreted with respect for the overriding requirements of the "common interest" reflected in Article 2.[445] Nevertheless, as the *Scrap* Judgments hold,[446] "it is by no means certain that all can be pursued, under all circumstances, simultaneously and in their entirety."[447] When full reconciliation is unattainable, then the High Authority may "afford one or the other of the goals the temporary pre-eminence *which may appear to the High Authority* to be required by the facts or economic circumstances ...."[448] As Advocate-General Lagrange concludes:

441 Opinion of the Court, 5 Rspr. 571, 580 (1958–59), discussed in text *supra*, p. 291f.

442 This defect was cured in the second proposal submitted to the Court. The condition for granting assistance, which the Court had found too broadly phrased – namely, in cases of "fundamental changes in marketing conditions" – was qualified by the phrase "... conditions, which are not directly bound up with the establishment of the common market." See ECSC Art. 56 § 2. The first proposal, however, was also struck down on other grounds.

443 Judgment 66/63, 10 Rspr. 1147, 1176f (1964), discussed in text *supra*, p. 283ff.

444 Conclusions of *Adv-Gen.* Lagrange, *ibid.*, p. 1204.

445 See text *supra*, pp. 255 and 256, esp. at notes 184 and 194.

446 Discussed in text *supra*, pp. 252–258.

447 *Meroni* Judgment 9/56, 4 Rspr. 9, 43 (1958), in text *supra*, p. 253f.

448 *Ibid.* Emphasis added. See also *Belges* Judgment 8/57, 4 Rspr. 231, 254 (1958), and Judgment 28/66 (*Netherlands* Case), 14 Rspr. 1 (1968), discussed in text *supra*, p. 265f.

Under the circumstances, ... the "economic situation" may be so differently evaluated that the judge can not responsibly substitute his judgment for that of the executive. This is forbidden not simply by Article 33, but, *even in its absence, by the elementary wisdom contained in the principle of the separation of powers.*[449]

The Court, however, does not simply abandon the field. It erects certain minimum standards of "reasonableness" and "due care."[450] These serve not to ascertain the concrete content of the "common interest" in a given case, but to prevent the High Authority from neglecting the interests of private parties in an "excessive or arbitrary way."[451] In the reconciliation of Treaty goals, therefore, the High Authority has been granted a "true discretionary power."[452]

In the Brandy Wine and Orange Import Cases,[453] the Court establishes a similar type of discretion for the Commission under the EEC Treaty. The issues arose with respect to those several viewpoints in EEC Article 29 which are to guide Commission decision-making.[454] Had the Commission unlawfully neglected certain of these viewpoints in rejecting the requests of the German Government for dispensations from the common Community tariff? Advocate-General Roemer believed so. While the Court *could not* "*prescribe exactly* the extent to which these viewpoints in Article 29 are to be respected in an individual case," he concludes, it could review

the Commission's train of thought and determine whether, according to all the recognizable and relevant economic and political factors, the *accent is correctly set.*[455]

The Commission had erred not only in its factual determination, but also in its exclusive emphasis on only certain of these viewpoints.[456]

449 Conclusions of *Adv-Gen.* Lagrange, in Cases 8–13/57, 4 Rspr. 317, 357f (1958). Emphasis added.

450 See *Chasse* Judgment 15/57, 4 Rspr. 159 (1958), discussed in text *supra*, p. 251f.

451 *Ibid.*, p. 195.

452 *Meroni* Judgment 9/56, *op. cit.*, p. 43.

453 Judgments 24/62 (*Germany* v. *EEC Commission*), 9 Rspr. 141 (1963), concerning brandy wine imports; and 34/62 (*Germany* v. *EEC Commission*), 9 Rspr. 287 (1963), concerning orange imports.

454 EEC Article 29 states guidelines for the "establishment of the common customs tariff" in Ch. I, Sec. 2 of the Treaty, including such goals as furthering commercial exchange, developing competitive conditions, ensuring the Community's requirements of supply, etc.

455 Conclusions of *Adv-Gen.* Roemer, in Case 24/62, *op. cit.*, p. 185; and in Case 34/62, *op. cit.*, p. 335. Emphasis added.

456 Case 24/62, *id.*, pp. 171f and 185f; and Case 34/62, *id.*, p. 355f.

The Court, however, refuses to accept even this moderate scope of review. In the Brandy Wine Judgment, it admits that a tariff dispensation might be justified by the conditions of Article 25, § 3.[457] Still, even if these conditions are met, "the Commission then 'can' further consider, in the light of the principles [of EEC Articles 2, 3 and 9] and of the viewpoints in Article 29, whether and to what extent a dispensation would be appropriate." These principles, including Article 29,

> characterize the frame of reference within which the Commission must exercise the *discretionary authority* granted it by Article 25 . . . [W]ithin these limits, which the Treaty draws and the Court must enforce, the Commission may freely exercise its discretionary authority and its decisions are not automatic.

Without further examination, the Court abruptly concludes: "It is not apparent that the Commission has infringed these Treaty principles.[458]

In the Orange Import Judgment, moreover, this reasoning is affirmed and developed. In language similar to the *Meroni* and *Belges* Judgments, just discussed, the Court points out:

> The viewpoints [in Article 29] refer to wholly different goals, which are at variance with each other and can not always be pursued simultaneously. The charge, that the defendants have not taken account of all of these guidelines, would only then be justified if they were all applicable in the case at bar.

But they are not and where they are, the Commission has taken them into consideration.[459] As to these specific EEC goals, therefore, the Court has refused the temptation of the Advocate-General to "set the correct accent." Instead, it has affirmed the discretionary authority of the Commission – as it did for the High Authority – to weigh and balance the conflicting goals subject to the outer limits of the fundamental Treaty provisions.

Even within the limits of Treaty provisions, however, the exercise of the Commission's discretion is not unrestricted. Thus, in the *Firma Beus* Decision, the Court granted the Commission certain discretion, under Article 11, paragraph 2, of EEC Regulation No. 23, in choosing the varieties of produce to be used in calculating the reference price for producers in the Member States. It noted, however, that this choice could

[457] EEC Article 25 § 3 permits the Commission to grant dispensations "provided that no serious disturbance in the market of the products concerned may result therefrom."

[458] Judgment 24/62, *op. cit.*, p. 154f. Emphasis added.

[459] Judgment 34/62, *op. cit.*, p. 318.

not be arbitrary.[460] On the broader level of Community policy, the Court went one step further and laid down a principle for determining priority among competing goals of the common agricultural market. It extrapolated a "so-called principle of 'Community preference' " from EEC Article 44 (2). Based on this principle the Treaty goals of lowering international trade barriers (EEC Article 110) and of guaranteeing Member State consumers regular supplies at reasonable prices (EEC Article 39(d) and (e)) were subordinated to the transitional protection of Community producers and the overall demands of establishing a common organization of agricultural markets (EEC Article 44).[460a]

This same result, it is submitted, could have been reached without the "preference" principle. Its introduction has the unfortunate consequence of hardening a delicate area of policy discretion into a *duty* to protect community agriculture for the time being against outside competition.[460b] Nevertheless, despite this judicial intrusion into the proper realm of Commission decision-making, the Court appears to be following a parallel course in both the EEC and ECSC.[460c] The Treaty goals admittedly are legally binding, but the scope of judicial review has been significantly restricted.

Finally, judicial review may be restrained by limiting the rights of appeal for certain categories of questions. In effect, the scope of review is restricted by the occasion for its exercise. The Treaties themselves, as Chapter II points out, expressly stipulate some major restrictions for private parties; the Court has announced, however, that "in case of doubt a provision granting legal redress is not to be interpreted restrictively to the detriment of the legal subject."[461] Nevertheless, in two major instances where the ECSC Treaty is far from clear, the Court has added additional restrictions on these rights. The first is implied in *Hamborner Bergbau AG and Friedrich Thyssen Bergbau AG* v. *High Authority*,[462] concerning the taxing power of the High Authority. While attacking an individual Decision of the High

[460] Judgment 5/67 (*Firma W. Beus GmbH. & Co.* v. *Chief Customs Office Munich*), 14 Rspr. 127, 145 (1968).

[460a] *Ibid.*, p. 147. See also the Conclusions of Adv-Gen. Gand, 14 Rspr. 151–53.

[460b] See Fuss, Case Note, 3 Europarecht 295, 297 (1968).

[460c] See, for instance, the more recent Judgment 1/69, (*Italy* v. *EC Commission*), where the Court grants the Commission a "broad scope of discretion" in shaping the freight and transportation conditions pursuant to EEC Article 80.

[461] Judgment 6/60, 6 Rspr. 1163, 1189 (1960). See also Judgments 7 and 9/54, 2 Rspr. 53, 86 (1955–56) ("The silence of the Treaty on this point can not be interpreted to the disadvantage of the enterprises and associations."); 32 and 33/58, 5 Rspr. 287, 312 (1958–59); 9/56, 4 Rspr. 7, 25–28 (1958); 25/62, 9 Rspr. 211, 237 (1963); and the Conclusions of *Adv-Gen.* Roemer, in Case 1/64, 10 Rspr. 899, 905 (1964).

[462] Judgment 41 and 50/59, 6 Rspr. 1025 (1960).

Authority refusing them dispensation from taxes for the year 1959–60,[463] the plaintiffs' real objective was the power of the High Authority to levy a tax at the then-fixed annual rate.[464] By the terms of ECSC Articles 49 and 50, the plaintiffs argued that the accumulated funds of the Community were already greater than those "required to carry out" the tasks of the High Authority. Further, this fiscal policy allegedly violated the Treaty requirements of "minimal burdens" on ECSC enterprises, of a strict "need" basis for taxation and of limited intervention. The very absence of parliamentary control over the High Authority's budget, they contended, made judicial review the more necessary.[465]

The Court never reaches these questions. By a "somewhat formalistic interpretation," as Bebr observes,[466] it rejects the appeal on procedural grounds. In brief, the plaintiffs could not reach the 1959–60 tax levy because it was not the legal basis of a possible tax dispensation; it "does not add any new normative provision to the High Authority's [prior] Decisions, as it *merely extends in force* the rate of levy fixed for the previous year."[467]

[463] The appeal came up, therefore, as an "exception of illegality" under ECSC Art. 36. See discussion of this appeal in text *supra*, p. 86f. The Decision itself was issued in the form of a Letter from the High Authority (July 24, 1959), in response to the plaintiffs' request.

[464] According to ECSC Article 50 § 2, the High Authority can levy a tax of up to 1% of the average value of coal and steel production. In 1952, the High Authority had imposed a levy, commencing at 0.3% and rising progressively to 0.9%, but the levy in the financial years 1958–59 and 1959–60 lay at 0.35%. The High Authority's long-announced policy was to maintain a $ 100 million loan guarantee fund and a special reserve fund to help finance workers' housing projects. Particular the former could be used not only to support industrial investment but also, due to its influence on the loan market, to channel and direct such investment in general. The plaintiffs challenged not so much the existence as the size of the funds. They were viewed as levers for a *dirigisme*, especially distasteful to the German firms who shouldered a major share of the tax burden. See Diebold, *The Schuman Plan*, 317–19 (1959); and Lister, *Europe's Coal and Steel Community*, 71f (1960).

[465] See Judgment 41 and 50/59, *op. cit.*, p. 1033ff, for contentions of the plaintiffs. This last argument, in particular, has been used to explain the extensive scope of judicial review in the Communities. See text *supra*, pp. 21, 51 and 71.

[466] Bebr, *Judicial Control of the European Communities*, 140, n. 8 (1962), referring expressly to the reasoning of *Adv-Gen.* Roemer, but equally applicable to that of the Court.

[467] Judgment 41 and 50/59, *op. cit.*, p. 1050f (emphasis added). But cf. Judgment 2/57, 4 Rspr. 133, 150 (1958), upholding the plaintiff enterprise's right to attack a general Decision of the High Authority continuing "an earlier Decision having the same effect."

As an alternative to dismissing the case on procedural grounds, Adv-Gen. Roemer further develops a view for restricting the scope of judicial review on the merits in regard to questions of tax policy. See his Conclusions, in Case 41 and 50/59, *id.*, p. 1077ff.

Nor does the Court then proceed "on its own motion," as it had in previous cases,[468] to examine these prior Decisions. Instead, it tacitly rejects what the plaintiffs had so fervently contended, namely, that there was an essential relationship between the level of an annual tax and a firm's application for dispensation. Given the practical impossibility for a firm, under ECSC Article 33, to attack the annual levy as a general act,[469] this Judgment secures the taxing policy of the High Authority against private appeal.[470]

Another and particularly striking example of such judicial self-restraint is found in the *Niederrheinische Bergwerk* Judgment.[471] There, the plaintiffs attacked a Decision of the High Authority,[472] designed to meet the mounting coal crisis by restricting and distributing Belgian coal imports. Since the Council of Ministers could not agree on measures for the ECSC as a whole,[473] Belgium was threatening "self-help" and the Dutch were considering retaliatory measures in return.[474] Amidst the political tensions, which are certainly not unusual for economic crisis situations, the High Authority resorted to its only practical alternative: an emergency measure under Article 37. Under this provision, the High Authority was not encumbered by the need for Council approval.

The difficulty was, as the plaintiffs were quick to point out, that Article 37 is for use only against those "fundamental and persistent disturbances in the economy" of a Member State which are *caused by* the action or inaction of

468 See, e.g., Judgment 14/59, 5 Rspr. 465, 492f (1958–59), concerning also an individual Decision challenged under ECSC Art. 36. For a review of the many cases in which the Court has proceeded "on its own motion," see Bebr, "Prozessmaximen," in *Zehn Jahre Rechtsprechung des Gerichtshofs der Europäischen Gemeinschaften,* 77, 81–98 (1965). Cf. also a later decision arising under the EEC "preliminary question" procedure, Judgment 5/67 (*Firma Beus* Case), 14 Rspr. 128, 144f (1968), in which the Court undertook without hesitation on its own motion to review and uphold the general Regulation No. 104/65 upon which the specific Regulation No. 144/65 rests, even though the court below had not questioned the former's validity. See comment by Fuss, 3 Europarecht 295, 304 (1968).

469 See Discussion in text *supra,* p. 81f.

470 Nor is it likely that the Member States or Council of Ministers would take up the cause for the enterprises, for the tax falls directly on the coal and steel producers.

471 Judgment 2 and 3/60 (*Niederrheinische Bergwerks-A.G. and Unternehmensverband des Aachener Steinkohlenbergbaues* v. *High Authority*), 7 Rspr. 281 (1961).

472 Decision No. 46–59 (Dec. 23, 1959), in Amtsblatt 1327 (Dec. 31, 1959), slightly amended by Decision No. 1–60 (Jan. 18, 1960), in Amtsblatt 103 (Jan. 28, 1960).

473 This excluded the resort to production quotas (ECSC Art. 58) as well as to any type of Treaty change (ECSC Art. 95). For discussion of the coal crisis, see Meade, Liesner and Wells, *Case Studies in European Economic Union,* 248ff (1962), and text *supra,* p. 41f and 248f.

474 See Europe CECA (Agence internationale d'information pour la Presse) 2f (Nov. 4, 1959).

the High Authority. Since the coal crisis was scarcely attributable to the High Authority, the plaintiffs contended in part that Article 37 had been improperly invoked, that its conditions had not been met and that, in any case, the measures taken violated the major Treaty purposes in Articles 2 through 5. The threshold question, however, was the permissibility of appeal. Article 37 explicitly provides for judicial review, but it does not specify the proper parties. Considering "the silence of the text," the Court began, "it is necessary to consider . . . whether there are cogent, logical reasons for restricting access to the Court."[475] The answer is yes!

The key to the Court's analysis lies in the nature of the questions at stake.

> The primary purpose of Article 37 is to make possible a reconciliation between the interests of the Member States, which are affected or endangered by fundamental and persistent disturbances, and the common interests of the Community.[476]

From the High Authority, the Court continues, this demands an "arbitral reconciliation" of interests "which is actually a grant of extra-ordinary powers." These "special powers," however, are not unlimited. The measures selected must not only be appropriate for combatting the economic disturbances, but also must secure "the essential interests of the Community."[472] As for the Court, it possesses "extremely far-reaching power" to review these measures, including "an assessment of the economic situation in the Member States" as well as a review of the necessity and appropriateness for the measures taken. In view of these considerations, an Article 37 appeal "concerns the political responsibility of the Member States and the High Authority" in achieving a legitimate reconciliation of the relevant interests.[478] "In truth," adds Advocate-General Lagrange,[479] "the frontier of administrative adjudication has been crossed and we find ourselves . . . much more in the sphere of federal constitutional law."

For this reason, Member States but not the ECSC enterprises themselves possess a right to appeal Article 37 measures. "In view of the importance of the possible interests at stake," the right of Member State appeal compensates for the lack of Council approval. Further, Member States are the most appropriate parties "to protect the public interests." They are "by their nature in a position to give all the information useful for thorough judicial

[475] Judgment 2 and 3/60, *op. cit.*, p. 308.
[476] *Ibid.*, p. 308f.
[477] *Ibid.*, p. 309.
[478] *Ibid.*, p. 309f.
[479] *Ibid.*, p. 326 and also 330.

review and, through their membership in the Council, to bear the responsibility for securing the essential interests of the Community."[480] Indeed, Lagrange observes, it would be not only unusual but "even somewhat shocking" to permit private parties to invoke the judicial review of fundamental economic disturbances in other Member States. Being unable to fully appreciate the circumstances, it would be incomprehensible for a single enterprise "to assume the role of Community defender when no State is prepared to do this."[481]

Moreover, the Court concludes, private parties can not derive a right of appeal from the general provisions in Article 33. "The conditions for applying Article 37 are intimately related to each other and cannot be examined separately." An Article 33 like an Article 37 appeal would force the Court to exercise its "extra-ordinary powers" of review. This may not be done "within the framework of the Court's general jurisdiction."[482] The fundamental nature of the questions at stake, therefore, dictates a restricted exercise of the Court's far-reaching powers of review.

These several cases demonstrate the latent leeway for self-restraint in Treaty interpretation. The Court, aware of its limited knowledge as to the questions raised, could restrict its scope in several ways. Although the presumption of constitutionality has been little applied, the Court has been particularly cautious in substituting its views of goal balancing for those of the High Authority and EEC Commission. The diverse and conflicting Treaty goals are directly binding, but their reconciliation lies largely at the discretion of the political organs of the Community. Further, the additional restrictions on the private right of appeal have considerably reduced the occasion for judicial review in the sensitive areas of taxation and Article 37 emergency measures. True, the Member States and the Community organs may still raise these questions, but they do not always share the interests of private parties.[483] This is apparent in the last two cases here reviewed: the measures in question were never attacked by the Member States, although the solution to the coal crisis in particular had foundered in the Council of Ministers. The Court has recognized, therefore, that its powers must be exercised with a prudent respect for the legitimate sphere of quasi-legislative authority in the Communities.

480 *Ibid.*, p. 310f. In its *mémoire* and *duplique,* the High Authority argued the application of the doctrine of "acte du gouvernement" to ECSC Art. 37 measures. The Court, however, does not expressly mention the term.

481 *Ibid.*, p. 329f.

482 *Ibid.*, p. 311.

483 This has been emphasized in text *supra,* p. 79f.

The Remanding Function

The modes of judicial restraint just discussed are more of doctrine than of tactic. The Court has, as a matter of principle, declared its unwillingness to examine certain questions or to make certain types of evaluations. Beyond this, there are also occasions when specific questions raised in litigation fall within the formal competence of judicial review but are not ripe for determination. That is to say, the fundamental issues at stake require clarification and further discussion before finally being resolved. This may occur of course, case-by-case, through "topical" reasoning: as in the Luxembourg Coal Levies Case, the Court raised the *topos* of "comparability" through *obiter dictum,* but left it for later development in the Rail Tariff and Miners' Bonus Cases.[484] These same *topoi* also may be presented and discussed within the broader but disciplined framework of Community institutions. Just such a procedure has been institutionalized in the "small Treaty revision," where all organs of the ECSC participate.[485]

On other occasions, the Court alone must initiate, force and sustain discussion among Community organs and Member States in the search for the underlying purposes of Community law. This requires a careful mixture of judicial activism and self-restraint. Depending on the context of a question, the only way to maintain legal development may be to avoid partially or fully a decision on the merits. In effect, the Court should focus discussion on the pertinent issue, but decide or perhaps dismiss the case on other grounds. This is tactic pure and simple, but tactic in service of the search for principle and of the overriding objective of legal development. Its function is to remand the issue to the appropriate governmental institution for reconsideration and renewed effort.[486]

What might be the nature of a "judicial remand" within the context of the Communities? It consists, above all, in carefully selecting those grounds of decision which keep open the course of legal discussion and development. In the very first Judgment on the Ruhr cartel problem, for instance, the

484 See discussion in text *supra,* p. 260f.

485 For discussion of this procedure, see text *supra,* p. 72f. Within the context of this procedure, the Court has not only made binding determinations, but also has offered a "suggestion" for rephrasing the language of a proposal in order to avoid certain future difficulties. In fact, the Council and High Authority incorporated the suggestion in their second proposal, which the Court accepted. See Opinion of the Court, 5 Rspr. 571, 581 (1958–59), and the follow-up Opinion, 1/60, 6 Rspr. 109 (1960).

486 See text *supra,* p. 214ff, for the theoretical justification of the judicial remanding function.

Court was called upon to determine whether price-setting powers under the ECSC Treaty could be employed to offset a distorted market structure.[487] It refused the unconditional application of the anti-cartel and anti-concentration provisions of Articles 65 and 66, but noted that such discretion of the High Authority was governed by the Transitional Convention. It thereby granted the High Authority the leverage and time needed to disband illegal cartels, but put the High Authority on warning that the issue could be raised again if delayed too long.[488]

Further, in the *Meroni* Judgment,[489] the Court nullified a Decision of the High Authority for an unconstitutional delegation of powers, but went on to focus attention on certain substantive issues. Although this further elaboration was not necessary for the outcome of the Judgment,[490] it pointed out the breadth of High Authority discretion in weighing and balancing conflicting Treaty goals. Ironically, what was widely heralded as an anti-diristic Judgment in terms of the case holding, was in substance a general outline of the vast powers of the High Authority in market intervention. Moreover, as the Court later notes, a nullification for unconstitutional delegation would not prejudice the merits of a High Authority decision.[491] It may, however, offer the Court an opportunity to express without committing itself on other points. The Court may thereby initiate a discussion which the legislative authority upon reconsideration of the measure can continue. At the same time, the Court reserves its "say" on the merits for a later date.[492]

A judicial remand, which does not prejudice the outcome of an issue, often must resort to procedural or other essentially formal grounds of decision. Perhaps the most flexible of these grounds in Community adjudication is that of inadequate motivation.[493] While the requirement of motivation is designed to protect the interests of the parties as well as to facilitate judicial review, it also by its nature constitutes a very general standard. As a result,

487 Judgment 6/54, 1 Rspr. 211 (1954–55), discussed in text *supra*, p. 246f.

488 The very absence of a time limit, for disbanding illegal cartels, in Article 12 of the Transitional Convention, the Court argues, makes clear the High Authority's discretionary power in this matter "during the transitional period." *Ibid.*, p. 234f.

489 Judgment 9/56, 4 Rspr. 9 (1958), discussed in text *supra*, p. 253f.

490 Judgment 108/63, 11–1 Rspr. 1, 15 (1965).

491 The Court subsumed the unlawful delegation under the ground of a *détournement de pouvoir*. See text *supra*, pp. 56–58. Although an examination of Treaty goals was quite proper under this broad ground, the Court had already determined the illegality of the Decision before proceeding so far.

492 See Bickel, *The Least Dangerous Branch: The Supreme Court at the Bar of Politics*, 181, 201 and 223 (1962), for a discussion of the delegation of powers concept in this sense.

493 This ground is discussed in text *supra*, p. 55 and *infra*, p. 480ff.

it permits the Court wide discretion in reviewing the legality of a particular Community act. Indeed, it may be difficult at times to distinguish qualitatively between motivations which the Court upholds and those which it rejects.[494] This has been amply demonstrated by the Court's reasoning in the *Geitling, Nold* and *Präsident* Judgments, discussed above,[495] concerning the gradual reduction and, finally, virtual elimination of the minimum trading requirements with the Ruhr sales agencies. There, the motivation requirement became the judicial vehicle for focusing attention and pressing discussion on the question of minimum access criteria. By means of it, the Decisions of the High Authority in the latter two of these cases were annulled and, in effect, remanded to the High Authority for renewed consideration without judicially prejudicing the ultimate resolution of the matter on the merits. Moreover, in the *Nold* Judgment, the Court took up this ground of annulment on its own motion, thereby broadening immeasurably the range for judicial maneuver.[496] The Community Court, therefore, possesses the ways and means for maintaining discussion before laying an issue to rest.

All this is not to say, however, that the Court either always consciously or willingly has employed judicial remand in fact. It simply serves to demonstrate that the conditions for its application potentially exist. Instead, in one crucial case, the Court failed unfortunately to take this course. This is the Road Tariff Publication Judgments,[497] where the "implied powers" reasoning was rejected for ECSC Article 70, paragraph 3. The wording of this provision may be seen as typical compromise language, uncertain as to the future needs of the Community. It requires, on the one hand, that transport rates "shall be published or brought to the knowledge of the High Authority." Considering that the costs of ECSC goods are transport-intensive – the price of coal, for instance, containing as much as 35% transport costs[498] – a full knowledge of transport tariffs is essential for a functioning price system.[499] It is a necessary corollary to the mandatory publication of product prices under Article 60 § 2, as well as crucial for the effective control of

[494] See Bebr, *op. cit.* (n. 466), p. 88; and Steindorff, *Rechtsschutz und Verfahren im Recht der Europäischen Gemeinschaften* 70 (1964).

[495] See discussion in text *supra*, p. 275f.

[496] See Bebr, *op. cit.* (n. 468), pp. 81–98, pointing up the Court's willingness to consider certain formal and procedural grounds "on its own motion."

[497] Judgments 20/59, 6 Rspr. 681 (1960); and 25/59, 6 Rspr. 743 (1960). See discussion in text *supra*, pp. 294–296.

[498] See Meade, *op. cit.* (n. 473), p. 336; Diebold, *op. cit.* (n. 464), pp. 155–58; and Lister, *op. cit.* (n. 464), p. 395.

[499] See Klaer, *Der Verkehr im Gemeinsamen Markt für Kohle und Stahl,* 94–101 (1961).

discrimination. "There is no need to elaborate," says Klaer,[500] that the prohibition of discrimination in transportation "can not be carried out if enterprises shipping across state lines do not know the domestic freight rates."

On the other hand, as the Court was quick to note, ECSC Article 70, paragraph 3, contains no details as to its implementation. This was to be decisive. Absent the appropriate language as well as all implication from other Treaty provisions and the context of the Treaty as a whole, the Court could find no legislative power for the High Authority as to the publication of transport tariffs. As a result, the High Authority was not only forced to return to the bargaining table, but more importantly expressly stripped of all leverage. It was required to resume the multilateral negotiations with the Member States which had, in the previous five-year period, failed to produce results. This stalemate, it should be recalled, lay in the negative vote of only one Member State.[501]

How should the Court have responded? Considering the importance of transport tariff publication for economic integration, its primary objective should have been to reopen the lines of negotiation. This was important for more than simply road haulage, since the solution to this issue would most likely set a precedent for the remainder of the transport sector.[502] It was necessary, first of all, to remand the issue *without prejudice* to the High Authority and Member States for serious reconsideration. The procedural grounds of decision for this were at hand. The Decision of the High Authority, which established the alternative forms for publishing road tariffs, had been issued as an Article 88 determination that the Member States had failed to meet their Treaty obligations under ECSC Article 70.[503] Seen solely in the light of Article 88, as the Court admits, the Decision constituted a major violation of procedure: the prescribed exchange of opinions between the High Authority and the Italian and Dutch Governments, prior to making such a determination, had not been properly observed. It does not justify, concludes the Court, "the grave step of declaring a State in breach of its

[500] *Ibid.*, p. 89. See also Ferron, *Le Problème des Transports et le Marché Commun*, 225f (1965).

[501] See Klaer, *id.*, pp. 274–76; and High Authority, Seventh Gen. Rep. 193f (German ed. 1958–59). All Member States, except Holland, had agreed in principle on the prior publication of maximum and minimum transport tariffs.

[502] This proved to be true in fact. Unable to issue a legislative Decision, the High Authority reverted to the mode of Recommendation, but extending it from road haulage alone to include transport tariffs in general. See note 511 *infra*, p. 315.

[503] Decision No. 18–59 (Feb. 18, 1959), Amtsblatt 287 (March 7, 1959).

Treaty obligation."[504] Or, seen solely in terms of motivation, as Advocate-General Roemer concludes, the Decision also is logically defective: while offering the Member States *three* alternatives for implementing their Article 70 obligation, the High Authority then condemns them for not having chosen either of the *first two* of these.[505] Considering the delicate nature of Member State negotiation, both these procedural deficiencies deserve emphasis. The Court, therefore, had ample reason for nullifying the Decision solely on procedural grounds. Without going to the merits of the issues, it should have remanded it for further consideration, admonishing the High Authority to reopen negotiations and seek a solution by voluntary agreement of the Member States.

In view of the failure of previous negotiations, however, something more was likely needed. It was necessary for the Court to strengthen – or at least not weaken – the High Authority's bargaining position vis-à-vis dissenting Member States.[506] How was such leverage to be supplied? The Court of course could simply have established, by necessary implication, a power of the High Authority to legislate in the field of tariff publication. While the ambiguous language of Article 70, paragraph 3, does not exclude this, the "implied powers" reasoning of the Court in other cases would tend to support it.[507] In particular, it was not doubted that Article 70 directly obligates Member States to publish their transport rates in some fashion or to bring them to the knowledge of the High Authority.[508] Price publication serves the goals of non-discrimination, price alignment and economic rationality – all of which have been recognized in other judgments.[509] In comparison to the prohibition of discrimination in the field of transportation, which the Court had absolutely affirmed, the power of the High Authority to legislate the alternative but uniform conditions for publishing transport tariffs in the

504 Judgment 20/59, *op. cit.*, pp. 715–17; 25/59, *op. cit.*, pp. 788–90. See also Bebr, "Prozessmaximen," *op. cit.* (n. 468), p. 93f. *Adv-Gen.* Roemer concludes also that these procedural irregularities had occurred, but believed that they amounted to an "infringement of legal hearing" only in the Dutch case. *Id.*, pp. 731–33 and 805–9, respectively.

505 Conclusions of *Adv-Gen.*, Roemer, in Case 20/59, *id.*, pp. 729f and 733–36. In Case 25/29, *id.*, having established an "infringement of legal hearing," Roemer did not go on to examine the question of adequate motivation.

506 While both Italy and Holland opposed the existence of a legislative power for the High Authority under Article 70, paragraph 3, Holland was the lone dissenter in the negotiations. See note 501 *supra*.

507 See text *supra*, p. 293ff.

508 It had, therefore, to be implemented. See Judgments 20/59 and 25/59, *op. cit.*, pp. 707 and 780, respectively.

509 See discussion in text *supra*, pp. 243ff.

Member States is quite modest. Far from challenging the reserved domain of the Member States, the demands of the High Authority were more of form than substance.

Nevertheless, the reluctance of the Court to imply Treaty powers in the sphere of transportation is understandable. The transport sector has not been integrated in the ECSC and transport policy is expressly reserved to the Member States.[510] In the peripheral sector of transportation, therefore, there is good reason to rely more on authentic interpretation by the Member States than on an unilateral interpretation by the Court of Justice. The dilemma between these two considerations could have been resolved by remanding the Decision to the High Authority for renewed negotiation, but making clear that a power by implication might be forthcoming at a later date. While the reluctance to imply a power may be justified, the Court should have been equally reluctant to fully exclude this possibility.

Whether this tactic would have been successful is another question. It would have given the Court the opportunity, however, to focus attention on the issue in all its urgency and to bring greater pressure to bear on the dissenting Member States. Even more important, it would have reopened the political process and paved the way for consensual agreement which is so crucial for legal development. Where judicial knowledge is uncertain, it is the better part of wisdom in constitutional adjudication to keep the discussion going.

Unfortunately, the course of the Court was one of stalemate. Unable to legislate by Decision the uniform conditions of tariff publication in the Community, the High Authority was forced to revert to the much less effective means of Recommendation. The Member States were simply ordered to take the necessary municipal measures, within the coming nine months, to meet the requirements of Article 70, paragraph 3.[511] In the face of a Dutch appeal, this time the Court upheld the High Authority.[512] Ironically, the reasoning of the Court is replete with all those basic considerations of Treaty purpose and values which it omitted in its previous Judgment. The damage, however, had already been done. Since a Recommendation could only repeat the goals of the Treaty and prescribe no means, transport tariffs will be published but will lack that important uniformity which the earlier Decision of the High Authority would have furthered.

Moreover, in the absence of a uniform standard, the individual measures

510 See text *supra*, p. 262f, and ECSC Art. 70, paragraph 5.

511 Recommendation No. 1–61 (March 1, 1961), Amtsblatt 469 (March 9, 1961).

512 Judgment 9/61 (*Netherlands* v. *High Authority*), 8 Rspr. 433 (1962).

of the Member States will not be so easily policed.[513] Each Member State alone will understandably be reluctant to publish more than its neighbors.[514] The result may well be a series of appeals against deficient measures in which the Court – through the gradual articulation of Article 70, paragraph 3 – will be required to establish that uniform standard which it denied the High Authority. A judicial standard, however, will be considerably less complete than a legislated one, determining only that minimum which does not violate the Treaty. What could not be done by Community legislation may well be undertaken, with a considerable loss of time, energy and effectiveness, by the Court. This would serve to demonstrate that the judicial remand – being at first glance a type of judicial activism – may be in the long run a means of self-restraint.

CONCLUSIONS

The judicial development of Community law, as this Chapter attempts to demonstrate, has proceeded largely teleologically through "topical" reasoning. In the sense used here, teleology is not a license for judicial legislation, but the methodological premise for understanding Treaty interpretation. It does not legitimate every act or decision expedient to a given purpose, but simply acknowledges that the continuing search for the purposes, values and principles underlying the Treaties is intrinsic to law and legal

[513] Immediately following Judgment 9/61, the High Authority asserted that the Member States were now clearly obligated "to ensure an appropriate publication by which all the Treaty goals can be attained. The mere communication of freight rates and conditions to the High Authority, without appropriate publication, would not constitute a satisfactory application of the Recommendation." Bearing in mind the limits of its recommending power, however, the High Authority made clear "that it did not intend to take a doctrinaire or formalistic position." High Authority, Eleventh Gen. Rep. 361–64 (German ed. 1962–63). Not until four years later, in 1966 after considerable negotiation (see the pertinent sections on transport policy in the Twelfth, Thirteenth and Fourteenth General Reports of the High Authority), was the High Authority able to gain Member State support for even minimal standards of rate publication. While all Member States now publish the fixed tariffs, such publication is often limited to maximum and minimum rates. Moreover, in France, Italy and the Netherlands, the use of special rates is widespread; these need not be published unless they deviate 5% (for coal) and 10% (for steel) from the official rates. High Authority, Fifteenth Gen. Rep. 171f (English ed. 1966–67), and the First Gen. Rep. 226f (English ed. 1967–68) of the new Commission.

[514] See conclusions of the High Authority, Twelfth Gen. Rep. 225 (German ed. 1963–64). Even as to 1968 and 1969, the Commission could only report: "It is therefore continuing its efforts to achieve adequate disclosure of rates and conditions of carriage in fields where transparency of the transport market is still insufficient or even non-existent." EC Commission, Second and Third Gen. Reps. 277f and 275f (English eds. 1968 and 1969).

development. The *topoi* themselves are the mode for pressing the judicial search. They do not determine but simply discipline judicial choice, embracing the continuing tension between the written norm and its ideal content. Taken substantively, they frame the given problem in terms of the relevant Treaty provisions and the purposes or values which they serve. Thus, through such *topoi* as "reasonable," "partial" and "normal," a given provision or concept is put in context and considered from the various standpoints of the Treaty as a whole. Beginning with the problem in question, they initiate a line of reasoning which is shaped and informed over the years with each new case. By this process, a judicial choice is continually tested and criticized in terms of accumulating judicial experience and the changing requirements of Community integration.

Taken institutionally, these same *topoi* also may frame a discussion among the several Community organs. This necessitates judicial self-restraint. Due to the limits of judicial knowledge, the Court on occasion must stay its hand in favor of other Community organs. It has done this permanently, where the judicial process is unfit to act, on matters concerning taxation and the exercise of emergency powers in the ECSC. On other occasions, it may couple techniques of temporary restraint with critical reasoning in order to initiate, force or maintain discussion on an issue not yet ripe for judicial determination or at least better left, if at all possible, for resolution by other organs of Community government. While the Court appears also to have recognized this facet of judicial interpretation in dealing with the minimum access criteria of the Ruhr sales cartels, it failed to employ it in the Road Tariff Publication Cases. Nevertheless, on balance, it has used its power most effectively to maintain the search for purpose in Community law.

CHAPTER VI

THE SEARCH FOR AUTHORITY

The second task of judicial interpretation lies in the uncertainties of supranational integration. These uncertainties, of course, may be due simply to the ambiguities of faulty draftsmanship. As to documents of a constitutional order, however, they will often reflect the limits of a community consensus. Textual ambiguity or incompleteness, for instance, may stem from the undesirability or impossibility of the parties concerned to achieve greater agreement at the time. Unable to reach agreement on specific questions, says Lauterpacht of international treaties,[1] the parties must often be content "to use an ambiguous or non-committal expression and to leave the divergence of views to be solved in the future by agreement or in some other way." This is the art of statesmanship; resolving those issues ripe for decisions and glossing-over others in favor of future developments. This is no less true for so fundamental and comprehensive documents as the European Community Treaties,[2] embracing a multitude of national and private interests. Perfection must give way to the demands of time and compromise lest the entire venture be forfeited.

Furthermore, the pace and difficulties of supranational integration, like that of a nation's history, may not always follow the original expectations of the founding parties. While this may, to some extent, be anticipated by escape clauses[3] or be corrected by subsequent agreements among the Member States,[4] the Treaties are constantly exposed to the strains and disintegrating

[1] Lauterpacht, "Restrictive Interpretation and the Principle of Effectiveness in the Interpretation of Treaties," 26 *Brit. YB Int. L.*, 48, 77 (1949).

[2] See, e.g., Hochbaum, *Das Diskriminierungs- und Subventionsverbot in der EGKS und EWG*, 33 (1962); and Wolf, "Auslegungsgrundsätze des Gerichtshofes," in *Zehn Jahre Rechtsprechung*, 193f (1965). Cf. also Reuter, *La C.E.C.A.*, 38f (1953).

[3] E.g., ECSC Arts. 37, 58, 59, 71, 74 and 95, and the particular protectionary measures for the various Member States in the Transitional Convention. See also EEC Arts. 8, 25(3), 36, 42, 44, 223, 224, 226 and 235.

[4] See the agreements of the Member States discussed *infra*, p. 372ff.

effects of private and national special interests. Indeed, the European Communities may be termed "a system in permanent crisis"; so long as supranational integration proceeds, these special interests in the Member States are continuously confronted with the overriding demands of the Communities.[5] In case of outright conflict, these interests may always take refuge in a nationalistic appeal or in the dualist doctrine of international obligations. In Belgium, Italy and to a lesser extent Germany, it has been noted,[6] this doctrine apparently dominates judicial practice; in the latter two States, it is buttressed by the institution of constitutional review. In France, the supremacy of treaties over municipal law is conditioned on reciprocity by the other signatory states. A truly unresolvable conflict between the Community and certain Member State legal orders, as Advocate-General Lagrange has concluded,[7] could well give rise to a chain reaction which would shake the very foundation of the Treaties. In the last instance, the course and pace of legal development in the Communities depends on the willingness of the Member States and their nationals to subject their interests to regulation by common Community procedures. The Treaty norms, therefore, can only imperfectly grasp the origin and growth of the consensus necessary for viable Community integration.[8]

Here is the source of that tension in Community law between reason and fiat, giving rise to the judicial search for authority. Legal authority, as Chapter III concludes,[9] is the "capacity for reasoned elaboration," relating action or, in this case, judicial decision to values. The values in question, discussed in the previous Chapter, are those primarily of the Treaties and the principles which they imply. Yet given the uncertainties of interpretation just mentioned, the very limits of practical reason which this implies and the evolutionary character of Community law, the Court can not be content simply with determinations of the law as it is or should be. Its reasoning

5 See Lindberg, "Decision Making and Integration in the European Community," 19 *Int. Organ.*, 56, 79f (1965); and his "Integration as a Source of Stress on the European Community System," 20 *Int. Organ.*, 233, esp. 235f (1966).

6 See text *supra*, p. 28f, for discussion of the relationship of Community and Member State law.

7 Conclusions of *Adv-Gen.* Lagrange, in Case 6/64, 10 Rspr. 1279, 1292 (1964).

8 A persuasive and insightful characterization of the relationship between the legal and political aspects of the Community Treaties is offered by von Simson, "Der politische Wille als Gegenstand der europäischen Gemeinschaftsverträge," in *Festschrift Riese*, 83 (1964). He concludes: "die Verträge enthalten die Unterwerfung der Staaten unter ein Prinzip der bedingten rechtlichen, und zugleich einer aus dieser und ihren Folgen hervorgehenden, und durch die ermöglichten, faktischen Unwiderruflichkeit." *Ibid.*, p. 97.

9 See text *supra*, p. 130f.

must offer persuasive insight that the values derived from the Treaties are not only well-founded *in law,* but also desirable and necessary for the venture at hand. The decisions of the Court must not only *be* correct, they must also *be believed* to be correct. The judicial reasoning considered now, therefore, is not so much that of the critical search for meaning, but of the rhetoric and argumentation of persuasion.

Nevertheless, the capacity to reason persuasively has real limits in a viable Community consensus. The nature and intensity of this consensus will vary of course from issue to issue. It may develop but only gradually and is constantly threatened by the retrogressive pressures of special interests. For the Court, it is especially evident – though not with mathematical precision – through the statements, conduct and shifting positions of the Member State governments and other Community organs. In a less wieldy but not less palpable form, it may also be reflected in local and national elections [10] and in public opinion polls.[11] While the degree of enthusiasm on an issue will often be difficult to determine if at all, adamant opposition is typically outspoken. And once it is clear that the limits of consensus have been reached, not even the clarity of the text can avail. The fiat of the Court is no greater than the consensus upon which it rests. The Court, therefore, is bound to a loyal interpretation of the Treaties, but this interpretation, to be effective, must respect the outer limits of Community consensus.

How has the Court responded to this second set of parameters? As in the previous Chapter, the judicial search for authority also will be analyzed under two perspectives. The first emphasizes certain modes of reasoning by which the Court may preserve and generate consensus for the Community legal orders. These modes, it is believed, are not unique to the Community Court, but may be found throughout the decisions of any court of a constitutional or international character. Within the peculiar context of supranational adjudication, however, they are of special importance to the search for legal authority. The second perspective, on the other hand, stresses this search within the institutional interplay between the Community Court and national tribunals. Here the potential conflict between competing legal orders is most poignantly reflected in the delimitation of Community from national jurisdiction. Within the framework of the "preliminary question" procedure, the Community Court is engaged in a dialogue aimed at resolving

10 Witness the French election returns of December 1965 in the light of former President de Gaulle's policy of the "empty chair." See Lindberg, *op. cit.,* 20 *Int. Organ.,* 240ff.

11 See, e.g., the poll of Gallup International, "Public Opinion and the European Community," 2 J. *Common Mkt Stud.,* 101 (1964), concerning various facets of European opinion as of February and March 1962.

this conflict without forfeiting the integrity of Community law. Indeed, whether clothed in the form of an institutional dialogue or not, this is the aim of both these aspects of the search for authority. To achieve this aim, as will be seen, the Court may employ various techniques of judicial activism and self-restraint.

1. JUDICIAL CONTRIBUTION TO CONSENSUS-BUILDING

The development of Community consensus may be analyzed from three points of view. As suggested in Chapter I,[12] these are procedural, substantive and result-oriented facets which need not always or necessarily harmonize with each other. To each of these facets also corresponds a mode of reasoning which the Court may employ to support its decisions and to strengthen the Community legal orders in general. The first of these facets is indispensable for preserving the impetus of economic integration. The most elementary requirement for promoting the authority of Community law is to maintain the integrity of the common Community procedures. This means viewing the Treaties not piece-meal but each as a functioning whole. The majority of litigation, however, centers on substantive issues. It is their authoritative settlement which contributes to the growth of the second facet of consensus. Here, judicial reasoning may be buttressed by that vast arsenal of persuasive techniques found in the sources of law. This is appeal to system, to tradition, to continuity and to predictability in the law. Finally, there is also a mode of judicial reasoning running parallel to the result-oriented facet of consensus formation. This is the not infrequent, but often disputed mode of reasoning from effects. Particularly in the search for authority, where the limits of logic and tradition are soon reached, reasoning from effects may be the sole means of persuasion. These three modes of reasoning by no means exhaust the repertoire of judicial argumentation.[13] They are simply selected to demonstrate how the Court, in a modest way, may contribute to furthering the authority of Community law.

[12] See text *supra*, p. 37ff.

[13] For an extended discussion of various modes of argumentation, which are open to courts as well, see Perelman and Olbrechts-Tyteca, *La nouvelle rhétorique: Traité de l'argumentation*, Pt. 3 (1958).

The Integrity of Community Procedures

The very minimum requirement of supranational organization is the maintenance of common decision-making procedures.[14] They force the Member States to solve their Community problems together, thereby intensifying interest and participation in the common venture and its success. Without a firm consensus at this point, the Communities would dissolve into more or less permanent councils of the six Member State Governments, acting essentially *ad hoc* as the situation demands. Such a council might well proceed – as does the Council of Ministers on many occasions – by simple or qualified majority vote, but dissenting Member States could always "go it alone." While this conception appeared to be at the heart of President de Gaulle's vision of Europe,[15] it is diametrically opposed to the fundamental tenets of the European Communities. Within their spheres of power the Treaties provide not only comprehensive procedures for Community action, but also procedures for approving deviations from individual Treaty norms by Member States in emergency situations. To a large extent, they reserve these decisions exclusively to Community organs.[16] These procedures ensure a minimum of independence for Community policy formation as well as a disciplined framework for legal development.

There are, of course, real limits even to this minimum consensus. They may lie, first of all, in a genuine dislike of supranational organization as such because it detracts from the sovereign sphere of traditional state power. This was at the root of France's month-long "empty chair" policy, ending in the Luxembourg Agreement of February 1966,[17] and was reflected in the various proposals to weaken the independent position of the EEC Commission.[18] Furthermore, such limits may stem from matters of substance, for the "title to rule" can not always be neatly insulated from the issues of the day. Thus, for the staunch supporters of a "free market" philosophy in Germany, su-

[14] See general discussion of Community decision-making procedure as buttressed by the Community legal orders in text *supra,* pp. 10ff, 19ff and 37–39.

[15] Beloff, "International Integration and the Modern State," 2 *J. of Common Market Studies,* 52, 59 (1964). See also the Press Conference of President de Gaulle (note *supra,* p. 41) and his television broadcast of April 19, 1963.

[16] In some instances, of course, Community procedures run parallel to the spheres of Member State powers. E.g., ECSC Art. 67.

[17] See text *supra,* p. 38f and literature cited there.

[18] The proposals, stemming from the French Government, were aimed both at reducing the Commission's role in international relations and at weakening its institutional independence by reducing the terms of office and electing the President on a revolving basis among Member States nationals.

pranationalism often appears to be a veiled threat of *dirigisme*.[19] Or, as is evident in the following cases, special national interests on given questions may run cross-purposes to Community procedures. Finally, and somewhat paradoxically, a full compliance with Community procedures simply may appear superfluous. Thus, where agreement on substance is fairly clear, Community organs and Member States may be tempted to avoid complex and time-consuming procedures which would only delay or hinder the desired action. However expedient such circumventive action may at first appear, it runs the danger of establishing precedents which detract from Community decision-making. In furthering the authority of Community law, therefore, the Court must above all secure the common framework of Community decision-making against the "self-help" measures of the Member States. Its opportunity to do so arises most typically within the framework of appeals against alleged Member State violation of Treaty obligations.[20]

I.

The importance of protecting Community procedures is most clearly reflected in the EEC. Given the essentially "skeletal" character of its Treaty,[21] a weakening of Community procedures could well compromise the whole attempt at economic integration. Well aware of this, the Court has carefully emphasized the exclusiveness of Community procedures for invoking emergency measures in the Member States. It has done this, moreover, within the context of Treaty provisions whose inviolability is the *sine qua non* of economic integration in the Communities. To do this, it has had to distinguish carefully between purely "program provisions," which require further Community action to be enforceable against Member State authorities, and those provisions which are immediately enforceable even by Member State nationals. In the course of these determinations, the Court not only has safeguarded Community procedures, but it also has affirmed Community standards for the establishment of the customs union and the common agricultural market. As to each of these areas, which will be examined in this Section, the Court has shaped the future course of economic integration.

19 See text *supra*, p. 40. Such skepticism has arisen within German industry especially vis-à-vis the High Authority financial policy. See note 464 *supra*, p. 306; and Kemmer, "Umstrittene Umstellung," in *Die Welt*, p. 9 (May 31, 1965).

20 This procedure is discussed in text *supra*, p. 63f.

21 See note 20 and discussion in text *supra*, p. 8.

The first area for judicial action deals with the removal of tariffs and equivalent Member State charges which impede the free movement of goods throughout the Community. Here the Court has had to weigh the exigencies of Member State economic and social policy against the Community requirement that any deviation from Community standards of free trade be channelled through the emergency procedures of Community decision-making. In the Pork Import Case,[22] one of the first to be adjudicated under the EEC Treaty, it squarely rejects all attempts to circumvene the emergency procedures of Article 226.[23] The Italian Government had informed the Commission of its new import restrictions on certain pork products from other Member States, but neglected to invoke Article 226 until the Commission formally established the existence of a Treaty violation.[24] Not until the Commission had laid the matter before the Court – and, in the meantime, had rejected the application of Article 226 – did the Italian Government rescind these import restrictions which, even if it did not deny, violated the Article 31 "stand still" obligation.[25] Nevertheless, Italy contended, since Article 226 had *always* been applicable, the Commission had erred in not taking it into consideration from the beginning. Further, the revocation of the restrictive measures – belated as this was – allegedly mooted the entire question. "In any case, according to a general principle of public law, every State is authorized in emergency situations to take the necessary temporary measures for counteracting seriously threatening events."[26]

The hand-writing was on the wall and the Court eradicated every jot of it. In the first place, the belated rescission of allegedly illegal measures can not moot an appeal by the Commission against a Member State. EEC Article 169 provides for a period within which the Member State can comply with the Opinion of the Commission. If this deadline is not met, the Commission

[22] Judgment 7/61 (*EEC Commission* v. *Italy*), 7 Rspr. 693 (1961).

[23] In certain cases of serious difficulties in Member State economies, EEC Article 226 establishes "an expedited procedure" by which "a Member State may ask for authorization to take protective measures for restoring the situation or for adapting the sector concerned to the economy of the Common Market." Cf. discussion in text *supra*, p. 72f.

[24] The restrictions were introduced in June 1960. Having received no answer to its letter of October 21, 1960, challenging them as Treaty violations, the Commission issued its "reasoned Opinion" on December 21, 1960, requiring the Italian Government to comply within one month.

[25] Judgment 7/61, *op. cit.*, p. 718. EEC Art. 31, par. 1 reads: "Member States shall refrain from introducing between themselves any new quantitative restrictions or measures with equivalent effect."

[26] *Ibid.*, p. 711 (Italy's argument as summarized by the Court). See also pp. 719 and 740.

cannot be denied the right to a judicial decision. The Court simply determines whether the violation occurred and not whether the defaulting Member State took the necessary steps to remove the Treaty violation.[27] Secondly, the two procedures for establishing a Treaty violation and for invoking emergency measures run parallel to each other. The outcome of the one need not await the other. In particular, the emergency procedure can be invoked only "on the basis of an express and clear application by the interested government."[28] Since no such application had been made until the Commission had issued its Opinion, the Commission had not failed to take the emergency situation into consideration.

Finally, the Court concludes, the Article 31 "stand still" obligation is absolutely binding. "It is generally known," as Advocate-General Lagrange puts it,[29] "that the Common Market is much more than a customs union; *in the first instance,* however, it is a customs union." Article 31, therefore, "permits of no exceptions, whether of a partial or temporary character." Otherwise, said the Court, "the way would be clear for unilateral actions of Member States, which would directly violate the Treaty goals in the area of free trade."[30] In emergencies, the only course for Member States is over Article 226. "The very existence of this procedure excludes every unilateral action by Member States. As a result, they can appeal neither to necessity nor the seriousness of the situation in order to circumvent this procedure."[31] The national problems of the Member States, urgent and temporary as they might be, can not obviate the fundamental obligation to Community procedures.

Almost exactly one year later, in the Lebkuchen Case,[32] the Court reemphasized these basic principles of the Common Market. At stake were certain "special levies" of Luxembourg and Belgium on Lebkuchen coming from other Member States. In point of fact, these were not customs duties, but they had an "equivalent effect" which violated the "stand still" obligation of EEC Articles 9 and 12. "From the clarity, certainty and unconditionality of Articles 9 and 12 and from the inherent logic of these provisions and of the entire Treaty," concluded the Court, any exceptions from these

[27] *Ibid.*, p. 715f. But cf. Judgment 7/69 (*EC Commission* v. *Italy*), 16 Rspr. 111, 117f (1970), where the Court with the parties apparently concurring found that an amendment to the national law in question required the filing of a new proceeding under EEC Article 169.

[28] Judgment 7/61, *id.*, p. 718f.

[29] *Ibid.*, p. 725.

[30] *Ibid.*, p. 718.

[31] *Ibid.*, p. 719.

[32] Judgment 2 and 3/62 (*EEC Commission* v. *Luxembourg and Belgium*), 8 Rspr. 867 (1962).

fundamental provisions "must be clearly stated and narrowly construed." [33] To show that the levies in question violate the Treaty, it is sufficient that they infringe the Community goals of free trade and undistorted competition [34] and "have been introduced not by way of the procedures provided for in Community law, but through a unilateral decision." [35]

Here, as in the previous case, the plaintiffs had adopted the tactic of delaying their request for emergency approval until the Commission had formally determined a Treaty violation. In view of the clear language in the Pork Import Judgment, however, the Commission took a more adamant stand: it was willing to delay Court action while considering the applicability of EEC Article 226, but only on condition that the levies were suspended until a decision could be reached. Since the Member States failed to respond, the Commission went to Court. Fully upholding this position, the Court reiterated that the mere application for exceptions from general Treaty provisions "could not vitiate the illegal character of unilateral measures taken in contradiction of these provisions, nor thereby retroactively validate the initial Treaty violation." Were it possible to hinder an Article 169 appeal against Member State Treaty violations simply by invoking the emergency procedures, "then this provision would become fully useless." [36]

More recently, in the Milk Products Case,[37] this judicial reasoning was extended generally to the Community sphere of agriculture. The nub of the issue: in the absence of a Community agricultural policy, are Treaty obligations negotiable? To some extent at least, it might appear in fact that they are. Shortly after the establishment of the Common Market, the governments of Luxembourg and Belgium introduced unilaterally certain levies on imported milk products, but the Commission did not condemn them formally until exactly three years later. Then ensued one-and-a-half years of discussion, including whether emergency measures would be authorized. As this proved fruitless, the Commission finally issued its final Opinion on April 1963 – fully four-and-a-half years after the violations had occurred.

[33] *Ibid.*, p. 881. The Court takes the same position as to EEC provisions regulating agriculture. *Ibid.*, p. 884f. See also Judgment 7/68, 14 Rspr. 663, 644f (1968); and Judgment 16/69, 15 Rspr. 377, 383 (1969).

[34] Judgment 2 and 3/62, *id.*, p. 882. The Court refers expressly to these goals as found in Part Two, Title I, Ch. 1 and in Art. 3 of the EEC Treaty.

[35] *Ibid.*, p. 882.

[36] *Ibid.*, p. 879f. See also Judgment 7/68, *op. cit.*, p. 642 (discussed in text *infra*, p. 478), where the Court refused to void Commission action against Italy for a Treaty violation on the basis that the Italian Parliament was about to undertake corrective measures.

[37] Judgment 90 and 91/63 (*EEC Commission* v. *Luxembourg and Belgium*), 10 Rspr. 1329 (1964).

In the meantime, the Council of Ministers had announced its intention, according to EEC Article 43, to establish a system of compensation levies for milk products by November 1, 1962.[38]

In view of this, the plaintiffs declared their willingness to comply with the Commission's Opinion *as soon as* an "adequate" alternative had been found to replace their national measures. In argument before the Court, they even contended that the failure of the Council to meet its own deadline justified Member States to take "self-help" measures in the interim. They were further adamant that the "stand still" requirement of EEC Article 12 did not apply to agriculture until a common Community policy had come about; any other view would undermine agricultural stability in the Member States. These delaying tactics, therefore, appear to be aimed not so much at the Commission as at pressuring the negotiations in the Council of Ministers. By the same token, it must be wondered if the delay of the Commission was not calculated to make this pressure felt.

Once the case had finally reached the Court, however, the table was turned and the States were on the defensive. Since the deadline of the Council for introducing regulations for milk products was no binding measure under EEC Article 189, the failure to meet it did not violate the Treaty. In any case, the violations of the plaintiff Member States considerably pre-date the Resolution of the Council of Ministers.[39] More importantly, in contrast to international law, the failure of the Community to meet a Treaty obligation would not justify non-compliance by the Member State.

Such a relationship between the obligations of the legal subjects can not be recognized for Community law. The Treaty not only creates reciprocal obligations between the several legal subjects to which it applies, but also establishes *a new legal order* fixing the powers, rights and duties of these subjects as well as the necessary procedure for determining and sanctioning eventual violations.

Absent an express provision to the contrary, therefore, "the Member States are prohibited from taking the law into their own hands." [40]

The same principle applies also to Community agricultural policy. Reasoning by implication, the Court extends the "stand still" requirement of

[38] Resolution of the Council of Ministers (April 4, 1962), Amtsblatt 1006 (April 20, 1962).

[39] *Ibid.*, p. 1345.

[40] Judgment 90 and 91/63, *op. cit.*, p. 1344. Emphasis added. See also the Conclusions of *Adv-Gen.* Roemer, *ibid.*, pp. 1357–59 and 1371f. See further the reasoning of the Court in its more recent Judgment 52 and 55/65 (*Germany* v. *EEC Commission*), 12 Rspr. 219, 263f (1966), that discriminatory treatment of the plaintiff by the Commission could not absolve a Member State of its Treaty obligations. See discussion of the Case in text *infra*, p. 479.

EEC Article 12, in Title I for the free trade in goods, to the agricultural sector regulated in Title II. While this Article does not constitute a measure of economic disarmament (for it leaves existing customs intact), it is

> as much *an indispensable condition* for replacing the several national markets by a common market as for replacing the national market orders with a common organization of agricultural markets.

Since Article 12 is "an essential provision" and deviations from it must be narrowly construed, the absence of any express exceptions to it in Title II make it equally binding for agriculture. Moreover, Article 44 suggests the same goal as Article 12: in case of emergency during the transitional period, Member States may introduce non-discriminatory minimum prices for agricultural products *only so far as* these prices neither reduce inter-State trade nor hinder its progressive expansion.[41] Unfortunately, no attempt was made to explore the essential differences between industrial and agricultural goods in the organization and integration of the Common Market.[42] The Court simply concludes that any difficulties arising for national markets during the transitional period could be met by the "special means and ways" expressly provided in the Treaty.[43] Had these been pursued, however, they apparently would have offered the plaintiffs a satisfactory alternative.[44]

Finally, with the gradual organization of the agricultural markets, the Court extended its reasoning in the Milk Products Case to encompass Member State interpretation of Community regulation. The occasion for this was a "preliminary question" reference in *Chief Customs Office Hamburg-Oberelbe v. Bollman,*[44a] dealing with the correct customs designation for imported turkey tails. Since the importer challenged the customs office's reclassification of the goods, the German Finance Court of Appeals asked whether Member States had the power to further interpret and define, through national laws, the designation of products covered by Community regulation. The Court rejected the action of the customs office, pointing out that the Regulation in question is directly applicable in all the Member

41 Judgment 90 and 91/63, *id.*, p. 1346f. Emphasis added.

42 Whereas EEC Article 38(2) provides for the application of the general rules of the Common Market to agriculture save where Articles 39–46 stipulate something else, Articles 39(2) and 40(2) make clear that agriculture has certain special needs which may require forms of organization other than the common rules of competition in Article 85ff.

43 Judgment 90 and 91/63, *op. cit.*, p. 1348; See esp. EEC Art. 44.

44 See the Conclusions of *Adv-Gen.*, Roemer, *ibid.*, p. 1371f.

44 See the Conclusions of *Adv-Gen.* Roemer, *ibid.*, p. 1371f.

States, notwithstanding any national provisions to the contrary.[44b] Indeed, Member States

are prohibited from adopting measures for the execution of the Regulation that are designed to alter the scope of that Regulation or amend its provisions. To the extent that the Member States have transferred their legislative powers in levy tariff matters to the Community, in order to ensure a proper functioning of the common agricultural market, they no longer have the power to enact normative provisions in this field.

As a result, Member States are required to do everything necessary to remove any obstacles that their laws may present to the application of the Regulation. In particular, that Regulation "does not permit the Member States to enact rules of their own that affect its scope." Nor are they authorized to issue binding rules of interpretation for the application of designations covered by subsequent Community Regulations.[44c] The Community organization of national agricultural markets, therefore, effectively preempts independent Member State action.

II.

This line of judgments, just considered, offers a much clearer defense of Community procedures than is to be found in the case law of the ECSC. This is not to say that ECSC procedures have been neglected. On the contrary, the Court has carefully scrutinized their observance and been willing, even "on its own motion," to consider inadequate motivation of High Authority acts and violations of the consultation requirements.[45] It has also nullified Community acts which violate the division of powers among Community organs[46] or unlawfully delegate Treaty powers.[47] More importantly, the Court has given no weight to arguments which would suspend or vitiate specific Treaty obligations of enterprises or Member States simply because the High Authority or *all* Member States have not fully complied with these

[44b] Regulation of EEC Council of Ministers (April 4, 1962), *Amtsblatt,* 159 (April 20, 1962).

[44c] Judgment 40/69, *op. cit.,* p. 80f.

[45] As to the requirement of motivation, see Judgment 18/57, 5 Rspr. 89, 114 (1958–59). As to the requirement of consultation, see Judgments 1/54, 1 Rspr. 7, 30f and 33 (1954–55); 6/54, 1 Rspr. 213, 233 (1954–55); 20/59 and 25/59, 6 Rspr. 681, 708 and 743, (1960); and 30/59, 7 Rspr. 1, 58 (1961). But cf. Judgments 111/63, 37/64 and 37/64, 11 Rspr. 919, 972 and 1013 (1965), construing the requirement for Council approval under ECSC Article 53(b) narrowly.

[46] See Opinion of the Court, 5 Rspr. 571, 581f (1958–59) (first proposal to amend ECSC Article 56 by "small Treaty revision" rejected), discussed in text *supra,* p. 291f.

[47] See Judgment 9/56 (*Meroni* Case), 4 Rspr. 9, 36–47 (1958), discussed in text *supra,* p. 253f.

Treaty provisions.[48] "This way of 'settling accounts' for alleged or actual breaches of the Treaty," Advocate-General Roemer points out,[49] "runs against the principles which the Court has developed in its jurisprudence."

Nevertheless, ECSC procedural requirements have not always been fully and consistently treated by the Court. The reasons for this may be seen in the peculiar nature of ECSC integration. While the powers of the ECSC are limited, within their own sphere they are thoroughly defined.[50] They thus establish a hard-core consensus on matters of substantive policy, whose margin, however, is quickly reached and broadly dependent on the willing cooperation of the Member States.[51] This two-fold character of partial integration has led – somewhat paradoxically perhaps – to a slackening of Community procedures at the core as well as the margins of ECSC powers.

At the core, the far-reaching normation of Community goals and means offers the ECSC a security and continuity in policy-making not found in the EEC. It establishes a basis of Community consensus extending far beyond the basic minimum of decision-making procedures. It is this that makes the "implied powers" reasoning viable judicial doctrine in Community legal development. Thus, in *Fédération Charbonnière,* despite the textual uncertainties of the Transitional Convention, the Court could rely on a general understanding of the purposes of this provision and at least on a passive consensus of the Member States on the question at hand.[52] (The same may be said of the Court's decision in the *Belges* Scrap Case.)[53] In its reasoning, however, the Court not only overlooks the absence of a consultation requirement which in other judgments was of considerable importance, but also fails to justify the use of "implied powers" within the broader context of Treaty revision.[54] This is not to condemn the doctrine as applied, for it may

48 See, e.g., the argument of the intervenors, recorded in the Conclusions of *Adv-Gen.* Roemer, in Case 9/61, 8 Rspr. 483, 493 and also at 467 (1962), claiming that if every Member State did not fully comply with transport tariff publication, discrimination would result. See also a similar argument by Community enterprises, in Case 36/64, 11 Rspr. 447, 454f (1965), and the comments of the *Adv-Gen. ibid.,* p. 471. The Court did not consider either of these arguments.

49 Conclusions of *Adv-Gen.* Roemer, in Case 36/64, *id.,* p. 471.

50 See text *supra,* pp. 7f and 14f and 288.

51 See discussion in text *supra,* pp. 298f.

52 See discussion of this case in text *supra,* p. 293f. See also Diebold, *The Schuman Plan,* 206 (1959); and Lister, *Europe's Coal and Steel Community,* 118 (1960), stating: "The Convention for the Transitional Provisions contained no explicit policy regarding the use to which the subsidy was to be put, although it was understood that the operators would do whatever was necessary to put the mines on their feet by February 1958."

53 Discussed in text *supra,* p. 298f.

54 See discussion in foregoing paragraph of text and the "implied powers" discussion in text *supra,* pp. 288–299.

be defended as a legitimate adjunct of an ongoing Community.[55] It is only to say that judicial initiative, however indispensable and unavoidable for legal development, may not be without a certain cost to Community procedures.

Beyond this core, at the margins of partial integration, Community consensus tends to weaken and with it the willingness of the Member States to submit national policy to Community review and approval. Here lies the second reason for the relaxation of ECSC procedures. This is most clearly reflected in the question of national restrictions on coal imports from nonmember countries. Like the EEC, the ECSC rests on the principle of free trade among the Member States. Article 4a) prohibits the levy of customs duties as well as quotas on ECSC goods.[56] Moreover, the High Authority early asserted that this principle was equally applicable to coal and steel products "which are *properly imported* into any country of the Community." Subject to this condition,

> no Member State of the Community has the right unilaterally to hinder the free movement of goods within the common market, either by customs duties or quantitative restrictions.[57]

Unlike the customs union concept of the EEC, however, Member States retain jurisdiction over their commercial policies *toward third countries* so far as the Treaty stipulates nothing to the contrary.[58] Thus, they conclude their own trade agreements and levy their own customs duties and quotas. Recognizing that these policies may well be incompatible with each other, the Treaty further envisages a Community policy of maximum and minimum limits on tariffs and other measures to coordinate licensing practices and even to impose common import restrictions in times of emergency.[59]

Still, the exercise of commercial autonomy by the Member States could well lead to disturbances within the Community. In particular, the differing import policies of the Member States invite circumvention: third-country goods could enter the country of least resistance and flow unhindered be-

55 See text *supra,* p. 298f.

56 As was pointed out *supra,* p. 6f, the principle of free trade *within* the Communities is somewhat broader for the ECSC as for the EEC.

57 High Authority, Fourth Gen. Rep. 137f (German ed., 1956). Emphasis supplied.

58 Cf. ECSC Art. 71, par. 1, with EEC Arts. 7, 12–37 and 110–116. See Lister, *op. cit.,* p. 339; and Meade, Liesner and Wells, *Case Studies in European Economic Union,* 406ff (1962). At the same time, EEC Articles 110ff provide that the "commercial policy" of the Member States in a narrower sense is subject only to coordinating action during the transitional period of the Treaty, to be replaced then by "a common commercial policy designed according to unified principles."

59 ECSC Arts. 72 through 75.

hind the trade walls of more restrictive Member States.[60] For this reason, ECSC Article 71 requires Member States to render each other "the necessary mutual assistance" to avoid such disturbances.[61] As the High Authority emphasized, the provision has a dual aspect. On the one hand, it establishes "the necessity and the duty [of the Member States] to act *in unison* and not unilaterally in removing the difficulties which might possibly arise." It specifically authorizes only those measures of assistance "which the High Authority has determined are consonant with the Treaty and binding international agreements."[62] On the other hand, this provision "in no way constitutes a procedure . . . at the discretion of the Member States." Rather, once the conditions for "mutual assistance" have been met, the applicant Member State has a "right" to this assistance from the other Member State governments.[63] Thus, while the free flow of third country goods *within* the Community may be restricted, these restrictions must be channelled through Community procedures.

From the beginning, France failed to comply with these procedures. The problem was not with customs duties, since at the opening of the common market these were practically non-existent in coal trade among the Member States.[64] The difficulty lay instead in the licensing restrictions of the governmentally-controlled French import agency, the Association Technique de l'Importation Charbonnière (ATIC). Its regulations, says Meade, were "opposed to the spirit if not the letter of the Treaty and . . . have no place in the economic union." They were "clearly incompatible with a full integration of the French coal market."[65] The High Authority was fully aware of this. "Even if import licenses are granted automatically," it remonstrated, they would hinder trade "by reason of the fact that the licenses must be requested and the applications reviewed."[66]

As early as 1953 and 1954, the High Authority had received charges from Antoine Vloeberghs SA – a Belgian dealer – that his sales of United States coal, properly imported under Belgian law, had difficulty entering

[60] Indeed, this possibility was to be the pressure for unifying the customs duties of the Member States. See Rapport de la Délégation française sur le Traité instituant la CECA 144 (1951).

[61] Cf. EEC Article 115 which makes this purpose expressly clear. See the discussion of this provision by Oppermann, "Die Schutzklausel des Artikels 115 des EWG-Vertrages," *AWD,* 97 (1964); and François, "La notion de détournement de trafic dans la CEE," *Rev. Marché Commun.* 127 (1964).

[62] High Authority, *op. cit.,* p. 138.

[63] *Ibid.,* p. 139.

[64] See Meade, *op. cit.,* p. 407.

[65] *Ibid.,* p. 235.

[66] High Authority, Third Gen. Rep. 112 (German ed. 1955).

France.[67] By 1958, as the coal surplus took on crisis proportions, this difficulty had become an impossibility. In contrast to Belgium, Germany and Holland, who had invoked the "mutual assistance" procedures of Article 71,[68] ATIC unilaterally barred all third-country coal whether imported directly or indirectly through other Member States.[69] Not until February 1961, after repeated censure for Treaty violation[70] and eight years of negotiation, was the French Government persuaded to remove those features of ATIC to which the High Authority most objected. Even then, the French expressly reserved ATIC's power to veto *all* coal imports of third country *origin.*[71]

Five months later, in July 1961, the Court handed down the *Vloeberghs* Judgment.[72] The plaintiff, after repeated complaints gone unanswered, charged the High Authority with the failure to censure the French Government for Treaty violation. Being essentially a dealer and not a producer of coal, however, he had no standing to attack directly the inaction of the High Authority.[73] Rather, by proving this inaction to be a *faute de service,* under ECSC Article 40, he could claim damages for the injurious effects of faulty administrative action.[74] Both Vloeberghs and Advocate-General Roemer adopted the early position of the High Authority, contending that once third-country coal had been "properly imported" into any Member State it enjoyed the right of free movement throughout the Community. The ECSC, reasoned Roemer, is "not a free trade zone, where the *origin* of the product is decisive but approximates a customs union such as that envisaged by the

[67] See the facts related in Case 9 and 12/60, 7 Rspr. 427, 436f and 513f (1961).

[68] *Ibid.*, p. 507f. See also High Authority, Seventh Gen. Rep. 73f (German ed. 1958–59.

[69] Since ATIC had avoided the recommended High Authority policy of concluding long-term import contracts, it was able to reduce its imports of United States coal in the first half of 1958 by 50% in comparison with the corresponding period in the previous year. The Community figure as a whole was 27%. See Lister, *op. cit.*, p. 327.

[70] See The High Authority Decision of June 22, 1956 (unpublished), which the French Government appealed in Case 5/56 (Amtsblatt 272 (September 24, 1956)) but withdrew several months later; and the High Authority Decision of December 18, 1957 (unpublished), which the French Government appealed in Case 2/58 (Amtsblatt 151 (March 17, 1958)), but also withdrew in an out-of-court settlement in February 1961. See generally, High Authority, Fourth Gen. Rep. 152–155 (German ed. 1955–56); Sixth Gen. Rep., vol. 2, pp. 109–113 (German ed. 1957–58); and Eighth Gen. Rep. 189 (German ed. 1959–60).

[71] The settlement is reported in the ECSC Bulletin 36–38 (February 1961).

[72] Judgment 9 and 12/60 (*Société Commerciale Antoine Vloeberghs SA* v. *High Authority*), 7 Rspr. 427 (1961).

[73] Thus, complaint 9/12 against an Article 35 "inaction" of the High Authority was rejected. *Ibid.*, p. 461f.

[74] *Ibid.*, pp. 462–65.

EEC."[75] Should the commercial policies of Member States be impaired by circumventive import practices, therefore, "the only recourse of Member States is to request mutual assistance."[76]

Nevertheless, France had never adopted this course. Since 1955, as other Member States realized the free trade principle, says Roemer, France's nonconformity constituted a Treaty violation and "a discriminating position within the Community." Even after a fair consideration of French commercial interest, "the toleration over the years of this illegal situation, which infringed the legitimate interests of coal dealers in other Member States, appears hardly defensible."[77] While the High Authority may enjoy some leeway in pursuing Treaty violations, "there is no reason to admit the existence of non-justiciable sovereign acts, subject only to political responsibility."[78] Rather, in view of all the circumstances, the inaction of the High Authority must be adjudged a *faute de service* – "a faulty non-exercise of essential supranational powers."[79]

The Court, however, follows the defense of the High Authority. It affirms the principle of free trade, as originally enunciated by the High Authority,[80] but denies Vloeberghs all rights to damages under Article 40. On the one hand, as a dealer for a third country producer, the plaintiff enjoys no *personal right* under the principle of free trade. While this principle extends to goods "properly imported" from countries, its purpose is

> not to protect these goods or their producers, but to avoid raising obstacles . . . which would in fact infringe or diminish free trade in Community goods.

Any rights of the plaintiff, in contrast to Community enterprises, are "only a 'reflex effect' of the guarantee which the Treaty extends to products produced in the Community."[81] On the other hand, while the High Authority is liable for damages arising from its malfeasance, the nature both of the transactions in question and of the plaintiff himself deprives him of Community protection. As to third country coal, Article 73 leaves the administration of import licenses to the Member States of destination. Such coal, if "properly imported," is of course protected by the principle of free trade; the coal of the plaintiff, however, "was never intended for trade in Belgium

75 Conclusions of *Adv-Gen.* Roemer, *ibid.*, p. 500.
76 *Ibid.*, p. 503f.
77 *Ibid.*, p. 513f.
78 *Ibid.*, p. 511f. The category of questions meant here are "political questions," i.e., "gerichtsfreie Hoheitsakte" or "actes du gouvernement."
79 *Ibid.*, p. 516.
80 *Ibid.*, p. 466f.
81 *Ibid.*, p. 467f.

or the Community in general, but solely for France." It is, in reality, a direct French import, "which has been given merely the appearance of a Belgian import."[82] Furthermore, Vloeberghs could not complain that the High Authority had failed to enforce the "mutual assistance" procedure of Article 71. This procedure "has not been created for the interests of third parties, but merely to protect the interests of the Community." The failure to invoke this procedure, therefore, can give a non-Community enterprise no right or judicial protection "to undertake the very practices which this procedure was intended to prevent" – i.e., the circumvention of Member State commercial policy.[83]

The Court's reasoning reveals a curious combination of abstract principle sharply reduced in application by the peculiar facts of the case.[84] This is accomplished, in the first place, by the criterion of "intended destination" heightened by allusion to fraud. For this and future cases, such a subjective criterion offers the Court considerable leeway in applying the principle of free trade to third country coal "properly imported" under Member State law. And yet, as Advocate-General Roemer contends, it endangers the principle of free trade itself. In international trade, "it is scarcely conceivable that a coal dealer would import larger quantities of coal, store it and only then decide on which markets he can sell it." Rather, as in the present case, the destination is usually already determined and the particular customers in prospect. To exclude these transactions from Community protection might well, as Roemer concludes, "leave no room to speak of for the application of free trade to indirect imports from third countries.[85]

Further, it is open to some doubt at least that Vloeberghs' transactions can be explained solely in terms of fraudulent circumvention. The origin of his coal was never concealed and his dealings with French customers above board. His location in Belgium may well have been dictated by a variety of sound business reasons having nothing to do with the circumvention of French commercial policy.[86] In particular, Vloeberghs' import contracts had been concluded *prior* to the dawn of the coal crisis, at a time when third country coal was moving freely throughout the Community – including

[82] *Ibid.*, p. 468f.

[83] *Ibid.*, p. 469.

[84] See Teitgen, "Jurisprudence récente en matière de droit économique et professionnel: Organisation du commerce du charbon dans la C.E.C.A.," 24 *Droit Social*, 525, 528 (1961).

[85] Conclusions of *Adv-Gen*. Roemer, *op. cit.*, pp. 500–2.

[86] E.g., nationality, established business contacts, proximity to other markets and matters of incorporation and taxation. The Court, however, considers none of these.

France.[87] At least until France invoked the "mutual assistance" procedure, therefore, Vloeberghs arguably had good reason to rely on Community protection.

Here lies the second, critical juncture in the Judgment. To what extent is Community procedure an inviolable condition precedent for Member State action? In the sphere of commercial policy, this requires weighing the general scope of Member State sovereignty against the "mutual assistance" exception to the Community principle of free trade. It is the conflict of partial integration in the ECSC, already encountered in terms of transport policy.[88] To have stressed Community procedures, as did the Advocate-General, would have been most consonant with a systematic interpretation of the Treaty. Otherwise, "this system of mutual assistance – at least in the area of quantitative import restrictions – would lose all meaning."[89] This approach would have led to a judgment of damages against the High Authority for a *faute de service,* implicating if not openly censuring the long-standing Treaty violation by France. Based on the standing of the plaintiff, however, the Court side-stepped this delicate issue. In an Article 40 appeal, it concluded, a non-Community enterprise is simply "not entitled to demand damages for an alleged violation of its rights arising out of the inaction of the High Authority."[90] In other words, where non-compliance with Community procedure is at issue, a non-Community enterprise is not the proper party to force the hand of the High Authority.

This reasoning of the Court demonstrates a prudent respect for the frailty of ECSC consensus on commercial policy. It neither resolves the issue of "mutual assistance" nor puts it beyond the reach of judicial review. Rather, by a peculiar tailoring of the facts and party standing, the Court simply reserves the question for another time when Community support is more apparent. It implies, moreover, that the resolution of such a fundamental question must await the initiative of interested *Community* parties.[91] In effect, the Court is following the lead of the High Authority just five months earlier, refusing to press France on the issue of "mutual assistance."[92] What

[87] See Case 9 and 12/60, *op. cit.,* pp. 436f, 513, and 518f.

[88] See discussion in text *supra,* pp. 260–270.

[89] Conclusions of *Adv-Gen.* Roemer, *op. cit.,* p. 503.

[90] Judgment 9 and 12/60, *op. cit.,* p. 469.

[91] It may be wondered, however, to what extent interested Community enterprises are in a position to challenge the inaction of the High Authority on this point. As recipients of third country coal, might they not also be estopped, by the subjective criterion of "intended destination" and fraud, from pressing a suit on the "mutual assistance" procedures? If so, then only the Member States remain a real threat.

[92] See text *supra,* p. 332f.

the High Authority had not accomplished in nine years of negotiations was the Court to achieve at the stroke of a pen?

The Court, moreover, could not rely on the willing support of other Member States. Considering the adamant French position, they had little to gain on this marginal question of procedure and would surely be reluctant to risk splitting the Community at a time when the coal crisis already had placed the efficacy of supranational procedures in doubt.[93] Even the Belgian Government, obviously annoyed at the Court's cavalier treatment of its import regulations, was content to ask merely for a revision of the Judgment, contending that the judicial reasoning misconceived Belgian import policy.[94]

In any case, the "mutual assistance" procedure and other such stop-gap measures were a very poor substitute for a Community commercial policy.[95] The failure of other Member States to press the issue, by subsequent court action, suggests their assent to this position. Absent a genuine interest within the Community to defend Community procedures, there is little that the Court can do alone. Judicial authority is at issue. As flagrant a breach as a Treaty violation might be, such flagrance would only be dramatized by further non-compliance with a judgment of the Court.

III.

When faced with the economic crisis in France in 1968, however, both the Commission and the Member States as well as the Court take a firmer view toward the integrity of Community procedures in the EEC and ECSC. That year, it may be recalled was one of turmoil for all of Europe. In France, student demonstrations and a nation-wide general strike, en-

93 See discussion in text *supra*, p. 41f.

94 See the Belgian Government's third party attack of Judgment 9 and 12/60, at 8 Rspr. 347 (1962).

95 From the beginning, the French were clear that, absent a common commercial policy, circumvention would be inevitable. See Rapport de la délégation française sur le Traité instituant la CECA 144 (1951). The EEC procedure in Article 115 to prevent "circumvention" by third country import has been invoked many times. See the articles cited in note 61 *supra*. At the time of the *Vloeberghs* Judgment, however, even the EEC with its comprehensive customs union basis had made only a hesitant start toward the goal of a common Community commercial policy. See Everling, "Rechtsprobleme der Gemeinsamen Handelspolitik in der EWG," in Erler (ed.), *Beiträge zum internationalen Wirtschaftsrecht und Atomenergierecht*, Bd. 1, Heft 5, p. 189, 191 (1965). Since that time, after five years of study and negotiation, it has passed the "origin of goods" Regulation No. 802/68, Amtsblatt Nr. I/148 (June 26, 1968), but has excluded from this Regulation the delicate question of petroleum products. See discussion of the *Albatros* Judgment *infra* in text, p. 410ff, concerning the French import monopoly on petroleum.

couraged currency speculation and near financial panic. Though the French were remaining firm on their pledge to complete the customs union by July 1, 1968, on June 25 the French government outlined to the Commission the steps it planned to take, beginning July 1, to meet the economic crisis. These consisted of import quotas in certain sensitive sectors, some import controls in others and export subsidies aimed at balancing the new wage increases. While these measures were said to be only temporary, they caught the Commission and the other Member States by surprise. They also caught the use of Community procedures up short. Indeed, France did not invoke the emergency procedure under EEC Article 226, which would have required formal action by the Commission. It relied instead on the less formal requirements of EEC Article 109 concerning safeguard measures for sudden crises in the balance of payments. Following round-the-clock meetings by the Commission, in an effort to preserve the appearance at least of Community procedures,[95a] the Commission approved retroactively the measures that had been implemented by the French government subject to certain limitations and correctives.

One of these limitations pertained to the "special rediscount rates" that France had announced for short-term export credit. In fact, since 1964 the Commission had been pressing the French government to discontinue its long-standing policy of granting preference interest rates for all export sales from France. Despite repeated contacts, the French government had refused to submit these rates to Community review and determination procedures. They allegedly resulted from monetary differences among the Member States, and were not intended to serve as an export subsidy. For this reason, the French government contended, the problem with preference rates had to await the harmonization of Member States' monetary and fiscal policies.[95b] When finally the French government indicated its willingness to consider the matter, the domestic crisis erupted and France announced instead its intention to decrease the preference rate. France further disregarded the Commission's intention to review the proposed decrease pursuant to the emergency procedures under EEC Articles 93 and 108 as well as ECSC Articles 37 and 67. On June 30, 1968, without waiting for a Commission Decision, the Banque de France reduced the preference rate from 3% to 2%, thus increasing the preference spread from 2 to 3 percentage points. Though the Commission subsequently approved this re-

95a See discussion, in *European Communities,* No. 115, p. 3ff (August 1968).

95b See Conclusions of Adv-Gen. Roemer, in Judgment 6 and 11/69, 15 Respr. 523, 546f (1969).

duction through October 31, it required that the preference spread be decreased from 3 to 1.5 percentage points thereafter. When in November France failed to comply, the Commission invoked the procedure against Treaty violations pursuant to EEC Article 169 and ECSC Article 88.[95c]

Upon appeal in both cases, judgment was for the Commission.[95d] In sharp contrast to the *Vloeberghs Judgment,* just discussed, the Court proceeds at every point from the procedural requirements of the Treaties. The central question for the Court is not whether as a matter of law the preference rates of the Banque de France violate Treaty prohibitions against State subsidies, but whether they accord with the Decision of the Commission on the matter and the Treaty procedures for reaching that Decision. From four different perspectives the Court examines whether "the Decision lacks all legal basis in the Community legal order"? In the first place, even granting the contention of the French government that EEC Article 104 reserves to the Member States responsibility for their overall balance of payments and monetary policy, Articles 105 and 107 still require them "to coordinate their economic policies" in achieving those goals. Indeed, the authorization and intervention procedures in paragraph 3 of both Articles 108 and 109 "would be meaningless if the Member States could deviate, unilaterally and free of Community control, from their Treaty obligations under the pretext that their actions fall exclusively within the sphere of monetary policy." The "mutual assistance" which Article 108 authorizes in cases of serious balance of payments difficulties is simply an extension of "that solidarity lying at the basis of the entire Treaty system" as set forth in Article 5. France may not, therefore, "take unilateral measures forbidden by the Treaty in exercising those powers reserved to the States." [95e]

EEC Article 92, moreover, forbids State aid of whatever kind which distorts or threatens to distort competition. Within the meaning of this provision, says the Court, "State aid" would include a preference rate for

[95c] For a discussion of these procedures, see text *supra,* pp. 63–65. In fact, when the Commission issued its decisions on December 18, 1968, alleging Treaty violations, France had reduced the preference spread to 2 percentage points. Just prior thereto, however, it had increased it to 4 points – in each case without following the procedure in EEC Article 93.

[95d] Judgment 6 and 11/69 (*France* v. *EC Commission*), *op. cit.* pp. 523–527. In Case 6/69, the Commission petitioned the Court that France had violated the EEC Treaty, and in 11/69 France attacked the Decision of the Commission establishing a Treaty violation. Cf. the case comment of Knöpfle, in 5 Europarecht 263 (1970), whose emphasis on the substantive issue of State aid overlooks the procedural significance discussed here.

[95e] Judgment 6 and 11/69, *op. cit.,* p. 540.

export credit which a Member State grants its export industries to assist them in competing with products in other Member States. Its character is not altered simply because the preference rate applies to all or only to export transactions, or because its aim is to decrease the difference between domestic and foreign rates. The prohibited character of "State aid" can only then be avoided, as set forth in Article 92(3), "in the event of a serious disturbance in the economy of a Member State, but only pursuant to the requirements of Article 93, i.e., only after a Decision of the Commission or possibly of the Council of Ministers." [95f]

The French government countered, however, that the preference rates in question actually constituted new safeguard measures in the sense of EEC Article 109. Since they became justified by the new balance of payments crisis in the fall of 1968, they could not be attacked on the basis of a Commission Decision which predated that crisis. The Court rejects this reasoning, pointing out that any unilateral measures taken by States under Article 109 "may be considered only as exceptional and provisional and, therefore, are valid only temporarily until their legal soundness can be examined." Further, since "it is a basic requirement for the functioning of the Common Market that Community institutions step in as soon as possible when States take unilateral measures which deviate from the Treaty," such measures must be reported immediately to the Commission and other Member States. France, however, did not observe these procedures. Its challenge to the Commission's action, therefore, is unfounded.[95g]

Finally, the French government attempted to defeat the action under ECSC Article 88 by reference to the reserved domain of the Member States. Since the preference rates apply to all export products and not just to coal and steel, it argued, they are not subject to the provisions of the ECSC Treaty. Even in the exercise of powers in their reserved domains, the Court responds, "Member States can escape the obligations of the Treaty only subject to the conditions set forth therein." Neither ECSC Article 4 which prohibits State aids and subventions "in whatever form they appear," nor Article 67 § 2 which authorizes the Commission to make exceptions to Article 4, however, allow for the distinction suggested by the French government. "A special rediscount rate for exports represents a subsidy, therefore, which must be authorized by the Commission under Article 67 so far as it affects the area of coal and steel." [95h] Since that authorization was

[95f] *Ibid.*, p. 540f. See also the more extensive discussion of "State aid" appearing in Judgment 47/69, rendered on June 25, 1970.

[95g] Judgment 6 and 11/69, *id.*, p. 541f.

[95h] *Ibid.*, p. 543f.

never forthcoming, the Commission's determination of a Treaty violation is upheld.

These several cases fully demonstrate the central role of judicial review in the preservation of Community procedures. In the EEC, where the procedural aspect is most crucial, the Court has constantly defended their integrity. It has, at the same time, emphasized certain inviolable principles of Community free trade without which a customs union would be untenable. Deviations from these principles, based even on national necessity, must be channelled through the Community and not left to the unilateral justification of the Member States. The same has been true essentially for the ECSC. The highly normative but limited character of its Treaty, however, offers instructive examples of the impact of consensus on Community procedures. On the one hand, where Community solidarity is great on particular issues, the creative leeway of the Court is understandably broader. The result is an increased flexibility for Community action which might otherwise have been delayed or frustrated by a more restrictive view of the judicial function. The *Vloeberghs* Judgment, on the other hand, demonstrates the real limits of a procedural consensus. The adamant position of France and the reluctance of the High Authority signaled the danger of pursuing the full logic of the letter and spirit of the Treaty. Instead, with great skill, the Court disposes of the case by reasoning which emphasizes the principle of free trade without resolving the procedural issue at stake. In effect, the Court is exercising its "remand function,"[96] this time in the search for authority. The matter was thrown back to the Member States and the High Authority, the main constituents of Community consensus. If a judicial settlement was desired, one of them would have to initiate Court action. In fact, just such a case arose with the French export preference rates in 1969. There, despite the strong views of France, the firm position of the Court on Community procedures is telling, since it could count on the support of the Commission and the other Member States. What the Court had left undone in the *Vloeberghs* Case was redeemed eight years later.

The Formation of Legal Sources

Beyond the sphere of Community procedures lies the vast realm of substantive issues for judicial determination. The contribution of the Court to the development of Treaty goals and powers, particularly of the ECSC, has been considered already in Chapter V. What remains to be considered here

[96] See text *supra*, p. 221f, discussing the "remand function" in the context of the "judicial dialectic."

are those legal sources which the Court has employed to reinforce its conclusions on Treaty content. As a matter of definition, the concept of "legal source" must be distinguished from other notions such as the "cause" and "basis" of law.[97] The "cause" of the Treaties, for instance, may be found in the various political and economic interests of the Member States in forming the Communities.[98] These, however, are not what usually is meant when referring to "sources" of law; they are simply the facts or motives behind state action and can not explain the origin of an obligation. Further, while the "basis" or authority of Community law – like all law – must be traced ultimately to the general consensus of its legal subjects,[99] the "source" itself is not this consensus. The "source" may contribute to the growth of consensus but can not ensure the latter's existence. Rather, "legal sources" are the social processes through which rules of law are created – or, as Esser puts it, "das 'fait social' . . . , mit dem die neue Rechtsnorm Wirksamkeit erhaelt."[100] This emphasis on process is crucial, for isolated statutes, decisions and behavior become meaningful and authoritative only within the larger context of the legislative and judicial processes.[101] Only within this context do these acts become integrated into the legal order and thereby a part of that common belief in their "binding" effect (opinio juris sive necessitatis) which is the "basis" of legal obligation.

The task of the following discussion is not to examine comprehensively the problem of sources in Community law.[102] Instead of three possible functions of legal sources in the development of law – to channel, to inform and to persuade – only the last will be considered here.[103] In light of the present stage of Community law, this emphasis is not unreasonable. The first or

[97] See e.g., Corbett, "The Consent of States and the Sources of the Law of Nations," 6 *Brit. YB. Int.*, L. 20 (1925); Ch. de Visscher, "Contributions à l'étude des sources de droit international," 3 *Rec. d'études Fr. Gény*, 389, 392f (1934); and Lauterpacht-Oppenheim, *International Law*, vol. I, p. 24f (8th ed. 1955).

[98] See the text *supra*, p. 42ff, discussing these "causes."

[99] See text *supra*, pp. 128ff and 189ff.

[100] Esser, *Grundsatz und Norm in der richterlichen Fortbildung des Privatrechts*, 137f (1956). See also Lauterpacht-Oppenheim, *op. cit.*, vol. I, p. 25, who speaks of legal sources as "the name for a historical fact out of which rules of conduct come into existence and legal force."

[101] Esser, *id.*, p. 138f. But cf. Corbett, *op. cit.*, p. 30; and Scelle, "Essai sur les sources formelles du droit international," in 3 *Rec. d'études Fr. Gény*, 400 (1934).

[102] For a comprehensive treatment of legal sources in the ECSC, see the early but insightful study of Mathijsen, *Le droit de la C.E.C.A.*, (1958).

[103] The usual conceptual classification of legal sources distinguishes simply between formal and material sources, the first two functions mentioned above. See, e.g., Jaenicke, "Völkerrechtsquellen," in Strupp-Schlochauer, *Wörterbuch des Völkerrechts*, vol. 3, p. 766f (1962) and Fitzmaurice, "Some Problems Regarding the Formal Sources of International Law," in *Symbolae Verzijl*, 153f (1958).

formal function of legal sources – namely, to channel or to identify and restrict the applicable law – has no basis in the Treaties. Unlike Article 38 of the Statute of the International Court of Justice, the Treaties are silent as to the proper sources of Community law and their hierarchy. They contain, at the most, only scattered references to "the observance of the respect for law in the interpretation and application of the Treaty,"[104] to the possible violation of "any legal provision relating to its application,"[105] to "general principles common to the laws of Member States"[106] and to the law of particular Member States.[107] Nor is there a sufficiently clear and recognized conception of Community organization, whether international, supranational or federal, from which to derive such a hierarchy.[108]

As to the second, the material or historical function of legal sources, the Court is of course free to inform itself about the law from all material at its disposal. Justice and morality and the requirements of public policy are the ultimate sources and *topoi* of judicial knowledge.[109] Their presence in the law, whether latent or express, is reflected in the gradual formulation of those fundamental legal principles discussed in Chapter V. Considering the innovationary character of the Communities, this knowledge may be borrowed from varying legal systems and traditions.[110] The only requirement is that it be appropriate for Community legal development in the light of the major Treaty purposes. It is this material which defines the categories of legal sources considered below.

There remains then the persuasive function of legal sources which will be emphasized here. Unfortunately, it has been given only passing attention in the literature. While it can not be isolated from the other two, it deserves special consideration because of its immense importance for the judicial development of law. Where norms are broad and ambiguous and uncertain of full compliance, as in the present stage of Community integration, the Court must not merely declare the law but must also obtain adherence to its

[104] ECSC Art. 31, EEC Art. 164, Euratom Art. 136.

[105] ECSC Art. 33, EEC Art. 173, Euratom Art. 146.

[106] See, e.g., EEC Art. 215, par. 2; Euratom 188, par. 2. For an exhaustive study of such references, see Bebr, *Judicial Control of the European Communities,* 27, n. 38 (1962); and Mathijsen, *op. cit.,* Ch. 3.

[107] See, e.g., ECSC Arts. 6, par. 3; 9, pars. 3 and 4; 21(1); 43, par. 2; 69(1); 73; and 92, par. 2. See also EEC Arts. 7; 37; 138(1); 177, par. 3; and 192, par. 2.

[108] See Migliazza, "La jurisprudence de la Cour de justice de Communautés européennes et le problème des sources du droit," 12 *Österr. Z. öff. R.,* 332f (1962–63).

[109] See Lauterpacht, "The Grotian Tradition in International Law," 23 *Brit. YB. Int. L.,* 1, 22f (1946); Fitzmaurice, *op. cit.,* pp. 161–68; and de Visscher, *op. cit.,* pp. 392–98.

[110] See Reuter, "Le recours de la Cour de justice des Communautés européennes à des principes généraux de droit," in *Mélanges Henri Rolin,* 263, esp. 271ff (1964).

pronouncements. This is the value of legal authorities whether in the form of the Treaty systems, generally recognized principles of law, a developing line of judicial decisions or the formation of practice or custom. As Charles de Visscher puts it: [111]

> This adherence of course is not, properly speaking, the final foundation of the law. Rather, it furnishes a point of intermediary support for legal norms which is even more palpable, more immediately accessible and better adapted to the practical needs of social life than the fundamental principle of justice whose realization they tend to secure.

This adherence, or persuasive quality, is the active contribution of legal sources to a developing Community consensus. It is the force of systematic reasoning, of analogy and tradition, of continuity and predictability in the law and, in the last instance, of the judicial recognition that a viable consensus must be a living or current consensus. The conscious formation of legal sources may well be the most lasting contribution of the Court to the development of authority in Community law.

I. The Treaty Systems

The Treaties, of course, are the primary source of Community law. They may, by the process of judicial interpretation, be elaborated and developed, but only within the reasonable limits of their provisions and within the context of the case at hand. A tortured treatment of their language not only does violence to the division of powers and the procedural framework upon which the Communities depend,[112] but also tends to undermine the respect for Community law and the influence of the Community Court in the search for authority. This need not mean, however, that absent a clear text the Treaties themselves offer no handholds for judicial interpretation. As Chapter V has demonstrated and the Court has recognized, the scope and content of Treaty articles must be determined "by the spirit of these provisions, by their systematic integration and by their terms." [113] This is reflected not only in the continuing search for the underlying principles of Treaty interpretation, already discussed, but also in a developing conception of a Community legal system. This judicial conception, as Tammes has shown for interna-

[111] de Visscher, *op. cit.* (n. 97), p. 393.

[112] See discussion in text *supra*, p. 323ff concerning the integrity of Community procedures.

[113] See text *supra*, p. 231f.

tional law,[114] will reveal the legal system as a source of law as well as the Court's view of its own function in the development of Community law.

Legal discussion surrounding the nature of the Treaties has been dominated by varying conceptions of the Communities. While Advocate-General Lagrange contends that such speculation is not for the judge (the judge, he states, "must view the Treaty as it is"),[115] the underlying question has not been so easily quieted. Treaty interpretation may be influenced by whether the Communities are conceived as federal, international, supranational or "L'Europe des patries." These alternatives, of course, do not exhaust the field. In fact, considering the present state of community development, the federal view would be premature and the international view insufficient.[116] The Court, for its part, prudently deferred this question, preferring to build its authority not on broad conceptions but primarily on a solid line of case determinations. Only after a full seven years of adjudication did it tackle the question head-on. The occasions for this – certainly no accident – were potential or real collisions between Community and Member State law. The direct confrontation with the Member State legal orders, as it were, called Community law to consciousness.

In the first confrontation of this sort, the *Humblet* Judgment of December 1960,[117] the Court reasoned from "a strict separation between the jurisdiction of Community organs and Member State authorities." The plaintiff contested Belgium's right to calculate his Community income in its assessment of joint-family tax liability. This allegedly violated Article 11 b) of the Protocol concerning the Privileges and Immunities of the ECSC. While agreeing, the Court refused to declare the national law in question invalid. "Community law," it said, "does not grant Community organs the authority to annul legislative or administrative acts of a Member State." Nor does it authorize the Court "to interfere directly with the legislation or administration of the Member States."[118] (And conversely, "neither Belgian legislation and case law nor the practice followed in analogous cases by the Belgian authorities can be decisive" for the interpretation of the Protocol.)[119] In the case of a Treaty violation by one of the Member States, ECSC Article 88

[114] Tammes, "The Legal System as a Source of International Law," 1 *Neth. Int. L. Rev.*, 374 (1953–54).

[115] Conclusions of *Adv-Gen.* Lagrange, in Case 6/64, 10 Rspr. 1279, 1285 (1964).

[116] See the conclusions in the text *supra*, p. 46ff.

[117] Judgment 6/60 (*Humblet* v. *Belgium*), 6 Rspr. 1163, 1184 and 1190 (1960).

[118] *Ibid.*, p. 1184f.

[119] *Ibid.*, p. 1192.

simply establishes a procedure, culminating in a judicial decision, for determining the existence of a violation.[120]

Nevertheless, subject to an Article 88 determination, the defaulting State should be led to withdraw the measure itself. Indeed, if the tax assessment in question is unlawful under the Treaty, "the Belgian Government would be obligated to take the measures necessary to annul it and to restore to the plaintiff the amounts collected." This obligation, established by ECSC Article 86, follows from both the Protocol and the Treaty, "which on the basis of their ratification have the force of law [Gesetzeskraft, force de loi] in the Member States and take precedence over national law."[121]

This strict separation of jurisdictions was then extended to the legal orders as a whole. This was the reason, in the *Bosch* Case, for refusing to consider certain alleged irregularities in the judicial procedure of a Dutch court. Community and Member State law, said the Court, "constitute two distinct legal orders independent of each other."[122]

The general justification for this extreme distinction was set forth, a year later, in the *van Gend & Loos* Judgment. The immediate question: was EEC Article 12 self-executing? In affirming this, the Court was led to consider the unique character of the Treaty:

> The purpose of the EEC Treaty is the creation of a common market whose functioning directly concerns individuals belonging to the Community. This means, at the same time, that the Treaty is *more than an agreement based on mutual obligations* of the contracting States. This view is confirmed by the Preamble of the Treaty, which is addressed not only to the Governments but also the peoples; and is confirmed even more concretely by the creation of institutions which have been transferred sovereign rights whose exercise touches Member States and citizens alike. Further, the nationals of the Member States, united by the Community, are called to collaborate in its functioning through the European Parliament and the Economic and Social Committee. Moreover, the task of the Court under Article 177, which is to ensure the unified interpretation of the Treaty by the national courts, is also proof that the States recognized that Community law could be invoked by their citizens before national courts.

From all this the Court concludes:

> the Community constitutes *a new legal order of international law* in whose favor the States have restricted – though within a limited framework – their sovereign rights; a legal order whose subjects are not only Member States but also individuals. Being independent of national legislation, therefore, Community law

[120] *Ibid.*, p. 1184.

[121] *Ibid.*, p. 1185f.

[122] Judgment 13/61 (*Kledingverkoopbedrijf de Geus en Uitdenbogerd* v. *Robert Bosch GmbH et al.*), 8 Rspr. 97, 110 (1962).

grants individuals rights just as it imposes on them duties. These rights arise not merely where expressly stipulated by the Treaty, but also on the bases of clear obligations which the Treaty imposes on individuals as well as Member States and Community organs.[123]

By the very nature of the EEC Treaty, as reflected in its specific provisions, therefore, a new "Community" legal order has been born.

This conception of an independent Community legal system is further unfolded in *Costa* v. *E.N.E.L.* Here too, the Court was led by "the wording and spirit of the Treaty."

In contrast to traditional international treaties, the EEC Treaty has created its own legal order which, by coming into force, has been received into the legal orders of the Member States and is to be applied by their courts. Thus, through the establishment of a Community unlimited in time – endowed with its own organs, with legal personality and capacity, with a competence to perform international acts and especially with genuine sovereign rights derived from the limitation of Member State jurisdiction or from the transfer of Member State sovereign rights – the Member States have restricted their sovereign rights, if only within a limited sphere, and thereby created a legal entity which binds them and their citizens alike.[124]

In the light of these three Judgments, therefore, the EEC Treaty has been characterized not by its relation to, but by its internal integrity and very independence of the traditional international and municipal legal orders.

This is no less true of the judicial conception underlying the interpretation of Community legislation. This became clear in its construction of the EEC Council's social security Regulation for migrant workers.[125] Here it was faced with a broad scala of approaches to Community law. To what extent did the phrase "worker or comparable person" – a key concept in applying the Regulation – take its content from the municipal laws of the Member States? Whereas the plaintiff argued for a unique Community content,[126] Advocate-General Lagrange viewed these terms simply as a *renvoi* to the conditions established by the particular Member State law. The Council, he

123 Judgment 26/62 (*N.V. Algemene Transport en Expeditie Onderneming van Gend & Loos* v. *Netherlands Finance Administration*) 9 Rspr. 1, 24f. (1963). Emphasis added. See also Judgments 28/67 (*Molkerei-Zentrale Westfalen/Lippe GmbH Trockenmilchwerk* v. *Chief Customs Office Paderborn*), 14 Rspr. 215, 230f (1968), which tacitly adopts the language of *Costa* v. *E.N.E.L.*

124 Judgment 6/64, 10 Rspr. 1251, 1269 (1964). See also 17/67 (*Firma Max Neumann* v. *Chief Customs Office Hof/Saale*), 13 Rspr. 591, 607f (1967).

125 Judgment 75/63 (*Unger* v. *Bedrijfsvereniging voor Detailhandel en Ambachten*), 10 Rspr. 378 (1964).

126 *Ibid.*, p. 390.

contended, "was not authorized to issue Community legislation on social security which displaces the various provisions of municipal law; nor had it intended to do so."[127] The EEC Commission and the German Government, on the other hand, took a more compromising position. In essence, said the latter, the Regulation "contains a uniform concept of 'workers and comparable persons,' but for determining the content of this concept it refers in large measure to national social security law."[128] As for the Commission: while the Regulation may coin Community terms and must be interpreted by reference to Community purposes, "the Treaty does not authorize the Community to legislate a unified social security law for all the Member States."[129]

This general opinion to the contrary, the Court adopts the position of the plaintiff. It is guided by the chief purpose of EEC Article 51, which is part of the "foundations" of the Community, namely, "to establish the broadest possible free movement of workers." In the first place, Articles 48 through 51 offer no indication that the content of the term "worker" should be determined by the municipal legal orders. Rather, the specific attributes of this concept, such as "employment" and "remuneration" mentioned in Article 48(2), "demonstrate that it is to be understood from the point of view of Community law." Of more importance for the Court, however: "Were the determination of the concept to be left to municipal law, every State would be in a position to alter the content of 'migrant worker' and to remove certain groups at will from the protection of the Treaty." This possibility, it concludes, "would rob Articles 48 through 51 of all importance and seriously endanger those Treaty purposes mentioned above." The concepts in question, therefore, are to be determined "not according to municipal but according to Community law."[130]

In thus stressing the independent and unique character of Community law, the Court has laid the basis for the inner dynamic of a new legal system. The Treaties are, on the one hand, the primary and unified source of Community law. They do not simply coordinate municipal law, but to a large extent establish a vantage point from which to evolve common and over-

[127] *Ibid.*, p. 412 and also 414.

[128] *Ibid.*, p. 391.

[129] *Ibid.*, pp. 392–94.

[130] *Ibid.*, pp. 395–97. See also Judgment 32/67, 14 Rspr. 68, 75 (1968), stressing the importance of uniformity in Community law as pertains to special tax levies by Member States on the compensation of Community officials; and Judgments 40/69 and 74/69, 16 Rspr. 69, 81 and 451, 459 (1970), to the same effect in respect to EEC Council Regulation No. 22–62, relating to the gradual establishment of a common market organization for poultry meat.

riding standards for Community integration. Such standards may be established by the Treaty provisions themselves or they may arise through Community legislation or by the special process of "harmonizing" certain areas of municipal law;[131] yet they may also be the product of judicial decision. As for the latter, the very emphasis on Treaty systems or "constitutions"[132] implies the prohibition of a *non liquet:* "that a court, otherwise endowed with jurisdiction, must not refuse to give a decision on the ground that the law is non-existent, or controversial, or uncertain and lacking in clarity."[133] The Court's conception of Community law, on the other hand, constitutes a radical separation of Community and Member State legal orders. It tends to stress the mutual independence rather than interdependence of both. While this has the virtue of screening the former against the paralyzing tendencies of divergent national practice, it also bears the mark of that dualist position which has so enfeebled the integrative effects of international law. Despite this rigorous formulation, as the remainder of this Chapter will show, the Court has been neither so restrained in asserting Community law nor unwilling to receive the principles and practices of the Member State legal orders. It is, therefore, well on its way to making the Treaty legal systems a self-constituting factor in the development of Community law. Herein lies their persuasive value.

II. General Principles of Law

A second and major source of Community law lies in those general principles of law common to other legal orders. They constitute a fund of knowledge, tried and tested by the municipal and international practice of States as well as by equivalent international organizations, which must be utilized if the Court is to escape "the reproach of a denial of justice"[134] and the stultifying effects of a *non liquet* on the development of Community law.[135] This is the elementary recognition, as expressed by Article 38 c) of the Statute of the International Court of Justice, of what has long been judicial

[131] See Stein, "Assimilation of National Laws as a Function of European Integration," 58 *Amer. J. Int. L.*, 1 (1964); and also his "Harmonisation of Law in the European Economic Community," Supp. No. 6 of the *Int. Comp. L. Qu.*, 27 (1963).

[132] See text *supra*, p. 20, n. 101, for citations.

[133] Lauterpacht, "Some Observations on the Prohibition of 'Non Liquet' and the Completeness of the Law," in *Symbolae Verzijl*, 196, 199 (1958). This is no less true for municipal legal systems (e.g., Art. 4 of the Code Napoléon and Art. 1 of the Swiss Civil Code) as for the international legal order. *Ibid.*, p. 198f. See also Schwarzenberger, *Manual of International Law*, 234 (4th ed., 1960).

[134] Judgment 7/56 and 3–7/57, 3 Rspr. 83, 118 (1957).

[135] See Mathijsen, *op. cit.* (n. 102), pp. 15–19, 90 and Ch. 4; and Bebr, *op. cit.* (n. 106), pp. 27–29.

practice[136] and, in a deeper sense, of the inherent requirements of legal interpretation itself.[137] This does not mean that any particular principles of another legal order – even those embodied in the constitutions of the Member States – are binding as such on the Community organs. The High Authority, said the Court, "is called only to apply Community law; it lacks the jurisdiction to apply the municipal law of the Member States."[138] Rather, the principles here in question simply offer authoritative evidence of an existing consensus upon which the Court may draw for persuasive support of its decisions. Seen from this perspective, they reflect a true *ius gentium* or common law which "est l'expression de la conscience commune des nations"[139] or, more concretely, of "a socially realisable morality."[140] Through their incorporation into Community law, they function as stabilizers of legal development, appealing to the continuity of existing practice and integrating judicial innovation with recognized legal doctrine.[141]

Considering the unique character of the Community legal orders, as conceived by the Court,[142] the general principles of international law may be expected to have little relevance and to be of little persuasive value in judicial decision. These principles not only minimize the role of the individual, but also offer meager direction for interpreting the institutional balance of Community powers as well as the economic subject matter of the Treaties traditionally reserved to the States.[143] Not surprisingly, therefore, the Court

[136] See Verdross, "Les principes généraux du droit comme source du droit des gens," in 3 *Rec. d'études Fr. Gény,* 383, 385 (1934); and Ch. de Visscher, *op. cit.* (n. 97), 389, 394f.

[137] This is Esser's thesis, discussed in text *supra,* p. 115ff, and confirmed by Chapter V of this text. See also del Vecchio, "Les principes généraux du droit," in 2 *Rec. d'études Fr. Gény,* 69, 72 (1934): "Ainsi, les règles particulières de droit ne sont pas vraiment intelligibles si on ne les place pas en rapport avec les principes d'où elles découlent; et cela, bien que ces principes puissent ne pas être, et ne soient effectivement pas, la plupart du temps, formulés dans les Codes."

[138] Judgment 1/58, 5 Rspr. 43, 63f (1958–59) (re Arts. 2 and 12 of the German Basic Law). See also Judgments 36–38 and 40/59, 6 Rspr. 885, 920f (1960) (re Art. 14 of the German Basic Law); and the Conclusions of *Adv-Gen.,* Roemer, in Case 18/57, 3 Rspr. 259, 266 (1957). For a rejection of the binding authority of international law, see Judgment 90 and 91/63, 10 Rspr. 1329, 1344 (1964); and the Conclusions of *Adv-Gen.* Lagrange, in Case 8/55, 2 Rspr. 231, 266f (1955–56) and of *Adv-Gen.* Roemer, in Case 6/54, 2 Rspr. 241, 244 (1954–55).

[139] Scheuner, "Les principes généraux du droit reconnus par les nations civilisées," 68-II *Rec. d. cours,* 95, 128 (1937).

[140] Lauterpacht, *The Development of International Law,* 172 (1958).

[141] See Esser, *op. cit.* (n. 100), pp. 298–306; and the conclusions of Jeanneau, *Les principes généraux du droit dans la jurisprudence administrative,* 184ff (1954).

[142] See text *supra,* p. 344ff.

[143] See the Conclusions of the *Adv-Gen.,* cited *supra,* note 138, in Cases 8/55 and 6/54.

has employed them rarely and then primarily as a means for strengthening the independence of the Community legal orders. Thus, the reception of the doctrine of "implied powers" into Community law emphasizes the autonomous development of these legal orders. There, the Court relies on "a rule of interpretation generally recognized in international as in municipal law." [144] And, in the *Humblet* Judgment, international practice was evidence *a contrario* of the Member States' intent to exempt Community employees from even indirect tax burdens on Community income.[145] Further, when Italy attempted to escape its Treaty obligations by reference to its rights under prior treaties with third countries, the Court responded in like manner:

According to the principles of international law, a state which undertakes a new obligation [meaning the EEC Treaty], in opposition to an earlier treaty, renounces *ipso facto* its rights thereunder so far as necessary to fulfill the new obligation.[146]

In this same spirit of strengthening Community autonomy, the Court has rejected Member State appeals to the "self-help" doctrine in the international law. While such doctrines may have their place in the rudimentary structure of international organization, "such a relationship between the obligations of the legal subjects can not be recognized in Community law." [147] In light of this uniform approach, the Court's reasoning in the Road Tariff Publication Cases [148] is all the more curious. There, the Court affirmed the general applicability of the "implied powers" doctrine to the Treaties, but found no basis for it in the provision in question. It then went on to consider whether the High Authority could derive any legislative powers from ECSC Article 88 procedure for establishing Member State Treaty violations. This procedure, said the Court,

goes a long way beyond the rules which up to now have been accepted in classic international law in order to ensure the execution of States' obligations. Article 88, *therefore,* must be interpreted strictly.[149]

Given the Court's insistence on the unique character of Community law,[150]

[144] Judgment 8/55 (*Fédération Charbonnière* Case), 2 Rspr. 297, 312 (1955–56), discussed *supra,* p. 293.

[145] Judgment 6/60, 6 Rspr. 1163, 1193f (1960).

[146] Judgment 10/61 (*EEC Commission* v. *Italy*), 8 Rspr. 1, 22f (1962).

[147] Judgment 90 and 91/63 (*EEC Commission* v. *Luxembourg and Belgium*), 10 Rspr. 1329, 1344 (1964), discussed *supra,* p. 327f.

[148] Judgments 20/59 and 25/59, 6 Rspr. 681 and 743 (1960), discussed *supra,* p. 312ff.

[149] *Ibid.,* pp. 713 and 785, respectively. Emphasis added.

[150] See discussion in text *supra,* p. 346f.

however, one could as well have expected the opposite conclusion. It is at least questionable whether international law has anything to say about the scope and function of particular Treaty provisions. This is not to say that the Court's conclusions were incorrect; for other reasons, which were also presented, Article 88 grants the High Authority no legislative powers. Rather, this ambiguous reference to international law must be viewed more as judicial rhetoric adapted to given conclusions rather than as consistent reasoning. In general, as has been seen, the Court has taken a much different approach in its use of general principles of international law.

In a few decisions, the Court has also drawn on parallel principles in other of the European Economic Treaties. Thus, by reference to the wording of EEC Article 184 and Euratom Article 156 in the Rome Treaties, the Court affirmed its liberal construction of private parties' right of appeal under ECSC Article 36. "Although not conclusive," it carefully pointed out, "these references support the above reasoning by showing that it is also accepted by the authors of the new Treaties." [151] And, in the *Humblet* Judgment, comparisons with the Rome Treaties supported the limited jurisdiction of the Community Court to review the compatibility of Belgian with Community law as well as the full exemption of Community income from Member State taxation.[152] Further, by reference to the regulation of competition in the EEC Treaty, the Court confirmed its interpretation of similar provisions for the ECSC. "Naturally," it said, "the decision in the present dispute can not be drawn from the EEC Treaty; it supports the thesis of the plaintiff, however, for Article 85(3) is concerned with material very similar to that in ECSC Article 65." The Court in fact assumes that "a similar viewpoint lies at the basis" of the two provisions.[153]

Such judicial comparisons, of course, in no way signal a fusion of the three Treaty systems. True, the Court has spoken of the need to construe Community law "in the sense of a functional unity which exists among the European Communities and the affiliated organs." [154] This conclusion, however, was drawn in the context of a dispute over the ECSC Personnel Statute and may not be extended, without more, to the Treaty systems as a whole.[155] In particular, the ECSC and Euratom spheres of jurisdiction are expressly

[151] Judgment 9/56, 4 Rspr. 9, 27 (1958).
[152] Judgment 6/60, 6 Rspr. 1163, 1184f and 1196 (1960).
[153] Judgment 13/60, 8 Rspr. 177, 214 (1962).
[154] Judgment 27 and 39/59, 6 Rspr. 819, 848 (1960).
[155] Unfortunately, this fact is not emphasized by Wolf, "Auslegungsgrundsätze des Gerichtshofs," in *Zehn Jahre Rechtsprechung,* 193, 194 (1965), who tends to stress the "functional unity" aspect too much.

guaranteed against changes arising from the EEC Treaty.[156] So too the Court has emphasized differences between the Treaty systems where they exist. This is true as to certain private rights of appeal,[157] as to periodic or unlimited contracts of employment[158] and as to considerations of regional economic policy in the calculation of discriminatory rail rates.[159] The Treaties, therefore, may be interpreted in the light of each other, but their fundamental structural differences must be preserved.

Recourse to general principles of municipal law, on the other hand, looms much larger in the Court's reasoning.[160] Not only does it correspond closely to the subject matter of Community regulation,[161] but it also will be most persuasive – because more familiar and trusted – for the bulk of legal opinion in the Member States. This does not mean that the Court must restrict its perspective to the Member State legal orders. Indeed, it has even been willing to consider the relevance of the United States Interstate Commerce Act for the ECSC regulation of discriminatory rail rates.[162] Still, at other times, it has been content to rest its reasoning simply on "generally recognized principles of administrative law,"[163] on the "public administration of many states,"[164] on "the most modern legal orders"[165] or on just "generally recognized principles of law."[166] These lapidary references, however, are less than convincing; they are to a large extent superfluous because the points at issue could as well have been resolved without them.[167] For the most part, judicial reasoning is most effective when the sources invoked are elaborated and their peculiar relevance pointed out.

Only rarely has the Court elaborated its references to general principles

[156] EEC Art. 232.

[157] Judgments 16 and 17/62, 8 Rspr. 961, 978 (1962); and 9–22/62, 8 Rspr. 1003, 1019f (1962).

[158] Judgment 43, 45 and 48/59, 6 Rspr. 965, 989 (1960).

[159] Judgment 27–29/58, 6 Rspr. 513, 540 (1960).

[160] The resort to such principles in the decisions of the International Court has been relatively infrequent. Their main function, says Lauterpacht, *op. cit.* (n. 140), p. 166, is "that of a safety-valve to be kept in reserve rather than a source of law of frequent application."

[161] See Conclusions of *Adv-Gen.* Lagrange, in Case 8/55, 2 Rspr. 231. 266f (1955–56).

[162] Judgment 3–18, 25 and 26/58, 6 Rspr. 373, 411 (1960).

[163] Judgment 1/55, 2 Rspr. 9, 29 (1955–56).

[164] *Ibid.*, p. 29.

[165] Judgment 7/56 and 3–7/57, 3 Rspr. 83, 127 (1957).

[166] Judgments 8/55, 2 Rspr. 297, 311 (1955–56); 32 and 33/58, 5 Rspr. 287, 313 (1958–59); 27 and 39/59, 6 Rspr. 819, 842f (1960); 43, 45 and 48/59, 6 Rspr. 965, 991 (1960).

[167] With the exception of the judicial reference in Judgment 8/55, *id.*, where the application of the principle of "proportionality" is not altogether clear.

of municipal law. It has done this, for instance, in the *Algera* Judgment where it considered the revocation of administrative measures[168] and, to a lesser extent, in the *Nold* and *Kloeckner* Decisions where it resolved certain civil law questions in the light of German law.[169] Most generally, the Court has preferred to rely – either expressly or impliedly – on the comparative research of the Advocates-General or on unstated studies of its own.[170] In striking contrast to the Court's decisions, the non-binding Conclusions of these fully independent judicial aides are rich in source material. Their comparative inquiries into Member State law – on such diverse questions as the concept of *détournement de pouvoir,*[171] contracts of employment[172] and the authority of public officials to verify tax statements[173] – reflect the influx of general principles of municipal law into the Community legal orders. The persuasive value and even the intelligibility of the Court's decisions, therefore, often depend on reading them in conjunction with the Conclusions of the Advocates-General.[174]

Above all, the appeal to Member States law is not automatic. It must be weighed carefully and selected in terms of its suitability to Community purposes.[175] The criteria for comparing legal concepts in varying legal systems, as Esser points out,[176] "can not be derived from their doctrinal role, but only from their common function in the several legal orders to which they belong." Thus, after some inquiry, Advocate-General Roemer refused to

168 Judgment 7/56 and 3–7/57, 3 Rspr. 83, 118ff (1957).

169 Judgments 18/57, 5 Rspr. 89, 110f (1958–59); and 17 and 20/61, 8 Rspr. 654, 690f (1962).

170 The apparent reliance of the Court on the expositions of the Advocates-General may be seen by comparing, for instance, in Judgments 7/56 and 3–7/57, 3 Rspr. 118f and 162 (1957) the opinions of the Court and the Conclusions of the Advocates-General (revocation of administrative measures); 42 and 49/59, 7 Rspr. 171f and 205ff (1961) (character of certain scrap transactions); 18/60, 8 Rspr. 418f and 427ff (1962) (meaning of "boycott"); and 17 and 20/61, 8 Rspr. 690f and 706ff (1962) (character of certain scrap transactions); and 4/68, 14 Rspr. 561, 574f (1968) (import of "force majeure" concept for Regulation No. 136/64). See also Judgments 5/68, 14 Rspr. 589, 599f (1968); 2/68, 14 Rspr. 654, 657–59 (1968); and 23/68, 15 Rspr. 43, 49–51 (1969), relying on general principles of Roman law in interpreting the concept of negligence by public officials as it relates to the Protocol on the Privileges and Immunities of the European Communities.

171 Conclusions of *Adv-Gen.* Lagrange, in Case 3/54, 1 Rspr. 157–78 (1954–55).

172 Conclusions of *Adv-Gen.* Lagrange, in Case 10/55, 2 Rspr. 433–35 (1955–56).

173 Conclusions of *Adv-Gen.* Roemer, in Case 31/59, 6 Rspr. 201–3 (1960).

174 See discussion in text *infra,* p. 362f and note 220.

175 See Lorenz, "General Principles of Law: Their Elaboration in the Court of Justice of the European Communities," 13 *Amer. J. Comp. L.,* 1, 7 (1964); Mathijsen, *op. cit.* (n. 102), pp. 5f and 141–43; Reuter, *op. cit.* (n. 110), p. 273f; and Migliazza, *op. cit.* (n. 108), p. 338.

176 Esser, *op. cit.* (n. 100), p. 339.

apply administrative law standards of the Member States to the distinction between general and individual acts of the High Authority. In the Member States, he concludes, this distinction has other implications as to administrative competence and the scope of judicial protection which, in addition to the terminological ambiguities, makes it of little value for the ECSC.[177] This is equally true for other spheres of Community law, e.g., market competition, discrimination and the division of powers among the Community organs, where parallels are either uncertain or simply lacking. The objective of comparative studies, warns Lagrange, "is not to create a synthesis or to lead to a sort of 'compromis juridique,' but rather to seek to determine the proper law of the Treaty."[178]

Furthermore, the rejection of such legal eclectics implies that the general principles adopted and adapted to Community law need not be common to all the Member States.[179] Nor may one speak of a "conquête du droit administratif français,"[180] despite the original importance of French administrative law in formulating the Community system of judicial review.[181] While a "common denominator" approach would seriously restrict the selection of legal principles,[182] the predominance of any one national legal order would violate the criterion of functionality as well as tend to alienate the remaining Member States. In fact, the decision of the Court and the Conclusions of the Advocates-General refer most frequently to German and French law. This is due undoubtedly in large part to the fact that the Advocates-General, being thus far French and German jurists, have simply drawn on the

[177] Conclusions of *Adv-Gen.* Roemer, in Case 7 and 9/54, 2 Rspr. 105, 122 (1955–56). See also the Conclusions of *Adv-Gen.* Gand, in Case 10/65, 11 Rspr. 643, 645 (1965) (re EEC Art. 95).

[178] Lagrange, "L'ordre juridique de la CECA vu à travers la jurisprudence de sa Cour de justice," 64 *Rev. dr. pub. sci. pol.*, 841, 857 (1958). See also his Conclusions, in Case 3/54, 1 Rspr. 152, 156 (1954–55). From the functional viewpoint stressed in the text and by Esser, however, Lagrange's comparative analysis is open to criticism. His study of the *détournement de pouvoir,* for instance, is very much concept- and language-oriented with little emphasis on the purpose and function of this ground of appeal in the Community system. See his Conclusions, in Case 3/54, *ibid.*, p. 157ff. The Court, it may be recalled, has not followed his narrow construction. See text *supra,* p. 81.

[179] Lorenz, *op. cit.*, p. 7f; Mathijsen, *op. cit.* (n. 102), p. 142; and the Conclusions of *Adv-Gen.* Lagrange, in Case 14/61, 8 Rspr. 557, 570f (1962), who rejects the resort to a "more or less arithmetical 'mean' between the different national solutions" as a source of Community law.

[180] This early contention of l'Huillier was early rejected by Mathijsen, *id.*, p. 141. See also Lagrange, *op. cit.* (n. 178), p. 857.

[181] See text *supra,* p. 51f.

[182] Lorenz, *op. cit.*, p. 13, points out, for instance, that "the minimum area of agreement existing among the national laws of the Community will rarely be sufficient to dispose of the problem of revocation" of administrative measures.

municipal law which they know best. It is also true, however, that these two legal systems in general tend to embody the most pronounced differences in conception and approach among the Member States. The emphasis, therefore, is not misplaced. In the selection of general principles of law, for the Communities as for the international legal order, what is necessary and reasonable is not their universal recognition but their uniform application in the main systems of national law.[183]

It remains to consider, in particular, the general principles found in Member State constitutional law. Does their authoritative position in Community law surpass the mere need to avoid a *non liquet*? When in doubt, in other words, should the Court interpret the Treaties in conformity with the general principles of Member State constitutions? On the one hand, as has already been noted,[184] the Court has refused to grant *specific provisions* of particular State constitutions binding effect. Thus, allegations that certain Decisions of the High Authority violated Article 14 (security of property) of the German Basic Law were rejected:

> In reviewing the legality of High Authority Decisions . . ., the Court is not authorized to ensure the respect for municipal provisions which are binding in one or the other of the Member States, even though they are constitutional laws.[185]

For either of two reasons, this position is thoroughly justifiable. For one, were the Court bound by the constitutional laws of the parties to the case, depending on their nationality, this would tend to undermine the unity of Community law.[186] In some States, such as Germany, judicial protection is comprehensive and individuals are safeguarded by a sweeping system of constitutional rights and judicial review.[187] To apply the standards of this system solely to German nationals would grant them a privileged status in the Communities, inconsistent with the Treaties,[188] and give rise to an un-

183 Lauterpacht, Private Law Sources and Analogies of International Law 89 (1927).

184 See text *supra*, p. 350, at note 138.

185 Judgment 36–38 and 40/59, 6 Rspr. 885, 920f (1960).

186 See Rabe, *Das Verordnungsrecht der EWG*, 128f (1963); Steiger, *Staatlichkeit und Überstaatlichkeit*, 107 (1966); and Tomuschat, *Die gerichtliche Vorabentscheidung*, 108 and 133 (1964). Further in international law, treaties are to be interpreted only according to general rules of jurisprudence and not by those applicable only to one signatory State. See Lauterpacht-Oppenheim, *International Law*, vol. 1, 956 (8th ed., 1955).

187 See, e.g., the German Basic Law of 1949, Arts. 1–20 (catalogue of individual rights), Arts. 21, 38, 79(3) and others (organizational prescriptions), and the scope of constitutional review defined in Arts. 93, 99 and 100 and § 90 of the Stat. of the German Constitutional Court.

188 Inconsistent at least with their spirit if not with their letter. See EEC Art. 7 and ECSC Art. 4. Wagner, however, considers such possible discrepancies according to

certain development of Community law varying with the nationality of the parties.

Or, if the Court is to avoid this, it would be forced to adopt the laws of those Member States where constitutional limitations on public power are greatest. This would establish a sort of "Gesetz des Minimums,"[189] meaning perhaps in some sense *in dubio pro libertate*. There is no basis, however, for believing that the Member States, particularly those without constitutional review, ever intended or desired this.[190] Even ignoring this fact, by what standards of comparison is the Court to make such fundamental and politically explosive determinations? Does the right to property mean more or less market competition? Is constitutional protection greater where the division of powers is stricter and how much stricter? It is not enough, as is often supposed,[191] simply to substitute one's own national brand of constitutional organization and protection as the applicable standard of comparison. It is noteworthy, therefore, that legal opinion in Germany over the past few years has tended to decrease its demands for the conformity of Community law with the German Basic Law. This constitutes, in particular, a growing awareness that the import and structure of supranational organization can not always be measured by a traditional or any national conception of constitutional organization.[192]

This conclusion, on the other hand, does not free the Communities from those general principles embodied in the Member State constitutions. The Court has undoubtedly cast its net too widely when, in rejecting the plaintiff's appeal to Article 14 of the German Basic Law, it concludes: the ECSC Treaty "contains neither a written nor an unwritten principle which forbids

nationality to be a legitimate aspect of federalism in the Communities. *Grundbegriffe des Beschlussrechts der europäischen Gemeinschaften,* 256 (1965).

189 This is Friauf's reference point for interpreting Community law in conformity with Member State constitutions. "Die Notwendigkeit einer verfassungskonformen Auslegung im Recht der westeuropäischen Gemeinschaften," 85 *Arch. öff. R.,* 224, 233f (1960).

190 See Rabe, *op. cit.,* p. 128; Steiger, *op. cit.,* p. 107; and numerous others of this opinion, cited by Tomuschat, *op. cit.,* p. 109, n. 410.

191 Behind the argument in Germany, for instance, for a "Gesetz des Minimums" or its equal lies the peculiar character of the German Constitution. See, e.g., Erler and Thieme, "Das Grundgesetz und die öffentliche Gewalt internationaler Staatengemeinschaften," 18 *VVdStRL,* 7, 8f, 24, 26f, 38ff and 50, 60ff (1960), emphasizing the minimum requirements, respectively, of structural homogeneity and the catalogue of constitutional rights. See also the more recent views of Friauf, *op. cit.,* 232f; Ehle, "Verfassungskontrolle und Gemeinschaftsrecht," 17 *N.J.W.,* 321, 322 (1964); and Wagner *op. cit.,* pp. 245–56.

192 See Kaiser and Badura, "Bewahrung und Veränderung demokratischer und rechtsstaatlicher Verfassungsstruktur in den internationalen Gemeinschaften," 23 *VVdStRL,* 1ff and 34ff (1966), and particularly the discussion which follows; and von

the infringement of acquired property."[193] On other occasions, the Court has had no difficulty finding unwritten principles of the same order, prohibiting the unlawful delegation of Community powers as well as "any excessive or arbitrary" injury to private parties by Community organs.[194] It would be an unbearable anachronism for constitutional thinking in the Member State were such principles not to guide Community law. Treaties, like constitutions, are not concluded in a vacuum, but against a background of general rules and principles.[195] While the Member States most certainly did not intend to incorporate the particular provisions of their individual constitutions into Community law, neither did they wish to jettison their most sacred legal traditions.[196] No more forceful testimony of this can be found than the substantive rights guaranteed by the European Convention for Human Rights.[197] While this Convention does not bind the Communities as such, it constitutes that broad core of constitutional rights recognized in all the Member States.[198] There is every reason, therefore, to affirm the interpretation of Community law in conformity with the general principles of law embodied in the Member State constitutions.[199]

Express judicial acknowledgement of this view is desirable not only to guide the development of legal content, but also for its persuasive support

der Groeben, "Über das Problem der Grundrechte in der Europäischen Gemeinschaft," in *Festschrift W. Hallstein,* 226 (1966). Cf. also Decision No. 98 (December 16, 1965) of the Italian Constitutional Court, discussed in text *infra,* p. 426ff.

[193] Judgment 36–38 and 40/59, 6 Rspr. 885, 921 (1960). This criticism goes to the Court's reasoning and not to its refusal to apply Article 14 of the German Basic Law.

[194] See Judgments 15/57 (*Chasse* Case) and 9/56 (*Meroni* Case), 4 Rspr. 159, 195 and 9, 44 (1958), discussed in text *supra,* p. 251ff.

[195] When in doubt as to the intention of the parties, says Lauterpacht, a treaty should be interpreted in conformity with the general principles of international law. *Op. cit.,* (n. 140), p. 27f. On the national level, the Supreme Court has often interpreted the United States Constitution with reference to its common law background. See, e.g., *Smith* v. *Alabama,* 124 U.S. 465, 478 (1888); and the further discussion and references in Ehmke, *Wirtschaft und Verfassung,* 207ff (1961).

[196] Even those who would reject a "Gesetz des Minimums" still maintain that the Court must follow those basic principles implied by democratic government and the "rule of law." See Badura, *op. cit.,* pp. 66–68; Steindorff, *Rechtsschutz und Verfahren im Recht der europäischen Gemeinschaften,* 57f (1964); and von der Groeben, *op. cit.* (n. 192), p. 233.

[197] See Arts. 2–15 of the Convention and the amending Protocol of March 20, 1952, concerning the protection of property.

[198] Of the six Member States, all but France have ratified the Convention; moreover, Belgium, Germany, Luxembourg and the Netherlands have accepted the compulsory jurisdiction of the Human Rights Court. See note 28 *supra,* p. 10 of the text. It is of no importance for this discussion that France has not ratified the Convention, since the principles which it embodies are fully a part of the French legal tradition.

[199] Cf. this with other type of constitutional conformity discussed in the text *supra,* p. 300f.

of judicial reasoning. *Stauder v. Ulm* offers a start at least in this direction. The complainant there argued that a Decision of the Commission addressed to the Member States violated his individual rights under Articles 1 and 3 of the German Basic Law as well as under general principles of Community law. Without referring to German constitutional practice or defining its terms more fully, the Court posits the existence of "basic individual rights embodied in the general principles of the Community legal order whose integrity the Court is bound to secure." Where doubt exists in the construction of the Commission's Decision, "the least burdensome construction should be given preference, if it is adequate to attain the goals which the Decision at issue is intended to serve." [199a] The precise nature and import of these "basic individual rights" remains to be determined.

General principles of law, therefore, are of particular importance for the development of Community law. Their reception is of course not automatic. Whether drawn from the international community, the other European Community Treaties, the Member State legal orders in general or their constitutional practice, they must be selected for their appropriateness to the aims of the Treaties. And where appropriate, they contribute to strenghtening and broadening the basis of consensus underlying Community law. This is especially true of the general principles of Member State constitutional law. Their incorporation into Community jurisprudence enables the Court to draw not only on a rich fund of knowledge, but also on the legitimacy and authority which this implies.

III. Judicial Decision and Precedent

A third source of Community law lies in the decisions of the Court of Justice. What is meant here is not "precedent," as a common lawyer might mistakenly regret,[200] for its binding authority is rejected in international law,[201] for the Community Court[202] and by continental legal theory in gen-

[199a] Judgment 29/69, 15 Rspr. 419, 424f (1969). See also text *infra* at p. 301.

[200] Stone, "Europäischer Gerichtshof in der Sicht eines amerikanischen Juristen," *Europäische Gemeinschaft*, 2, 3 (May 1964).

[201] See Arts. 38 d) and 59 of the Statute of the International Court of Justice. Judicial decisions, however, are not without considerable authority in practice. Lauterpacht, *The Development of International Law*, 8ff, esp. 13f (1958); and Rosenne, *The Law and Practice of the International Court*, 611f (1965).

[202] See, e.g., Dumon-Rigaux, "La Cour de justice des Communautés européennes et les juridictions des Etats membres," 19 *Ann. dr. sci. pol.*, 7, 38 and 59 (1959); Donner, "The Court of Justice of the European Communities," Supp. No. 1 of the *Int. Comp. L. Qu.*, 66, 68 (1961); and Tomuschat, *Die gerichtliche Vorabentscheidung*, 187 (1964). But cf. Mathijsen, *La C.E.C.A.*, 105–8 (1958); and Bebr, "Prozessmaximen," in *Zehn Jahre Rechtsprechung*, 78, 79f (1965).

eral.[203] Nor should judicial decision, as a legal source, be confused with the now fashionable "Grundsatzentscheidung" in German law; the latter is neither "leading case" nor binding precedent in common law language, but an attempt in a particular case to generalize an irregular or perhaps contradictory series of decisions into a basic principle.[204] And, finally, the authority of judicial decision should not be reduced to custom, for the formative force of the courts in legal development does not depend necessarily on long and uniform usage.[205] True, judicial decision in all legal systems is subject to the needs of continuity, stability and predictability in the law, but as Holmes so scathingly puts it: "it is revolting to have no better reason for a rule than that it was laid down in the time of Henry IV."[206]

In the last instance, the authority of judicial decisions, like that of *stare decisis,* depends on the persuasive reasoning which those decisions bring to bear on the problem at hand.[207] No legal doctrine, says Lauterpacht, "can save a precedent based on bad or obsolete law from being disregarded directly or by the less conspicuous but equally effective process of distinguishing."[208] Even in the common law, therefore, prior judicial decisions are authoritative only insofar as "they are not plainly unreasonable and inconvenient."[209] This is simply the presumption, elementary to justice, that all men in like circumstances be treated alike. Parity of reasoning in concrete cases, whether formally binding or not, is one of the most forceful methods of judicial argumentation.

The extent to which judicial decision may become a true source of legal authority, however, is not simply a matter of doctrine but also of judicial style. "The very substance of reasoning, of its development," says Rivero of the Community Court, "depends to a large extent on the form in which it

[203] See, e.g., the critical discussion of Germann, "Praejudizielle Tragweite höchstinstanzlicher Urteile," 68 *Z. schweiz. R.*, 297, 300 (1950); Esser, *Grundsatz und Norm,* 83, 119f, 252 and 275 (1956); and Ermacora, *Verfassungsrecht durch Richterspruch,* 24ff (1960).

[204] See Esser, *id.*, pp. 26, 244, 267f, 277f and 282, who points out that this represents a breach in the ideology of a complete and perfected system of code law.

[205] Germann, *op. cit.*, pp. 429–44 and esp. p. 433. See also Esser, *id.*, p. 23f, notes 68 and 69, and pp. 83f and 138–40; and Gény, *Méthode des Interprétations*, vol. II, p. 39 ff. (2nd ed. 1954). But cf. Ermacora, *op. cit.*, p. 27 f.

[206] Holmes, "The Path of the Law," 10 *Harv. L. Rev.*, 457, 469 (1896–97).

[207] See Allen, *Law in the Making,* 264f, 281 (5th ed. 1956); Esser *op. cit.*, pp. 200, 275f, 281, 284 and 292f; Llewellyn, the *Common Law Tradition,* 426 (1960); and Lauterpacht, *The Development of International Law,* 18, 37ff (1958).

[208] Lauterpacht, "The So-called Anglo-American and Continental Schools of Thought in International Law," 12 *Brit. YB Int. L.*, 31, 55 (1931). See also his "The Development of International Law," *id.*, pp. 13–15.

[209] See Allen, *op. cit.*, p. 225, quoting Parke J., in *Mirehouse* v. *Rennell,* 1 Cl & F 527, 546.

takes shape."[210] Thus, the style of opinion-writing may be succinct or extensive, highly formalized or pragmatic, abstract or concrete and fact-oriented, highly technical or simple and mundane, declarative or argumentative. Taken in context, these contrasting adjectives of style will characterize a particular conception of the judicial function.[211] They will suggest, for instance, who comprises the audience of the courts: the parties, jurists, the nation as a whole? What is the framework of the decision: a highly consolidated doctrinaire system or primarily the problem at hand? And, what is the mode of conflict resolution: *fiat* based on a well-established *raison d'état* or persuasion within a continuing dialogue between governmental institutions and between the courts and the public?

None of these characteristics, of course, is present in pure form in any legal system. Further, the style and context of judicial opinion-writing will exemplify such characteristics as these only imperfectly and then to varying degrees. At one extreme, perhaps, lies the highly formal, succinct and rigorous opinions of the French courts which, as Lawson says, "are often so laconic as to be almost unintelligible, or at least to give rise to interminable discussion among the jurists."[212] This reasoning, which one may hesitate to call "reasoned," is addressed primarily to jurists and not to the parties and particularly not to the lay public.[213] At the other extreme is the relaxed, personal atmosphere of the English courts, where a continuing dialogue occurs between bench and bar and where judicial decisions are a series of argumentative opinions.[214] In between lie the German and American opinions, more scientific than the English but less formal and more extensive than the French; yet while the former are solemn and final *Staatsakte*, por-

210 Rivero, "Le problème de l'influence des droits internes sur la Cour de Justice de la CECA," 4 *Ann. franç. dr. int.*, 295, 298 (1958).

211 See Wetter, *The Styles of Appellate Judicial Opinions*, Chs. 2, 3 and 4 (1960), who offers an insightful analysis and comparison of the Swedish, French, German, English and American styles. In his endeavor to make "style" an independent method of judicial analysis, however, he fails to distinguish clearly the different meanings which "style" might imply, i.e., form of writing, atmosphere of judicial work (relaxed, bureaucratic, etc.), institutional framework (i.e., among courts and between the courts and other governmental institutions), and style as a concept of law or way of legal thinking. See also Llewellyn, *op. cit.*, pp. 62ff and 446ff.

212 Lawson, *Negligence in the Civil Law*, 233f (1950), speaking of the Cour de Cassation. As to the opinions of the Conseil d'Etat, Hamson writes that "it is a real intellectual pleasure to come to judgments of this brevity after the meanderings of some of the pronouncements of the English courts. But it also requires a considerable art to read these judgments intelligently; they are almost a concatenation of formulas." *Executive Discretion and Judicial Control*, 119 (1954).

213 Wetter, *op. cit.*, pp. 28–31.

214 *Ibid.*, pp. 32–35.

traying a single and unified decision of the court,[215] the latter are more personal, argumentative, at times discursive and often, in concurring and dissenting opinions, even challenging the reasoning of the court's decisions.[216]

On the constitutional level, moreover, despite the absence of dissenting opinions, the German style tends to be more argumentative and even more extensive, paralleling in many aspects the approach of the United States Supreme Court. Opinions of the International Court of Justice and its predecessor have also followed this pattern, which Lauterpacht has argued is essential to the persuasive development and elaboration of international law.[217] This is important, for it would indicate that where, by its nature, the law is less system- and more problem-oriented and is less sure of a forthcoming consensus, courts are more conscious of the need for persuasion.[218] At this level, they can not rely on the highly integrated doctrine of a code, but must be concerned to preserve a viable legal system whose problems reach far into the unresolved realm of political theory.

It is perhaps not accident, therefore, that the Community Court has adopted in general not the brief "attendu" form of the French courts, but the more extensive judicial style of Germany and Italy. The one, says Rivero, "places the accent on its authority to pronounce the law, the other on its concern to persuade and to obtain, if possible, the adherence of the two parties."[219] Only rarely does the Court simply state a general principle from which then derives a solution for the case at hand. By and large, it argues its views, often marking its agreement or disagreement with the par-

[215] See Beyer and Luettig (eds.), *Bericht, Gutachten und Urteil,* 204 (24th ed. 1963): "Das Urteil ist ein Staatsakt. Der Richter spricht als Organ des Staates, wenn er das Urteil erlässt. Daraus ergibt sich, dass die Sprache einfach und klar sein muss, würdig, streng und gemessen im Ausdruck." See also McWhinney, *Constitutionalism in Germany,* 22–25 (1962); Wetter, *op. cit.,* pp. 26–28; and Esser, *Grundsatz und Norm,* 282, note 216 (1956), speaking of "die 'obrigkeitliche' Sprache des deutschen 'Urteilsstils.'"

[216] Nadelmann, "The Judicial Dissent," 8 *Amer. J. Comp. L.,* 415 (1959); and his "Non-Disclosure of Dissents in Constitutional Courts: Italy and Germany 13 *Amer. J. Comp. L.,* 268 (1964), comparing the practice of dissenting opinion in various States and presenting the arguments for and against it. These articles are translated and reprinted in 86 and 90 *Arch. öff. R.,* 39 and 440 (1961 and 1965), respectively.

[217] Lauterpacht, *The Development of International Law,* Chs. 3 and 4, esp. pp. 39–43, 61f and 66–71 (1958).

[218] This is no necessary proposition. The opinions of the Conseil Constitutional of the Fifth French Republic, for instance, are very brief. Its subject matter is uniquely limited, however, and its norm control is preventive and not repressive. It performs more an *ad hoc* arbitral than a continuing adjudicative function. See Eisenmann and Hamon, "La juridiction constitutionnelle du droit français," in Mosler (ed.), *Verfassungsgerichtsbarkeit in der Gegenwart,* 231, 255ff (1962).

[219] Rivero, *op. cit.* (n. 210), p. 299f. He distinguishes between two judicial forms, which correspond to two intellectual attitudes: "avec la forme 'attendu,' le juge se borne à s'expliquer, avec la forme 'dissertation,' il se justifie."

ties and the Advocates-General. Quite often, however, references to these views are only brief, vague, implicit or even lacking. For a full understanding of the Court's reasoning and emphasis as well as of the context of the case as such, it is usually necessary to consult the summarized arguments of the parties and, especially, the Conclusions of the Advocates-General,[220] which are published together with the judicial decisions. In particular, the Conclusions of the Advocates-General tend to form a functional unity with the decisions of the Court. Their reasoned positions not only offer the Court independent arguments against which to test its own conclusions, but they present the Community as a whole with concurring or dissenting views which may well influence the future development of the law.[221] While the Court's opinions, therefore, reflect a certain compromise between two differing continental judicial styles,[222] the emphasis is on persuasion rather than assertion.

Given the fact that both in theory and style the Court's decisions may be a formative force in the development of legal authority, to what extent has this been recognized in practice? Needless to say, 17 years of litigation over so broad a field as the Treaties is scant time in which to build a continuing practice. Nevertheless, where this has occurred, as for certain issues of procedural rights, of the scrap compensation program, of regulating competition and of the EEC "stand still" provisions, the Court has often cited prior decisions and even case headnotes. It has done this, however, not with that frequency and elaboration which is found in the Conclusions of the Advocates-General, but more often by mere reference with bare or no comment.[223] While such reference may be a helpful hint to the pursuing lawyer, it is of very little persuasive value for the decision at hand and does less to awake a consciousness of the continuity and constancy of judicial reasoning. Only occasionally, as in the *"Geitling," "Mausegatt" and "Präsident"* Judgment,[224] has the Court bothered to make the parallel clear.

[220] See the case comments of Ipsen, in 1 Europarecht 55, 60 (1966). This applies to an even greater extent to the decisions of the French Conseil d'Etat. "It would on occasion be virtually impossible," says Hamson, *op. cit.* (n. 212), p. 119, "to grasp the real point of a decision without collating the Commissaire du Gouvernement's 'conclusions'."

[221] See discussion in text *supra*, p. 23. Otto Riese, former Justice of the Community Court, has declared himself in favor of dissenting opinions. See his "Erfahrungen aus der Praxis des Gerichtshofs der EGKS," *Deutsche Richter Z.* 270, 273 (1958); and again in "Über den Rechtsschutz innerhalb der europäischen Gemeinschaften," 1 *Europarecht*, 24, 50f (1966) with references to other views on the question.

[222] Rivero, *op. cit.* (n. 210), p. 299f.

[223] See, e.g., Judgments 1/58, 5 Rspr. 43, 71 (1958–59); 2/57, 4 Rspr. 133, 149f (1958); 14/59, 5 Rspr. 465, 496 (1958–59); 1 and 14/57, 3 Rspr. 213, 235 (1957; 73 and 74/63, 10 Rspr. 1, 26 (1964); and 66/63, 10 Rspr. 1147, 1180 (1964).

[224] Judgment 13/60, 8 Rspr. 177, 228f (1962), discussed in text *supra*, p. 278ff.

In one earlier Judgment, however, it not only elaborated a previous judicial decision, but also reprimanded the High Authority for not applying the rule developed there to all firms accross-the-board. In a 1959 Judgment,[225] the Court had denied the firm SNUPAT an exemption from the scrap program levies.[226] It indicated the conditions under which an exemption would be lawful, but expressly refused to consider whether other exemptions granted by the High Authority fell within the scope of this reasoning.[227] Soon thereafter, SNUPAT challenged the failure of the High Authority to withdraw these exemptions to other firms, which it alleged were equally ineligible. Despite the fact that the period for attacking the acts in question had run, the Court granted an appeal of inaction against the High Authority. Its prior Judgment, it said,

> places the exemptions in a new light; it should have led to a review of their legal basis and then to the release of a Decision concerning their legality. In other words, on the basis of that Judgment, the High Authority should have reviewed its earlier position; it should have examined whether in light of the principles established in that Judgment the exemptions in question could be maintained, for it was *now obligated* to take account of these principles . . . .[228]

Since in the prior Judgment these other exemptions most expressly had not been in question, this obligation could have arisen only by the prejudicial effect of the Court's reasoning. Not even in reliance on ECSC Article 34[229] would the Court have been authorized to pronounce *ultra petitio.*[230]

To what extent is case precedent authority for the Community Court? Two differing views appear in the jurisprudence of the Court, represented by the Advocates-General Lagrange and Roemer. Lagrange, on the one hand, has affirmed the strict rule of "relativity," whereby judicial decisions are binding only *inter partes* and for the cause(s) of action decided in a given

225 Judgment 32 and 33/58 (*Société Nouvelle des Usines de Pontlieue Aciéries du Temple (SNUPAT)* v. *High Authority*), 5 Rspr. 287 (1958–59).

226 For a discussion of this program, see text *supra*, p. 250f.

227 Judgment 32 and 33/58, *op. cit.*, p. 322, hinting that the High Authority might have given the exemption category too broad a construction.

228 Judgment 42 and 49/59 (*SNUPAT* v. *High Authority*), 7 Rspr. 109, 162f (1961). Emphasis added.

229 According to ECSC Art. 34, the High Authority "must take the necessary measures in order to give effect to the judgment of annulment." This would apply presumably by analogy to judgments condemning the inaction of the High Authority, but only as to that particular judgment in question.

230 Bebr, *Judicial Control of the European Communities*, 130 (1962). The Judgment 42 and 49/59 might, of course, be isolated as a mere attempt to open up the acts in question to judicial review. Whether this would be acceptable or fully supportable under ECSC procedure will not be considered here.

case.[231] The judicial nullification of governmental measures, as is permitted in certain cases in Germany and France,[232] constitutes simply an exception to the rule and is permissible only by way of express provision. Further, as a corollary to this rule, Lagrange distinguishes between the Court order (dispositif, Tenor) and the reasoning (motifs, Gruende) of the decision.[233] In accordance with continental practice generally,[234] only the former has binding effect. This "golden rule of relativity," Lagrange contends,[235] guards the Court against over-committing the future. It –

> prevents the Court from taking shelter behind prior judgments . . . and requires it to remain aware of its responsibility, namely, to test anew in every case the legal rule with reality. This can lead the Court eventually to recognize its errors in the light of new facts, of new arguments or of a spontaneous search of conscience, or, what more frequently occurs, to *vary* [nuancer] its position without abandoning it in principle. And so, in the light of experience and of the further development of legal theory as well as of economic, social or other phenomena, the Court may contribute to that which one has called the evolution of case law.

The Court, of course, must exercise self-restraint in using this freedom, lest it endanger certainty in the law. In the last instance, however, "it is by the *moral* authority of its decisions, and not by the legal authority of the object judged, that a court such as ours must prevail.[236]

Roemer, on the other hand, has viewed more liberally the legal authority of the Court's decisions. In keeping with the practice of the German Constitutional Court,[237] he sees the *ratio decidendi* as partaking of the binding effect of the judgment. Thus, in *Barge* v. *High Authority*,[238] Roemer pointed out: "The legal authority of a judgment of annulment arises from the order [Entscheidungstenor] in the case, as derived from the *ratio decidendi* [tragende Entscheidungsgruende]." Further, while all else constitutes mere *obiter dicta,* even its importance for the evaluation at hand "could not be

[231] Conclusions of *Adv-Gen.* Lagrange, in Case 28–30/62, 9 Rspr. 85, 88 (1963).

[232] *Ibid.*, p. 88f.

[233] See his Conclusions, in Case 5/55, 1 Rspr. 197, 303f (1954–55).

[234] *Ibid.;* See, e.g., Art. 5 of the Code Napoléon which forbids the judge to lay down general principles in the cases decided. But cf. text *supra* at note 204.

[235] Case 28–30/62, *op. cit.*, p. 91f (Fr. ed., p. 84f).

[236] *Ibid.* Cf. also, on this point, *Gény, op. cit.* (n. 205), p. 47f.

[237] The German Constitutional Court appears to proceed from the view that the *ratio decidendi* partakes of the binding effect of a judgment, although precisely what this means is not discussed. See 1 BVerfG 14, 37 (1952); 3 BVerfG 261, 266 (1954); 6 BVerfG 309, 325 (1957). This apparently would exclude *obiter dicta.* See Maunz, *Deutsches Staatsrecht,* 244 (13th ed. 1964).

[238] Judgment 14/64, 11–4 Rspr. 1 (1965).

doubted." In any case, he ascribes to the prior judgment a "prejudicial effect" on the Court's reasoning in the present case.[239]

On another occasion, Roemer attempts to support his Conclusions, in part, by reference to *obiter dicta* in the Road Tariff Publication Judgments.[240] There, the Court had denied the High Authority all power to legislate the form of rate publication, but added: "if the High Authority wishes to remind the States of their obligations, it can proceed only by means of a Recommendation without being able to impose upon them its own choice of means for complying with these obligations."[241] Accordingly, the High Authority resorted to a Recommendation, issuing it to all Member States, whether or not parties to the dispute, and as to all aspects of transportation, trucking and rail alike. Upon appeal,[242] it defended its action in part by reliance upon the Court's previous statements. While the Court made no reference to this argument, the Advocate-General took it seriously. It was unnecessary to determine, he said, "where the *ratio decidendi* stops and possible *obiter dicta* begins . . . . [A]ll statements in the text of the Judgment are borne by the will of the Court." When, therefore, the Court rejects a Decision and suggests a Recommendation, it is to be assumed "that precisely in that context the Court considers a Recommendation to be permissible and appropriate." Then, after examining the context and making certain reservations, Roemer concludes: "in the present case, Judgments 20/59 and 25/59 and their remarks can be recognized as the *legal basis* for issuing the Recommendations . . . without disturbing the Treaty system."[243] The "Treaty system," apparently, establishes the outer limits of such authority.

The Court makes no clear choice between these two views. It has, on occasion, applied the rule of "relativity" with all strictness[244] as well as – for instance, in the *SNUPAT* Judgment just mentioned[245] – ascribed obligatory effect to its *ratio decidendi*. More often, however, it has simply cited relevant decisions without comment and taken no position on principle.[246] This is closer to international practice, where precedent is not formally binding but previous decisions are frequently cited and quoted in support of judicial

239 Conclusions of *Adv-Gen*. Roemer, *ibid.*, p. 18.

240 Discussed in text *supra*, pp. 294f and 312ff.

241 Judgments 20/59 and 25/59, 6 Rspr. 681, 711 and 743, 784 (1960).

242 Case 9/61 (*Netherlands* v. *High Authority*), 8 Rspr. 433 (1962).

243 Conclusions of *Adv-Gen*. Roemer, *ibid.*, pp. 493 and 495. Emphasis added.

244 In Judgments 33/59 and 46 and 47/59, 8 Rspr. 765 and 835 (1962), the Court reviewed anew claims of malfeasance against the High Authority, although these had been rejected in a previous Judgment.

245 See text *supra*, p. 257f.

246 See note 223 *supra*, p. 363.

reasoning.[247] Nor, as discussed at the beginning of this subsection,[248] would such a compromise by the Court be incompatible with the fundamental considerations guiding Lagrange's view; the tension in the law between the goals of predictability and constant reappraisal exists equally for the rule of "relativity" as for that of "precedent." In the last instance, both are subject to the overriding demand that judicial reasoning be persuasive for the case at hand.

Once the Court has acknowledged the authority of its prior decisions, the distinction between *ratio decidendi* and *obiter dictum* becomes important. While the latter may be of immense value for the understanding of the case and for the law,[249] if unskillfully handled it may also tend to overcommit the future of Treaty interpretation or raise false hopes among the parties. Not only Roemer, the Court also has recognized this distinction[250] and has used its *dicta* at times, if not always wisely, to give a certain direction to the law.[251] Contrary to Roemer, however, the Court need not – indeed, should not – ascribe so far-reaching authority to its *dicta*. By the spirit but not the doctrine which Lagrange sets forth, the Court must maintain its full potential for a creative contribution to legal development. While judicial decision in the Communities is an unquestionable source of legal authority, therefore, it also is an authority which must be applied selectively.

IV. Acts and Practices of Interpretation

A final source of Community law may be seen in the interpretative acts of Community organs and Member States. These may range from the conduct of Community officials in developing procedures and precising Treaty

[247] See Lauterpacht, The Development of International Law 8–15 (1958). "In fact," he says, "the practice of referring to its previous decisions has become one of the most conspicuous features of the Judgments and Opinions of the [International] Court." While the Court is "not fettered by the rigidity of the formal doctrine of precedent, it has, as shown, largely adopted its substance." *Ibid.*, pp. 9 and 13f. See also Rosenne, *The Law and Practice of the International Court,* 611ff (1965).

[248] See text *supra,* p. 359f.

[249] See Esser, *Grundsatz und Norm,* 284 and also 199f, 205f (1956).

[250] See Judgment 5/55, 1 Rspr. 275, 291 (1954–55) (appeal for the interpretation of a judgment); and the case comment of Cavaré, in *Hommage au Président Basdevant,* 96, 111 (1960).

[251] Besides the Road Tariff Publication Cases, just mentioned, see also the use of *obiter dicta* in the Luxembourg Coal Levies Judgment, discussed in text *supra,* p. 259f, and the "suggestion" of the Court in its first "small Treaty revision" Opinion on ECSC Article 56, discussed in note 46 *supra,* p. 329. While these are arguably justifiable, the Court's gratuitous remarks in Judgment 5/55, *op. cit.,* p. 292, could well have undesirably prejudiced the future. There, although the Court held the requested interpretation of its earlier Judgment to be unnecessary, it went on to state that the High Authority's reliance on that Judgment had been erroneous. See critique of Riphagen, "The Case Law of the ECSC Court of Justice," 2 *Neth. Int. L. Rev.,* 384, 393f (1955).

content to supplementary agreements among the signatory States. Whereas the former are typically defined as "practice" and the latter may assume the proportions of "authentic interpretation," the line dividing the two is not easily fixed.[252] Nor, for purposes of this study, need it be. It is necessary only to conclude, with Reuter, that these acts contribute to the growth of Community law.

> To exclude the possibility of important developments of custom in Community law would make an abstraction of the very special traits of the Community experiment. However carefully the text may be drafted, it inevitably contains a great number of gaps, of contradictions and imperfections.[253]

Given this, the question now is the extent to which the Court has and should incorporate such practices and agreements into Community law. Their incorporation, on the one hand, generates persuasive support for the Court's determinations. It constitutes recognition of the *status quo,* whether as reflected in the practice of Community officials or in the more recently expressed intent of the Member States. So long as this accords with a loyal interpretation and development of the Treaties, such practices and agreements form a natural complement to legal sources.[254] Difficulty arises, on the other hand, when they contradict or radically alter the original or underlying conceptions of the Treaties. At that point, the *status nascendi* is confronted with the expressions of a new *status quo.* The search for purpose and the preservation of certain Community procedures may be in conflict with the search for authority. How should the Court meet this dilemma?

Despite the brief period of Community adjudication, the Court has recognized the formative contribution of executive practice to Community law. Thus, in the more recent *Lemmerz* and *Mannesmann* Judgments, it was not unlawful for the High Authority and its agencies to supplement

[252] For discussion and references, see Bernhardt, *Die Auslegung völkerrechtlicher Verträge,* 44f, 126ff and 168ff (1963). Cf. also Ch. de Visscher, *Problèmes d'interprétation judiciaire en droit international public,* 20ff and 121ff (1963).

[253] Reuter, *La CECA,* 39 (1953). See also Mathijsen, *Le Droit de la C.E.C.A.* 103–5 (1958).

[254] The relevance of subsequent practice or conduct of signatory States for the interpretation of treaties has been recognized both by national and international tribunals. See Bernhardt, *op. cit.,* p. 126ff; de Visscher, *op. cit.,* p. 121ff; and UN Int. Law Comm., Draft of "Law of Treaties," Arts. 68 and 69 § 3(b), UN Doc. A/CN 4/L 107 (Jan. 7, 1965). There is much less agreement, however, whether this practice may work law-creatively and particularly whether international organizations, through their practices and decisions, may engage in substantive auto-interpretation which is binding upon the member States. See Bernhardt, *id.,* p. 131f and 168ff, who correctly affirms this capacity.

scrap program legislation of the ECSC Council. In the former Judgment, the plaintiff had argued that the High Authority could not levy interest on payments in arrears to the scrap compensation fund: the unanimous consent of the Council, as required by ECSC Article 53 b), had never been given for such measures. This consent was not necessary, said the Court, for the measure in question

> appears necessary to prevent individual enterprises from suffering unjust disadvantages through delays in payment by others. This measure does not change the basis of the compensation program. It was introduced so that the program can function correctly and attain the goals set by the Council.[255]

Against similar objections by Mannesmann, the Court also upheld the formula of the scrap *Caisse* for calculating currency exchange rates of payments due. The Decision in question, it concluded, "does not alter the purpose and functioning of the *Caisse* . . . ; on the contrary, it would logically extend the earlier measure to cases where the rate of exchange fluctuates over time."[256] At least interstitially, therefore, Community executive organs appear to possess an independent capacity to develop Community law.

On other occasions, the Court has drawn on the previous procedures or positions of Community organs in order to support its reasoning. Such references, as there are, reveal their essentially instrumental value to the Court. They are employed not so much to ascertain the proper content of a legal provision, but to confirm a decision based on other grounds[257] or to refute opposing arguments of Community organs by reference to their contradictory practice.[258] Above all, the references demonstrate the very secondary importance of such practices for judicial interpretation and the unquestioned supremacy of the Treaty texts. Thus, the Court has lent the interpretations by Community officials – including the President of the Court and the Committee of the Presidents[259] – of Community acts, the

[255] Judgment 111/63 (*Lemmerz-Werke* v. *High Authority*), 11 Rspr. 893, 919 (1965).

[256] Judgment 37/64 (*Mannesmann AG* v. *High Authority*), 11 Rspr. 951, 971 (1965).

[257] See Judgment 13/61, 8 Rspr. 97, 112 (1962) (implementing Regulation confirms Court's construction of EEC Arts. 85 and 86).

[258] See Judgments 1/54, 1 Rspr. 7, 27f (1954–55); and 20/59 and 25/59, 6 Rspr. 681, 709f and 743, 782 (1960), where earlier Decisions of the High Authority are cited to contradict its present position.

[259] See ECSC Article 78 § 3, § 5 and § 6 for the function of this Committee, composed of the Presidents of the High Authority, the ECSC Council, the Court of Justice and the European Assembly. For a discussion of this "merkwürdigste europäische Instanz," see Donner, "Der Einstimmigkeitsgrundsatz in dem nach Artikel 78 des EGKS-Vertrages gebildeten Ausschuss der Präsidenten," in *Festschrift Otto Riese*, 123 (1964).

Personnel Statute and other measures no particular legal authority.[260] According to ECSC Article 31, it reasoned,

> the Court ensures the respect for law in the interpretation and application of the Treaty. It would not be bound, therefore, by the view of the Committee of the Presidents nor by the wording of the Personnel Statute, should a decision in the present dispute require a choice between the two views just presented.[261]

Nor, in determining the existence of a binding Community act, were the formal requirements issued by the High Authority decisive; while they desirably enhance the predictability of procedures, the Court went on to base its reasoning on fundamental policy considerations drawn from the Treaty.[262] Finally, the Court has rejected an attempt to establish a *détournement de pouvoir* by reference to conflicting statements of High Authority goals published in earlier memoranda. "[T]he legality of the Decision challenged," it said, "does not depend upon its conformity with the memoranda . . . , but solely upon its agreement with the Treaty."[263]

Beyond the area of Community "practice" lies a great variety of agreements concluded by the Member States. Some, like the appointment of nationals to Community executive organs and to the Court of Justice, are expressly foreseen by the Treaty[264] and are not of importance here. Others, like the protocols annexed to the tariff Agreement of March 2, 1960, on List G goods, constitute "authentic interpretation" in the truest sense: they do not simply fix the duties for the goods in question, as provided by EEC

260 See Judgments 7/56 and 3–7/57, 3 Rspr. 83, 125 (1957); 53 and 54/63, 9 Rspr. 517, 536f (1963); 15/60, 7 Rspr. 239, 258f (1961); and 102/63, 10 Rspr. 1471, 1502 (1964). See also the Conclusions of *Adv-Gen.* Roemer, in Case 90 and 91/63, 10 Rspr. 1351, 1362ff (1964), rejecting the attempt of the defendant Member States to rely on previous OEEC, Spaak and EEC Commission reports in determining the meaning of "market organization" for agricultural products under the EEC Treaty.

261 Judgment 7/56 and 3–7/57, *id.*; Further, in Judgment 53 and 54/63, *id.*, the Court said that the statements of Community officials "could not in any case influence the construction of High Authority decisions, if by omitting these statements the interpretation achieves a clear result." There remains, however, the negative pregnant.

262 Judgment 23, 24 and 52/63, 9 Rspr. 467, 483–85 (1963). Further, in Judgment 6/54, 1 Rspr. 213, 233 (1954–55), the Court took note of the High Authority's Decision – reporting that the Consultative Committee and the ECSC Council had been consulted – but did not allow this to relieve it of the duty to make an independent inquiry into the matter.

263 Judgment 15/57, 4 Rspr. 159, 201 (1958). In another case, Judgments 9/56 and 10/56, 4 Rspr. 9, 35f and 51, 74f (1958), the Court found it unnecessary to consider plaintiff's charge that the failure of the High Authority to respect at least three of six recommendations of the ECSC Council for the administration of the scrap program constituted a *détournement de pouvoir*.

264 ECSC Arts. 10, 11 and 32b; EEC Arts. 158, 161 and 167; and Euratom Arts. 127, 130 and 139.

Article 20, they also attempt to regulate the application of certain exception and emergency provisions of the Treaty. Further, although concluded subsequent to the EEC Treaty, this Agreement with its protocols was ratified by the Member State parliaments and possesses, therefore, a formal validity equal to the Treaties themselves.[265]

In the Brandy Wine Case,[266] the German Government supported its argument for a tariff dispensation under EEC Article 25 by reference to the "final clauses" of that Agreement. Since the Signatory States, it contended, had failed at the time to reach full agreement, they and the Commission took express notice of Germany's intent to receive tariff dispensations on certain goods.[267] Advocate-General Roemer acknowledged the legally binding authority of this formal declaration, for "the Member States clearly intended more than a mere reference to the applicability of Article 25 (3)." While it could not be assumed, without more, that they wished to alter the Treaty, they did intend

> to give the Commission concrete binding directives ... which are to receive special weight within the framework of the general discretionary considerations which the Commission is obligated to respect under Article 25 (3).

It was for the Court, then, "to examine whether the Commission has kept within these directives."[268]

The Court, however, refused this approach. Article 25, it said, "confers *on the Commission* the task of reviewing the market conditions for the goods in question and the difficulties which hinder the supply of the complaining Member State."[269] This evaluation was to be guided by the basic Treaty norms in Articles 2, 3 and 9 as well as by the totality of those considerations mentioned in Article 29. "This legal situation," the Court concluded without more,[270] "is not affected [nicht beruehrt, non affectée] by the declaration of March 2, 1960. . ."

In a second case, two years later, the Italian Government supported its demand for a tariff dispensation from the common EEC customs by re-

265 This Agreement of March 2, 1960, for establishing the common tariffs for List G goods is published in *Amtsblatt* 1825 (Dec. 20, 1960).

266 Judgment 24/62 (*Germany* v. *EEC Commission*), 9 Rspr. 141 (1963), discussed in text supra, p. 303f.

267 *Ibid.*, p. 152. In *Amtsblatt, op. cit.*, p. 1869, this declaration reads as follows: "As concerns the List G agricultural products in Appendix II of the Treaty, the Member States take notice [zur Kenntnis nehmen] of the intention of the Federal Republic of West Germany to receive tariff dispensations for the following goods: . . ."

268 Conclusions of *Adv-Gen*. Roemer, in Case 24/62, *ibid.*, p. 181f.

269 Judgment 24/62, *ibid.*, p. 154f. Emphasis added.

270 *Ibid.*, p. 154.

ference to this same Agreement.[271] In Protocol VIII of that Agreement, "the Member States endorse [befuerworten, expriment un préjugé favorable] the application of Article 226 of the Treaty in the form of an isolation" of the Italian silk market during the following six years for those products where "this isolation appears necessary."[272] Although the Commission had granted certain dispensations, the Italian Government attack them as insufficient.[273] This time, in light of the foregoing Judgment, Advocate-General Roemer took a more restrained view of the Agreement. The authorization for such dispensations, he pointed out, rests solely on the legal basis of the emergency provisions of Article 226. "In particular, it would be erroneous to view Protocol VIII of the Agreement . . . as additional and broader authorization." In endorsing the application of Article 226, the Member States simply express "the factual recognition of the necessity to take protective measures in favor of the Italian economy" for certain goods.[274] "The fact that Protocol VIII cites Article 226 of the Treaty and refers to its particular conditions and modalities of application is decisive."[275]

In even clearer language, the Court held that the language of "endorsement" was not legally binding. "The Commission must endeavor to take account of these directives, but is not bound to any certain legal duty." Absent this binding effect, on the one hand, the original discretion of the Commission under Article 226 is "unaffected." The Protocol "could neither alter Article 226 nor replace it by a special provision for Italian silk products." Nor was this intended, for by referring to Article 226 the Member States "evidence their desire to remain within its boundaries."[276] On the other hand, the Court does not totally abandon the field. Should the Commission, in evaluating the economic circumstances on the Italian silk market, "seriously violate its duties" under Article 226, it could be censured.[277] Such a violation, however, would apparently not be measured by the declarations in the Protocol. In either case, therefore, the Court defended Commission discretion primarily in terms of Treaty norms. It was little inclined to give special weight to the "authentic interpretation" of the Member States, at least when their intent to bind the Community organs had not been made unmistakably clear. At the same time, it took no

271 Judgment 32/64 (*Italy* v. *EEC Commission*), 11 Rspr. 495 (1965).
272 *Amtsblatt, op. cit.*
273 Judgment 32/64, *op. cit.*, p. 501.
274 *Ibid.*, p. 514.
275 *Ibid.*, p. 507f.
276 *Ibid.*, p. 507f.
277 *Ibid.*, p. 508.

principled position as to the authority of such interpretation within the context of Community law. This question was left open.

The Court's position appears to have hardened considerably, however, when Italy raised the question again five years later. The context lay in the Decision of the EEC Council to accelerate formation of the customs union. Due to favorable economic developments in the Common Market, it may be recalled, the Council took action under EEC Article 235 to move the completion goal forward to July 1, 1968, a full 18 months ahead of schedule.[277a] During the discussions in the Council that preceded this Decision, however, the Italian Delegation had expressed its unwillingness to accept such an early termination date for existing tariff dispensations on tin and lead. As a result, when the Commission refused to extend these tariff dispensations Italy refused to comply and was sued by the Commission for violation of the Treaty.[277b] In its defense, Italy contended that the acceleration Decision of the Council was based on "negotiations in which the contracting parties exercised autonomy resulting from their sovereignty." Whatever its form it stated, the "Decision" was in substance an international agreement equal in rank to the EEC Treaty itself. Consequently, the expressed views of the Italian Delegation constituted a reservation to the Decision under principles of international law and a limitation to its application in the case at hand.

The Court, however, rejects this view three-fold. The acceleration Decision, it reasons, was adopted within the framework of EEC Article 235, a procedure for supplementing the Treaty provisions. As such, the Member States did not act merely as a group of States, but as the Council of Ministers and as an organ of the EEC in light of the established goals of the Treaty. The Council Decision, therefore, could not be characterized as an "international agreement." Further, "the scope and effect of the acceleration Decision must be interpreted according to its wording, and may not be restricted by means of reservations or declarations which were expressed while the measure was being worked out." [277c] Nor would there be any basis for consulting the *procès-verbal* of the Council. Finally, the Court grants, while the Commission might have deviated from the import of the acceleration Decision, it did this only via the emergency procedure of EEC Article 226. Whatever economic and social policy arguments the Italian government may have had, therefore, should have been considered

277a Judgment 38/69 (*EC Commission* v. *Italy*) 16 Rspr. 47 (1970).

277b EEC Council Decision No. 66–532 (July 26, 1966), *Amtsblatt*, 2971 (Sept. 21, 1966).

277c Judgment, 38/69 *op. cit.*, p. 57.

at that time. Once again, the Court leaves open the possibility that the decisions of the Commission might be challenged within the framework of the emergency procedure.[277d] It makes clear, however, that the basis of this challenge must be the existing economic and social conditions in Italy and not uncertain references to unformalized commitments.

Finally, there remain numerous agreements of Member State representatives concluded *in* Council but *not by* the Council or its three predecessors. Although usually, but not always, published in the Official Journal of the Communities, they demonstrate certain characteristics which clearly distinguish them from regular acts of the Council. For one, their form of publication – not at all uniform – is at variance with that of the latter.[278] They may be signed or unsigned, designated as "acts," "resolutions," "declarations," "decisions" or "conventions" and concluded by the "Conference of Representatives of Member State Governments" or by the "Representatives of the Member State Governments in Council Assembled." For another, their subject matter often lies at the margins or outside the strict competence of the Council, but may also compete with existing Community jurisdiction. Of the 63 odd agreements listed by Kaiser,[279] 43 concern such varying matters as the application and implementation of specific Treaty provisions, the establishment of auxiliary organs, particular tariffs and the accelerated formation of the common customs union as well as the implementation of treaties between the Member States and associated states. Among these may also be listed the Luxembourg Agreement – concerning the voting procedure in the EEC Council and certain forms of cooperation between the EEC Council and Commission – which attempts to restrict Community policy-making flexibility.[280] With the entry of the EEC into its final phase, the number and importance of these agreements will most certainly increase.

Above all – and here is the danger – these agreements expedite decision-making by circumventing Community procedures and, at times, even the

[277d] *Ibid., p. 58.*

[278] Kaiser, "Die im Rat vereinigten Vertreter der Regierungen der Mitgliedstaaten," in *Festschrift Carl F. Ophuels,* 107, 115f (1965).

[279] *Ibid.,* p. 108–114. The other 20 agreements concern those appointments discussed in text *supra,* p. 370 at note 264.

[280] See Mosler, "National- und Gemeinschaftsinteressen im Verfahren des EWG-Ministerrats," 26 *Z. ausl. öff. R.,* 1, 7–9 and 10–12 (1966), who argues persuasively that this Agreement is simply an attempt to regulate those rules of procedure which the Council is authorized to establish under EEC Art. 151. Such regulation, however, is restricted by the obligations of the Council under the Treaty. For the text of the Agreement see Europ. Parl. Sitzungsdok., Anlage zu Dok. 18 of 7 March 1966 (1966–67).

ratification procedures of the Member State parliaments.[281] Their tendency is to undermine the participation of the Community organs in favor of *ad hoc* agreements among the Member State governments. What is involved, therefore, are "Mischformen gemeinschaftlichen Handelns,"[282] emphasizing the element of reciprocal bargaining among the Member State representatives in Council.

What is the status of these agreements in Community law? The answer can not be, as Carstens and Wagner would have it:[283] the Member States remain "masters of the Treaties" and, therefore, their governments may alter them at will by unanimous agreement. This would be to confuse the Member States and their parliaments as founders of the Communities with their existing governments. Certainly the Treaties in no way authorize the governments alone to make fundamental changes in their Community obligations. Instead, they not only prescribe special provisions for minor Treaty revisions,[284] but also stipulate that any major amendment be ratified in accordance with the constitutional procedures of the Member States.[285] To date, at least, this means parliamentary ratification. It is irrelevant,

[281] See Houben, *Les Conseils de Ministres des Communautés européennes,* 96f (1964); Buerstedde, *Der Ministerrat im konstitutionellen System der Europäischen Gemeinschaften,* 135f (1964); Wagner, *Grundbegriffe des Beschlussrechts der Europäischen Gemeinschaften,* 229–32, 242 (1965); and Kaiser, *op. cit.*, p. 120f.

[282] Buerstedde, *id.*, p. 134f. See also Kaiser, *id.*, p. 120; Wagner, *id.*, p. 228–237; Mosler, *op. cit.*, p. 7; and Meibom, "Zur rechtlichen Systematik der Beschlussfaehigkeit der Organe der europaeischen Gemeinschaften," 14 *Betriebs-Berater,* 583, 584 (1959).

[283] Carstens, "Die kleine Revision des EGKS-Vertrags," 21 *Z. ausl. öff. R.*, 1, 6–8 and 37 (1961); Wagner, *id.*, pp. 235ff. See also Waelbroeck, "Contribution à l'étude de la nature juridique des Communautés européennes," in *Mélanges Henri Rolin,* 506, 514–16 (1964). Cf. Wohlfarth, "Europäisches Recht: von der Befugnis der Organe der EWG zur Rechtsetzung," 9 *JB int. R.*, 12, 29 (1959–60); and Scheuner, "Die Rechtsetzungsbefugnis internationaler Gemeinschaften," in *Festschrift Alfred Verdross,* 229, 237 (1960), who, although cited in this context, would scarcely accept the extreme consequences drawn by Carstens and Wagner. In particular, Scheuner points out that the legal basis for Community decisions "kann nicht ohne weiteres durch eine Zustimmung der Regierungen aller beteiligten Länder ersetzt werden, wenn diese nicht vertragliche Form annimmt." *Ibid.*, p. 237 and note 42. Among those who reject these extreme consequences, see also Mosler, *op. cit.* (n. 280), p. 5, note 8; Lambers, "Les clauses de révision des traités instituant les communautés européennes," 7 *Ann. franç. dr. int.*, 593, 601–7 (1961); and van Naters, "La révision des traités supranationaux," 6 *Neth. Int. L. Rev.*, 120, 129–31 (1959).

[284] See ECSC Art. 95, EEC Art. 235 and Euratom Art. 203. In its Opinions concerning the "small Treaty revision" of ECSC Article 56, the Court concluded that Article 95, at least tacitly, forbid revisions which would alter the relationships between the Community and the Member States. Opinions of the Court, 5 Rspr. 571, 576 (1958–59); and 1/60, 6 Rspr. 109, 117 (1960).

[285] See ECSC Art. 95 and 96, EEC Arts. 235 and 236, and Euratom Arts. 203 and 204.

therefore, that international law might otherwise give these governments a free hand to cancel or modify the Treaties.[286]

Furthermore, the neglect of Community procedures through governmental agreements on a few occasions[287] is not sufficient to work their desuetude. The authority of these procedures has been constantly reaffirmed by voluminous Community legislation, including Treaty alterations,[288] over the years. In fact, the Member State parliaments have not always accepted these *ad hoc* agreements of their governments unchallenged.[289] In any case, it would be fully incongruous with the fundamental importance of the Treaties for the peoples in the Member States to assume that basic alterations in the procedures or substance of the Communities could be undertaken without the publicity and debate of parliamentary ratification. Such deliberation on major issues is the essence of constitutional government, whether on the national or supranational level. As the Court has said, the EEC Treaty "is more than an agreement based on mutual obligations of the Member States . . . [for it] is addressed not only to the Governments but also to the peoples . . ."[290]

This does not mean, however, that governmental agreements which neglect Community procedures are of no authority for the Community Court. If, on the one hand, they have been ratified through the constitutional procedures of *all* the Member States, they have met essentially the Treaty requirements. Other requirements, such as that of consultation with the

286 Wagner, *op. cit.* (n. 281), p. 236, stresses the fact that, according to international law, nothing requires treaties to be altered or cancelled only via the identical procedures by which they came into being.

287 Indeed, Carstens *op. cit.*, p. 8, bases his broad conclusion simply on cases of procedural neglect under the ECSC Treaty. Moreover, they concern agreements ratified by Member State parliaments.

288 See, e.g., the "small Treaty revision" of ECSC Art. 56 discussed in the text *supra*, p. 291f, and also the Decisions issued by the ECSC Council under Art. 95, par. 1, during the coal crisis. Discussed by Hellwig, "Die supranationalen Vollmachten der Hohen Behörde," in Zellentin (ed.), *Formen der Willensbildung in den europäischen Gemeinschaften*, 31, 42f (1965).

289 Witness, for instance, the proceedings in the German Bundestag leading to the ratification of the "acceleration Decision" of May 12, 1960 (discussed by Houben, *op. cit.* (n. 281), p. 94f); and the rejection by the Dutch parliament of their Government's assertion during the Saar Treaty debate that the ECSC Treaty could be revised by the Member States without respecting the Treaty procedures (discussed by van Naters, *op. cit.*, (n. 283), p. 124f).

290 Judgment 26/62 (*van Gend & Loos* Case), 9 Rspr. 1, 24f (1963), discussed in text *supra*, p. 346f, and *infra*, p. 402f. Even accepting the extreme thesis of Carstens and Wagner, is it factually true that the Member State governments are "masters of the Treaties?" Does not the Luxembourg compromise, for instance, reflect as much the French election results of December 1966 as the resolute position of the remaining five Member State governments?

European Parliament and, where appropriate, with the Commission,[291] are not serious checks on resolute Member States in any case. As has just been argued, on the other hand, the same reasoning can not apply to governmental agreements simply among the heads or the representatives of the Member State governments.

Nevertheless, these agreements can not be relegated, as mere facts, outside the sphere of Community law and adjudication.[292] They are instead clear evidence of the current state of consensus among the Member States and, as such, of that *opinio necessitatis*[293] which underlies the development of Community legal authority in practice. Thus, should the occasion arise, the Court could scarcely ignore the restraints on Treaty voting procedures as unanimously adopted by the Member State governments in the Luxembourg Agreement.[294] If, in contravention of this Agreement, the Member States would attempt to impose a majority solution on "very important" French or other Member State interests without first endeavoring "for a reasonable time" to achieve unanimity, the EEC might well be faced with another boycott.[295] Under these circumstances, a judicial rendering of the Treaty [296] might well harden the political fronts, making no solution at all feasible. This is to say that such agreements are an undeniable formative force in the development of Community law and, within the outer limits

[291] See EEC Art. 236 and Euratom Art. 204; and cf. ECSC Art. 96.

[292] Such a position, however, appears to be that of Mosler, *op. cit.* (n. 280), p. 24f and also pp. 10–12 and 23–25; and of Meibom, *op. cit.* (n. 282), p. 584.

[293] For a discussion of *opinio necessitatis* in custom and practice, see Simonius, "Quelles sont les causes de l'autorité de droit?" in 1 *Rec. d'études Fr. Gény*, 204 (1934); and Guggenheim, "L'Origine de la notion de l'opinio juris sive necessitatis comme deuxième élément de la coutume dans l'histoire du droit des gens," in *Hommage au Président Basdevant*, 258, 259 (1960), defining the term as "the belief in the obligatory quality of the rule" existing in prolonged and constant practice.

[294] The first paragraph of the first of the two declarations to this Agreement, *op. cit.* (n. 280), reads: "Where, in the event decisions may be taken by majority vote upon proposal by the Commission, *very important interests* of one or more Member States are at stake, the members of the Council will endeavor *within a reasonable time* to reach a solution which is acceptable to all members of the Council while respecting their mutual interests and the interests of the Community in accordance with Article 2 of the Treaty." Emphasis added. This Agreement, as Mosler points out, *op. cit.*, p. 12, is not by itself a violation of the EEC Treaty. It would be, however, if it led to compromising certain Treaty goals by Council inaction. *Ibid.*, p. 24f.

[295] See, e.g., the appraisals of President de Gaulle's strategy and tactics by Hoffmann, "De Gaulle, Europe and the Atlantic Alliance," 18 *Int. Organ.*, 1 (1964); and Lindberg, "Integration as a Source of Stress on the European Community System," 20 *Int. Organ.*, 233, esp. 254f (1966).

[296] Court action, for instance, could take the form of an appeal by a Member State or the EEC Commission against the inaction of the Council (EEC Art. 175) or against the refusal of France to comply with a Council Decision (EEC Arts. 169 and 170).

of the spirit of the Treaties, must be recognized as a source of law.[297] To ignore them is to trifle with important, if not indispensable elements of current Community consensus and the very basis of legal authority.

In conclusion, the tension between the *status quo* and the *status nascendi* in Treaty interpretation need not necessarily mean judicial capitulation before the *ad hoc* agreements of the Member State governments. The value of such agreements as a source of legal authority, like that of case law and general principles of law,[298] is their persuasive force within the context of the Community legal systems. To the extent possible, the Court should strive – as it did in its Judgments on the tariff Agreement concerning List G goods[299] – to integrate the current will of the Member State governments into the broader context of the Treaties. This implies the positive contribution of governmental practice to the development of Community law. Where these agreements are seriously at odds with fundamental Treaty provisions, however, the Court must either reject them outright and present a persuasive case for all the Community to hear or at least avoid approving them. As to the latter, there are judicial techniques for avoiding decision or for narrowing its scope in favor of a decision on the question at a more propitious time.[300] Which of these several possible courses should be chosen is a matter for judicial statesmanship in light of the issue at hand. An untimely decision or overextended reasoning may only perpetuate the disunity among the Member States or lead to an irreconcilable breach in Community consensus. As the "guardian of Community law," the Court must seek to avoid this breach and preserve the continuous development of Community law. This is the overriding goal of the judicial search for authority.

Reasoning from Probable Effects

A third mode of judicial reasoning, in furtherance of Community consensus, is essentially utilitarian. It is based neither on the systematic integri-

297 See Kaiser, *op. cit.* (n. 278), p. 124; and Wagner, *op. cit.* (n. 281), pp. 236–42. Lambers, *op. cit.* (n. 283), p. 606f, concludes, in sum, that the Court can not enforce such agreements, but it also can not annul them. "Il s'agit donc d'une obligation, mais d'une obligation dépourvue de véritable sanction. Ce caractère de lex imperfecta n'a rien d'exceptionnel dans le droit de la Communauté européenne. Il marque bien la place qu'elle occupe dans le développement de la société internationale: entre une union des Etats et un Etat fédéré."

298 See text *supra*, pp. 359f and 367–380.

299 See text *supra*, pp. 370–372.

300 See discussion of such techniques in text *supra*, pp. 177ff, 299ff, 334–337, 413f, 480ff, and 496–499.

ty of Community procedures nor on the formation of a continuing jurisprudence through reference to recognized legal sources, but on an assessment of the effects, good or bad, which follow from a given Treaty construction. These effects, of course, are typically more hypothetical than real, for practical reasoning in the law is rarely susceptible to unambiguous, demonstrable proof. Indeed, the very value of reasoning from effects is to circumvent inconclusive legal construction and other arguments by focusing attention on more palpable and generally persuasive events. As Perelman puts it:[301]

> The unity between a cause and its consequences may be perceived with such poignancy that an immediate emotive transfer inexplicably occurs from one to the other, such that one believes to be accepting something for its own value when in reality this is due to the consequences.

This is pragmatism pure and simple. The correctness of a legal construction is measured by its probable effects. It constitutes essentially "bootstrap" reasoning, for it assumes an accord on the cause and the evaluation of those very effects from which it proceeds. Here lies both its strength and weakness.[302] Absent this accord, it is readily open to attack. Given this accord, the tangible expression of probable consequences and their relation to legal constructions may be highly persuasive.

This mode of reasoning may be demonstrated by three examples from the Court's jurisprudence. In the first place, it has been employed to strengthen the scope of Community policy over that of the Member States. This is not the end-means reasoning of the "implied powers" doctrine, discussed above in Chapter V,[303] but a balancing of competing jurisdictions at their margins. Thus, in the *Barbara Erzbergbau* Case,[304] the plaintiffs attempted to support the use of certain German discriminatory rail rates by the requirements of regional economic policy. Since this question had been nowhere expressly regulated in the Treaty, they relied on the goals in ECSC Article 2, paragraph 2, and Article 3(a), (d), (e) and (g) as well as on Article 70, paragraph 5, which reserves transportation policy generally to the Member States. In contrast to Advocate-General Lagrange,[305] the Court fully rejected this view, seeing in Articles 4 and 70, paragraph 4, an absolute prohibition on such discrimination. If the Member States had re-

301 Perelman and Olbrechts-Tyteca, *La nouvelle rhétorique: Traité de l'argumentation,* 359 (1958), who style this mode of reasoning "l'argumentation pragmatique."
302 *Ibid.,* p. 358ff.
303 See text *supra,* p. 288ff.
304 Case 3–18, 25 and 26/58, 6 Rspr. 373 (1960), discussed in text *supra,* p. 261ff.
305 *Ibid.,* p. 458f.

tained the jurisdiction to pursue such policies, it reasoned, "this could frustrate the realization of the common market, particularly because of . . . [their] differing transport policies." [306]

This mode of reasoning also has been employed to ascribe to Community law provisions a uniform content. As already has been discussed above, the Court was faced with several alternative approaches to Community law in interpreting the social security Regulation for migrant workers.[307] Should it give the Regulation a unique Community content, rely in large part on national practice or establish simply a *renvoi* to the Member State law of the national in question? Only the first of these alternatives, concluded the Court, was consonant with the EEC Treaty goal of free labor mobility. "If national law were free to determine and change unilaterally the content of the terms in question, [EEC] Articles 48–51 would be robbed of all meaning and the previously mentioned goals of the Treaty would be seriously endangered." [308]

Thirdly, this reasoning has also been used to assert the supremacy of Community law over all Member State law prior and subsequent. It is instructive in this respect to consider the reasoning of Advocate-General Lagrange and the Court in the *E.N.E.L.* Case.[309] The former proceeds, implicitly at least, from a dualist conception of Community obligations; the Member States are obligated under the Treaties, but the internal effect of these obligations depends on their respective constitutions. He emphasizes, however, "the disastrous – that word is not too strong – consequences" which this might have "for the functioning of the constitutional systems created by the Treaty and, as a result, for the future of the common market . . ." [310] The Court, moreover, goes one step further and draws concrete conclusions from these consequences for the supremacy of Community law. "If Community law could have different effect from one State to the other, depending on subsequent national legislation," it concludes, "the realization of the [EEC] Treaty goal in Article 5, paragraph 2, and the prohibition of discrimination in Article 7 would be endangered." And further, "no type of municipal law can take precedence over the law created by the Treaty . . . , without denying its character as Community law and placing in doubt the legal basis of the Community itself.[311]

306 *Ibid.*, p. 413.

307 Judgment 75/63, 10 Rspr. 378 (1964), discussed in text *supra*, p. 348f.

308 *Ibid.*, p. 396. See also the sequel to this, Judgment 100/63, 10 Rspr. 1213, 1231 (1964), where reasoning from effects is employed to reject certain matters of form as conditions precedent to the enforceability of a Treaty Regulation.

309 Case 6/64, 10 Rspr. 1251 (1964) discussed in text *supra*, p. 347 and *infra*, p. 405ff.

310 *Ibid.*, p. 1291.

311 *Ibid.*, p. 1269f. See also the reasoning of the Bundesfinanzhof, Decision of April 25, 1967, reported in 2 Europarecht 239, 244 (1967).

All three of these uses of reasoning from probable effects are drawn together by the reasoning in the Dye-stuff Case.[312] There the Court was called upon to determine the relationship between Community and national antitrust law where actions were proceeding concurrently and independently of each other under each legal system against the same defendants. Taken in its strict sense, an application of the prevailing "double barrier" theory of antitrust law in the EEC would have allowed the unqualified cumulative application of the provisions of each system. Since under certain circumstances national law might be inconsistent with Community law, the Court could not accept this. "To recognize a right of the Member States to adopt or retain measures that are likely to jeopardize the benefits of the Treaty," the Court reasoned, "would be contrary to the nature of the Community legal order." Moreover, to allow the mandatory force of Community law "to vary from State-to-State based on national legal acts would impair the effect of the Community legal order and endanger the realization of Community objectives." Consequently, any conflict must be resolved by giving priority to Community over Member State antitrust law.

This type of reasoning, as Carstens correctly points out,[313] does not establish the binding quality of Community law. For that matter, nothing short of an unambiguous Treaty provision, stipulating the supremacy of Community law, would convince those proceeding from a strict dualist view of Treaty obligations. Moreover, it must be admitted that such reasoning is more hypothetical than real. Despite the fact that the constitutional practice in all Member States does not acknowledge the absolute supremacy of Community law, the feared consequences have not in fact occurred. Nevertheless, this mode of reasoning is not stripped thereby of all authoritative value. The literature as well as the Court employs it.[314] Even Carsten, ironically enough, resorts to it in order to reject it.[315]

In a real sense, reasoning from probable effects is simply another aspect

[312] Judgement 14/68 (*Wilhelm et al. v. Federal Cartel Office*), 15 rspr. 1, 14 (1969). See also the discussion at p. 502ff *infra*.

[313] Carstens, "Der Rang europäischer Verordnungen gegenüber deutschen Rechtsnormen," in *Festschrift Otto Riese*, 65, 69 (1964).

[314] See, e.g., the arguments of Ipsen, "Das Verhältnis des Rechts der europäischen Gemeinschaften zum nationalen Recht," in *Aktuelle Fragen des europäischen Gemeinschaftsrechts*, 1, 20ff (1965); and his remarks on the same question at an October 1964 conference, recorded in 23 *VVdStRL*, 134 (1966). There he argues the supremacy of Community law from the requirements of a functioning and viable Community system.

[315] Carstens, *op. cit.*, p. 69f, argues not only that the feared consequences have not in fact occurred, but also that the continued and unchallenged functioning of the Communities on the basis of Member State agreements, concluded counter to Treaty procedures, demonstrates that the Member States remain supreme over the Treaties.

of the method of effective interpretation, discussed in Chapter V.[316] While there it focuses primarily on the developing Treaty purposes within the framework of Treaty powers, here it is concerned with elucidating the need to respect them in practice by showing the futility of any other conclusion. The Court does not confuse *de facto* with *de jure* authority in recognizing that were the Member States not to treat their Treaty obligations *as* binding obligations, the Communities could not long exist. The failure of any one Member State to do so could well induce or even make it politically necessary for others to follow suit. Precisely this far-sighted calculation or enlightened self-interest on the part of the Member States can contribute over time to the unconditional recognition of the supremacy of Community law.[317] The Court does well to argue the necessity of this conclusion if the Communities are to succeed. In this insight lies the persuasive value of reasoning from effects.

Taken as a whole, these procedural, substantive and result-oriented perspectives suggest the potential contribution of judicial decision to strengthening Community consensus. This potential has been realized most fully in arguing the integrity of Community procedures; even where, as in the *Vloebergh*s Judgment, the Court has appeared to retreat, its reasoning has been narrowed and the way kept open for the reassertion of procedural values at a later date. The Court has been equally willing to employ the more controversial mode of reasoning from effects. By comparison with the former, its persuasion is not the logic of system, but the far-sighted consideration of consequences inimical to the Communities as going ventures.

The formation of legal sources by the Community Court, on the other hand, has proceeded surprisingly slowly and rarely has been fully exploited. The weakness is one more of quality than of quantity: although the judicial reference to prior decisions, Community practice and the general principles of other legal orders are not infrequent, they are all too often unexplained and vague as to context and import. As a result, a great deal of potential authority lies fallow. Fortunately, the style of the Court's opinion-writing is both extensive and argumentative, reflecting a full awareness of the need to persuade. In particular, the Court has been building a conception of

316 See discussion in text *supra*, p. 234f.

317 See the conclusions of Simson, "Der politische Wille als Gegenstand der europäischen Gemeinschaftsverträge," in *Festschrift Otto Riese*, 83, 97f (1964); and Bülow, "Das Verhältnis des Rechts der europäischen Gemeinschaften zum nationalen Recht," in *Aktuelle Fragen des europäischen Gemeinschaftsrechts* 28, 46 and 52f (1965), who speaks of the gradual development of the supremacy of Community law from now existing "de facto supremacy" by way of the principle of effective interpretation.

Community law, emphasizing independent Treaty legal systems which establish more than mere reciprocal obligations between the Member States. True, Community law is not so independent of the Member State legal orders as the Court would appear to be saying, but the conception itself is a valuable argument for securing the primacy of the Treaties against the centrifugal tendencies of divergent national interests and legal traditions. This conception further establishes the frame of reference for selecting and applying the other legal sources.

2. THE DIALOGUE BETWEEN THE COURTS

In the Communities, the search for authority focuses largely on the tension between the Community and Member State legal orders. The Court itself has affirmed their strict separation: they "constitute two distinct legal orders independent of each other."[318] This means, on the one hand, that the Communities are not bound by Member State Law and, on the other, that the Court cannot nullify acts of Member States which violate the Treaties.[319] While the Court may determine, in a proper proceeding, that a Member State has violated its Treaty obligation, the judgment is not self-executing.[320] Nor is there an express provision to regulate the supremacy of the one legal order over the other. As a matter of both fact and law, Community integration has not progressed so far. The resulting conflicts, as Advocate-General Lagrange has noted,[321] are "the unavoidable consequence of competing legal orders."

It now remains to place this tension in an institutional context in order to appreciate more fully its impact on the judicial development of Community law. Nowhere is this impact more clearly evident than in the litigation arising under EEC Article 177 "preliminary question" procedure. Within this framework, as described in Chapter II,[322] questions of Community law raised in cases before national courts may be certified to the Community Court for determination. Unlike other forms of Community adjudication, there are no parties, but only "participants";[323] specific ques-

318 Judgment 13/61 (*Bosch* Case), 8 Rspr. 97, 110 (1962), discussed *supra*, p. 346.

319 See text *supra*, p. 345 (*Humblet* Case) and p. 351 at note 145.

320 See discussion in text *supra*, p. 65.

321 Conclusions of *Adv-Gen.* Lagrange, in Case 13/61, *op. cit.*, p. 146. See also Batailler, "Le juge interne et le droit communautaire," 9 *Ann. franç. dr. int.*, 735, 736–43 (1963); and discussion in text *supra*, p. 25ff.

322 See text *supra*, pp. 67–70 and 84f.

323 As Article 20 of the Statute of the Court provides, the "participants" in a proceeding – whether the Member States, the Community organs or the parties themselves

tions and not the case itself are the subject of referral. Not the parties themselves but the national court selects the questions to be referred and receives the answer of the Community Court. This is a procedure designed to secure unity in the interpretation of Community law while leaving its application in the concrete case for the national courts. This gives rise, says Lagrange, "to a genuine and fruitful collaboration between the national courts and the Court of Justice subject to the mutual respect for the jurisdiction of each."[324]

Thus, the stage is set for a dialogue between the courts. The purpose of the following discussion is not to examine comprehensively the "preliminary question" procedure as such, but to demonstrate how this procedure may frame a dialogue which furthers the search for authority in Community law. To this end, the procedure will be examined at three critical junctures, each reflecting the tension between the Community and national legal orders. The first concerns the threshold questions by which the dialogue is initiated. When is a question of Community law raised which must be submitted for determination? What is the Court's duty to answer? Secondly, once a question is submitted and accepted, what is the scope of the Community Court's interpretation? How to draw the delicate line between interpretation and application in the concrete case? Thirdly, even given the Court's determination, the issue of authority has not been thereby resolved. The application of Community law in the concrete case may conflict with Member State law. What is the responsibility of the national courts in such cases? At each of these three junctures, there is a potential if not real confrontation between Community and Member State legal orders. The immediate question for determination may vary from case to case, but it can not conceal the constant theme of the search for authority and respect for Community law. The task of the Community Court is, so far as possible, to maintain control of this dialogue and to turn it in favor of Comunity law.

Disciplining the Dialogue

The key to disciplining the dialogue lies in the threshold requirements for invoking the "preliminary question" procedure. When must it be invoked and the issue in question be determined? The language of the Treaty

– are entitled to submit memoranda or written comments to the Court. But this right extends only to those expressly designated in Article 20. Judgment 19/68, 14 Rspr. 707, 716f (1968).

324 Conclusions of *Adv-Gen.* Lagrange, in Case 13/61 (*Bosch* Case), 8 Rspr. 119 (1962).

is not unequivocal. According to EEC Article 177, the Community Court "is competent to make a preliminary decision concerning [in part] the interpretation of the Treaty" and "the validity and interpretation of the acts of Community organs." Except for the German version, all Treaty languages speak explicitly in this general and permissive term of "competent to." [325] Must the Court decide on every question laid before it or has it discretion to precise and select the issues or even to delay or refuse an answer? The Article then continues: where "any such question [of interpretation or validity] is raised in a case" pending before a national court of last appeal, that court "shall refer the matter to the Court of Justice." Accordingly the referral is mandatory, but conditioned on a question being "raised." (Since lower courts may – but need not – submit such questions, that aspect of the procedure is not acute for the following discussion). At first reading, therefore, the requirements of both the Community and national courts for invoking the "preliminary question" procedure are not without a certain ambiguity. The answers to the questions which this raises must be sought within the broader framework of the Treaty as a whole and its institutional context.

I.

Proceeding chronologically, the first question concerns the national courts. When is a question "raised," which they are obligated to submit to the Community Court? That determination cannot, in the first place, be the automatic result of a party's request to submit a question to the Community Court. The "preliminary question" procedure was not designed to make the Court an appellate division of national courts, but simply to secure the unity and integrity of Community law.[326] This goal must be achieved by a coordination between the courts which respects the delicate balance of national and Community jurisdiction and avoids frivolous questions of the parties aimed primarily to delay judicial proceedings.[327] Nor, in the second place, is the decision to certify in any sense mechanical. A national court, for instance, must determine whether under the circum-

325 The Court of Justice, these versions state, "est compétente pour statuer," "è competente a pronunciarsi" and "is bevoegd . . . een uitspraak te doen" a preliminary decision. The German version states simply: "Der Gerichtshof entscheidet . . ."

326 See text *supra*, p. 67f. In Judgment 31 and 33/62, 8 Rspr. 1027, 1042f (1962). the Court rejected an attempt by the parties to invoke directly the "preliminary question" procedure. See also Judgment 44/65 11 Rspr. 1267, 1275 (1965).

327 See Conclusions of *Adv-Gen*. Lagrange, in Case 6/64, 10 Rspr. 1279, 1293 (1964).

stances it is a court of last appeal, whether a question of Community law has been put at all and whether that question concerns the case before it. Thus, in deciding to submit a preliminary question in the *Puttershoek* Case, the Hague court of appeals assumed that *fondantmasse* is an export good which is subject to EEC Article 12, and that the tax on it had the same effect as a customs duty and was, therefore, contrary to the Treaty. This reasoning, said the Community Court in accepting the question for interpretation, shows that the Dutch court "has not independently interpreted Article 12, but has held to the interpretation which the Community Court gave this Article in its previous Judgment . . ." [328]

What is the nature and scope of this primary decision which national tribunals of last appeal must make? Two types of criteria are often suggested by the literature: that of "relevance' 'and that of "dubiousness." [329] As to the first, it is certainly indispensable that the question certified be "relevant" for determining the immediate dispute before the national court.[330] Otherwise, the decisions of the Court could be transformed into mere advisory opinions which are incompatible with its general jurisdiction [331] and might involve the Court in disputes where no real Community interest is at stake. The determination by a national tribunal that Community law is in some way "relevant" does not, of course, imply either its supremacy over Member State law or its decisive importance for the case at hand. It means simply, in the words of Advocate-General Roemer: the national courts "form an opinion on the solution of a municipal law dispute and consider at what points their legal and factual train of thought should be complemented with the aid of a binding Article 177 Treaty interpretation." [332]

More important, however, is the criterion of "dubiousness." It has been

[328] Judgment 73 and 74/63 (*N.V. Internationale Crediet- en Handelsvereniging "Rotterdam" and Coöperatieve Suikerfabriek en Raffinaderij G.A. "Puttershoek" v. Minister for Agriculture and Fisheries in the Hague*), 10 Rspr. 1, 13f (1964).

[329] See the analyses, for instance, of Tomuschat, *Die gerichtliche Vorabentscheidung,* 113ff and 154ff (1964); and Dumon, "Le renvoi préjudiciel," in *Collège d'Europe, Droit communautaire et droit national,* 197, 233ff (1965).

[330] This appears to be generally undisputed in the literature. See, e.g., Knopp, "Über die Pflicht deutscher Gerichte zur Vorlage von Auslegungsfragen an den Gerichtshof der Europäischen Gemeinschaften," 16 *Juristen Z.,* 305, 310 (1961); van den Heuvel, *Prejudiciële vragen en bevoegdheidsproblemen in het Europees recht,* 49, 64 (1962); Wohlfarth, "Anfänge einer europäischen Rechtsordnung und ihr Verhältnis zum deutschen Recht," 3 *Juristen JB,* 241, 259 (1962–63); Samkalden, *Comment on Judgment,* 28–30/62, 11 *Soc. Econ. Wetgeving,* 227, 230 (1963); Dumon, *id.*, p. 234f; and Tomuschat, *id.*, p. 124, with further references.

[331] See text *supra,* p. 73f, emphasizing the generally "binding" character of the Court's decisions.

[332] Conclusions of *Adv-Gen.* Roemer, in Case 26/62, 9 Rspr. 30, 39f (1963).

developed by those who emphasize the term "question" in the text of Article 177, paragraph 3,[333] or who otherwise seek to narrow the obligation of national courts.[334] As a condition to invoking the "preliminary question" procedure, in other words, must some doubt exist as to the validity or meaning of a Community law provision? This can be affirmed without difficulty for questions as to the validity of a Community act under the Treaties. On this point, the criterion of "dubiousness" possesses a large degree of built-in objectivity; it entails an either – or judgment. Taking "validity" to encompass both the formal and substantive standards of legality,[335] therefore, a question need only then be submitted if a national court seriously considers not applying an act of a Community organ because it violates the Treaty in some way. A national court may err of course in favor of a provision's validity under the Treaty, but this is no threat to Community law.

For the question of interpretation, on the other hand, there is no such clear standard which would adequately ensure an evenhanded application by national courts. This is true, for instance, of the "acte clair" doctrine. It has its origins in the practice of certain Member States[336] and enjoys considerable support among Community literature.[337] As developed in France, in respect to the strict division of jurisdiction between the civil and administrative courts, a question of interpretation need only then be submitted by the former to the latter if it raises "une difficulté réelle . . . de nature à faire naître un doute dans un esprit éclairé."[338] Absent this, there is nothing to be interpreted but only applied.

This view has been adopted by the Conseil d'Etat, France's highest administrative court, in refusing to certify certain questions of EEC Treaty interpretation to the Community Court. Thus, in *Société de pétroles Shell-Berre and Others,*[339] the Conseil d'Etat acknowledged its obligation under

[333] See, e.g., Knopp, *op. cit.*, p. 310; and Dumon, *op. cit.*, p. 236ff.

[334] See, e.g., Tomuschat, *op. cit.*, pp. 114–18, who rejects the first alternative.

[335] See the Conclusions of *Adv-Gen.* Roemer, in Case 73 and 74/63, 10 Rspr. 33, 42–44 (1964). Cf. Tomuschat, *op. cit.*, p. 110f.

[336] Besides France, the doctrine is also applied in Belgium and Luxembourg. See Tomuschat, *op. cit.*, p. 95.

[337] Dumon, *op. cit.*, p. 236f, ascribes it the majority view. See also the literature cited by Tomuschat, *op. cit.*, p. 117.

[338] This is the classical formulation of Laferrière, *Traité de la juridiction administrative,* vol. I, p. 498 (1896). See Pépy, "Essai d'une vue d'ensemble sur l'application de l'article 177 du Traité de Rome," *Rec. Dalloz: Chron. juris.* II, p. 9, 11 (1964); and Tomuschat, *op. cit.*, p. 95f.

[339] Decision of June 19, 1964, reprinted in 80 *Rev. dr. pub. sci. pol.,* 1034 (1964). See also the excerpts and comment by Wenner, in *AWD,* 261 (1964). See also the

Article 177, in accordance with Article 55 of the 1958 French Constitution, but only

si une "question" relative à l'interprétation du Traité est "soulevée" dans cette affaire,

and then only

dans le cas où il existe un doute sur le sens ou la portée d'une ou plusieurs clauses du Traité applicables au litige principal et si, de la solution de cette difficulté, dépend l'issue du litige.[340]

Since, it concluded, the French import restrictions under attack fell plainly (clairement) within the purview of EEC Article 37, whose purpose is clearly (d'une manière claire) to establish a special *régime* of regulation during the transition period for state monopolies of a commercial character, they are excluded from the application of general Treaty provisions. Further, there was nothing to indicate that paragraph 2 of Article 37, which clearly (il est clair) forbids introducing new and intensifying existing discriminatory measures between nationals of the Member States, had been infringed by the recent French decree.[341] In contrast to the Hague court in the *Puttershoek* Case, therefore, the Conseil d'Etat sovereignly interprets the Treaty in order to reject its application.[342]

Whatever its place in municipal law, the doctrine of "acte clair" presents a serious threat to the unity and integrity of Community law.[343] It permits Member State judges to evade Community law interpretation or even to undertake it on their own. In the first place, an "acte clair" determination,

implicit recognition of this position in German, Dutch and French cases, including other more recent decisions of the Conseil d'Etat, cited *supra* in notes 97 and 98, p. 69.

[340] *Shell-Berre* Case, *id.*, p. 1039.

[341] While the discrimination, in fact, was between French distributors of oil products, restricting the opening of new gas stations, it favored companies selling Sahara oil products to the detriment of imports from other petroleum sources, including the other Member States.

[342] In its conclusion, the Conseil d'Etat stated: "Considérant que de tout ce qui précède il résulte que les sociétés requérantes ne sauraient se prévaloir utilement, à l'appui de leurs conclusions subsidiaires ci-dessus analysées, de ce que l'arrêt litigieux pourrait être contraire ... à certaines clauses du Traité de la CEE ..." *Shell-Berre* Case, *op. cit.*, p. 1040. After weighing the problems involved, the Commissaire du gouvernment also adopted the "acte clair" view for reasons of efficient judicial administration. 80 *Rev. dr. pub. sci. pol.*, 1019, 1030f (1964).

[343] See text *supra*, p. 68f, Bebr, *Judicial Control of the European Communities*, 193f (1962); Pépy, *op. cit.* (n. 338), and his more extensive article, "L'article 177 du Traité de Rome et les juridictions françaises," 52 *Rev. crit. dr. int. privé*, 475, 501 and 695, 701–6 (1963).

like that of "sens clair," is the result and not the starting point of judicial reasoning.[344] While the doctrine properly counsels judges against unnecessarily searching out obscurities not present in the text, it too requires a decision that the language in question *is* unambiguous. "[L]a ligne de démarcation entre le clair et l'obscur," muses Pépy,[345] "est parfois difficile à fixer." Logically, this determination belongs to the process of interpretation and must at least be confirmed by the Community Court. Secondly, Member State courts are ill-equipped to make an "acte clair" determination of Community law. While the Community Court has reasoned occasionally in "sens clair" terms,[346] this in no way speaks for national courts within the framework of the "preliminary question" procedure. Not only is the EEC Treaty binding in four different languages, but its terminology must be uniformly interpreted according to the needs of supranational regulation. Its meaning cannot be left to the vagaries of divergent national practice; except where the Treaties expressly provide, in no case is Community law, for instance, French law in France and German law in Germany. Where national practice is relevant, as in the interpretation of such concepts as "discrimination," it must be sifted through comparative studies in terms of Community needs.[347] In its reasoning, however, the Conseil d'Etat did not – and is scarcely the proper authority to – undertake such studies.[348] Indeed, on other occasions, national courts have shown a definite lack of knowledge on basic Treaty structure.[349]

[344] See Esser, *Grundsatz und Norm*, 123–25 (1956); and Lauterpacht "Restrictive Interpretation and the Principle of Effectiveness in the Interpretation of Treaties," 26 *Brit. YB Int. L.*, 48, 53–55 and 83f (1949).

[345] Pépy, *op. cit.* (n. 338), p. 11, quoting Batiffol. See also the discussion of Daig, "Aktuelle Fragen der Vorabentscheidungen nach Art. 177 EWG-Vertrag," 3 *Europarecht*, 259, 285–89 (1968).

[346] See, e.g., Judgment 5/55, 1 Rspr. 277, 291 (1954–55); See also the Conclusions of *Adv-Gen.* Lagrange, in Case 5/55, *ibid.*, p. 304; 8/55, 2 Rspr. 231, 267f (1955–56); 6/60, 6 Rspr. 1205, 1213f (1960); 28–30/62, 9 Rspr. 85, 95f (1963). And also the Conclusions of *Adv-Gen.* Roemer, in Cases 26/62, 9 Rspr. 31, 51 (1963).

[347] See text *supra*, pp. 349–351 and 354, and the study of "discrimination" and "subvention" by Hochbaum, Das *Diskriminierungs- und Subventionsverbot in der EGKS und EWG*, 30–48 (1962).

[348] See critique of Wenner, *op. cit.* (n. 339), p. 261f; and also Colin, *Le Gouvernement des juges dans les Communautés Européennes*, 100f (1966).

[349] The French Court of Appeals in Amiens (3rd Ch.), for instance, considered an EEC Article 177 referral unnecessary, because conflicts between Community and Member State law were not to be settled through this procedure, but must be overcome by the harmonization of Member State laws via EEC Arts. 100–102. *Nicolas and Soc. Maison Brandt Frères* (May 9, 1963), reported in *Rec. Dalloz: Chron. juris.*, 556 (1963), and in 1 *C. M. L. Rev.*, 359 (1963–64). For critical comment, see Hémard, *Rec. Dalloz: Chron. juris.*, 559 (1963).

Further, in the *E.N.E.L.* Decision, discussed *infra*, p. 405ff, the Italian Corte Costitu-

Finally, the very tension between Member State and Community legal orders speaks strongly in favor of a strict Article 177 obligation for national courts. Certainly the analogy to the French legal system fails to take this into consideration. The "preliminary question" procedure is not part merely of a division of competences between civil and administrative courts within a unified legal system. It is an attempt to coordinate competing legal orders and to overcome the initial reserve and uncertainties of the Member States and their authorities toward the new body of Community law.[350] Nor is this procedure bedded in a consolidated legal order whose educational patterns and tradition help discipline the judicial dialogue. Just to the contrary: national judges are being asked to give up national ways of thinking and acting in favor of the Communities. Their knowledge, contact and sympathy as to the new legal orders may be minimal or even lacking.[351] Considering the innovatory character of the Communities and their potential conflict with national law, therefore, the "acte clair" doctrine offers national courts an all-too-tempting "escape hatch" for delicate questions of interpretation. It is incompatible with the requirements of Community law.

These objections are equally valid for other, even more specific standards of "dubiousness." Tomuschat, for instance, would require national courts of last instance to refer provisions for interpretation to the Community Court only if there is some subjective or objective doubt as to their meaning.[352] Subjective doubt exists when a national court indulges in protracted reasoning in order to determine the meaning of a Community law provision. Like the "acte clair" doctrine, however, this standard is easily evaded; a court which does not or refuses to recognize the difficulties of Community law interpretation will scarcely find such reasoning necessary. To avoid this weakness, Tomuschat adds an objective standard. However free of subjective doubt, a Community provision must still be referred for interpretation if the meaning which a national court wishes to adopt is at variance with the decisions of higher courts in other Member

zionale referred to the EEC Commission as the "Commissione consultiva" (advisory Commission) – an expression to be found nowhere in the Treaty. See 116 Giurisprudenza Italiana 533 (1964).

350 See text *supra*, p. 385f.

351 See, e.g., the comments of Pépy, in *Collège d'Europe, Droit communautaire et droit national,* 191f (1965). The French judges, he remarks, "ne baignent pas dans une atmosphère "communautaire" comme certains de leurs confrères étrangers. Le "règlement communautaire" leur apparaît donc comme une notion assez obscure sinon bâtarde et ils le dépouillent de tout le prestige et l'autorité propres au Traité."

352 Tomuschat, *op. cit.* (n. 329), p. 121f.

States, respected views in the literature or the official positions of Community organs. Even given the uncertain premise that national courts have the time, expertise and facilities to make the careful surveys which such a standard implies, what results when existing opinion is scant or lacking on a question? Are decisions *primae impressionis,* which may point the way for other courts, to be left to national courts on a "first come, first serve" basis? This solution would threaten the very policy of "painless accomodation" which Tomuschat sees as the guarantee of the "preliminary question" procedure.[353] The Community Court would only then be called upon after the divergencies, which this procedure was meant to prevent, had become a fact of national practice. Certainly at this stage in Community legal development, where the uncertainties of interpretation are so great, there is need of a stricter presumption in favor of the Court's jurisdiction.

Apart from the criterion of "dubiousness," however, there are occasions when the submission of a question of interpretation would appear to be superfluous. This is the case when a question raised before a national court has already been settled – whether in a general appeal or via the "preliminary question" procedure – by the Community Court.[354] The Court appears to have recognized this possibility. Thus, on the one hand, in the *SNUPAT* Judgment discussed above,[355] it ascribed obligatory effect to its *ratio decidendi.* While far from establishing the doctrine of "precedent" in Community law as a matter of principle, this and other cases evidence the prejudicial authority of prior decisions of the Community Court.[356] The danger of drawing on such general authority, of course, lies in the fine and often uncertain distinction between *obiter dictum* and *ratio decidendi.* The unskilled application of the Court's decisions by national tribunals, as pointed out above,[357] can lead to unintended results which overcommit Community law. The danger is all the more real for Member State judges who are unacquainted with Community law and unused to drawing such distinctions. Still, if held within its proper limits, the application of such general authority by national courts would contribute to efficient judicial administration without endangering the unity of Community law.

As to prior "preliminary question" decisions of the Court, on the other hand, this danger is not acute. Here, in contrast to judicial decisions in other forms of Community appeals, the holding itself contains the Court's

[353] *Ibid.,* pp. 13 and 103.

[354] See Bebr, *op. cit.* (n. 343), p. 194; and Tomuschat, *op. cit.* (n. 329) p. 190f. Certainly all those supporting the "acte clair" position would not object to this.

[355] See text *supra,* p. 563.

[356] See text *supra,* p. 563ff.

[357] See text *supra,* p. 366f.

formula of interpretation. By reference to this holding and the question certified for interpretation, the decisions of the Court may be easily circumscribed and tested as to their adequacy for the case before the national court. The Judgment of the Court in *Da Costa en Shaake*[358] affirms this view. There, faced with identical questions of a national tribunal presented in a prior "preliminary" proceeding,[359] it granted the request for interpretation but simply referred the Dutch Tariefcommissie to the holding of its previous Judgment. Although Article 177, it reasoned, "unconditionally obligates" national tribunals of last appeal to submit all questions of Community law for interpretation,

> still the effect of an interpretation by the Court in a previous Article 177 proceeding can vitiate the justification for this obligation in a particular case and make it appear senseless. This is especially true when the question submitted is identical to a question already the object of a preliminary decision in a case analogously situated.[360]

The request, therefore, would be granted but in answer the national court was referred to an earlier judgment of the Community Court. The question posed as well as the circumstances involved in both cases were identical.

As the Court noted in passing, however, national courts would not be prevented from certifying a question anew, "if they judge this to be appropriate."[361] This occurred recently in a referral by the German Finance Court of Appeals (BFH). Though the self-executing character of EEC Article 95, paragraph 1, had been affirmed in a previous judgment of the Community Court,[362] the BFH nevertheless raised the question again under

[358] Judgment 28–30/62 (*Da Costa en Shaake N.V. and Others* v. *Netherlands Finance Administration*), 9 Rspr. 63 (1963).

[359] While the specific questions are identical, the complaining parties and certain facts giving rise to the complaint are different.

[360] Judgment 28–30/62, *op. cit.*, p. 80f. See also Judgments 13/67, 14 Rspr. 281, 293 (1968), and 24/67, 14 Rspr. 363, 372 (1968), where "similar kinds" of preliminary questions are answered by reference to earlier 'preliminary question' decisions of the Community Court.

[361] Judgment 28–30/62, *id.*, p. 82. Certifying a question anew would be "appropriate," for instance, if the national court wished to deviate from a prior interpretation of the Community Court or if a prior interpretation were inadequately worded to meet the needs of the immediate case. See Bebr, *op. cit.* (n. 343), p. 194; and Tomuschat, *op. cit.* (n. 329), p. 191f. In Judgment 29/68, 15 Rspr. 165, 178f (1969), the Court held the national courts bound to the interpretation which they rendered, but acknowledged their right to resubmit it if greater clarity were necessary.

[362] Judgment 57/65 (*Firma Alfons Lütticke* v. *Chief Customs Office of Saarlouis*), 12 Rspr. 257 (1966).

new circumstances.[363] The self-executing effect of that Article, it reasoned, would create immense difficulties in calculating the amount of turnover tax due on imports which the German tax courts could not adequately handle. In fact, more than 200,000 claims for refunds had been made with German authorities, out of which approximately 15,000 suits had grown. While the Community Court did not change its mind, neither did it dispose of the matter, as in the *Da Costa en Shaake* Case, by reference back to its previous decision. Rather, it arrived at its conclusion only after careful review of the new circumstances and considerations of practicability raised by the BFH in its referral.

Summing up, therefore, all "relevant" questions of Community law coming before national courts of last appeal should be certified to the Court of Justice for "preliminary" interpretation. There should be no category of "actes clairs," however defined, which can escape this unconditional obligation. While "settled" or repeat questions need not be certified for interpretation, this assumes that they are identical with ones already submitted *and* that they are raised in cases analogously situated. This is true particularly where the authoritative interpretation is drawn not from prior "preliminary question" decisions but from opinions of the Community Court in other types of proceedings. In the latter case, the interpretation as such is not set forth in the Court's order but must carefully be extrapolated from the entire body of the decision. A less strict obligation would permit national tribunals to expound upon the Court's interpretation and thereby endanger the unity of Community law. The value of this strict rule of referral is its manageability, allowing for the greatest degree of Community control over the unity and development of Community law.

It may be countered that such a strict obligation would flood the Court with "preliminary question" proceedings and overtax Community judicial administration.[364] At this early stage in Community history, however, this fear is more speculation than fact. Since the end of 1966, when referrals by national courts under the EEC Treaty rose sharply in number, the Community Court has rendered preliminary decisions at the rate of only 12-15 per year. This represents less than half of the Court's annual case load. While this rate of "preliminary" decisions may well increase in the

363 Judgment 28/67 (*Molkerei-Zentrale* v. *Chief Customs Office Paderborn*), 14 Rspr. 215, 231–233 (1968). In its opinion, the BFH noted from presenting the same question in another case that the *Lütticke* Judgment was binding only for the case before the certifying national court; it would not prevent another court from presenting the same question in another case.

364 See Tomuschat, *id.*, p. 117.

coming years, this is scarcely an unexpectedly large or too burdensome a case load under the circumstances. In any case, as Advocate-General Lagrange points out, the natural tendency of judges is to exercise their jurisdiction fully rather than abdicate it in favor of another tribunal.[365] More importantly, even should the evil of overtaxing the Court's capacity materialize, it should not be tackled by a doctrine – whether "acte clair" or any other – which would shift the solution of the problem largely to the discretion and divergent practice of national courts.[366] Instead, if the unity of Community law interpretation is to be secured, the solution must be a Community solution: either by expanding the number of judges and dividing the court into chambers, or by formulating Community rules or judicial doctrine to deal with the selection of cases. In other words, if discretion is to be used in selecting questions for "preliminary" decision, it should be exercised by the Community Court.

II.

Unclear as yet is the extent to which the Court wills to exercise discretion in the selection of cases for "preliminary" decision. It has refused, for instance, to delay its decision or to dismiss a question where the propriety of a "preliminary" referral by a Hague court was being appealed under Dutch law. Due to the strict separation and independence of the Community from the national legal orders, it reasoned, the Treaty is simply not concerned with the course of judicial appeal in the Member States. Just so, on the other hand, the Treaty

> conditions the decision-making authority of the Community Court solely on the existence of an Article 177 request, without requiring it to determine whether the decision of the municipal court is legally enforceable according to provisions of national law.[367]

Nor, by the same token, does the Community Court appear willing to review the determination of national courts that a particular question of Community law is "relevant" to the concrete case. The only requirement for its jurisdiction, it said in *van Gend & Loos,* is that the question presented "clearly concerns" the interpretation of the Treaty.

365 Conclusions of *Adv-Gen.* Lagrange, in Case 28–30/62, 9 Rspr. 85, 94f (1963), just discussed.

366 As Tomuschat, *op. cit.* (n. 329), p. 117, n. 438, the discussion of the "preliminary question" procedure in the literature often reflects the particular solutions in Member State practice.

367 Judgment 13/61 (*Bosch* Case), 8 Rspr. 97, 110 (1962), discussed in text *supra,* p. 346 and *infra,* p. 401f. See Judgment 19/68, 14 Rspr. 707 (1968) (Court not authorized to determine whether Member State had jurisdiction over action in point).

The considerations on which the national court has based its formulation of the question as well as the importance which it attaches to the question within the context of the case before it are barred from judicial review.[368]

Or, as was concluded in the *E.N.E.L.* Judgment, the Court is not authorized "to review the reasons and aims of the request for interpretation."[369]

Does it necessarily follow, however, that the Court must decide all questions laid before it by national courts? Although some have affirmed this as a duty of the Community Court,[370] that in no way follows necessarily from the Judgments just cited. In those decisions, the Court was concerned to reject arguments of the Member States designed to oust Community jurisdiction; in the latter two Judgments, Member States had objected that the only question involved was one of their own constitutional law. While refusing to review the considerations behind national courts' decisions to refer, the Court did not say that other circumstances and other independent reasons of Community policy would not justify altering, denying or delaying a decision in any given case. The argument that Community and Member State legal orders are distinct and independent of each other cuts two ways: just as the Community Court may not review the decisions of national courts requesting preliminary interpretation, neither may the latter control the exercise of the former's jurisdiction. The language of EEC Article 177, it should be recalled,[371] authorizes but does not expressly require an interpretative decision by the Community Court. The duty to request need not be identical with the duty to answer.

Where might this identity fail? In the first place, the mutual respect for Community and Member State legal orders may require the Court at times to precise, restrict or even expand "preliminary" questions. EEC Article 177 offers no specific form for such questions; it is sufficient, concluded the Court in the *Bosch* Case, that national courts "formulate the questions in a concrete and simple manner." If, as a result, the question is phrased too broadly, the Court will decide it "only within the limits of its jurisdiction, i.e., only so far as the question concerns Treaty interpretation."[372] Similar-

368 Judgment 26/62, 9 Rspr. 1, 23f (1963), discussed in text *supra*, p. 346f. See also the Conclusions of *Adv-Gen*. Roemer, *ibid.*, p. 40: and Judgments 28/68, 10/69 and 13/68, 5 Rspr. 125, 135 and 309, 315f and 679, 690 (1969), respectively.

369 Judgment 6/64, 10 Rspr. 1251, 1269 (1964), discussed in text *supra*, p. 347 and *infra*, p. 367ff. See also the Conclusions of *Adv-Gen*. Lagrange, in Case 75/63, 10 Rspr. 403, 406 (1964); and Judgment 56/65, 12 Rspr. 281, 301 (1966).

370 See Dumon, *op. cit.* (n. 329), p. 256; and Tomuschat, *op. cit.* (n. 329), p. 137 and 158f esp. n. 552.

371 See text *supra*, p. 385.

372 Judgment 13/61, 8 Rspr. 97, 110 (1962), discussed in text *supra*, p. 346, and *infra*, p. 401f.

ly, in the *E.N.E.L.* Judgment, the Court refused to consider the validity of an Italian nationalization law under the EEC Treaty, but asserted its power "to extract from the imperfectly phrased request of the national court those questions which concern Treaty interpretation."[373] And, conversely, the specific request of a Luxembourg court was expanded to include the interpretation of "all other provisions in the light of which the disputed question can be answered." In order to ascertain the scope of this catch-all clause, the Court examined both the reasoning and holding of the national court's judgment.[374] In either event, whether expanding or trimming the preliminary questions, the efforts of the Court are directed at avoiding a formalism which would only delay judicial proceedings and be "inappropriate for that very special area of judicial cooperation" between national courts and the Community Court.[375]

Even given the formal requirements of jurisdiction, moreover, there may be overriding policy considerations which behoove the Court to delay its decision in a specific case. This, it may be recalled, has been a favored tactic of the German Constitutional Court: keeping the case before it, but postponing a decision until other cases have accumulated or other avenues of conflict resolution have been given a chance.[376] Thus, a certain delay may permit the accumulation of preliminary referrals on a difficult question of Community law coming up through other national courts. Rather than determine the issue piecemeal, the Court may enlighten its perspective by the multiple insights of parties and cases variously situated. Not only may this contribute to judicial efficiency, but also judicial decisions based on this broadened experience are most likely to produce mature and persuasive rules of Community law. Furthermore, delay may be employed to avoid delicate issues which may better be resolved by other processes of decision-making. It may favor the settlement of disputes, for instance, by parties out-of-court or by political decision in the Communities or Member States. While settlements are not unusual in the history of Community adjudication,[377] the Court has – and rightly so – refused to moot charges of Treaty

373 Judgment 6/64, 10 Rspr. 1251, 1268 (1964), discussed in text *supra*, p. 347, and *infra*, p. 405ff. See also Judgment 20/64, 11–3 Rspr. 1, 8 (1965).

374 Judgment 101/63 (*Wagner* v. *Fohrmann and Krier*), 10 Rspr. 417, 431f (1964). See also the Conclusions of *Adv-Gen*. Lagrange, *ibid.*, p. 442.

375 Judgment 16/65, 11 Rspr. 1151, 1165 (1965).

376 See discussion in text *supra*, p. 184.

377 See the list of cases withdrawn before judgment in Valentine, *The Court of Justice of the European Communities*, vol. II, p. 839ff (1965), the discussion in Scheingold, *The Rule of Law in European Integration*, 301ff (1965); and Korsch, "Prozessmaximen," *Zehn Jahre Rechtsprechung des Gerichtshofes der Europäischen Gemeinschaften*, 122, 132ff (1965). The ATIC settlement between the High Authority and the

violation merely because of a Member State's belated compliance.[378] But it has also refused to postpone a decision on a question of parliamentary immunity even for a few days, although fully aware that the European Parliament was about to deal with the matter.[379] Nevertheless, within the framework of the "preliminary question" procedure, judicial restraint may at times be indispensable. For private parties may raise issues going to the heart of Member State Treaty obligations,[380] and force a judicial commitment which lacks the support of an effective Community consensus.

It is also conceivable, partially for the same reasons, that the Court should refuse a decision altogether on a preliminary question. This does not necessarily require the existence of a broad discretion to pick and choose cases, such as that enjoyed by the United States Supreme Court through its *certiorari* jurisdiction.[381] An exceptional power such as that, generally unknown on the Continent, ought not be assumed without express provision. There are, however, certain doctrinal bases which the Court may develop in order to avoid unnecessary decisions and their potential conflict with the Member State legal orders. One such basis is the category of "repeat" questions. As in *Da Costa en Shaake*,[382] they may be summarily dismissed by reference to prior judgments. And whether a question is "repeat", i.e., is "identical" and arises in a case "analogously situated", is a decision of the Community Court. As adjudication accumulates and certain aspects of Community law become more settled, the Court's leeway in making this decision may be expected to increase. Moreover, for reasons which Advocate-General Roemer calls "Rechtsmissbrauch,"[383] a referral may be so inherently contradictory, may so offend general priciples of law or so misconstrue clearly settled questions of municipal law that it must be

French Government is a good example of political compromise. See text *supra*, p. 333f at ns. 69 and 70.

378 See discussion in text *supra*, pp. 324–327.

379 Judgment 101/63 (*Wagner* v. *Fohrmann and Krier*), 10 Rspr. 417, 431 and 426–28 (1964). See also the Conclusions of *Adv-Gen*. Lagrange, *ibid.*, p. 443f.

380 See, e.g., Judgments 26/62 (*van Gend & Loos* Case), 9 Rspr. 1 (1963); 10/65 (*Deutschmann* v. *Germany*), 11 Rspr. 365 (1965); and 106 and 107/63 (*Toepfer KG and Getreide-Import-Gesellschaft* v. *EEC Commission*), 11 Rspr. 546 (1965).

381 See United States Supreme Court Rules 38, 39 and 41, reprinted in Hart and Wechsler, *The Federal Courts and the Federal System*, 1394f (1953). Almost as many as nine-tenths of the cases reaching the Supreme Court may be denied review on the basis of the Court's *certiorari* discretion. See, e.g., the annual overview of the business of the Supreme Court, published in 79 *Harv. L. Rev.*, 106f (1965) (1964 term).

382 See text *supra*, p. 392f.

383 Conclusions of *Adv-Gen*. Roemer, in Case 26/62, 9 Rspr. 31, 40 (1963). See also Tomuschat, *op. cit.* (n. 329), p. 156f.

dismissed. These are obvious substantive legal considerations which no court can ignore.

Finally, what of referrals which are clearly irrelevant for a determination of the case before a national court? While the Court has refused to review the "reasons and aims" of a national court's request for interpretation,[384] neither is it authorized to give purely theoretical decisions without all binding effect. Such decisions, says Advocate-General Lagrange,[385] "could concern very important questions or lead to serious conflicts with national courts." Thus, more recently, the Court has indicated that its jurisdiction may not be invoked to review Treaty provisions which "obviously have been drawn-on erroneously." [386] In order to avoid unnecessary tension between Community and Member State legal orders, therefore, the general rule must have its exception: manifestly irrelevant referrals must be rejected.

This analysis has been concerned with the threshold questions of the "preliminary question" procedure. They are the key to disciplining a dialogue between the Community and Member State legal orders. Due to the existing tension between these legal orders and the need to promote the unity and integrity of Community law, emphasis has been laid on a strict obligation of referral. National courts are thereby pressed to engage in Community problems, to participate step-by-step in the building of a Community and to consciously submit themselves to instruction by the Community Court. For the same reason, it is necessary to lodge whatever discretion is appropriate for limiting preliminary referrals in the hands of the Community Court. In this way, the Court can maintain maximum control over the development of Community law and its interpretation through national tribunals. At the moment, the Court has little flexibility in controlling the flow of preliminary referrals. Not only are its doctrinal bases very limited, but the current needs of the Community are both to encourage rather than check the use of preliminary referrals by national courts and to build a settled body of Community law. This, however, does not obviate the existing tensions between the legal orders. It merely shifts their impact to another level – the level of judicial interpretation itself.

[384] See text *supra*, p. 395 at note 369.

[385] Conclusions of *Adv-Gen.* Lagrange, in Case 6/64, 10 Rspr. 1279, 1284 (1964).

[386] Judgment 13/68, 14 Rspr. 679, 690 (1968) (where the Court stated the principle but only to reject out-of-hand the objection of the Italian Ministry of Foreign Trade that because the question presented in fact concerned trade with third countries and not between Member States, the interpretation requested was unwarranted). But cf. the position of Tomuschat, *op. cit.* (n. 329), pp. 113ff and 154ff, and Judgment 10/69, 15 Rspr. 309, 315f (1969) in conjunction with the views of the Commission (p. 313f) and of Adv-Gen. Roemer (p. 321).

The Scope of Interpretation: A Most Delicate Matter

The tension between the Community and Member State legal orders is also reflected in the very substance of the Court's "preliminary question" decisions. These decisions, due to the strict separation of competing jurisdictions, have been bisected into the tasks of interpreting and of applying Community law. As if to emphasize this distinction, Advocate-General Lagrange speaks of "abstract" interpretation in contrast to "concrete" application.[387] The former is relegated to the Community Court, while the application of Community law to the concrete case is reserved to the national judge. Within the framework of the "preliminary question" procedure, the Court may neither interpret, much less apply, national law nor determine its compatibility with Community law.[388] Treaty violations by Member State authorities, including national courts, must be attacked directly via other judicial procedures.[389] The distinction, therefore, is not simply theoretical, but of great practical importance. And this is precisely the difficulty. "The delimitation of application from interpretation," avows Lagrange, "is certainly one of the most delicate problems which EEC Article 177 raises. This is especially true because the boundary line between them at the same time divides the jurisdiction of the Community Court from that of national courts and no court is authorized to determine cases of conflict." [390]

It must be asked first to what extent this distinction is viable in practice. In the first place, a wholly abstract interpretation would offer national courts very little guidance for preserving the unity of Community law. If, as is generally asserted,[391] the "preliminary" interpretation is to avoid the improper application of Community law, then the Court's instructions to national courts must be fairly concrete. Further, the full severance of appli-

387 See the Conclusions of *Adv-Gen.* Lagrange, in Cases 13/61, 8 Rspr. 119, 135 (1962); 75/63, 10 Rspr. 403, 406f (1964); and 101/63, 10 Rspr. 437, 441 (1964).

388 See Judgment 6/60 (*Humblet* Case), 6 Rspr. 1163, 1184f (1960), discussed in text *supra*, p. 351f; and the Judgments cited in note 101 *supra*, p. 69. See also Jaenicke, "Das Verhältnis zwischen Gemeinschaftsrecht und nationalem Recht in der Agrarmarktorganisation der Europäischen Wirtschaftsgemeinschaft," 23 *Z. ausl. öff. R.* 485, 533f (1963); and Ipsen, "Das Verhältnis des Rechts der europäischen Gemeinschaften zum nationalen Recht," in *Aktuelle Fragen des europäischen Gemeinschaftsrechts,* 1, 5–7 (1965); and Münch, "Compétence des juridictions nationales, leur tâche dans l'application du droit communautaire," in *Collège d'Europe, Droit communautaire et droit national,* 173, 176–82 (1965).

389 See, e.g., the procedures provided in EEC Arts. 169 and 170, discussed in text *supra*, pp. 63–65.

390 Conclusions of *Adv-Gen.* Lagrange, in Case 6/64, 10 Rspr. 1279, 1283 (1964).

391 See text *supra*, p. 67f, and the literature references in the sources cited there.

cation from interpretation would have disastrous results for the development of Community law. "The "content" of positive law," concludes Esser, is determined only by means of case decision."[392] The Court is not engaged in a mere "academic exercise",[393] but in decision-making on the text, disciplined and enriched by the pecularities of the case at hand. To ignore this is to ignore the insights and limits of practical reason and to lose contact with reality and the changing needs of Community integration.[394] Finally, as guardian of the integrity of Community law, the Court can not be indifferent to the context or outcome of the particular case. The potential conflict between Community and Member State law – implicit in many of the preliminary questions so far submitted – will face even the most cooperative of national courts with the difficult problem of competing loyalties. Were the Court to neglect this factor in formulating its decisions, it would run the danger of abdicating its legitimate and persuasive influence over Member State courts or even of overtaxing the developing Community consensus. For these three reasons, a strict separation between interpretation and application in the "preliminary question" procedure can not be maintained.[395] It constitutes a legal schizophrenia anathema to the respect for Community law.

Fortunately, the Court has not been blind to this danger. While repeatedly disclaiming all jurisdiction over the application of Community law to the concrete case, it has exercised considerable discretion from case-to-case in determining the scope and concreteness of its interpretation. To some extent, of course, the varying precision of the Court's decisions is due

[392] Esser, *Grundsatz und Norm*, 285 (1956), in reliance on Gény. "Die Norm," says Esser at another point (*ibid.*, p. 85, n. 244), "ist weder 'da,' noch wird sie frei 'geschöpft,' sondern sie wird allenthalben aus der Interdependenz von aktueller Fallgerechtigkeit und bisher erkannter Zielsetzung als 'rule' neu integriert. See also his discussion at pp. 7, 119, 253f, 261 and 306f.

[393] See the Conclusions of *Adv-Gen.* Lagrange, in Case 8/55, 2 Rspr. 231, 234 (1955–56).

[394] See the Conclusions of *Adv-Gen.* Lagrange, in Case 28–30/62, 9 Rspr .85, 92–94 (1963), discussed in text *supra*, p. 392. In Case 75/63, 10 Rspr. 403, 407 (1964), Lagrange further suggests that EEC Art. 177 procedure is always part of a legal dispute whose "particular circumstances very frequently contribute considerably to elucidating the abstract question of interpretation, in the same way that an example supports a theory . . . ." This metaphor, however, is weak if not misleading, for cases are constitutive and not merely illustrative of the law and case-law is more real than any theory. See discussion in text *supra*, pp. 117f and 158–162.

[395] Tomuschat, *Die gerichtliche Vorabentscheidung*, 103f (1964), is able to maintain this distinction only by giving "interpretation" a broad construction which does not restrict the "concreteness" of the Court's conclusions. This, however, solves nothing because the question is: how concrete can an interpretation be without anticipating the application in the case at hand and usurping the jurisdiction of the national courts?

to the nature of the questions put by the national courts. At other times, however, its flight into abstraction reflects a prudent respect for the political sensitivities of the Member States. These sensitivities are real limits to judicial authority and the developing Community consensus. Nevertheless, they do not prevent the Court from speaking – and speaking persuasively – for the supremacy of Community law in the Member States. In this way, the Court may supply national courts and, indeed, the Community of jurists as a whole with cogent reasons and appropriate techniques for preferring Community law in conflict resolution. These reasons and techniques may be mere hints or extensive *dicta,* speaking beyond the case to the Community as a whole but no less important for stimulating discussion and pressing the development of Community consensus. By a prudent combination of activism and self-restraint, therefore, the Court may employ its "preliminary" interpretation to further and preserve the authority of Community law.

I.

In the very first preliminary question, presented by the *Bosch* Case, the Court was clearly reluctant to inquire at all into the underlying facts of the dispute. While affirming, in principle, the direct application of EEC Article 85 to agreements in restraint of trade and competition, it refused to decide whether the Bosch agreement fell within the meaning of that provision.

> This [latter] question can not be viewed as a pure matter of Treaty interpretation *because* the entire text [of the Bosch agreement], containing the concisely phrased restraining clause, has not been reproduced in the request for a preliminary decision. The Court could not answer the question without first making inquiries which are not authorized by Article 177 of the Treaty.

For this reason, the Court rather superfluously concludes, "it is not impossible" that the Bosch agreement is covered by Article 85.[396] The reasoning is most curious, for the Court is authorized by Article 21 of its Statute to "request Member States and institutions not parties to the case to supply all information which the Court considers necessary for the proceedings."[397] This surely must include the referring court itself, for it is typically

[396] Judgment 13/61, 8 Rspr. 97, 115 (1962) (emphasis supplied), discussed in text *supra,* p. 394.

[397] The language of the German text is even stronger, authorizing the Court to "demand" (verlangen) the necessary information. Tomuschat, *op. cit.,* pp. 127 and 150, believes such information to be indispensable for the Court's interpretation, but – without mentioning the Court's Statute – can find no authority in the text of the Treaty which would permit the Court to make such requests.

the chief source of such information. It would be strange indeed, if the Court's jurisdiction under Article 177 could be paralyzed by an oversight "preliminary question" procedure as well as to the basic opposition of the Court appears self-induced, due perhaps to the uncertainties of this new "preliminary question" procedure as well as to the basic opposition of the French Government to the Court's jurisdiction over the question at hand.

The Court, however, has not always been so restrained in formulating its "preliminary" decision. This is evident two-fold in the *van Gend & Loos* Judgment.[398] In the first place, the Court establishes the self-executing effect of Article 12 by reference not only to its terms and the Treaty as a whole, but also to the nature and function of law in the EEC. This broad reasoning, cited earlier in this Chapter,[399] lays down a fundamental conception of the Community legal orders. Still, the Court avoids the sweeping assertion of the EEC Commission that Community law is supreme over the national legal orders.[400] It concludes simply: EEC Article 12 "establishes individual rights which the national court must respect."[401] Secondly, in stark contrast to the *Bosch* Decision, the Court then goes into the particular legal problem facing the Dutch Tariefcommissie. Does Article 12 prohibit an increase in tariffs on Dutch imports which result not from a rise in the rate of duty but from a re-classification of products? Despite the protests of the Dutch and Belgian governments, the Court holds this to be a question of Treaty interpretation and not of application. Article 12, it concludes, forbids all "actual increases" in duties whatever the cause.

When, after the Treaty takes effect, a Member State product is subjected to a higher rate of duty, it is of no importance how this tariff increase has been accomplished.[402]

Such an increase, the Court states in its holding, "can result from a reclassification of tariffs, which places the product in a higher tariff category, as well as from an increase in the applicable rate of duty."[403] While the Court expressly reserves this factual determination for the Dutch tribunal,[404] the very wording of its decision made the outcome of the case a foregone conclusion.

On other occasions also, while holding to its strict distinction between

398 Judgment 26/62, 9 Rspr. 1 (1963), discussed in text *supra*, p. 346f.
399 See text *supra*, p. 394f.
400 Judgment 26/62, *op. cit.*, pp. 14–16.
401 *Ibid.*, p. 25f.
402 *Ibid.*, p. 28.
403 *Ibid.*, p. 30.
404 *Ibid.*, p. 28.

interpretation and application, the Court has gone on to give the national court very concrete guidelines for the case at hand. Thus, in its first Judgment interpreting the social security Regulation for migrant workers in the EEC,[405] it took pains to state the conditions under which Community law would be violated. Article 19(1) of this Regulation

> opposes municipal laws which subject the guarantee of the benefits in question . . . to stricter conditions than those which would [otherwise] be applicable had the party concerned become sick within the territory of the State to which the social security institution is subject.[406]

And, in another Judgment on this Regulation, the Court concluded that benefits "like those, which are the object of the present submission" of the Berlin court, are not payment in kind (Sachleistung) in the sense of Community law.[407] For that reason, the question of the national court was answered negatively.

Finally, in the *Deutschmann* Judgment, the Court employed the specific findings of a Frankfurt court to determine the factual characteristic of the German administrative charges in question. Since they were levied exclusively on the distribution of import licenses, it concludes, "EEC Article 95 is not applicable to *these charges.*" [408] Further, in both *Firma Milchwerke Wöhrmann* and *Firma Kunstmühle Tivoli*, the Court gives its interpretation "in light of" the national fees and factual matters at issue.[408a] The questions here turned on the characterization under Community law of fees within the framework of Member State turnover taxes. At times, therefore, the "pre-

[405] Judgment 75/63 (*Unger* v. *Bedrijfsvereniging voor Detailhandel en Ambachten*), 10 Rspr. 379 (1964). For the text of Regulation No. 3 of the EEC Council, here in question, see *Amtsblatt*, 561 (Dec. 16, 1958). See also discussion in text *supra*, p. 348.

[406] *Ibid.*, p. 399. See also Judgment 15/69 (*Württembergische-Milchverwertung-Südmilch-AG v. Ugliola*), 15 Rspr. 363, 369f (1969) (Court spells out with particularity the type of national requirements for military service which must be applied equally to nationals of all Member States wherever they are employed within the Community).

[407] Judgment 33/65 (*Dekker* v. *Federal (German) Insurance Institution for Employees*), 11 Rspr. 1185, 1191 (1965). See also Judgment 61/65 (*G. Vaassen-Göbbels* v. *Beambtenfonds voor het Mijnbedrijf*), 12 Rspr. 583, 604 (1966), where the Court found it necessary to review in brief the provisions of the Dutch law and to cite certain admissions of the defendant as to Dutch law in order to interpret the EEC Social Security Regulation. As Advocate-General Gand pointed out, in his Conclusions, it would be difficult to interpret the one "without at the same time indulging more or less in an interpretation" of the other.

[408] Judgment 10/65 (*Deutschmann* v. *Germany*), 11 Rspr. 635, 642 (1965). Emphasis supplied.

[408a] Judgments 7/67, 4 Rspr. 267, 277 (1968), and 20/67, 14 Rspr. 299, 308 (1968). Cf. also Judgment 25/67, 14 Rspr. 311, 329f (1968).

liminary" interpretations of the Community Court have been very concrete, if not to the point of anticipating the determination of the case before the national court.

II.

If this reasoning appears simply a logical and integral part of Community law interpretation, then the position of the Court in the *E.N.E.L.* and *Albatros* Cases is all the more striking. These two, in contrast to the cases just discussed, concern not the rather low level interests of isolated tariff duties, administrative charges or social security coverage for migrant workers, but the highly sensitive area of state monopolies. At the opening of the EEC, such monopolies controlled the import of certain products into France, Germany and Italy.[409] Due to their importance to the fiscal interests and market systems of these Member States, they were subjected to special regulations in EEC Article 37.[410] "These monopolies," said the Commission with cautious ambiguity in its Third General Report, "constitute to some extent a reserved area which is more or less excluded from the normal market rules."[411]

The dismantling of these monopolies – in contrast to other types of quantitative import restrictions regulated in the same Chapter of the Treaty – was not to be dictated by Commission Directives. It could be encouraged only by non-binding Recommendations.[412] In the general language of Article 37(1), paragraph 1, they are to be phased-out by the Member States

> in such a manner as will ensure the exclusion, at the date of expiration of the transitional period, of all discrimination between the nationals of Member States in regard to conditions of supply or marketing goods.

This means, for one, abstaining from any new measures of discrimination, especially those based on import restrictions tied to marketing outlets on the national market, on favorable sales prices for national products or on conditions of distribution.[413] Even more, this means that the removal of all existing discriminatory measures be timed in keeping with the general abolition of other quantitative restrictions. This timing is of the essence, as

[409] See EEC Commission, Third Gen. Rep. 96–98 (German ed. 1959–60).

[410] Wohlfarth *et al.*, Die EWG: Kommentar zum Vertrag, Bem. 1 zu Art. 37 (1960).

[411] EEC Commission, *op. cit.*, p. 95f.

[412] Cf. EEC Art. 33(7) with Art. 37(6). This demonstrates, say Wohlfarth et al., *op. cit.*, Bem. 10 zu Art. 37, that the commercial monopolies are of more serious importance for the Member States than the other quantitative restrictions.

[413] See EEC Commission, Fifth Gen. Rep. 48f (German ed. 1961–62). See also the "stand still" provision of EEC Art. 37(2).

the Commission early recognized, for without it the removal of quotas and customs duties would simply be replaced by monopolistic marketing practices.[414] For this reason, paragraph 2 of Article 37 (3) also provides indirect means for sanctioning unlawful delays. So long as a Member State fails to make these adjustments, "the Commission may authorize the other Member States to take . . . protective measures whose conditions and particulars it stipulates." What the Commission can not control directly, therefore, it may offset by retaliatory mandates to injured Member States.[415] It may also, of course, press charges of Treaty violation under EEC Article 169 against the delinquent Member State.

This brief sketch of EEC Article 37 suggests the great number of problems open for judicial clarification. The first occasion for this arose in *Costa* v. *E.N.E.L.*[416] The plaintiff had refused payment of his electricity bill and lodged a suit before a Milan court, alleging that the recent nationalization of the production, distribution and sale of electricity in Italy was unconstitutional as well as infringed EEC Articles 102, 93, 53 and 37. In response to these allegations, the Milan court suspended proceedings and submitted these questions, respectively, to the Italian Corte Costituzionale and the Community Court for decision. In a Judgment of March 7, 1964, the former rejected the contention of unconstitutionality as unfounded.[417] Article 11 of the Constitution, it reasoned, by which Italy "agrees to the limitation of her sovereignty" in favor of certain international organizations,[418] is only a "permissive norm" to be implemented by ordinary laws. Article 11 can "endow the ordinary law which makes the Treaty operative

[414] The dismantling of quotas, said the Commission in its Fourth General Report 45f (German ed. 1960–61), "would not enable the exchange of goods to develop if an unlimited state monopoly exists, i.e., if the state itself not only determines the level of imports but is also the single importer. From this it necessarily follows that the transformation of these monopolies must be coordinated with their import function, if one wants to attain that goal, namely, the removal of every discrimination in the supply and marketing conditions between the nationals of the Member States by the end of the transitional period. See also the Commission's Third Gen. Rep. 96 (German ed. 1959–60); and Wohlfarth et al., *op. cit.*, Bem. 6 zu Art. 37.

[415] Such an approach to Community sanctions is not unusual. See, e.g., ECSC Art. 67 § 2, para. 3.

[416] Judgment 6/64, 10 Rspr. 1251 (1964), discussed in text *supra*, pp. 339 and 371.

[417] Judgment No. 14 of La Corte Costitutionale italiana (March 7, 1964), cited in text *supra*, p. 32, note 165.

[418] Art. 11 of the Italian Constitution of 1948 reads: "Italy renounces war as an instrument of offense to the liberty of other peoples or as a means of settlement of international disputes, and agrees, on conditions of equality with the other states, to the limitations of her sovereignty necessary to an organization (alle limitazioni di sovranità necessarie ad un ordinamento) which will assure peace and justice among nations; and will promote and encourage international organizations constituted for this purpose."

[in Italy] no greater legal effect than that which inheres in its legal source." While Italy of course must respect its international obligations, the Constitution does not vitiate subsequent laws, contrary to the Treaty, which withdraw restrictions on Italian sovereignty. There was no need, therefore, either to consider the character of the EEC and its consequence for Italian law or to review any alleged violations of the Treaty. For the same reason, it was unnecessary to consider the plaintiff's request for a "preliminary" interpretation by the Community Court.

Just three months later, on July 15, 1964, the Community Court handed down its "preliminary" decision on the *E.N.E.L.* matter. Its reasoning was unavoidably prejudiced by the *fait accompli* of the nationalization law itself [419] and the position of the Corte Costituzionale. Assuming that the nationalization were contrary in some sense to Community law, it could not be examined in detail within the limited scope of the "preliminary question" procedure.[420] And if attacked directly by the Community Court, there were no certain prospects that a law so freighted with emotion would be altered or revoked. Yet even if the nationalization were not contrary to the Treaty, the Court could scarcely leave the reasoning of the Corte Costituzionale unchallenged. In Germany too, where the dualist view is also dominant, a pending submission before its Constitutional Court was challenging the constitutionality of the EEC Treaty in general.[421]

In his Conclusions, Advocate-General Lagrange addressed himself directly to this problem, but only affirmed the dualist position. His answer was one of hedged optimism, that these two countries would not confront the Communities with a truly irresolvable conflict. In flattering tones, he concludes:

> Not for one moment do I believe that Italy, who has always stood in the forefront of furthering the idea of Europe – that Italy, the land of the Messina Conference and of the Rome Treaty, would not find the constitutional way which enables it to live in full agreement with the principles of the common Charter.[422]

The Court's reasoning, on the other hand, reflects an attempt to reply in

[419] The EEC Commission, apparently, had not been informed of the coming nationalization or consulted as to its possible implications for the EEC. See Judgment 6/64, *op. cit.*, p. 1263.

[420] The appropriate form of appeal for such an examination is the Treaty violation procedure of EEC Articles 169 or 170, which can be initiated only by the Commission or a Member State. See discussion in text *supra*, pp. 63–65 and 82f.

[421] See the decision of the Rhineland Palatinate Finance Court of November 14, 1963, reprinted in Aussenwirtschaftsdienst des Betriebs-Beraters 26 (1964); and discussed by Ophuels, *ibid.*, p. 65.

[422] Conclusions of *Adv-Gen.* Lagrange, in Case 6/64, 10 Rspr. 1279, 1292 and also 1289–91 (1964).

principle to the Corte Costituzionale while, at the same time, avoiding a direct confrontation on the specific issues in question. It is an unusual combination of judicial activism and self-restraint.

The reply itself takes the form of *obiter dictum*.[423] Its pretext is a defense of the "preliminary question" procedure. The Italian Government had argued vehemently – as had other Member State governments in previous "preliminary" proceedings – that the question submitted by the Milan court concerned not Treaty interpretation but the application of municipal law. For its part, the Commission had affirmed the Court's jurisdiction, noting simply that the aspect of interpretation could be extracted from the question submitted. Instead of following this approach of the Commission, as it had on previous occasions,[424] the Court answers by arguing the supremacy of Community law.

The judicial reasoning picks up where it left off in the *van Gend & Loos* Decision.[425] The Court examines the nature of the EEC and the law on which it is based, but expands its reasoning to draw the consequences for the relationship between Community and Member State law.

> Due to the reception of Community law into the law of each Member State and, more generally, the wording and spirit of the Treaty, it is impossible for the State to introduce subsequent measures unilaterally against a legal order which they have accepted on the basis of mutuality. Such measures, therefore, do not deny the application of the Community legal order. If the Community law could have different effect from one State to the other, depending on subsequent national legislation, the realization of the Treaty goals in Article 5, paragraph 2, and the prohibition of discrimination in Article 7 would be endangered. The obligations, which the Member States have undertaken in the Treaty . . . , would not be absolute but only contingent, if they could be placed in doubt by later legislative acts of the signatory States.

Then, after a brief reference to the Community procedures and legislation which replace the unilateral action of the Member States, it concludes:

> no type of municipal law can take precedence over the law created by the Treaty and thereby derived from an autonomous legal source, without denying it its character as Community law and without jeopardizing the legal foundation of the Community itself. In transferring . . . rights and duties, which were up till then subject to national legal orders, to the Community legal order, the Member States have established a lasting limitation on their sovereign rights which can-

423 In contrast to the Conclusions of *Adv-Gen.* Lagrange, however, the Court's reply avoids all mention of the particular Member States in question.

424 See text *supra*, p. 395.

425 See text *supra*, pp. 346f and 402.

not be revoked subsequently by unilateral measures inconsistent with the concept of the Community.[426]

This reasoning, of course, proceeds wholly from the viewpoint of Community law, ignoring the dual obligation of national courts to their own constitutions. It attempts to persuade primarily by arguments of cause-effect,[427] based on the nature and purposes of the EEC. Whatever the merits of these arguments, the reasoning of the Community Court clearly oversteps those limits of "preliminary" interpretation, repeatedly drawn in previous Judgments.[428] For it is addressed to and expressly restricts the authority of national law. "If this is the correct interpretation," as Stein points out, "it is perhaps the first time in history that a court established by an international treaty has asserted its power to determine, with effect not only in the "international" (or Community) legal order but also in national law, the hierarchical value of the very norm to which it owes its existence."[429]

By contrast with these sweeping conclusions on the authority of Community law, the Court modestly trims its reasoning when coming to specific Treaty provisions. Not once, in fact, does it consider or even mention the question of nationalization which gave rise to the *E.N.E.L.* dispute. EEC Articles 102 and 93, it concludes in the first place, are not self-executing and cannot, therefore, be relied upon by private parties in a "preliminary question" proceeding.[430] Article 53, on the other hand – prohibiting Member States from "introducing any new restrictions on establishment[431] in their territories by nationals from other Member States" – does create rights for private parties. Seen in the context of the preceding Article 52, it requires "only that the establishment of nationals from other Member States is not subjected, through new measures, to stricter provisions than apply to native nationals." Apparently but not unambiguously, this Article also extends to nationalization, for the Court adds: "this [requirement] applies

[426] Judgment 6/64, *op. cit.*, pp. 1269–71.

[427] See discussion in text *supra*, p. 380f.

[428] See the Judgments cited in note 101, *supra*, p. 69f and discussed in text *supra*, pp. 399–403. Indeed, at the opening of its Judgment 6/64, *op. cit.*, p. 1268, the Court concludes: Article 177 "preliminary question" procedure "authorizes the Court neither to apply the Treaty to the individual case, nor – as it could in the Article 169 procedure – decide on the agreement of municipal measures with the Treaty."

[429] Stein, "Toward Supremacy of Treaty-Constitution by Judicial Fiat in the EEC." 48 *Rev. Dir. int.*, 3, 24 (1965).

[430] Judgment 6/64, *id.*, pp. 1271–73.

[431] The "freedom of establishment," as defined in EEC Article 52, includes "the right to engage in and carry on non-wage-earning activities, and also to set up and manage enterprises . . ."

without regard to the legal form of the enterprise."[432] The Court does not say, however, whether nationalization in any particular form would infringe the establishment provisions.

The reasoning is even less concrete as to the contents and scope of EEC Article 37. This provision, says the Court, contains both active and passive obligations for the Member States: the transformation of existing State monopolies during the transitional period, and the prohibition of all new measures of discrimination.[433] The latter, which is the only one relevant to the *E.N.E.L.* question, "is binding on the States and concerns their nationals directly; these [nationals] can derive rights from it which are to be respected by the national courts."[434] In essence, Article 37 (2) prohibits

> all new monopolies or arrangements in the sense of Article 37(1) so far as they introduce new discriminations in supply and marketing conditions. The task of the [national] court in the main proceeding, therefore, is first to consider whether this goal is actually contravened, i.e., whether the measure in question introduces or leads to a new discrimination in the supply and marketing conditions between the nationals of the Member States.[435]

However, even new discriminatory measures, the Court emphasizes, are prohibited only

> if, on the one hand, they are directed at the sale of commercial products in regard to which competition and interstate trade is possible, and if, on the other hand, they are of actual significance for this trade.[436]

But what constitutes "discrimination," "interstate competition" and a "monopoly in commercial products?" And when could this discrimination be of "actual significance" for Community trade? Of these crucial concepts nothing more is said. With only the vaguest of hints as to the relevant criteria, these determinations are expressly reserved for the national court.[437]

The *E.N.E.L.* reasoning, therefore, demonstrates the broad scope of judicial flexibility within the framework of a "preliminary question" interpretation. The Court, on the one hand, has assumed the role of an advocate, arguing in unconditional terms the supremacy of Community law. To consider its position binding on national courts would simply ignore the do-

432 Judgment 6/64, *op. cit.*, p. 1274.
433 *Ibid.*, p. 1274f.
434 *Ibid.*, p. 1275.
435 *Ibid.*, p. 1275f.
436 *Ibid.*, p. 1276.
437 *Ibid.*

minant dualist view in the constitutional practice of certain Member States. Rather, its reasoning rests wholly on a particular conception of Community law and from this perspective only is it conclusive.[438] Nevertheless, the undiminished value of the Court's reasoning lies in putting forthrightly and clearly the question of Community authority, in arguing its case persuasively and in engaging the national courts in a dialogue on the issue. This reasoning has been employed, though in abbreviated form, in subsequent judicial decisions.[438a]

On the other hand, the Court has also exercised self-restraint. In contrast to the judgments just previously discussed, it has left certain key concepts undefined. Considering the widely varying views especially of "discrimination" in Member State practice,[439] it must seriously be doubted that this very restricted scope of interpretation can ensure the unity of Community law. Still, the Court has not closed the door to a determination of these issues in future cases. While it was understandably reluctant to provoke a quarrel with the Italian Government for the sake of the plaintiff's electricity bill, the nationalization question could always be raised by the Commission of a Member State in an appeal of a Treaty violation. The *E.N.E.L.* reasoning, like that in the *Albatros* Case to follow, clearly depicts the extent to which the Court may fashion its decisions to avoid delicate questions of the moment.

III.

A further example of judicial restraint – this time by a strict narrowing of the "preliminary" question submitted appears in *Albatros* v. *SOPECO*.[440] In question was a French import monopoly on petroleum and oil products (Régime d'importation du pétrole), allegedly violating the Treaty provisions

[438] See the discussion of Frohwein, "Zum Verhältnis zwischen dem EWG-Recht und nationalem Recht aus der Sicht des Gerichtshofes der Europäischen Gemeinschaften," *AWD*, 233, 234–36 (1964).

[438a] See, e.g. Judgment 28/67 (*Molkerei-Zentrale*), 14 Rspr. 213, 230 (1969): "The Community represents a new legal order for the benefit of which States have, although to a limited degree, restricted their sovereign rights ..."; Judgment 13/68 (*Salgoil*), 14 Rspr. 679, 693 (1969); EEC Articles 31 and 32, par. 2, obligate Member States and especially their competent courts "to safeguard the interests of any violation of those provisions by guaranteeing them a direct and immediate protection of their interests, regardless of the relationship under internal law between those interests and the public interests in question"; and Judgment 14/68 (*Wilhelm* v. *Bundeskartellamt*), 15 Rspr. 1, 14 (1969): "EEC Article 87, par. 2(e), by giving a Community institution the power to define the relationship between national law and Community law on competition, confirms the preeminence of Community law."

[439] See the conclusions of Hochbaum, *Das Diskriminierungs- und Subventionsverbot in der EGKS und EWG,* 21 and 30 (1962).

for eliminating quantitative restrictions between the Member States.[441] It was established by a law of March 30, 1928, regulating oil imports through a system of selective and restrictive licensing. In French terminology it constitutes a *monopole délégué*,[442] reserving the basic decisions to the government while transferring their execution to private French firms. Since the opening of the Common Market, its implementing regulations have been altered by several decrees: one of September 24, 1958, extended the quotas of certain licensees for a period of three years; another of January 3, 1959, extends the licensing restrictions to the erection of gasoline stations and, in effect, sets a *status quo* for existing licensees in favor of companies handling Sahara petroleum products;[443] the third and even more controversial decrees of October 16, 1961 and February 27, 1963, grant "French or comparable (Sahara) petroleum" special privileges in opening gasoline stations.[444]

When in April 1959 the French firm SOPECO was denied an import license, it informed the Italian firm Albatros that it could not accept its purchases of gasoline. While SOPECO might have challenged the Government's decision before the French administrative courts,[445] it waited until sued by Albatros before a Rome civil court and then interposed the defenses of impossibility of performance and *erreur substantielle de droit*. Both defendant and plaintiff also believed that the French decision and the *Régime* upon which it rests (and, in particular, the decree of September 24, 1958) infringe EEC Articles 31, 32, 33 and 37. On this basis, they persuaded the Rome court to submit a preliminary request for interpretation to the Community Court.

This request touched a sensitive nerve in the Community. Not only was an Italian court directly questioning the legality of a French law, but it was doing so before the French courts had had an opportunity to speak on the matter.[446] When, just five months later, the Conseil d'Etat did address itself

440 Judgment 20/64 (S.A.R.L. *Albatros* v. *Société des pétroles et des combustibles liquides* (SOPECO)), 11–3 Rspr. 1 (1965).

441 See EEC Articles in Part Two, Title I, Chapter 2 of Treaty.

442 See also the conclusions of the Conseil d'Etat in the *Shell-Berre* Decision, 80 *Rev. dr. pub. sci. pol.*, 1034, 1039f (1964), discussed in text *supra*, p. 388f.

443 This is the decree challenged, but in vain, by the plaintiffs in the *Shell-Berre* Case before the Conseil d'Etat. See text *supra*, p. 388f.

444 The factual background of the *Albatros* Case is examined by Fourré and Wenner, "Der EWG-Vertrag in der Gerichtspraxis (Artikel 37 und 177)," *AWD*, 149, 150 (1965).

445 See the *Shell-Berre* Case, discussed in text *supra*, p. 388f.

446 The substance of the preliminary questions reads as follows: (See the abbreviated phrasing of *Adv-Gen*. Gand, in Case 20/64, *op. cit.*, p. 13, and the original in the Judgment, *ibid.*, p. 4).

to one aspect of the *Régime*, it relied on the "acte clair" doctrine and rejected the request for a "preliminary question" decision. In its opinion, there was no Article 37 "discrimination" to be complained of.[447] Further, the Community was split as to the effect of Article 37 on Member State commercial monopolies. Holland and Belgium, neither of which possess such monopolies, argued not only for a strict "stand still" obligation in such cases, but also for a step-by-step removal of existing monopoly discrimination in coordination with the elimination of other quantitative restrictions.[448] For France, on the other hand, the *Régime* accounted alone for 15% of its gross imports and constituted the most important French import monopoly.[449] It rejected fully the Dutch-Belgian view, contending that monopolies of an Article 37 character are subject to special regulation independent of the general provision for eliminating quotas. In particular, it also denied the relevance of the September 1958 decree for the case at hand as well as the jurisdiction of the Rome court to pronounce on French laws.[450]

The Commission too supported essentially the French view. Despite its previous position – that the removal of monopoly discrimination must be harmonized with the general elimination of quotas[451] – it now excluded EEC Article 37 from the impact of Article 33.[452] Indeed, this position had long been reflected in the pace at which the French, following generally the Recommendations of the Commission, had been dismantling their monopoly restrictions. According to the original goal of Article 33 (3), every quota was to equal not less than 20% of national output by the end of the tenth

A. Is Article 30, in conjunction with Articles 3, 31, 32 and 35, of the Treaty to be interpreted such that it nullifies the prior French legal provisions, especially the law of March 30, 1928?
B. Must the content of Articles 31 and 32, in conjunction with Article 5, of the Treaty be given precedence over the decree of September 24, 1958, by which the law of March 30, 1928, has been amended and altered?
C. In case questions A and B are answered negatively, has Article 33, in conjunction with Article 5, of the Treaty nullified the French *Régime* at any time subsequent to the opening of the Common Market?
D. Does Article 37, in conjunction with Article 5, of the Treaty contain a step-by-step prohibition of state commercial monopolies such as that operating under the French laws concerning petroleum imports?

447 See the *Shell-Berre* Case, discussed in text *supra*, p. 378f. It concerned, however, not the decree of September 24, 1958, here in question, but of January 3, 1959.

448 See Judgment 20/64, 11–3 Rspr. 1, 5 and 7 (1965).

449 EEC Commission, Third Gen. Rep. 97 (German ed. 1959–60).

450 Judgment 20/64, *op. cit.*, p. 6f.

451 See text *supra*, p. 403f, esp. note 411.

452 Judgment 20/64, *op. cit.*, p. 6f. See also the Commission's Answer 4, para. 4, to Question No. 51 of Burgbacher, in *Amtsblatt*, 390, 392 (1965).

year of transition; yet, by the end of the fifth year, the French import quota on crude oil and oil products from other Member States amounted to no more than 1.4 million annual tons, or 4.7% of total French consumption.[453] By 1964, with the time period half expired, this quota had increased to just 1.65 million annual tons.[454]

Moreover, this discrepancy was aggravated even more by the acceleration Decision of the EEC Council on May 12, 1960. According to it,[455] the existing quotas on industrial goods were to be fully abolished by December 31, 1960. At that time, the Commission had pointed out the need for an exact program for dismantling monopolies which would abolish existing discriminations in the shortest time possible.[456] Still, as late as January 1965, it had apparently not completed this program and could not precisely evaluate the discriminations of the French oil monopoly.[457] Even in its July 1966 report to the Council, the Commission only emphasized the existing difficulties with the French policy and hoped that they would not "lead to the isolation of the French market"[458] In its memorandum to the Court, therefore, the Commission not unexpectedly defended the discretion of the French Government in dismantling its monopoly restrictions. As a result, it concluded, the obligation of Article 37 (1) becomes binding only at the end of the transitional period.[459]

On February 4, 1965, with this record of Community and French policy before it, the Court handed down its decision in the *Albatros* Case. By narrowly restricting the scope of its reasoning, it manages to avoid almost every question in issue. In the first place, the Court declares itself incompetent to examine French import regulations. As a result, it flatly refuses to determine whether the French *Régime* falls within the aegis of Article 37.[460] By implication, at least, this was also the reason for not considering whether the decree of September 1958 infringes the Article 37 (2) prohibition of new discriminatory measures.[461] This restraint is more in keeping with the

453 EEC Commission, Sixth Gen. Rep. 47 (German ed. 1962–1963).

454 EEC Commission, Eighth Gen. Rep. 47 (German ed. 1964–1965).

455 See the EEC Commission's Third Gen. Rep. 29ff, esp. 39 (German ed. 1959–60).

456 *Ibid.*, p. 33f.

457 See the Commission's Answers 5. and 7. to Question No. 51 of Burgbacher, *op. cit.*, p. 392. See also its Answer to Question No. 52 of Pedini, in *Amtsblatt*, 2237 (1963).

458 EEC Commission, "Erste Aufzeichnung der Kommission an dem Rat über die Politik der Gemeinschaft im Bereich von Erdoel und Erdgas," in Sonderbeilage zum *Bulletin der EWG*, No. 7, pp. 11f, 16f (July, 1966).

459 Judgment 20/64, 11–3 Rspr. 1, 6 (1965).

460 *Ibid.*, p. 9.

461 *Ibid.*, If, as the French Government had asserted, the decree were irrelevant to the present case, the Court could have applied Advocate-General Lagrange's formula, mentioned in text *supra*, p. 388f. According to it, patently irrelevant questions may be

Bosch and the second-half of the *E.N.E.L.* Judgments than with the more concrete analysis in the *van Gend & Loos* and *Deutschmann Cases* and those concerning social security and turnover taxes in the EEC.[462] Certainly in the *Deutschmann* and social security decisions the Court had not been unwilling to determine whether the charges and benefits in question fall within the scope of Community law. It could take consolation in the fact, however, that the Conseil d'Etat itself had affirmed the application of EEC Article 37 to the French *Régime* in question.[463] This presumably would be followed by the Rome court in the present case.

Secondly, the Court also narrows its decision by a singleminded concentration on one fact of the case. In effect, it ignores the questions of the Rome court by formulating one of its own. Did the stipulated provisions of the EEC Treaty *in 1959,* when the import license was refused, have the effect *ipso jure* of nullifying the national restrictions in question? The Court's answer is a clear "No." The pace for dismantling existing monopoly restrictions "can not be determined abstractly for the future." Rather, the Treaty "simply prohibits the introduction of restrictions and discriminations of all kinds as well as requires the step-by-step removal of existing restrictions and discriminations, so that at the end of the transitional period they are fully abolished." [464] There is no need to decide, therefore, whether the application of Article 37 is exclusive of all other Treaty provisions concerning the elimination of quantitative restrictions or whether its application is directly enforceable in the Member States.[465] The Court merely determines that existing restrictions of an Article 37 type were not automatically abolished at the opening of the Common Market and "that none of the Articles [in question] obligated the States by 1959 to remove fully these barriers." [466]

This answer, as in the *E.N.E.L.* Judgment, is little more than a reiteration of the Article 37 text itself. The Court simply points out the outer limits of its application: while monopoly restrictions and discrimination of all kinds must be abolished by the end of the transitional period, Member States had not been obligated *ipso jure* to do this fully in 1959, at the opening of the Common Market. The questions, however, as to whether the Treaty nullified the French *Régime* at any period prior to the end of the transitional

rejected by the Court in order to avoid unnecessary conflict with national courts. Cf. the Conclusions of *Adv-Gen.* Gand, *ibid.*, pp. 14f and 21.

462 See discussion in text *supra*, p. 402f.

463 See text *supra*, p. 388f.

464 Judgment 20/64, *op. cit.*, p. 9f.

465 *Ibid.*, p. 10.

466 *Ibid.*, p. 10f.

period and as to what would be a reasonable pace for its dismantling were left unanswered. By clinging to the 1959 date, the one fact not stressed by the Rome court,[467] the Court could ignore the subsequent five years of developments surrounding the French *Régime*. This stress on certain facts of the case – stepping clearly beyond the narrow limits of an abstract interpretation – allowed the Court to avoid the really delicate issues put by the Rome court. As Europe CEE reported, "the Court endeavored to define as little as possible the legal issue of French legislation in the sphere of petroleum imports."[468]

Does this mean, then, that the Court – like the Commission – is leaving the dismantling of the oil import monopoly largely to the discretion of the French Government? This can not be answered with certainty.[469] In one enigmatic passage, it suggests that the parties concerned were not without future judicial relief. If injured by unlawful measures of a Member State, they could

> secure their rights and interests at any time by appealing these measures before a competent national court of that State . . . , subject to the right and duty of that court to invoke the Article 177 procedure . . . .[470]

If emphasis is placed on "that State,"[471] the Court may simply be admonishing the parties for going "forum shopping." Or, it also may be a hint that the Rome court should follow the decision of the Conseil d'Etat in so far as it is relevant.[472] In the Community of Member States, it might be argued, it is inappropriate for one national court to question the legality of another Member State law, at least before the courts of the latter have had an opportunity to consider the question.[473] All direct attacks on Mem-

[467] See the statement of the Rome court's questions in note 446 *supra*.

[468] Europe CEE (Agence internationale d'Information pour la Presse), p. 6 (Feb. 4, 1965).

[469] Fourré and Wenner, *op. cit.* (n. 444), p. 151, see the failure of the Court to consider the legality of the September 1958 decree under the Treaty as strong evidence that, at least at the date of the *Albatros* Judgment (Feb. 4, 1965), EEC Article 37 had no effect *ipso jure*. This, however, need not follow at all from the Judgment.

[470] Judgment 20/64, 11–3 Rspr. 1, 10 (1965).

[471] This is Fourré's and Wenner's view, *op. cit.* (n. 444), p. 152.

[472] See *Shell-Berre* Decision in text *supra*, pp. 388f and 411, n. 445.

[473] See Neri, "Le juge italien et le droit communautaire," in Donner et al., *Le Juge national et le Droit communautaire*, 77, 89 (1966), who suggests that normally a judge should see that the parties have exhausted the existing remedies of the foreign state before considering the legality of that state's law. Münch rightly suggests, however, that in case of conflict between Community law and the law of a Member State other than that of the forum, the national court may make an exception of *ordre public* and refuse to apply that Member State law. "Compétence des juridictions nationales, leur tâche dans l'application du droit communautaire," in *Collège d'Europe, Droit communautaire et droit national*, 173, 186f (1965).

ber State laws, therefore, would be reserved for the Treaty violation procedure of EEC Articles 169 and 170.

On the other hand, this passage may be read as stressing the parties' remaining right of appeal at a later time. If so, then the Court may be warning the Commission and the French Government alike of judicial control to come, should the dismantling of monopoly discriminations not proceed apace. A preliminary question, originating in a case of later date, might yield a more concrete answer. Once again, therefore, the Court has held Article 37 open for future determination. Considering the French resistance, the reluctance of the Commission and the absence of a direct judicial attack from another Member State, as Fourré and Wenner conclude, "should the Court then have been able to reach another conclusion?" [474]

This second phase of the dialogue reflects the delicate problems of Community law which private litigants may raise by way of the "preliminary question" procedure. They reflect the latent tension at work in the Communities between judicial interpretation of the Treaties and the limits of consensus among the Member States. Like the High Authority in the *Vloeberghs Case*,[475] these limits often have been writ large in the shifting position of the EEC Commission. Here, as there, the Court's reasoning demonstrates a sensitive feel for these limits and the skill to find a timely solution which will not prejudice the future development and strengthening of Community law. In resolving this tension, the Court has had to struggle with its apparent inflexible duty to accept all preliminary referrals, even those attacking fundamental economic policies of the Member States, as well as with the at times unrealistic "abstract" limit on the scope of its interpretation.[476]

To this end, two parallel lines of judicial reasoning have been developed – one self-restrained and one activist. The first, found in the *Bosch, E.N.E.L.* and *Albatros* Judgments, permits the Court to avoid issues presented by national courts. This has been accomplished by reference to the inadequacy of information, by flights into abstractions and ambiguities and by an exaggerated reserve toward Member State laws. The second, reflected in the *van Gend & Loos, Deutschmann,* social security and turnover tax decisions, acknowledges the need for concrete guidelines oriented to the facts of the particular case before the national courts.[477] In its ex-

474 Fourré and Wenner, *op. cit.* (n. 444), p. 152.
475 See discussion in text *supra*, p. 330ff and esp. 330f and 336f.
476 See discussion in text *supra*, pp. 394f and 399.
477 The Court's emphasis on the 1959 date of the *Albatros* Case may also be seen as

tended form, appearing as *obiter dicta* in the *E.N.E.L.* Judgment, it may carry the Court beyond the limits of the specific case and into a general defense of Community legal authority. Here, the Court demonstrates with all clarity that its mission is not simply legal interpretation in the narrow sense, but to advocate and strengthen the Communities themselves. At this point, the Court becomes a conscious initiator of discussion with national courts, the Member State governments and jurists in general in the search for authority in the law.

On Judicial Responsibility

This emphasis on dialogue is not mere metaphor. The "preliminary question" procedure establishes the framework for a disciplined and continuing discussion between Community and Member State courts on questions of Community law. True, the questions in issue may vary from case to case and must be initiated by national courts. Still, the recurrent underlying theme remains the search for authority in Community law. And once submitted, as the foregoing paragraphs have shown, these questions may be shaped by the Community Court and used as springboards to argue the supremacy of Community law. The Court, therefore, is an active participant in this dialogue, presenting national courts with the Community alternative.

Nevertheless, the dialogue itself is no answer to the potential conflict between Community and Member State law. The resolution of this conflict lies outside the "preliminary question" procedure. It is, in the last instance, a question of law application in concrete cases by national courts.[478] They,

an attempt to direct the attention of the Rome court away from the broader Community issues toward the original context of that case.

[478] See Ipsen, "Das Verhältnis des Rechts der europäischen Gemeinschaften zum nationalen Recht," in *Aktuelle Fragen des europäischen Gemeinschaftsrechts,* 1, 5–7 (1965); and Münch, "Compétence des juridictions nationales, leur tâche dans l'application du droit communautaire," in *Collège d'Europe, Droit communautaire et droit national,* 173, 176–82 (1965). But cf. Ophüls, "Die Geltungsnormen des europäischen Gemeinschaftsrechts," in *Festschrift Otto Riese* 1, 22–26 (1964), who recognizes that the application of two often competing legal orders by the national judge implies a "split personality," but sees his salvation in the procedures against Treaty violation and for a "preliminary question" decision. In the latter case, the Community Court "entscheidet nicht unmittelbar über die Gültigkeit oder Ungültigkeit der staatlichen Regelung, bestimmt sie aber *modo obliquo*: denn *logisch* ergibt sich aus der Gültigkeit der Gemeinschaftsnorm als Komplement notwendig, dass die staatliche Norm materiell ungültig ist, . . . dass der nationale Richter verpflichtet ist, diese logisch gebotene Schlüsse zu ziehen . . ." *Ibid.,* p. 25f. This assumes, however, that as to the question of legal authority, the logic *of the Treaties* is conclusive.

as much as the Community Court, stand astride the two legal orders and are responsible for the realization of Community law. If the Communities are to succeed, therefore, national courts must exercise "the greatest restraint" dictated by "a genuine spirit of cooperation between the national courts and the Community authorities." [479]

To fully appreciate the dialogue, then, it must be traced back to the Member States and their tribunals. Here is evidence that the Court's views, as expressed in the *van Gend & Loos* and *E.N.E.L.* Judgments, are not without impact on national thinking. Here also is evidence that the dialogue is not restricted to the referring national court alone or to the specific question referred, but will often extend to a general discussion on Community legal authority among other national tribunals, the parliaments, the literature and jurists in general. And finally, here is evidence of the central guiding role of constitutional courts in furthering the respect for Community law in the Member States. Primarily for this latter reason, the following examples will be drawn from Germany and Italy, the only two Member States with the institution of judicial review.

I.

The potential breadth of the dialogue is well reflected in the discussion surrounding a decision of the German Finance Court of Rhineland/Palatinate. Holding Regulation 19 of the EEC Council to be unconstitutional, the Finance Court suspended its proceedings on November 14, 1963, and referred the matter to the German Constitutional Court.[480] Its reasoning, if affirmed, would constitute a serious challenge to the viability of the European Communities, at least as transitional organizations of supranational integration. Voicing the doubts of German jurists in previous years,[481] it found the political structure of the EEC to be so incongruous with the requirement of the division of powers set forth in the German Basic Law

479 Conclusions of *Adv-Gen.* Lagrange, in Case 13/61 (*Bosch Case*), 8 Rspr. 119, 146f (1962).

480 Decision of November 14, 1963: III 77/63, reprinted in *Entscheidungen der Finanzgerichte,* 22 (1964); 17 *Die öff. Verw.,* 306 (1964), *AWD,* 26 (1964), and 1 *C. M. L. Rev.,* 463 (1963–64). Basing itself on Art. 18, par. 1, and Art. 20, par. 1, of the Regulation 19, the plaintiff had attacked the authority of the German Government to levy a turnover tax on certain grains imported from other Member States.

481 See the discussion paper especially of Erler, "Das Grundgesetz und die öffentliche Gewalt internationaler Staatengemeinschaften," in 18 *VVdStRL,* 7, 8f, 24, 26f and 38–45 (1950), at the Erlangen Conference in October 1959; Bucher, "Verfassungsrechtliche Probleme des Gemeinsamen Marktes," 10 *N.J.W.,* 850 (1957); and Kruse, "Strukturelle Kongruenz und Homogenität," in *Festschrift Herbert Kraus,* 112 (1954).

that it could no longer be justified as a "transfer of sovereign rights" under Article 24 (1) of that law.[482] In particular, the quasi-legislative power of the EEC Council, as a purely executive organ, was said to violate the delegation of powers restrictions in Article 80 of the Basic Law. As a result, German constitutional requirements could be satisfied only if EEC Regulations were issued through the regular channels of German parliamentary procedure *or* if the Member States were to establish a full and operational European Parliament with legislative powers. As it stood, however, the structure of the EEC violated an inviolable provision of the Constitution. "It leads not toward, but introduces a development," the Finance Court concluded, "which diverges from the rule of law."

One month later, issue was joined as the Administrative Court of Frankfurt expressly rejected the conclusions of the Finance Court.[483] The transfer of sovereign powers, it reasoned, is constitutional so long as the EEC guarantees the rule of law, the "same basic conception" of political organization and the "same scope" of individual rights as found in the German Basic Law. While the transfer was limited by the Basic Law, these limits apparently had not been infringed. In the ensuing months, while awaiting the decision of the Constitutional Court, the conclusions of the Finance Court were sharply attacked in the literature,[484] repudiated by a Resolution of the German Bundestag[485] and implicitly rejected by the reasoning of the Community Court and its Advocate-General in the *E.N.E.L.* Judgment of July 15, 1964.[486]

Then, just three months later, at the Kiel Conference of October 1964 a dramatic change was registered in the thinking of German public lawyers.[487]

[482] Whereas Article 20(2) of the German Basic Law provides that governmental power will be "exercised through special legislative, executive and judicial organs," Article 79(3) excludes this division of powers from constitutional amendment. Further, while Article 24(1) authorizes the German Federal Government to "transfer sovereign rights by legislation to international organizations (zwischenstaatliche Einrichtungen)," Article 129(3) forbids the delegation of legislative powers.

[483] Decision of December 17, 1963: II/1 – 636/63, reprinted in *AWD*, 60 (1964); 17 *Die öff. Verw.*, (1964); and 2 *C.M.L. Rev.*, 102 (1964–65).

[484] See, e.g., Klein, Case Note, 17 *Die öff. Verw.*, 308 (1964); Ophüls, "Deutsches Zustimmungsgesetz zum EWG-Vertrag teilweise verfassungswidrig?" *AWD*, 65 (1964); and Ipsen and Nicolaysen, "Haager Kongress für Europarecht und Bericht über die aktuelle Entwicklung des Gemeinschaftsrechts, 17 *N.J.W.*, 339, 344 (1964).

[485] On June 24, 1964, following an examination and initiative of the "Legal Committee," the Bundestag passed a resolution holding the ratification law on the EEC to be in accord with the German Constitution. Deutscher Bundestag, Sitzungsberichte 6501B (132. Sitzung: 4. Wahlperiode, 1964).

[486] See discussion in text *supra*, p. 347 and 406.

[487] See the discussion papers of Kaiser and Badura, in 23 *VVdStRL*, 1 and 34 (1966), and the following discussion, esp. the summarizing remarks of Scheuner. *Ibid.*, p. 106ff.

In stark contrast to a similar conference five years earlier, there was now general agreement that Community law should be granted a position independent of Member State constitutions and must be understood in terms of its own needs and conceptions. While the dominant dualist position of international obligations was not abandoned nor the need for certain basic constitutional restrictions on Community powers rejected, the Conference did break with the view that the Communities had to be images of German constitutional structure.

Nevertheless, when in March of the following year the Finance Court of Rhineland/Palatinate again was faced with the application of the same EEC Regulation, it refused to revise its earlier position.[488] It was obviously impressed – if not somewhat baffled – by the shift in legal opinion, but remained unconvinced. "It is clear," it concluded in no uncertain terms, "that the main task of all the lawyers and politicians involved must be to find ways of removing these [unconstitutional] discrepancies . . . not just by refined legal arguments, but by reorganizing the European Communities." The demand was more for revolution than evolution in Community organization.

The challenge was plain, the long-feared confrontation had arisen. Yet almost four years passed until the Federal Constitutional Court rendered its decision. It appears to have employed its familiar delay tactic,[489] keeping the case before it and biding its time for decision until the issue had been thoroughly discussed in the literature and legal opinion had tended to consolidate.[490] Those four years constituted almost a full generation in the life of the EEC; during that time, the *E.N.E.L.* Judgment was tendered by the Community Court, the common market for agricultural products was established and President de Gaulle's boycott of the EEC Council finally ended in the Luxembourg Agreement of February 1966. Moreover, the technique of decisional delay allowed the Constitutional Court to inform itself from the ongoing social debate of the issue. Conversely, it also permitted the dialogue to continue toward a consensus of legal opinion, unhindered by judicial fiat. The technique is passive but the Court maintains maximum control, for at any time it may step in, render its judgment and redirect the

See also Vogel, "Die Verfassungsentscheidung des Grundgesetzes für eine internationale Zusammenarbeit," in Heft 292/293 *Recht und Staat in der Geschichte und Gegenwart,* 24–26 and 42–48 (1964).

488 Decision of March 25, 1965: III 46/65, reprinted in *Entscheidungen der Finanzgerichte,* 342 (1965), and 5 *C.M.L. Rep.,* 67 (1966).

489 See discussion in text *supra,* p. 184.

490 As to the impact of this delay on discussion in Germany, see Ipsen, Case Comment, 2 Europarecht 358f (1967).

dialogue. Considering the import of the question for Germany as for the Communities as a whole, this caution of the Constitutional Court was eminently justified.

Indeed, the delay tactic of the Constitutional Court had the more immediate salutary effect of forcing other German courts to face up to the challenge of the Finance Court. Thus, just two months prior to the decision of the Federal Constitutional Court, the Finance Court of Appeals (BFH) took the initiative on its own. It could wait no longer due to the backlog of cases.[491] The immediate issue was whether the countervailing charge levied by the Commission on imported poultry from Poland infringed the taxing powers of the Member States? The BFH could have taken the tack of the lower Finance Court and pressed for a decision on the constitutionality of the EEC; on the other hand, it might have reserved all constitutional questions for later and simply requested a decision of the Community Court on the validity of the EEC measure under the Treaty. It took neither approach as such. Rather, it submitted a preliminary question to the Community Court *and* in doing so, like the Administrative Court of Frankfurt before, thoroughly reviewed and expressly affirmed the constitutionality of the EEC. In the course of its opinion, the BFH concluded:

> The political unification of Europe, to which the Basic Law is committed, can be realized only step-by-step under the [prevailing political] circumstances. The EEC represents a significant step in this direction .... Article 24 of the Basic Law, therefore, should be interpreted to mean that the transfer of sovereign powers to the EEC ... can not be measured by the strict standards which apply to the exercise of these sovereign powers by the constitutional authorities within the State itself.[492]

Whatever questions might arise as to the constitutionality of an EEC norm under German law, there was no doubt as to the constitutionality of the Treaty itself. The doubts of the lower Finance Court were squarely rejected.

Two months later, on July 5, 1967, the Federal Constitutional Court also rejected the conclusions of the Finance Court of Rhineland/Palatinate.[493] It did so, however, not on the merits but by a hairslim 4-3 decision on pro-

[491] Decision of April, 25, 1967 – VII 198/63, reported in 2 Europarecht 239 (1967). The preliminary request to the Community Court which that Decision embodied, concerning the legality of an EEC supplementary levy, was answered in 17/67 (*Firma Max Neumann* v. *Chief Customs Office of Hof/Saale*), 13 Rspr. 591 (1967).

[492] 2 Europarecht 244. See also the Saar Treaty Decision, discussed in text *supra*, p. 193f, whose language the Constitutional Court employed to justify taking account of the "political realities" in the nature of the EEC and its relation to German law.

[493] 22 BVerfG 134 (1967), reported in 2 Europarecht 351 (1967).

cedural grounds. No constitutional question was presented, it reasoned, because the Treaty provisions at issue do not conflict with the German turnover tax in point.[494] While recognizing without concluding that the quasi-legislative authority of EEC Article 189 *might* constitute an unconstitutional delegation of power, the Constitutional Court nevertheless maintained that this would not taint the entire Treaty. The decision disappointed those who had hoped for reasoning of the type offered by the BFH. Non-committal as it was, however, the decision focused public attention on the pro-Community views of the German Federal Government and Bundestag. It further drew expressly on the jurisprudence of the Community Court which had developed on the Treaty provisions in question during the time the referral was before the Constitutional Court.[495] That jurisprudence permitted the Constitutional Court to sidestep a potentially embarrassing constitutional conflict with the Treaty.

The constitutional question was not to be put off so easily. A number of German trading companies appealed the constitutionality of similar EEC Regulations directly to the Federal Constitutional Court.[496] The Regulaitons, they contended, infringed their individual rights under the Basic Law to life and liberty, equality before the law, free choice of occupation and security of property,[497] as well as violated other basic constitutional principles and certain norms of Community law themselves. Once again the Court rejects the question on procedural grounds. Community Regulations are not "acts of German public authorities," pursuant to § 90 of the Statute of the Court. Their constitutionality can not be appealed directly by individuals.[498] The Court thereby effectively disarms private litigants as the prime movers for attacking the constitutionality of Community acts.

By recourse to *obiter dicta,* on the other hand, the Constitutional Court clearly recognizes the unique "supranational" character of the EEC:

[494] The turnover tax, concluded the Constitutional Court in reliance on prior decisions of the Community Court, is an "internal charge" within the meaning of EEC Article 95ff and not a charge having the equivalent effect of a custom and proscribed by EEC Article 12.

[495] Judgment 57/65 (*Firma Alfons Lüticke GmbH* v. *Chief Customs Office Saarlouis),* 12 Rspr. 258 (1966), concluding that EEC Article 95, paragraph 1, has self-executing effect in the Member States.

[496] Decision of October 18, 1967, reported in 3 Europarecht 134 (1968). EEC Regulations No. 135 of the Commission (*Amtsblatt,* 2621 (1962)) and 159/66 of the Council (*Amtsblatt,* 3286 (1966)), which plaintiffs challenged, concerned EEC supplementary levies on imported poultry, fruits and vegetables.

[497] Arts. 2(1), 3(1), 12(1) and 14, respectively, of the German Basic Law.

[498] The Court, however, refused to say what the result would be if content identical to the Community acts were embodied in German laws. 3 Europarecht 137.

The organs of the EEC exercise sovereign powers which the Member States have renounced in favor of the Community which they established. The Community itself is neither a state nor a federal union. It is a unique type of Community in the process of a progressive integration: a "zwischenstaatliche Einrichtung" in the sense of Article 24, paragraph 1 of the Basic Law, to whom the Federal Republic of Germany, like the other Member States, has "transferred" certain sovereign rights.

As a result, it continues citing opinions of the Community Court,

a new public authority has arisen which is independent of Member State authorities; its acts, therefore, *neither need be ratified by the Member States nor can they be nullified* (aufgehoben) *by them*. The EEC Treaty represents, as it were, the *constitution of the Community*. The laws issued by the Community organs within the framework of Treaty powers, the "secondary Community law," forms a legal order of its own whose norms are neither international law nor the national law of the Member States. Community law and the municipal law of the Member States constitute "two distinct legal orders independent of each other"; the law created by the EEC Treaty originates from an "autonomous legal source." [499]

The parties, therefore, are referred to the "system of legal protection" established by the Treaty. As if to caution against an undue extension of its *dicta,* however, the Court expressly reserves the question of whether and to what extent Community law could be measured against the constitutional standards of the Basic Law in a differently situated controversy.

The Federal Constitutional Court appears to have taken a page from the *E.N.E.L.* Judgment of the Community Court. While restraining its hand on the merits, it has nevertheless taken the opportunity to speak over the heads of the parties to the nation at large. It has affirmed *in principle* that Community law, within the framework of the Treaty powers, can not be nullified by the Member States. Its reasoning on this point, it should be noted, proceeds not by argument from probable effects or by way of such Treaty provisions as EEC Article 189, paragraph 2,[500] but rather from the unique and independent character of the Community which the Member States established. It has in effect adopted the product of ten years of probing

[499] 3 Europarecht 136. The different approaches to these two decisions by the Constitutional Court can be explained partly by their differing posture and partly by the fact that in each case a different bench of the Court rendered the opinion. While the one bench publishes the result of its judicial vote, the other maintains secrecy in that regard.

[500] But cf. Ipsen's comment thereto, 3 Europarecht 140 (1968), who seeks to imply such an argument from the Court's reasoning. As to the argument of "probable effects," see discussion in text *supra*, p. 378ff.

debate on the question within Germany, including the gradually emerging positions of the German government, the Bundestag and the now dominant segment of juristic opinion.[501] The Constitutional Court, however, has not said either that Community law is supreme over national law or even that it supersedes subsequent conflicting national legislation. Nor has its reasoning on this point been more than *obiter dicta.* It says simply that because the Community and Member State legal orders are independent of each other, the laws of the one can not be nullified by the laws of the other. The concept of "independent legal orders" is a two-edged sword which applies equally to the Member States as to the Communities. It does not entail a supremacy rule for the resolution of conflicts.

At the same time, the Federal Constitutional Court holds *specific* questions of constitutionality in abeyance. That is to say, while Community and Member State law rests on "two distinct legal orders independent of each other," it does not necessarily follow either that their constitutional requirements are mutually exclusive or that the Member State authorities have renounced their supervision of those requirements. This crucial point distinguishes the *dicta* of the Constitutional Court from the less restrained reasoning of the BFH. As the Constitutional Court correctly senses, a Community still in the process of integration and without either a bill of rights or a full-fledged parliamentary system ought not be given carte blanche authority even as to its functionally limited sphere of powers.[502]

In resolving the question as to the authority of Community law, therefore, the Constitutional Court has prudently and wisely refused at every point along the way to legislate from on high. Instead, it has delayed decision on an earnest and debated question and thereby encouraged continuing discussion and an ever-broadened participation of professional and public opinion. Even when confronted with the issue, it has carefully restricted the right of private appeal and thus resisted the great temptation to attempt to "settle" the issue by judicial fiat. This restraint has given the civil courts their head and allows them to form a cutting edge for developing a consensus of constitutional opinion within Germany. As has been seen, both the Administrative Court of Frankfurt and the Finance Court of Appeals ac-

501 See discussion of views set forth in the Decision of the Constitutional Court, cited *supra* note 493, at 2 Europarecht 352f. It should not be forgotten that however critical one may regard the contrasting views of Professor Ipsen, as an advocate of the supremacy of Community law, and of the Finance Court of Rhineland/Palatinate as the devil's advocate, both have contributed immensely to the discussion and the fruit which it has brought forth.

502 See discussion in text *supra,* p. 356ff, concerning the application of general principles of Member State constitutional law to the Communities.

cepted this challenge in good style. Further, once a developing consensus in support of Community law was clearly evident, the Court consolidated these gains through *obiter dicta* while noting further questions and holding them up for continuing discussion.

As a result, the Federal Constitutional Court has succeeded in encouraging and guiding the growth of consensus within Germany on crucial questions of Community legal authority. This is reflected notably in subsequent decisions of the Finance Court of Appeals (BFH). Thus, in applying the preliminary question decision of the Community Court in *Max Neumann*,[503] the BFH echoes the language of the Constitutional Court. In a detailed analysis of the relationship between Community law and German customs regulations, it emphasizes the existence of two parallel and independent legal orders; yet at the same time, it concludes that the court is bound by the preliminary decision of Community law declaring the validity of EEC Regulation No. 135-62 governing the levies on imported fowl. This reasoning is carried one step further in applying the preliminary decision of the Community Court in *Molkerei-Zentrale,* a judgment rendered the following day.[503a] In affirming the direct application of EEC Article 95 to German turnover tax levies, the BFH states: "To the extent that there is a conflict in the application of Community law, the court must consider the *supremacy of Community law.*" The effect in that event, it continues, would be not to nullify the national provision in point, but only to make it inapplicable to the extent of the conflict. In neither of these cases, however, does the court assert the unconditional supremacy of Community law. Indeed, in the *Max Neumann* Case, the court takes great pains to measure the Community Regulation in question against provisions of the Basic Law.[503b] While the BFH has shown itself repeatedly as the advocate of Community law, therefore, it has proceeded from a dualistic view of Community-Member State obligations. It also has been as reluctant as the Federal Constitutional Court itself to absolve Community law from the requirement of German constitutional law.

[503] Decision of July 10, 1968 – VII 198/63, reported and commented on in 4 Europarecht 255 (1969). This Decision constitutes an application of Judgment 17/67 (*Firma Max Neumann* v. *Chief Customs Office Hof/Saale*), 13 Rspr. 591 (1967).

[503a] Decision of July 11, 1968 – VII 156/65, reported in 3 Europarecht 394 (1968). This Decision constitutes an application of the Judgment 28/67, (*Firma Molkerei-Zentrale Westfalen/Lippe GmbH Trockenmilchwerk* v. *Chief Customs Office of Paderborn*), 14 Rspr. 215 (1968).

[503b] See also the Decision of the BFH of July 10, 1968, to this same effect reported in 4 Europarecht 158 (1969).

II.

A parallel trend in legal opinion appears to be afoot in Italy, though it has not progressed as far as in Germany. It is visible, above all, in the recent Decision of the Corte Costituzionale, upholding certain ECSC Treaty provisions which deviate from the requirements of the Italian Constitution.[504] There, certain Italian steel firms which had been fined by the High Authority for failing to report the amount of their electricity consumption, attacked the constitutionality of Community judicature and the judicial protection which it affords private parties. The special jurisdiction of the Community Court, combined with its limited accessibility for private litigants, allegedly violated the requirements of Articles 102 and 113 of the Italian Constitution.[505] Based on the reasoning of the Corte Costituzionale in its previous *E.N.E.L.* Decision,[506] the lower court concluded that the Treaty was equal in rank only to national legislation. Treaty provisions, therefore, were subject to constitutional review.

Without abandoning the dualist position it assumed in the *E.N.E.L.* Decision, the Corte Costituzionale rejects this conclusion and the reasoning upon which it rests. The Treaty provisions in question are excluded from the operation of Articles 102 and 113. In reaching this result, it adopts implicitly the conception of the Community Court in the *van Gend & Loos* and *E.N.E.L.* Judgments,[507] asserting the unique and independent character of Community law. The ECSC, concludes the Corte Costituzionale,

> constitutes a legal order which is distinguished in every way from the municipal legal order; the latter recognizes the legal order of the Community not merely to inject it into its own legal system, but rather in order to fashion effectively international cooperation within the framework of Community purposes and to determine the cases in which the authorized activity of Community organs has municipal effects.[508]

The unique character of the ECSC, therefore, would appear to entail the coexistence of mutually exclusive legal orders.[509]

[504] Decision No. 98 of the Italian Constitutional Court (Dec. 16, 1965), reprinted in 1 Europarecht 146 (1966).

[505] While Art. 102 of the Italian Constitution provides that judicial control will be exercised only through "magistrati ordinari" and forbids the use of "special courts," Art. 113 guarantees legal protection against acts of public authorities.

[506] See discussion in text *supra*, pp. 347 and 405.

[507] See discussion in text *supra*, pp. 347f, 402 and 406ff.

[508] 1 Europarecht 148.

[509] This position has been taken also by Ophüls, *op. cit.* (n. 478), p. 23, reiterating

For this reason, the prohibition of special courts under the Italian Constitution simply does not apply to the Community legal order. Tribunals on the national level, the Corte states,

> are not authorized to review the legal acts of ECSC organs, for these organs are not subject to the sovereign authority of the Member States nor do they lie within the legal order of any one of these States: their acts simply form the material for a lawful qualification under the individual legal orders insofar as the obligation exists to grant them legal effect.[510]

Nor need the guarantees of judicial protection in the ECSC, moreover, "imitate exactly those of the Italian legal order which are not suitable in every way for an organ with international structure." In any case, the Community Court is pledged to ensure the rule of law in the interpretation and application of the Treaty, and "has been organized and operated pursuant to rules which correspond to the basic characteristics of the Italian legal order." Because of this correspondence in fact as to the judicial rights of the parties in question, there was no need to consider whether the constitutional guarantees of judicial protection in Article 113 also applied to organs of the ECSC.[511]

Like the Federal Constitutional Court of Germany, therefore, the Italian Corte Costituzionale also has been struggling with the dualist view of international obligations. It too, though not by express reliance on the jurisprudence of the Community Court, has recognized the unique and independent character of Community law. Unfortunately, the parallel ends here at the moment for, unlike the Federal Constitutional Court, the Corte Costituzionale prejudiced its position adversely at the very outset by meeting the issue head-on at a relatively early period in Community integration. It employed neither the tactics of delay and avoidance nor the strategy of *obiter dictum* which has served the former so well in encouraging discussion and pressing the growth of a constitutional consensus favoring the authority of Community law. Indeed, it even failed to delay its initial decision in the *E.N.E.L.* Case long enough (a matter of three months) to allow the Community Court to interpret the relevant Treaty provisions.[512] Had it done so, the Corte Costituzionale might well have been able to reconcile the Italian

his views expressed at the Second International Conference at The Hague on The Law of the European Communities (1963); and Lagrange, "La primauté du Droit communautaire sur droit national," in *Collège d'Europe, Droit communautaire et droit national,* 21, 23–26 (1965).

510 *Ibid.*

511 *Ibid.*

512 See discussion in text *supra,* p. 405f.

nationalization decree at issue with the rather vague guidelines set forth by the Community Court.

The more recent decision of the Corte Costituzionale suggests a new judicial tack in the offing. The Corte appears to be addressing itself to the underlying premises of the Community legal orders, while restraining its opinion where possible on specific issues. It further evidences a willingness to grant the Communities greater independence and flexibility within their own spheres of operation.[513] This undoubtedly reflects in no small way the creative initiative of the Community Court in the *E.N.E.L.* Judgment.[514] The questions still remain, however, as to precisely what is the exclusive sphere of Community law, and to what extent it is free of the idiosyncrasies of Italian constitutional standards. Above all, the Corte Costituzionale still must deal with the dualist view of treaty obligations which it imprudently applied in the first place to Community law.

III.

Despite these recent developments in constitutional practice, the dominant dualist view in the Member States has not been overcome.[515] Except for the Netherlands and Luxembourg, the potential conflict between the Community and the Member State legal orders has not been obviated.[516] Though conflict may be minimized or avoided in specific cases through rules of interpretation favorable to international obligations,[517] direct confrontation may still occur. Even the relaxation of specific constitutional

[513] For a rather optimistic view of what this portends for Italian constitutional practice, see the Case Comment of Glaesner, 1 Europarecht 149, 151f (1966).

[514] *Ibid.*, p. 151; and Neri, "Le juge italien et le droit communautaire," in Donner et al., *Le Juge national et le Droit communautaire*, 77, 93–96 (1966). See in particular the epilog to the *E.N.E.L.* Case in the Decision of May 4, 1966 by the Milan court of first instance. It refused to apply the Italian nationalization law, on the basis of which the plaintiff had been charged a $ 3 electricity bill, because it violated Community law. It not only based itself on the Community Court's reasoning in the *E.N.E.L.* Judgment (text *supra*, p. 406ff), but went on to draw further-reaching conclusions as to other Treaty articles which that Court itself had been unwilling to draw. The Decision is reported and noted in 1 Europarecht 360 (1966).

[515] Indeed, it is well to note that all the solutions in the Member States, including the much-praised Netherlands Constitution favoring the supremacy of Community over subsequent national law, proceed from a fundamentally dualist view of international obligations. See also the conclusions of Pescatore, "Die unmittelbare Anwendung der europäischen Verträge durch die staatliche Gerichte," 5 Europarecht 56, 78f (1970). Few have been willing to argue, as does Ophüls, *op. cit.*, (n. 478), p. 23f, that law takes precedent *simply because* it is Community law.

[516] See discussion in text *supra*, p. 38f.

[517] See discussion in text *supra*, p. 35f.

standards, as applied to the Communities, does not remove the threat of subsequent national legislation. Moreover, attempts to extrapolate a conflicts rule from the uncertain language of the Treaties alone[518] ignores the crucial fact that arguments as to the authority of the Treaties rest on consensus of opinion rather than on the hidden logic of the text. Basis disagreements as to the supremacy of Community law can not be removed or bridged so simply. In the end, nothing less than a constitutive act of the Member States, whether singly or in concert and whether by representative assembly or through the evolution of judicial decision, can assure the ascendence of Community law.

Until that act has occurred, what is the overriding responsibility of national tribunals – and especially of constitutional courts – when confronted directly and unavoidably with national legislation that contradicts pre-existing Community law? Because of the dominant dualist view in the Member States, the answer must be found if at all within the framework of the national legal systems. In such cases Steindorff, for instance, attempts to imply a presumption of supremacy based on the ratification laws of the Member States to the Community Treaties.[519] Subsequent national legislation, he reasons, which conflicts with Community law but does not expressly repudiate this presumption, is not to be applied. Only express repudiation by the particular law itself would overcome this presumption. In the last instance, therefore, the legislature must win with respect to *any single piece* of legislation. Since the resolution of the conflict can not be expected from the national judge of the defaulting Member State,[520] the matter must be attacked through the Community procedures against Treaty violation.[521]

Steindorff's answer has the advantage of being nationally based, but it is no stronger than the statutory authority which it presupposes. In particular, it is not evident why the presumption which he implies from the ratification laws would have any greater force than the converse implication that subse-

[518] E.g., Ipsen, *op. cit.* (n. 478), p. 17ff, relying on EEC Art. 189, par. 2. See note 137 *supra*, p. 27. But cf. the conclusions of Münch, *op .cit.* (n. 478), p. 181, in this respect.

[519] Steindorff, *Rechtsschutz und Verfahren im Recht der europäischen Gemeinschaften*, 53ff (1964). Cf. also Hayoit de Termicourt, "Le Conflit 'Traité-Loi interne,' " 8 *Journal des Tribunaux*, 481, 486 (1963); and Bülow, "Das Verhältnis des Rechts der europäischen Gemeinschaften zum nationalen Recht," in *Aktuelle Fragen des europäischen Gemeinschaftsrechts* 28, 52f (1965).

[520] Steindorff, *id.*, p. 54.

[521] See ECSC Art. 88, EEC Arts. 169 and 170, and Euratom Arts. 141 and 142. These are discussed in text *supra*, pp. 63-65.

quent conflicting national legislation repudiates any presumption of supremacy. *Gesetz ist Gesetz*!

An answer to the question of judicial responsibility in the Member States must go deeper. Indeed, it reaches constitutional proportions and, therefore, lies peculiarly within the province of constitutional courts wherever they exist. Its roots are not any specific constitutional provision or doctrine – although these may well be present in some form – but simply the overriding objective of responsible government.[522] This objective says, in a word: in the sphere of international affairs, parliament is sovereign to take on and dissolve itself of international obligations, but its action must be considered action, must be deliberate and deliberated and in some measure proportional to the magnitude of the decisions taken. Where this relationship is crassly lacking, such action is presumably arbitrary and the decisions are not to be taken at full value.

What would this mean concretely for the European Communities? The Treaties, it may be argued, establish Communities of far-reaching importance and impact for the nationals of Member States. Their laudatory goals of economic and ultimately political integration in the interest of peace and liberty accord with the purposes for which such international organizations originally were authorized in the Member State constitutions.[523] Essentially, these Communities are characterized by an identification of specific with common Community interests and by the integral functioning of specific Treaty norms as part of broader Treaty procedures and objectives. Individual Member States can not negate any single norm without jeopardizing the uniform and non-discriminatory operation of the Communities in the other Member States.[524] This is the unique element of "community." Just as the

[522] Cf., for instance, Article 20 of the German Basic Law, concerning the nature of the German Federal Republic as a democratic government whose authority is exercised within a division of powers and, in its exercise, bound to the constitutional order and the overriding principles of law.

[523] See, e.g., Art. 11 of the Italian Constitution of 1948, and the Preamble and Art. 24 of the German Basic Law.

[524] See Steindorff, *op. cit. (n.* 519), pp. 51f and 48, emphasizing the need for uniformity in the enforcement of rules of competition; Ipsen, *op. cit.* (n. 478), p. 20f emphasizing the principle of effectivity in the EEC; and Simson, "Der politische Wille als Gegenstand der europäischen Gemeinschaftsverträge," in *Festschrift Otto Riese,* 83, 93f (1964): "So wie der rechtsstaatlich verfasste Staat einen Verstoss gegen die Rechtsstaatlichkeit wohl begehen könnte, aber eben nicht, ohne damit vor aller Augen seine Rechtsstaatlichkeit in Frage zu stellen, so kann auch – das ist die eigentliche Bindungskraft der Verträge, die in diesem Sinne einer Verfassung, d.h. der Identifizierung einer Gemeinschaft mit einer bestimmten Lebensform entsprechen – der einzelne Staat sich von der gewählten Rechtsordnung in keinem einzelnen Punkte lossagen, ohne das Ganze aufzugeben."

Community Court is guardian of this larger perspective against the centrifugal pull of divergent national interests,[525] so the constitutional courts in the Member States also must defend it within their national contexts.[526] Their overriding task, like that of the Community Court, is to draw clear lines of responsibility for national authorities. In isolated cases of conflict between the legal orders, whether express or implied, this means ignoring national laws. Otherwise, the subordination of Community law might trigger a chain reaction or disillusionment among the other Member States and possibly a disintegration of the Communities themselves. This is not a decision to take lightly.

In effect, the national court is exercising its remand function.[527] It is calling for reconsideration of the legislative position without depriving parliament of the ultimate choice. That is to say, Member State parliaments are free to reject in full – just as they only could accept in full – their obligations under any one of the Community Treaties. For the sake of any one special interest, however, they may not negate the Treaties piecemeal.[528] Only on this basis can responsible governmental action be presumed or, to put it another way, can the legislature be presumed to have intended the far-reaching consequences which a rejection of specific Community laws might entail. Only on this basis can the importance of the Communities for the lives of the peoples of the Member States fully be appreciated and respected. Should a Treaty ever be revoked in full by a Member State parliament, then the national courts have reached the limits of their powers and proper function. For then the issue has been clearly drawn, the political decision deliberately taken, the responsibility consciously accepted. The people have chosen.

CONCLUSIONS

It may be concluded that the Community Court has been active in the search for authority in Community law. By its emphasis on the integrity of

[525] See Simson, *id.*, p. 94f; and the discussion of the Community Court's jurisprudence in text *supra*, pp. 323ff and 345ff.

[526] See, e.g., the case comment of Brändel, 4 Europarecht 51, 55f (1969), who supports the authority of the German Federal Constitutional Court to overrule other German courts which misconstrue their obligation under Community law. Since the Community Court is not in a position to do this, he concludes: "Constitutional courts of the Member States are insofar the sole guardians of the EEC Treaty."

[527] Discussed in text *supra*, pp. 310 and 423f.

[528] See Bülow, *op. cit.* (n. 519), p. 51, contending that Germany would only then avoid the supremacy of Community law if the Communities were dissolved or Germany left the Communities.

Community procedures, on a unique conception of Community law and, to a lesser extent, on the need to develop supporting legal sources and its reasoning from effects, the Court has sought to build a lasting base for the Treaty constitutions. At the same time, it has not been unaware of its leading and limited role in the formation of a general Community consensus. The Court has been conscious in the *Vloeberghs* and *Albatros* Judgments of the real limits on its authority when faced with the unwillingness and indifference of the High Authority or Commission and the Member States. It has quite prudently avoided issues which might better be resolved at a future date. Nevertheless, it has gone out of its way – if only by *obiter dicta* – to advocate the supremacy and integrity of Community over national law. In recognizing its overriding responsibility to the search for authority, it has demonstrated a skill and sensitivity for the legitimating power of a court exercising judicial review. This initiative, it would appear, has not been without salient effect on Member State authorities and legal opinion. This has been evident particularly in Italy and Germany. It is with those authorities that the responsibility ultimately rests for the success or failure of the European Communities.

CHAPTER VII

THE SEARCH FOR PRACTICABILITY

The third task of the Court of Justice lies in the search for practicability. It arises, as has already been discussed,[1] from the continuing tension in the law between the almost infinite multiplicity and complexity of social facts and patterns and the need to develop clear and general guides of conduct. Without an appreciation of this tension and of the demands which it places on the articulation of legal rules, the Court runs the danger of oversimplification or, at the other extreme, of a dissolution of the law into the casuistry of an endless line of cases. Both extremes signal a loss of legal control. The one because high levels of abstraction, however profound or logical or systematic, tend to lose contact with social realities and do not meet the practical needs and expectations of an ongoing society. The other because highly individualized rules are of little predictive value and the law loses accordingly in the certainty it can offer legal relationships. Negatively speaking, therefore, the search for practicability requires the judicial avoidance of these two extremes.

Stated positively, the task of the Community Court is to articulate workable or manageable rules of conduct which guide as they control. To achieve this, legal rules must orient on those key points in the underlying systems and pattern of social action from which adjustments in conduct can effectively be made. This often requires a unique ordering of the social factors at work and an assessment of their effects within the stated or implied framework of Community law. Moreover, as Llewellyn has so well phrased it,[2] the well-shaped rule carries its reasoning on its face, offering insight into its scope and goal. The judicial approach which practicability entails has been termed "pragmatic": the good rule is that which works, which is an efficient and effective means to attain specific Treaty goals and values – whether procedural or substantive, implied or express. What is efficient and effective,

1 See text *supra*, p. 133ff.
2 See text *supra*, p. 138f.

as a means to an end, depends in turn on the ability to guide and control those whom the law addresses. The identity of these addressees of the law varies from Community to Community and, more importantly, from rule to rule. Thus, the most workable rules for regulating competition in the oligopolistic coal and steel markets may not be effective in the more competitive markets of household appliances or in the highly regulated and subsidized sectors of agriculture and atomic energy. Further, such rules must not only reflect the kinds of personal motives at work in a market economy, but also the various forms of company organization and management or of business and consumer practices in the Member States. For this reason, pragmatic reasoning in judicial decision demands an intimate understanding of the persons and practices which the law seeks to control. Its aim is not to revise the law, but to give Treaty provisions the most effective articulation in practice.

There is a close relation of the pragmatic reasoning in mind here with the "implied powers" reasoning and the "reasoning from probable effects" discussed in Chapters V and VI. The "implied powers" reasoning is also ends-means reasoning within the framework of the teleological method of interpretation.[3] It is concerned, however, with the existence of a power as implied from the common purposes and text of the Treaties and not with the practical effects or exercise of this power in fact. Just the opposite is true of the "reasoning from probable effects" which is an aspect of the search for authority.[4] It focuses not on the proper scope of Treaty powers, but on the supremacy of these powers over competitive legal orders. It attempts to establish the need to respect the exercise of these powers. It proceeds not from the text, but from the probable consequences to the text resulting from loss in authority. Pragmatic reasoning also looks to effects. The effects in mind, however, are essentially not the responses of power centers in the Communities, although the willing cooperation of legal subjects may be a condition for practicability – and vice versa. Rather, pragmatic reasoning is the attempt to find the rule which will workably bind together both text and the social facts and patterns which it aims to control. Effect and ends-means reasoning, therefore, may be employed in different contexts.

Finally, like the other tasks of the Court, the search for practicability also has an institutional aspect. This has been discussed in terms of the real limits to rule practicability in the judicial process.[5] These are the limits to rule individualization, to a stable or controllable context for rule operation as

[3] See discussion in text *supra*, p. 288ff.
[4] See discussion in text *supra*, p. 378ff.
[5] See text *supra*, p. 198ff.

well as to judicial expertise in many areas of the law. When these limits are reached, the Court may ameliorate its deficiencies to some extent. Yet where this is not possible, it must be prepared to withdraw in favor of other Community organs better suited to the task. This institutional aspect will be discussed in Section 2 of this Chapter. To be considered first, however, is the fundamental task of rule formulation.

1. THE WELL-SHAPED RULE

The Treaties, as may be expected, rarely offer concrete rules of law ready for unambiguous case application. This is true to only a lesser degree of Community legislation. "The normation of economic facts," observes Advocate-General Roemer in an early case,[6] "is a difficult task. It is impossible to avoid the use of concepts which require value judgments and can be grasped only through the knowledge and evaluation of economic relationships." Indeed, the Treaties have gone quite far in attempting such normation. What is even more difficult, however, is the articulation of rules making these concepts workable in practice. There are limits to the inventiveness of the Court to combine all the relevant economic facts in an intelligent and operational statement. There are also demands of administrative efficiency, of clarity and certainty or simply of time pressure, which may call for a rule capable of minimizing or avoiding certain of the complexities or difficulties of a problem. In such cases, conciseness becomes an instrument in the search for practicability. Whether clothed in the form of a legal fiction or of the *prima facie* presumption of a *per se* rule, there has occurred to some extent an intentional and selective distortion of the factual circumstances. The following paragraphs will consider more closely some representative examples in the use and misuse of these forms of judicial rule-shaping.

The Lure of Simplicity

The uses of legal fiction are numerous. As Fuller has so admirably shown, they range all the way from techniques of convenience and persuasion to judicial innovation. By definition, a fiction is "either (1) a statement propounded with a complete or partial consciousness of its falsity, or (2) a false statement recognized as having utility."[7] That is to say, the utility of legal fictions lies in the conscious use of false statements. As a matter of convenience only, which is of interest in this Chapter, fictions are useful shortcuts

[6] Conclusion of *Adv-Gen*. Lagrange, in Case 6/54, 1 Rspr. 241, 245 (1954–1955).
[7] Fuller, *Legal Fictions*, 9 (1967). See his ch. 2 for the motives of legal fiction.

in rule formulation. They confer upon unwieldy and complex or unascertainable factual situations a simplicity which does not exist in fact. As one German writer states:

> We can only regard reality as a Heraclitean flux of happenings, and our thinking itself would be fluid and would run together if it were not that by fiction we obtain imaginary standpoints and boundaries by which we gain control over the flow of reality.[8]

Thus, "constructive notice" avoids the need to prove actual delivery, and the vast and varied resources and economic organization of an enterprise may be subsumed under the guise of a unified "corporate personality". Such fictions offer the Court operative and workable facts or concepts. In employing them, however, it is important to keep their original context and purpose in mind. Only in this way, as Fuller's definition indicates, is it possible to guard against transferring them inappropriately to unrelated fields. Furthermore, the immediate advantage to the Court in adopting such shortcuts must always be weighed against the possible danger of oversimplification in the law.

Precisely this danger was ignored in the judicial decisions reviewing the High Authority's formula for calculating scrap levies. These levies, it will be recalled,[9] were used to compensate the higher cost of scrap purchased on the world market. By this program, the High Authority hoped to ensure a stable market and an adequate supply of scrap at going Community prices without disrupting the market mechanism itself.[10] The compensation program, as the Court made clear in upholding it,[11] influenced market prices only indirectly, but no less affected the price level and other typical market factors, including the supply and demand of related products. Indeed, the surcharge levied on increased scrap consumption by steel-producing enterprises was designed to encourage the adoption of scrap-saving steel-producing processes. It was of the greatest importance, therefore, that the formula for assessing the scrap levy be compatible with the general Treaty

[8] Vaihinger, *Die Philosophie des Als Ob,* 411 (4th ed., 1920), cited and translated by Fuller, *id.,* p. 108f.

[9] See discussion in text *supra,* p. 250f.

[10] In describing the ECSC Art. 53 arrangements, Reuter, "Les interventions de la Haute Autorité," in 5 *Actes Officiels du Congrès Stresa,* 7, 15 (1957), speaks of "un procédé de nivellement des conditions de la concurrence qui s'introduit dans le marché commun"; and Schüle, "Marktinterventionen der Hohen Behoerde und finanzielle Einrichtung," 19 *Z. ausl. öff. R.* 464, 475 (1958), considers them as "immer auf den Markt bezogen."

[11] Judgment 8/57, 4 Rspr. 231, 251 (1958). See text *supra,* p. 254ff.

standards of market control, including non-discrimination[12] and normal competition,[13] as well as with the specific Treaty goals of the scrap program itself.

In Decision No. 2-57 of the High Authority and Council,[14] which revised the scrap program, the scrap levies were based essentially on the "purchased scrap" of Community enterprises. The "own resources" or salvage scrap of these enterprises, on the other hand, were tax-exempt.[15] In practice, unfortunately, these terms were far from clear. Although apparently self-explanatory, being nowhere defined in the Decision itself, they became the source of considerable litigation. In effect, the Court was delegated the task of defining, delimiting and shaping them into workable rules adapted to a functioning scrap compensation program.

Before proceeding further, it is instructive and consistent with topical reasoning[16] to consider three alternative perspectives for analyzing these terms. They are suggested, but not sufficiently developed, by Advocate-General Lagrange.[17] Each of them – conceptual, technical and economic – is reflected in the Court's reasoning and offers one or more points of reference for applying the scrap levy. The *conceptual approach* is the most comfortable, because the most familiar, to the jurist. It permits the Court to equate the terms "purchased scrap" and "own resources" with more traditional concepts of the legal order. Thus, while acknowledging the limitations, Lagrange suggests the possibility of defining "purchased scrap" in the civil law sense, i.e., as scrap "acquired by way of sale." Not the legal nature of the enterprise in question but the character of the business transaction would be decisive. Such a definition is obviously open to manipulation,

[12] See discussion in text *supra* pp. 251 and 259ff.

[13] See discussion in text *supra*, p. 270ff.

[14] *Amtsblatt*, 61 (Jan. 28, 1957).

[15] The first two paragraphs of Decision No. 2–57 read:

"1. The total consumption of scrap during a specified period shall be equal to the sum of the tonnages of:
- its total own resources, and
- its deliveries of purchased scrap,

increased by the reduction of stocks, or decreased by the increase of stocks, and reduced, where applicable, by the amount of scrap sold and/or assigned.

"2. The consumption of purchased scrap during the accounting period shall be equal to the quantity mentioned in the proceeding paragraph decreased by:
- its total own resources,
- the decrease in its stocks."

[16] The method of topical reasoning is discussed in text *supra*, pp. 214ff, 233f and 257–260.

[17] See the Conclusions of *Adv-Gen*. Lagrange, in Case 20/58, 5 Rspr. 187, 200ff (1958–59). The complaint itself, however, was dismissed by the Court on procedural grounds.

varying with the form of business transaction elected. Although this definition is implied in the very wording of the term, Lagrange too rejects it as an exclusive criterion.[18]

The High Authority, on the other hand, chose to emphasize the concept of "ownership" in conjunction with the legal nature of "enterprise." When requested by the Scrap Office to define "own resources," it held to the "natural meaning of the term," e.g., the "legal ownership of these resources at the time of their being salvaged." This meant, it continued,

> that an enterprise, which is delimited in all respects by its legal personality, may consider as its own resources any scrap salvaged by itself in such works as are owned by the same legal entity as itself.[19]

According to this view, the scrap salvaged and consumed in a purely steel-producing enterprise would clearly be tax-exempt. But the definition further suggests – causing a flurry of litigation – that scrap arising in manufacturing plants will *only then* be exempt if consumed by steel-producing plants which are vertically integrated on the basis of outright ownership of assets. In contrast to *concerns* of firms controlled by stock ownership, only these *consolidated companies* would possess a single legal personality. Advocate-General Lagrange was clear that, in terms of this definition, the system would obviously lack in logic and be not altogether satisfactory in effect.[20] The question then is whether such illogic is compatible or indeed a necessary compromise with economic realities.

Even the High Authority, however, was not willing to rely exclusively on this conceptual approach. In a letter to the Scrap Office, it drew a special exemption for two steel-producing enterprises whose plants were "integrated locally with one or more plants not belonging to them, but in which scrap is salvaged." The salvaged scrap of all these plants could be considered the "own resources" of the two enterprises. The exemption was based not on the existing organizational ties, but on "the 'local integration' of a single industrial group within which scrap circulates in the same way as in a single enterprise."[21] To some extent – as Lagrange would have it[22] – this

[18] *Ibid.*, pp. 200, 204f.

[19] Letter of the High Authority to the Scrap Office (Dec. 18, 1967, in *Amtsblatt*, 45 (Feb. 1, 1958).

[20] Conclusions of *Adv-Gen.* Lagrange, *op. cit.*, pp. 210–12.

[21] Letter of the High Authority to the Scrap Office (April 17, 1958), reproduced in the Conclusions of *Adv-Gen.* Lagrange, *ibid.*, p. 193f.

[22] Conclusions of *Adv-Gen.* Lagrange, *op. cit.*, p. 200f, distinguishing simply between scrap arising within (chutes propres) and outside (ferrailles d'achat) the locally integrated complex of plants.

exemption is based on a *technical analysis:* the plants in question form an integrated complex whose industrial processes are interdependent. The High Authority's viewpoint, however, is as much geographical as technical. Moreover, in terms purely of the techniques of steel production and manufacture, plants need not be adjacent for their industrial processes to be technically interdependent or coordinated. Rather, from a technical standpoint, it would be much more useful to define "own resources" in terms of the particular industrial process in which it arises, e.g., steel production, steel processing and refining or the manufacturing of steel products. As indeed Lagrange and the Court later point out,[23] scrap circulates continuously through the various stages of production and manufacture. The question is, technically speaking, in which of these several stages is it tax exempt? Considering that the ECSC possesses jurisdiction solely over enterprises "engaged in the production" of coal and steel, "own resources" could logically be limited to scrap arising in the course of steel production. The power to exempt, it may be argued, can reach no further than the power to tax.

A third perspective of analysis emphasizes the *economic* goals and impact of the scrap levy. If, as has been noted above, the scrap program is an indirect means for influencing the market price while preserving the market mechanism, then the rules for applying the concepts of "purchased scrap" and "own resources" must be shaped to this end. Advocate-General Lagrange acknowledges this, but attempts a highly doubtful distinction between market scrap and firm scrap. The scrap program, he says, "concerns only scrap acquired on the market; scrap, which is not on the market, is not part of the program."[24] The key to his distinction is the flow of scrap according to a market price. Thus when, as is typical of scrap moving between the subsidiaries of a concern, the sales or bookkeeping price "at least nearly approaches the market price so that the former is influenced by the latter," then this is sufficient proof of "purchased scrap."[25] On the other hand, the scrap circulating within locally integrated plants – like the "own resources" of a consolidated company – "is normally withdrawn from every influence of the market."[26]

However attractive, the logic of this distinction is deceptive and scarcely compatible with a competitive market mechanism. It neglects the impact of "opportunity costs" – i.e., the cost of opportunities foregone, of doing one

[23] Judgment 42 and 49/59, 7 Rspr. 109, 167 (1961); and Conclusions of *Adv-Gen.* Lagrange, in Case 17 and 20/61, 8 Rspr. 699, 705, (1962).

[24] Conclusions of *Adv-Gen.* Lagrange, in Case 20/58, 5 Rspr. 187, 202 (1958–59).

[25] *Ibid.*, p. 204f.

[26] *Ibid.*, p. 209.

thing rather than another with a particular resource – on allocation decisions within an enterprise. In a competitive market system, as Fellner points out,[27] this principle of efficient resource allocation "is of general applicability to the operations of the enterprise." Aside from short-run constraints and given the goal of profit maximization, no enterprise would consume its own salvaged scrap knowing that an alternative use would bring a higher price.[28] The impact of this principle on allocation decisions is the same whether the enterprise then sells its salvaged scrap, because cheaper sources are at hand,[29] or simply consumes less by introducing scrap-saving steel-producing processes. In both cases, as is certainly the working assumption behind the scrap program, market price is the measure of the alternative use and of the opportunity costs to the firm. For this reason, *all scrap consumed* in the production of steel – whatever its source – bears an express or implied market price and is economically relevant. From an economic viewpoint, therefore, the scrap levy must be based strictly on steel consumption, i.e., on the decision of a firm to allocate scrap to steel production. Any exemptions must adhere closely to the standards of efficient firm performance lest they distort market competition.

Given these three viewpoints, how did the Court mould them into a concrete rule? Its reasoning unfolds in the course of three appeals, here known as the *SNUPAT* I, *SNUPAT* II and *Klöckner* Cases. The plaintiff in *SNUPAT* I[30] – Société Nouvelle des Usines de Pontlieue-Aciéries du Temple – is a fine steel-producing French enterprise, whose shares are owned 99.7% by the automobile manufacturing firm Régie Renault. The latter is the chief consumer of SNUPAT's steel production and furnishes it with large quantities of salvaged scrap. Moreover, technically, financially and organizationally the two have long been subject to a unified control. The plaintiff, therefore, considered the salvaged scrap of Régie Renault to be its "own resources," attacked the attempt of the High Authority to clas-

[27] Fellner, *Emergence and Content of Modern Economic Analysis,* 207 (1960).

[28] For an analysis of "opportunity costs" and the premises which underlie it, see Müstermann, "Die Bedeutung der Opportunitätskosten für die unternehmerischen Entscheidungen," 36 *Z. Betriebswirtschaft: 1. Ergaenzungsheft,* 18 (1966). Fellner, *id.,* however, notes in practice that enterprises do not usually include interest in the costs of using, for instance, internal funds. Nevertheless, such quirks can scarcely be made the basis of analysis and policy aimed at the Treaty goal of economic rationality. For a discussion of this goal, see text *supra,* p. 236ff.

[29] Due to transportation costs, for instance, a steel-producing enterprise would most rationally purchase the scrap salvaged in a second nearby manufacturing enterprise rather than turn to the more remote "own resources" of its own manufacturing plants.

[30] Judgment 32 and 33/58 (*Société Nouvelle des Usines de Pontlieue Aciéries du Temple* (*SNUPAT*) v. *High Authority*), 5 Rspr. 287 (1958–59).

sify it as "purchased scrap" and argued, in the alternative, that it fell within the exception of "local integration" which the High Authority had recognized for other enterprises. It contended, in effect, that scrap arising within the individual plants of a vertically integrated steel-producing and manufacturing concern (so-called "concern scrap") should be treated no differently than if these same firms were part of a consolidated company.

These contentions are rejected, but judicial reasoning is restricted to a bare minimum. It is of no importance, the Court commences, that the transfer of salvaged scrap from Régie Renault to SNUPAT, as the plaintiff has asserted, takes place without reference to the scrap market. While the scrap program is designed "to keep scrap prices at a reasonable level," the costs must be borne by the scrap consumer. "The scrap payments, therefore, rest not on participation in the scrap market, but on scrap consumption."[31] True as this may be, it is misleading: it suggests that scrap consumption is not an integral part of the market mechanism. Yet the preservation of the market mechanism and the competitive impulse which it embodies is a basic premise of the scrap program. Thus, at the very outset, the economic grounds of judicial analysis are subject to doubt.

Unfortunately, the Court fails to redirect its reasoning in considering the exemption of "own resources." This exemption, it concludes, is basically a question of double taxation. The circulating scrap of steel-producing enterprises, within Community jurisdiction, "could be subjected to payments to the subsidy fund only at the risk of twice taxing the same quantity of scrap. This clearly would be inequitable."[32] Just why this would be inequitable, however, is not at all clear. From an economic viewpoint, based purely on scrap consumption, double taxation would not work inequitably on steel-producing firms, but simply be passed on to steel consumers in the form of increased steel costs. At the most, it would burden those steel-producing processes which are more scrap-intensive, for the scrap salvaged as a by-product of these processes would contain a large percentage of taxed scrap. In terms of the revised scrap program, however, this is no objection. The very aim of the penalty levy was to stimulate the introduction of scrap-saving steel-producing processes by Community enterprises.

Nevertheless, by reference to the Treaty requirement of non-discrimination, the Court then attempts to justify and limit this exemption. It is justified, on the one hand, for it stimulates internal economies in a firm without disturbing the interplay of competition. It encourages increases in produc-

[31] *Ibid.*, p. 318.
[32] *Ibid.*, p. 319.

tivity by "a kind of competition known in Germany as Leistungswettbewerb," and thereby accords with the Treaty.

> A steel-producing and scrap-consuming enterprise, which consumes its own salvaged scrap, re-introduces one of its own by-products into the production cycle. Consequently, within the production process of steel from scrap, this re-use clearly leads to an increase in the quantity of steel produced from that scrap which has already been subject to the scrap levy and, therefore, to an increase in productivity.[33]

The Court is apparently assuming that – except for the exemption – an enterprise would not be so intent on salvaging scrap arising in its own plants. This proposition remains unproven. As such, considering the importance of scrap to steel production and its scarcity in the Community, this premise is seriously open to doubt.[34] Moreover, as Advocate-General Lagrange points out in a later case,[35] scrap never constitutes 100% of the raw material of steel production. Indeed, it may account for no more then 50% of inputs in an SM furnace and as little as 25% in a blast furnace. This means, in effect, that goodly portions of scrap salvaged and consumed in a company's own mills are subject to no scrap levy at all – much less a double levy. These portions are further increased by the amounts of scrap arising in a steel producer's manufacturing plants, but salvaged from the steel acquired from third enterprises.[36] Far from simply stimulating internal economies in an enterprise, therefore, the exemption of "own resources" severely discriminates against enterprises possessing no or fewer scrap-producing plants.

The Court then attempts, on the other hand, to limit "own resources" by excluding "concern scrap." To equate "concern scrap" with "own salvage scrap" (chutes propres), it argues, would both violate the basis of the exemption and discriminate against steel-producing enterprises which are not part of a scrap-producing concern. This would not only tend to increase the difference in production costs between these two types of enterprises, as forbidden by ECSC Article 67, but it would do so as the result of "accidental geographical, administrative or financial ties which are basic to the notion of 'concern'." Such "chance links" (liens contingents), concludes the Court, run counter to the Treaty concept of "productivity" (rendement),

33 *Ibid.*, p. 319f.

34 See Steindorff, "Finanzielle Einrichtungen," in *Zehn Jahre Rechtsprechung des Gerichtshofs der Europäischen Gemeinschaft,* 437, 454 (1965).

35 Conclusions of *Adv-Gen.* Lagrange, in Case 42 and 49/59, 7 Rspr. 179, 201 (1961).

36 See Conclusions of *Adv-Gen.* Lagrange, in Case 17 and 20/61, 8 Rspr. 699, 709 (1962), raising this point without elaboration.

"which refers only to the results of efforts made by individual enterprises" and not to measures – whether public or private – which would "artificially modify the normal interplay of competition." Indeed, the variations in the legal structure of a concern over time are said to "demonstrate the arbitrary and changing character of its structure" and can not be viewed, therefore, as "typical factors of efficiency in the steel-producing enterprise."[37] And yet, it must be wondered why the legal structure of a concern, especially one possessing virtually 100% of its subsidiaries' shares, is any more the product of "chance links" than a vertically consolidated company. The Court sees no need to answer this, for it concludes that the exemption of "concern scrap" from the scrap levy would constitute a *per se* discrimination in violation of ECSC Article 4.[38]

Having failed to obtain an exemption for itself, SNUPAT attacks the exemption of "local integration" in a second suit.[39] Could a group of steel-producing and manufacturing firms, which are technically integrated with and geographically adjacent to but legally independent of each other, exempt their salvaged scrap from the scrap levy? After first rebuffing the High Authority for ignoring the reasoning of *SNUPAT* I,[40] the Court goes on to equate the exception of "local integration" with its previous assessment of "concern scrap." To exempt the one, like the other, from scrap payments would be discriminatory under the Treaty because based on "essentially geographical and, thus, chance links."[41] Due to the costs of transportation –

> It would be unjust as well to subject the scrap circulating between two different companies to differing regulations, depending on whether their plants lie closely adjacent or far from each other .... This could increase artificially the differences in production costs, which would run counter to the Treaty as well as to the basic principles of the compensation program.[42]

This is simply a logical extension of the reasoning in *SNUPAT* I.

The Court then shifts its emphasis markedly from an economic to a strictly legal analysis. Neither of the two groups of firms in question is said to constitute "a single enterprise." Within the meaning of the Treaty,

> the concept of "enterprise" coincides with the legal concept of natural or legal personality, for the Treaty employs that concept primarily for the purpose of designating persons having rights and duties.[43]

37 Judgment 32 and 33/58, 5 Rspr. 287, 320f (1958–59).
38 *Ibid.*, p. 321.
39 Judgment 42 and 49/59 (*SNUPAT* v. *High Authority*), 7 Rspr. 109 (1961).
40 *Ibid.*, p. 162f.
41 *Ibid.*, p. 164.
42 *Ibid.*, p. 165.
43 *Ibid.*, p. 164.

Absent a Treaty provision to the contrary, it continues, there is no basis for assuming that two distinct companies could form a single enterprise. Otherwise, it would be frequently impossible to identify those "enterprises" designated in ECSC Article 80. Even total local integration, where the enterprises' production is economically interdependent, can not change the fundamental fact that different juridical personalities are represented. He who chooses a particular legal form, admonishes the Court, for whatever advantages he expects to gain, must also be prepared to accept whatever disadvantages come with it.[44]

In the course of the *SNUPAT* Judgments, therefore, the concept of "own resources" has been defined wholly in terms of legal personality. Absent the exception of "local integration", this is essentially the position of the High Authority first cited. The Court has fully abandoned the technical and economic viewpoints in favor of the conceptual approach. The scrap arising in various steel-producing, steel-processing and manufacturing plants will be exempt from the scrap levy, depending simply on whether these plants are part of a consolidated company subject to Community jurisdiction. True, at one point, the Court appears prepared to limit the source of "own resources" to steel-producing plants only. Under the ECSC Treaty, it says, such firms "can never form a single enterprise" with their locally integrated manufacturing firms, because Article 80 concerns only those enterprises "engaged in production in the field of coal and steel."[45] This technical formula, unfortunately,[46] is suggested only by way of negative pregnant and is rejected by other language in the Judgment. At one point, for instance, not the technical analysis but simply the legal identity between the salvager and buyer of scrap is emphasized.[47] And at another, it is decisive that the salvaged scrap was "from the beginning the property of an enterprise within the meaning of the Treaty," i.e., "had the same owner, in the strict sense of that word, from the point of its 'production' to the point of its consumption."[48] It appears that the Court is irretrievably wedded to the standard of legal personality.

It is well to consider just why the Court felt compelled to adopt such a conceptualized definition of "own resources." Certainly, the Treaty makes this nowhere clear.[49] Its provisions touch the Community coal and steel

44 *Ibid.*, p. 165.

45 *Ibid.*

46 See text *supra*, p. 438.

47 Judgment 42 and 49/59, 7 Rspr. 109, 166f (1961).

48 *Ibid.*, p. 167f.

49 As Frieur concludes in his *La CECA: Activité et Evolution* 260 (1963), the High Authority has adopted differing criteria of "enterprise" depending on the material in question.

enterprises from a variety of viewpoints – market regulation,[50] price publication,[51] information,[52] financial aid[53] and judicial control[54] – none of which is expressly delimited by the concept of legal personality. For this reason, as Richemont has pointed out,[55] the definition of "enterprise" depends in large part on the concrete application of the Treaty provisions. And, as has just been seen, the attempt to draw strict distinctions between law and economics may have serious and undesirable consequences.

The Court apparently recognized the difficulty, but was not clear how to overcome it. In the *Klöckner* Case,[56] decided just a year after *SNUPAT* II, it further defends its conceptualist position. As in *SNUPAT* I, here too concerns were challenging the levy on scrap drawn from their own subsidiaries; their overall integration, the plaintiffs insisted, was so complete as to justify equating this scrap with the "own resources" of a single enterprise. The issues are basically the same. The primary difference is simply that here not the steel-producing subsidiaries but the parent companies themselves are leading the attack. What is involved, in the words of Advocate-General Lagrange, is "a kind of withdrawal action" by the plaintiff holding companies.[57] Yet, instead of disposing of the appeal in short, by reference to its previous judgments, the Court takes the pains once again of attempting to justify its position in full.

At the very outset, it sets forth the underlying problem as one of rule practicability. Community financial arrangements, on the one hand, must be planned –

> to take account of the economic realities to which they must be applied, so that the desired goals can be reached on the most favorable conditions and with the least sacrifice for the interested enterprises.[58]

On the other hand, this principle of justice "must be harmonized with the principle of legal certainty, which in turn rests on the requirements of justice and economy." The Court then outlines its approach to reconciling these two competing ends of the law:

[50] ECSC Arts. 4, 65 and 66.
[51] ECSC Art. 60.
[52] ECSC Arts. 47 and 86(4).
[53] ECSC Arts. 54–56.
[54] ECSC Arts. 33–36.
[55] de Richemont, "La notion d'entreprise dans le droit des Communautés européennes," *Le droit européen,* 306, 314 (1963).
[56] Judgment 17 and 20/61 (*Klöckner-Werke AG and Hoesch AG* v. *High Authority*), 8 Rspr. 653 (1962).
[57] Conclusions of *Adv-Gen*. Lagrange, in Case 17 and 20/61, *ibid*., p. 701.
[58] Judgment 17 and 20/61, *ibid*., p. 686.

> By virtue of the complex and changing character of economic life, the institution and functioning of a financial arrangement – designed to guarantee the equilibrium on the common market – require the application of clear and objective criterion to a great number of cases with certain common basic traits. It is not possible to take account of all the differences which may exist in the organization of the economic units subject to the High Authority without otherwise hindering the activity of the Authority and its effectiveness.[59]

The very shaping of the rule, therefore, entails a selective treatment of the underlying economic realities subject to regulation.

This selective treatment is then applied to the concept of "purchased scrap." The word "purchased" is to be given a broad interpretation. It does not entail all the conditions of a sales contract but simply "the transfer of scrap for a price by an outsider to a scrap-consuming enterprise." [60] This means that "every movement of scrap between different enterprises is taxed, even in cases which from an economic standpoint represent no actual transfer of value." [61] Thus, neither Klöckner's attempt to characterize the scrap transfers as simply "exchange transactions" between subsidiaries,[62] nor the attempt of Hoesch's steel-producing subsidiary to reserve property rights in the scrap of the steel transferred to manufacturing subsidiaries, could alter the character of "concern scrap" and exempt it from the levy.[63]

It remained only to define the concept of "scrap-consuming enterprise." By similar reasoning, the court also avoids an economic interpretation of this concept.

> An enterprise consists of the unified organization of personnel, material and intangible factors, which belong to a distinct legal subject and are directed for a prolonged period toward certain economic goals.[64]

As a matter of fact, however, "the unity of economic activity does not entail unity in the legal sense." Rather, "by the mere fact of creating an independent legal personality, the law recognizes the formal autonomy and individual responsibility of enterprises." By this means, regardless of the economic realities, "individual subsidiaries are attributed by law the direction and business risks of their activities." [65] This would be no less true for a highly integrated concern, concludes the Court, since "its activity unfolds between

[59] *Ibid.*
[60] *Ibid.*
[61] *Ibid.*, p. 688.
[62] *Ibid.*, p. 690.
[63] *Ibid.*, p. 691.
[64] *Ibid.*, p. 687.
[65] *Ibid.*

those entities [subsidiaries] which legally are the parties to economic exchange."[66] Nor does it matter that the High Authority may have defined the concept of "enterprise" differently within the framework of its investment or general taxation programs. These go to other areas of Community regulation and are not decisive for the scrap program.[67] The strictly legal concept of "enterprise," therefore, was considered to be a permissible criterion for determining those subject to the scrap levy.

This criterion certainly is, in the words of the Court, "clear and objective." Indeed, it was believed to be "justified by the practical advantages which a simple and clear criterion of distinction entail."[68] Another criterion, of course, might well be more favorable to industrial concerns. In view of the difficulty of drawing sharp distinctions between the numerous types of industrial concerns possible, however, such a criterion "could produce very serious uncertainty in its practical application." It could, therefore, "have created an obstruction to the proper functioning of the scrap program and, in certain circumstances, a source of discrimination itself."[69]

Practicability alone, of course, cannot be the whole answer. Even a "clear and objective" criterion, as Advocate-General Lagrange admonishes the High Authority,[70] also must be legally justified. To demonstrate this, the Court turns once again to a discussion of discrimination. It does not deny that its concept of "enterprise" – as the plaintiffs contend – leads to "noticeable disadvantages" for concerns in competition with consolidated companies. This fact, however, was not sufficient to establish discrimination under the Treaty. Discrimination can only be established

> if the High Authority has treated comparable situations differently and thereby injured certain parties, without being able to justify this difference in treatment by objective distinctions of some importance.[71]

In other words, while ignoring certain similarities in the production conditions of concerns and consolidated companies, these two types of enterprises could justifiably be distinguished on the basis of "their legal struc-

66 *Ibid.*, p. 687f.

67 *Ibid.*, p. 689.

68 *Ibid.*, p. 694. The strictly legal concept of "enterprise" as the decisive criterion for measuring the scrap levy has been affirmed most recently in Judgment 50/65 (*Acciaierie e Ferriere di Solbiate* v. *High Authority*), 12 Rspr. 509, 521 (1966).

69 Judgment 17 and 20/61, *op. cit.*, p. 694.

70 Conclusions of *Adv-Gen.* Lagrange, *ibid.*, p. 713. See also Börner, "Diskriminierung und Subventionen," in *Zehn Jahre Rechtsprechung*, 216, 227 (1965).

71 Judgment 17 and 20/61, *id.*, p. 692f. Börner, *id.*, p. 229, criticizes this statement as self-contradictory. This need not follow, however, if the first clause is read as a general statement of logic and the second as the applicable value standard.

ture."[72] The Court, unfortunately, does not specify what justifies this basis of distinction. Clearly not the Treaty standards of economic rationality and market competition mentioned in *SNUPAT* I. From an economic point of view – as the plaintiffs provocatively suggest[73] – legal structure is simply another of those "chance links" which were rejected in *SNUPAT* I and II. And from the viewpoint of competition, the market policies of highly integrated concerns as well as of consolidated companies are equally subject to unified control.[74] Nor, as has already been noted,[75] is there any reason to limit the Treaty goal of economic rationality to enterprises operating as a single legal personality.

The Court, therefore, has never satisfactorily established the nexus between its conceptual approach and the goals of the scrap levy. It has failed to shape the concepts of "purchased scrap" and "own resources" into rules consonant with the technical and economic underpinnings of the compensation program. In short, its approach – as that of the High Authority – has been conceptualistic rather than functional. Having concentrated on the notion of "enterprise" rather than on the activities of scrap consumption and steel production, it has followed the High Authority into a legal dead-end. No matter how the concept of "enterprise" is twisted and turned, whether excluding or including industrial concerns, some types of enterprises were to be put at a competitive disadvantage. This disadvantage rests not upon criteria of economic rationality, as the Treaty requires, but upon the "chance links" of legal structure. Moreover, such links may be subject to manipulation: one lawyer reports that as the trend of the Court's reasoning became clear, three or four holding companies altered their organizational structure to avoid similar liabilities in the future.[76] The Court, therefore, erred in the extreme of simplicity. It unnecessarily adopted a concept which was inappropriate, in terms of the scrap program and the more general Treaty goals, as a point of adjustment for the actions of scrap-consuming enterprises. While it expressly recognized the general requirement of practicability in Community law, it failed to shape a workable rule in practice.

[72] Judgment 17 and 20/61, *id.*, p. 693.
[73] *Ibid.*
[74] See Börner, *op. cit.*, p. 224.
[75] See discussion in text *supra*, p. 440f.
[76] Pinckernelle, "Finanzielle Einrichtungen," in *Zehn Jahre Rechtsprechung des Gerichtshofs der Europäischen Gemeinschaften*, 456, 457 (1965).

Per se Analysis

The use of *per se* rules has long been an integral part of market regulation in United States antitrust law. That is to say, certain kinds of business conduct have come to be viewed as illegal, independent of an examination of their market effects in the particular case or of the circumstances which led to them.[77] In the past, the Supreme Court has applied this standard to price-fixing and market-sharing agreements as well as to boycotts or concerted refusals to deal. Where applicable, as Kaysen and Turner point out,[78] *per se* rules have the advantage of administrative simplicity; they are relatively clear and to a great extent self-enforcing, for they avoid the need to evaluate complex market effects and conditions. They tend, therefore, to lessen the volume and complexity of legal proceedings as well as the uncertainty in economic regulation.

By their own logic, on the other hand, these rules must be limited to types of market practices and behavior which can readily be identified. They lack the flexibility and sophistication to deal with the more complex economic situations where the value balance may shift from case to case. From the very beginning, therefore, the prohibited practices must entail fairly clearly a significant degree of harm for the market mechanism. These practices, to summarize the alternatives of Kaysen and Turner, must be either always harmful, sometimes harmful and sometimes neutral or at least – where the consequences tend to vary from situation to situation – far more harmful than beneficial in the aggregate.[79] Indeed, the most rudimentary standards of justice require that the element of arbitrariness, which the strictness of *per se* analysis implies, be justified by the generally harmful effects which the forbidden practices are believed to cause. For these reasons, the advantages of administrative simplicity must be weighed against the need for a more flexible analysis of market effects.

At first glance, the Treaty provisions regulating competition do not appear to permit *per se* determinations. ECSC Article 65 § 1 and EEC Article 85 (1) both condition the prohibition of restrictive practices among enterprises on their tendency to impede or distort competition on the common markets. In practice, however, the Community Court has employed con-

[77] This is the definition of Kaysen and Turner, *Antitrust Policy: An Economic and Legal Analysis,* 142 (1959). Cf. Neale, *The Antitrust Laws of the U.S.A.*, 21 (1962), who describes the *per se* rule more as a rule of construction or evidence which establishes an irrefutable presumption of illegality when certain facts are proven.

[78] Kaysen and Turner, *id.*, p. 142f.

[79] *Ibid.*

cepts and presumptions in a manner akin to *per se* rules. In the *Geitling* Case, as has already been observed,[80] the Court struck down a tying clause in the trading regulations of the Ruhr sales agencies, requiring minimum purchases by coal wholesalers who wished to trade with any one of these agencies. In doing so, it declared:

[A]ny limitation upon the number of wholesalers allowed as direct customers restricts or distorts competition between the wholesalers, however many of them there may be.[81]

This proposition was not developed further by later cases.

In subsequent cartel judgments, moreover, the Court adopts two other rather simplifying presumptions. Thus, in one case, it defines the "relevant market" under ECSC Article 65 § 2 c) in a very conceptualistic fashion. Instead of attempting to draw the effective geographical limits of Ruhr coal competition, based on transport costs and other factors, it simply employs a Community-wide territorial boundary.[82] It then goes on, at another point, to employ a countervailing power theory in determining the permissible size of "benevolent" coal cartels. In highly oligopolistic markets, reasons the Court,

the influence of a selling organization depends not so much on the product quantities which it controls as on those controlled by rival organizations.[83]

The reorganization of the Ruhr from three into two sales cartels is lawful, therefore, since each is no larger than the Charbonnages de France. Each of the two "is confronted in the same coal field and in other areas of the common market with economic units approximately equal in strength."[84]

However valid for the ECSC, this rather conceptualistic approach to market analysis is of little general value in the context of the EEC. The Common Market, while restricted to "interstate trade", covers a whole variety of industries and economic sectors whose market structure is not always or so apparently oligopolistic as that of the coal and steel market. More typically, competition will exist among one or more large firms and a scattering of smaller ones, all attempting to protect their market shares by

80 See discussion in text *supra*, pp. 272–274.

81 Judgment 2/56 (*"Geitling" Ruhrkohlen-Verkaufsgesellschaft mbH et al.* v. *High Authority*), 3 Rspr. 9, 43 (1957). Emphasis added.

82 Judgment 13/60 (*"Geitling," "Mausegatt" and "Präsident" Ruhrkohlen-Verkaufsgesellschaften mbH* v. *High Authority*), 8 Rspr. 177, 231f and 235 (1962), discussed in text *supra*, p. 278ff.

83 *Ibid.*, p. 233.

84 Judgment 66/63 (*Netherlands* v. *High Authority*), 10 Rspr. 1147, 1182 (1964), discussed in text *supra*, p. 283ff.

the whole gamut of monopolistic tactics at their disposal. As the Chief of Germany's Antitrust Division has argued, the Common Market as an economic and political goal of the Rome Treaty should not be identified with the narrower concept of the "relevant market." This, he asserts, is clear from the language of EEC Article 85 (1) c), prohibiting "the division of markets or sources of supply." The "relevant market" must simply be larger than any one area of a Member State.[85]

The fact remains, however, that the Court is faced in the EEC with the application of Treaty provisions not unlike those in the ECSC Treaty. Indeed, EEC Article 85 has been said to be unmistakably an extrapolation of ECSC Article 65.[86] Thus, like its ECSC counterpart, that Article begins with a general statement of prohibited practices:

(1) The following practices shall be prohibited as incompatible with the Common Market: all agreements between enterprises, all decisions by associations of enterprises and all concerted practices which are capable of affecting trade between Member States *and* which are designed to prevent, restrict or distort competition within the Common Market *or* which have this effect.[87]

In particular, this proposition is then said to include direct or indirect price-fixing, market-sharing, discriminatory and tying practices as well as production, market, technical development and investment controls or limitations. All these practices, according to Article 85 (2), are "automatically null and void." Under the conditions in Article 85 (3), however, the prohibition in 85 (1) may be declared inapplicable in the case of:

- any agreement or category of agreement between enterprises,
- any decision or category of decisions by associations of enterprises, and
- any concerted practice or category of concerted practices

which helps to improve the production or distribution of goods or to promote technical or economic progress, whilst allowing consumers a fair share of the resulting profit and which does not:

(a) subject the enterprises in question to any restrictions which are not indispensable to the achievement of the above objectives; or
(b) enable such enterprises to eliminate competition in respect of a substantial part of the goods concerned.

[85] Günther, *Relevanter Markt im Recht der Wettbewerbsbeschränkungen*, in 47 Jurist. Studiengesellschaft Karlsruhe 21 (1960).

[86] Riesenfeld, "Protection of Competition," in Stein and Nicholson, *American Enterprise in the European Common Market*, vol. II, p. 197, 327 (1960).

[87] The translation is that of Graupner, *The Rules of Competition in the EEC*, 198 (1965). Emphasis added.

Like ECSC Article 65, therefore, EEC Article 85 sweepingly prohibits anti-competitive practices, but provides dispensation under specific conditions for those practices which have an overall salutary effect.

The first opportunity for the Court to examine this provision came up in the *Bosch* Case, decided in April 1962.[88] The case arose by way of "preliminary question" from The Hague Court of Appeals. In the original proceeding, the Bosch refrigerator manufacturing enterprise in Germany, together with its exclusive dealer in Holland had obtained a judgment against the Dutch firm de Geus for interfering with an export prohibition which Bosch had laid upon its German dealers. At the urging of the defendant upon appeal, The Hague Court requested the Community Court to determine whether the prohibition was null and void under EEC Article 85 (2), so far as it concerned export to the Netherlands. As Advocate-General Lagrange remarks,[89] the request touched "the functioning of a particularly sensitive area of the Common Market where it is most necessary to reconcile the common interest with legal certainty." Legal certainty was at issue, but only within a distinctly limited context. Rather than address itself to the particular export clause in question, the Court restricts its answer to the "pure question of Treaty interpretation."[90] This was, in its mind, determining the legal effect of Article 85 and establishing a practicable relationship between its three paragraphs.

In a clear and reasoned judgment,the Court affirms the "self-executing" character of Article 85.[91] This is implied by Articles 88 and 89, granting Member State authorities the right to enforce Article 85 from the moment the Treaty took effect. Due to the provision for granting dispensation to certain otherwise prohibited practices, however, the legal effect of 85 (2) had to be carefully differentiated. In particular, by implication of Article 89, dispensation for otherwise prohibited practices under Community law would only then be in order with the passage of the first implementation Regulation to Article 85.[92] To void such practices automatically before the machinery for their exemption could take hold, declared the Court, "would contradict the general principle of certainty in the law." As a result, until the passage of this Regulation, those practices prohibited by Article 85 (1) are

[88] Judgment 13/61 (*Kledingverkoopbedrijf de Geus en Uitdenbogerd* v. *Robert Bosch GmbH and N.V. Maatschappij tot Voortzetting van de Zaken der Firma Willem van Rijn*), 8 Rspr. 97 (1962).

[89] Conclusions of *Adv-Gen*. Lagrange, *id.*, p. 123f.

[90] Judgment 13/61, *id.*, p. 115. See discussion in text *supra*, p. 401f.

[91] *Ibid.*, p. 111f.

[92] This was to occur within three years after the Treaty came into force. See EEC Art. 87(1).

only then void when so declared by the Commission under Article 89 (2) or by Member State authorities under Article 88. Moreover, even when this Regulation comes into force, the existing practices of Community enterprises and associations are not void, if duly registered. Rather, they have "temporary validity" *until* and insofar as the Commission or Member State authorities refuse them approval. Those otherwise prohibited practices not duly registered, on the other hand, are null and void from the time the first implementation Regulation takes effect.[93] This solution runs fully parallel to that adopted by the Court for ECSC Article 65.[94] As to the practice of exclusive dealing in particular, however, the Court was less than clear. "It is not impossible," it concludes laconically,[95] that the export clause in question falls within the purview of Article 85 (1).

Even with the enactment of Council Regulation 17, the first implementing Regulation to EEC Articles 85 and 86,[95a] the "self-executing" effect of Article 85(1) still raised questions. For instance, would the registration of a standard agreement with the Commission be effective as to all such agreements concluded contemporaneously or subsequently to the registration? The Court affirmed this in the *Bitsch* Case, noting that the registration put the Commission on notice of the contract's existence and "allowed it to obtain more complete information at any time." [95b] Further, since the Regulation did not apply to all potentially prohibited agreements, what of agreements expressly exempted from registration? As the *Bilger* Case demonstrates, an exclusive dealing contract (between a German brewery and an innkeeper) might not be subject to registration because it involves "neither imports nor exports between Member States"; yet due to the broader language in EEC Article 85(1), it could be said to "affect trade between Member States." As in *Bosch,* the Court again emphasizes the need to avoid any solution that "would seriously jeopardize legal certainty." In the absence of any Community regulation, it reasons, Member State authorities (including their courts) remain competent to apply EEC Article 85 in accordance with Article 88. Since parties to such exempt agreements, "which are scarcely capable of affecting trade between Member States," could "reasonably assume that their agreement would to this extent have the same effect as registered agreements," the Court concludes that agree-

[93] Judgment 13/61, *op. cit.*, p. 113f.

[94] See Judgment 1/58 (*Friedrich Stork & Co.* v. *High Authority*), 5 Rspr. 43, 67ff (1958–59).

[95] Judgment 13/61, *op. cit.*, p. 115.

[95a] Council Regulation No. 17–62 (Feb. 6, 1962). *Amtsblatt,* 204 (Feb. 21, 1962).

[95b] Judgment 1/70 (*Parfums Marcel Rochas Vertriebs-GmbH* v. *Bitsch*), 16 Rspr. 515, 522–524 (1970).

ments which are exempt from registration and are not registered remain fully valid so long as their invalidity has not been established.[95c]

The *Bosch* Decision also left undecided the civil law effect of registered agreements. Would an agreement be enforceable among the parties, pending a determination by the Commission whether the dispensation provisions in EEC Article 85(3) are applicable? This question was raised in the *Smith Corona* Case, where one party attempted to justify its breach of an exclusive distributorship agreement by reference to the prohibitions in EEC Article 85(1). In a decision arising under the "preliminary question" procedure, the Court in effect disallowed this defense. Registered agreements, which may be prohibited by Article 85(1), are fully valid so long as the Commission has not issued a decision pursuant to Article 85(3). The Court based its reasoning once again on the demands of practicability in the law. Since, as presently constituted, the parties had no right to accelerate the Commission's consideration of the agreements under Article 85(3), it "would contradict the general principle of certainty in the law" to conclude that such agreements were not fully effective until the Commission's decision was rendered. While this position might create some "practical hardships" under some circumstances, "the difficulties which could result from the uncertainty of the legal relationships based on registered agreements would be even more harmful." [95d]

In none of the above decisions, however, did the Court reach the substance of exclusive dealing arrangements. In fact, four years elapsed after the *Bosch* Decision before the Court spoke again on the matter. By that time a number of cases had collected and substantial Community legislation had evolved.[96] The first step in this direction was Regulation 17, which was adopted in February 1962 with special regard for the dispensation provisions of EEC Article 85(3).[97] It was designed "to meet the need of ensuring effective supervision by means of the simplest administrative

[95c] Judgment 43/69 (*Brauerei A. Bilger Söhne GmbH* v. *Jehle*), 16 Rspr. 127, 137 (1970).

[95d] Judgment 10/69 (*S.A. Portelange* v. *S.A. Smith Corona Marchant International et al.*) 15 Rspr. 309, 316 (1969).

[96] For a survey of this legislation, Van Damme, "La mise en oeuvre des Articles 85 et 86 du Traité de Rome, *Cah. dr. européen,* 35 (esp. at p. 38 n. 10), 279, 402 and 602 (1966) and 49 (1967). In particular, the EEC Council limited the application of the rules of competition in the sectors of agriculture and transportation.

[97] Regulation No. 17–62 (Feb. 6, 1962), *Amtsblatt,* 204 (Feb. 21, 1962). Its reference to EEC Art. 86, concerning the misuse of market power, will not be discussed here. See Van Damme, *id.*, p. 422ff.

control." [98] To achieve this, it required Community enterprises, who wished to take advantage of the dispensation provisions, to notify the Commission of their agreements, decisions and concerted practices.[99] Then, subject to review by the Community Court, the Commission was given exclusive power to grant the exemptions.[100] The Commission was concerned, however,

> that such agreements, decisions and concerted practices are probably very numerous and cannot, therefore, be examined at the same time and, on the other hand, that a number of them have special features which may make them less of a threat to the development of the Common Market.[101]

As a result, it appeared desirable "to introduce a more flexible system" for processing certain groups of practices, "without, however, prejudicing the question of their validity under Article 85." Accordingly, certain groups of practices of lesser economic importance need not be registered with the Commission, although they fall within the aegis of Article 85 (1).[102] Moreover, in all other cases, where doubt exists as to the legality of a practice, interested enterprises can request the Commission to issue a "negative clearance." It states, in effect, that on the facts known the Commission had no grounds for intervening with a specific practice.[103] These procedures were then implemented by subsequent Regulations of the Commission.[104]

As a matter a fact, this emphasis on efficient and workable procedures was not exaggerated. The EEC Commission was soon inundated by a flood of agreements, decisions and concerted practices, and requests for dispensation. Within two years after the passage of Regulation 17 – by April 1964 –

[98] Regulation No. 17–62, *id.*, Motivation, para. 3. Moreover, besides the major aspects mentioned in the text, the Regulation also establishes fines and penalties for offenses, regulates the jurisdiction between the Commission and Member State authorities, grants a right of hearing to third parties interested in Commission Decisions and provides the Commission with investigative powers.

[99] Regulation No. 17–62, *op. cit.*, Arts. 4 and 5. The deadlines for notifying existing agreements are set in Arts. 5(1) and 7(2).

[100] *Ibid.*, Art. 9.

[101] *Ibid.*, Motivations, par. 5.

[102] *Ibid.*, Arts. 4(2) and 5(2), and Motivations, par. 6. See text *supra* at note 95c.

[103] *Ibid.*, Art. 2, and Motivations, par. 7.

[104] See EEC Commission Regulation No. 27–62 (May 3, 1962), *Amtsblatt*, 1118 (May 10, 1962) (re notification procedures and application for "negative clearance"); Regulation No. 153–62 (Dec. 21, 1962), *Amtsblatt*, 2918 (Dec. 24, 1962) (introducing notification procedures for certain types of exclusive dealing contracts); and Regulation No. 99–63 (July 25, 1963), *Amtsblatt*, 2268 (August 20, 1963) (re the rights of the parties concerned and of third parties to a hearing).

they had reached the appalling figure of 37,000.[105] Of these, 25,000 were applications for "negative clearance" and for dispensation, which the Commission had just begun to process in 108 instances. The remaining 12,000 were straightforward exclusive dealing contracts without further competitive restrictions. Since they were believed to contain "no clauses particularly likely to distort competition within the Common Market," a simplified procedure was provided for their registration.[106] At least in stimulating the registration of practices, therefore, Regulation 17 appears to have been a resounding success. If, however, these practices were to be processed with that dispatch and predictability required of certainty in the law, the Commission would have to develop a set of clear, easily applicable standards.

Part of the way was paved by the use of legally non-binding "announcements" in the Official Journal of the Communities. Under the heading "Communications," the Commission declared its opinion that exclusive dealing contracts with commercial agents and certain types of patent licensing agreements were beyond the pale of Article 85 (1).[107] Moreover, it announced its intention to grant group dispensation – at least for the time-being – to more simple types of exclusive dealing arrangements.[108] Due to political oppositions from certain Member States as well as legal doubts from other quarters,[109] however, the Commission turned to the Council for the express and general authority to grant such dispensations.[110] This mandate was not forthcoming. Instead, in Regulation 19, the Commission was given a more limited power. On the basis of experience gathered from individual Decisions, it was authorized to define the specific conditions under which certain types of exclusive dealing arrangements and contractual restrictions for the protection of commercial and industrial property rights would be exempt from the application of Article 85 (1).[111] Upon appeal, the Community Court affirmed the legality of this power for these agreements.[112] While the Court did not decide whether and which of these agree-

105 See EEC Commission, Seventh Gen. Rep. 71ff (German ed., 1964). See also p. 62ff and p. 62f of the Eighth and Ninth Gen. Reps. (German eds., 1965 and 1966).

106 See EEC Commission Regulation No. 153–62, *op. cit.*, Motivations, para. 4.

107 See *Amtsblatt,* 2921–23 (Dec. 24, 1962).

108 See *Amtsblatt,* 2627–29 (Nov. 9, 1962).

109 See Deringer and Tessin, "Gruppenausnahmen im EWG-Kartellrecht in Aussicht," *AWD,* 71f (1964); Gleiss and Hirsch, *EWG-Kartellrecht,* 247f (2d ed. 1965); and EEC Commission, Sixth Gen. Rep. 69 (German ed., 1963).

110 See the draft of this Regulation, in *Amtsblatt,* 3318 (Nov. 30, 1964).

111 See Regulation No. 19–65 (March 2, 1965), *Amtsblatt,* 533 (March 6, 1965).

112 Judgment 32/65 (*Italy* v. *EEC Council and Commission*) 12 Rspr. 457 (1966). The plaintiff, believing that these agreements fell without the purview of Article 85(1) and, therefore, beyond the power of dispensation, had lost the vote in the Council of Ministers and carried its case to the Court.

ments would be prohibited by Article 85 (1), it did imply approval of the commission's view that exclusive dealing arrangements with business agents were not of this type.[113]

A way had been opened, therefore, for simplifying the administration of antitrust regulation in the EEC. The procedure of group dispensation would have the dual effect of automatically eliminating a great number of agreements registered from further examination[114] and, by implication, of obviating the need for agreements of this type to be reported in the future.[115] Before this could be attained, however, the Commission had to arrive at a set of clearly definable characteristics which met the requirements of Article 85 (3). This it did in a series of five applications for dispensation concerning various types of exclusive dealing contracts. Of these, three contained no further anticompetitive restrictions, a fourth and fifth forbid the sale of competitive products and the fifth, in addition, included a "closed territory" clause.[116] All but the last were exempted from the application of Article 85 (1). These individual Decisions and their motivations reveal the Commission's view that exclusive dealing contracts on the whole tend to improve the distribution of goods to the benefit of consumers. In particular, such agreements enable the exclusive dealer to maintain a well-stocked line of products, spare parts and accompanying services and to cater to the pecularities of a given market. They facilitate entry into foreign markets and the acquisition of specialized knowledge as well as simplify the complex marketing operation as a whole. As a result, consumers benefit by better and quicker service at not excessive prices. Indeed, due to the increased demand which such arrangements stimulate, the resulting increase in production may lower fixed costs and thereby product prices. Absent market-sharing, price-setting and other further-reaching restrictions on competition,

[113] *Ibid.*, p. 485f. See also Judgment 56 and 58/64 (*Grundig-Consten* Case), 12 Rspr. 321, 387f (1966).

[114] In effect, those 12,000 exclusive dealing agreements registered with the Commission by the simplified procedure. See text *supra* at note 106 and the discussion in Gleiss-Hirsch, *op. cit.* (n. 109), pp. 248 and 357ff.

[115] As is pointed out by Spormann, "Die Gruppenfreistellung zweiseitiger Alleinvertriebsvereinbarungen," *AWD*, 333 (1966), this conclusion can be gathered from the context of the provisions of Regulation 19 and the Motivations of the Commission's draft proposal upon which this Regulation is based.

[116] These are, respectively, the individual Decisions of the EEC Commission: D.R.U.-Blondel, *Amtsblatt*, 2194 (1965); Hummel-Isbeque, *Amtsblatt*, 2581 (1965); Jallatte-Voss and Jallatte-Vandeputte, *Amtsblatt*, 37 (1966); and Grundig-Consten, *Amtsblatt*, 2545 (1964). These Decisions are published, respectively, in *AWD*, 256 and 356 (1965), 63 (1966) and 329 (1964). For a review of them, see in particular Spormann, *id.*, p. 334; and Schluep, *Der Alleinvertriebsvertrag – Markstein der EWG-Kartellpolitik*, 114ff (1966).

therefore, the Commission considered exclusive dealing contracts "at the present indispensable" for a better distribution of goods on the Common Market.[117]

These Decisions being made and the experience gathered, the time was ripe for implementing Regulation 19. Besides the appeal of the Italian Government just mentioned,[118] however, two other cases were up for judgment. The Commission, therefore, withheld publishing the draft of its implementing Regulation until the Community Court had a chance to speak.[119] The first of these two judgments, *Société Technique Minière* (LTM) v. *Maschinenbau Ulm GmbH* (MBU),[120] was handed down in a "preliminary question" procedure initiated by the Court of Appeals of Paris. The plaintiff, seeking to void a minimum requirements obligation, charged that the exclusive dealing agreement violated Article 85 (1). Under the terms of the contract, MBU promised to make delivery within two years and then only to LTM in France. For its part, LTM agreed to maintain a good functioning and well-stocked repair service and not to deal in competitive products without prior consent. The contract contained no "closed territory" provision, so that LTM could re-export UBM's products at will to other countries.[121]

The Community Court restricted its decision to a high level of abstraction. Nevertheless, its reasoning gives insight into judicial method and the position of exclusive dealing contracts within the general framework of Article 85. As to method, the Court begins by rejecting a *per se* prohibition of exclusive dealing agreements under paragraph 1 of that provision. Agreements between Community enterprises are only then prohibited,

> if they fulfill diverse conditions which have less to do with their legal nature than with their relationship to "trade between the Member States" and "competition." The Treaty provision in question, therefore, rests on a two-fold economic evaluation of the effects of agreements.

Despite the absence of a *per se* prohibition, "the existence of particular circumstances or of especially strict clauses for the protection of exclusive

[117] See the Motivations of the last three Decisions of the Commission listed *supra*, note 116.

[118] See text *supra* at note 112.

[119] In *Amtsblatt*, 849 (March 25, 1967), the Commission published the implementing Regulation No. 67–67 of March 22, 1967, by which certain more limited types of exclusive dealing arrangements are freed from the application of the Article 85(1) prohibition until December 31, 1972.

[120] Judgment 56/65, 12 Rspr. 281 (1966).

[121] The plaintiff contended, however, that a *de facto* division of territories did exist by virtue of an obligation arising from commercial usage. *Ibid.*, p. 295.

dealing rights" *can bring* a contract within the purview of Article 85 (1). Only in this case might an agreement be prohibited and required to be registered with the Commission for purposes of 85 (3) dispensation. Whether such an agreement *is* prohibited "depends solely on whether, in the light of the circumstances of the particular case, it objectively fulfills the enumerated criteria of Article 85 (1)."[122]

The Court then proceeds to these enumerated criteria. As to the first, the agreement in question must of course be "between enterprises." Although the Court does not consider the point, it would seem to be referring to the legal concept of "enterprise" developed in the case law of the ECSC Treaty.[123] Thus, in later Judgments, the existence of a contract between two independent "legal persons" – and not simply between an enterprise and its agent – distinguishes the application of EEC Article 85 from Article 86.[124] The Court is clear, however, that Article 85 (1) applies to agreements between enterprises whether on the same (horizontal) or on different (vertical) levels of the economic process.[125] The dispute which long surrounded this question, therefore, has been laid to rest.[126]

Secondly, the agreement must be "capable or affecting trade between Member States." In sharp contrast to much of the literature and the Conclusions of Advocate-General Roemer,[127] this requirement is viewed less as a substantive than as a functional criterion. It –

> marks off the sphere of application of the Article 85(1) prohibition in such a way that it requires a prospective evaluation whether the agreement in question *can* obstruct the erection of a unified market between the Member States.

Only insofar is Article 85 applicable. This requirement is then met –

> when on the basis of all the objective elements of law or fact, it can be predicted with an ample degree of probability that the agreement directly or indirectly, actually or potentially, *can* influence trade between the Member States.

[122] *Ibid.*, p. 302. See also Judgment 23/67 (*S.A. Brasserie de Haecht* v. *Wilkin-Janssen*), 13 Rspr. 543, 555f (1967), which avoids the *per se* illegality under EEC Article 85(1) of exclusive purchasing agreements in the brewery industry.

[123] See discussion in text *supra*, p. 443f.

[124] Judgments 56/65, 12 Rspr. 457, 485f (1966); and 56 and 58/64, 12 Rspr. 321, 387f (1966), discussed in text *supra* at note 113.

[125] Judgment 56/65, *op. cit.*, p. 302f.

[126] See the discussion of Gleiss and Hirsch, *op. cit.* (n. 109), p. 96ff; and of Schluep, *op. cit.* (n. 116), p. 84f. See also Judgment 23/67, *op. cit.*, p. 554f.

[127] See the Conclusions of *Adv-Gen.* Roemer, Case 56/65, *op. cit.*, p. 314: and the discussion of Gleiss and Hirsch, *id.*, p. 109ff; of Schluep, *id.*, p. 85f; and Deringer, *Das Wettbewerbsrecht der EWG:* Kommentar Art. 85(1), Anm. 39ff (1965).

For an exclusive dealing contract to fall within the meaning of Article 85 (1), therefore, it is necessary – although not sufficient – that it "*can* erect trade barriers between the Member States and thereby impede the economic interpenetration intended by the Treaty."[128] Not the fact but the probability of impeding interstate trade, therefore, is decisive. The Court appears to be rejecting the view that the effect on interstate trade must be adverse. If so, then the interstate trade clause serves primarily to delimit the jurisdiction between the EEC and the Member States in the field of antitrust regulation. The question remains, however: just what is "an ample degree of probability" of influencing trade?

The only really substantive criterion of Article 85 (1), then, is whether the agreement in question is "designed to prevent, restrict or distort competition within the Common Market" *or* to "have this effect." These are, said the Court, alternative and not cumulative tests of legality. The one, based on the term "designed," refers to "the actual object of the agreement" in light of "the economic context of its operation." The prohibited distortion of competition "must result from the whole or part of the provisions of the agreement."[129] Should this "objective intent" be lacking, then the effects of the agreement are to be examined. Whereas LTM contended that "even the most negligible" anticompetitive effect brought an agreement within the pale of Article 85 (1),[130] the defendant, the Commission and especially Advocate-General Roemer took a more circumstantial view of the Treaty provision. The agreement in question would not then be prohibited, they argued respectively, if "effective horizontal competition" still exists, unless the agreement results in "a noticeable infringement" of competition or unless the facts prove or indicate a marked infringement of competitive conditions."[131] The Court follows the latter two views:

> For an agreement to be prohibited, the existing conditions must have the total result of noticeably preventing, restricting or distorting competition. The measure of this is the competition which would exist in the absence of the disputed agreement.[132]

Precisely for agreements necessary to the penetration of new markets, the Court continues, "there can be doubt that a distortion of competition ex-

128 Judgment 56/65, *op. cit.*, p. 303. Emphasis added. See also Judgments 23/67, *op. cit.*, p. 556; and 5/69, 15 Rspr. 295, 302 (1969).

129 Judgment 56/65, *id.*, p. 303.

130 *Ibid.*, p. 297.

131 *Ibid.*, pp. 293, 290 and 315, respectively.

132 *Ibid.*, p. 303f.

ists." For this reason, whether an exclusive dealing contract is illegal – due to its purpose *or* its effect – depends on the particular circumstances. That is to say, the Court must consider the nature and amount of the products covered by the disputed agreement, the market power of the parties, whether the contract stands alone or is part of a pattern of agreements and whether it is further protected by territorial restrictions.[133] As to exclusive dealing agreements in general – but particularly for those necessary to the penetration of new markets – the Court adopts a flexible and differentiated approach.

In the *Grundig-Consten* Judgment of just two weeks later,[134] however, this approach was considerably restricted. In both cases, a German producer made the French firm its exclusive distributor in France; yet two factors serve to distinguish this Judgment essentially from its predecessor. In contrast to the *LTM-MBU* Case, the Court is not faced with a "preliminary question" and could not restrict itself, therefore, to an abstract interpretation. The plaintiffs, supported by the Italian and German governments, were attacking an individual Decision of the EEC Commission which condemned their exclusive dealing contract as contrary to Article 85 (1) and ineligible for dispensation under Article 85 (3).[135] Moreover, beyond imposing minimum requirements and reciprocal exclusive dealing obligations, the agreement was part of Grundig's overall "closed territories" approach to distribution on the Common Market. Consten was obligated not to re-export Grundig products (radio, television, tape-recording and dictating equipment) to other Member States. It had also agreed to undertake a reasonable promotional program, to maintain a well-equipped repair and guaranty service and not to deal in competitive products. For its part, Grundig had granted Consten in effect the "closed territory" of France, by laying re-export prohibitions on its exclusive dealers in the other Member States. This protection was reinforced by the issue of the Grundig International trademark "GINT," which all Grundig products in Europe (including Germany) bore and which was registered in France in Consten's name.

The implications of such "closed territory" clauses and their supporting agreements, like exclusive dealing arrangements in general, for the maintenance of competition are far from certain.[136] On the one hand, they insu-

[133] *Ibid.*, p. 304.

[134] Judgment 56 and 58/64 (*Consten S.A.R.L.* and *Grundig-Verkaufs-GmbH* v. *EEC Commission*), 12 Rspr. 321 (1966).

[135] See the Commission's Decision of Sept. 23, 1964, in *Amtsblatt*, 2545 (Oct. 20, 1964). See discussion in text at note 116 *supra*.

[136] That is to say, as one writer puts it: "limitations on competitive activity in one direction *may* strengthen competitive forces in another." Preston, "Restrictive Distribu-

late the exclusive dealer in a given territory from intra-brand competition and, depending on the strength of the brand name on that particular market, increase his monopolistic leverage. "Grundig" is obviously a well-known brand name and some of its products, at least the tape-recording and dictating equipment, supplied about 17% of French sales.[137] In addition, for certain Grundig products, the Commission found actual prices to be running as much as 20% higher in France than Germany. This differential arose at the wholesale level.[138] On the other hand, such vertical territorial restrictions allegedly increase the dealer's readiness to press inter-brand competition as well as to introduce and push new brand names and products on the market. This is of no small importance for entering foreign markets where consumer tastes and business habits are unknown or unfamiliar. Particularly those manufacturers, who lack both a well-known brand name and sufficient credit or capital, may be able to reach the market and maintain their competitive position only by virtue of a risk-splitting venture with distributors. And, for those who can afford it, the prohibition of such arrangements may simply lead manufacturers to integrate forward, thus permanently foreclosing their competitors from existing dealers. These general considerations, however, are only of limited value in the abstract. Their truth depends largely on the concrete circumstances of the case and the existing market structure.[139] There may be good reason, therefore, for avoiding hasty generalizations on the legality of "closed territory" arrangements.

tion Arrangements: Economic Analysis and Public Policy Standards," 30 *Law and Cont. Prob.*, 506, 508 (1965). For a discussion of the underlying business considerations and the economic context of such restrictions, see Preston, *id.*; Schluep, *op. cit.* (n. 116), pp. 42–78 and 166–74; Düsberg, "Wirtschaftliche Analyse der zweitseitigen Alleinvertriebsverträge," 16 *Wirtschaft und Wettbewerb*, 463ff (1963); Champaud, "La concession commerciale," 16 *Rev. trim. dr. comm.*, 451, 453–64 (1963); Travers and Wright, Restricted Channels of Distribution under the Sherman Act," 75 *Harv. L. Rev.*, 795f and 809ff (1962); and Holton, "The Role of Competition and Monopoly in Distribution: The experience of the U.S.," in Miller (ed.), *Competition, Cartels and their Regulation*, 263ff (1963).

137 See the Conclusions of *Adv-Gen.* Roemer, in Case 56 and 58/64, 12 Rspr. 401, 413 (1966).

138 Decision of September 2, 1964, *op. cit.*, p. 2546f. The Commission's analysis, however, has not gone uncriticized. See, in particular, the Conclusions of *Adv-Gen.* Roemer, *id.*, p. 433f.

139 Thus, the decision of the United States Supreme Court in *White Motor Co.* v. *United States*, 372 U.S. 253, 261 (1963) (concerning client as well as vertical territorial restrictions), in remanding the case for trial: "We know too little of the actual impact of such territorial restrictions . . . ," cautioned Justice Douglas, "to reach a conclusion on the bare bones of the documentary evidence before us." As a result, absent price-fixing and given adequate sources of alternative products to meet the needs of the unfranchised, "closed territory" arrangements adjudicated subsequently in the federal courts have been tested in light of the "rule of reason." See *Snap-On Tools Corp.* v.

The Community Court was not of this opinion. Like the EEC Commission,[140] it appears to have been led single-mindedly by the objective of developing clear-cut rules which both meet the need for administrative simplicity and further economic integration. The guiding aim of economic integration is emphasized at the very opening of the Judgment, as the Court once again rejects the view that Article 85 (1) applies only to horizontal agreements between Community enterprises. Agreements between producers and distributors, it concludes,

> which tend to restore the national divisions in trade between Member States, could well thwart the most basic goals of the Community. The Treaty, whose Preamble and text aim at suppressing the barriers between States and which opposes their reintroduction in several strict provisions, cannot allow enterprises to create new barriers of this type.[141]

(This same emphasis can be found in a second Judgment of the same day, upholding the power of the Council and Commission to grant certain types of agreements group dispensation from the application of Article 85 (1). The immediate goals of Article 85, to remove existing trade barriers and ensure honest competition, said the Court, in turn serve "the establishment of a unified market," one of the main objectives of EEC Article 2.)[142]

FTC, 321 F 2d 825 (7th Cir., 1963) (absent evidence that petitioner could monopolize or was monopolizing tool sales, the restriction of distributors but not purchasers of petitioner's products to exclusive territories did not have effects which were "significantly anti-competitive"); *Sandura Co.* v. *FTC*, 339 F 2d 847 (6th Cir., 1964) (since, according to trial court, petitioner's closed territory distributorships increased "the competitive good that flows from interbrand competition without any showing of detriment to *intra*brand competition," the only justified conclusion "is that elimination of the closed territory arrangement would impair competition, rather than foster it"); and *United States* v. *Arnold, Schwinn & Co.*, 388 U.S. 365 (1967) (though subjecting products *sold* to distributors to territorial restrictions upon resale is a *per se* violation of the Sherman Act, this does not necessarily follow where manufacturer retains ownership of the goods "and there is nothing in this record – after elimination of the price-fixing issue – to lead us to conclude that Schwinn's program exceeded the limits reasonably necessary to meet the competitive problems posed by its more powerful competitors"). See also Jordan, "Exclusive and Restricted Sales Areas under the Antitrust Laws," 9 *UCLA L. Rev.*, 111, 155 (1962); and Preston, *op. cit.* (n. 136), p. 508f, who points out: "The present state of economic analysis does not, in general, permit us to specify the impact of changes at one of several vertically related market levels upon structure and behavior at another."

140 See discussion in text *supra*, p. 453f, and EEC Commission, First, Second, Third and Seventh General Reports 62, 82, 116 and 64f (German eds., 1958, 1959, 1960 and 1964), respectively.

141 Judgment 56 and 58/64 (*Grundig-Consten* Case), 12 Rspr. 321, 388 (1966).

142 Judgment 32/65 (*Italy* v. *EEC Council and Commission*), 12 Rspr. 457, 483 (1966).

The Court then develops its reasoning in light of this overriding Community objective. As in the *LTM-MBU* Judgment, the threshold requirement of Article 85 (1) that the agreement in question be "capable of affecting trade between Member States," is reduced to a purely jurisdictional standard. The views of the plaintiffs, the German Government and Advocate-General Roemer, that the agreement must be shown *on balance* to impede interstate trade,[143] are swept aside. In lieu of this, the Court asks

> whether the agreement directly or indirectly, actually or potentially, is capable of *endangering freedom of trade* in a manner which *can impair* the attainment of the *goals of a unified interstate market.*[144]

Thus, the "predictive" test in the previous Judgment,[145] that the agreement is able to impede economic interpenetration among the Member States, has been retained. Here, however, the emphasis has been placed almost exclusively on the freedom of individual enterprises to trade across State lines.[146] As a result, even though the Grundig-Consten agreement might lead to a "considerable increase in the volume of trade between the Member States," it still can fall within the purview of Article 85 (1). It does indeed, the Court concludes, by impeding the import and re-export of Grundig products to and from France. These territorial as well as trademark "limitations on freedom of trade" suffice to bring the Grundig-Consten agreement within the scope (but not yet the prohibition) of Article 85 (1).[147]

This judicial emphasis and approach is followed next in developing and applying the criterion of restrictions on competition. In sharp contrast to the approach of the plaintiffs, the German Government and the Advocate-General,[148] the Court makes no attempt to determine the specific economic effects of the agreement in question on inter-brand competition. Its method is to limit analysis purely to the "intent" test of Article 85 (1). On the one hand, it reasons, competition between producers

> might be generally more obvious than that between distributors of the same brand. This does not mean, however, that an agreement which restricts intra-brand competition would escape the prohibition of Article 85(1) merely because it strengthens inter-brand competition.

143 See Judgment 56 and 58/64, *op. cit.*, pp. 370f, 411f and 414f.

144 *Ibid.*, p. 389.

145 See the *LTM-MBU* Case in text *supra*, p. 459.

146 Cf. the views of Catalano, *Manuel de droit des Communautés Européennes,* 430 (1964); and Verloren van Themaat ,'Gedanken zur Wettbewerbspolitik im Gemeinsamen Markt," *Wirtschaft und Wettbewerb,* 555, 559 (1963).

147 Judgment 56 and 58/64, *op. cit.*, p. 389f.

148 *Ibid.*, pp. 341, 355–60, 364–69, 411–14 and 441–45.

On the other hand,

> once it appears that an agreement is aimed at restricting, preventing or distorting competition, there is no need for purposes of Article 85(1) to consider its concrete effects. In the Decision in question, therefore, the failure of the Commission to examine the effects of the agreement on inter-brand competition is not in itself a legal defect.

The existence of this "aim" or "intent" was obvious to the Court. By means of the re-export restriction and the trademark protection, within the entire context of Grundig's "closed territories" network, the plaintiffs "wanted to remove every possibility of competition in Grundig products on the wholesale level within the contract area."[149] In other words, despite the unconditional language of Article 85 (1), the "relevant market" may be restricted solely to the Grundig products in question. An application of the "intent" criterion, therefore, apparently obviates the need to consider both the economic effects of the agreement and the broader context of inter-brand competition.

To this extent, a conclusive presumption has been erected equal in kind to *per se* illegality. And the Court does not shy from stating the economic considerations upon which it rests. The Grundig-Consten exclusive dealing arrangement, it declares in summary fashion,

> effects an *insulation of the French market* and allows, for the products in question, the imposition of *prices* which are *subject to no effective competition.*

Moreover,

> the more producers are able to distinguish clearly their brand name from other brands in the eyes of consumers, inter-brand competition will tend to diminish.[150]

For this reason, where distribution constitutes a considerable part of total costs, competition between dealers should be encouraged. This, in turn, the

[149] *Ibid.*, p. 390f. The plaintiffs also contended, but to no avail, that in considering the entire "closed territory" network of Grundig within the Community, the Commission had decided "ultra petita" and infringed the "right to be heard" of Grundig dealers in other Member States. *Ibid.*, pp. 353f, 391 and 394f. Indeed, in the more recent *Brasserie de Haecht* decision, cited *supra* in note 122, the Court affirmed that the existence in the same market among other firms of similar exclusive purchasing agreements was "one of several elements to be considered" in determining whether competition had been impaired.

[150] *Ibid.*, p. 391f. Emphasis added.

Court asserts, stimulates the dealers to greater (inter-brand?) competition.[151] Since the agreement in question aims both "at insulating the French market for Grundig products and at artificially maintaining separate national markets within the Community for a very widespread brand name, it distorts competition on the Common Market." [152]

With these few bare economic recitals the Court ends its inquiry. There is no need, it insists, to consider such economic facts as the price differences between France and Germany, the amount of distribution costs borne by Grundig as the *quid pro quo* of territorial protection or the representative character of the factual determinations made by the Commission. Neither these, nor the correctness of the viewpoints chosen by the Commission to compare German and French market conditions, nor even the possible favorable effects of the agreement in other respects, are relevant. Given the competitive restrictions mentioned above, "none of these circumstances could lead to another solution within the framework of Article 85 (1)." [153] The limits to this approach, however, lie in the extreme economic assumptions of the Court's reasoning. These assumptions are subject to serious questioning. If it were true, for instance, that the prices of Grundig products in France were "subject to no effective competition," [154] Grundig-Consten would in fact have a monopoly of the French market. Yet the Court offers no evidence to support such a rash assertion.[155] Nor, in the alternative, does it demonstrate with any greater cogency the economic validity of limiting the "relevant market" to Grundig products.[156] Rather proceeding from the "intent" criterion, the Court infers the most far-reaching consequences of competitive restrictions, which themselves must

[151] The language of the Court is, in fact, this ambiguous: "Because distribution constitutes a considerable part of total production costs, it seems important that competition between dealers also be encouraged. The dealers are stimulated to greater efforts precisely through competition between distributors of the same brand products." *Ibid.*, p. 392. Either the second sentence refers to "efforts" in inter-brand competition or it is simply a repetition of the first.

[152] *Ibid.*, p. 391f.

[153] *Ibid.*, p. 392. In the more recent *Parke, Davis* decision, cited *infra*, in note 159, the Court also concludes that "the fact that the price of the patented product is higher than that of the non-patented product does not necessarily constitute an abuse."

[154] Quoted in context in the text at note 150 *supra*.

[155] Indeed, the evidence presented suggests no more than a minor degree of market control by Grundig products in France.

[156] See Gleiss and Hootz, "Alleinvertriebsverträge mit absolutem Gebietsschutz und EWG-Kartellrecht," *AWD*, 307, 311 (1966): "Der Gerichtshof geht von einem lebensfremden Wettbewerbsmodell aus." See also Schluep, *op. cit.* (n. 116), p. 152; and Hennings, in *Die Welt* (August 18, 1966), criticizing the atomistic, if not perfect model of competition from which the Court proceeds.

rest on highly uncertain – if not unrealistic – premises. This reasoning, concludes Schluep sharply, "is a shocking example of confusing economic considerations with a juristically motivated expedient for facilitating the application of the law." [157]

Having established the illegality of the "closed territory" clause,[158] the Court then turns to the trademark protection. The crucial distinction implicit in its analysis lies between the existence of a trade mark right, as the creature of national law, and the exercise of that right in concert with others.[159] While under French law Consten is regarded as the original holder of the "GINT" trademark, this is only by virtue of the agreement with Grundig aimed at the restriction of competition. This agreement, coupled with a similar exclusive use of the "GINT" trademark in other countries, "permits the control and hindrance of parallel imports." Such agreements which violate the prohibitions of Article 85 (1), are not protected by those Treaty provisions reserving certain "police powers" and the institution of property to the regulation of Member States.[160] "This prohibition would be fruitless if Consten could use the trademark to pursue a purpose already recognized in the agreement as unlawful." [161] The plaintiffs must also be enjoined, therefore, from asserting rights arising from national trademark protection against parallel imports from other Member States.

Nor was the Court more sympathetic to the plaintiffs' claim to dispensation, under Article 85 (3), from the prohibition of Article 85 (1). This is an aspect of Article 85, it will be recalled, which was not considered in the *LTM-MBU* Judgment. Before proceeding to the merits of the issues, therefore, the Court clarifies the nature of this provision. In the first place, Article 85 (3) entitles enterprises to an adequate review of their applications. "The Commission may not simply require enterprises to establish the exis-

[157] Schluep, *id.*, p. 152.

[158] The Court trimmed down the Commission's Decision, which had nullified the whole of the Grundig-Consten agreement, to include the "closed territory" aspects of the exclusive dealing arrangement only.

[159] Judgment 56 and 58/64, *op. cit.*, p. 393f. This distinction is more clearly drawn and developed in Judgment 24/67 (*Parke, Davis and Co.* v. *Probel, Reese, Beintema – Interpharm and Centrafram Co.*) 14 Rspr. 85 (1968), concerning the application of EEC Articles 85 and 86 to national patent rights. While the rights of a patent holder as such are not subject to those EEC provisions, the Court concludes, the exercise of those rights by way of an agreement, decision or concerted practice (Art. 85) or in order to exploit a dominant market position (Art. 86) might well be.

[160] Judgment 56 and 58/64, *id.*, p. 393f. As to the "police powers" and property rights, see EEC Articles 36 and 222. The Court also concludes that EEC Article 234, which protects the rights of third countries arising from (trademark) conventions with Member States, is not applicable.

[161] *Ibid.*, p. 394.

tence of conditions for dispensation, but must contribute according to principles of good public administration and through its own resources to ascertaining the material facts and circumstances."[162] Furthermore, in performing its task, the Commission must make difficult evaluations of economic circumstances. Judicial review must respect this character of these evaluations "by restricting itself to the correctness of the facts upon which they rest and of their subsumption under the concepts of the applicable law. Its primary function is to examine the motivations of the Commission's Decisions which should set out the relevant facts and considerations.[163]

On the merits, the focus of attention is the term "indispensable" in Article 85 (3) (a). Does the agreement impose "any restrictions not indispensable to the attainment of the objectives" stated in Article 85 (3)[164] or, as the Commission put it, would the improvement in the distribution of goods by virtue of the exclusive dealing contract no longer be attainable if parallel imports are permitted?" Not every advantage accruing to the contract parties, reasons the Court, constitutes such an improvement and the basis for Article 85 (3) dispensation.

> The subjective method, by which the concept of "improvement" depends on the particularities of the contractual relations in question, would not conform with the aims of Article 85. Moreover, the very requirement of the Treaty that the competitive restriction be "indispensable" for the improvement discussed here, clearly indicates the importance of this improvement. In particular, it must entail noticeable objective advantages which are able to compensate for the accompanying impediments to competition.[165]

As the Court sees it, then, the standard of "indispensability" serves to distinguish between the mere special advantages of the parties and the general improvements to the market system. Since these improvements are purchased at the cost of competitive restrictions, however, they can be justified only in terms of the Treaty objectives defined in Article 85 (3).[166]

[162] *Ibid.*, p. 395f.

[163] *Ibid.*, p. 396. For a discussion of the requirement of motivation, see text *infra*, p. 480ff.

[164] These specific goals, it may be recalled (see text *supra*, p. 451), are the improvement of production or distribution of goods and the promotion of technical and economic progress, whilst allowing consumers a fair share of the resulting profit.

[165] Judgment 56 and 58/64, *op. cit.*, p. 396f.

[166] Because Article 85(3) is aimed at promoting certain specific economic goals, rather than a workable and effective mechanism of competition, it would be well to refrain from characterizing it as a "rule of reason." It performs essentially a welfare function, which Schluep, *op. cit.* (n. 116), p. 163, prefers to call a "gemeinschafts- oder wirtschaftspolitische Rule of Reason."

None of the alleged advantages of the "closed territory" clause, the Court concludes, meet this standard. The competition from parallel imports, for instance, may well enhance the uncertainty of Consten's sales predictions; "yet such risk is inherent in all commerical activity and, insofar, deserves no special protection." Nor is a division of territories essential to ensure a guarantee and after-sales service in keeping with the high reputation of Grundig products. As a rule such free servicing is given only by the dealer who made the sale; despite the handicap of challenging an established dealer, there is no evidence that Consten's chief competitor in France UNEF has provided a servicing detrimental to this reputation. In any case, nothing prevents Consten from informing consumers of the advantages they may reap by purchasing through official Grundig distributors. It is not true, therefore, that Consten's advertising must necessarily benefit parallel importers. Finally,[167] Consten need have no fear that the results of its efforts at market research will benefit parallel importers. Since *it* is the sole concessionaire of Grundig in France, only it will receive equipment adapted specially to that market. For all these reasons, the "closed territory" clause is not "indispensable" to the aims of Article 85 (3), and fails to meet one of the essential requirements for dispensation.[168]

Putting these cases into perspective, then, what can be said of the Court's approach to EEC Article 85? For one, it is obviously wedded to a view of the regulation of competition which best serves major Treaty goals. In effect, the concept of competition has become a function of the overriding policy of economic integration. Speaking generally, this is really nothing new: those who drafted the EEC Treaty recognized from the beginning that a system of competition is the necessary complement of a customs union in order to create an effective Common Market. What is new, however, is the attempt to give this general policy concrete expression in shaping specific rules. Rather than Community integration being the by-product of a developing system of competition, that system is to be developed in terms of the needs of integration. This is reflected in the interpretation of Article 85 (1), for instance, through judicial emphasis on "freedom to trade" instead of on the "maintenance of competition." As demonstrated in the *Grundig-Consten* Judgment, the pure test of market foreclosure – of excluding dealers from *any* portion of the market for the goods in question – serves to condemn an

[167] In a rather left-handed fashion the Court also rejects the contention of the plaintiffs that territorial protection was necessary to amortize the costs of introducing Grundig products into France. The factual basis of this argument, said the Court, had never been established and, even if established, would have nothing to do with the improvement of the distribution of goods. Judgment 56 and 58/64, *op. cit.*, p. 398.

[168] *Ibid.*, pp. 397–99.

agreement, whatever its impact for an effective and developing system of competition. The question then remains, at least for the "intent" criterion applied in that Judgment, whether room still exists for a "rule of reason" which would prohibit only those territorial restraints in exclusive dealing arrangements which are significantly or unduly restrictive of competition.

At the same time, the method of analysis followed by the Court in the *Grundig-Consten* Judgment manifests a sensitivity toward the need for practicability in the law. As such, it not only echoes the view of the Commission, stated in the motivations to Regulation 17, but also recognizes the immense administrative problems of processing the thousands of restrictive agreements registered with the Commission since February 1962. It has, in effect, paved the way for Regulation 67 of the Commission which in turn has granted a four year moratorium on EEC Article 85 (1) to a large majority of the exclusive dealing arrangements presently registered with the Commission.[169] Lest the Community system of antitrust regulation become mired in a morass of detail, some categories of broad application had to be developed.

Rule simplicity, of course, is often and necessarily purchased at the price of neglecting certain material facts. Thus, the flexible and differentiated approach outlined by the Court in the *LTM-MBU* Case gave way in the *Grundig-Consten* Judgment to a *per se* rule of restrictive intent. Unfortunately, the Court failed to present cogent reasoning – whether in terms of economic policy or of the actual harmful effects on competition – for adopting such a stringent rule as to "closed territory" clauses at this early stage in economic integration. Nor is legal and economic opinion so settled as to obviate such an inquiry. The Court, it must be concluded, has been both somewhat hasty in its generalizations as well as lax in examining and in forcing the Commission to consider more precisely the facts and economic evaluations underlying the Grundig-Consten Decision.

Indeed, the subsequent decision in *Völk* v. *Ets J. Vervaecke s.p.r.l.*[169a] suggests that the Court may be having second thoughts on the matter. In that case, coming up by way of the "preliminary question" procedure, the defendant challenged the validity of an exclusive dealing agreement with the German firm. Vervaecke allegedly was granted a closed territorial concession for plaintiff's washing machines and dryers in Belgium and

[169] See Regulation No. 67–67, cited *op. cit.* (n. 119). It has been estimated that it exempts approximately 30,000 of the 40,000 restrictive agreements now on file with the Commission from the application of EEC Article 85(1). Commerce Clearing House, Common Market Reporter § 2726.15 (current edition).

[169a] Judgment 5/69, 15 Rspr. 295 (1969).

Luxembourg. Since plaintiff's market share amounted to only 0.2% of German production in 1963 when the contract was executed, and had steadily declined to 0.05% in 1966 when suit was brought, the German Court understandably wanted to know whether this affected the application of Community antitrust law. Does the application of EEC Article 85 (1), it asked, depend on "the market share of the plaintiff which was actually attained or aspired to in the Member States, particularly in the closed territories of Belgium and Luxembourg?" In answering this question affirmatively, both the Commission and Advocate-General Gand felt obliged to restrict the application of the *Grundig-Consten* reasoning. The statement there that there is "no need for purposes of Article 85 (1) to consider the concrete effects" of an agreement aimed at restricting, preventing or distorting competition, must be interpreted in light of the peculiar facts of that case. It cannot mean, they contended, that the intensity of the effects does not matter, or that agreements may be measured by different standards, based sometimes on their purpose and sometimes on their effect. Nor can it mean that EEC Article 85 (1) applies to a purely theoretical restriction of competition. Rather, in reliance on the *LTM-MBU* Judgment, they conclude, there must be a "noticeable infringement of competition." [169b]

The Court appears to accept these conclusions, but with precious little reasoning. It begins by adopting word-for-word the formula of *LTM-MBU* for determining whether the agreement is "capable of affecting trade between Member States." It then turns to the question of whether the agreement constitutes an anticompetitive arrangement. The standards of Article 85, it states, must be understood "in light of the factual circumstances accompanying the agreement in question." For this reason, an agreement will not fall within the scope of that Article,

> if in light of the weak position of those participating in the market of the products in question, it impairs the market only insignificantly. As a result, possibly even an exclusive dealing agreement with closed territorial protection would not be subject to the prohibition of Article 85 (1) in view of the weak market position which the participants have for their products in the closed territory.[169c]

If this somewhat cryptic language is construed in terms of the reasoning of the Commission and the Advocate-General, then the Court has added a much needed proviso to *Grundig-Consten*. It will have restricted the latter to its facts and opened up exclusive dealing arrangements to more

[169b] *Ibid.*, pp. 299f and 304–306. See discussion in text *supra*, p. 460.
[169c] *Ibid.*, p. 302.

probing economic analysis. If, on the other hand, the Court is merely establishing a *de minimis* limit to the application of Article 85 (1), then the uncertainty created by the stringent language of *Grundig-Consten* still haunts the field of exclusive dealing arrangements.[169d]

By comparison with adjudication under ECSC Article 65,[170] the Court has followed a familiar pattern in interpreting EEC Article 85. Paragraphs 1 of these two Articles, in the lead-off Judgments of *Geitling* and *Grundig-Consten,* respectively, received a *per se* treatment. Indeed, in both cases, the Court expressly spurns an analysis of the economic facts and circumstances in question. The alternative criterion of illegality, set out in the *LTM-MBU* Case – that should the "intent" test prove inconclusive, the Court would go on to examine the economic effects of an allegedly restrictive practice – has simply not been reached. Rather, thus far this type of judicial analysis has been reserved for the dispensation provisions of these two Articles. They are the reservoir of certain overriding Treaty goals to which the system of competition must adapt itself, so long as a minimum of competition remains.[170a]

Nevertheless, in interpreting these provisions, the Court has exerted considerable self-restraint. In the Ruhr Coal Cartel Cases, arising under the ECSC Treaty,[171] its reasoning is often conceptualistic and concerned more with the general structure of oligopoly in the Community coal industry than with the precise impact of the cartel agreements on a workable system of competition. The language of the *Grundig-Consten* Judgment, moreover, is even more restrained. The Court not only restricts expressly the scope of judicial review under EEC Article 85 (3), but then fails to exercise even that authority. Thus, the Court accepts the Commission's conclusions not so much on a specific analysis of the supporting facts and circumstances of

169d In any case, the Commission has followed the lead of the Court in an apparent attempt to reduce the number of requests it receives for clearance and dispensation. Eleven months after the *Völk* Decision was rendered, it published a "Communication" setting forth a *de minimis* rule for practices which do not fall within the scope of EEC Article 85 (1). It was careful to note, however, that the (non-binding) rule of the Commission remains subject to the developing jurisprudence of the Court. EC Commission, Announcement of May 27, 1970, *Amtsblatt,* No. C 64/1 (June 2, 1970).

170 See discussion in text *supra,* pp. 273f and 449f.

170a See Judgment 14/68 (*Walt Wilhelm* v. *Federal Cartel Office),* 15 Rspr. 1, 14 (1969), stating that these provisions enable "the Community authorities to exercise some positive, albeit indirect action, in order to promote a harmonious development of economic activities throughout the Community, in accordance with Article 2 of the [EEC] Treaty."

171 See text *supra,* esp. pp. 281ff.

the case, but by reference to a few considerations of economic policy and general commercial practice. This may well mean, as it has for the ECSC, that in the regulation of competition the Court by and large will follow the lead of the Commission.

The foregoing discussion has focused on two judicial techniques of rule formation, the legal fiction and the *per se* rule. Both have manifold forms not treated here. Nor are the examples here selected more than representative either of the Court's practice or of the techniques available to it in the search for practicability in the law. Nevertheless, these examples demonstrate that the Community Court is quite sensitive to the demands of rule manageability. Indeed, the *Klöckner* Judgment openly discusses the methodological quandary which the Court faces. It can scarcely be doubted, moreover, that these same considerations underlie the reasoning of *Grundig-Consten*. Unfortunately, the Court too readily has mistaken conceptualistic simplicity for rule practicability. This is particularly true of the Scrap Levy Cases where the rule adopted runs cross-purposes with the financial program. The *per se* analysis of *Grundig-Consten*, on the other hand, should be criticized less for its conclusion – which rightly appreciates the pressure of time and administrative efficiency – than for the confusing and highly abstract rationale underlying the construction of EEC Article 85 (1). In sum, the Court fails to elaborate a rule whose reason *and* scope are clear on its face. Predictability in this important area of Community law has greatly suffered and interested parties are forced to second-guess the Court and the path of the law.

2. OF RULE AND DISCRETION

Till now, the discussion of practicability has centered on the task of judicial rule articulation. This creative task has been measured solely by the high standard of clear and intelligible rules which carry their reasoning on their face in order to guide as they control. This standard is the basis for certainty and predictability in the law. As set out above,[172] however, the search for practicability also has its institutional aspects. Not every legal problem, to put it bluntly, is a proper subject for the judicial rule shaping function. Lacking in expertise, in broad discretionary authority and in the power to initiate action and to undertake comprehensive programs, the Community Court – like all courts – is not always equipped or even best suited to treat the issues properly before it. It may, on the one hand, attempt

172 See discussion in text *supra*, p. 198ff.

to ameliorate its deficiencies by the articulation and application of concepts and rules with built-in flexibility. In such cases, the Court itself provides the institutional basis for simplifying complex problems and circumstances, and for developing standards which permit a high degree of case individualization. Such standards, as will be seen of the motivation requirement, vest the Court with certain, albeit rather limited spheres of discretion.

On the other hand, there are times when even this degree of judicial flexibility is not sufficient to treat the problems at hand. Other Community organs or Member State authorities, with the capacity and power to plan, supervise and initiate action are better suited or the only ones able to do the job. This is particularly true for certain aspects of economic regulation which, as Steindorff points out, "lends itself only very imperfectly to legal normation." It must often be left, therefore, to administrative officials.[173] Indeed, the Treaties are replete with indefinite legal concepts which are meant to preserve the necessary leeway for economic judgment, prediction and reassessment. Should the Court attempt to harden these concepts into firm rules of law, it could well paralyze the development of workable Community regulation. This does not tell the Court to fully abandon the field, but more often restrict itself to a review of the minimum requirements of due process. In any case, the specific exercise of judicial self-restraint, says Steindorff, "depends on whether the judge or the administrative official is better able to make the decision."[174]

The following discussion will attempt to show the extent to which the Court has recognized these institutional aspects of the search for practicability. It is arranged so that the position of the Court may be tested. in the first place, vis-à-vis the proper sphere of the Community executive organs and, secondly, vis-à-vis Member State authorities.

The Court and Community Organs

The legislative and executive organs of the Communities have benefited most often from the exercise of restraint in judicial rule-making. And this perhaps for no better reason than that their acts are the grist of Community adjudication. That is to say, in part, when questions have arisen as to the appropriateness or expediency of Community measures or as to the assessment or prediction of economic facts and circumstances, the Court has been willing to recognize a certain sphere of discretion for the Community organ concerned. It would be exaggeration at this point to speak of settled patterns

[173] Steindorff, *Die Nichtigkeitsklage,* 116f and also 100 and 134 (1952).
[174] *Ibid.*, p. 109.

of judicial opinion on the matters, but there is strong evidence in the case law of this direction. Thus, while the Court as a rule proceeds by presuming the legality of Community acts,[175] in addition it has declined on occasion to review materially relevant factual determinations underlying these acts which are not absolutely decisive for the issues at hand.[176] Similarly, there has been judicial reluctance to review economic evaluations of Community organs even when this is expressly permitted by the Treaty.[177] Only rarely has the Court been willing to make fact-finding inquiries on its own.[178] Nor has it responded favorably to charges that particular measures, though otherwise within the law, could be improved or are inappropriate for attaining Treaty goals. "The Court can only then object to the selection [of measures] when the High Authority has overstepped the objective limits to its activity established in the Treaty."[179] These aspects, however, have been elaborated by other writers[180] and need not be pursued further here.

Perhaps less discussed is the leeway which the Court has allowed the Community executive authorities in three other areas. These are the timing and decision to enforce Community law, the requirement of motivation and the retroactive effect of invalidating Community acts. The considerations underlying judicial reasoning in each of these areas are grounded, in part or wholly, in the notion of practicability and the limits which it sets to the exercise of judicial rule-shaping. At the same time, an examination of the motivation requirement reveals the judicial development of a standard with a unique sphere of built-in flexibility. Moreover, all three areas discussed

175 See, e.g., Judgment 7/56 and 3–7/57, 3 Rspr. 83, 126 (1957): "The issue of an administrative act establishes a presumption of its validity. This can be removed only through nullification or recall so far as these measures are permissible." This is simply a presumption of *de facto* validity, however, and is not the rule of statutory interpretation favoring a constitutional construction. See text *supra*, p. 300f.

176 See, e.g., Judgments 13/60, 8 Rspr. 177, 220 and 232 (1962); 34/62, 9 Rspr. 287, 320f (1963) as compared to the Conclusions of *Adv-Gen*. Roemer, *ibid.*, p. 340ff; and 14/61, 8 Rspr. 511, 546 (1962).

177 See, e.g., Judgments 6/54, 1 Rspr. 213, 237f (1954–55); and 8/57, 4 Rspr. 231, 255 (1958). But cf. Judgment 106 and 107/63, 11 Rspr. 547, 556–58 (1965) (Court refutes view of the EEC Commission that certain grain imports would seriously threaten the stability of the German grain market).

178 Thus, in Judgment 24 and 34/68, 6 Rspr. 589, 616 (1969), the Court relied on the findings of an expert inquiry which it had instituted in order to determine whether, in light of the rates charged by water carriers, the rail rates had been properly set. In the Miner's Bonus Judgment, on the other hand, the Court was obviously unwilling to inquire with precision to what extent the bonus had in fact been offset by other charges. Judgment 30/59, 7 Rspr. 1, 60 (1961).

179 Judgment 17 and 20/61, 8 Rspr. 655, 694f (1962).

180 See, e.g., Bebr, "Prozessmaximen," in *Zehn Jahre Rechtsprechung*, 77, 100ff (1965).

demonstrate an attempt by the Court, in a show of self-restraint, to delineate the proper sphere of executive discretion. In the third group of cases, this attempt at delineation develops into an institutional interplay, a type of judicial remand, between the Court and the High Authority.

1. Discretion in Timing and Enforcement of the Treaties

Four cases will serve to demonstrate the sensitivity of the Court to the necessity for executive discretion in the timing and decision to enforce Community law. In its very first judgments, the Price Publication Cases,[181] the Court was requested to condemn the "Monnet rebate" not only as a violation of the Treaty, but also as a *détournement de pouvoir*. While it struck down that act on the first count by a rigidly literal interpretation which denied the High Authority all discretion to determine the conditions of publication, it rejected the charge of *détournement de pouvoir*. At first glance, this appears quite strange. There was considerable uncontested evidence that the more flexible rule of the "Monnet rebate" had been introduced primarily because the strict requirement of prior price publication had proven inefficacious in practice.[182] Prices had been falling on the steel market and, as may be expected in competition among-the-few, steel enterprises preferred to sell below published prices rather than tip off their competitors and set off a further round of price reductions. Violations had been widespread.[183] Indeed, the High Authority freely admitted the apparent existence of a concerted effort among steel enterprises to publish higher than actual prices.[184] Despite this, no sanctions had been imposed.[185] Rather, the "Monnet rebate," the High Authority hoped, would not only introduce greater flexibility in price schedules, but also "induce enterprises to adjust their lists to the prices actually charged." [186]

Are such concessions not a *détournement de pouvoir* in the purest sense, namely, the exercise of a Treaty power "for an objective other than the one for which the powers were granted?" [187] Did not the High Authority, in other words, alter the price publication requirement precisely because un-

181 Judgments 1/54, 2/54, 3/54 and 4/54. Discussed in text *supra*, p. 349ff. Since the relevant parts of the Judgments are substantially identical, all citations from Judgment 1/54, 1 Rspr. 7 (1954–55).

182 See the Conclusions of *Adv-Gen*. Lagrange, *ibid.*, pp. 75f and 123, and the statement of the High Authority cited in the following text.

183 See note 116 *supra*, p. 244.

184 See Conclusions of *Adv-Gen.*, Lagrange, *op. cit.*, p. 75.

185 *Ibid.*, pp. 75f and 123.

186 High Authority, Second Gen. Rep. 94f (English ed. 1964).

187 See text *supra*, p. 55f.

der existing market conditions firms would not cooperate and, in the alternative, because it was not willing to press prosecution? The answer was "No". While the "Monnet rebate," reasons the Court, "may have been inspired partially" by the need for a more efficacious rule, "it is clear that above all it intended to achieve the objectives referred to in the Treaty." [188] This doctrinal distinction between the "partial" and "essential" motive or object of an act[189] leaves immense leeway for judicial determination in specific cases *and,* if so desired, judicial self-restraint.

Advocate-General Lagrange, however, was more candid:

> Your Honors, we know the real aim [of the "Monnet rebate"]; it consisted in fashioning the *most appropriate conditions* for publication, in order to ensure [High Authority] control of non-discrimination in the light of market conditions and, at the same time, to further free price formation.[190]

And part of what is "appropriate" consists in knowing when to apply "the delicate and dangerous means" for Treaty enforcement in ECSC Article 65 § 5, which are "dangerous for those who make use of them and not only for those affected." To have applied those sanctions in the case at hand "would have amounted to a declaration of war on the producers at the very opening of the common market. This is a *political* consideration which falls within the competence of the High Authority."[191] The Court's doctrinal distinction referred to above, therefore, was essentially a means for safeguarding the proper sphere of executive discretion.

Judicial restraint in reviewing the timing and decision to enforce Community acts can also be detected in three other varying situations. In one early Judgment, already discussed,[192] the High Authority was permitted to postpone dismantling obviously illegal coal cartels while it sounded out their respective positions, assessed the economic circumstances and developed an overall strategy of competitive regulation for the coal industry. "Since

188 Judgment 1/54, *op. cit.,* p. 34. Further: "Even if an unjustified motive, namely, the desire to avoid sanctioning defaulting enterprises, is present together with motives which, of themselves, justify the action of the High Authority, the Decisions would not, on this account, be vitiated by a *détournement de pouvoir,* provided that they do not infringe upon the essential aim, which is the prohibition of unfair competitive practices and discrimination." *Ibid.*

189 This distinction exists also in French administrative law. Says de Laubadère, *Traité élémentaire de Droit administratif,* vol. I, sec. 905 (1963): "Lorsque l'auteur de l'acte a poursuivi plusieurs buts, il suffit que l'un de ces buts soit legal pour que la mesure soit correcte." See also Duez-Debeyre, *Traité de droit administratif,* 393 (1952).

190 Conclusions of *Adv-Gen.* Lagrange, in Case 1/54, *op. cit.,* p. 76.

191 *Ibid.*

192 Judgment 6/54 (*Netherlands* v. *High Authority*), 1 Rspr. 211, 234 (1954–55), discussed in text *supra,* p. 247f.

Article 12 of the Transition Convention specifies no time limit for the prohibition of these cartels," said the Court, "the High Authority enjoys a discretionary power during the period of transition." This judicial gloss on a purely procedural provision justified the use of ceiling prices to compensate for the lack of effective competition.

By the same token, the Court sustained the power of the Commission in a more recent case in deciding when to file a suit against a Member State under EEC Article 169. In a reasoned opinion, issued July 24, 1964, the Commission noted that the Italian Government, in violation of EEC Article 16, was imposing a progressive charge on objects of artistic, historic, archaeological or ethnographic interest exported to other Member States. In response, the Italian parliament convened a committee to study the problem. The Commission set December 31, 1965 as a deadline. Although a bill did emerge from this study, and was adopted by the Italian Senate, it had not been considered by the Chamber of Deputies before its adjournment on March 11, 1968. Several days earlier on March 6, in an apparent effort to spur such consideration, the Commission filed suit against Italy on the matter. Because the bill was still pending before parliament, Italy maintained that the suit was inadmissible. It allegedly violated the spirit of the Treaty as set forth in EEC Article 2, namely, "to promote throughout the Community a harmonious development of economic activities...." The Court, like Advocate-General Gand flatly rejected this defense. The Italian Government, it noted, had been given ample warning. In any case, "it is for the Commission to decide when to bring suit before the Court of Justice. The considerations behind this decision cannot affect the admissibility of the suit, since the latter depends solely on objective criteria." [193]

Furthermore, in its first and negative Opinion on the proposed "small Treaty revision" to ECSC Article 56, the Court refused to consider whether the difficulties which the revision was designed to combat were not in fact due to the failure of the Community to use the powers which it already possessed. "Such an examination would be legally conclusive," it said, "only in a contentious proceeding which greatly exceeds the scope of Article 95." [194] Nevertheless, as the Court itself recognized, Article 95 grants it "full jurisdiction as to all matters of fact and law" in determining whether the alleged difficulties "necessitate a revision of the Treaty provisions ...." Certainly, whether the existing powers were sufficient to meet the difficulties would have been a relevant consideration in determining whether their revision was "necesssary."

193 Judgment 7/68 (*EEC Commission* v. *Italy*), 14 Rspr. 633, 642 (1968).
194 Opinion of the Court, 5 Rspr. 571, 580 (1958–59).

Finally, in the recent case of *Germany* v. *EEC Commission,*[195] the Court refused to condemn the Commission for the selective enforcement of EEC Articles 13 and 14 among the Member States. Paragraph 2 of that Article empowers the Commission, in part, to fix the time for the progressive abolition of charges in force between the Member States having an effect equivalent to customs duties on importation. The Commission, admittedly, had proceeded against certain administrative charges on German imports, but not against similar charges of all the Member States. It argued, however, that it simply had attacked those violations which were more important from the viewpoint of competition and was awaiting the outcome of the present judicial test before proceeding further.[196]

The Court does not assess these arguments. In rejecting Germany's complaint of a *détournement de pouvoir* because of discriminatory treatment, it determines simply that, as to time order, Article 14 (2) and (3) is "less strict" for the administrative charges in question than for tariffs themselves. To be sure, "a certain harmony must be maintained" in abolishing these charges and tariffs, but the Commission's procedure in the present case reveals no Treaty violation. Moreover, while "a certain time order must be observed, the Commission is not prevented from determining itself the details of the progressive abolition of these charges." Then, in a show of *obiter dictum,* the Court concludes:

> Even if the Commission had not met its obligations toward the other Member States, this could not vitiate the obligation of a Member State imposed by the lawful application of the Treaty.

The proper and only recourse for the latter in such case is to call upon the Commission, if necessary by judicial appeal, to take action against the remaining delinquent Member States.[197]

The self-restraint of the Community Court in these cases should be generally applauded. On the supranational level, where economic regulation is in many ways innovatory, experimental and plagued by hard questions of coordination, the timing and decision to enforce the Treaties entails – as Advocate-General Lagrange suggests – both "delicate and dangerous" aspects. Only exceptionally does the Court possess the tactical insight as well as the ability to formulate workable rules on these matters. Moreover, that potentially powerful ground of judicial review, the *détournement de pou-*

195 Judgment 52 and 55/65, 12 Rspr. 219 (1966).
196 See the Conclusions of *Adv-Gen.* Roemer, *ibid.*, pp. 253–55, which reject these arguments as unconvincing.
197 Judgment 52 and 55/65, *ibid.*, p. 237.

voir, should as a rule be exercised with great caution. "Only prudent restraint in many cases," says Steindorff of the French Conseil d'Etat,[198] "could have made such an extensive power of judicial control bearable." Certainly, in the first and third cases examined, there was no need for the Court to consider the question of timing and enforcement, since the Decisions and proposed Treaty revision had already been rejected on other grounds or for other reasons. And, in the second case discussed, the need for executive discretion was clearly justified. The difficulties in dismantling the coal cartels were immense, requiring nothing less than the establishment of a new economic order for the industry.

The last of the judgments just considered, however, has been attacked with some vehemence.[199] After all, equal treatment on matters of tariffs and similar charges between the Member States is an essential one-half of a customs union. Even in the exercise of discretion, there is no room for arbitrariness.[200] The reasoning of the Court, therefore, should have emphasized and not minimized the principle of equal treatment. The *obiter dictum* of the Court nevertheless should be affirmed. When the Commission fails to enforce the Treaty uniformly, the answer is not to vitiate or postpone the enforcement of Treaty standards, but to compel the Commission to meet its obligation. The standards of the Treaty, as the Court has so well recognized,[201] are the minimum and not the maximum conditions for economic integration.

II. Individualization in the Motivation Requirement

The difficulty of demarcating the proper spheres of judicial review and executive discretion is well demonstrated by the standard of motivation. Articles 15, 190 and 162 of the ECSC, EEC and Euratom Treaties, respectively, require that binding acts of Community organs[202] "be supported by

198 Steindorff, *Die Nichtigkeitsklage,* 77 (1952).

199 See, in particular, the "Observations" of Frowein, in *Cah. dr. européen* 301ff (1967).

200 See the Conclusions of *Adv-Gen.,* Lagrange, in Case 15 and 29/59, 6 Rspr. 31, 37 (1960): "Discretion does not mean arbitrariness. The High Authority must observe the Treaty and general principles of law." See also Llewellyn's "Law of Lawful Discretion": "*no* discretion has any business to be wholly free; *no* discretion has any business to be truly unique in exercise .... To be *right* discretion, ... the action so far as it affects any man or group adversely must be undertaken with a feeling, explicit or implicit, of willingness, of readiness, to do the like again, if, as, and when a like case may arise." *The Common Law Tradition: Deciding Appeals,* 217 (1960).

201 See in particular the discussion in text *supra,* p. 322ff.

202 This generalization requires some reservations. While ECSC Article 15 applies to

reasons and shall refer to any proposals or opinions which are to be obtained pursuant to the Treat[ies]."[203] This means, in practice, that these acts are prefaced by the facts and considerations which justify their promulgation. However, as the Court early pointed out, these provisions "contain no more precise definition of the form or scope of this obligation."[204] They constitute, on the one hand, a highly abstract and purely procedural standard not going to questions of substance.[205] This has forced the Court in no small way to articulate, through its case law, both the major purposes as well as the general guidelines of this standard. On the other hand, due to the highly individualized nature of the motivations, the Court possesses great leeway in the application of these guidelines to specific Community acts. Here it becomes apparent just how difficult it is, despite the purely procedural nature of this standard, to apply it meaningfully without considering the substance of the motivation. What, for instance, constitutes adequate and reasoned support of a specific Community act? Adjudication of the motivation standard, therefore, may sensitively reflect the views of the Court toward the proper sphere of executive discretion in Community decision-making.

What are the purposes of this standard? While proceeding cautiously at first, by 1963 the Court had established four major purposes which are summarized in the Brandy Wine Judgment. The requirement of motivation, it states,

> does not fulfil merely a formal function, but seeks to give the parties an opportunity to defend their rights, the Court an opportunity to exercise its control and the Member States, as well as their interested nationals, an opportunity to ascertain the way in which the Commission has applied the Treaty.[206]

These purposes, unfortunately, are nowhere more fully developed. It is perhaps useful, therefore, to attempt a somewhat more comprehensive list of potential functions for this standard.

The classical one, suggested by Plato in the *Laws*, is that of persuasion. Like the preface to a law, the motivation is a means of exhortation, of creating good-will in its addressees and, therefore, of making a governmental

the binding acts and opinions of the High Authority only, the corresponding provisions of the Rome Treaties say nothing of opinions but do extend the motivation requirement to the Council of Ministers as well as to the Commission and, in addition, mention the need to refer to the proposals as well as the opinions which must be obtained in the course of decision-making. For a discussion of the acts which are binding in each of the Communities, see text *supra*, p. 73f.

203 As *Adv-Gen*. Roemer contends, there appears to be no reason why these three provisions do not constitute the same standard. Case 24/62, 9 Rspr. 159, 167 (1963).

204 Judgment 6/54, 1 Rspr. 219, 232 (1954–55).

205 See the discussion in text *supra*, p. 311f.

206 Judgment 24/62 (*Germany* v. *EEC Commission*), 9 Rspr. 141, 155 (1963).

act more ecceptable to them.[207] This function may well be of little value for complex economic regulations administered by an impersonal bureaucracy. The second function, that of information, is more promising and suggested by the fourth purpose mentioned above by the Court. Considering the complexities and innovationary character of Community regulation, the motivation offers a useful thumbnail sketch of the legal and factual basis of the act in question, its aim and perhaps even its moving cause. In short, the act is made more intelligible to interested parties.

Most important, however, is the third, the control function of the motivation requirement. It has three aspects. For one, it furthers self-criticism by Community organs of their acts. The need to account for each step of the reasoning leading to a decision helps these organs to identify and control otherwise inarticulated assumptions and evaluations.[208] While the immediate impact of such self-scrutiny obviously should not be exaggerated, it is the kind of self-discipline exercised by every conscientious law-giver. Particularly in areas of discretionary judgment, Advocate-General Roemer points out,[209] the motivation "may be seen as an indication of the conscientiousness with which the Decision has been reached." In such cases, says Llewellyn, "character becomes a part of law."[210] In another and perhaps broader sense, the requirement of motivation opens up Community acts to public criticism. It forces Community organs to compete on a more equal footing with the best legal and economic minds in the Member States in justifying Community acts. It also permits the national legislatures as well as the European Parliament to debate and review them more intelligently.[211] Considering the rudimentary character of political control in the Communities, such criticism should play an important role.

Finally, and in the more concrete sense which the Court has recognized, the requirement of motivation renders Community acts more accessible to judicial attack and review. Most obviously private litigants, with limited knowledge and means at their disposal, can more readily test the cogency of the reasoning behind an act and develop grounds of attack. As for the Court, it is better able to check the authenticity of the defense presented by Community organs at trial. Indeed, were it to follow French judicial practice in the matter, the Court might consider Community acts to be bound by the scope and content of their motivations and subject to nullification should

[207] Plato, *Laws,* IV 723 (Jowett trans.).

[208] Ipsen in discussion, *Zehn Jahre Rechtsprechung,* 511 (1965).

[209] Conclusions of *Adv-Gen.* Roemer, in Case 34/62, 9 Rspr. 327, 336 (1963).

[210] Llewellyn, *The Common Law Tradition: Deciding Appeals,* 217 (1960).

[211] See the Conclusions of *Adv-Gen.* Lagrange, in Case 36–38/59 and 40/59, 6 Rspr. 933, 941f (1960).

their motivations be legally faulty or factually in error.[212] In any case, it should be emphasized, of all the purposes which the motivation serves only this last has to do directly with judicial control.

However clear these several purposes might be, they provide only very general guidelines for determining the proper content and scope of motivations. For this reason, the Court has tried, but with only limited success, to develop more specific rules.[213] In order to satisfy the three latter purposes which it set out above, the Court has declared:

the Decision need only set out the most important legal and factual considerations upon which it is based and which are necessary to understand the reasoning which led the Commission to its Decision. This can certainly be done in a concise manner, so long as clarity and cogency are not impaired.[214]

Still, the question remains: just which are the most important considerations "necessary to understand the reasoning" of the Commission? Further, what constitutes sufficient clarity and cogency? Such questions can not be answered generally. They must be left largely for determination in the specific case.

On occasion, the Court has attempted to propound some rules-of-thumb for testing the adequacy of a motivation. Thus, as just quoted, a motivation may be brief but not vague,[215] at least not so vague that it can not be understood or the relevant Treaty provisions known from its context[216] or by reference to sources known to the addressee of the act.[217] That is to say, the

[212] See Steindorff, *Die Nichtigkeitsklage,* 56f, 70f and 143f (1952); and Waline, *Droit administratif,* 473–78 (9th ed. 1963). As the latter points out, at p. 488, with the increasing reluctance of the Conseil d'Etat to annul an administrative act on the basis of a *détournement de pouvoir,* there has been a corresponding strengthening of the motivation requirement. Although at one point, during the series of Ruhr cartel Judgments, the Community Court appeared to be moving in this direction (see note 227 at p. 485 *infra*), it by and large has not followed this course. See the Judgments cited *supra* in notes 177 and 178 as well as those discussed in text *infra,* p. 489ff. See also Steindorff, *Rechtschutz und Verfahren im Recht der europäischen Gemeinschaften,* 71 (1964).

[213] See generally the valuable discussion of le Tallec and Ehlermann, "Die Begründungspflicht für Rechtsakte der Europäischen Gemeinschaften," *AWD,* 149 (1966).

[214] Judgment 24/62, 9 Rspr. 141, 155 (1963). See also Judgments 6/54, 1 Rspr. 213, 232 (1954–55); 2/56, 3 Rspr. 9, 37 (1957); and 66/63, 10 Rspr. 1147, 1174 (1964).

[215] See Judgments 24/62, *id.,* pp. 154–57; and 66/63, *id.,* p. 1174.

[216] See Judgments 6/54, 1 Rspr. 213, 232f (1954–55); 2/56, 3 Rspr. 9, 37 (1957); and 66/63, *id.,* p. 1175.

[217] The Advocates-General have rejected the possibility that the requirement of motivation could vary depending on the addressee's ability to inform himself from sources outside the Decision. See their Conclusions in Cases 4–13/59, 6 Rspr. 295, 317 (1960); 24/62, 9 Rspr. 159, 167f (1963). While the Court has not answered the question head-on, it has taken the position, with one exception (Judgment 1/63, 9 Rspr. 653,

motivation must present "the reasons with sufficient clarity to permit the Court and all the parties concerned to determine that the pertinent provisions have been correctly applied."[218] This does not mean that each article of an act must be independently motivated, if its motivation may be gathered from the context of the entire Decision.[219] Moreover, while the Community organs must mention that they have fulfilled the required consultations and other procedural requirements, they need not consider the particular opinions expressed there.[220] Nor is it necessary to list all the arguments which would justify a Decision[221] or to refute possible or even known objections to the Decision.[222] Finally, it does not matter whether the views stated in the motivations are correct in law, so long as they are not self-contradictory.[223] And, in developing their reasoning, Community organs can restrict themselves to an evaluation of the concrete case before them.[224] They need not write a "scientific monograph" on the matter[225] or develop a general theory covering the Treaty provisions in question.[226] Such rules, however, set only very minimal requirements at the outer limits of the motivation standard.

As a result, when it comes to determining the adequacy of specific motivations, the Court possesses a very flexible tool. Part of this flexibility has been employed to vary the stringency of the motivation requirement as to different categories of Community acts.[226a] Thus, following the French prac-

678 (1963)), that inadequate motivations of *individual* Decisions could be healed through sources known or made known in the Decision to the addressee. See Judgments 1 and 14/57, 3 Rspr. 213, 233 (1957); 35/62 and 16/63, 9 Rspr. 423, 444 (1963); 78/63, 10 Rspr. 787, 812 (1964); 80/63, 10 Rspr. 837, 868 (1964); 108/63, 11–1 Rspr. 1, 14 (1965); 36/64, 11 Rspr. 446, 461 (1965); and 1/69, 15 Rspr. 277, 285 (1969). This indicates at least that the aim of facilitating judicial review is not the central purpose of the motivation requirement. Cf. le Tallec and Ehlermann, *op. cit.*, p. 152f.

[218] Judgment 8–11/66, 13 Rspr. 99, 113 (1967), nullifying a Decision of the EEC Commission under Article 15 of Regulation No. 17–62 (re competition) for inadequate motivation. See also Judgment 3/67, 14 Rspr. 37, 47 (1968), upholding an individual Decision of the High Authority under the scrap levy program.

[219] See Judgments 2/56, 3 Rspr. 9, 37 (1957); and 18/62, 9 Rspr. 561, 602 (1963).

[220] See Judgments 4/54, 1 Rspr. 189, 208.

[221] See Judgment 3–18, 25 and 26/58, 6 Rspr. 379, 417 (1960).

[222] See Judgments 2/56, 3 Rspr. 9, 37 (1957); 34/62, 9 Rspr. 287, 314f (1963); 21/64, 11 Rspr. 241, 260 (1965); 29/67, 14 Rspr. 391, 416f (1968); and 3/67, Rspr. 37, 48 (1968).

[223] See Judgment 2/56, 3 Rspr. 9, 38 (1957); and 24/62, 9 Rspr. 141, 156f (1963).

[224] See Judgment 3–18, 25 and 26/58, 6 Rspr. 379, 417 (1960).

[225] See the Conclusions of *Adv-Gen.* Roemer in Cases 108/63, 11–1 Rspr. 19, 25 (1965); and 4 and 13/59, 6 Rspr. 295, 317f (1960).

[226] See Judgment 3–18, 25 and 26/58, 6 Rspr. 379, 417 (1960).

[226a] Judgment 5/67, 14 Rspr. 127, 144 (1968): "The extent of the duty to furnish reasons as laid down in EEC Article 190 depends on the legal nature of the measure in issue."

tice mentioned above, the exercise of essentially discretionary powers by the Commission must be thoroughly motivated. While broad discretionary powers are exceptions in the Treaties, though more frequent in the ECSC, many Decisions are at least in part the product of executive discretion. As the Court has reasoned in the *Präsident* Judgment, the approval of "benevolent cartel" agreements under ECSC Article 65 § 2

> involves by its nature an assessment of the situation based on the economic facts and circumstances and, therefore, falls partly outside the jurisdiction of the Court. Due to this limitation on judicial review and to the fact that the approval depends on a determination by the High Authority [new Commission] that all the conditions prescribed by Article 65 § 2 are fulfilled, an extensive motivation is indispensable and this requirement must be unconditionally observed. The motivation must enable interested and, where the occasion arises, also the judge to determine the circumstances on the basis of which the High Authority arrived at its conclusion that the required conditions were met, so that the factual and legal soundness of these considerations may be reviewed.[227]

As the scope of judicial review decreases, therefore, the requirement of motivation is correspondingly strengthened. This suggests the complementarity between the judicial and non-judicial control aspects, discussed above, of the motivation standard.

The *Präsident* Judgment of course represents more than a doctrinal development of the motivation standard. It also depicts, as has already been pointed out,[228] the imaginative use of that standard to effect a judicial remand of the minimum access criteria of the Ruhr coal cartels to the High Authority for reconsideration. Thus, while doctrinally it may well appear, as Bebr suggests, that the Court in *Präsident* "actually strives for an economic evaluation,"[229] the opinion has a sound functional justification. The Court simply must not become a captive at a later point of doctrine developed with another purpose in mind. To impose stringent standards of

[227] Judgment 36–38 and 40/59, 6 Rspr. 885, 922 (1960). See also Judgments 18/57 (*Nold* Case), 5 Rspr. 89, 114–16 (1958–59) (High Authority Decision approving trading requirements under ECSC Art. 65 § 2 inadequately motivated); 25/62 (*Brandy Wine* Case), 9 Rspr. 141, 154–56 (1963) (EEC Commission Decision refusing full amount of requested customs dispensation inadequately motivated); and 56 and 58/64 (*Grundig-Consten* Case), 12 Rspr. 321, 396 (1966) (re motivation and proper sphere of executive discretion under EEC Article 85(3)). Similar positions have been taken on personnel decisions of Community organs in Judgments 27/63, 10 Rspr. 271, 293f (1964); and 94 and 96/63, 10 Rspr. 645, 672 (1964). While *Adv-Gen.* Roemer advocates more stringent motivation requirements as discretionary powers increase (e.g., Case 24/62, 9 Rspr. 159, 167 (1963), *Adv-Gen.* Lagrange pursues the opposite course (e.g., Cases 36–38 and 40/59, 6 Rspr. 933, 943 (1960); and 103/63, 10 Rspr. 1187, 1191 (1964)).

[228] See discussion in text *supra*, pp. 275f and 311f.

[229] Bebr, *Judicial Control of the European Communities*, 87 (1962).

rationality on the motivation of complex economic judgments could in fact restrict the proper sphere of executive discretion and stultify administrative action.

The Court as well as the Advocates-General also have distinguished between the motivations of general and individual Decisions. General Decisions of the High Authority, said the Court, have the character of EEC Regulations and "require no special motivation for provisions which are clear and conform without difficulty to the whole of their decisional context."[230] Individual Decisions, on the other hand, must be more thoroughly motivated, especially those which set financial obligations for private parties. A levy of payment by the High Authority under the scrap program, for instance, must be prefaced by "an exact and detailed breakdown of each item of the debt." Otherwise the parties are "left in ignorance as to how their debt has been calculated" and the Court can not review the Decision.[231]

Furthermore, there is every reason to impose a strict requirement of motivation on Commission decisions, especially under the ECSC Treaty, which condemn Member States for Treaty violations.[232] While in the EEC such condemnations are binding only after judicial decision, in the ECSC they bind the Member State upon issue but may be appealed.[233] Due to the still delicate questions of sovereignty at stake, it might be argued, the High Authority and Commission should be required to consider in their motivations the essential contentions of the States concerned.[234] Although the Court has not taken a definite position on this as yet, it has attempted to preserve all stages of the pre-appeal condemnation procedure[235] and a full

230 Judgment 18/62, 9 Rspr. 561, 602 (1963). See also the Conclusions of *Adv-Gen.* Lagrange, *ibid.*, p. 613, and of *Adv-Gen.* Roemer, in Case 108/63, 11–1 Rspr. 19, 25 (1965); and Judgment 5/67, 14 Rspr. 127, 144 (1968). But cf. Steindorff, *op. cit.* (n. 212: Rechtsschutz), p. 73.

231 Judgment 9/56, 4 Rspr. 9, 30 and 32 (1958). See also Judgments 10/56, 4 Rspr. 51, 70 (1958); 1/63, 9 Rspr. 653, 678 (1963); and 18/62, 9 Rspr. 561, 602 (1963), concerning levy of payments under the scrap program. And see 67/63, 10 Rspr. 321, 352f (1964), concerning the High Authority's Decision to withdraw its prior approval of a wholesaler's continued association with the Oberrheinischen Kohlenunion.

232 See Bebr, "The Development of a Community Law by the Court of the ECSC, 42 *Minn. L. Rev.*, 845, 873 (1958); and discussion in text *supra*, p. 64f.

233 Compare ECSC Art. 88 and EEC Arts. 169 and 170; and see discussion in text *supra*, p. 63f.

234 See the Conclusions of *Adv-Gen.* Roemer, in Case 20/59, 6 Rspr. 719, 735 (1960).

235 See, e.g., Judgment 20/59 and 25/59, 6 Rspr. 681, 714–17 and 743, 787–90 (1960), comparing regular Decisions of the High Authority with those condemning Member State violations; and Bebr, "Prozessmaximen," in *Zehn Jahre Rechtsprechung*, 77, 92–94 (1965).

correspondence between the reasons given in the motivation and the Community's contentions on appeal.[236]

Finally, the special character of personnel decisions suggests a further basis of distinction. Not only is this requirement of motivation written specially into the Personnel Statute,[237] but it also concerns procedures, judgments of character, performance and personality as well as other confidential matters which in some respects give it a flavor all its own. The peculiarities of this field of Community law will not be pursued here.

Nevertheless, try as one might to harden the Court's case-by-case reasoning into solid doctrine,[238] these categories are plagued by exceptions and irregularities.[239] Such things might of course be written off simply as random deviations due to the eccentricities of the particular cases. Even then, they would indicate the high degree of built-in flexibility of the motivation standard. It is conceivable, however, that something more is at work: that because of this flexibility the motivation standard is highly sensitive to the delicate balance between judicial rule-making and administrative discretion.[240] Four examples may serve to demonstrate this. Since each concerns individual Decisions, the preceding discussion indicates that the standard would be strictly applied. Furthermore, since all except the last of these examples involves the exercise of an important degree of administrative discretion, there is additional reason for requiring a most thorough motivation. Nevertheless, the Court fails in each case to demand just this.

The first two cases arise from individual Decisions of the High Authority directed at two different steel enterprises. In *Acciaieria e Tubificio di Brescia v. High Authority*,[241] an exercise of the ECSC discovery procedure was under attack. The Community powers under ECSC Article 47 (1) are rather broadly defined: "The High Authority may collect the information necessary to carry out its duties. It may take the necessary steps to verify such information." Being a mixed steel enterprise *and* manufacturer, the plaintiff feared that the permissive language of the High Authority's Decision would empower the inspector, at his discretion, to review both aspects of its activi-

236 See Judgment 45/64, 11 Rspr. 1123, 1137f (1965), rendered under EEC Art. 169.

237 Personnel Stat. Art. 25, published in *Amtsblatt*, 1385 (June 24, 1962).

238 This has been the attempt of le Tallec and Ehlermann, *op. cit.* (n. 213).

239 Emphasized by Steindorff, *op. cit.* (n. 212: Rechtsschutz), p. 70.

240 See Institut royal des relations internationales, "Les recours en annulation et en cas de carence dans le Droit de la CECA," 13 *Chron. pol. étr.* 291, 325 (1960); Bebr, *op. cit.* (n. 228), pp. 87–89; Steindorff, *id.*, p. 70; and Colin, *Le gouvernement des juges dans les Communautés européennes*, 260f (1966).

241 Judgment 31/59, 6 Rspr. 159 (1960).

ties. The latter, of course, lies beyond the jurisdiction of the ECSC.[242] While Advocate-General Roemer condemned the Decision and its motivation for being unnecessarily vague and for failing to specify more precisely the scope of the examination and the information it aimed to procedure,[243] the Court blandly concludes:

> . . . [T]he examination [of plaintiff's books, etc.] carried out by the High authority in obtaining information may direct it to further inquiries which could not be set out in detail in the motivation. . . . [O]nly the aim pursued may serve as a criterion [of need] and not a predication of the results expected which . . . can alter as the result of the examinations made.[244]

If indeed, as the Court affirms, "the discovery powers of the High Authority are confined *in principle* to those activities of enterprises within the sphere of coal and steel production,"[245] then it is reasonable to require a fairly specific account of the kinds of documents and facts being sought – *at least* in areas beyond the Community's jurisdiction. In view of the extremely vague language of the High Authority's Decision,[246] the Court's reasoning comes close to authorizing a "fishing expedition."

By the same token, in *Société des usines à tubes de la Sarre* v. *High Authority,*[247] the Court also upheld a most vaguely motivated investment Opinion. The High Authority is authorized, under ECSC Article 54 (4), to "issue a reasoned Opinion on those projects within the framework of the goals of Article 46," including in particular programs of modernization and the expansion of productive capacity. While such an Opinion is not legally binding, if unfavorable it could well affect an enterprise's credit-rating and even result in a loss of credit on a particular investment.[248] In this case, the High Authority refused to approve the plaintiff's plan to install an electro-steel furnace. In one short paragraph, absent all remnant of facts, the High

[242] This jurisdiction is definied in ECSC Arts. 80 and 81.

[243] See the Conclusions of *Adv-Gen.* Roemer, *op. cit.*, pp. 206f, 209 and 214f.

[244] Judgment 31/59, *id.*, p. 181. See also the Report of Wuerdinger, in *Das Auskunftsrecht gegenüber Unternehmen und Unternehmenszusammenschlüssen innerhalb internationaler Gemeinschaften*, 7, 18–20 (1964); and the language of the Court in Judgment 5–11 and 13–15/62, 8 Rspr. 917, 943 (1962): "Since Article 47 of the Treaty, in granting the High Authority the power to "collect the necessary information," uses a very broad formula, the demand to send the documents to Luxembourg need not be specifically motivated."

[245] Judgment 31/59, *id.*, p. 181.

[246] Reported in the Conclusions of *Adv-Gen.* Roemer, *id.*, p. 194.

[247] Judgment 1 and 14/57, 3 Rspr. 213 (1957).

[248] See Bebr, *op. cit.* (n. 229), p. 50. But cf. the Conclusions of *Adv-Gen.* Lagrange, *id.*, p. 245.

Authority simply expressed its views that investments of this type would endanger the supply of scrap on the common market.[249] Although this Opinion, said the Court, "contains only a very brief motivation, it is an adequate one."[250] It was sufficient that the High Authority had made reference to two previous but non-binding policy statements, which were by then one and two years old.

There is no doubt, of course, that the High Authority can exercise its Article 54 powers to influence and coordinate private investment in terms of the lawful goals of the scrap program.[251] Considering the breadth of these powers, their significance for the business opportunities of individual enterprises and the absence of judicial review on the merits, however, there is good reason for requiring a more thorough and reasoned motivation. Certainly, the fate of business investments is worthy of as much attention as the levy of payments due under the scrap program.[252] Yet for reasons left unstated, the Court declined to demand even the most minimal requirements of motivation.

In the two concluding examples, the Court is reviewing Decisions directed not at private enterprises but at one Member State. The first concerns the Brandy Wine and Orange Import Judgments, rendered within a span of two weeks and representing two attacks of the German Government on the refusal of the EEC Commission to approve certain dispensations from the common tariff wall. In both cases, the Commission was faced with the delicate task of weighing the general good in maintaining the common tariff schedules on brandy wine and oranges against the exceptional and not unjustified needs of Germany for third country imports.[253] Under EEC Article 25 (3), as the Court affirms in these cases, the Commission possesses a sphere of "discretionary authority" for suspending, in whole or in part, certain customs restrictions, provided that this would cause no "serious disturbance" on the market of the products concerned.[254] This discretion was utilized to trim down considerably the amount of dispensation requested for brandy wine and to reject altogether a dispensation on third country orange imports for the year 1962. The motivations of both Decisions are based to a large extent on fairly general economic models and both employ equally abstract reasoning. Yet in contrast to Advocate-General Roemer, who con-

249 The Decision and its motivation are reprinted by the Court, *id.*, p. 223f.
250 *Ibid.*, p. 233.
251 These goals are discussed in text *supra*, p. 249f.
252 See discussion in text at note 231 *supra*.
253 For a discussion of the Member State interests at stake, see Bülow's case comments in AWD 276–281 (1963).
254 See discussion in text *supra*, p. 303f.

demned them both for this reason,[255] the Court struck down the first and upheld the second.

In the Brandy Wine Judgment, the motivation in question was censured both as "contradictory" and "summary."[256] On the one hand, the Court reasoned, the Commission had asserted the adequacy of existing supply, on the basis of a more limited dispensation than requested, without "giving a more extensive justification and the amount and trend of the surplus available." On the other hand, the Commission had claimed that a higher dispensation could lead to "serious disturbances" on the market without either "describing the danger more closely or showing how the one necessarily leads to the other."[257] The Commission, it should be pointed out, had listed the trends in brandy wine imports – although not the surpluses available – from third countries and Member States. What the Court demanded, apparently, was specific justification for cutting-off third country imports at one particular level rather than another. Abstract considerations and conclusions were not sufficient.

Nevertheless, in the Orange Import Judgment[258] the Court fails to take the Commission to task for the lack of just such precision. The Commission had rejected Germany's application for a dispensation during 1962 on third country imports of oranges. In its Decision,[259] the Commission justified the absolute inviolability of existing customs schedules on oranges as necessary to protect the fledgling orange crops of Italy, then in the process of expansion, as well as non-citrus fruit production in the Member States. Since, as Germany was quick to point out,[260] these new Italian orchards would not yield fruit for 5 or 6 years and, even then, not enough to supply the needs of Germany, the Commission's case rested primarily on the cross-elasticities of demand in Germany between third country oranges and the non-citrus fruits of Community origin. The dispensation in question, reasoned the Commission, would affect adversely the Community price level of fruit *because of* the substitutability of the fruits in point. This in turn would *tend to* decrease investment in storage capacity for non-citrus fruits, which at present were in oversupply. As a result, a dispensation *would frustrate* the

255 Conclusions of *Adv-Gen.* Roemer, in Cases 24/62 and 34/62, 9 Rspr. 159, 170f and 327, 337–39 (1963).

256 Judgment 24/62 (*Germany* v. *EEC Commission*), 9 Rspr. 141, 156f (1963). See the Decision of the EEC Commission (May 11, 1962), in *Amtsblatt*, 1368 (June 9, 1962).

257 Judgment 24/62, *id.*, pp. 155–57.

258 Judgment 34/62 (*Germany* v. *EEC Commission*), 9 Rspr. 287 (1963).

259 Appended to plaintiff's complaint.

260 See Conclusions of *Adv-Gen.* Roemer, *op. cit.*, p. 331f.

realization of the Community agricultural policy, particularly the goals prescribed in EEC Articles 29 a) and d) and 39 (1) d) and e).

To attribute such vast consequences to a mere year's dispensation to Germany for oranges, as the Court itself grants,[261] is something of an exaggeration. Even assuming the cogency of this reasoning, the Decision is scarcely justified by the very general remarks upon which its rests. In reading the Decision, says Advocate-General Roemer,

> one can not avoid the impression that the Commission, on the basis of general agricultural policy, has seen fit to apply the requirements set out in the general Treaty rules without examining the actual economic situation and the consequences of the tariff dispensation for the year 1962. Yet such an examination is necessary if Article 25 is to fulfill its corrective function.[262]

It must be concluded, therefore, that the specific kind of reasoning demanded of the Commission in its Brandy Wine Decision was no longer in vogue two weeks later for the motivation of the orange import Decision.

Finally, a fourth variation on the motivation standard as developed by the Court is depicted by the *Firma Schwarze* Case.[263] In this Case, coming up by way of "preliminary question" procedure, the Decision of the Commission under attack is devoid literally of all reasoning and factual basis.[264] It consists simply of a schedule fixing the "free-to-frontier price" for barley imported by Germany from Holland prefaced only by reference to the Treaty, a previous Decision of the Commission and certain "price offers made known to the Commission." (On the basis of this schedule, German authorities determine the additional amount they may levy on imported grain in order to compensate for higher domestic German prices). Stating neither the source of the "price offers," the quantities and qualities in question nor the specific calculations by which the revised price schedule had been reached, the Decision seemed to the plaintiff to fail for lack of motivation.

Nevertheless, both the Court and the Advocate-General held the motivation to be fully adequate. In the first place, reasons the Court, reference to the previous Decision gave sufficient notice of the procedure and general

261 Judgment 34/62, *id.*, p. 321.

262 *Ibid.*, p. 338f.

263 Judgment 16/65 (*Firma C. Schwarze* v. *Einfuhr- und Vorratsstelle für Getreide und Futtermittel*), 11 Rspr. 1151 (1965).

264 See the Conclusions of *Adv-Gen.* Gand, *id.*, p. 1175. The Decisions themselves are not published but attached as a supplement to the weekly agricultural information.

criteria upon which the motivation was based.[265] Secondly and most importantly, the absence of specific calculations in the motivation – as are required, for instance, of the scrap levy Decisions – is justified squarely by the demands of administrative practicability. Due to the function of the "free-to-frontier prices," they must be closely attuned to the changing market; if necessary, they must be recalculated and published anew each Friday. The Commission receives the raw data Thursday afternoons on the various products and has about 24 hours to process it for each of the Member States. The specificity of motivation sought by the plaintiff would require the Commission to assess and publish a mountain of data not for just one, but for hundreds of such prices. This simply is not feasible:

> In view, first, of the time available for issuing the Decision and, secondly, of the number of prices to be set, the machinery envisaged in Regulations 19 and 89 would not be able to function properly. The preparation and editing of such motivations would consume so much time that the price set would run the danger of antedation before being issued.[266]

As a result, the Court concludes, the requirement of motivation "must be adapted to the realities, the time and the technical facilities available for making the Decision."[267] In ascertaining the accuracy of the Commission's determination, interested parties must be content to compare the prices quoted with those published in previous Decisions and the general criteria already known. Any doubts would then be resolved upon appeal to the Court, when the Commission would reveal the data in question. In this way, adequate judicial control and legal protection for the parties concerned would be preserved, while meeting the needs of administrative effectiveness[268]

The requirement of motivation, as these cases well demonstrate, provides a most flexible standard of judicial review. Though essentially procedural in character, its purpose is to test the facts and considerations upon which a Community act rests. By its very nature, this requires the application of an abstract standard to a highly individualized set of circumstances. As a result, the Court may vary widely the requirement in practice without unduly prejudicing its future application.

This built-in flexibility may be employed either in restraint of judicial

[265] See Decision No. 63 of the EEC Commission of December 21, 1962, in *Amtsblatt,* 121 (January 24, 1963), and Regulation No. 19–62 of the EEC Council of April 4, 1962, in *Amtsblatt,* 933 (April 20, 1962) to which the former refers.

[266] Judgment 16/65, *op. cit.,* p. 1168.

[267] *Ibid.,* p. 1167.

[268] See Judgment 16/65, *id.,* p. 1168.

rule-making or to strengthen judicial control. While this control is not on the merits, the judicial condemnation of a particular motivation can be so worded and employed as to force the critical reappraisal by Community organs of the Decision in question or to bring its inarticulated premises into the open. This was the effect of the *Präsident* Judgment. More frequently, as in the areas of Community investigative powers, investment policy and agricultural import restrictions, however, the Court has used its leeway in rule application to limit the motivation requirement. The *Firma Schwarze* Judgment, moreover, squarely acknowledges the impact of considerations of administrative practicability in the application of that requirement to customs decisions. In short, the motivation requirement may become a potent instrument of judicial policy. This is not to condemn it, but to put the Court on guard against an exaggerated requirement which would impinge on executive discretion and stultify administrative action. The motivation standard, says Steindorff,[269] "must steer its way between the Scylla of completely unsubstantiated motivations and the Charybdis of a requirement approaching the specificity of case pleadings."

III. Retroactivity and Certainty in Executive Decisions

A third group of cases demonstrates the institutional interplay between the Community Court and the High Authority in the search for rule practicability. Being a sequence to the Scrap Levy Cases discussed previously in this Chapter,[270] they begin where adjudication on the scrap payment formula leaves off. The High Authority, it will be recalled, exempted the circulating scrap of legally independent but "locally integrated" enterprises from payments under the scrap program. Upon appeal in the *SNUPAT* II Case, however, the Court rejected this exemption as incompatible with the principles and goals of the ECSC Treaty. Accordingly, it faulted the High Authority for not acting on plaintiff's request to revoke all such exemptions. The remaining question was one of remedy, to be answered under ECSC Article 34. Could the High Authority simply revoke retroactively individual Decisions under which certain enterprises had acted for well over three years? A delicate balance of values was at stake: between certainty in the law and the general demand of administrative legality. As a reflection of this, the laws of the Member States are divided on the question. While Belgium, France and Italy recognize in principle the retroactive revocation of illegal administrative acts which benefit the parties, legal opinion in Ger-

269 Steindorff, *Die Nichtigkeitsklage*, 70 (1952).
270 See text *supra*, p. 436ff.

many and Holland tends to look more at the particular circumstances.[271] Apparently inclined toward the latter position, the Court chose to defer determination and set the stage for a dialogue with the High Authority.

The Court proceeds, in the first place, by outlining the values to be considered. The steel firms who benefited from the exemption had asserted their reliance on administrative acts. Such a claim, replies the Court, fails to recognize "that the undoubtedly important principle of legal certainty is not absolute, but is applicable only in conjunction with the principle of administrative legality." Which of these principles takes precedence in a particular case depends on "balancing the public interest against the private interests involved." In the present case, these are:

– on the one hand, the interests of those benefited and, above all, the fact that they were permitted to believe in good faith that they need not pay charges on the scrap in question, and that in the operation of their business they could rely on the continuance of this position;
– on the other hand, the interest of the Community is the orderly functioning of a compensation program which rests on the solidarity of all scrap consuming enterprises. This interest requires that everything be done in order that the illegal exemption of some enterprises does not lead to a lasting financial disadvantage for their competitors who are subject to the tax.[272]

The Court, however, remains silent on the precise balance to be drawn. It does note that the scrap levy accounts had been settled only temporarily at the present time, so that it still would be possible to collect any back payments by instalments.[273] It even suggests that, in accordance with Member State law, administrative acts based on false or incomplete information of the parties concerned could be revoked retroactively.[274] This fact might be relevant for the present case, it believed, because both steel firms in question had taken exemptions on scrap salvaged in the "locally integrated" manufacturing plants, even though derived from steel produced in plants outside this industrial grouping.[275] Nevertheless, the Court concludes, "it is primarily the task of the High Authority to assess these facts, weigh up the various interests concerned and decide accordingly whether or not the

271 See Wiesner, *Der Widerruf individueller Entscheidungen der Hohen Behörde der EGKS*, 94–98 (1966).

272 Judgment 42 and 49/59 (*SNUPAT* v. *High Authority*), 7 Rspr. 107, 172f (1961).

273 *Ibid.*, p. 173.

274 As Wiesner, *op. cit.*, pp. 62f and 94ff, points out, however, only if the administrative act were obtained by fraud of the parties concerned.

275 Judgment 42 and 49/59, *op. cit.*, p. 173. It is somewhat ironic that the Court should emphasize this fact at this time, when it preferred to ignore it as to scrap consumed by fully consolidated companies. See text *supra*, p. 443f.

illegal exemptions are to be revoked retroactively. This was purportedly a decision which the Court could not take "in lieu of the High Authority, a determination that it must make under Article 34."[276] Accordingly, the High Authority was obliged to revoke the exemption, but whether *ex nunc* or *ex tunc* would depend on the balance of Community and private interests struck by the High Authority.

This conclusion of the Court, it should be emphasized, does not follow with such apparent logic from the language of Article 34. That Article says, referring primarily to the annulment action under Article 33 rather than to the appeal for non-action under Article 35: "In case of annulment of a Decision or Recommendation of the High Authority, the Court shall remand the matter to the High Authority. The latter shall take the measures which that judgment of annulment entails."[277] This language does not say, as the conclusion of the Court seems to suggest, that the High Authority shall take measures which *it deems* in its discretion to accord with the judgment of the Court. Moreover, it can be argued with good reason that the question of the retroactive revocation of an administrative act is properly for the Court and not the High Authority.[278] Certainly the relevant facts and considerations are available equally to the Court as to the High Authority. And the question of retroactivity is scarcely a matter peculiarly dependent on an economic evaluation by the High Authority. Instead, as the Court itself points out, it requires a balance between the Community interests in the orderly functioning of the scrap program and the reliance interest and injury of illegally exempted enterprises. Neither these concepts nor the balance to be struck belongs peculiarly or exclusively to the sphere of administrative judgment. Indeed, courts are faced daily with both aspects in almost every field of adjudication.

Not surprisingly, therefore, the Court stops short of placing the question of retroactivity wholly in the sphere of administrative discretion. Despite disclaimers of judicial competence in *SNUPAT* II, it draws no sharp distinction between the proper spheres of judicial and administrative power. Rather, as the subsequent case shows, this curb on the judicial rule-shaping

[276] *Ibid.*, p. 174.

[277] The German and French versions read as follows: "Im Falle der Nichtigerklärung verweist der Gerichtshof die Sache an die Hohe Behörde zurück. Diese hat die Massnahmen zu ergreifen, die sich aus dem Nichtigkeitsurteil ergeben"; "En cas d'annulation, la Cour renvoie l'affaire devant la Haute Autorité. Celle-ci est tenue de prendre les mesures que comporte l'exécution de la décision d'annulation."

[278] Wiesner, *op. cit.*, p. 108, contends that the standard of "public interest" raised by the Court in *SNUPAT* II is not simply a matter of administrative discretion, but an indefinite legal concept which the Court must assist in defining.

function serves to initiate a continuing discussion between the Court and the High Authority on the merits of the question. The dialogue begins immediately after the judgment in *SNUPAT* II, as the High Authority reviews its position on the exemptions granted in light of the Court's reasoning. It is satisfied, upon investigation and after consultation with the enterprises concerned, that they can not be charged (as the Court had suggested) with having given false or incomplete information.[279] Then, following the interests-balancing approach laid down by the Court, the High Authority revokes the exemptions retroactively.[280] Like the Court, it too in reaching this conclusion neither rejects the *ex nunc* nor adopts the *ex tunc* effect in principle.

In *Koninklijke Nederlandsche Hoogovens en Staalfabrieken N.V.* v. *High Authority,* one of the exempted enterprises challenges that Decision of the High Authority. While upholding the latter's position, the Court does not simply accept uncritically the reasoning of the High Authority as might have been expected had the question been one purely for administrative discretion. Instead, at the very outset it flatly rejects an argument of the High Authority designed to oust the Court's jurisdiction on the question. Though *SNUPAT* II "referred the appraisal of the facts back to the High Authority," it points out, "this does not prevent judicial review of the legality of that Decision as in the present case."[281] Indeed, the Court goes on to review the essential facts and considerations behind the Decision as well as the counter-arguments of Hoogovens, asking whether the High Authority had "correctly weighed the public interest against the private interest in question."[282]

Two main lines of argument are carefully scrutinized. The first is a variation of arguments on the theme of *de minimis* injury. Plaintiff charged that the illegal exemptions injured other enterprises as well as the scrap program only insignificantly, particularly when compared to the injury plaintiff now would suffer if it had to pay past scrap levies. In fact, the assertion went uncontradicted that Hoogovens' contribution to the scrap fund would amount to no more than 0.37% of total charges. Nevertheless, replied the Court, the amount in question was some 5 to 6 million Dutch florins; to accept such an argument not only would reward the plaintiff with an unjust enrichment, but would always exclude retroactive cancellation of illegal exemptions, for the comparison of one man's obligations to the whole would necessarily appear *de minimis*.[283] Nor could plaintiff complain because a

279 See Judgment 14/61, 8 Rspr. 511, 544f (1962), discussed immediately below.

280 High Authority Decision of June 14, 1961, appearing in part in Judgment 14/61, *id.*, p. 519–22.

281 Judgment 14/61, *id.*, p. 544.

282 *Ibid.*, p. 551.

283 *Ibid.*, p. 545.

change in the sheet metal market prevented him, unlike his competitors in previous years, from passing the scrap payments on to the consumers in the form of higher product prices. Present disadvantages, said the Court, are offset by previous advantages: while others were paying additional costs, Hoogovens was making extra profits, either at higher prices or at lower prices but expanded production.[284] Finally, the Court was unimpressed that 97.3% of plaintiff's immediate competitors in sheet metal production were integrated and, therefore, could not be harmed by an *ex nunc* revocation because they already received exemptions on their "own resources."[285] The remaining competitors, it countered, should not have to pay for Hoogovens' illegal exemptions. In any case, not even the integrated ones could fully be excluded, for they had to go outside their enterprises for some scrap.[286]

Secondly, the Court tests plaintiff's claim of injurious reliance. The High Authority, Hoogovens contended, could not revoke retroactively an exemption on which it had relied in good faith for 3½ years.[287] Without denying the soundness of the proposition itself, the Court concludes that the alleged reliance was not justified under the circumstances. While a "reasonable time" for revoking the illegal exemption might well have long since run, this depends on the type of Community act in question. In the present case, the Decision to grant exemptions to "locally integrated" enterprises had no "constitutive" but only "declaratory" effect, i.e. did not create personal rights for the plaintiff.[288] Indeed, the High Authority had "no power to grant exceptions or exemptions from the duty to contribute to the compensation

[284] *Ibid.*, p. 546.

[285] *Ibid.*, p. 546f.

[286] *Ibid.*, p. 547. Cf. criticism in note 275 *supra.*

[287] The time sequence is as follows: By a published Decision of December 18, 1957, the High Authority withdrew its initial objections to the unanimous decision of the Scrap Fund Office (October 30, 1957), which defined as "own resources" scrap recovered by Breedband from its works and delivered to plaintiff. In a letter of April 17, 1958, the High Authority published its rationale of "local integration" as the basis for the exemption. *SNUPAT* II, the Judgment of the Court condemning the exemption, was rendered on March 22, 1961, and as of June 14 of that year the High Authority cancelled the exemption with retroactive effect.

[288] As to this distinction, see the Conclusions of *Adv-Gen.* Lagrange, Case 14/61, *op. cit.*, pp. 186–88. Lagrange states that personal or vested rights arise only where "the right derives from the act," such as the appointment of an official or the grant of authority by the administration. This does not arise, on the other hand, where "the right derives solely from the statute or regulation, and the act does no more than apply the statute or regulation, interpreting it if need be." Such would be the case for the financial relations, debts and credits of the state or of public authorities, or for contested revenue claims.

program, but only to declare that the obligation to pay the levy does or does not exist."[289]

Moreover, though the basis of any reliance may be said to lie in the High Authority Decision of December 1957, Hoogovens could not "feel certain at any time" that the distinctions drawn there would be upheld by the Court. It knew of the "marked tendency" to litigate the scrap program from all angles and "particularly to make issue of situations in which there was, or appeared to be, an element of discrimination."[290] By the same token, the High Authority cannot be charged with negligence in granting the exemption and then waiting until *SNUPAT* II before revoking it. Not only is plaintiff estopped by its own conduct from making this charge, but as he well knows "the correct interpretation of the basic Decision on the distinction between purchased scrap and salvaged scrap has proven to be very debatable."[291] In any case, due to the obvious prosperity of Hoogovens, the Court was unwilling to conclude that plaintiff would suffer a serious injury by reimbursing the scrap fund for past exemptions.[292]

These cases evidence how the investigative and individualizing functions of administrative fact-finding and discretion can be harnessed to the rule-shaping task of the Court. The question of retroactivity, as defined by the Court, does not lend itself to a strict separation but rather to a unique amalgamation of the administrative and judicial functions. This is particularly true where, as here, the Court is searching for a suitable rule and, lacking the advantages of a lower trial court level, can supplement, test and precise its reasoning through the insight and experience gained by the High Authority in reaching its own decision. The technique employed is a type of judicial remand. The Court sets out the parameters which are to guide the High Authority, but without foreclosing the latter's decision upon further review. Indeed, though the remand is phrased in the traditional language of administrative discretion, the Court upon subsequent appeal makes a detailed, substantive analysis of the considerations underlying the High Authority's

289 Judgment 14/61, *id.*, p. 551. See also the subsequent Judgments 111/63, 11 Rspr. 893, 911f (1965) (no justifiable reliance on an order of the Scrap Fund which erroneously excluded the plaintiff from scrap payments); 37/64, 11 Rspr. 951, 974 (1965) (retaining a Regulation, which unjustifiably granted some enterprises advantages over others, would be discriminatory and infringe the goals of the scrap program); and 54/65, 12 Rspr. 529, 544–46 (1966) (exemptions based on "mere declarations" of the High Authority cannot create reliance).

290 Judgment 14/61, *id.*, p. 550.

291 *Ibid.*, p. 551.

292 *Ibid.*, p. 553. For *Adv-Gen.* Lagrange, an injury to the plaintiff would only then be relevant if it amounted to something bordering on economic collapse. *Ibid.*, p. 576.

decision. Thus, a show of judicial restraint became the entrée for an institutional interplay. What began as an apparent delineation of powers was consummated as a dialogue between the Court and the High Authority.

At the Edge of Community Jurisdiction

The institutional limits on judicial rule-shaping are reflected also in the powers reserved to the Member States and their authorities. The very attempt to establish the Communities along functional lines, rather than on the basis of plenary powers, creates delicate problems of coordination between the Community and Member State legal orders. Thus, as a matter of principle, Community law and Member State law have been deemed to "constitute two distinct legal orders independent of each other." [293] Not only has the Community Court no express authority to construe national law, it further has refused at times to draw on national law for the interpretation of the Treaties.[294] This position of course provides the Court with a certain leverage for advancing the uniform application and independent authority of Community law in the Member States. At the same time, it enables the Court to avoid embarrassing confrontations with Member State authorities as well as entanglements in the niceties of national law.

From an administrative viewpoint, the Communities simply have not been equipped with the line organization necessary to implement the Treaties independent of Member State authorities. As a result, the relatively small staff of the new Commission, approximately 5,000 members as presently combined since July 1, 1967,[295] must rely heavily on close cooperation with national administrative machinery. In nine out of ten cases, as Donner points out,[296] the final execution and implementation of Community law lies with national agencies and officers. The problem for the Court is to formulate rules which respect the limits of Community jurisdiction while affording an effective coordination with Member State law. Two cases, one in the field of customs duties and the other in the field of antitrust, well

[293] Judgment 13/61 (*Bosch* Case), 8 Rspr. 97, 110 (1962), discussed in text *supra*, p. 346f, together with the *van Gend & Loos* Judgment.

[294] See discussion in text *supra*, p. 347f (*Unger* Case), p. 350, particularly at n. 138, and pp. 356–359.

[295] See Knöpfle, "Organisation und Arbeitsweise der Gemeinsamen Kommission der Europäischen Gemeinschaften," 3 Europarecht 30, 46–59 and 53 (1968), who notes that the merger of the Community executive organs may decrease this combined staff to 4,000. See also the discussion by Coppe, "Eurocrat's 'Identity,'" *European Community* 10 (No. 131, February 1970).

[296] Donner, *The Role of the Lawyer in the European Communities* 164f (1968).

illustrate the Court's sensitivity and sound approach to this problem of rule practicability.

I.

The first case, *EEC Commission* v. *Italy*,[297] turns on an apparent ambiguity in the formula for determining the applicable customs duty on Italian imports of radio-electronic equipment. Which of two customs duties – the one actually applied or the one lawfully applicable – should serve as the "basic duty" for calculating successive tariff reductions under EEC Article 14 (1). That Article stipulates:

For each product, the basic duty to which the successive reductions shall apply shall be duty applied on January 1, 1957.

On that date, alternative custom rates were applicable on imports to Italy of radio-electronic equipment from the other Member States. The one rate originated with the Annecy Tariff Conference of 1949, the other stemmed from the Sixth Protocol to the Geneva Conference which Italy signed on May 23, 1956. Pending parliamentary ratification of that Protocol, Italian customs officials were ordered by executive decree to apply the rate more favorable to the importer.

The Italian Government sought to take the new Geneva rates as its "basic duty." These not only worked most advantageously for Italian manufacturers, they also allegedly were the only lawfully existing rates at the time. Thus, by presidential decree of July 2, 1956, the new rates were given effect subject only to temporary application of the alternative Annecy rates in the event they were lower. This alternative was viewed simply as a special dispensation to foreign exporters pending ratification of the Geneva Protocol by the Italian Parliament. Though ratification did not occur until January 2, 1958, the President of the Republic nevertheless was empowered to enforce it from signatory date. In signing the Geneva Protocol, therefore, Italy became bound to the new rates and, except for special dispensation by executive order, the existing duties under the Annecy convention became ineffective.

Moreover, Italy contended, the new rates were protected expressly by EEC Article 234. Under that provision, "the rights and obligations arising from agreements concluded between one or more Member States and . . .

297 Judgment 10/61 (*EEC Commission* v. *Italy*), 8 Rspr. 1 (1962).
298 EEC Art. 234, par. 1. Emphasis added.

third countries before this [EEC] Treaty came into force shall not be affected by the provisions of this Treaty." [298] Since this Article relates to the time the convention is concluded, rather than to the time of its ratification, Italy was not only authorized but obligated to apply the Geneva rates to the products in question.

As a matter of law, therefore, Italy appeared to have built a strong case for the new rates. The Court rejected both arguments, however, adopting in each case the more practicable views of the Commission. Thus, Italy could not invoke EEC Article 234 in derogation of its Treaty obligations. The rights protected there are those of third countries, not of the Member States. "Under principles of international law, a State assuming a new obligation, which is contrary to the rights it possesses under a previous treaty, relinquishes those rights to the extent necessary for the fulfillment of the new obligation." [299] By carefully distinguishing between prior rights and prior duties, the one with respect to third countries and the other as to Member States, the demands of the Rome Treaty could be squared with the Geneva Protocol.

The more difficult question concerned the applicable rate of duty. While the text of EEC Article 14 (1) referring to "the duty *applied* on January 1, 1957," argues in favor of the duty applied in fact, it is not conclusive. What if the duty actually applied were unlawful or erroneously calculated under Italian law? On the other hand, as Advocate-General Lagrange well notes, the Court "would go too far in demanding or allowing a test of legality or even of constitutionality with respect to the duty levied." This would carry judicial review into the realm of interpreting national law. It would also require judicial scrutiny of each rate appealed to the Court. In order to avoid such "inextricable complications," said Lagrange, it was necessary to find "a rule whose application was simple and to a certain extent automatic." [300]

The Court too acknowledged these competing considerations. Italy's line of argument, it said, "would oblige the Commission, and eventually the Court, to inquire in each specific case into the validity of domestic administrative measures with respect to the law of the interested Member State." Such an inquiry would exceed the mandates of both Community institutions, and "would lead to inacceptable consequences." [301] For this reason, the Court held to a literal interpretation of the Treaty, looking to the customs rate actually applied on January 1, 1957, as reflected in the uniform application

299 Judgment 10/61, *op. cit.*, p. 22f.
300 Conclusions of *Adv-Gen.* Lagrange, *ibid.*, p. 31f and also p. 41.
301 Judgment 10/61, *ibid.*, p. 21.

by the Italian customs administration of the official tariff tables then in effect. The legality of these tariff rates of course must be presumed, but the presumption has an operational basis in the national legal systems. The burden of assuring the legality of the actual rates is left with the domestic importers and their competitors, namely, with the persons most immediately affected by erroneous or unlawful tariff schedules. So long as these persons had not successfully attacked or were content with the legality of the official tariff tables, the Court too could rely justifiably upon them. In this way delicate issues of Italian law would be avoided. The Court offered a rule, therefore, which respected both the requirements of practicability and the independence of Member State law.

II.

In the Dyestuff Case, decided on February 13, 1969, the Court faced an issue going to the very basis of the EEC as a common market.[302] What is the relationship between Community and Member State law in the face of concurrent proceedings against alleged illegal practices? The question was prompted by a submission from the Berlin Court of Appeals under EEC Article 177, based on penal action by the German Federal Cartel Office against four German dyestuff manufacturers (Badische Anilin und Soda-Fabrik AG, Farbenfabriken Bayer AG, Farbwerke Hoechst AG and Casella Farbwerke Mainkur AG) and three of their managers for illegal price-fixing under Sections 1 and 38 (1) No. 1 of the German antitrust statute.[303] The questions submitted did not go to the substance of the case. Rather, since the EEC Commission concurrently had opened proceedings in the same case for violation of EEC Article 85, they concerned essentially jurisdiction. Under these circumstances, the Berlin court asked: (1) Is it compatible with EEC Article 85 and their implementing Regulations to apply the prohibitions of Community and Member State law cumulatively? (2) Or does the risk of dual penalties in that case preclude cumulative application? (3) Is cumulative application of Community and Member State laws contrary to EEC Articles 3(f) and 5 and Article 9 of Regulation No. 17 (on cartels), which call for the establishment of a system ensuring undistorted competition in the Common Market? (4) Is it contrary to EEC Article 7, prohibiting discrimination on grounds of nationality, that one

[302] Judgment 14/68 (*Wilhelm, et al.* v. *Federal Cartel Office*), 15 Rspr. 1 (1969).

[303] Decision of November 28, 1967, reprinted in *Wirtschaft und Wettbewerb* 407 (1968).

State's nationals are adversely affected by the measures of its cartel authority in relation to the nationals of other Member States who are similarly situated?

The Court heard arguments not only by the defendants, but also by the governments of France, Germany and the Netherlands and by the EEC Commission. The three governments, together with Advocate-General Roemer, adhered to the prevailing "double barrier" theory: anticompetitive practices of Community enterprises may be subject to the independent and cumulative application of both Community and Member State law.[304] The EEC Commission, on the other hand, took a more conciliatory position. As a matter of principle there was nothing, in its view, to prevent a concurrent application of Community and national antitrust prohibitions, provided that the "uniform application and enforcement of Community law" was not thereby impaired. Only the defendants argued that, where EEC Article 85 applied, it preempted the field and excluded the application of German antitrust law.[305]

The Court followed the lead of the Commission. As its point of departure, it acknowledged the possibility that "the same cartel may, in principle, be the subject of two parallel proceedings, one before the Community authorities under EEC Article 85 and the other before the national authorities under internal law." Thus, while it admitted that, "because of the possible interdependence between economic circumstances and the legal situation," a distinction between Community and national law might not always be justified, nevertheless these legal systems may "take different approaches to antitrust matters." The first views them from the standpoint of interstate trade, the latter from the peculiar and widely varying perspectives of Member State policy.[306] Moreover, since EEC Article 87(2)(e)

[304] For a discussion of the "double barrier" theory, see its originator: Koch, "Das Verhaeltnis der Kartellvorschriften des EWG-Vertrages zum Gesetz gegen Wettbewerbsbeschraenkungen," Der Betriebsberater 241 (1959). See also Niederleithinger, "Deutsches Kartellrecht und das Gemeinschaftsrecht," 14 AWD 371 (1968).

[305] For a discussion of this approach, see Mestmäcker, "Parallele Geltung von Verbotsnormen des deutschen und europaeischen Rechts gegen Wettbewerbsbeschraenkungen," Der Betriebsberater 1297 (1968).

[306] Judgment 14/68, *op. cit.*, p. 13. As to the varying approaches of Member State antitrust law, see the brief overview of Markert, "The Dyestuff Case: A Contribution to the Relationship Between the Antitrust Laws of the European Economic Community and its Member States," 14 Antitrust Bulletin 869, 870-72 (1969); and the more extensive analyses of Riesenfeld, "The Protection of Competition," in Stein and Nicholson, *American Enterprise in the European Common Market,* vol. II, p. 207ff (1960), and Blake (ed.), *Business Regulation in the Common Market Nations,* vols. I, II and III (1969).

empowers the Council to issue Regulations "to determine the relationship between national laws and the provisions of EEC Articles 85 and 86," the concurrent application of Member State antitrust law must have been intended.[307] Insofar the "double barrier" theory was affirmed.

Had the Court stopped here, it would seriously have weakened the effectiveness of Community antitrust law. Application of Community law, especially in situations where a fine balance of economic and legal factors exists, could be undermined on either of two levels by conflicting national decisions. The primary objective of Community law, the Court points out, is "to remove obstacles to the free movement of goods in the Common Market and to ensure and strengthen the unity of that market." Thus, EEC Article 85 (1) prohibits certain anticompetitive practices of every enterprise in the Community. Beyond this, however, the Commission is also authorized "to exercise some positive, albeit indirect control for the furtherance of a harmonious development of economic activity throughout the Community, in accordance with EEC Article 2." Thus, pursuant to EEC Article 85 (3), The Commission may under certain conditions grant dispensation to cartels which help to improve the production or distribution of products or to promote technical or economic progress." [308] EEC antitrust regulation, therefore, reflects positive aspects of policy implementation as well as the negative prohibitions of anticompetitive practices.

Contrary to the original understanding of the "double barrier" theory, therefore, the concurrent application of Community and Member State laws may result in more than simply cumulative penalties on the same prohibited practice. Serious cases of conflict could arise. For this reason, the Court qualified its initial statement by an important proviso:

> Because the general definitive character of the Treaty must be respected, this parallel application of the national system is permissible only insofar as it does not jeopardize the uniform application of Community antitrust law and the full effectiveness of its implementing measures throughout the Common Market. Any other solution would be incompatible with the objectives of the Treaty and the nature of its rules of competition.[309]

Further the Court drew the necessary implication of this proviso and concluded that in such cases any conflict between Community and national law "must be resolved by applying the principle of priority of Community law." [310] This means, the Court concludes, that until Community Regu-

[307] Judgment 14/68, *id.*
[308] *Ibid.*, p. 14.
[309] *Ibid.*, p. 13f.
[310] *Ibid.*

lations under EEC Article 87(2)(e) provide otherwise, or unless the uniform and effective application of Community law is jeopardized, national authorities may proceed under internal law against enterprises faced with concurrent action by Community authorities. Further, it rejects defendant's view that EEC Article 7 prohibits Member State action in such cases. The Community prohibition in Article 7 against discrimination "does not apply to possible disparities in treatment and distortions that arise out of difference between the laws of the Member States, where such laws affect all persons subject to them according to objective criteria and without regard to nationality." [311]

In searching for a workable conflicts rule the Court wisely has made perfectly clear that there are no easy solutions. The parallel and competing nature of Community and Member State legal orders permits no automatic preemption of national law in the realm of antitrust application, at least not until the Council of Ministers has exercised its authority to the contrary under EEC Article 87(2)(e).[312] The concept of what constitutes "prejudice" to the "full and uniform application of Community law and the effectiveness of measures issued or to be taken for its implementation" is left for future judicial determination.[313] For the interim, the Court sets out two guidelines. As a general principle, "should the Commission, during the course of a national proceeding against the same cartel, reach a decision which would not be compatible with the effects of the decision of the national authorities, then these authorities must take the appropriate measures." [314] More specifically, as regards the application of EEC Article 85 (1) prohibitions, "so far as cumulative penalties would result from dual prosecution, general considerations of equity – expressly found in ECSC Article 90 (2) – require that any determination of penalties take into account the prior penalties." [315] Presumably, this should guide national courts as well as the Community Court, although the latter could not prescribe this result for the former.

The importance of the Dyestuff Case is that it offers a workable framework for pursuing the complex questions involved in the relationship be-

311 *Ibid.*, p. 15f.

312 When asked by a member of the European Parliament whether, in light of the Community Court's decision the time had not come for Council regulation of Community-Member State antitrust laws pursuant to EEC Article 87(2)(e), the Council replied that this would require a thorough study by the authorized Community institutions. Written Question No. 260/9, *Amtsblatt* No. C5. (January 13, 1970)

313 Judgment 14/68, *op. cit.*, p. 17.

314 *Ibid.*, p. 14.

315 *Ibid.*, p. 15.

tween Community and national antitrust law.[316] Rather than grasp for hasty solutions, it sets the outlines of the problem, draws the minimum requirements for the effective application of Community law and opens the door to continuing discussion on the remaining questions.

CONCLUSIONS

The search for practicability in the law, discussed in this Chapter, demands large amounts of imaginative craftsmanship from the Court of Justice. Highly complex sets of social facts and patterns, peculiar to economic regulation in the Communities, must be reduced to manageable rules of conduct. In the Scrap Levy Cases, the Court comes face to face with this requirement, expressly relying on the need for simplicity and clarity in rule-shaping in order to avoid uncertainty in rule application. The few examples considered in this Chapter, moreover, further reflect the need to reach below the facade of legal concepts into the underlying economics or sociology of the behavioral problems which the law seeks to regulate. Pragmatic reasoning seeks to elaborate a rule which can orient and guide such conduct in terms of specific ends of the law. Unfortunately, as the Scrap Levy and *Grundig-Consten* Cases amply demonstrate, the Court has failed to press its inquiry sufficiently toward these underlying rationale and operative factors. As a result, the rule runs the danger both of missing its mark and lacking the insight necessary to further predictability in the law.

From an institutional perspective, the judicial search for practicability sensitively reflects the delicate balance in the law between rule and discretion. The Court fully embraces the latter aspect not only in its shaping of the relevant facts, but also in the application of abstract concepts to highly individualized fact situations. The motivation requirement, for instance, exemplifies both a widely varying application in practice as well as a valuable tool of judicial policy. There are limits, however, even to this type of judicial discretion and, more generally, to effective rule-shaping. The court has recognized these limits by deferring to executive discretion in the timing and decision to enforce treaty obligations. Such determinations can not easily be dictated by standardized conditions. Further, when faced with the complexities of national law, the Court has endeavored to adopt a rule which respects the limits of Community jurisdiction while deferring the underlying questions of legality to the legal processes in the Member States. Finally, as

[316] See, for instance, the thorough discussion and suggestions offered by Markert *op. cit.*, pp. 886-94.

has been true in other respects in the preceding Chapters, the limits on judicial rule-shaping also have given rise to the mode of judicial remand. In an epilogue to the Scrap Levy Judgments, the Court and the High Authority engaged in an exchange of views which laid the basis for determining the legality of the retroactive cancellation of Community acts. By the same token, the Dyestuff Case carefully established the minimum requirements for Community jurisdiction in antitrust regulation; yet it also set the framework for continuing discussion with national authorities of the complex relationship between Community and Member State law. For the various reasons peculiar to the judicial search for practicability, therefore, the Court clearly has recognized the third type of institutional constraint on the full exercise of the judicial power.

CONCLUSIONS

The first seventeen years of the European Communities, beginning with the establishment of the Coal and Steel Community in the early 1950's has witnessed the emergence of innovatory legal orders. Though not belonging to the traditional spheres of either national or international law, these new legal orders are in essence constitutional. Thus, despite their Treaty basis, the limited powers granted them encompass fundamental areas of economic regulation and reach far into the domain traditionally claimed for national sovereignty alone. The authorized acts as well as the self-executing provisions of the Treaties directly bind Member State nationals and their enterprises. They apply also to the laws and authorities of the Member States. In stark contrast to the international community, moreover, Community powers are exercised and Community law develops within the disciplined, institutionalized framework of a division and balance of governmental functions. This organizational framework embraces the play of powers not only among Community institutions, but also between the Communities and the Member State governments as represented in the Council of Ministers. As a result, while the Communities lack the political and organizational solidarities of a federal governmental structure, from an institutional viewpoint they still possess the essential elements for independent policy formation and the building stones for a future European government. By the same token, they offer the necessary drive and impetus for challenging the Member States to continued economic and political integration.

Within this constitutional framework the Court of Justice is called to be both guardian of the Treaties and arbiter of the balance of powers in the Communities. As guardian of the Treaties, it must preserve the unity and integrity of Community legal orders in the face of divergent special interests of individual enterprises and Member States. To this end, the Court has been endowed with broad powers of judicial review. Thus, its mandatory jurisdiction may be invoked against Community organs in violation of the Treaties by other Community organs, Member States and Member State nationals. It similarly may be invoked against defaulting Member States by such parties, though not by Member State nationals except through the "preliminary question" procedure or, in the ECSC, via the appeal against non-action of the Commission. Moreover, the Court repeatedly has required Member States, who allegedly faced emergency situations, to comply with Community decision-making procedures before increasing import restrictions on products from other Member States. The notion of "self help" for States, as it is known in international law, has no place in the Community legal structure.

The Court, on the other hand, also assumes an arbiter function as its decisions touch the more delicate, and typically fundamental, questions of Community law. At those points the highly political premises of the Communities become visible. Such questions, thus far, have not been raised so much as to the balance of powers between Community organs, perhaps because of the rudimentary structure of this balance and of the great influence of Member State governments in the Communities. Rather, they have touched primarily the scope and limits of Community powers vis-à-vis the Member States. Thus, in the Luxembourg Coal Levies, the Rail Tariffs and the Miners' Bonus Judgments, the Court's decisions turned in large part on the character of partial integration in the ECSC. The overriding Community objective of economic rationality had to be weighed against the primary responsibility of Member States for their general economic policy. By the same token, the "implied powers" reasoning of the Court amply demonstrates that a plenary Community power does not necessarily exist for every Treaty objective. Indeed, its necessary implication may depend largely upon whether, as to the area in question, there exists a hard core consensus on substantive Community policy among the Member States. For this reason, the Court at times may weigh in prudence the necessity for the Community power in question against the expected reluctance of Member States to subject their policies to Community review and control. This is not to say that the question in such cases is less fit for judicial determination, but only that the underlying element of consensus clearly takes on added weight in legal development.

These diverse aspects of judicial review in reality constitute just one judicial function, the immensely creative function of judicial interpretation. It originates essentially from a teleological view of judicial decision whose major ingredients are the search for purpose, for authority and for practicability in the law. These ends of law not only frame the rationality of judicial decision, but also establish the evolutionary basis for legal development. In the search for purpose, for instance, the Court rejected a fixed hierarchy of Treaty norms. Instead, through the self-critical discipline of topical reasoning, the Court pressed its inquiry beyond the literal meaning of the Treaty norms toward an economic philosophy of workable competition in the ECSC which would permit a balanced realization of potentially conflicting Treaty goals. Such *topoi* as "reasonableness," "common interest," "discrimination," "subvention" and "normal conditions of competition" became the rhetorical means for focusing judicial analysis in the ECSC on the problems of a common price system, orderly markets, special burdens and benefits to industry and a minimum degree of competition. At the same time, the Court has recognized the inherent limits on judicial knowledge. It has granted Community organs considerable discretion in the formulation of Community policy, so long as they respect those minimum standards of substantive due process which are basic to the rule of law.

The Court, moreover, has carefully supplemented its self-critical development of Community law by the persuasive reasoning inherent in the search for authority. Not only must the law be worthy of respect, society also must believe that the law is worthy of respect. This fact becomes particularly acute for the newly emerging Community legal orders. For this reason, the Court has been aware of the need to preserve and further a developing Community consensus. This means, as already noted, that the Court secure the integrity of fundamental Community procedures against the centrifugal tendencies of national interests. It also means developing rhetorical techniques by which to build a common body of Community law and, with it, the basis to engender widespread support for isolated and sometimes unpopular judicial pronouncements.

As in the search for purpose, here too specialized *topoi* have become the focal points and the bearers of judicial reasoning. Their function, however, is not so much to inform as it is to persuade the interested public. Clearly the Court's reasoning from probable effects is of this type. It has helped bridge the gap between the absence of a supremacy clause in favor of Community law and the working necessity for Member States to respect that law if the Communities are to continue intact.

Other *topoi* also, traditionally subsumed under the category of legal sources, contribute to continuity and predictability in the law. Ultimately, they form a broad residue of generally accepted judicial reasoning. Unfortunately, the formation of these legal sources, particularly that of judicial precedent, has proceeded quite slowly. While prior decisions are occasionally cited, they are rarely elaborated in a meaningful way. As a result, a great deal of potential judicial authority lies fallow. The style of the Court's opinion-writing, on the other hand, is by and large extensively reasoned and aimed at persuading rather than merely declaring the law. In particular, the Court has been careful to build a concept of Community law which emphasizes the autonomous character of the Treaty legal systems and the interdependency of Member State obligations. Despite certain weaknesses in its approach, therefore, the Court has accepted the basic premise of the search for authority in Community law.

Finally, the teleological methodology of the Court is enriched by the pragmatic reasoning inherent in the search for practicability in the law. The Court must shape concrete rules of application which bind together in workable effective fashion the Treaty language with the business behavior and social patterns that the law is intended to control. While the Court has expressly acknowledged these demands of practicability, it has not always accepted their dictates in practice. This was notably true in the Scrap Levy Cases where the judicial formula for assessing the scrap levy fell short of the market policies underlying the compensation program itself. A more thoroughly reasoned topical analysis, focusing on functionally related rules rather than isolated legal concepts, would have led the Court to a less rigid and arbitrary definition of "enterprise" and to a more economically sound formula for assessing the scrap levy.

By the same token, the *per se* reasoning in the *Grundig-Consten* Judgment reflects the pressures of time and of administrative efficiency on judicial rule shaping. While the Court failed to deal in depth with both the facts and the economic theory behind the closed territorial arrangement in question, rule manageability was the recognized order of the day. Unfortunately, in the area of economic regulation, the Court's jurisprudence has been plagued generally by its failure to analyze and present the facts and underlying theory in the detail necessary to assure to a reasonable extent that the resulting rule will be both manageable and capable of attaining the Treaty goals. The ambiguity in judicial reasoning, that on occasion has served so well the search for authority, often impedes the search for practicability in Community law. As a result, while the Court's style of opinion-writing reveals extensive reasoning, the reasoning itself too often lacks adequately detailed and technical analysis.

These three tasks of creative judicial decision do not necessarily lead to a harmonious conclusion in a particular case. The most workable rule does not always allow the most just solution, nor will the most just solution always have sufficient support among the governing powers, or the real public, in the Communities. Various facets of these internal conflicts appeared in the Scrap Levy Cases, the *Vloeberghs* Judgment and the *Grundig-Consten* Decision. Such "preliminary question" decisions as *Albatros,* moreover, suggest that the absence of active support for Community norms among the Member States and Commission may stifle the search for purpose in the law. The proper approach in such cases, as the Court expressly recognized in the Scrap Levy Cases, is not to gloss over these conflicts, but to give them a candid hearing. Above all, the Court must seek so far as possible in each decision to accommodate these conflicting tasks. Paradigm examples of this accommodation may be found in the German and French Rail Tariff cases, in the *Vloeberghs* Judgment and in *EEC Commission* v. *Italy* concerning the Geneva Protocol on basic duties. In each case, the Court worked out a rule of the case which adequately resolved the conflicts arising within the search for purpose, authority and practicability in the law.

Despite this tension and the actual conflicts which may result, these three tasks of the Court also reflect a more fundamental and enduring characteristic of Community law. They contribute to an evolving consensus on constitutional values in the European Communities, for the reason and consent which they combine are the twin roots of a developing legal order. Thus, the new insights which are gained through the self-critical, persuasive and pragmatic reasoning of the Court are tested continually against the empirical standard of consent as defined by specific types of publics. In this way, through the exercise of judicial review, the Court can help ensure that the fundamental values which evolve as part of the constitutional consensus not only are authoritatively accepted throughout the Communities, but also are just in their objective and translated concretely into workable rules.

By the same token, this evolving consensus offers the Court a viable basis for its legitimating power. It forms a fertile admixture of the governing powers and publics of the Communities in which judicial reasoning may be planted and by which acceptance may be generated for the Court's decisions throughout the Communities. Thus, the Court has relied on the legitimating mode of tradition by reasoning from the established principles of the international and national legal orders. It has appealed also to the unity and integrity of Community law, to basic notions of justice in the law and to the ongoing process of integration in the Communities, and in that way identified itself charismatically with the ultimate goals of the European Communities themselves. Finally, in reasoning from the requirements of rule simplicity and of administrative necessity and effectiveness, and from the literal meaning of the Treaty text, the Court has drawn on the legitimating mode of legality. As a result, within the methodological framework of the search for purpose, authority and practicability in the law, the jurisprudence of the Court has contributed uniquely to the maintenance and development of a consensus underlying Community law.

Institutionally viewed, however, the power of the Court is limited. The Court has no monopoly over legal development, either in the search for purpose, authority or practicability in the law. Instead, Community government reflects a continuum of decision-making among all governmental authorities, in which the Court is qualified to determine only certain issues, and then often only some one facet of the particular issue in question. For this reason, the Court has carefully delineated its jurisdictional authority when challenged. More significantly, as in the *Hamborner Bergbau*, the *Niederrheinische Bergwerk* and the *Vloeberghs* Judgments, it has employed its power of interpretation to restrict the standing of private litigants to attack the exercise by the High Authority of its taxing and emergency powers as well as the failure of the High Authority to proceed against defaulting Member States. On other occasions, as the Scrap Judgments and the Brandy Wine and Orange Import Cases well demonstrate, the Court has expressly restricted its own scope of review in favor of the quasi-legislative prerogative of other Community organs. And, in the *E.N.E.L.* and *Albatros* Decisions, the extremely abstract and truncated reasoning of the Court on the Treaty articles at issue reflects a prudent attempt to avoid potentially embarrassing confrontations between Community and Member State policy. In this way, the Court has manifested a keen awareness of the real limits of its power in the development of Community law. These limits extend beyond the formal lines of the Court's jurisdiction and encompass its institutional capacity to treat adequately the issues before it. The Court not only acts, therefore, it is also acted upon.

Above all, the exercise of judicial power is not restrained for its own sake. The principle of judicial moderation is an integral part of the judicial style characterized by the dialectic of judicial decision. Rather than risk the danger of cutting-off constructive discussion, of prematurely polarizing opinion or of blunting the development of a well-shaped rule, the Court often is best advised to stay its hand permanently, or for a time, as to those aspects of a question which are better resolved by or with the assistance of the insight and procedures of other branches of government. Not only may the Court stay its hand, but also by resort to the techniques of judicial remand it may focus the issues and press discussion among the Community organs and the Member States. Thus, although the Court unfortunately failed to take this approach in the Road Tariff Publication Judgments, its reasoning in the *Meroni* Judgment and in the *Geitling, Nold* and *Präsident* series of Judgments well illustrates how the Court may force the High Authority to reconsider the underlying substantive issues of a case by nullifying Community Decisions on essentially procedural grounds. Or, as in the *SNUPAT* II and *Koninklijke Nederlandsche Hoogovens* Cases, the Court worked in concert with the High Authority to shape a rule to govern the retroactive revocation of illegal Community Decisions. Similarly, within the disciplined framework of the "preliminary question" procedure, the Court initiated a dialogue with Member State courts by the liberal use of obiter dictum and visibly furthered the authority of Community law. In each instance, the exercise of judicial restraint became the occasion for involving other Community organs in discourse on vital questions in the development of Community law.

The dialectic of judicial decisions represents the capstone of judicial review. As a judicial style, it portrays an acute awareness of the limits on judicial knowledge and on the law as an instrument of social control. It further demands an in-depth appreciation of the relative strengths and weaknesses of the principal institutions of government. These institutional realities in turn must be woven, as the Court has done to a large extent, into finely crafted, extensively reasoned decisions which are technically sound as well as statesmanlike well-balanced judgments. The dialectic, moreover, contributes to an evolving consensus on constitutional values in the Communities. It not only disciplines discussion on these values, but offers continuity and direction for such discourse. It expands the rationality of judicial decision to include the combined wisdom of the principal organs of Community and Member State governments. Above all, the dialectic of judicial decision strengthens that loyalty to the law without which law cannot exist. That is to say, it stresses not primarily adherence to rules as such, but rather to the overriding search for purpose, authority and practicability in the law.

In terms of the standards of judicial decision examined here, therefore, the Court of Justice has contributed greatly to the responsible development of Community law. Both as a matter of substance in the realm of trade and competition and as a matter of procedure in the formation and implementation of Community policy, its jurisprudence has raised and dealt with many questions which are fundamental to the European Communities as ongoing enterprises. In doing so, the Court not only has shaped constitutional values in the Communities, it also has consolidated a constitutional framework for their continuing evolution. Herein lies its enduring contribution to European economic integration. The evolving consensus on values, which underlies successful integration, must continually be structured within the context of the Community legal orders as a whole. At the same time, the structuring of these values must not foreclose, but must be permitted to generate further legal development. The creative tasks of judicial decision in the search for purpose, authority and practicability in the law offer a rationality for stimulating this legal development. They also allow the Court to operate fully, intelligibly and responsibly within the real limits of the peculiar institutional context of Community government. Most importantly, they portray a legal development based ultimately on reasoned choice. As a result, the creative tasks of the Court embrace and further the objective of economic integration.

BIBLIOGRAPHY

The bibliography is divided into two main parts: the first lists the literature dealing with the European Communities, while the second lists that concerning the theory of judicial decision generally.

1. LITERATURE ON THE EUROPEAN COMMUNITIES

Documents

ECSC, High Authority Bulletin. Luxembourg, serial.

– High Authority, General Reports on the Activities of the Community, with annexes. Luxembourg, annual.

European Community, Official Journal (= Amtsblatt, Journal Officiel) of the European Communities. Brussels, serial.

– Court of Justice, Reports of Judgments (= Sammlung der Rechtsprechung, Recueil de la Jurisprudence). Luxembourg, serial.

– European Parliament, Documents of Proceedings (= Sitzungsdokumente). Strassburg, serial.

EEC, Commission, "Erste Aufzeichnung der Kommission an dem Rat über die Politik der Gemeinschaft im Bereich von Erdöl und Erdgas," in Sonderbeilage zum Bulletin der EWG No. 7. Brussels, July 1966.

– Commission, General Reports on the Activities of the Community, with annexes. (German ed.) Brussels, annual.

Federal Republic of Germany, Entwurf eines Gesetzes über die Gründung der EGKS vom 18. April, 1951, Begründung des Vertragswerkes (Anlage 3), Drucksache No. 2401. Deutscher Bundestag, I. Wahlperiode, 1949.

– Entwurf eines Gesetzes zu den Verträgen vom 25. Maerz 1957 zur Gründung der EWG und der Euratom, Drucksache No. 3440. Deutscher Bundestag, 2. Wahlperiode May 4, 1957.

– Ergänzung zu dem Entwurf des Gesetzes (just cited), Drucksache No. 3615. Deutscher Bundestag, 2. Wahlperiode, June 13, 1957.

France, Ministère des Affaires Étrangères, Rapport de la Délégation Française sur le Traité instituant la CECA. 1951.

Treaties of the European Communities with texts, protocols, conventions, annexes and Statutes of the Court of Justice, in particular:

Treaty Establishing the European Coal and Steel Community – Paris, April 18, 1951.
Treaty Establishing the European Atomic Energy Community – Rome, March 25, 1957.
Treaty Establishing the European Economic Community – Rome, March 25, 1957.
Convention Relating to Certain Institutions Common to the European Communities, of March 25, 1957.
Treaty Establishing a Single Council and a Single Commission of the European Communities, together with the Protocol on the Privileges and Immunities of The European Communities, the Final Act and The Decision by the Representatives of the Governments of The Member States Relating to The Provisional Installation of Certain Institutions and Services of the Communities, of April 8, 1965.

Books and Monographs

Actes Officiels du Congrès sur la C.E.C.A. Stresa, 1957.
Alder, C. Die Befugnisse der Organe der EWG gegenüber Mitgliedstaaten und Privatunternehmen. Basel, 1962.
Bächle, H-U. Die Rechtsstellung der Richter am Gerichtshof der Europäischen Gemeinschaften. Berlin, 1961.
Balassa, B. The Theory of Economic Integration. London, 1962.
Ballerstedt, K. Uebernationale und nationale Marktordnung. Tübingen, 1955.
Bandilla, R. Das Klagerecht der Mitgliedstaaten der Europäischen Gemeinschaften gegen Durchgriffsakte. Hamburg, 1965.
Bebr, G. Judicial Control of the European Communities. London, 1962.
Becker, P. Der Einfluss des französischen Verwaltungsrechts auf den Rechtschutz in den Europäischen Gemeinschaften. Hamburg, 1963.
Beloff, M. Europe and the Europeans. London, 1957.
Benoit, E. Europe at Sixes and Sevens: The Common Market, The Free Trade Association and the United States. Columbia Univ. Press, 1961.
Berie, H. and Miller, R. Gemeinsamer Markt und Euratom. Berlin 1959.
Bernhardt, R. Die Auslegung völkerrechtlicher Verträge. Berlin, 1963.
Bindschedler, R. Rechtsfragen der Europäischen Einigung. Basel, 1954.
Blake, H. M. Business Regulations in the Common Market Nations. III Vols. New York and London, 1969.
Boehmer, G. Der völkerrechtliche Vertrag im deutschen Recht. Cologne and Berlin, 1965.
Bok, D. The First Three Years of the Schuman Plan. Princeton Univ. Press, 1955.
Bonaert, A. et al. Fragen der Nichtigkeits- und Untätigkeitsklagen nach dem Recht der EGKS. Frankfurt, 1961.
Bonnefous, E. L'Europe en face de son destin. Paris, 1952.
Bowett, D. W., The Law of International Institutions. London 1963.
Breitner, F. Der Gerichtshof der Montangemeinschaft und seine Anrufung bei fehlerhaften Organakten. Hamburg, 1954.

Buerstedde, S. Der Ministerrat im konstitutionellen System der Europäischen Gemeinschaften. Brussels, 1964.
Bülow, E. and Ipsen, H-P, Aktuelle Fragen des Europäischen Gemeinschaftsrechts. Stuttgart, 1965.
Catalano, N. Manuale di Diritto delle Comunità Europee. Milan, 2d ed. 1965.
– La CEE e l'Euratom. Milan, 1957.
Colin, J-P. Le Gouvernement des juges dans les Communautés Européennes. Paris, 1966.
Collège d'Europe, Droit communautaire et droit national: Semaine de Bruges. Brussels, 1965.
Commission d'étude interuniversitaire de l'Institut royal des Relations internationales. Les Conséquences d'ordre interne de la participation de la Belgique aux organizations internationales. The Hague, 1964.
Dahm, G. Völkerrecht, Stuttgart, Vol. I (1958), Vol. II (1961), Vol. III (1961).
Davis, K. C. Administrative Law Treatise. St. Paul, 1958.
Delvaux, L. La Cour de justice de la CECA. Paris, 1956.
Deringer, Arved, Das Wettbewerbsrecht der EWG: Text und Kommentar. Düsseldorf, 1965.
Diebold, W. The Schuman Plan. New York, 1959.
Donner, A. M. et. al., Le Juge national et le Droit communautaire. Leyden, 1966.
– The Role of the Lawyer in the European Communities. Northwestern Univ. Press, 1968.
Duez, P. and Debeyre, G. Traité de droit Administratif. Paris, 1952.
Eagleton, C. International Government. New York, 3rd ed. 1957.
Feld, W. The Court of the European Communities. The Hague, 1964.
Fellner, W. Emergence and Content of Modern Economic Analysis. New York-Toronto-London, 1960.
Ferguson, C. E. A Macroeconomic Theory of Workable Competition. Duke University Press, 1964.
de Ferron, O. Le Problème des transports et le Marché commun. Geneva, 1965.
Friauf, K. Die Staatenvertretung in supranationalen Gemeinschaften. Marburg, 1960.
Galbraith, J. K. American Capitalism: The Concept of Countervailing Power. Boston, 1952.
Ganshof van der Meersch (ed.), Droit des Communautés européennes. Brussels, 1969.
Gleiss, A. and Hirsch, M. EWG-Kartellrecht: Kommentar. Heidelberg, 2d ed. 1965.
Graupner, R. The Rules of Competition in the EEC. The Hague, 1965. v.d. Groeben, H. and v. Boeckh, H. Kommentar zum EWG-Vertrag. II Vols. Bonn and Frankfurt, 1958.
Haas, E. The Uniting of Europe. London, 1958.
Hallstein, W. Der Schuman-Plan. Frankfurt, 1951.
– United Europe, Challenge and Opportunity. Harvard Univ. Press. 1962.

v.d. Heuvel, H. Prejudiciële vragen en bevoegdheidsproblemen in het Europees recht. Antwerp, 1962.
Hochbaum, M. Das Diskriminierungs- und Subventionsverbot in der EGKS und EWG. Baden-Baden and Bonn, 1962.
Hoffman, W. Zusammensetzung und Befugnisse des Parlaments der Europäischen Gemeinschaften. Bonn Univ. Dissertation, 1961.
Houben, P-H. Les Conseils de Ministres des Communautés européennes. Leyden, 1964.
Jeanneau, B. Les principes généraux du droit dans la jurisprudence administrative. Paris, 1954.
Jerusalem, F. Das Recht der Montanunion. Berlin and Frankfurt, 1954.
Kapp, E. The Merger of the Executives of the European Communities. Bruges, 1964.
Kaysen, C. and Turner, D. F. Anti-Trust Policy: An Economic and Legal Analysis. Harvard Univ. Press, 1959.
Kiss, A-C. L'abus de droit en droit international. Paris, 1953.
Klaer, W. Der Verkehr im Gemeinsamen Markt für Kohle und Stahl. Bonn, 1961.
Klinger, H. Kommentar zur Verwaltungsgerichtsordnung. Göttingen, 1960.
Kovar, R. Le pouvoir réglementaire de la CECA. Paris, 1964.
Krawielicki, R. Das Monopolverbot im Schuman Plan. Tübingen, 1952.
Laferrière, E. Traité de la juridiction administrative. II Vols. Paris, 2d ed. 1896.
de Laubadère, A. Traité élémentaire et de droit administratif. Vol. I. Paris, 1963.
Lauterpacht, H. Private Law Sources and Analogies of International Law. Londen, 1927.
– The Development of International Law. London, 1958.
– The Function of Law in the International Community. Oxford, 1933.
– and Oppenheim, L. International Law. Vol. I. London, 8th ed. 1955.
Lindberg, L. The Political Dynamics of European Economic Integration. Stanford Univ. Press, 1963.
Lister, L. Europe's Coal and Steel Community. New York, 1960.
McDougal, M. and Associates. Studies in World Public Order. Yale Univ. Press, 1960.
McNair, L. The Law of Treaties. Oxford, 1961.
v. Mangoldt, H. and Klein, F. Das Bonner Grundgesetz: Kommentar. Berlin and Frankfurt, 2nd ed. 1957.
Marjolin, R. Europe and the United States in the World Economy. Duke Univ. Press, 1953.
Mathijsen, P. Le Droit de la C.E.C.A. The Hague, 1958.
Maunz, T. Deutsches Staatsrecht. Munich, 13th ed. 1964.
– and Dürig, G. Grundgesetz Kommentar. Munich and Berlin, 2nd ed. 1966.
Meade, J., Liesner, H., and Wells, S. Case Studies in European Economic Union. London, 1962.
Mercier, P. Effets internationaux des jugements dans les États du Marché commun. Geneva, 1965.
Miller, J. P. (ed), Competition, Cartels and Their Regulation. Amsterdam, 1962.
Moser, B. Die überstaatliche Gerichtsbarkeit der Montanunion. Vienna, 1955.

Mosler, H. Das Völkerrecht in der Praxis der deutschen Gerichte. Karlsruhe, 1957.
– Verfassungsgerichtsbarkeit in der Gegenwart. Berlin and Cologne, 1962.
Much, W. Die Amtshaftung im Recht der EGKS. Frankfurt, 1952.
Neale, A. D. The Antitrust laws of the U.S.A.: A Study of Competition Enforced by Law. Cambridge Univ. Press, 1962.
Newhouse, J. Collision in Brussels: The Common Market Crisis of 30 June 1965. New York, 1967.
Osterheld, H. Die Vollstreckung von Entscheidungen der EGKS in der Bundesrepublik Deutschland. Frankfurt, 1954.
Philip, A. L'Europe unie et sa place dans l'économie internationale. 1953.
Pigorsch, W. Die Einordnung völkerrechtlicher Normen in das Recht der Bundesrepublik Deutschland. Hamburg, 1959.
Polanyi, K. The Great Transformation. Boston, 1944.
Rabe, H-J., Das Verordnungsrecht der EWG. Hamburg, 1963.
Reuter, P. La C.E.C.A. Paris, 1953.
de Richemont, J. La Cour de justice – Code annoté. Paris, 1954.
Robertson, A. European Institutions. London, 1959.
Rosenne, S. The Law and Practice of the International Court. 2 Vols. Leyden, 1965.
Ross, A. A. Textbook of International Law. London, 1947.
Roulet, J-D. Le Caractère artificiel de la Théorie de l'abus de droit en Droit international public. Neuchâtel, 1958.
Rupprecht, W. Die Nachprüfungsbefugnis des europäischen Gerichtshofes gegenüber Ermessenshandlungen der Exekutive in der Montanunion und der EWG. Kiel Univ. Dissertation, 1962.
Sannwald, R. and Stohler, J. Wirtschaftliche Integration. Tübingen, 1958.
Scheingold, S. The Rule of Law in European Integration. Yale Univ. Press, 1965.
Schilling, J. Völkerrecht und Staatliches Recht in Frankreich. Hamburg, 1964.
Schluep, R. Der Alleinvertriebsvertrag: Markstein der EWG-Kartellpolitik. Bern, 1966.
Schmitt, C. Der Nomos der Erde im Völkerrecht des Jus Publicum Europaeum. Cologne, 1950.
Schwartz, B. French Administrative Law and the Common Law World. New York Univ. Press, 1954.
Schwarzenberger, G. Manual of International Law. London, 4th ed. 1960.
Steiger, H. Staatlichkeit und Ueberstaatlichkeit. Berlin, 1966.
Stein, E. and Nicholson, T. American Enterprise in the European Common Market: A Legal Profile. Univ. of Michigan Press, 1960.
Steindorff, E. Die Nichtigkeitsklage im Recht der EGKS. Frankfurt, 1952.
– Rechtsschutz und Verfahren im Recht der europäischen Gemeinschaften. Baden-Baden, 1964.
Strauss, W. Fragen der Rechtsangleichung im Rahmen der europäischen Gemeinschaften. Frankfurt, 1959.

Tomuschat, C. Die gerichtliche Vorabentscheidung nach den Verträgen über die europäischen Gemeinschaften. Cologne, 1964.

Tosato, G. L. I Regolamenti delle Comunità Europee. Milan, 1965.

Toynbee, A. The World and the West. London, 1953.

Valentine, D. The Court of Justice of the European Communities. II Vols. London, 1965.

de Visscher, C. Problèmes d'interprétation judiciaire en droit international public. Paris, 1963.

de Visscher, P. Le Droit public de la C.E.C.A. Liège, 1956/57.

Vogel, K. Die Verfassungsentscheidung des Grundgesetzes für eine internationale Zusammenarbeit. Heft 292/293 Recht und Staat in der Geschichte und Gegenwart. Tübingen, 1964.

Wagner, H. Grundbegriffe des Beschlussrechts der europäischen Gemeinschaften. Cologne, 1965.

Waline, M. Droit administratif. Paris, 9th ed. 1963.

Wetter, J. The Styles of Appellate Judicial Opinions. Leyden, 1960.

Wiebringhaus, H. Gerichtshof für Europa? Leyden, 1967.

Wiesner, W. Der Widerruf individueller Entscheidungen der Hohen Behörde der EGKS. Hamburg, 1966.

Wohlfarth, E. and Everling, Glaesner and Sprung. Die EWG, Kommentar zum Vertrag. Berlin and Frankfurt, 1960.

Zehn Jahre Rechtsprechung des Gerichtshofs der Europäischen Gemeinschaften. Cologne, 1965.

2. LITERATURE ON THE THEORY OF JUDICIAL DECISION: BOOKS AND MONOGRAPHS

Abraham, H. The Judiciary: The Supreme Court in the Governmental Process. Boston, 1965.

Adler, M. Dialectic. New York, 1927.

Allen, C. Law in the Making. Oxford, 5th ed. 1956.

Anscombe, G. E. M. et al. New Essays on Plato and Aristotle. New York, 1965.

Aristotle's Nicomachean Ethics, On the Motion of Animals, Prior and Posterior Analytics, Rhetoric and Topics. Britannica Great Books translations.

Arnold, T. The Folklore of Capitalism. Yale Univ. Press 1961.

Austin, J. Jurisprudence. Lectures on Jurisprudence or the Philosophy of Positive Law. 2 Vols. London, 4th ed. 1873.

Bachof, O. Verfassungswidrige Verfassungsnormen? Heft 163/164 Recht und Staat in Geschichte und Gegenwart. Tübingen, 1951.

Bäumlin, R. Staat, Recht und Geschichte. Zürich, 1961.

Bergbohm, K. Jurisprudenz und Rechtsphilosophie. Leipzig, 1892.

Beveridge, A. The Life of John Marshal. Vol. 4. Boston and New York, 1919.

Beyer, G, and Luettig, P. Bericht, Gutachten und Urteil. Berlin and Frankfurt, 24th ed. 1963.

Bickel, A. The Least Dangerous Branch: The Supreme Court at the Bar of Politics. New York, 1962.

– Politics and the Warren Court. New York, 1965.

Black, C. L. The People and the Court. New York, 1960.
Braybrooke, D. and Lindblom, C. A Strategy of Decision – A Policy Evaluation as a Social Process. London, 1963.
Das Bundesverfassungsgericht. Karlsruhe, 1963.
Cahn, E. Confronting Injustice. Boston, 1966.
– The Moral Decision: Right and Wrong in the Light of American Law. London, 1959.
– Sense of Injustice. New York Univ. Press, 1949.
Cardozo, B. The Growth of the Law. Yale Univ. Press, 1924.
– The Nature of the Judicial Process. Yale Univ. Press, 1921.
– The Paradoxes of Legal Science. Columbia Univ. Press, 1928.
Carlston, K. Law and Structures of Social Action. Columbia Univ. Press, 1956.
Cohen, M. R. Law and the Social Order. New York, 1933.
Coing, H. Die obersten Grundsätze des Rechts. Heidelberg, 1947.
– Grundzüge der Rechtsphilosophie. Berlin, 1950.
Commager, H. Majority Rule and Minority Rights. German ed. Wiesbaden, 1947.
Corwin, E. The Constitution and What it Means Today, 12th ed. 1958.
Dahl R. and Lindblom, C. Politics, Economics and Welfare. New York, 1953.
Ebenstein, W. Die rechtsphilosophische Schule der Reinen Rechtslehre. Prague, 1938.
Ehmke, H. Wirtschaft und Verfassung. Karlsruhe, 1961.
Ehrlich, E. Grundlegung der Soziologie des Rechts. Munich and Leipzig, 1929.
– Die Juristische Logik. Tübingen, 2d ed., 1925.
Eichenberger, K. Die richterliche Unabhängigkeit als staatsrechtliches Problem. Bern, 1960.
Ermacora, F. Verfassungsrecht durch Richterspruch. Karlsruhe, 1960.
Esser, J. Grundsatz und Norm in der richterlichen Fortbildung des Privatrechts. Tübingen 2nd ed. 1964.
The Federalist Papers. New American Library Ed. Paperback 1961.
Forsthoff, E. Lehrbuch des Verwaltungsrechts. Vol. 1. Munich and Berlin, 8th ed. 1961.
– Recht und Sprache, Prolegomena zu einer richterlichen Hermeneutik. Halle, 1940.
Frank, J. Courts on Trial. Princeton Univ. Press, 1949.
Freedeman, C. The Conseil d'État in Modern France. Columbia Univ. Press, 1961.
Friedmann, W. Law in a Changing Society. London, 1959.
– Law and Social Changes in Contemporary Britain. London, 1951.
Friedrich, C. Man and his Government: An Empirical Theory of Politics. New York, 1963.
– and Chapman, J. W. (eds.). Nomos VI: Justice. New York, 1964.
– (ed.). Nomos VII: Rational Decision. New York, 1964.
– The Philosophy of Law in Historical Perspective. Univ. Chicago Press, 1963.
– Zur Theorie und Politik der Verfassungsordnung. Heidelberg, 1963.
Fuller, L. Legal Fictions. Stanford Univ. Press, 1967.
– The Morality of Law. Yale Univ. Press, 1964.
Gadamer, H-G. Wahrheit und Methode. Tübingen, 2d ed. 1965.

Garlan, E. Legal Realism and Justice. Columbia Univ. Press, 1941.
Gény, F. Méthode d'interprétation et sources en droit privé positif. II Vols. Paris, 2nd ed. 1954.
– Science et Technique en droit privé positif. IV Vols. Paris, 1913.
Grote, G. Aristotle. Vol. I London, 1872.
Haines, C. G. The American Doctrine of Judicial Supremacy. Univ. of Calif. Press, 2d ed. 1932.
Hall, J. Studies in Jurisprudence and Criminal Theory. New York, 1958.
Hamson, C. J. Executive Discretion and Judicial Control. London, 1954.
Hand, L. The Bill of Rights. Harvard Univ. Press, 1960.
Hart, H. L. A. The Concept of Law. Oxford, 1961.
Hauriou, M. Principes de Droit public. Vol. I. Paris, 2nd ed. 1916.
Hofmann, H. Legitimität gegen Legalität. Berlin, 1964.
Holmes, O. W. Collected Legal Papers. New York, 1920.
– The Common Law. Boston, 1881.
– Holmes-Laski Letters. Vol. I. Harvard Univ. Press, 1953.
– Holmes-Pollock Letters. Vol. I. Harvard Univ. Press, 1941.
v. Ihering, R. Der Zweck im Recht. Leipzig, 4th ed. 1904–1905.
Jackson, R. The Supreme Court in the American System of Government. Harvard Univ. Press, 1958.
Jahrreiss, H. Mensch und Staat. Cologne and Berlin, 1957.
Jeanneau, B. Les principes généraux du droit dans la jurisprudence administrative. Paris, 1954.
de Jouvenel, B. De La Souveraineté. Paris, 1955.
Kägi, W. Die Verfassung als rechtliche Grundordnung des Staates. Zürich, 1945.
– Zur Entstehung, Wandlung und Problematik des Gewaltenteilungsprinzip. Zürich, 1937.
Kant. Die Metaphysik der Sitten. Vorlaender Edition.
Kapp, E. Greek Foundations of Traditional Logic. Columbia Univ. Press, 1942.
Keller, A. Die Kritik, Korrektur und Interpretation des Gesetzeswortlautes. Wintherthur, 1960.
Kelly, A. and Harbison, W. The American Constitution. New York, 1955.
Kelsen, H. Hauptprobleme der Staatsrechtslehre. Reinheim, 2nd ed. 1960.
– General Theory of Law and the State. Cambridge, 1949.
– The Law of the United Nations. London and New York, 1950.
– Pure Theory of Law. Univ. of Calif. Press, 1967. A translation from the 2nd revised and enlarged German edition by Max Knight.
– Reine Rechtslehre. Vienna, 2nd ed. 1960.
– What is Justice – Collected Essays. Univ. of Calif. Press, 1960.
Klein, F. Bundesverfassungsgericht und richterliche Beurteilung politischer Fragen. Münster, 1966.
Krislov, S. The Supreme Court in the Political Process. New York, 1965.
Laband, P. Staatsrecht des Deutschen Reiches. Aalen, 5th ed. 1964.
Larenz, K. Kennzeichen geglückter richterlicher Rechtsfortbildungen. Karlsruhe, 1965.
– Methodenlehre der Rechtswissenschaft. Berlin, 1960.
Laski, H. The American Democracy. London, 1949.
Lauterpacht, H. The Development of International Law. London, 1958.

Lawson, F. Negligence in the Civil Law. Oxford, 1950.
Lee, H. D. P. Zeno of Elea. Cambridge Univ. Press, 1936.
Legal Institutions Today and Tomorrow. Columbia Univ. Press, 1959.
Llewellyn, K. N. The Bramble Bush. New York, 2nd ed. 1951.
- The Common Law Tradition: Deciding Appeals. Boston, 1960.
- Jurisprudence: Realism in Theory and Practice. Univ. of Chicago Press, 1962.
de Malberg, R. Carré. Contribution à la Théorie générale de l'État. Vol. I. Paris, 1920.
McDougal, M. and Associates. Studies in World Public Order. Yale Univ. Press, 1960.
McWhinney, E. Constitutionalism in Germany and the Federal Constitutional Court. Leyden, 1962.
-Judicial Review in the English-Speaking World. Univ. of Toronto Press, 2nd ed. 1960.
Mannheim, K. Ideologie und Utopie. Frankfurt, 3rd ed. 1952. Trans. by Heinz Maus from Ideology and Utopia. London.
Mason, T. Harlan Fiske Stone. New York, 1956.
de Montesquieu, C. Considérations sur les causes de la grandeur des Romains et de leur décadence, 1734.
- De l'Esprit des Lois. Britannica Great Books translation.
Morgenthau, H. J. Politics Among Nations. New York, 1956.
Mosler, H. (ed.). Verfassungsgerichtsbarkeit in der Gegenwart. Berlin and Cologne, 1962.
Murphy, W. Congress and the Court – A Case Study in the American Political Process. Univ. of Chicago Press, 1962.
- and Pritchett, C. Courts, Judges and Politics. New York, 1961.
Perelman, Ch. The Idea of Justice and the Problem of Argument. New York, 1963. Translated by John Petrie.
- Justice et Raison. Collected Essays. Presses Universitaires de Bruxelles, 1963.
- and Olbrechts-Tyteca, L. La nouvelle rhétorique: Traité de l'argumentation. II Vols. Presses Universitaires de France, 1958.
- Rhétorique et Philosophie pour une Théorie de l'argumentation en philosophie. Collected Essays. Presses Universitaires de France, 1952.
Plathner, G. Der Kampf um die richterliche Unabhängigkeit bis zum Jahre 1848. Breslau, 1935.
Plato, Laws and Phaedrus. Britannica Great Books translations.
Polanyi, M. The Logic of Liberty. Chicago Univ. Press, 1951.
Pound, R. An Introduction to the Philosophy of Law. Yale Univ. Press, 1959.
- Jurisprudence. Vol. III. St. Paul, Minn., 1959.
Radbruch, G. Der Geist des Englischen Rechts. Heidelberg, 4th ed. 1956.
- Der Mensch im Recht. Collected Essays. Göttingen, 1961.
- Einführung in die Rechtswissenschaft. Stuttgart, 9th ed. 1952.
- Rechtsphilosophie. Leipzig, 3rd ed. 1932.
Radin, M. The Law and Mr. Smith. New York and Indianapolis, 1938.
Ripert, G. Le déclin du droit: études sur la législation contemporaine. Paris, 1949.
Rosenblum, V. Law as a Political Instrument. Garden City, New Jersey, 1955.
Ross, W. D. Aristotle. London, 5th ed. 1949.

Rostow, E. The Sovereign Prerogative - The Supreme Court and the Quest for Law. Yale Univ. Press, 1962.
Rousseau J-J. Du Contrat social. Paris, 1946.
Sabine, G. H. A History of Political Theory. New York, 1954.
Scharpf, F. Grenzen der richterlichen Verantwortung. Karlsruhe, 1965.
Scheuner, U. Die Auslegung verfassungsrechtlicher Leitgrundsätze. Rechtsgutachten. Wetzlar, 1952.
Schmidhauser, J. The Supreme Court as Final Arbiter in Federal-State Relations 1789–1957. Univ. of North Carolina Press, 1958.
Schmitt, Carl. Der Begriff des Politischen. Berlin, 1963.
– Die Lage der europäischen Rechtswissenschaft. Tübingen, 1950.
– Legalität und Legitimität. Munich and Leipzig, 1932.
Schneider, H. Gerichtsfreie Hoheitsakte. Heft 160/161 Recht und Staat in Geschichte und Gegenwart. Tübingen, 1951.
Schubert, G. Constitutional Politics. New York, 1961.
Shapiro, M. Law and Policies in the Supreme Court. London, 1964.
Siorat, L. Le problème des lacunes en droit international: Contribution à l'étude des sources du droit et de la fonction judiciaire. Paris, 1958.
Smend, R. Staatsrechtliche Abhandlungen und andere Aufsätze. Berlin, 1955.
Stone, J. Human Law and Human Justice, London, 1965.
– Law and the Social Sciences in the Second Half Century. Univ. of Minn. Press, 1966.
– Legal System and Lawyers' Reasoning. Stanford Univ. Press, 1964.
– The Province and Function of Law. Sidney, 1950.
Strauss, L. Natural Right and History. Univ. of Chicago Press, 1953.
– What is Political Philosophy? Free Press Glencoe, 1959.
Swisher, C. American Constitutional Development. Boston, 1943.
Swisher, C. B. Roger B. Taney. New York, 1935.
– The Supreme Court in Modern Role. New York Univ. Press, 1958.
Thayer, J. John Marshall. Boston, 1901.
Thoma, R. Die Rechtsstellung des Bundesverfassungsgerichts. Gutachten. Bonn, 1953.
Toulin, S. E. The Uses of Argument. Cambridge Univ. Press. 1958.
Triepel, H. Staat und Politik. Heft 1, Beiträge zum ausl. öff. Recht. Berlin, 1927.
Truman, D. The Governmental Process: Political Interests and Public Opinion. New York, 1951.
del Vecchio, G. Die Gerechtigkeit. Basel, 2nd German ed. 1950.
Viehweg, T. Topik und Jurisprudenz. Munich, 1963.
de Visscher, C. Theory and Reality in Public International Law. Princeton Univ. Press, 1957.
Vose, C. Caucasians Only. Univ. of Calif. Press, 1959.
Warren, C. The Supreme Court in U.S. History. Vol. II, Boston, 1926.
Wasserstrom, A. The Judicial Decision: Toward a Theory of Legal Justification. Stanford Univ. Press, 1961.
Weber, M. The Theory of Social and Economic Organization. Free Press Glencoe, 1947.
– Wirtschaft und Gesellschaft. 2 Vols. Tübingen, 1956.

Wechsler, H. Principles, Politics and Fundamental Law. Harvard Univ. Press, 1961.

Welzel, H. An den Grenzen des Rechts: Die Frage nach der Rechtsgeltung. Cologne, 1966.

– Naturrecht und Materiale Gerechtigkeit. Göttingen, 4th ed. 1962.

Wengler, W. Der Begriff des Politischen im Internationalen Recht. Heft 189/190 Recht und Staat in Geschichte und Gegenwart. Tübingen, 1956.

Wieacker, F. Gesetz und Richterkunst: zum Problem der aussergesetzlichen Rechtsordnung. Karlsruhe, 1958.

– Privatrechtsgeschichte der Neuzeit. Göttingen, 1952.

Winckelmann, J. Legitimität und Legalität in Max Webers Herrschaftssoziologie. Tübingen, 1952.

Wolf, E. Verfassungsgerichtsbarkeit und Verfassungstreue in den Vereinigten Staaten. Basel, 1961.

ABBREVIATIONS

Adv-Gen.	Advocate-General of the Court of Justice of the European Communities
Amer. Bar Assoc. J.	American Bar Association Journal
Amer. J. Comp. L.	American Journal of Comparative Law
Amer. J. Int. L.	American Journal of International Law
Amer. Pol. Sci. Rev.	American Political Science Review
Amtsblatt	Amtsblatt (= Journal Officiel) der Europäischen Gemeinschaften = Official Journal of the European Communities
Ann. dr. sci. pol.	Annales de droit et de sciences politiques
Ann. Dig.	Annual Digest
Ann. franç. dr. int.	Annuaire français de droit international
Arch. VR.	Archiv des Völkerrechts
Arch. öff. R.	Archiv für öffentliches Recht
Art.(s)	Article(s)
AWD	Aussenwirtschaftsdienst des Betriebs-Beraters
Ber. deutsch. Ges. VR.	Bericht der deutschen Gesellschaft für Völkerrecht
BFH	Bundesfinanzgerichtshof
BGH	Bundesgerichtshof
BGHZ	Bundesgerichtshof für Zivilsachen
Brit. YB. Int. L.	British Yearbook of International Law
Bull. Soc. franç. Phil.	Bulletin de la Société française de philosophie
BVerfG	Bundesverfassungsgerichtshof
Cah. dr. européen	Cahiers de droit européen
Ch.	Chapter
Chic. L. Rev.	Chicago Law Review
Chron. pol. étr.	Chronique de politique étrangère
C.M.L. Rep.	Common Market Law Reports

C.M.L. Rev.	Common Market Law Review
Colum. L. Rev.	Columbia University Law Review
Deutsche Richter Z.	Deutsche Richter Zeitung
Die öff. Verwaltung	Die öffentliche Verwaltung
Dir. int.	Diritto internazionale
EC	European Communities
EEC = EWG = CEE	European Economic Community
ECSC = EKSG = CECA	European Coal and Steel Community
Euratom = EAG = Euratom	European Atomic Energy Community
Europa-Arch.	Europa-Archiv
European YB.	European Yearbook
f, ff	page(s) following
Gen. Rep.(s)	General Report(s) of the High Authority (ECSC) or Commission of the European Communities
Harv. L. Rev.	Harvard Law Review
ICJ, ICJ Stat.	International Court of Justice, Statute of the Internation Court of Justice
Int. Comp. L. Qu.	The International and Comparative Law Quarterly
Int. Labour Rev.	International Labour Review
Int. Organ.	International Organization
J. Common Mkt. Stud.	Journal of Common Market Studies
J. Pub. L.	Journal of Public Law
JB. int. R.	Jahrbuch für internationales Recht
JB. öff. R.	Jahrbuch für öffentliches Recht
Juristen JB.	Juristen Jahrbuch
Juristen Z.	Juristenzeitung
Law and Cont. Prob.	Law and Contemporary Problems
Law Soc. Gaz.	The Law Society Gazette
Minn. L. Rev.	Minnesota Law Review
Modern L. Rev.	Modern Law Review
Monatss deutsches R.	Monatsschrift für deutsches Recht
n.	footnote
Natural L. Forum	Natural Law Forum
N.J.W.	Neue Juristische Wochenschrift
Neth. Int. L. Rev.	Netherlands International Law Review
No.	Number
Nouvelle rev. écon. contemp.	Nouvelle revue de l'économie contemporaine
N.Y.U.L. Rev.	New York University Law Review

Österr. Z. öff. R.	Österreichische Zeitschrift für öffentliches Recht
Ohio St. L.J.	Ohio State Law Journal
Proc. Amer. J. Int. L.	Proceedings of the American Journal of International Law
Pas. Lux. Juris.	Pasicrisie Luxembourgeoise: Jurisprudence
Qu. J. Econ.	Quarterly Journal of Economics
Rabels Z.	Rabels Zeitschrift
Rec. d. Cours.	Recueil des Cours de l'académie de droit international
Rec. Dalloz: Chron. Juris.	Recueil Dalloz: Chroniques jurisprudence
Rec. d'études Fr. Gény	Recueil d'études sur les sources du droit en l'honneur de François Gény
Rev. crit. dr. int. privé	Revue critique de droit international privé
Rev. dr. int. sci. pol.	Revue de droit international de sciences diplomatiques, politiques et sociales
Rev. dr. pub. sci. pol.	Revue de droit public et de la science politique
Rev. écon. pol.	Revue d'économie politique
Rev. int. franç. dr. gens.	Revue internationale française du droit des gens
Rev. Marché Commun	Revue du Marché Commun
Rev. trim. dr. com.	Revue trimestrielle de droit commercial
Rev. trim. dr. europ.	Revue trimestrielle de droit européen
Riv. dir. int.	Rivista di diritto internazionale
Rspr.	Sammlung der Rechtsprechung (= Recueil de la Jurisprudence, Reports of Judgments) of the Court of Justice of the European Communities
Soc. Econ. Wetgeving	Sociaal Economische Wetgeving
Stan L. Rev.	Stanford University Law Review
Stat.(s)	Statute(s)
U.C.L.A. Intra L. Rev.	University of California (Los Angeles) Intramural Law Review
U.C.L.A. L. Review	University of California (Los Angeles) Law Review
U. Chi. L. Rev.	University of Chicago Law Review
U.N.	United Nations
U. Pa. L. Rev.	University of Pennsylvania Law Review
Villanova L. Rev.	Villanova L. Rev.
VVdStRl	Veröffentlichungen der Vereinigung der deut-

	schen Staatsrechtslehrer
Vol.(s)	Volume(s)
Yale L. J.	Yale Law Journal
Z. ausl. int. Priv. R.	Zeitschrift für ausländisches internationales Privatrecht
Z. ausl. öff. R.	Zeitschrift für ausländisches Recht und Völkerrecht
Z. Betriebswirtschaft	Zeitschrift der Betriebswirtschaft
Z. ges. Handels- und Wirtschaftsrecht	Zeitschrift für das gesamte Handels- und Wirtschaftsrecht
Z. schweiz. R.	Zeitschrift für schweizerisches Recht

INDEX OF COURT DECISIONS
(*Alphabetical*)

This index lists both alphabetically and by case number the judgments of the Court of Justice of the European Communities which are cited or discussed. Page numbers denote case citations only, while italic type indicates pages where case is also discussed.

INDEX OF COURT DECISIONS
(*Case Number*)

INDEX OF TREATY ARTICLES

ECSC Treaty

Article

(ECSC)

ECSC Transitional Convention

Article

EEC Treaty

Article

INDEX OF SUBJECT AND AUTHOR

Both substantively and from an institutional perspective, the Court has contributed uniquely to European economic integration through the continuing search for purpose, authority and practicability in Community law. This is due as much to prudent judicial self-restraint as to the exercise of judicial power. Not only has the Court shaped Community values and concrete rules through its jurisprudence, it also has consolidated a constitutional framework for their continuing evolution.

About the author: Born 1935 in California. B.A. (summa cum laude) from Wabash College 1957. L.L.B. and M.A. in economics at Yale University 1963. Dr. jur. (magna cum laude) from University of Bonn 1967, where he served as Assistant to the Director of the Institute for International Law.
He is a member of the Indiana (1963) and Ohio (1968) bars and practiced law in Cleveland, Ohio, until becoming Assistant General Counsel in 1972 of the International Operations of Sears, Roebuck and Co.

ISBN 978-94-011-8679-7

GPSR Compliance

The European Union's (EU) General Product Safety Regulation (GPSR) is a set of rules that requires consumer products to be safe and our obligations to ensure this.

If you have any concerns about our products, you can contact us on ProductSafety@springernature.com

In case Publisher is established outside the EU, the EU authorized representative is:

Springer Nature Customer Service Center GmbH
Europaplatz 3
69115 Heidelberg, Germany

Batch number: 10830943

Printed by Printforce, the Netherlands